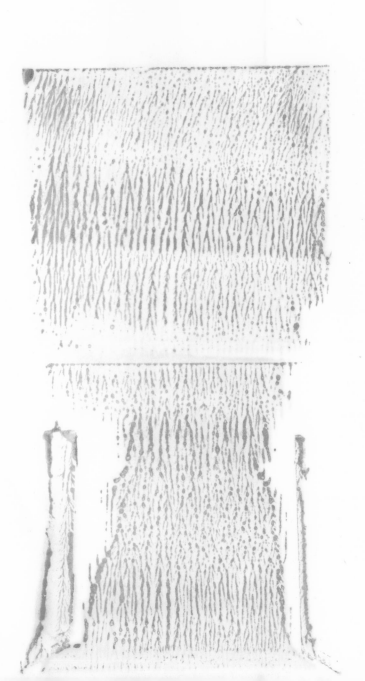

The
Coevolution
of Climate
and Life

The Coevolution of Climate and Life

Stephen H. Schneider

Randi Londer

Sierra Club Books · San Francisco

for Rebecca and Adam,
whose generation deserves a chance
to work for a sustainable future

S H S

for my loving parents,
Shirley and Morton Londer

R L

QC
981.8
.C5
S358
1984

Copyright © 1984 by Stephen H. Schneider and Randi Londer
All rights reserved.
No part of this book may be reproduced
in any form or by any electronic or mechanical means,
including information storage and retrieval systems,
without permission in writing from the publisher.

Library of Congress Cataloging in Publication Data

Schneider, Stephen Henry.
    The coevolution of climate and life.

    Bibliography: p.
    Includes index.
    1. Climatic changes. 2. Life (Biology) I. Londer,
Randi. II. Title.
QC981.8.C5S358 1984   551.6   83-610
ISBN 0-87156-349-5

Jacket design by Larry Ratzkin
Book design by Wolfgang Lederer
Printed in the United States of America
10   9   8   7   6   5   4   3   2   1

Contents

Preface

The Coevolution of Climate and Life explores the earth's climate history and some possible scenarios for its future; the mechanisms of climate change; and the political and ethical implications of the discoveries of climatologists.

We'll cover a vast time scale here, ranging from what the weather may have been at the very origin of the earth and the beginnings of biological evolution to the likelihood and timing of the next Ice Age. Sharp climatic effects resulting from cataclysmic events are also touched on. For example, a massive earth/asteroid collision some sixty-five million years ago is believed by many to have cast up a vast pall of debris in the atmosphere for several months, enough to have blocked out the sun and temporarily dropped the climate below freezing, wiping out most life greater in size than small mammals. This put the final nail in the coffin of the dinosaurs. Such theories have a bizarre modern application. Some who study the potential aftermath of a nuclear war argue that the blasts and fires started in the wake of such a terrible human catastrophe could put huge amounts of debris in the atmosphere. Such debris could cause effects comparable to those that apparently occurred at the time of the disappearance of the dinosaurs. It may seem absurd to study potential climatic consequences following such a horrendous multi-megaton exchange, but these environmental consequences must be borne in mind by those who persist in talking of winning such a war; they must be understood by the several billion non-combatants, bystanders whose food growing capacity could be dramatically curtailed in the climatic aftermath of such a war.

Even without human intervention, of course, it is obvious that climate exercises powerful constraints over the kinds and numbers of living things that can exist on earth. This is graphically illustrated by the wide geographic differences in the distribution of climate types and life forms of today. But what is probably much less well appreciated is the fact that life, as it multiplied and evolved over the aeons, altered the land, air and seas—enough to have changed markedly the very climatic conditions from which earlier life emerged. In a sense, climate and life grew up together, each exerting fundamental controlling influences on the other. Climate and life have *coevolved*, to borrow a term developed by population biologists Paul Ehrlich and Peter Raven.* Today, the balance of mutual influence between climate and life is shifting radically. If we include mankind's social and technological juggernaut as part of the definition of life, then one side effect of our collective footprint on the face of the earth is significant climate modification.

Carbon dioxide is a good example of our influence. This gas, which is involved in life processes and nonlife chemistry as well, has aptly been called the most important substance on earth by noted environmental scientist Roger Revelle.† Not only has CO_2 been a primary agent for the long-term recycling of the earth's crust through the weathering process, but CO_2 in the atmosphere and oceans is a primary nutrient for most plants. Furthermore, CO_2 helps to determine the temperature of the earth's surface through the process popularly known as *the greenhouse effect*.

Each year the CO_2 concentration in the air undergoes a cycle caused by the growth and decay of seasonal plants. Scientists have been monitoring atmospheric CO_2 concentration at the Mauna Loa Observatory in Hawaii for more than twenty-five years. They have discovered that superimposed on this annual cycle is a long-term upward trend of some 9 percent over the twenty-five-year period of record since 1958. This trend is widely believed to be a result of human activities, and it could cause significant global climatic changes if it continues. The links between CO_2, climate, and society are excellent examples of why our future well-being may require that, at the very least, we talk more—and with greater knowledge— about the weather than we have been accustomed to in the past. In these pages we will deal with not just the CO_2 connections between climate and life, but interactions between climate and food, water, energy and health as well.

Considerable evidence suggests that we are modifying climate at a faster rate than we can understand or predict the consequences.

*Ehrlich, P. R. and Raven, P. H., 1965, Butterflies and plants: A study in co-evolution, *Evolution 18:* 586–608.
†Carbon atoms that combine with other elements during life processes (such as photosynthesis or animal metabolism) are *organic carbon*. But it is not only the organic compounds of carbon that are important to us. Carbon comes in a ubiquitous *inorganic* form—carbon dioxide (CO_2).

How serious is this predicament? To explore that question we'll draw relevant information from astrophysics, chemistry, geophysics, and evolutionary biology to reconstruct some of the very early conditions of climate and life. Knowledge from geology, paleontology, ecology, and glaciology is then used to chart the developments of continents, oceans, ice sheets, the atmosphere, and expanding life. When humans finally appear much, much later on, we sample findings from archaeology, history, botany, and dendrochronology (tree-ring analysis), among other disciplines. Next, the more familiar modern disciplines of meteorology, oceanography, chemistry, biology, physics and computer science are tapped to help explain what has caused—and might yet cause—major climatic shifts.

In *The Coevolution of Climate and Life* we will also describe how climatologists work, how scientists from many other related fields gather and interpret their data, stressing not only their findings but their disagreements. Like other people, scientists are not immune to prejudice and special interest; but over time their collective belief in evidence and verification of tentative theories usually overcomes entrenched interests.

Finally, we will explore these important questions:

- How seriously does our pollution and abuse of the land affect climatic conditions?
- How vulnerable are we to natural climatic variations?
- Can we cope with plausible future climatic changes—from either natural or human causes?

To peer into our climatic future and to estimate what impact climatic changes might have on humanity means trying to understand and predict human behavior as much as atmospheric behavior. When you consider that taking action to deal with climatic change will generally mean pitting the interests of one group against another, you will probably agree that some discussion of the political and social sciences is called for. Therefore, our trail will pass through the agricultural sciences, hydrology, energy systems engineering, sociology, political science, economics, strategic planning, and ethics. In essence, to explore the coevolution of climate and life requires that we look simultaneously at many facets of nature—including people.

Ecologists have long recognized the interconnectedness of the myriad components of nature. In view of this, it is an impossible task to explain fully all relevant issues, even in the limited realm of weather and climate. We simply aren't up to it; nobody is. But philosophers have long known that full scientific understanding of any segment of nature is never possible; we must be satisfied with continuing refinements.* Thus, our aim here is more modest: we simply hope to provide a good deal of information for those who want an interpretive, state-of-the-art sample of most of the important issues we believe bear directly on the coevolution of climate and life. In particular, our hope is that these pages will prove helpful to a wide spectrum of decision makers—and to the citizens who choose them. We will all have to decide—even if by default—how to minimize the adverse effects of looming climatic hazards and how to maximize emerging climatological opportunities. We believe that the best way to foster more rational actions in the face of changing climates is to place the decision making processes on a firmer base of knowledge. It is our hope that *The Coevolution of Climate and Life* contributes to this base.

Because of the potentially diverse readership of this book, a number of editorial trade-offs had to be made. First, we have tried to use both metric and approximately equivalent English units when hard numbers are given. Second, we have strived to define basic concepts and to avoid specialized jargon, perhaps to a point that may seem a bit patronizing to some readers already knowledgeable in certain fields discussed here. We believe this is a trade-off worth making, however, so that our subject is more accessible to that ill-defined but omnipresent educated layperson. Even so, there are considerable numbers of facts, counter facts and ideas from more than a dozen disciplines presented here. Although digesting the whole presentation shouldn't require any specialized training, following all the pathways of admittedly complex sets of arguments will likely call for more than a casual reading from most readers—but then a good mystery also requires careful reading to catch most of the clues or unravel a complex plot.

Despite the large number of issues raised and the hundreds of references cited, many specialists in each of the dozen or so disciplines covered here will undoubtedly wonder why we treated *their*

---

*For example, see the discussion in Schneider, S. H., and Morton, L., *The Primordial Bond: Exploring Connections Between Man and Nature Through the Humanities and Sciences* (New York: Plenum), 1981.

specialities so sparsely in comparison to the others—at least this was the gripe we got from a number of our prepublication specialist readers. To such specialists we can only say that *The Coevolution of Climate and Life* does not attempt to provide a detailed or balanced history of who contributed what to each of the many disciplines we discuss. Rather, we have been selective, basing our choice of topics and contributors on how easily they provide relatively clear, representative examples of important issues that each discipline has to offer to our overall theme.

Finally, we had to choose an effective way to draw on the backgrounds and experiences of a climatologist and a science journalist. Although both of us have often crossed over these lines of responsibility in this work, clearly the principal responsibility for the scientific content—and opinions—largely fell to the scientist, just as much of the draft writing and organization fell to the journalist. Many scientific events and research works are cited in which Stephen Schneider has been a personal participant. The frequent reporting of these experiences and offerings of his interpretive opinions on many issues here have led us to use the first person style in many places; to be sure, "I" is a less awkward, more economical construction than the repeated use of "the author who is a climatologist . . ."!

A broadly interdisciplinary work such as this would necessarily tax the research abilities and other resources of any set of authors. We are no exception. Therefore, we owe a great debt to those who read—and sometimes reread—various drafts in order to keep us honest in different fields of expertise. Even in those developing areas where new knowledge will rapidly make any present assessments soon obsolete, we have worked hard to present the state of the art as of 1983. Our many manuscript readers helped us toward this goal. In particular, we wish to thank Starley L. Thompson, H. Nüzhet Dalfes, John S. Perry, Curt Covey, William F. Ruddiman, Andrew McIntyre, and Suzanne Lipsett for reading and criticizing the entire manuscript in sometimes more than one of its early incarnations. We also deeply appreciate the critical reviews of various chapters from Jesse H. Ausubel, Eric J. Barron, Robert S. Chen, Robert E. Dickinson, Ronald L. Gilliland, Judith Jacobson, James Kasting, Maria Krenz, Diana Liverman, Amory and Hunter Lovins, Michael Rampino, Carl Sagan, Samuel and Doris Schneider, and Stephen G. Warren. In addition, discussions or helpful suggestions from many others are gratefully acknowledged. Typing aid from

Mary Rickel, Ursula Rosner, Verlene Leeburg, Jan Stewart, Barbara McDonald, Eileen Boettner, Suzanne Parker, and Beverly Chavez is appreciated, as is the reference assistance we received from NCAR librarian Gayl Gray and the work from Justin Kitsutaka and his colleagues in the NCAR graphics group. The patience, encouragement and editorial and other publication assistance from James Cohee, our editor at Sierra Club Books, has also left its mark on this book. We thank A. Brewster Rickel for compiling the index. We also gratefully acknowledge the many people and institutions who gave us permission to use their illustrations or other copyrighted material, original references which are cited for the convenience of the readers at the place in the book where the materials are first used.

Without a myriad of cheerful and efficient services from Mary Rickel—ranging from typing illegible notes, to editing, to collating several "final" drafts, to looking up references, to handling numerous phone calls from various scientists and the publisher—this work might never have been finished. Finally, Cheryl K. Schneider not only made significant comments at all stages of this project, but put up with endless meetings at odd hours and countless other disruptions of normal life for over four years, while all the time providing gentle encouragement—and an occasional bit of pressure—to get it done once and for all! We sincerely hope our efforts will prove worthy of all the help we have received.

Stephen H. Schneider
National Center
for Atmospheric Research*
Boulder, Colorado

Randi Londer
New York, New York

*The National Center for Atmospheric Research is sponsored by the National Science Foundation. Any opinions, findings, conclusions, or recommendations expressed herein are those of the authors and do not necessarily reflect the views of the National Science Foundation.

PART I

FOUR BILLION YEARS OF WEATHER: THE EARTH'S CLIMATE HISTORY

1 Climate Before Man

Before trying to explain the present climate or attempting to predict its future course and influence on life, we must first describe what the climate has been in the past—that is, explore the field of *paleoclimatology*. This necessitates a long look backward over geologic time to determine what climate was like when life began on earth, when single-celled creatures flourished, when vegetation evolved, when animals crawled out of the sea, when fossil fuels formed, when dinosaurs came and went, when ice ages reigned, and when human civilizations eventually emerged. These coevolutionary developments, as explained in the preface, have taken place over the four and a half billion years of geologic history. Since the past is often the best key to the future, we'll begin by exploring our climatic roots.

Paleoclimatologists use geologic evidence to reconstruct climates of the past. Thus, it is appropriate to begin an examination of climate with a survey of the fundamental tools available to scientists who wish to interpret the earth's history.

An immense amount of geologic time passed before humans inhabited the earth. The few records we have of the climate of that time have long since been buried. We are referring to ancient rocks or other remnants whose structures contain clues to past conditions. Of particular importance to the connections between climate and life are those geological remains containing direct evidence of past life. Surprisingly, such fossils (from *fossilis,* Latin for "dug up") were not widely recognized for their importance to geology until the mid-eighteenth century and to climatology until much later.

Dating the Age of the Earth

How do scientists determine the age of the various remains they work with? More interestingly, how do they calculate the earth's age?

Theologians were among the first to hazard a guess as to the earth's age, and in some cases it was heresy to contradict their answers. In 1654, using the Bible as a reference, the Irish Archbishop of Armagh, James Ussher, announced that the creation had taken place on October 26, 4004 B.C., at 9:00 A.M.* But by the nineteenth century it had become obvious to most geologists that the archbishop's date could not possibly be correct.

In the 1700s, Scottish geologist James Hutton and some of his contemporaries believed that the physical and chemical processes that shaped the earth's surface provided clear evidence that the planet was at least tens of millions of years old. They based this estimate on a geologic principle known as *uniformitarianism,* which held that geologic processes in the past were essentially the same as those at work today (a concept that will crop up repeatedly in these pages). For instance, Hutton noted that the manner in which clay and silt were being deposited at the mouth of a river was observable. By studying new layers of sediments and how they solidified into shale and siltstone, he could infer how long it took the old layers to build up. By assuming that the same processes of sedimentation occurred over millions of years in the past,[1] he could estimate the age of similar formations and hence the approximate age of the earth.† This method of using rock deposits as age indicators, however, depended on many variables that were too complex to measure. For example, climatic changes or differences in land elevation could both alter erosion rates.

Geologic Periods: Relative Dating

Geologic periods are named for some feature of the geographical areas in which they were first studied. For instance, a nineteenth-century English geologist named Adam Sedgwick described a sequence of rock strata in northern Wales. He suggested

---

*One technique for "dating" the origin of the earth by Judaeo-Christian traditions is to "count begats" backward in time. This fundamentalist approach typically takes one back some 5000 to 10,000 years or so. Creation myths from other religions however, have put the date—or the most recent date within an endless cycle of creations—as far back as billions of years.

†As evolutionary biologist Stephen Jay Gould (*Natural History, 91,* p. 9, May 1982) noted, Hutton believed "that God had ordained a beginning and would devise an end" to the earth. But in between these end points, "God rested and permitted the world to run by the natural laws that he had established." Thus, Gould reports, Hutton felt no contradiction between his belief in God and his scientific findings.

4

that this rock system be named the Cambrian system, *Cambria* being a Latin form of the native Welsh name for Wales. Meanwhile, in southern Wales, Sedgwick's Scottish colleague Roderick Murchison was studying a rock system close in age to that of the Cambrian. Murchison chose the name Silurian for his strata after an ancient tribe named the Silures that had inhabited the area at the time of the Roman conquest. Discovered independently, these two rock systems overlapped. Murchison believed that a portion of Sedgwick's Cambrian period really belonged in his Silurian. Sedgwick disagreed and a feud erupted between the two men which the scientific community did not settle until after their deaths.[2]

In 1879, English geologist Charles Lapworth proposed that an intermediate period be introduced between the Cambrian and the Silurian. He suggested the name Ordovician after a tribe called the Ordovices that had once occupied northern Wales. All three names were later adopted as part of the standard geologic time sequence. Each era in this sequence is subdivided into periods, and these are further subdivided into epochs. Where geographic names are not used, an epoch denotes the early, middle, or late part of a period.

Table 1.1 shows the geologic time sequence now established, based on modern dating techniques. It should be noted that in the nineteenth century, while geologists did not know the absolute age of the rocks they studied, they had an idea as to the relative age of a stratum. They determined this by comparing the position of lower and therefore older rock strata. This principle is called the Law of Superposition.

Geologists have also devised a system of nomenclature for the composition and age of various rock strata. This system consists of divisions of time and names for the rocks deposited during those times. The time units are simply subdivisions of geologic time. The three major eras of recent geologic time are the Paleozoic, Mesozoic, and Cenozoic, during which most life forms evolved.* The fossilized remains of these forms have been used extensively to determine relative ages and to subdivide the eras into periods or epochs. Because the rapid evolution of life leaves a detailed record

---

*The entire block of time between now and 570 million years ago, including the three eras shown in Table 1.1, has collectively been referred to as the Phanerozoic Eon.[3] Similarly, because of their near-billion-year length, the Proterozoic, Archean, and Hadean intervals have also been referred to as eons. (These first four billion years of geologic time are often referred as the Precambrian or the Prepaleozoic.) Here, however, we will refer to an *aeon* as a time unit of one billion (10^9) years.

5

Table 1.1 The Geologic Time Scale

Era	System or Period (rocks) (time)	Series or Epoch* (rocks) (time)	Approximate Absolute Age (Beginning of unit)
Cenozoic (recent life)	Quaternary	Holocene	10,000
		Pleistocene	2 to 3 million
	Tertiary	Pliocene	7 million
		Miocene	22 million
		Oligocene	40 million
		Eocene	55 million
		Paleocene	65 million
Mesozoic (intermediate life)	Cretaceous ("abounding in chalk")	Many series	140 million
	Jurassic (Jura Mountains, France)		195 million
	Triassic (from a three-fold division in Germany)		230 million
Paleozoic (ancient life)	Permian (Perm, a Russian province)		280 million
	Carboniferous (from the abundance of coal)		325 million
	†Pennsylvanian		
	†Mississippian		350 million
	Devonian (Devonshire, England)		400 million
	Silurian (the Silures, an ancient British tribe)		440 million
	Ordovician (the Ordovices, an ancient British tribe)		500 million
	Cambrian (*Cambria*, a Latin form of the native Welsh name for Wales)		570 million
Precambrian or Prepaleozoic	Proterozoic Age	Many local systems and series are recognized, but world-wide correlation is much more difficult to establish for very old remains, since there are only a few. Also, beginning and ending dates for these eras vary among some authors.	2.5 billion
	Archaen Age		3.8 billion
	Hadean Age		4.6 billion (?)

*Periods of the Mesozoic and Paleozoic are typically subdivided into early, middle, and late epochs, which correspond to lower, middle, and upper series (rock strata).

†These are common alternative names for subdivisions of the Carboniferous Period.

in the sediments, fossils have been used in geologic cross dating—matching rocks from different places that were deposited at the same time. Time-rock units consist of the strata deposited during that period or epoch. Since we are dealing primarily with climatology, we need not concern ourselves with the details of rock strata systems or series per se. In the course of this book, however, we will discuss some of the fossils these systems contain insofar as these fossils are indicators of past climates.

Paleomagnetic Records

The earth's magnetic polarity has reversed itself many times in the past 4.6 billion years,* and such magnetic reversals have been recorded by rocks that became permanently magnetized when they were formed.[4] Igneous lava flows magnetize as they cool from a molten state. In so doing, the magnetized materials in the rock align themselves with the current direction of the earth's field. Scientists can use this alignment in samples to pinpoint when geological events occurred in relation to each other. However, determining the absolute dates when the magnetic reversals occurred requires one or more of the methods discussed below.

Absolute Dating Methods

By the nineteenth century geologists had established time sequences of rock strata from fossils. Although this sequence solved the problem of relative dating, absolute dating techniques were being sought to pin down more precisely the age of each stratum. For instance, one scientist thought that by calculating all the sodium salts in the oceans plus the amount added each year from igneous rock erosion, he could determine an accurate age for the earth. This method, however, failed to account for chemical and biological reactions that help to create a salt balance in the oceans.

---

*These shifts may in fact have affected the climate. The flip-flopping has lowered the strength of the earth's magnetic field, thereby exposing the atmosphere to cosmic radiation of higher intensity. This increased bombardment could have influenced the composition of the upper atmosphere, thus altering the climate. Some researchers have even noted that the magnetic reversals coincided with the extinction of particular species, suggesting a possible link between the magnetic shield, atmospheric composition, and the evolution of life.[5]

7

Nor did it cover the deposition of salt in the oceans during evaporation. Historical geologists needed a method of dating that was independent of such uncertain variables. Finding a reliable clock to reconstruct the geological calendar became a major pursuit.

Thermodynamic Dating Method Two hundred years after James Ussher proclaimed the earth's age, Lord Kelvin tried to formulate an answer scientifically. The Scottish scientist, who was one of the most influential theoretical physicists of his day, used the known principles of thermodynamics to determine the age of the earth. He assumed that the planet began as a molten body, at about 3850°C (7000°F). From past explorations of deep mines and observations of lava flows from the earth's interior, he knew that the interior of the earth was hotter than the surface. By examining the temperature change between the earth's surface and its interior (what is called the geothermal gradient), Lord Kelvin hoped to infer the earth's age. His calculations suggested that the time needed for the geothermal gradient to reach its present value was close to 100 million years.[6] That, he asserted, was the age of the earth. This estimate set off a flurry of controversy among the theoretical physicists, who backed Lord Kelvin, and the geomorphologists (geologists who look at land forms), who did not. The latter believed that some features of the earth's surface indicated the planet was much older than 100 million years. Their theories, however, failed to explain the greater age indicated by these observed features, and many physicists then rejected the geologists' contentions, since they were based on observations alone and not on theoretically sound explanations.

Radioactivity Dating Methods Sometimes in science new insights or discoveries lead to a reconciliation between seemingly conflicting theories and observations. Such was the case in this controversy: the question of the earth's age became moot when radioactivity was discovered around 1900, some fifty years after Lord Kelvin based his estimate of the earth's age on the nonradioactive thermodynamic theory. Radioactivity, which provides a source of heat generated by the decay of radioactive substances in the earth's interior, was unknown to theoretical physicists in Lord Kelvin's time. Their ignorance of its influence caused them to underestimate the age of the earth. Radioactivity also provided an

8

independent benchmark that geologists needed for dating.* The elements for a reliable clock had been found.

A radioactive atom disintegrates over time, whereas a stable atom can maintain its composition indefinitely. The disintegration rate of radioactive atoms is believed to be constant; it is virtually unchanged by chemical or physical alterations of the compounds in which the atoms are contained (such as rock, water, or air). The decay rate of a radioactive element is expressed in terms of its *half-life*—that is, the time it takes for half the atoms originally present to decay into *daughter* products. A radioactive element becomes a daughter product by spontaneously emitting mass and energy. This rate of emission, or decay, is unaffected by temperature or pressure. If we know at what constant rate daughter products are formed, all we need to find in order to determine a rock's age is the ratio of original element to daughter product. This knowledge enables scientists to calculate when the mineral containing the original radioactive element was formed. Using radioactive decay in rocks as a guide, geologists can determine the absolute age of rocks, and hence of various strata of the earth.† This technique is called *radiometric dating*.

Several radioactive elements are used to date rocks. Among them are uranium isotopes,‡ which can decay (with half-lives between 700 million and 4.5 billion years) to isotopes of lead;

---

*Polish scientist Marie Sklodowska-Curie discovered radioactivity in various elements, including uranium and radium. Her work probably contributed to her death. She died at age 67 in 1934 of leukemia, which was likely accelerated and possibly even induced by overexposure to radioactive substances. Incidentally, Curie received the Nobel Prize twice—in 1903 for physics and in 1911 for chemistry. But she was nevertheless rejected for membership in the French Academy of Sciences because of her sex.

†There are sources of possible error, however. Some of the decay products such as argon are gases and can escape rocks or minerals; other decay products are water soluble and can leach out of samples; and some daughter products, thought to result from decay, could actually have been present when the sample crystallized.

‡An isotope is any one of the varieties of an element. Isotopes of the same element differ from one another by the number of neutrons their atomic nuclei contain. For example, hydrogen has three isotopes, or varieties: the most common is ordinary hydrogen, which has one proton and no neutrons in the nucleus of its atom; another is deuterium, with one proton and one neutron; the third is tritium, which has one proton and two neutrons. Here we are referring to radioisotopes (or radioactive isotopes), which are isotopes whose atoms have *unstable* nuclei—that is, the atom decays into another element by emitting a particle. There are also stable isotopes, such as deuterium, oxygen-18, and oxygen-16 (both of the latter two with eight

9

rubidium, which decays (with a half-life of 50 billion years) to strontium; and potassium, which decays (with a half-life of 1.3 billion years) to argon. Scientists experimenting during this early phase (from 1900 to 1938) of radiometric dating were hampered by crude analytical methods and an inadequate knowledge of the nuclear processes involved. But they were able to make rough estimates by measuring lead-uranium ratios in uranium minerals and helium-uranium ratios in a variety of rocks and minerals. Because of long half-lives, the rubidium-strontium and potassium-argon techniques are among the most reliable and can span the entire history of the earth—now put at about 4.6 billion years. However, radioactive elements with shorter half-lives are needed for dating more recent events, such as those of the past few thousands of years.

Radiocarbon Dating   In 1947, the American chemist Willard Libby discovered an indispensable dating tool that enabled climatologists, oceanographers, geologists, and archaeologists to reconstruct accurately climatic change, geological events, and animal and cultural evolution.* Libby and his co-workers found a way to estimate the age of the remains of plants and animals that died within the past 40,000 years or so. Such materials include wood and other plant remains (such as peat beds), marine and freshwater shells, and groundwater and ocean waters in which carbon has dissolved.

Carbon-14 (C^{14}) is one of the three naturally occurring isotopes of the element carbon, which is abundant in the atmosphere-ocean-biosphere reservoir. Unlike carbon-12 and carbon-13, which are stable isotopes, C^{14} is unstable; but its atmospheric concentration is replenished by a fairly continuous stream of cosmic rays imping-

---

protons, but one with eight and one with ten neutrons). Since the relative abundance of these stable isotopes can reflect temperature or other environmental factors at the time sediments or fossils were laid down, they provide important clues to both climatic and biological conditions in the geologic past. We discuss this more later.

*Libby's original thesis was published in 1952 in a slim volume entitled *Radiocarbon Dating* (University of Chicago Press). In 1969, Libby participated in the twelfth Nobel Symposium held at the Institute of Physics at Uppsala University, Sweden. The proceedings of the symposium include Libby's "Ruminations on Radiocarbon Dating," in which he said that "some of the original assumptions need further thought" (such as the constancy of the radiocarbon concentration in the biosphere, and the rate C^{14} mixes in the atmosphere and oceans).

ing on nitrogen molecules in the atmosphere and turning them into C^{14}. Through photosynthesis, atmospheric carbon (including C^{14}) is converted into organic carbon compounds. While the plants are alive, there is a relative equilibrium in the amount of C^{14} in their tissues, since they are always replenishing their supply of C^{14} by photosynthesizing atmospheric carbon. Because animals are always eating live or recently dead plants (or plant eaters), they also contain a C^{14} level that is in close equilibrium with the atmosphere. But when the plant or animal dies, the radioactive C^{14} in their tissues decays, since no further C^{14} is taken up.

Like all radioactive elements, C^{14} has a half-life—5730 ± 40 years. Thus, it takes approximately 5730 years for half of a given number of C^{14} atoms to undergo radioactive decay. Since this rate of decay is not influenced by outside conditions, the rate of disappearance of C^{14} from a sample has an absolute relation to the time it was incorporated into the sample. Therefore, scientists can determine the age of a sample—approximately, at least—by measuring the relative amount of C^{14} it contains.[7]

Climatologists use carbon-14 dating along with the traditional technique of recording the strata of fossils to help establish a chronology of climatic changes. By using C^{14} dating to determine the ages of samples from trees plowed under by ice masses, we can recreate the chronology of the continental glaciers' advance. The radiocarbon dating of peat samples from bogs and driftwood from lake shorelines has also yielded glaciation timetables. The C^{14} content of shells of different planktonic animals found in deep-sea sediments enables us to date fluctuations in oceanic conditions conducive to each animal's abundance. In this way, we are able to infer temperatures and related climatic conditions. Climatologists have been able to use Libby's dating tool to obtain a worldwide picture of climate for about the past 40,000 years. Radiocarbon dates of charcoal from the hearths of cave dwellers have helped us sketch human history and its relation to climatic fluctuations.

In addition to radiometric dating, other absolute dating methods are available to scientists. These methods are described briefly in the following sections.

Fission Track Dating Spontaneous uranium fissions occur within most rocks; that is, fragments of the nuclei of uranium atoms fly apart and travel a fraction of a centimeter, leaving a submicroscopic trail of altered material where atoms have been bumped from their normal positions. If one starts with an assumption that there is a certain amount of fissionable material in a sample and if one knows the theoretical decay rate of that material and the initial concentration of radioactive material, then the number of decay trails should tell how long it has been since the material was formed. These trails are made detectable by a chemical process that dissolves the altered material, making the trail visible under an ordinary microscope or even with the naked eye. Fission track dating is an advantageous method for several reasons: most minerals contain at least a trace of uranium with the abundant isotope U^{238}, which fissions spontaneously; measurements can be made on extremely small specimens; and it covers a very broad time span from fewer than 100 years up to 4.5 billion years.

Amino Acid Dating   Another dating technique now being refined is based on chemical changes that occur in proteins over time. The molecular structure of amino acids can change with time and temperature, so a scientist who, by some other method, knows the temperature history of an amino acid sample can estimate the sample's age. Conversely, if one knows independently the age, one can infer a sample's temperature history. This technique, which may provide an independent check on dating schemes such as radiocarbon methods, is still in a fairly early stage of testing for paleoclimatic purposes.[8]

Climates of Past Geologic Eras

Having briefly surveyed the tools available in geology to determine the age of the remains available to us, we can begin to apply these tools to the subject at hand: the earth's climate. In this section we describe the most climatically significant events that have taken place across geologic time. (See Table 1.1 for an outline of the geologic time scale.)

The Precambrian Era

There are several lines of geologic evidence useful for paleoclimatic inference. Of these, only one—sedimentary rocks—seems to have any applicability back into the early part of the Archean Age (somewhat arbitrarily taken to be between 3.8 and 2.5

billion years ago). However, other evidence, such as well preserved sediments; diverse fossilized forms of simple one-celled bacteria that lack cell nucleii (known as *prokaryotes*); preserved soil profiles; chemical deposits indicative of intense evaporation zones (known as *evaporites*); and more diverse old rocks indicative of the growth of continents all stretch back more than 2 billion—and sometimes more than 3 billion—years. Most of the Archean Age appears to have been marked by the presence of shallow oceans. This is primarily because there is little evidence that would indicate there had been continents. Evaporite deposits appear at the end of the Archean, when significant continental growth is believed to have begun. From that time on the record is potentially very good "for paleoclimatic reconstruction," says planetary scientist James Walker. But, he laments, "there has been little analysis yet about what that record may tell us about climatic factors."[9]

The lack of empirical data makes speculative nearly all climatic reconstructions of this important time when life was being established on earth. However, the dearth of hard information does allow those scientists—myself among them—who enjoy using their intuition to guess how nature may have operated. The risks of this scientific gamesmanship occur later on, of course, when data piles up and most of these imaginative, intuitive theories wither in the bright light of newly acquired information. (By analogy, theorizing on the nature of moon rocks was a relatively safe and enjoyable scientific game for a number of scientists until the Apollo astronauts brought a few samples of lunar reality back to earth!)

From the meager evidence now assembled, it appears likely that Precambrian climates were, on average, not dramatically different from those ranges of temperatures found over most of the past 600 million years—that is, not well below freezing nor much above the current high temperatures in deserts. Quite simply, over several billion years it was neither too cold nor too hot for the prokaryotic cells to have thrived over at least part of the earth; in the late Proterozoic Age, some 1 billion years ago, conditions were equable enough for a dramatic biological change to have occurred: the evolution of nucleated organisms such as micro-animals, plants or fungi known as *eucaryotes*. "The differences between these groups" (prokaryotes versus eucaryotes), explained evolutionary theorists Lynn Margulis and James Lovelock, "are far greater than the differences between animals and plants."[10] Indeed, these early life types, many varieties of which still exist, became the cellular building

13

blocks for multicelled organisms known as *metazoa*. These forms began to appear some 800 million years ago, shortly before the end of the Prepaleozoic Era. The metazoa, in turn, became an evolutionary foundation for more modern life forms. While climatic conditions may well have been extreme in parts of the world in the Precambrian—as they are in some places today—they still had to have been equable in enough places to have allowed the bacteria to continue to survive and the more complex biota to have evolved.

Other more direct evidence of environmental conditions, such as beds of ancient evaporites, tells us that there were some existing land or coastal shelf areas or enclosed basins that were arid at one time. It was the dryness that created these intense evaporation-induced deposits. Although some geological remains have been found, suggesting a few prolonged glacial periods (see the two Precambrian temperature dips in Figure 1.1), there is little evidence of widespread glaciation in the early earth history. It isn't clear, however, whether the relative absence of evidence indicates there was usually no ice present. It is possible that early glacial clues were either destroyed over time or simply haven't yet been found in the Precambrian geologic record.

A great deal of climatic inference has yet to be made from several available lines of geological evidence. But the very existence of a clear record showing the expanding evolution of life is the best—albeit indirect—proof we have that ancient climates over the first 3 to 4 billion years of earth history were not radically different from subsequent times. However, there is abundant evidence for relatively small changes of average surface temperatures—ranging from a few up to a few tens of degrees Celsius—that emerges from the rich geological records of the most recent billion years. These climatic changes were certainly important to the various organisms living through the fluctuations, since each species required an appropriate ecological niche in which to avoid extinction. Thus, although paleoclimatologist L. Frakes has sketched in his guess for global temperatures in the first 2 billion years of earth history in Figure 1.1, the range could well have been tens of degrees C warmer or colder on average than at present.

The Paleozoic Era

Although modern radiometric techniques tell us that the earth is more than 4 billion years old, we've already seen that

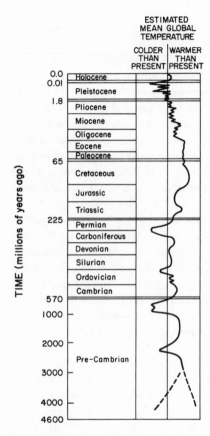

ESTIMATED MEAN GLOBAL TEMPERATURE

COLDER THAN PRESENT | WARMER THAN PRESENT

TIME (millions of years ago)

Figure 1.1

Generalized surface temperature changes of the earth over its geological history. Only relative departures from today's conditions are suggested, particularly for Precambrian times. [Source: L. A. Frakes, 1979, Climates Throughout Geologic Time *(Amsterdam: Elsevier), p. 261.]*

our knowledge of the planet's climate much before 600 million years ago is relatively scanty. Ancient life proliferated—that is, the kinds of species and the population of each type became increasingly numerous—during the Cambrian, the earliest period of the Paleozoic Era, although there are remains extant of very primitive life (mostly single-celled organisms) some 3.5 billions of years old. However, it wasn't until the Devonian Period, some 400 million years ago, that enough fossil evidence accumulated to provide much of a climatological interpretation. Figure 1.1, compiled by Frakes, summarizes the general climatic picture over geologic time.*

It was some 430 million years ago, during the Silurian Period,

---

*However, as noted by Frakes, this picture of paleotemperatures is very sketchy, "and relative values only are suggested."[11]

that plants appear to have emerged from the sea and established themselves on land.[12] The early Devonian land plants, while small and simple, were widely distributed: they ranged from the Falkland Islands to Spitsbergen to the interior of Asia and North America.* Given this range, either these primitive plants could tolerate wide temperature differences or the earth's surface temperature was much more uniform during the Devonian Period than it is today. If the latter was true, was the earth's temperature uniformly warm or cold? Most believe the answer is probably warm, since we find the earliest amphibians (during the late Devonian) widely distributed and we know that modern amphibians can only tolerate a very limited range of warm temperatures. If paleoclimatologists can compare early life to modern species and thereby assume "biological uniformitarianism," then the climate in eastern Greenland some 340 million years ago must have been quite temperate. We should note that drawing inferences about climate by comparing ancient life to life today is not easy. The continents were not in the same places they are today. More importantly, many organisms that lived during the Paleozoic Era are now extinct. Hence, it is difficult to judge what their ecological requirements were—and thus it is not clear to what extent biological uniformitarianism is a valid assumption.

Primitive jawless fish, which are characteristic of the Devonian Period, give further confirmation of the uniformity of climate.[13] These animals appeared widely, if not consistently, in parts of northern Europe, eastern Greenland, North America, Australia, and Antarctica. Given that information, one interpretation is that environmental conditions were probably about the same all over.

Amphibians dominated during the subsequent geologic period —the Carboniferous. The term Carboniferous means "abundance of coal." This abundance was noted early in what are now the states of Mississippi and Pennsylvania, hence two subperiods of the Carboniferous Period are called the Pennsylvanian and Mississippian. (Only in North America are the late and early Carboniferous referred to as the Pennsylvanian and Mississippian, respectively.) The continuing presence of amphibians during this period suggests that

---

*The Falkland Islands are located in the south Atlantic Ocean east of the tip of Argentina—as most people learned from banner headlines of war in 1982. Spitsbergen is east of Greenland; it is currently the northernmost inhabited land on earth. Coal is mined by its inhabitants. The presence of coal attests to the likelihood of warmer climate in the past.

fundamentally the climate changed very little—that is, warm temperatures continued. But the most significant evidence for a protracted warm period is the explosion in plant evolution and biomass in North America and Europe; this resulted in widespread coal, oil, and natural gas, the fossil fuel deposits.[14]

While the Northern Hemisphere seemed to remain warm beyond the Carboniferous Period (as evidenced by the continuing Carboniferous-type flora), the Southern Hemisphere experienced a long ice age during the late Carboniferous/early Permian Period, some 280 million years ago. Ice sheets covered portions of east-central South America, Antarctica, South Africa, peninsular India— then in the Southern Hemisphere—and Australia. Nevertheless, reptiles were apparently able to flourish; they were the most abundant land animals during the Permian, and adapted to the changing climatic (as well as geologic) conditions.

The Mesozoic Era

Continental land masses began to break apart in the late Triassic. This phenomenon, known as continental drift, is discussed later in this chapter. This breakup has been connected with a number of climatic events, also to be discussed. Flora in the Triassic Period, which followed the climatically nonuniform Permian, indicate a widespread return to warmer temperatures. Reptiles and amphibians continued to evolve and disperse widely, another indication of milder and more even climates.

Dinosaurs dominated the Jurassic and Cretaceous Periods [65 to 195 million years ago (mya)]. Their large size and nearly worldwide distribution in the fossil record suggest continued mild climates. By this time no substantial accumulations of ice appear to have been present on earth, even in the polar latitudes. In fact, during the Jurassic Period, coal (evidence of abundant plant life) was formed on what is now Mt. Weaver in Antarctica. As further evidence of mildness and lack of ice, sea levels were approximately 300 meters (960 feet) higher 100 million years ago than today, in part because the water was not tied up on land in huge ice sheets, as it is today.

By the late Cretaceous Period, many of the genera of modern trees and shrubs had appeared. The forerunners of modern corals were also living during the Cretaceous; they offer some of the best evidence for warm temperatures. By employing stable isotope

17

chemistry (discussed in detail in Chapter 2), paleoclimatologists can estimate the water temperatures in which these organisms lived, and hence the climate.

Paleo–Sea Levels: A Controversy
over Science and Business

If all ice on earth melted today, sea levels would rise some 70 meters (230 feet). At the height of the last ice age enough water was contained in the big ice sheets to lower sea level some 100 meters (328 feet). Thus, all the ice of the recent past could account for only 170 meters or so of sea level change, something like half of the 300- to 400-meter-higher sea levels found for the mid-Cretaceous, some 100 mya. However, the major reason usually cited for large sea level changes in the Mesozoic was the altered shape—and volume—of ocean basins associated with sea floor spreading and continental drift, which we will discuss shortly. Something of a major geological controversy has sprung up over this issue of paleo–sea levels.

The slow processes of ocean basin volume change have been compiled over the past two decades from the geologic record by a number of scientists.[15] These have been collected by L. Frakes and

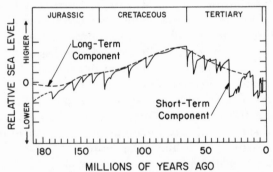

Figure 1.2

Estimates of sea-level changes over the past 180 million years, showing both long- and short-term components. [Sources: L. A. Frakes, 1979, Climates Through Geologic Time *(Amsterdam: Elsevier), pp. 208–210; and P. R. Vail, R. M. Mitchum, Jr.,*

and S. Thompson III, 1979, Seismic stratigraphy and global changes of sea level, Part 4: Global cycles of relative changes of sea level, in C. Payton (ed.), Seismic Stratigraphy— Applications to Hydrocarbon Exploration, *American Association of Petroleum Geologists Mem. 26:83–97.]*

are seen as the smoothly varying dashed line labeled "long-term component" in Fig. 1.2.[16] However, in 1977 something of a bomb-shell was dropped on the geological community by Exxon Produc-tion and Research Company scientist Peter Vail.[17] Because of their company's multibillion dollar petroleum exploration program, the Exxon researchers had access to many seismic studies and records of sedimentary rocks deposited on continental margins. Their ana-lyses of these data from all over the world led to the highly fluctuat-ing sea level reconstruction in Figure 1.2 labeled "short-term com-ponent." This result produced instant controversy for two reasons. First, it suggested that large, rapid sea level drops occurred during periods thought to be both warm and relatively ice-free. Such rapid lowering of sea levels was claimed to be comparable to or greater than changes occurring from ice ages to interglacial times more recently. For example, according to the Exxon results, an abrupt sea level fall occurred about 50 million years ago, which Frakes notes "coincides with a time of warming according to isotopic paleo tem-peratures."[18] Uncertainties in the methods of various conflicting researchers combine with missing data to leave most of these dis-putes over the short-term component still unsolved.

The second point of controversy over the Vail curve involves a clash of differing perspectives between academics and business ex-ecutives. Because these data can be quite helpful in pointing petro-leum explorers towards fossil deposits, a for-profit venture like Exxon is necessarily concerned with maintaining a competitive edge in its industry. Therefore, the Exxon scientists would only release their results and discuss their general methods, but withheld the supporting detailed evidence as proprietary. Academic scientists, while generally welcoming the Exxon work as a potentially major contribution, expressed considerable annoyance at being shielded from the underlying data since it could help to resolve some of the scientific controversies generated by the new findings. Science writer Richard Kerr, after talking to a large number of geologists, noted that "although appreciative, those outside of the oil industry have been frustrated . . . 'about not seeing the data'."[19]

The Cenozoic Era

In the late Cretaceous Period through the Eocene Epoch, some 55 million years ago, the earth underwent major changes. As shown later in this chapter, the continents were shifting and their present shapes and positions were emerging, mountain ranges were building, the continental seas were receding, and the era of mammals had taken hold. The dinosaurs—for reasons discussed more fully later on—and many other species disappeared suddenly at the end of the Cretaceous, but the smaller, more persistent Mesozoic reptiles—crocodiles and turtles, for example—hung on, as did many plants. Some mammals lived on the high plains, where temperatures could be extremely harsh, thus indicating that mammals are often ambiguous climatic indicators since they frequently tolerate a wide temperature range. During the Cenozoic Era, large climatic differences from place to place were established, defining the zones or ecological niches in which modern species could survive. All these kinds of evidence provide some general indicators of global climatic conditions over the past half billion years. Various estimates have been collected and generalized in Figure 1.1. Note the planetary cooling trend since mid-Cretaceous times indicated in this figure, and the onset of rapid fluctuations in the climate of our last geological period. Owing to the relative lack of sufficiently high-resolution paleoclimatic data sources, it is as yet unclear whether there were similarly large and rapid climatic fluctuations in the Tertiary, although the Exxon sea level curve has been so interpreted by some. Also, some fragmentary recent evidence suggests that fluctuating ice age/interglacial cycles may have occurred and that Antarctica may have been extensively glaciated before the conventionally accepted dates—13 to 16 million years ago—when most paleoclimatologists believe the transition from relatively unglaciated to a glaciated earth occurred. This has led to something of a controversy between oceanographers, who interpret the marine sediment record to support conventional beliefs, and some continental geologists, who find evidence for Antarctic glaciation ten or so millions of years earlier. "In the absence of overwhelming evidence from either the ocean or the Antarctic continent," Richard Kerr remarked, the debate is likely to continue.[20] It underscores for us how important it is to gain sufficient verifying data to eliminate incorrect hypotheses. There is abundant evidence to suggest that, as large volumes of permanent ice became established at the poles—shepherding in the recent geologic period—rapid alterations between ice ages and warm interglacials dominated the climatic picture.

This brings us up to the increasingly changeable climates of the recent geological past, the last epoch of which has seen the evolution of human societies. It is the mineral legacies—in particular fossil fuels—of our geologic and paleoclimatic past that have powered the development of modern industrial societies. Let us look briefly, then, at some of the climatic and other environmental factors responsible for our endowment of hydrocarbon fuels.

The Origin of Fossil Fuels

The origins of the fossil fuels we use today were deposits of organic matter—that is, former life. The first requisite for producing large organic deposits is high biological productivity, which in turn is enhanced by moderately warm and humid climates and high concentrations of CO_2 in the atmosphere. Both of these conditions appear to have been sufficient for high productivity for long periods during the past half-billion years.

Climate is not the only factor in the production of fossil fuels. But during the Carboniferous it was very favorable to their formation: there was sufficient precipitation and warmth to sustain lush and diverse vegetation. Russian climatologist Mikhail Budyko believes that atmospheric CO_2 concentrations from the Devonian right up to recent epochs was many times greater than it is today, an interesting but controversial opinion.[21] If it were true, the CO_2 would have enhanced photosynthesis and biological productivity as well as helping to maintain the warm climate through the greenhouse effect.

Starting at least 300 million years ago, when land plants were undergoing their rapid evolution, there were periods in which much of the world was covered with lush vegetation whose remains suggest that the climate was frequently warm and humid. There was an explosion of plant evolution; vegetation flourished in widespread regions of apparent tropical climate, accumulating and decomposing in bogs, swamps, delta plains, and shallow seas. Such swamps might have been similar to today's Okefenokee Swamp in Georgia or the Florida Everglades, although the species of plant or animal life were mostly different.

Production of Organic Matter

Most of the weight of living material is made when organisms convert inorganic carbon dioxide to sugar or starches (organic carbon compounds) by photosynthesis in green plants. For photosynthesis to be successful, appropriate nutrients (like nitrogen or phosphorus) and proper environmental conditions (like adequate sunlight, temperature, or salinity) must be available for each species. The energy to combine the CO_2 molecules with hydrogen molecules (which come from water, the other essential ingredient in photosynthesis) is supplied by the Sun's radiation. Later on, when a dead leaf decays or is burnt, for example, its organic hydrocarbon remains "giveback," as heat, the solar energy that during photosynthesis originally had combined the CO_2 and H_2O molecules into the C, H and O molecules (that is, the hydrocarbons). Some of the original CO_2 and H_2O are also returned to the environment in decay or burning, along with a host of other chemical compounds (like methane, carbon monoxide, and nitrogen or sulfur oxides).

Preservation of Organic Matter

Most of the organic matter formed as a result of photosynthesis is later decomposed by microbial action, and, as mentioned, the heat, H_2O, CO_2, and other decay products are then returned to the environment, becoming available to repeat the photosynthesis/decay cycle. However, if the organic matter falls to a place where there is little available oxygen to facilitate decay, it can be preserved longer than in an oxygen-rich environment. Such anoxic (that is, with little oxygen) environments are found today in the bottom of some deep lakes, in swamps, in some soils, or in some parts of the oceans. It is likely that only a small fraction (probably less than 1 percent) of the total photosynthetic production of past life is preserved today as fossil organic carbon compounds. These fossil fuel remains of paleolife were probably spared total decomposition because they were deposited in sufficiently anoxic environments before they had a chance to decay completely and thus be recycled into the paleoenvironment.

Burial of Organic Matter

Over millions of years, a rain of both organic and inorganic materials has built up sediment layers all over the earth. Many areas of land now well above sea level contain fossil remains that fell into shallow seas or bogs that existed in the geological past.

These deposits remind us how different environmental conditions have been, inasmuch as these strata of buried organic matter are often found today in the center of continental mountain ranges.

At present, sediment accumulates in the oceans at an average rate of about 40 meters (131 feet) per million years. The weathering, or erosion, of continents is a principal factor in determining the sedimentation rate. It also helps make available the nutrients needed to produce the marine plants whose remains make up the bulk of fossil fuels buried beneath the sea floor. The sedimentation rate has varied considerably in time and from place to place over geological history in a complicated, poorly understood way. Climate variations, life forms, and the location of continents are also important factors in this rate. For our purposes here, though, it is sufficient to point out that burial of organic matter is as important to the formation of fossil fuels as is the biological formation of organic carbon and its preservation in anoxic environments.

Trapping of Organic Fuels

Before any buried organic matter becomes a recoverable hydrocarbon fuel, it needs to be preserved in an appropriate rock formation long enough to be transformed to fuels. For oil and gas to be economically recoverable, there usually must be a geologic structure that can serve as an underground reservoir into which the mobile fossil fuels can migrate. Exploration geologists search for such rock structures, which may trap oil or gas in accessible reservoirs.

Here is one way that the sea level curve developed by Exxon researchers (labeled "short-term component" in Figure 1.2) can help find oil. Rising sea level results in a layer of sediment that laps onto the continental margin. When sea level retreats, this layer may be partly exposed to erosion that removes a portion of it. If the next rise in sea level covers the layer with mud, which later becomes a hard impermeable shale layer, then a potential trap exists for petroleum. Now suppose an offshore Exxon test well indicates that a particular rock formation were a likely source of petroleum. The combined knowledge of sea level variations (where potential traps may exist) and the seismic records would allow the exploration geologist to trace this formation up the slope to where a shale cap may have trapped the mobile fossil fuel.

23

Carbon Dioxide and Fossil Fuels:
Coevolutionary Links to Climate

As the debris accumulates and is buried, rising pressure and temperature causes chemical changes to the unoxidized plants' hydrocarbon molecules. Coal, oil, and gas—the hydrocarbon fossil fuels—are thus created. This process takes millions of years and has been occurring over the past several hundred million years. But in a matter of a century or so, people are unlocking these fossil fuels and releasing the stored carbon atoms and chemical energy to the atmosphere. Hence, as we've just seen, much of the carbon dioxide and solar energy used for photosynthesis and plant growth that were taken out of the paleoenvironment over hundreds of millions of years are merely being returned to the present environment, but at a much faster rate. Thus, CO_2 is building up in the atmosphere; and heavily industrialized regions, where heat from fuel burning is concentrated, are generally warmer than surrounding areas. Carbon dioxide and fossil fuels comprise a bridge that quite literally ties our climatic future to a half-billion years of the climatic, biologic, and geologic past. A common element of all three has been mentioned already several times: continental drift.

Continental Drift

We noted earlier that the rates of formation, preservation, and transformation of organic matter to fossil fuels depended on CO_2 concentration, the climate, sea levels, and continental positions over geologic time. One of the most exciting discoveries of modern geology connects all four: the concept of continental drift. Not only is this finding an intellectual achievement, but it has economic and political significance in our own time since it is central to strategies used by petroleum explorers, who spend billions of dollars each year to search for fossil fuels. Just as maps of sunken treasure guided legendary characters to riches, so are modern maps of paleogeography and paleoclimate clues to nature's buried fossil fuel treasures.[22] Although there are many missing details and unanswered questions—and even a few doubters besides biblical fundamentalists—we can be relatively certain that the view of geological history shaped by the notion of continental drift is reasonable, since a mass of evidence exists for drifting continents.[23] This view of geological history is described briefly below.

Paleocontinental Positions

Very little evidence is available with which to reconstruct maps of continental sizes or positions much before several hundred million years ago. It was probably not until the end of the Archean Age, some 2.5 billion years ago, that the earth's surface was covered by much of anything other than water. Undoubtedly, volcanic islands and other relatively temporary land masses must have been present over the early part of the Precambrian, but not until the end of the Precambrian is there much evidence left to go on. Let's go over some of the findings for the past 200 million years or so, for which a great deal of evidence is available.

About 200 million years ago (mya) the continents were closely joined as Pangaea, or "all lands," a supercontinent that was surrounded by Panthalassa, "all seas", which was the ancestral Pacific. A small ocean wedged between the continents has been called the Tethys Sea, named for the wife of Oceanus, who in Greek myth was the mother of the seas. Tethys, the ancestral Mediterranean, separated what was to become Africa and a conglomerate called Eurasia. After some 20 million years of drift (about 180 mya), the northernmost continents, known collectively as Laurasia, split away from the southern group, Gondwana, named after a geological province in east central India. Through the Jurassic Period, the North Atlantic widened considerably. It can just be seen on the map showing continental positions 160 mya in Figure 1.3.[24] The shaded areas on this map were above the sea level then. Present latitude and longitude lines are drawn on the continents to indicate how the continental positions have changed over time.

Gondwana started to break up around this time too, at the end of the Jurassic, some 140 mya. India, discernible near the bottom of the map for 160 mya in Figure 1.3, moved toward Asia during the period from 140 to 100 mya, with Madagascar attached. Africa-South America was becoming isolated from Antarctica-Australia. The South Atlantic was about to be created. Rotating clockwise, relative to Africa, the Eurasian landmass had begun to cut off the eastern end of the Tethys Sea. South America separated from the west coast of Africa at about 124 mya, at the beginning of the Cretaceous Period. In the middle of the Cretaceous, some 100 mya,

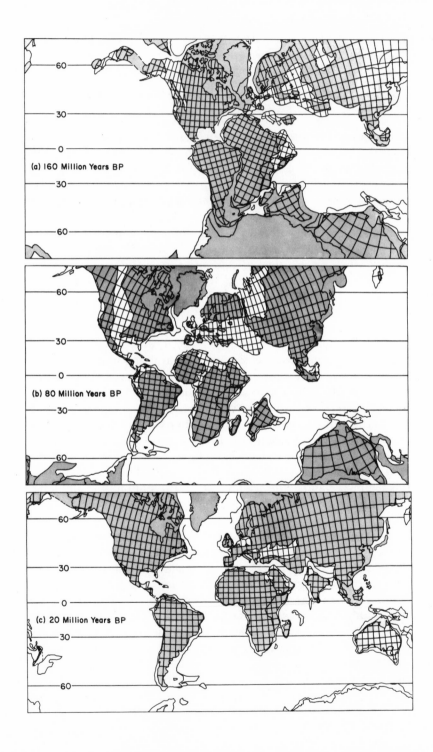

(a) 160 Million Years BP

(b) 80 Million Years BP

(c) 20 Million Years BP

Figure 1.3

Three "snapshots" of paleocontinental positions reconstructed from geological data on continental drift. The shaded areas were above sea levels at the times for each reconstruction. Present latitude and longitude lines are drawn on the continents to indicate how the conti- *nental positions have changed over time. [Source: E. J. Barron, C. G. A. Harrison, J. L. Sloan, II, and W. W. Hay, 1981, Paleogeography, 180 million years ago to the present, Eclogae Geologicae Helvetiae 74 No. 2:443–470, plates 2, 6, and 9.]*

about a quarter of the land now above sea level in the Northern Hemisphere was submerged in shallow seas, including the middle of North America, near what today is called the mile-high city of Denver, Colorado. (Such former shallow seas, incidentally, are ideal potential locations for fossil fuels.)

Toward the end of the Cretaceous, the South Atlantic established itself as a major ocean and the Mediterranean Sea became recognizable as well. India continued its northward drift. Madagascar became isolated from India between 80 and 100 mya. A very important climate-related feature can be seen on the map for 80 mya in Figure 1.3. The continental margins of Antarctica and Australia and South America are touching, blocking any significant flow of water around Antarctica. Today an ocean current flows all around the polar continent, isolating it thermally from warm-water flows in the South Atlantic and South Pacific. At 80 mya, those warm currents could have flowed unimpeded all the way to the margins of Antarctica, warming it just as the Gulf Stream warms the British Isles today. But Australia remained connected to Antarctica until about 55 mya, and the Antarctic Peninsula was attached to South America until more recent times.

The continents have continued to shift since the end of the Cretaceous Period, 65 mya, when the dinosaurs, as well as many other species, mysteriously became extinct. During the geologically brief era from 65 mya to the present, nearly half the present ocean floor was created. Also, large quantities of fossil fuels were deposited in the last half of the Cretaceous, some of them in the shallow seas of such now-high lands as the Rocky Mountain region of the United States. These mountain states didn't rise much above sea level until about 60 mya. By 20 mya, India's northward drift had caught up with Asia. This relatively recent collision resulted in the building of today's highest mountains, the Himalayas. Australia and South America parted from Antarctica, leaving that continent isolated and centered roughly on the South Pole.

The Evidence for Continental Drift

Although there are many remaining uncertainties, the concept of continental drift revolutionized earth sciences in the 1960s when its basic principles became widely accepted by both geologists and geophysicists. Yet the original proponent of the concept, German meterologist and geophysicist Alfred Wegener (who also coined the word Pangaea), first introduced it in the 1920s.*

Continental drift had been a widespread notion for centuries before Wegener. When maps of the Old and New Worlds were drawn, geographers noticed what a close jigsawlike fit some of the continents, such as South America and Africa, would make—if only they could be moved! And, throughout the nineteenth century, geologists discovered similar rock and mineral layers, fossils, and other peculiar matches in corresponding places on different continents. For example, there are signs of the Permian glaciation in Southern Hemisphere countries such as South America and Africa, now an ocean apart (see Figure 1.3), which led some to wonder whether these continents were once joined as part of Gondwana, positioned and glaciated near the South Pole.[25] The evidence includes similar patterns of rock grooves etched by glaciers dragging boulders along the rock pavement. From these grooves scientists have been able to determine the direction in which the paleoglaciers moved. Normally, continental ice sheets move seaward or downslope, but relative to the present continental positions, the glaciers appear to have moved inland or upslope, which is contrary to glacial physics (and gravity). If the southern continents are adjusted to their Permian-Era positions, however, the direction of glacial movement is indeed mostly toward the sea or away from the pole.

Skeptics scorned such proof and the theory the evidence supported. In the 1920s the president of the American Philosophical Society in Philadelphia proclaimed continental drift as "utter damned rot!"[26] And there the matter stood until after World War II. As it turned out, two more revolutionary developments were needed to give Wegener's ideas credibility: direct physical proof that the continents had moved (and that they are still moving), and an explanation of that movement.

*Wegener is generally considered the first to offer a fairly complete set of arguments for the concept of continental drift, although others before him had similar but less developed ideas.

Sea Floor Spreading   Physical evidence for movement of continents came with the discovery in the 1950s of a midocean ridge system, some 65,000 kilometers of submarine mountain ranges that virtually circled the globe.* This mountain chain was shown to have a narrow, deep rift along its center line. Up through that rift wells the earth's hot magma, which, as it solidifies, spreads outward and forms new crustal material. This process is called sea floor spreading, and by the 1960s it was verified by paleomagnetic techniques. As new rocks form, they become permanently magnetized, aligning their magnetic fields in the direction the earth's field is pointing at that particular time. When the earth's field reverses, as it does periodically, these reversals show up on the sea floor in parallel stripes on both sides of ocean ridges. Oceanographers can determine just how fast the sea floor is spreading by measuring the distance from the rift to the magnetic reversals whose ages are approximately known. (Such estimates of sea floor spreading rates were used to derive the long-term component of sea level change shown in Figure 1.2.)

The paleomagnetic evidence was gathered when magnetometers were dragged through the water by research ships back and forth over the sea floor "stripes" to determine their polarity. This is still proxy evidence for sea floor spreading. Direct evidence was obtained in the late 1960s when the *Glomar Challenger* extracted cores from the Mid-Atlantic Ridge as part of the Deep Sea Drilling Project. As predicted, the ocean floor was youngest at the rift, and progressively older farther away on either side of the divide.[27]

What happens to old crust when new crust is formed? And how does this renewal of crust affect the continents? The second revolutionary development that gave credibility to Wegener's theory—plate tectonics—resulted from attempts to answer these and other questions.

The Theory of Plate Tectonics

A distinction needs to be made between the observed facts supporting the existence of drifting continents and hypotheses

---

*Other direct evidence can be found by measuring the relative north-south separation of landmarks on either side of the fault system that parallels the California coast. Mt. Diablo on the American plate is drifting several centimeters each year southward relative to Mt. Tamalpais on the Pacific plate, just a few dozen kilometers to the west.

to explain the causes of these facts. A similar distinction can be made in the example of biological evolution. The *fact* of evolution is backed up by literally millions of bits of fossil and other more modern evidence, even though the *mechanism*—Darwin's natural selection being the classical scientific theory—is still very much debated by scientists (and certainly challenged by creationists).[28] The fact that the theories explaining the processes of these phenomena are not nearly complete does not negate the vast amount of evidence supporting the existence of the phenomena themselves. In a March 29, 1982 cover story, *Newsweek* magazine quoted evolutionist Stephen Jay Gould on this point: "Evolution is a fact, like apples falling out of trees. Darwin proposed a theory, natural selection, to explain that fact. Newton's theory of gravitation was eventually superseded by [Einstein's] general relativity. But apples didn't stop in midair while physicists debated the question." Similarly, regardless of how correct the theory of plate tectonics turns out to be, the evidence for continental drift is so pervasive that its existence is accepted by nearly all knowledgeable geologists and geophysicists.

The notion of drifting plates was introduced by Toronto geophysicist J. Tuzo Wilson in 1965.[29] According to the theory of plate tectonics, the earth's crust is divided into huge segments or plates that travel on its pliable mantle. These plates of continental and oceanic crust are thousands of kilometers wide and up to 130 kilometers (80 miles) thick. When the plates move away horizontally from one another, they form fissures (the midocean ridges) through which new crust can well up. When such fissures occur on land (one example is the Afar rift in Africa), continents begin to split. When plates collide, one of two things happens: they either buckle to form a mountain range or one *subducts*—dives under—the other. Heat and pressure then melt some of the subducted material, which eventually reforms and upwells at fissures as new crust.

It is generally the ocean crustal plate that gets buried and recycled, because it is denser and thinner than continental crustal plate. Whenever the two kinds of plate collide the lighter, continental one overrides the oceanic plate and forces it to subduct. Hence, oceanic crust is continually being buried and recycled, which accounts for the young age of the sea floor relative to the age of the continents —the average age of the ocean floor is only 106 million years, while the oldest terrestrial rocks have been dated at almost 4 billion years ago. When plates of continental crust collide, as India and Asia have, mountain ranges are formed, in this case the Himalayas.

Earthquakes also occur much more frequently at plate boundaries than elsewhere, which provides further support of the theory. Indeed, both the existence of continental drift and the theory of plate tectonics enjoy wide acceptance from geophysical scientists.

Continental Drift and Climate

The important point for our purposes is that the surface of the earth is constantly evolving. Earlier, we implied that continental drift was somehow connected to the era of more frequent ice ages. At least one climatic coincidence can be linked to the rearrangement of the continents—the isolation and subsequent glaciation of Antarctica.

Through much of the first half of the Tertiary Period, some 35 to 65 mya, which was before Antarctica was isolated, many species of deciduous (seasonal) and coniferous (evergreen) trees were present there.[30] Wood fragments on the West Antarctica islands attest to this fact. Hence, temperatures in Antarctica—or at least at the margins of the continent, for that is where the fossils have been found—were much warmer than today, by perhaps 10° to 15°C (18° to 27°F).[31] In fact, as Pangaea was just beginning to break up some 200 million years ago, there was apparently a much smaller difference in temperatures between the equator and the poles than exists today—that is, there was a relatively low equator-to-pole thermal gradient.

However, 55 million years ago, Australia began to separate from Antarctica, which prefaced a marked climatic change on the latter continent. A circum-Antarctic ocean current of major significance began to develop around 30 million years ago. The flow of this current around the continent has been unimpeded since the Drake Passage between South America and the Antarctic Peninsula opened up, and a seaway was created between Australia-Tasmania and East Antarctica. Again, the Deep Sea Drilling Project provided evidence of sea floor spreading in this connection. Cores were taken in this area to date the sea floor and find out when shallow-water barriers to the circum-Antarctic flow were eliminated.[32] This circular flow tends to isolate warmer waters to the north, which, as mentioned earlier, probably led to colder waters surrounding Antarctica. The development of Antarctic sea ice almost 40 mya and an ice cap later on are thus probably more than coincidental with the isolation of Antarctica. By 4 million to 7 million years ago, Antarctica was certainly heavily glaciated, although some think it may have been ice covered tens of millions of years earlier; the ice there today ties up enough water to coincide with about a 55-meter (180-foot) decline in sea level.

Along with the evidence for the glaciation of Antarctica and the intense development of the Antarctic circumpolar current at this time, evidence exists for intensification of another major ocean current—the Gulf Stream. The velocity of this current, a major feature of North Atlantic Ocean circulation, has fluctuated in the past. (We discuss the Gulf Stream more fully in Chapter 4.) Evidence of its changing strength over millions of years lies in the varying rates of erosion of the Blake Plateau off the coast of Florida, over which the Gulf Stream flows.[33]

While the currents were intensifying and the continents rearranging themselves to approximately their present positions, sharply differentiated climatic zones were being established between the equator and the poles. Individual plant and animal species that had once been widely distributed settled into more restricted regions with appropriate warmer or cooler climates, depending on their ecological requirements (which also change as species evolve biologically). The high biological productivity that helped to create coal and oil beds so prevalent in the Cretaceous Period waned with the planetary cooling—and possible reduction in CO_2 concentration—that arose in the transition to our era. Thus the earth eased into the Quaternary—the 2-million- to 3-million-year period in which major ice expansions and contractions have recently recurred roughly every 100,000 years.* We are currently living through an interglacial epoch (the Holocene) within the Quaternary —an episode that many believe is already sinking back down to another glacial age. Since continental positions have shifted relatively little over the past few million years, some other explanation must be sought if we are to understand the causes of the many ice ages during the Pleistocene. There is no lack of hypotheses, as Chapters 2 and 7 will show. Next, we take a close look at how scientists reconstruct the climates of the last half-million years, during which ice ages came and went and from which civilizations ultimately emerged.

*If the Exxon curve for the short-term component of sea level fluctuations (shown in Figure 1.2) is even partially correct, and if it reflects rapid glaciation events rather than other nonclimatic causes, then the earth "eased" into the Quaternary only in the sense of the long-term component shown in Figure 1.2 or the generalized temperature trends shown in Figure 1.1.

2 The Coming of Ice: The Pleistocene

Piecing together a picture of Pleistocene climates is like assembling a puzzle in which there is no cover picture on the box, some pieces are missing, and many of the pieces are made of different materials. The missing pieces are bits of evidence that have been lost or are yet to be discovered; the pieces made of varying materials represent the different types of evidence paleoclimatologists search for, such as ancient ocean sediments, soil deposits, ice layers, fossil insects, and pollen. In this chapter we will select a number of examples of these kinds of evidence to illustrate how the history of the Pleistocene can be reconstructed from these fragments of climatic history. We also hope to show how formidable challenges have been met and overcome by scientists working with very limited information. Like other kinds of historians, paleoclimatologists holding the same facts nevertheless may disagree over many details on what the past was like; and they have much different visions of what the puzzle's missing pieces may be like.

After reviewing some of the history of heated controversy over the portrayal of the Pleistocene, we will turn to the principal techniques paleoclimatologists use to piece together the climatic past. In order to show—not just state—how reliable inferences from each of these techniques are, we will need to discuss a few fairly complicated methods in some detail. But only if we know what the composite strength of the evidence is can we put together a confident overview of the ice age climates. And, if history remains, as it so often does, the key to predicting the future, then it is imperative that we develop some understanding of what has happened and why in order to estimate what will happen next.

33

The Historical Debate

The idea that the earth experienced a glacial age—that in fact some 30 percent of the earth's total land area was once covered by ice—was one not quickly embraced by early geologists. *Erratic boulders* appearing in places far from their points of origin and piles of unsorted rocks and sediments were interpreted by eighteenth-century geologists as having been transported and deposited by the biblical flood. The idea that, thousands of years ago, rocks were dragged over the landscape by glaciers, scratching deep grooves along the way, was ridiculed. The scratches were more likely made by a "cart . . . wheel . . . the day before yesterday," one satirist wrote.[1]

Some early geologists, however, did not subscribe to the "great flood" theory. Ironically, one Swiss skeptic of the biblical theory was a minister. In 1787, Bernard Friederich Kuhn asserted that huge erratic boulders could not have been transported hundreds of miles by a flood. Rather, he said, they were evidence of an ancient glaciation. James Hutton, the Scottish geologist, agreed with Kuhn, and several other scientists developed glacial theories independently.

In the early 1800s, simple observation had already convinced those who lived near still-existing glaciers that more extensive ice sheets had once covered large areas. Swiss mountaineer Jean-Pierre Perraudin noted that glaciers, which were then found only in the higher, southern regions of the Val de Bagnes, had once filled the whole valley. As a compromise between the advocates of flood and the advocates of ice, English geologist Charles Lyell suggested in the 1830s that icebergs and ice rafts laced with boulders had drifted along in the great flood.*

Yet Lyell's theory was doubted, too, because almost no marine fossil shells existed among the material he said was deposited by the biblical flood. However, some drift deposits (debris transported and dumped by glaciers) did contain such fossils; they became known as *shelly drifts*. These drifts were disturbing evidence to advocates of glaciation, for they bolstered the theory of the marine origin of rock transport. Self-made Scottish scientist James Croll gave a creative

---

*It was Lyell who coined the word Pleistocene, which became synonymous with ice age. However, Lyell intended the term to refer to an interval, from which many of the fossils represent species living now.

twist to the interpretation of the problematic shelly drifts; in 1865 he explained them by hypothesizing that ice sheets had once moved over areas now covered by shallow seas. Scraping the remains of the shallow ocean floor, the ice sheets had picked up the shells and deposited them at their current locations. The marine fossils, Croll decided, were simply erratic boulders on a smaller scale.

However, it took the persistence of Louis Agassiz to finally convince nineteenth century geologists of the glacial theory. Like Perraudin, Agassiz was firmly convinced that glacial ice masses had once blanketed the Swiss mountains. So in 1837 he assembled a group of his skeptical colleagues and took them to the Jura Mountains, where rock pavement has been polished smooth by a glacier. The spot Agassiz chose was miles from any existing ice; he was sure that the rocks there were conclusive evidence of past glaciation.

Scientists of the Swiss Society of Natural Sciences derided Agassiz's notion of past glaciation. Nevertheless, Agassiz dramatically pressed his theory:

> The ground of Europe, previously covered with tropical vegetation and inhabited by herds of great elephants, enormous hippopatami, and gigantic carnivora became suddenly buried under a vast expanse of ice . . . sunrays rising over the frozen shore . . . were met only by the whistling of northern winds and the rumbling of the crevasses as they opened across the surface of that huge ocean of ice.[2]

Such a catastrophic view was in keeping with the geological outlook of the times. Many believed that earth history was a series of epochs, each of which ended with some incredible disaster. Agassiz's version of the catastrophe theory was that the epochs were closed by the ice ages.

While Swiss scientists would not agree with this theory, Agassiz did get some backing from Reverend William Buckland, an Oxford geologist. But the rest of the British geological community took another twenty years to accept Agassiz's view. Most geologists could not imagine ice sheets of the magnitude Agassiz described. The potential for huge ice sheets was accepted only after the extent of Greenland ice was mapped in an 1852 expedition. Later in the nineteenth century, the Antarctic ice sheet's dimensions were also established. More and more polar expeditions and observations of valley glaciers helped seal the acceptance of the glacial theory.

By the mid-1860s, Agassiz's glacial theory had become generally accepted.

During the affluent Victorian era, geologists hunted worldwide for glacial evidence. They were able to map the extent of the ice age in North America, for example, by finding deposits of till—an unsorted mixture of debris and rocks ranging in size from boulders to pebbles. Till is deposited at the snout, or terminal end, of the glacier in what is known as an *end moraine*.* The end moraine of the last Pleistocene glacier complex in North America was found to be a ridge that stretched intermittently from eastern Long Island to the state of Washington. This ridge, which defined the southernmost margin of the ice sheet, reached some 50 meters (164 feet) at some points.

Glacier Formation, Movement, and Connection to Sea Level

Glaciers come in three general types that can be distinguished by their size and location. The smallest occur in tropical- or temperate-latitude mountainous areas such as the Alps, Rocky Mountains, and Himalayas. These *mountain glaciers*—also called *valley glaciers*—carve out rounded U-shaped valleys, whereas valleys with rivers flowing through tend to be V-shaped. Medium-sized glaciers are referred to as *ice fields*. They typically occur between mountains on highland plateaus, as in southeastern Alaska and on Baffin Island in Canada. The third and largest type of glacier is the *ice sheet*, which at its largest covers continents. Today, continental-scale ice sheets exist in the polar regions on Antarctica and Greenland. During the ice ages, ice sheets covered large parts of North America, Asia, and Europe.

By observing active glaciers, geologists were able to deduce how glacial ice is formed. Layers of snow that fall on the glacier are compacted under the weight of succeeding snowfalls; neighboring ice crystals then grow together to become single, larger crystals. This happens especially fast if the ice is at the melting point, as it is in a temperate glacier. When subjected to sufficient pressure, ice

---

*There are also *ground moraines*, which, like end moraines, are composed of till. However, ground moraines are not as pronounced as end moraines; they are usually thinner and have gentler slopes.

flows, but slowly, of course, relative to liquid water. As the ice thickness builds, it begins to flow outward under its own weight. As it flows, the glacier accumulates loose rocks along the way, freezing them in its lower layers. It is this transport of rocks in the lower layer that is responsible for smoothing or scratching the rock pavement over which the glacier moves. When the glacier melts, it releases as till its cargo of trapped materials, some of which has been transported for long distances.

Glaciologists have studied the physics of glaciers and discovered their sizes and shapes are governed by certain internal-flow laws and external influences.[3] For instance, the ultimate size of a glacier depends on the geography of the land on which it forms and flows, and how much ice melts (or breaks off as icebergs, should the glacier end at the sea).

Oceans provided the huge amounts of water needed to build the ice sheets. Scottish geologist Charles Maclaren was probably the first to recognize this connection. He hypothesized in 1841 that the water "necessary to form the . . . ice would depress the ocean about 800 feet" (245 meters). Maclaren's colleagues considered his estimate to be wild speculation. Today we know that in fact sea level 20,000 years ago was below present levels by some 100 meters (328 feet) or so. Scientists still debate the precise figure; the bulk of the estimates range from about 50 to 200 meters (164 to 656 feet). Several land bridges between continents were exposed by fallen sea levels, and these allowed land animals, including people, to migrate to otherwise isolated places. These bridges—and perhaps a solid covering of sea ice—afforded connections between England and Ireland, Alaska and Siberia, Siberia and Japan, Australia and New Guinea, Australia and Tasmania, and India and Sri Lanka (Ceylon).

Changing land forms (such as coastlines) during the Pleistocene were not solely a result of ocean water being tied up in or released from the ice sheets. Several other factors were involved. The weight of the glaciers had an effect too. These thick ice sheets exert tremendous pressure; they depress the land, making the area underneath them subside. Changing the shape of the land then alters the flow rate of the glacier, which has proved to be an important factor in ice age cycles (see Chapter 7).

This subsidence also forces the land to alter its position relative to the seas, causing shorelines to change relative to the sea level. Rubber rafts floating in a swimming pool make a good analogy to the continents. If we were to place dome-shaped blocks of ice in the middle of the rafts they would sink slightly in the middle and bulge out and rise slightly at the sides, and the water level on the sides would change because of this distortion. If we removed the ice, the middle of the rafts would spring back up and the sides would return to their original positions. Such effects occur on the continents over geologic time—that is, very slowly. For one thing, the ice is not suddenly lifted; it melts—or even surges—rather slowly. Thus, the continents rebound slowly, a process that can go on for many thousands of years after the ice has disappeared.[4] Geologists call this phenomenon *glacial rebound* or *isostatic adjustment.* In the Scandinavian Gulf of Bothnia, for example, glacial rebound is still occurring. The once depressed land is regaining its contour at the approximate rate of 1 centimeter (0.39 inches) per year.

The vertical movement of the earth's crust in the Gulf of Bothnia makes the Baltic Sea level *appear* to be dropping. This is known as a *relative* change in sea level; such a change is local or regional and is recorded in relation to the land, which may be either uplifting or subsiding. Worldwide changes in sea level—which occur when sea water is locked up in extensive ice sheets, for example—are called *eustatic* sea level changes. Just as glaciers have weight, so does water. Removing sea water can result in rebound of the sea floor, which in turn can affect sea level. When the amount of water is altered in the ocean, the sea floor and continental margins adjust to the changing weight by moving up or down. This movement can change the volume of ocean basins, thus further altering sea levels.

To recapitulate, there are actually three major factors that contribute to global sea levels: the shape of the ocean basins and continental margins; the volume of world sea water; and the distribution and amount of ice. Hence, we can see that when observing sea level fluctuations from our landed vantage point we must consider several factors. For instance, when a glacier melts at least two things occur: the water once locked in the glacier returns to the sea, raising its volume, and the land under the former ice begins to rebound, making the sea level at nearby coastlines appear to fall. The net effect varies considerably from place to place, although a rapid, large-scale melting is generally experienced everywhere as sea level rises.

As geologists had known for some time that more than one glacial advance had occurred during the Pleistocene, it is natural that some would have assumed that oscillations occurred in sea levels as well.[5] But direct physical evidence for the magnitude and timing of sea level changes came only in the past few decades. Changing sea levels of the Pleistocene are recorded in layers, or *terraces,* of coral reefs that form in the shallow waters off coastlines.

Coral Reef Terraces: A Record of Fluctuating Sea Level

Corals primarily live in shallow water—less than 100 meters (328 feet) or so deep—because their symbiotic partners, one-celled algae called zooxanthellae, require sunlight for photosynthesis.[6] The photosynthetic products are a major food supply for the coral organisms, which in return provide the algae with a secure physical shelter.

The shallow waters inhabited by corals have fluctuated over geological time, sometimes exposing and killing coral reefs, at other times submerging them so far below the surface that not enough sunlight for photosynthesis reached the zooxanthellae so that the corals died with the algae. Thus, the fossil remains of ancestral coral reefs are potential clues to the climatic past, or at least to fluctuations in sea levels.

Like all fossil indicators, coral reef terraces are imperfect measures of climatic variations. Their remains do not correlate exactly with past sea level. Still, scientists can find useful relationships—for example, between notches in existing reefs and periods of constant sea levels: waves at a constant level tend to lap against the same part of an above-sea-level fossil coral reef and help to erode away a wedge. More importantly, researchers can also relate rising or lowering sea levels to terraces or steps of coral reefs where a succession of old shorelines is left behind.

While these remains may seem like direct evidence of past sea level variation, quantitative results depend on which theory of reef formation is used. One hypothesis states that islands such as Barbados, where there are a number of distinct coral reef terraces, intermittently rise out of the sea. Each time such a tectonically active island rises significantly, one reef section is exposed to the air and dies. Then, another terrace develops along the new shoreline at a lower spot on the island. Hence, each terrace represents a separate incidence of reef growth at a certain sea level at a certain time. Climatic change enters the discussion when we consider that the combination of island uplift and sea level changes can occur simultaneously. In that case, scientists can deduce the history of sea level changes from the elevations of the terraces—provided that they know the rate at which the island has risen out of the sea.

A second theory of reef terrace formation postulates that terraces have been carved out of a continuously growing reef by the action of waves. This process is appropriately called erosional, for as the island rises, erosion carves out a new terrace at each new uplift stage. In whatever way they form, terrace levels are identified stratigraphically—that is, by their overlapping and relative positioning. The terraces are dated using carbon-14 and thorium-uranium methods. Unfortunately, C^{14} dating is only reliable for up to 40,000 years or so, and thorium-uranium dating, while promising, still has many technical problems.[7] Because of the uncertainties involved in relating reefs to past sea levels, the evidence at one set of reefs must be compared with terraces at other locations as well as with other reconstructions of sea level using other techniques.

In 1971, a group of American and Australian scientists traveled to New Guinea to collect coral samples from the Huon Peninsula for later laboratory dating. Pounding with sledgehammers and axes, they broke off "hundreds of protrusions from promising ledges."[8] They dated several terraces, each terrace, the scientists concluded, representing an indication of a high sea level stand at the time it was built. Major terraces were dated—or dates simply assumed—as follows, beginning with the youngest, nearest the present coast: 5 to 9 thousand years ago (kya); 29 kya; 35 to 42 kya; 61 kya; 85 kya; 107 kya; and 125 kya. The researchers concluded that sea level oscillations recorded on the peninsula resulted from eustatic sea level changes caused by glacial changes. (Terraces implying sea level oscillations are also seen at other sites around the world, an example of which we will discuss below.)

Interpreting the volume of worldwide sea level change based on reef terraces is complicated, we noted, because such absolute change is superimposed on the relative sea level changes due to tectonic uplifting of the island. The Huon Peninsula is tectonically active, and tremors have been known to be associated with lifting island coasts up from the sea.[9] In order to interpret by how much sea levels altered to create each terrace, geologists must assume how much the islands were rising over time. It is not even clear, although it usually is assumed, that uplift has been constant—at a relatively slow rate of about 1 millimeter (0.039 inches) or less per year.[10] This represents an uplift of 100 meters (328 feet) in 100,000 years. Sea level variations from glacial changes occur typically at

40

rates ten times faster. Thus, reef terraces up to 100 meters or so in height can record several large sea level fluctuations that occurred over the past 100,000 or so years.

The results from the Huon terraces would be more convincing if the sea level rises suspected in New Guinea were correlated with similar evidence in different parts of the world. Thus researchers have looked to other islands for confirmation. Barbados is one.

Like New Guinea, Barbados is tectonically active, a factor that must be taken into account in the measurement of its sea level changes. Correlations can be made between these islands since it is highly unlikely that the two, in opposite hemispheres and different oceans, would be moving vertically in concert. Barbados sits about 240 kilometers (150 miles) east of the string of Windward Islands in the Caribbean Sea. Three distinct coral reef terraces there suggest that high sea levels occurred around 82,000 years ago, 105,000 years ago, and 125,000 years ago.[11] This evidence correlates broadly with the dates of the three major Huon terraces. But again, assumptions of uplift rates and the difficulties in interpreting each terrace's date still keep scientists arguing over the meaning of the results, particularly by how much and when the sea level changes occurred.

Nevertheless, such estimates have been made. For example, by assuming from other evidence that sea levels were about 6 meters (20 feet) higher 125,000 years ago than today, and by assuming a constant uplift rate, Barbados terraces that formed about 82,000 and 105,000 years ago would have represented separate high stands of sea level still some 13 meters (42.7 feet) below present levels.[12] For similar assumptions, New Guinea terraces for the comparable dates suggested comparable sea levels.[13]

Researchers must make certain assumptions about the rates of change in uplift rates. In order to minimize errors in such guess work they must check changes in a number of places using vastly different techniques. We explore a number of these methods shortly. However, we will now mention one independent corroboration, at least for the 125,000-, 105,000-, and 80,000-year-old high sea level stands inferred from Barbados and New Guinea data. A variety of lines of evidence suggests that these dates and sea levels inferred from the two tectonically active islands are reasonably in line with independent findings in Bermuda, which is tectonically inactive.[14] However, the quantitative inferences are still subjects of debate.

41

Paleoclimatic Evidence Using Stable Isotopes

It is imperative to compare reconstructions from independent techniques in order to gain confidence in climatic inferences from single lines of evidence. Shortly we will do this. But first it is necessary to explain a powerful tool common to many of these independent techniques. It ranks near radiometric dating in importance as a principal method for paleoclimatologists to decipher the geological record.

It is fortunate for paleoclimatologists that some 570 million years ago marine organisms all over the world began secreting calcium carbonate (limestone, $CaCO_3$) shells. These shells, sometimes called walls or external skeletons, served as protection against predators. As it turned out, they became invaluable for scientific research. In 1947, geochemist Harold Urey, then at the University of Chicago, reasoned that it should be possible to use the oxygen atoms incorporated in these shells as an indicator of past ocean temperatures. Urey had demonstrated (theoretically at least) that the amount of the heavier oxygen isotope (O^{18}) that the organism extracts from the surrounding sea water depends on the temperature of the water; the colder the water, the greater the preference for O^{18} compared to the lighter isotope, O^{16}.* Hence, Urey figured that past water temperatures could be determined by measuring the O^{18}/O^{16} ratio in fossil $CaCO_3$ skeletons. These are called *isotopic temperatures*. [15]

Paleoclimatologists use an oxygen isotope ratio index, δO^{18}, which is simply the relative difference between the ratio O^{18}/O^{16} of the water, ice, or silicate or carbonate fossil sample and this ratio for today's standard conditions.† δO^{18} is a small number, typically a few tens of parts per thousand or less. If it is negative, it means there is relatively less O^{18} in the fossil sample than for today's

---

*The natural abundance of the three oxygen isotopes are: O^{16}, 99.76 percent; O^{17}, 0.04 percent; and O^{18}, 0.20 percent.

†The formula is

$$\delta O^{18} = \left\{ \frac{(O^{18}/O^{16}) \text{ sample}}{(O^{18}/O^{16}) \text{ standard}} - 1 \right\} \times 1000\%o$$

The relative differences between sample and laboratory standard ratios of O^{18}/O^{16} are typically one to ten or so parts per thousand [or per mil—represented by the

standard conditions; and the reverse if δO^{18} is positive. To apply Urey's suggestion in a practical example, paleoclimatologists have measured δO^{18} in fossil carbonate shells. In the mid-Cretaceous, for example, δO^{18} was usually more negative than in late Cretaceous, suggesting a cooling trend.* Indeed, isotopic temperatures helped to derive the generalized temperature curve shown in Figure 1.1.

Oxygen Isotopes as Ice Volume Indices

There are, however, circumstances that can vary the isotopic composition of the water itself and hence that in the secreted shell. This would confuse interpretation of δO^{18} values as paleotemperatures. For example, when water evaporates molecules containing O^{16} are more readily vaporized. This more common isotope is preferentially evaporated from the ocean just because it is lighter. Thus, colder temperatures discriminate against the evaporation and in favor of the precipitation of heavier O^{18} molecules. Rain or snow at colder temperatures is relatively depleted in O^{18}, in part because less O^{18} is evaporated in the first place from colder water.† Thus, when glaciers are forming on land the cold precipitation is depleted in O^{18} relative to that in the oceans. And if the glacier builds up to great heights, then the high altitude to which the water vapor is forced in order to condense into snowfall further reduces the O^{18} content of the glacial snow.[16] As a result, the ocean in an ice age will become "enriched" with O^{18} because O^{16}-abundant water will be "locked up" in the glaciers. Because of this, ice volume can be reconstructed by tracing δO^{18} in fossil ocean-dwell-

---

symbol ‰, which is why the formula contains the factor 1000 in the definition of δO^{18} (which is read "del O^{18}")]. In 1953, a team of scientists at Chicago found that an increase in δO^{18} of only 1 per mil in calcite shells corresponds to a water temperature decrease of about 4°C.

*Unfortunately, chemical changes known as *diagenesis* occurring over millions of years in rocks or sediments distort the climatic significance of the δO^{18} record. Oxygen atoms in water in the pores of the sediments can be exchanged with oxygen atoms in the calcite shells of millions-of-years-old fossil forams. It is essential to correct for the diagenetic process before valid climatic inferences can be made on such time scales. (See, for example, J. S. Killingley, *Nature 301:*594–597, 1983.)

†There is an additional complication. The temperature at which evaporated water subsequently condenses also has a great bearing on the O^{18}/O^{16} of the precipitation. If the water vapor is carried high aloft to colder temperatures, then it would become even further depleted in O^{18} than if the condensation occurred at a lower, warmer altitude.

ing creatures. When δO^{18} in the oceans is relatively positive, this means—other factors being constant—that ice volume is relatively large because O^{16}-rich water is tied up in the ice.

At the same time, the snowfall builds glaciers that are relatively O^{18}-poor. Because colder temperatures cause greater O^{18} depletion in snowfall, this allows scientists to estimate paleotemperatures by examining δO^{18} in fossil ice—a method we will elaborate on later. Unfortunately, the two effects—temperature change and ice volume changes—are *simultaneously* present in most fossil samples from the oceans used for isotopic analyses. This means great care is needed in interpreting δO^{18} in fossil shell samples as either ice volume or temperature records, for in reality the δO^{18} value reflects both effects mixed together.[17]

Wolfgang Berger and J. Gardner of the Scripps Institution of Oceanography have estimated that "variations of up to 1 per mil from the average are not uncommon" in oceanic surface waters, suggesting an uncertainty of perhaps several degrees Celsius in temperatures inferred from δO^{18} analyses.[18] This corresponds to variations in the local salinity of ocean water, often caused by evaporation. Another alteration to salinity occurs when ice sheets on land grow substantially, as salt is then left behind in the oceans and their salinity increases. This is a global effect, whereas evaporation/precipitation patterns cause regional effects. Rhodes Fairbridge of Columbia University has estimated that at the height of the last ice age, when sea levels had dropped some 100 meters (328 feet) or more, ocean salinity increased by some 3 percent, "comparable with the Southern Red Sea today."[19]

Because the ratio of O^{18} to O^{16} is not uniformly distributed in the oceans—since evaporation, precipitation, and runoff are not uniform among the oceans at any given time—the O^{18}/O^{16} ratio is different at different parts of the ocean surface. The ratio also varies with depth, reflecting the fact that deep waters mix slowly—a cycle that may not be completed for up to several thousand years. Thus, local trends of O^{18}/O^{16} could be displaced in time by several thousands of years from trends of globally averaged O^{18}/O^{16}.

Consider an example. Suppose a sudden warming melted part of the Greenland ice sheet in a short period of time. The resulting meltwater would be O^{16}-rich relative to the sea. Almost immediately the surface waters of the North Atlantic would become O^{16}-rich as well, and this would be reflected in the remains of the animals that dwelled at the surface during the melting. However, it would take hundreds of years before the O^{16}-rich water mixed to the bottom of the whole Atlantic and perhaps several thousand years before it diffused more uniformly around the world's oceans.

Although the event we just hypothesized would show up in the strata that make up the geological record all over the globe, important differences in O^{18}/O^{16} ratios can occur in time and from place to place because of mixing and other local factors such as evaporation and runoff. These difficulties confuse dating and climatic interpretation of individual records, particularly for small or short-term climatic fluctuations.

Berger and Gardner studied three additional complications to the interpretation of δO^{18} records in fossil shells. One deals with so-called *vital effects*, in which different organisms take up oxygen isotopes in differing proportions. Taken together, uncertainty over all these complications "introduces errors which are . . . [about] 2° to 3°C," they believe.

Although isotopic chemistry is complicated and we've seen that many uncertainties infiltrate δO^{18} interpretations, enough careful experimentation has been done that many scientists are nonetheless fairly confident of the gross temperature or ice volume estimations that the technique yields.* Indeed, it is probably the single most important technique for reconstructing the comings and goings of Pleistocene ice ages.

Proxy Evidence of Climatic Change

Since the Victorian era, when geologists examined the most overt physical evidence for glaciers, other clues have been uncovered that tell us where, when, and to what degree climatic changes took place during the Pleistocene. Our modern descriptions of past ice ages could hardly come from geological surveys or data from meteorological instruments dutifully recorded and archived by national weather services over the past 20,000 years. Rather, our reconstructions of the Pleistocene are based on evi-

---

*The nonuniform nature of O^{18}/O^{16} in the oceans and a strong dependence of evaporation and condensation on temperature is also characteristic of an alternative set of stable isotopes useful for paleotemperature reconstruction: deuterium (contained in "heavy water" molecules) and hydrogen (contained in regular water molecules). Thus, the so-called "D/H ratio" can be used for paleoclimatic inferences.[20]

dence largely proxy by nature, and, as we will see in some detail, each one still generates considerable controversy. But these pieces of proxy evidence are worth studying, nonetheless, for they may well be a key to understanding climate change—not only in the past, but also in the future.

The history of the Pleistocene is written in layers—of ocean sediments, marine shorelines, bog and lake sediments, ancient terrestrial soils, limestone in caves, or snow accumulation long since transformed into still-existing glacial ice. In the following subsections we will look at some examples of these different kinds of layers, which are Nature's written record—the so-called proxy record—of past climates. We will discuss how the layers are dated and explore the climatic indicators they have preserved. We have had to be selective in choosing which proxies to cover, and the data discussed here represent just some of the efforts made to reconstruct paleoclimate. Hence, many important classic and recent works are either briefly noted or omitted. Our purpose is to illustrate by concrete examples how the evidence is obtained and how reliable it might be, not to catalog all attempts by all investigators.

Beetle Proxies

We mentioned earlier that Pleistocene climatic fluctuations resulted in extensive plant and animal migrations. This was especially true for insect populations such as Coleoptera—beetles. There are at least 200,000 known species of Coleoptera, the largest order of the insects. The ubiquitous beetle responds quickly to changes in its environment, most notably the climate. Because they can leave an area rapidly when the climatic conditions no longer suit them, beetles don't necessarily have to perish or adapt.

Of course, climate is not the only factor controlling the habitat of a certain species of beetle. Competition for food with other species, predators, available vegetation, and other factors all contribute to the population dynamics of beetles as well as other insects and animals (see Figure 2.1).[21] Moreover, these factors are not independent, since climate can influence biotic factors such as vegetation, habitat, or predator populations. Climate also determines the temperature or moisture conditions that limit a particular species physically. Thus, climate is mixed in with other *limiting factors* in checking the population size of a species. If one examines not a

46

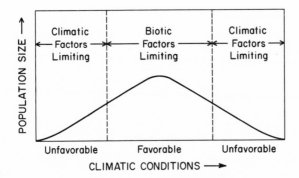

Figure 2.1

The relative numbers of some species are shown schematically against a background of climatic conditions. For extreme climatic environments, population density is low and climate can be considered a limiting factor. Where climatic conditions are favorable, other factors, such as species' *competition, are more important than climate in determining population size. Thus, interpreting climatic conditions from the relative population sizes of various animals or plants requires considerable knowledge of both climatic and other biotic factors that could limit each species population.*

single species but the simultaneous populations of many species (called an *assemblage*), then many of the complicating factors controlling the population size of individual species can be separated from climatic factors. For example, if assemblages of "warm-loving" beetle species shift southward (in the Northern Hemisphere), the response is more likely to be climatically induced than if only a few of the warm-loving species migrated. However, reconstructing the history of migrations of beetle assemblages is a painstaking labor.

British entomologist G. Russell Coope meticulously counted the fossil remains of some 200 different species of beetles and the number of times they occurred in layers of lake sediments at, for example, Low Wray Bay in Windermere, England.[22] Coleoptera have sturdy outer parts that can survive intact and in great numbers as fossils. Several thousand still identifiable specimens have been found in a few kilograms of peat bog silt, after having been buried thousands of years. Coope has identified Quaternary-age beetles by dissecting male genitalia from their abdomens. These genitalia are a perfect morphological (that is, shape) match to modern counterparts. Physiologically, the beetles appear to have varied little over hundreds of thousands of years (which supports the doctrine of biological uniformitarianism on this time scale). The host plants they inhabited during the Pleistocene also appear to be the same as those observed today. Even when Arctic cold threatened, the beetles could maintain their physiological needs by migrating en masse to other, warmer areas with similar surroundings. To a large extent, as Coope put it, "beetle species kept the same company in the past as they do today."

Thus, Coleoptera assemblages make good climatic indicators and, as we mentioned, have been used to determine climatic changes in lowland central Britain. Coope looked in particular at the remains of those species for which climate was the principal limiting factor, although he examined many species assemblages across the range. Using radiocarbon techniques to date the soil in which the fossil remnants were found, Coope was able to determine the variation over time of beetle assemblages. From them he reconstructed temperature fluctuations over the past 50,000 years.

Coope found that toward the end of the ice age, between 13,000 and 14,000 years ago, an unusual warm period occurred which he refers to as the Windermere Interstadial. These warm temperatures did not last long enough for the flora and fauna to adjust and establish a biological equilibrium. Without such an equilibrium, climatic interpretation of the beetle assemblage data becomes less reliable.

The Windermere Interstadial is so named for the sediment samples Coope took from deposits at Low Wray Bay in Windermere, in the central British Isles. Of these samples he says, "Even at the base of interstadial deposits there are none of the . . . arctic-alpine species that were so characteristic an element of the pre-interstadial faunas. In their place is a suite of species that would be quite at home in the Windermere area today and which includes a number of species that are either absent from the more northerly parts of Europe or else very rare there."[23]

Just as rapidly as they appear, the relatively southern species seemingly disappeared from the upper part of the interstadial sequence. In their place, Coope reports, is the first arrival of the more northern species, heralding "the truly arctic faunas" of the following climatic period. Thus, by means of beetle proxies we see that at least in Windermere the record of climate is not always a long, cold period replaced by warmth that gradually shifts to cold. More rapid large climatic fluctuations are precedented.

48

Pollen Proxies

While Coleoptera are a rough climate indicator and serve as a tangible example of the use of animals as paleoclimatic proxies, plants are usually more reliable proxy evidence. Many species have left a legacy of pollen for palynologists to study. These scientists examine different species of pollen and other small organisms preserved in the sediment. Pollen data have been a chief source of climatic information on land for the Pleistocene since Swedish botanist Lennart von Post first introduced the technique of pollen analysis in 1916. The technique is based on the steady accumulation of sediments in lakes and bogs to form organically rich deposits. These deposits can be recovered by the use of hand-driven corers, and the sediment layers dated with radicarbon techniques. In some cases where annual layers are intact, they can actually be counted year by year back thousands of years.

Like the beetles, pollen grains have tough outer parts. These walls are produced by some plants in order to protect the inner sperm-producing cell during reproduction. The durable walls also help preserve the microscopic pollen grains in sediments.

In Figure 2.1 we saw that the largest beetle populations tend to exist in the middle range of environmental conditions; in this range population sizes are determined by many agents, not just climate. Hence, making *climatic* interpretations of fossil population counts becomes complicated. The same is true for pollen. One could, of course, neglect most midrange species and concentrate on species in the climatically limiting ranges in order to reconstruct the climate. But to do so would be to disregard much information and to base the reconstruction on fewer fossil samples. However, in recent years a way of accounting for population variations in more species has been discovered, even in some of those in the middle of the range. This method, called *transfer function analysis,* can integrate information from dozens of species and use their variations to infer climatic history. The integration process manipulates vast quantities of data on many species, something that no one person could do by hand or head for more than a few species. Before the technique was employed, such scientists as von Post could only look at a few species, particularly those constrained largely by climate.

Transfer function analysis is a mathematical technique. A mathematical relation, called a regression equation or transfer function, links present climatic variables such as temperature to present biological variables such as the relative abundance of certain types of pollen or insects. The investigator obtains a formula by correlating data on present climatic variables to data on present biological variables. Then, invoking the notion of uniformitarianism, he or she assumes that past biological variables were influenced by climatic variables in the same way. Thus, the investigator uses the formula derived from today's conditions to estimate past climates by "plugging in" fossil biological variables, such as the changing amount of one kind—or a whole assemblage—of fossil pollen. To the extent that uniformitarianism holds and the environmental conditions today are close enough to conditions in the past, the technique works well.

The development and use of transfer function analysis for climatic reconstruction from biological proxies requires an interdisciplinary effort that includes geologists, botanists, entomologists, climatologists, geochemists, and mathematicians. All these specialists are needed to gather, date, and interpret the climatic significance of field evidence. Brown University researcher Thompson Webb is one of those who works with pollen proxies. He discusses some difficulties in interpreting pollen evidence as follows:

> Pollen changes at individual sites can result from a variety of non-climatic factors including soil changes, forest fires, human disturbance, local infilling of the site, and invasions by new species. In general, if any of these factors are the main cause for changes in pollen values, these changes will vary greatly among nearby sites and show no large scale patterns. The local nature of these changes will thus contrast with pollen changes influenced by shifts in the broad scale climate. The changes induced by climate will have similar trends over broad regions.[24]

To appreciate how difficult it is to analyze the data, let's look at an example. Webb, then a graduate student at the University of Wisconsin, and his advisor, the well known climatologist Reid Bryson, analyzed pollen data compiled from all over the midwest, including a place called Kirchner Marsh, south of Minneapolis (see Figure 2.2). The marsh lies near the prairie/forest border, a marginal area that lends an advantage to climatic reconstruction.*

*It is marginal in the sense that relatively small changes in climate can cause large percentage changes in the types of plants, since the site is near the prairie/forest boundary.

50

When moisture decreased across Minnesota, the prairie/forest border moved eastward; when moisture conditions increased, the border moved back westward. These changes are reflected in the relative abundance of various pollen species—in this case, pollen from trees or plants that thrive in drier conditions relative to those that thrive in wetter conditions.

The pollen evidence from Kirchner Marsh is useful for climatic trends over hundreds to many thousands of years. Such pollen records, buried as they are in well-mixed sediment layers, are sampled at intervals of 200 to 500 years. This mixing tends to blur out shorter-term climatic events. If mixing were absent, sampling could be done at closer intervals, yielding information on shorter-term climatic trends. But there are strict requirements for this type of high-resolution sampling. Since dating the pollen sediment layers in which the pollen lies requires more precision than the 400- to 1000-year uncertainties inherent in radiocarbon techniques applied to these sediment layers, the pollen samples must be contained in unmixed sediments or annual layers (called *varves*) in order to obtain the necessary time resolution. Also, the pollen sites must be in regions where at least several varieties of pollen are highly sensitive to the more rapid climatic changes being studied. Nevertheless, as Figure 2.2 shows, we can already see that fossil pollen counting can be a useful climate proxy, even at low-resolution sampling. As we will explain in Chapter 3, the annual varved layers of some lake sediments can provide closer interval samplings and a wealth of climate information. But first we return to our selective look at the proxies for the Pleistocene and its ice ages.

Loess Proxies

Although parts of Europe, Asia, and North America escaped glaciation over the past few million years, their climates were nevertheless affected by the encroaching ice elsewhere. This phenomenon too is recorded in layers—in this case, layers of a fine, windblown, yellowish-brown dust, a fertile soil that German farmers call *loess*. German geologist Ferdinand von Richthofen explained the windblown origin of loess in 1879. When the southern boundary of ice sheets began to melt, he postulated, large amounts of very fine grain sediments were deposited. Since little vegetation existed at the glacial margin to hold the silt, it was picked up by winds, carried away, and deposited in adjacent areas.

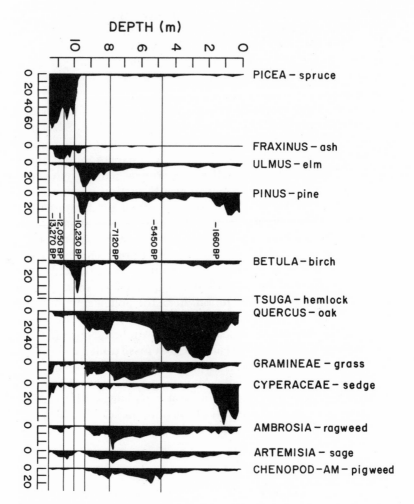

Figure 2.2

The percent of total pollen found in the soil to a depth of ten meters at Kirchner Marsh, Minnesota is shown for a variety of species. Since these species vary with climatic changes, analysis of the relative fractions of pollen for each of them can help researchers reconstruct the climate at this site. Note, for example, the large fraction of spruce pollen below 10 meters depth. This indicates ice-age-like conditions that dominated the site earlier than 12,000 years before the present (BP). Today, spruce trees are typical of the boreal forest far to the north. Similar pollen talleys *have been constructed at sites all over the world to help piece together what climate has been like over the past hundred thousand years or so.* [Source: H. E. Wright, T. C. Winter, and H. L. Patten, 1963, Two pollen diagrams from southeastern Minnesota: Problems in late-glacial and post-glacial vegetation history, Geological Society of America Bulletin 74:*1371–1396.]*

Observations of modern Alaskan glaciers support this theory. During the Alaskan summer large amounts of silt can often be seen at the terminus of a quick-melting glacier. The silt dries and is blown to grasslands where it enriches the soil. Soil in the North American midwest owes some of its fertility to loess blown from the terminus of the North American ice sheet from the last ice ages. In some places in Europe, loess has built up some hundreds of meters, while in other areas only thin patches exist. In Czechoslovakia, deposits of loess were used in brickmaking. In a quarry pit near the city of Brno, Czechoslovakian geologist George Kukla (now at Lamont-Doherty Geological Observatory of Columbia University) found ten distinct layers of soil and loess. These types of soil layers can be seen at construction sites, for instance, where earth has been cut away to reveal strata laid down years before; they are a visual record of climatic history.[25]

Kukla knew that the nonglaciated regions of Czechoslovakia were ideal for recording Pleistocene climate fluctuations. When the ice sheets were extensive, central Europe was cold and semiarid— dry, windswept, and covered with loess. But when the glaciers were diminishing, Czechoslovakia's climate was perhaps even warmer and wetter than today. In a temperate environment, forests of broad-leafed trees flourished and fertile soils formed. These changes were recorded (among other places in eastern Europe) in the Brno brickyard where Kukla had been digging since the late 1950s.

The layers Kukla found were not a simple alternation of soil and loess. Rather, the cycle was composed of three types of soil and the loess. The first soil in the sequence indicated a warm and moist forest-type climate. The second layer was a black soil containing fossils such as snails that suggested a somewhat cooler and drier climate. In the third layer, above the black soil, was a layer of brown soil much like that found in temperate parts of Arctic regions today. But the layer that indicated the coldest climate was the fourth layer —the loess—which completed the cycle.

From this sequence, Kukla deduced that the cooling phase of climate lasted much longer than the warming phase. He dated repetitions in the Brno soil-loess cycle, fixing the occurrence of Pleistocene ice ages at every 100,000 years.

Kukla also found that the transitions from the cold to warmer phases were very abrupt. Distinct *marklines* among the layers clearly divided the cycles, and could be used to correlate with climatic changes in other regions.

For paleoclimatology, these findings provided a very important corroboration: they pointed to a 100,000-year ice age/interglacial cycle, a period confirmed by other scientists who studied ocean sediments, another kind of Pleistocene layer.

Ocean Sediment Proxies

James Croll, the clever Scot who interpreted shelly drifts, had the foresight to recognize that the geological record on land was inadequate for a complete study of climate. He wrote, "In the deep recesses of the ocean, buried under hundreds of feet of sand, mud and gravel, lie multitudes of the plants and animals which . . . were carried down by rivers into the sea. And along with these must lie skeletons, shell, and other exuviae of the creatures which flourished in the seas of these periods."[26]

Scientists today agree. Columbia University paleoclimatologist James Hays told a group of scientists gathered for a 1976 workshop on solar variation and long-term climatic change that "in general, this record [deep-sea cores of ocean sediment layers] has the advantage of being far more continuous and less disturbed than the continental record, and the oceanic record more closely approximates global changes in climate than does the record from bits of the continents."[27]

Croll's idea of excavating the sea floor was first attempted in 1872 by the British HMS *Challenger* (whose modern namesake is the *Glomar Challenger*). During a round-the-world voyage lasting three and a half years, the scientists aboard HMS *Challenger* found that a blanket of sediment did indeed cover the sea floor; in the deep ocean away from the coasts they found an ooze, much of which is made up of the fossilized remains of microscopic plants and animals.* The *Challenger* biologists discovered that the source of the

---

*Marine sediments originate partly as terrestrial materials. For example, constant erosion of the earth's surface soils and rocks sends millions of tons annually into the oceans. This is one aspect of the biogeochemical cycles that we discuss in Chapter 4. Some material that becomes part of the marine sediments is windblown and falls out over the oceans. Rivers also transport chemicals that are vital to the plankton, such as silica, calcium, nitrogen, and phosphorus. These chemicals are absorbed by the tiny organisms so that they can build their shells—the hard parts that survive in the oceanic sediments for the "climate record." In regions of high biological productivity, there are high sedimentation rates (that is, 10 centimeters or more of sediment are laid down every thousand years). In such places sediments are largely biological oozes. In places where few nutrients are available to foster

minute fossils was plankton (a term derived from a Greek word meaning "wanderer"). Some of the numerous living plankton were captured in nets dragged through the surface waters by the scientists. The live plankton matched the remains found on the sea floor surface. It became apparent that the sea floor ooze had formed over a long period of time and was fed by the slow rain of planktonic skeletons to the ocean bottom.

Ocean Bottom Fossils The ocean bottom sediments that consist largely of organic fossil remains are primarily of two types: one composed of calcareous (that is, calcium carbonate) shelled organisms such as foraminifera (sometimes called forams), which are especially prevalent in warmer waters; and one composed of siliceous-shelled organisms such as radiolaria and diatoms, the latter mainly found in colder surface waters where there is a sufficient supply of nutrients.* A third type of sediment is made up mostly of inorganic compounds such as clay, which itself is largely composed of falling atmospheric dust and particles from river runoff. Clays exist everywhere in the oceans but are only a small fraction of sediments where biological productivity is high and organic remains dominate. Where clay-dominated sediments occur they contain very few fossil carbonate organisms, because they are below what is known as the *calcium carbonate compensation depth (CCD)*—that is, the chemical boundary below which exposed carbonate shells raining down are efficiently dissolved. At the CCD the amount of dissolution equals the amount of exposed calcite shells raining down.

The average calcium carbonate compensation depth is some 4000 meters (13,120 feet), but it varies from ocean to ocean and over time. Acidity, carbon dioxide, and the increasing pressure and decreasing temperature that come with varying ocean depth all contribute to the dissolution rate of fossil skeletons. But not all calcite is dissolved below the CCD. Some of the remains of forams eaten by other marine organisms above the CCD are excreted in

---

planktonic growth, there are low sedimentation rates (less than a few centimeters per thousand years). In these places the bottom ooze is largely clay minerals that were carried by winds or rivers. [See Schopf, T. J. M., 1980, *Paleooceanography* (Cambridge, Mass.: Harvard University Press) as a general reference on this topic.]
*These colder waters are nutrient rich primarily because colder waters high in nutrients upwell from below.

fecal pellets. These pellets sink to the sea floor, thus allowing the foram skeletons to cross the CCD boundary and become preserved in the sediments. Silica shells, on the other hand, are more prone to dissolution near the surface than at depth. Thus, those silica fossils that do make it to the bottom are typically well preserved.

Foraminifera are neither plants nor animals, but rather primitive organisms called *protista.* They have a variety of forms—shapes like miniature snails, rice grains, kidneys, or golf balls—and live in all parts of the oceans. Those that are freefloating are called *planktonic.* Other forams are *benthic,* living on the bottom of the ocean to forage for food that drifts down. Foram species tend to be less diversified in cold water; for example, polar seas are dominated by one planktonic form—the *Globigerina pachyderma.*

Radiolaria are planktonic animals, and their shapes are delicate: long spines with lacy geometric designs characterize this order. Diatoms, on the other hand, are one-celled plants. These algae live in all the oceans but mainly in the nutrient-rich upwelling zones. The diatoms are basic to the food chain, since the nutritious water they live in also attracts larger animals that feed on them. Most diatoms have a distinctive feature: a siliceous shell made up of two halves that fit together like a pillbox. Thousands of species of those plants fashion a variety of architectural shapes from propellers to domes to stars—as well as pillboxes.

Plankton are sometimes closely adapted to temperature: most species live in a certain ocean climate and can tolerate no other. If the temperature changes much, they either adapt, migrate, or are replaced by species better adapted to the new conditions. Those that do *not* adapt well are good paleoclimatic indicators; a change in their relative abundance often signifies a change in climate. Thus, like beetles or pollen remains, fossil assemblages of these tiny creatures found in the ocean sediments reflect the temperature of the water and air overhead at the time the organism lived.

Ocean Coring Techniques   The relation of some planktonic species to climate can, as explained earlier, be measured by oxygen isotope ratios of their remains. Millions of years' worth of ocean bottom sediment has built up, creating a chronological record of climatic changes that must be deciphered. Initial attempts to extract a cross-section of this record were quite crude. It wasn't until 1947 that the early corers were improved upon by Swedish oceanographer Björe Kullenberg. He devised a piston corer that could extract samples 10 to 15 meters (33 to 49 feet) long from hard sediments without disturbing the record. More recently, a team of Scripps Institution of Oceanography engineers developed hydraulic corers that can draw out samples up to 100 to 200 meters (330 to 650 feet) long even in unconsolidated soft sediments.[28] This allows paleoclimatologists to look farther back in climate history.

Reading for climatic meaning in a sea core can be difficult. It may be some 30 meters (100 feet) long with every few centimeters representing as many as 1000 years of climatic history. Hundreds of different species of plankton may be present, representing a number of fossil assemblages. One way to read and interpret these assemblages is by comparing them to modern ones. It is assumed that if an organism lives in a certain temperature range now, it always lived in that kind of climate—again, the principle of uniformitarianism. And as we have said, for each temperature range particular assemblages can be identified.

However, counting these tiny organisms can be a tedious process. A mud sample from a core is sifted for these organisms, which are then counted by hand while viewed under a microscope. Computers are then used to analyze the abundance of each species and compare it with that of every other species. The differing abundances of various species seem to be the crucial factor; their relationship with various properties of the surface waters, including summer and winter temperature and salt content, is expressed by mathematical equations in a technique called *multiple factor analysis.* The use of mathematical techniques in treating plankton assemblages is like the transfer function analysis described earlier, which has been used for the climatic interpretation of large volumes of data on pollen assemblages.

Bioturbation However, researchers ran into a problem when dating sea cores.[29] Instead of finding that the top layers dated from the present, they discovered that the first 10 centimeters (4 inches) or so were typically 3000 years old. It was unlikely that these data indicated that no sediments had formed in the past three millenia! So some paleoclimatologists assumed their coring devices were losing the top few layers in the samples. Considerable effort went into figuring out how to redesign coring devices to prevent the suspected loss of the core tops. As it turned out, biologists had the answer to the problem, and no major redesign was needed.

The ocean floor, where these sediments are deposited, is the habitat for a number of bottom-dwelling animals: crabs, octopi, clams, sea cucumbers, crustaceans, and worms are among those that forage there for food. In the process, these animals burrow, leave tracks and trails (and their excrement), and make holes and mounds in the sediment. While they are reworking the bottom ooze, these organisms are smearing out the climatic evidence. Darwin understood as long ago as 1881 that burrowing earthworms play an important part in mixing the top layers of soil. Similar effects can be observed in any shallow-water environment, and are found in the deep ocean as well. Researchers have dubbed this process *bioturbation,* a contraction of "biological perturbation." Thus, the bottom dwellers mix sediments several centimeters deep (and thousands of years old) with freshly deposited layers. This mixing—known as a *postdepositional process*—gives the surface mud an average age of several thousand years and limits the time resolution of sea cores at all depths, smearing out the accompanying climate information by a similar number of years. This complication has led to considerable difficulties in interpreting climatic changes from some oceanic core sites, as we'll see later on.

The 100,000-Year Cycle:
Evidence from the Oceans

Thousands of cores have been gathered from the oceans since the late 1940s. One large collection is stored at Columbia University's Lamont-Doherty Geological Observatory in Palisades, New York. At Lamont-Doherty, cores raised from the Caribbean Sea in the late 1960s were analyzed by geochemists Wallace Broecker and Jan van Donk.[30] Building on earlier work of Cesare Emiliani, they found evidence for the 100,000-year climate cycle—also found by Kukla—by studying the oxygen isotope ratios in small fossil organisms. It took many years, several disciplines, and dozens of scientists before these cycles and the stages in which they fell were finally ascertained; even now there is some argument over many of the details. What follows is a brief review of how paleontologists, geochemists, climatologists, geologists, and geophysicists pinned down the general pattern of major late Pleistocene climatic fluctuations and thus arrived at the 100,000-year ice age beat.[31]

Early Works

We mentioned earlier that scientists had many problems extracting columns of sea sediments before the advent of the Kullenberg corer. Despite these obstacles, Wolfgang Schott, a German paleontologist, examined in the early 1930s a group of cores about a meter long raised from the equatorial Atlantic by the German *Meteor* expedition of 1925–1927. Schott first mapped twenty-one planktonic foram species as they were distributed on the present sea bed. Then he took a census of the forams at regular intervals along the cores and found three distinct layers. The top first and third layers matched the current sea floor sediments—that is, warm-loving species were present. A middle layer exhibited the same species, but there was a higher proportion of the cold-loving variety. Schott concluded that the layers could be correlated to ice ages and interglacials by determining whether cold or warm loving foram species dominated the sediment. This discovery so captivated paleontologists that they wanted longer cores. They knew that if a meter-long core extended through the last ice age, much more climatic evidence could be found in a core 10 meters (32.8 feet) long.

Gustaf Arrhenius, of the Scripps Institution of Oceanography in California, chemically analyzed cores from the Pacific and found that the concentration of calcium carbonate in sediments rose and fell cyclically. Arrhenius thought that these variations resulted from the Pacific Ocean circulation changing in intensity during the ice ages. In any case, Arrhenius' work showed that chemical as well as paleontological evidence in the oceanic sediments could be used to study Pleistocene climates—at least in the Pacific.

Chemical analysis techniques were getting another boost around this time from Harold Urey, who theorized, as explained earlier, that isotopic composition of foram shells could be used to determine past ocean temperatures. The theory was developed and applied by Samuel Epstein (now at the California Institute of Technology) and Cesare Emiliani, who came to the University of Chicago in 1949.

Emiliani investigated Pleistocene deposits using chemical analysis techniques refined by Epstein. In 1955, Emiliani—now a well-known paleoclimatologist at the University of Miami—published what is considered a landmark paper.[32] Among the conclusions reported was that isotopic variations in cores taken from the Caribbean and the equatorial Atlantic indicated several complete glacial/ interglacial cycles over the past 300,000 years.* Emiliani also reported that temperature of surface waters in the Caribbean dropped about 6°C (10.8°F) during glacial periods. This estimate has led to a keen dispute over the size of the temperature decrease in tropical waters during the ice ages.

Meanwhile, Columbia University researchers were taking a much different approach, one based on Schott's method of counting forams. To keep up with the influx of some 200 cores a year, David Ericson devised a simple laboratory procedure that pinpointed the few species he considered especially sensitive to climatic changes.

A debate brewed: Whose method was more reliable? In order to find out, Emiliani and Ericson decided to examine the same samples from three Caribbean cores, each using his own method. Emiliani's technique translated oxygen isotope ratios *quantitatively* into degrees Celsius, while Ericson's species counts only revealed qualitative estimates of general temperature trends. Emiliani enumerated his inferred temperature variations in seventeen stages from the top down.†

Temperature Versus Ice Volume: Interpreting the Oceanic Record

It was unclear whether Emiliani's isotopic curve or Ericson's *menardii* curve offered a more realistic climate history. The U.S. National Science Foundation (NSF) agreed to sponsor a two-day symposium in January 1965 to help resolve the controversy. Both Emiliani and Ericson were to present their evidence.[33] Ericson argued that the isotope variations measured by Emiliani could not be correlated with ocean temperatures, because Emiliani neglected changes in ice volume. Emiliani criticized Ericson for just relying on one species of forams; he also argued that the Pleistocene glaciers

---

*Prior to Emiliani's contribution, moraines in Europe were used as evidence of glaciations, of which only four had been identified. As new glaciers destroyed old evidence, traces of only the largest previous advances remained intact as moraines. The ocean record showed these large advances as well as lesser glacial/interglacial events.

†*Stages* are designated as layers thought to have formed between two boundaries during the same time period all over the world. To geologists, a stage is a stratigraphic subdivision of rocks, but the concept also applies to sea sediments. In the case of fossil forams, *biostratigraphy* can tell us at what boundary a certain species appeared, and at what boundary it disappeared. The layer in between is the stage.

may not have been as rich in O^{16} as some of the geochemists thought.*

At the time of the meeting, John Imbrie, then a professor of geology at Columbia, had been studying benthic (bottom-living) fossils and using them as paleoclimatic interpreters for more than ten years. He suggested using statistical techniques on the assemblages in order to separate the temperature effect from other environmental influences, and eventually he decided to try this himself.

By the summer of 1969, Imbrie and his student Nilva Kipp were confident enough about their technique to put the Ericson-Emiliani controversy to a test. They did so by analyzing the Caribbean core V12-122 (so-called because it was extracted by the now-retired Lamont-Doherty research vessel *Vema* on the twelfth cruise at the one hundred and twenty-second station). According to Imbrie and Kipp's method, the temperature of the Caribbean surface water during the last ice age had not dropped the 6°C (1.8°F) that Emiliani had postulated, but only 2°C (3.6°F). As Imbrie had suspected, his results suggested that other effects had indeed affected the foram population. Thus, temperature changes were not the only factor. By attributing all faunal isotope variations to temperature, Imbrie later wrote, "Emiliani had overestimated the magnitude of the temperature change." If Imbrie and Kipp were right in their estimate of a 2°C lowering of Caribbean temperatures during the last ice age, a significant conclusion could be drawn: much of the isotopic variation must be due to changes in factors other than ocean surface temperature; principal among these are changes in the volumes of the ice sheets. English geophysicist Nicholas Shackleton had simultaneously concluded that the δO^{18} signal was largely that of changing ice volume. Also, in March of 1969 Danish glaciologist Willi

---

*This controversial opinion is supported by at least one independent paleoclimatic proxy: the D/H ratio of a few fossil tree rings analyzed by Yapp and Epstein.[34] In this study it was suggested from the δD of these tree-ring remains that the last ice age was marked by a North American ice sheet with δO^{18} *less* negative than δO^{18} is today at Greenland. If true, this result for δD suggests that δO^{18} in the North American glacial ice 18,000 years ago reflects *warmer* conditions than can be found now on Greenland or Antarctica. The discrepancy between this and most classical assumptions and observations for ice age δO^{18} in glaciers is not yet resolved, but may, for example, be due to a vital effect related to seasonal tree growth and seasonal precipitation. One could also be misled if the few tree-ring remains sampled to estimate the 18,000-year-old δO^{18} received their moisture from a source other than glacial meltwater, and that source had a relatively high value of δD (and by implication δO^{18} as well).

Dansgaard and his colleague Heinrik Tauber independently reported that "at least 70 percent of the oxygen-18 variations found
in shells of planktonic foraminifera from deep sea cores between
times of glacial maximums and minimums are due to isotopic
changes in ocean water, and at most 30 percent to changes in ocean
surface temperature."[35] We will review the Danish scientist's glaciological method later on.

The Problem of Dating

Shackleton was later to confirm Emiliani's Caribbean
stages in his own isotopic curves for core V28-238, this one from
the equatorial Pacific. Recall that in our definition of stages, we said
that these subdivisions occur between boundaries of differing
materials in successive sediment layers. Before the boundaries in
the Pleistocene layers could be revealed and the stages placed between them, two more pieces of evidence had to be used. The first
was a discovery made years earlier by geophysicist Bernard
Bruhnes. While in a French brickyard in 1906, he found that as a
newly baked brick cools, its iron particles align themselves parallel
to the direction of the earth's magnetic field at the time. Cooling
lava flows, it turns out, do the same thing. Hence, they contain
information about the history of the earth's magnetic field, which
has reversed itself many times.

With this in mind, Bruhnes measured the direction of magneti-
zation in several ancient lava flows; he was amazed to discover that
some of the flows were magnetized in directions opposite from that
of the present magnetic field. Twenty years later a Japanese geophysicist confirmed Bruhnes' discovery. After studying a succession
of lava flows in Japan and Korea, Motonori Matuyama concluded
that the earth's magnetic field has reversed itself at least once during
the Pleistocene Epoch some 730,000 years ago. Field reversals had
occurred many times during geological epochs much older than the
Pleistocene. Hence, nature had provided a way to correlate worldwide dates of widely separated deposits, and the boundaries in
which to place stages, Pleistocene stages in particular.

In the 1960s, geologists with the U.S. Geological Survey named
the late Pleistocene Epoch of "normal" polarity the Bruhnes Epoch,
and the earlier period of reversed polarity the Matuyama Epoch.
Since a magnetic reversal is a "globally synchronous" event, it oc-

curs everywhere simultaneously and provides a cross check on relative dates of layers in different deep sea cores.*

In 1966, geophysicist Christopher Harrison and geologist Brian Funnel at the Scripps Institution found evidence of the 730,000-year-old Bruhnes-Matuyama boundary in two Pacific cores. Some 3000 Lamont cores teeming with potential climatic information were waiting to be cross-dated in the context of this chronology—a framework provided by the calendar mark from the magnetic reversal.

Neil Opdyke, who was then at Lamont, is a specialist in rock magnetism. He and his colleagues found that the magnetic signal was clearly marked in the cores they examined. Their discovery made it possible for the first time to correlate and date climatic events in any core that recorded the paleomagnetic reversal. However, what was still lacking was a relative time scale for Pleistocene events between magnetic reversals. And the 730,000-year-old magnetic reversal event, though globally synchronous, was not a precise absolute date. It is uncertain to a few tens of thousands of years. Even a firm date for the beginning of the Pleistocene Epoch was unknown.†

What was needed was a reliable measure of globally synchronous variations (that is, stages) in the sediment record. As Imbrie noted, the "most urgent task was to subdivide the 730,000-year-long Bruhnes Epoch into stratigraphic zones—that is, into layers that could be recognized and correlated from core to core. Only if

---

*Beware of taking the term globally synchronous too literally. Geologists are hard pressed to prove (with one exception being a flip in the magnetic field) that most events, such as an ice age or a change in the abundance of forams, occurred *everywhere* at exactly the same time. Geologists deal with very long time scales, something we must bear in mind when discussing such events as a "global" variation of O^{18} and O^{16} in the oceans. During the Pleistocene, for which dating is becoming fairly accurate, one distinct O^{18}/O^{16} event may be termed "globally synchronous" only in the sense that it happened everywhere within less than a few thousand years. But in the Cretaceous Period, for which the time record is much more fuzzy and dating less precise, a "globally synchronous" event such as an O^{18}/O^{16} variation might be one that occurred everywhere within several million years—still a fairly short time compared to the tens of millions of years between periods.

†Because the appearance and disappearance of various fossil forams are not necessarily cosynchronous in different parts of the world, there is still a considerable confusion in dating the beginning of the Pleistocene by this technique (see Obradovich *et al.*, 1982, *Nature 298:*55–59).

such a stratigraphic scheme were available would it be possible to recognize . . . local distortions of the climatic record. Once recognized, these distortions could be avoided or corrected."[36] If found, such stratigraphic zones would occur in *all* oceans.

The CLIMAP Era

Further support came after Shackleton and Opdyke analyzed a long core that penetrated the 730,000-year-old magnetic reversal boundary. They developed a curve (see Figure 2.3) that reflected variations in the isotopic composition of the fossil forams that had been living on the sea floor—that is, benthics; the stages found in the upper part of the core corresponded to those of Emiliani for the surface-dwelling forams.[37] This finding helped prove that major climatic cycles in the late Pleistocene were global events, which were indeed about 100,000 years long. Their results also helped to foster CLIMAP*—the major 10-year international, interdisciplinary effort initially launched to reconstruct details of the maximum of the last ice age 18,000 years ago. (Its maps of surface temperature differences between today's climate and that reconstructed for 18,000 years ago are given in Figure 2.4).[38] John Imbrie, a CLIMAP leader, recounts how the Shackleton and Opdyke finding was received:

> Shackleton's colleagues were therefore delighted to discover that his second curve—which reflected variations in the isotopic composition of foraminifera living on the sea floor— was identical to that of the planktonic curve. And as Shackleton pointed out, oceanic bottom water—always close to freezing—could not have been much colder during an ice age . . . And, because sea water was mixed rapidly by currents, any chemical change in one part of the ocean would be reflected everywhere within a thousand years.[39]

A Few Caveats on CLIMAP We should point out a few difficulties still bothering a number of paleoclimatologists about climatic inferences such as those quoted in the last passage or derived from the results shown in Figures 2.3 and 2.4. First, as seen in Figure 2.3, no dates are indicated between the only two firmly cosynchronous times: the present and about 730,000 years

*CLIMAP stands for Climate: Long-Range Investigation, Mapping and Prediction.

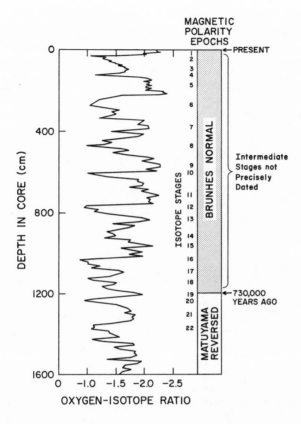

Figure 2.3

Variation in the oxygen isotope ratios in the shells of fossil forams living near the ocean floor taken from a deep sea core in the Pacific Ocean. If all other factors are constant, less negative values of this oxygen isotope ratio index (δO^{18}) indicate colder climates corresponding to increased ice volumes. However, a decrease in bottom-water temperature would also cause a less negative δO^{18}. Each major change of direction in the oxygen isotope ratio curve is called a stage, as indicated on the figure. Inasmuch as similar stages are found from deep sea cores taken all over the world, many paleoclimatologists believe that these major shifts in oxygen isotope ratio index indicate a record of global climatic change over the past million years or so. The only certain globally synchronous dates, however, are the present and the time when the earth's magnetic polarity reversed roughly 730,000 years ago. [Source: N. J. Shackleton and N. D. Opdyke, 1973, Oxygen isotopes and paleomagnetic stratigraphy of equatorial Pacific core v28-238: Oxygen isotope temperatures and ice volumes on a 10^5 and 10^6 year scale, Quaternary Research 3:39–55.]

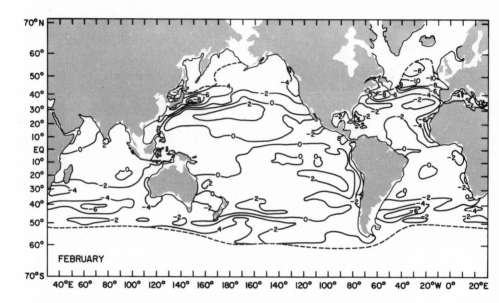

FEBRUARY

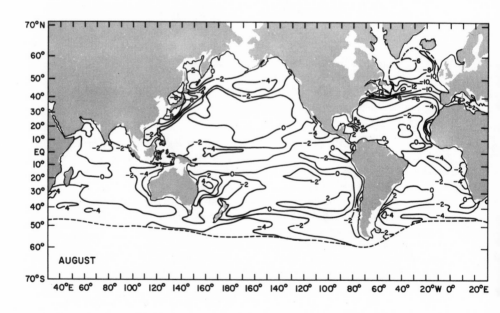

AUGUST

Figure 2.4

CLIMAP project reconstructions of ocean surface temperatures at the last glacial maximum (about 18,000 years ago) compared to modern sea surface temperatures for the months of February and August. The shaded areas show continental outlines for today's sea levels, whereas the solid lines indicate the coastal position at the last glacial maximum when mean global sea level dropped by some 100 to 150 meters (330 to 500 feet). The global average sea surface temperature change estimated by CLIMAP scientists is about 1.7°C (3.1°F) cooler in August and about 1.4°C (2.5°F) in February. Note that Ice Age
sea surface temperatures estimated here were particularly cooler in the North Atlantic in August and off the coast of Japan in February. The dashed lines are CLIMAP's estimates of sea ice extent, which was (18,000 years ago) increased by some 50 percent over the present in the Southern Hemisphere and extends below Iceland and off the British Isles and the North American coast, even in the summer. [Source: CLIMAP Project Members (Andrew McIntyre, leader), 1981, Sea surface temperature anomaly maps for August and February in the modern and last glacial maximum, Geological Society of America map and chart series M-36, maps 5A and 5B.]

ago, time of the magnetic reversal. Since uranium/thorium dating is not yet entirely reliable, and carbon-14 dating fades after 40,000 years or so, dating intermediate stages is still approximate.* What scientists do instead is match the O^{18}/O^{16} stages from core to core in order to compare the climatic events recorded at one core to events at others. Of course, such matching is legitimate only if the isotopic stages are distinct on each core and are occurring at the same time. The belief that these stages are truly globally synchronous events is virtually a canon among most paleoclimatologists today. Indeed, Imbrie's remark that "because sea water was mixed rapidly by currents, any chemical change in one part of the ocean would be reflected everywhere within a thousand years" seems to justify such a belief. However, while it is true *now* that ocean currents mix up most of the sea water within a thousand years or so, only by assuming paleo-oceanographic uniformitarianism can we conclude that the same was true, for example, 18,000 years ago, at the height of the last ice age. If the physical and chemical mechanisms responsible for mixing the oceans were different in the past from those today, which is not very unlikely, then mixing times would also have been different—perhaps by many thousands of

*Except, perhaps, for the 125,000-year-old high sea level stand (dated as cosynchronous to within a few thousand years) on several islands, as mentioned earlier.

years. If so, then many oxygen-isotope stages in different core locations may not have been globally synchronous events; rather they could have been "synchronous" only to within several thousand years of each other.

Consider a second example of implicit uniformitarianism creeping into the interpretation of Shackleton's results. In our quotation, Imbrie cited Shackleton's belief that "oceanic bottom water—always close to freezing—could not have been much colder during an ice age." If this were so and the bottom-water temperature were relatively unchanged, then the primary interpretation of the variations in the isotopic record of benthic forams is changing ice volume —although there are other possible sources of errors, as we noted earlier. Thus, CLIMAP scientists interpreted the benthic foram isotopic record largely as a measure of ice volume and not temperature change. Recall that this is the point on which some of them criticized Emiliani. But the statement that bottom-water temperatures are relatively constant over time is just an assumption that is not yet proven.

Water does not just sink from the top of the ocean to the bottom all around the globe. Most sinking water occurs in a few limited geographic regions of the world—particularly off Antarctica and off Norway, where relatively dense cold or salty waters are found. When the water sinks, it reflects the surface temperatures at those locations—that is, the bottom water is nearly the same temperature as sinking surface water. When these plumes of sinking water hit the bottom they spread out horizontally, eventually covering the ocean floor globally. This process can take up to thousands of years.

Water in the Norwegian Sea sinks at an average temperature of 2°C (35.6°F), whereas the water in the Antarctic region sinks at a colder temperature, -2°C (28.4°F). This is because Arctic water is saltier than Antarctic water and salty water tends to be heavier. Thus, it sinks at a higher temperature than fresher water. Interestingly, the relative saltiness of the North Atlantic is not a local effect; it can be traced to the Mediterranean Sea. The Mediterranean region is not very rainy. Hence, evaporation far exceeds precipitation there. Since evaporation leaves the salt behind, the Mediterranean is a relatively salty sea. This dense, salty water flows out through the Strait of Gibraltar to the North Atlantic where it gets caught up in Atlantic currents, such as the Gulf Stream, and some of it ultimately ends up in the Norwegian Sea. There, the surface waters are cooled so that at about 2°C they become heavy enough to sink to the bottom. Indeed, there is evidence from deep sea cores that North Atlantic deep water formation was sharply curtailed in glacial epochs.[40]

Globally averaged bottom-water temperatures are about 0°C (32° F). The reason is that similar amounts of water sink in each hemisphere—in the north at +2°C and in the south at −2°C. The average temperature, then, is 0°C. But this doesn't mean that bottom-water temperatures *locally* are always 0°C—they depend on how close the location is to either the northern or southern zones of sinking.

Let's tie all this back to the debate as to whether Emiliani's record measured temperature or global ice volume. We have just showed that salinity and surface temperature combine to determine where water sinks and at what temperature it sinks. These factors may have been significantly different during different times in the Pleistocene—for example, when the Norwegian Sea was covered with sea ice, as in Figure 2.4. Not only could each part of the ocean have had bottom water of significantly different temperatures, but even the globally averaged value may have changed by a few degrees Celsius with time. If so, these changes would, as we discussed in the O^{18}/O^{16} section earlier, confuse the quantitative interpretations of both reconstructed temperatures and ice volumes (or sea levels) and the global synchroneity of Emiliani's seventeen—or the twenty-two in Figure 2.3—stages.

Another potential problem in interpreting the oxygen isotope record as sea level changes was suggested informally by Wallace Broecker. He reminded paleoclimatologists that if considerable sea ice buildup occurred, this part of global ice volume would not contribute to sea level drops, since the weight of floating ice is already displaced by the water (Archimedes' famous principle).[41] If the O^{18}/O^{16} ratio in sea ice were the same as the open oceans, then any changes in sea ice volume would not affect the sediment fossils' O^{18}/O^{16} ratios, nor would they affect sea levels. But if sea ice discriminated in favor of one isotope—say O^{16}—then extensive sea ice buildup would increase δO^{18} in sea water, thereby giving a false impression that the ice volume on land was more than it really was. In view of some recent theories of ice buildup and decay (to be discussed in Chapter 3), which rely heavily on sea ice and floating ice shelves, Broecker's concern may prove to be significant for the climatic interpretation of O^{18}/O^{16} records in benthic forams, depending on what the O^{18}/O^{16} record generally was for the floating ice. This, in turn, would depend on how and where the floating ice was formed.

What motivated Broecker to raise these caveats in the first place is the discrepancy in the inferences from coral reefs and O^{18}/O^{16} curves in deep sea cores for sea level changes between glacial maximum and interglacial minimum ice volumes. You can see from Figure 2.3 that δO^{18} varies by about 1.5 units (the units are parts per mil) from glacial to interglacial extremes. CLIMAP members assumed that a 1.0 ‰ increase in deep sea benthic forams' δO^{18} is equivalent to about a 100-meter (328-foot) sea level drop. (We will show how to derive this figure later on.) Thus, oceanic cores where δO^{18} varies by some 1.5 ‰ suggest sea level drops of some 150 meters (some 500 feet) from interglacial to glacial extremes. But the physical evidence from the reef islands or Bermuda suggested sea level differences some 30 to 80 meters or so *less* than the differences inferred from, say, Shackleton and Opdyke's benthic foram O^{18}/O^{16} record on Figure 2.3. As Broecker noted, a bottom water cooling of 2°C would account for 0.5 ‰ of the 1.5 ‰ O^{18}/O^{16} difference between glacial/interglacial extremes. This would imply a reduction in inferred sea level variations from ocean core O^{18}/O^{16} in fossil forams of about 50 meters. This one-third reduction would bring the sediment core proxy sea levels closer in line with the proxy evidence from the islands—and with Dansgaard and Tauber's estimate of ice volume changes mentioned earlier.

Finally, a prominent CLIMAP contributor, William Ruddiman, pointed out (in collaboration with his Ph.D. student Alan Mix) a further caveat in interpreting the O^{18}/O^{16} curves as a time history of continental ice volume. They noted that O^{16}-rich snowfall locked up in glaciers at the beginning of ice ages might be less O^{18}-poor than colder snowfalls occurring much later on.[42] This would confuse the timing between O^{18}/O^{16} changes measured in cores and actual changes in ice volumes. In 1982, Curt Covey (then a postdoctoral fellow at NCAR—the National Center for Atmospheric Research) and I took the Ruddiman/Mix point a bit further. We argued that it is very difficult to be confident as to what precise value of δO^{18} would be representative for all major ice sheets in the glacial ages, since, you recall, this value depends critically on both the temperature of evaporation *and* condensation of the water vapor that produced the snow. In other words, we can't simply apply a formula for δO^{18} versus temperature derived from today's conditions over the Greenland Ice Cap to the glaciers of the last ice age without making further—and hard to verify—assumptions. The most critical uncertainties involve where the moisture came from, the meteorological pathways the water vapor followed before it fell as snow on the big North American and Scandinavian ice sheets, and the δO^{18} flow through the glaciers.[43]

Of course, we cannot yet say the extent to which the recent CLIMAP interpretations would be seriously altered even if the caveats raised here turn out to be important. And there is a good deal of consistency across many different proxies, which suggests that present interpretations are at least qualitatively valid. But, it is important to understand the basic causal mechanisms of those climatic changes. Once all these are well understood, better verification can be made of present inferences that rely on various assumptions in order to make quantitative climatic statements from the proxies.

CLIMAP's global maps showing ocean temperatures and the extent of glaciation at the height of the last ice age (Figure 2.4) are a remarkable achievement, despite the quantitative arguments over the details, which will probably take place for decades among paleoclimatologists. They have amassed sufficient evidence so that no one knowledgeable disputes that this period saw a vastly different climate from today. Likewise, it is clear that global climatic changes occurred many times during the Pleistocene.

As we pointed out in the caption for Figure 2.4, ocean temperatures averaged about 1.5° to 2°C (2.7° to 3.6°F) colder—perhaps 10° C (18°F) colder in the higher midlatitudes—18,000 years ago, a conclusion that follows directly from CLIMAP's extensive evidence. However, temperatures on *land* were generally 5° to 15°C colder than today, particularly in higher latitudes. This was determined through other—largely pollen—kinds of proxy evidence. Thus, it seems virtually certain that many CLIMAP inferences will hold up over time, even if their published numbers do change somewhat.

Dunes and Other Precipitation Proxies

Dozens of investigators around the world have collected pollen analyses as well as other data to reconstruct temperature and rainfall patterns for the continents as they are believed to have been about 18,000 years ago. Although temperatures varied from place to place, one extensive compilation of the pollen evidence suggests that near the Great Lakes regions, in Turkey, Iran, and central Russia average temperatures were as much as 15°C colder than currently.[44] Temperatures were perhaps 5° to 10°C colder in southern Australia, New Zealand, the western United States, South America, Africa, and Asia.

A few sites in central Africa, on the California coast, and in northern Australia were perhaps only a few degrees colder than today. But these sites are generally near enough to oceans probably to have been influenced by milder oceanic cooling.

The analysis mentioned above of pollen assemblages also provides estimates of precipitation variations. The continental record suggests generally drier conditions throughout central Africa, central South America, Alaska, southeastern United States, India, and much of Australia. Notable exceptions appear to have been extreme northern Africa, central south Africa, and the southwestern and central United States, where evidence for wetter land surfaces appears.

There is corroborative evidence for these conclusions from techniques other than pollen analyses. One method used is to analyze sediments in arid regions in a search for signs of extinct lakes. Let's consider the case of central south Africa, which, as we said, appears to have been wetter during the height of the last ice age.

I. N. Lancaster at the University of the Witwatersrand in Johannesburg, South Africa investigated rainfall patterns in the central Kalahari desert watershed where a belt of *pans,* or small, dry lakes, extends.[45] His analysis of sediments in these areas suggests that at the end of the glacial period 17,000 to 15,000 years ago, "the Kalahari, now a semi-arid area with little or no surface drainage, was a region of widely distributed small lakes as a result of substantial increase in rainfall." But how could Lancaster be sure that it was increased rainfall rather than decreased evaporation that was responsible for these lakes?

Assuming that temperatures were some 5°C (9°F) lower at that time than today, Lancaster computed an evaporation decrease due to the cold temperatures. "Even allowing for this," he argues, "rainfall increases of 1.5 to 2 times present amounts would have been necessary to sustain permanent lakes in the region." If there were substantial runoff as well, the needed amounts of rainfall would have to have been even higher.

We elaborate on a few of the details of this case because it demonstrates the kinds of techniques and their uncertainties that are implicit in paleoclimatic reconstructions of precipitation. For example, the calculation of evaporation is based on a formula that is only approximate. More importantly, to compute evaporation accurately requires some knowledge not only of what the temperature was then, but also the seasonal extremes of temperature, the variations in windiness, and even cloudiness.[46] Clearly, we cannot know these meteorological data for the period 15,000 to 17,000 years ago with great precision. Moreover, some available evidence dates from about 19,000 years ago, other evidence from 15,000 years ago, and so on. Some cover averages over these times. Hence, care must be used in constructing maps of the climate of the "18,000-year-ago glacial maximum." This is simply because it is not clear to what extent conditions dated at 19,000 or 16,000 years ago (ya) also would apply at 18,000 ya. The clear meaning of this discussion is essentially that *the more consistent the various lines of evidence, the more confidence we can have*—a restatement of the scientific method.[47] That is why the search for more evidence in the Pleistocene layers is continuing.

Another kind of evidence of what conditions were like around 18,000 years ago is data on dunes. As we have seen, the layers of Pleistocene soils include loess, which serves as a climatic indicator. We can also analyze the Pleistocene soils for the spread of dunes, a clear indication of aridity. German scientist Michael Sarnthein has investigated considerable evidence on dunes. He has compiled some 350 references, evidence that includes archaeological clues such as shells, bones, charcoal, and chunks of wood that were radiocarbon dated.[48] He also used paleosoils and lake deposits with pollen profiles. With this information, Sarnthein concluded that dunes were very widespread relative to today in much of central Australia, northwest India, Africa, and central South America during the height of the last ice age. Sarnthein also cited evidence that the southwestern United States was wetter at that time. Hence, despite the buildup of glaciers during the last ice age, climates were drier in most places.

The extent of dunes as reconstructed by Sarnthein for 18,000 ya is shown in Figure 2.5. Also shown are the present distribution of dunes and an additional map indicating decreased aridity during a warm period about 6000 ya. This *climatic optimum* will be discussed in detail later.

Today, some 10 percent of the land area between 30°N and 30°S is relatively arid. The structures of the dunes in these areas indicate

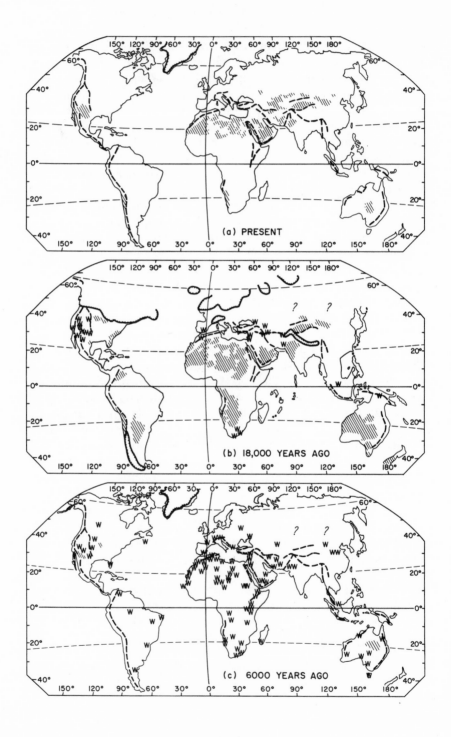

(a) PRESENT

(b) 18,000 YEARS AGO

(c) 6000 YEARS AGO

Figure 2.5

A comparison of (a) major dune-covered areas of the world today, (b) at the height of the glacial maximum 18,000 years ago, and (c) at the climatic optimum 6000 years ago. W indicates fossil evidence of wet stands. Heavy lines show glacial ice sheet borders; the dashed lines are mountain ranges or rift zones. Despite considerable uncertainties in many details, these maps agree broadly with many other paleoclimatic reconstructions that suggest the Ice Age climate was generally more arid than present and the climatic optimum generally wetter. [Source: Modified after M. Sarnthein, 1978, Sand deserts during glacial maximum and climatic optimum, Nature 272:43–46.]

the degree of aridity, strength of surface winds, and prevailing wind direction. Sarnthein's study of the 18,000-ya period indicates that some 50 percent of the land between 30°N and 30°S was covered by dunes in two vast belts; they spanned the tropical margin of the Sahara, southern Arabia, northwest India, and the northern part of South America. Meanwhile, in the Southern Hemisphere, dune fields and dry steppe regions advanced poleward of 35°S in south Australia. Northern Patagonia (in Argentina), Paraguay, and southwest Brazil were also apparently dry and dune covered. Today's total human population would be unable to survive in such a climate, since total food production would be seriously reduced.

Presumably, lowered temperatures during the glacial maximum resulted in less evaporation. This factor alone would have meant a wetter surface. But, Sarnthein argues, the reduction in precipitation was even greater than the reduction in evaporation. Hence, the net effect was a generally drier climate during the ice age. This difference between evaporation and precipitation is referred to as the *moisture deficit.*

As we noted in discussing Lancaster's results, there are other complicating factors in determining a moisture deficit. We know that after a rainstorm, the wet streets will dry more quickly if the temperature is high than if it is low. But windiness figures in (blowing air aids evaporation), and the relative humidity is a factor too (the drier the air, the faster water can be evaporated into it).* These complications render *individual* reconstructions of precipitation

---

*Relative humidity is the amount of humidity in air of a certain temperature relative to how much it can potentially contain at that temperature. The warmer the air, the more absolute amount of water vapor it can sustain. When the air becomes saturated (that is, relative humidity equals 100 percent), fog or clouds or dew typically occur.

75

highly tentative. Only when an ensemble of data is examined can coherent patterns begin to emerge. Sarnthein's analysis of many records strongly suggests that his overall conclusions of aridity around 15,000 to 18,000 ya are correct. Other independent studies tend to agree.[49] But again, not all these data are from the same time period, and more digging is needed.

Ice Proxies

So far in this chapter we have looked at proxy indicators from forams to pollen to beetles to sand dunes in order to infer, among other things, the extent of ice during the last glacial maximum. But we haven't looked much at the ice itself. There are Pleistocene layers in existing ice that contain clues about its past character and extent.

In 1966, at a site called Camp Century in northern Greenland, U.S. Army engineers drilled through about 1370 meters (4400 feet) of ice to reach bedrock. In the 1970s, several additional cores were taken in different parts of Greenland. In 1968, a core 2160 meters (6912 feet) long was obtained at Byrd Station in West Antarctica. The Byrd Station and Camp Century cores, for example, contain information that can be used to reconstruct a climate record extending back at least 100,000 years. Intact cores from the center of each of these continents would hold even longer records; in Antarctica they might go back some 500,000 years or more. A record that long could yield invaluable and detailed information, and would help verify the shorter cores.

For paleoclimatologists, one advantage of studying ice layers is that single years of climatic history can be distinguished stretching back over some thousands of years. In some places in Greenland, for example, up to half a meter of snow falls each year. In cold, dry parts of Antarctica, annual snowfall can be as little as a few centimeters. However, this still compares favorably to the compact sediments found in the ocean, where 1000 years of natural history is typically squeezed into several centimeters of a deep sea core. The narrowness of the span and the effects of bioturbation tend to obliterate the short-term details. However, small layers become a problem in ice cores too, for as the annual snowfall layers become buried and compacted, they become transformed into ice layers. These are much thinner than the thickness of annual snowfall layers; but this compaction also allows for a much longer record. For example, at Camp Century the core is some 1400 meters long and covers some 140,000 years of ice history. This implies that on average, each centimeter of ice represents one year of record. Actually, at the top of the core the first few thousand years is comprised of much thicker annual layers, but the bottom part of the core represents a greatly compressed and distorted longer record. Depending on what one is looking for in the ice record, this situation can be an advantage or a disadvantage. In any case, ice provides independent information so vital to corroborate inferences from deep sea proxies. Thus, scientists have looked to ice cores extracted from the Greenland and Antarctic ice sheets—the most dramatic of the permanent features of the Pleistocene.

Obtaining continuous cores proves to be difficult because drilling technology for ice cores is still evolving. Keeping the cores free from contamination is another problem: lubricating fluid is often needed to keep the ice from seizing or blocking the drill bit. Such "antifreeze" chemicals can taint the sample.

Yet another problem lies in the behavior of the ice. While ice layers are not subject to bioturbation, blowing snow can mix near the surface before the snow is compacted into ice. This *aeroturbation* process eliminates the distinction of annual snow layers in some core sites where annual snowfall is very little and no melting occurs at any time throughout the year. In parts of Greenland, however, conditions are such that distinguishable annual layers go back several thousand years. In addition, ice layers everywhere become distorted as they flow under their own weight. This distortion affects the cross section as it is revealed in an ice core. So, as with bioturbation in deep sea cores or diagenesis in ancient sedimentary rocks, glacial scientists must take this post-depositional motion into account when examining their cores for climatic evidence.

The most extensive study of this kind was done on the Greenland core by a group headed by the Danish geophysicist Willi Dansgaard.[50] He characterized various layers representing glacial or interglacial periods by measuring the oxygen isotope ratios of the ice, as is done in sea cores. In ice, we noted earlier, greater relative amounts of the lighter isotope O^{16}, or a deficit of heavier O^{18}, is generally indicative of a colder period.* Conversely, more O^{18} in ice

---

*Remember that δO^{18} in ice depends in a complex way on both temperature at the site of the snowfall and the pathway followed by the water vapor from the initial phase of evaporation to final condensation and precipitation on the ice cap.

77

relative to O^{16} indicates an interglacial. Assigning ages to the layers was a more complicated task for Dansgaard's team. In principle, the layers of snow accumulation could be viewed as an absolute chronology, much like the annual growth rings of a tree. But another way to establish a time scale had to be devised for the reasons discussed earlier. One of those reasons is that seasonal layers of snow in the lower section of the ice sheet merge as they become ice, distorting the year-by-year chronology. More importantly, the ice sheet itself is distorted as it flows outward under its own weight. Ice deep down at any spot actually came from a place well upstream and many thousands of years earlier. Dansgaard employed J. F. Nye's mathematical model of glacier flow in order to calculate estimated age-depth relationships.[51]

First, the Dansgaard team estimated when ice at a given depth had been laid down in the past. This was done by mathematically simulating how the glacier flows, using the Nye model. Unfortunately, this calculation cannot be very accurate, since many ele-

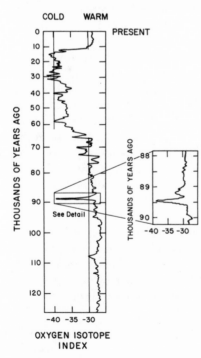

Figure 2.6

An ice core taken at Camp Century, Greenland provides a climatic record back some 120,000 years or so. When the oxygen isotope ratio index (δO^{18}) is large and negative, it suggests a relative absence of the isotope O^{18}, indicating relatively cold conditions. One of the most interesting—and controversial—features of this record is the apparently rapid switch from warmer to glacial-like conditions in δO^{18} shown in the detail. However, this and other details have been revised by subsequent analyses. [Source: W. Dansgaard, S. J. Johnsen, H. B. Clausen, and C. C. Langway, Jr., 1971, Climatic record revealed by the Camp Century ice core, in K. Turekian (ed.), Late Cenozoic Glacial Ages *(New Haven and London: Yale University Press).]*

ments of ice dynamics are poorly understood. Thus, the date of ice layers becomes more uncertain the deeper into the ice we go—that is, the further back in time we go.

As can be seen in Figure 2.6, Dansgaard and his colleagues did date the Greenland ice core back at least some 140,000 years. From 140,000 to about 75,000 years ago they found that O^{18} was generally relatively abundant in the ice ($\delta O^{18} \approx -25\%o$), suggesting a warm period. From then until about 10,000 years ago, less O^{18} ($\delta O^{18} \approx -40\%o$) suggests an ice age.

In Figure 2.6 it can also be seen that at about 10,000 years ago there was a fast shift to relatively more O^{18}, indicating a sharp warming. Of course, this is in broad agreement with other paleoclimatic evidence suggesting that for tens of thousands of years prior to 10,000 years ago the earth was in generally colder conditions.*

Paleo-Sea Level Differences Based on Ice Cores, Deep Sea Cores, and Coral Reefs

We referred several times earlier to the differences in interpretation of paleo-sea level extremes between δO^{18} records in ocean sediment cores like Figure 2.3 and coral reef proxies—or other such direct physical evidence on islands. Let's put this debate into the perspective of the independent results from a Greenland ice core like Figure 2.6.

The value of oxygen isotope index (δO^{18}) from the Camp Century ice core is between -40 and $-25\%o$, the latter figure corresponding to slightly more O^{18} in the ice, which is indicative of interglacial times. The former number ($\delta O^{18} = -40\%o$) is suggestive of ice-age-like conditions, where there is even less O^{18} in the ice. But δO^{18} in the oceanic benthic forams varies in the opposite sense. For example, δO^{18} on Figure 2.3 ranges from about -2.5 to $-1.0\%o$; but this time the less negative number ($\delta O^{18} = -1.0\%o$) is appropriate for glacial condition when relatively more O^{18} is in the seas and relatively less in the ice. Let's connect these two sets of δO^{18} records by estimating the effect on oceanic δO^{18} of melting

*The overall picture of inferences obtained from Dansgaard's early work represented in Figure 2.6 is relatively unchanged, although the details have undergone significant revisions in the fifteen years since the Camp Century results were first published.[52]

the *present* ice caps. Oceanic waters today have an average depth of about 4 kilometers (2.5 miles). If all ice on Greenland and Antarctica today were to melt, it would raise sea levels some 75 meters (250 feet). This represents about a 2 percent increase in the volume of ocean water. Since the δO^{18} of today's ice (including Antarctica) is something like $-40\%o$, melting all of it would drop the δO^{18} value of sea water by about $0.8\%o$ (which is about 2 percent of the $-40\%o$ or so difference between δO^{18} in today's ice and today's ocean water). This simple exercise tells us that if δO^{18} of todays' ocean water drops (i.e., becomes more negative) by $0.1\%o$, then there would be—all other factors being constant—about a 10-meter sea level rise.

Most paleoclimatologists use this relation (an $0.1\%o$ drop in oceanic δO^{18} implies a 10-meter sea level rise) to be roughly valid over the time frame of the last glacial age, even though it is derived from *today's* conditions. So, let's consider the ice age conditions. If one assumes a value for δO^{18} of the excess ice in glacial times as compared to today and one estimates the volume of this excess ice from various lines of geologic evidence, then one can make a straightforward, independent estimate of how δO^{18} should have changed in the oceans in the last ice age. Willi Dansgaard and Heinrik Tauber, as mentioned earlier, made just such a calculation in 1969. Based on their estimates of the volume of glacial ice and its O^{18}/O^{16} value, Dansgaard and Tauber concluded that δO^{18} in the oceans should have been about $1.2\%o$ higher (that is, have a less negative value) 18,000 years ago than now. This is about 70 percent or so of the $1.5\%o$ variation of δO^{18} between glacial/interglacial extremes found in the Shackleton/Opdyke core (Figure 2.3). The remaining variation could, the Danish scientists suggested, reflect cooling in bottom-water temperature of about 2°C—very close to independent estimates made later on by Broecker and others based on differences between sea levels inferred from reef proxies and those inferred from δO^{18} changes shown in Figure 2.3.

Although there are still considerable uncertainties in the assumed values of δO^{18} in glacial age ice—and for the assumed volume of glacial ice as well—these uncertainties are probably measured in a few tens of percent, not 50 to 100 percent. We say this because analyses from ice cores do corroborate—qualitatively at least—the general inferences that CLIMAP and other scientists made from oceanic proxies.

The Pleistocene Climate:
A Brief Recap

Figure 1.1 showed that the past million years or so appears to have had a very different character from previous periods.* A principal feature of the Pleistocene was its repeated fluctuations of mean air temperatures. The cold extremes are commonly called *glacial periods* (or *ice ages*), and the warm periods are known as *interglacials*. The record is marked by repeated invasions of mid-latitude regions by glaciers and sea ice, by fluctuations in sea level, and by extensive plant and animal migrations.

During the Pleistocene the earth was marked by the continuous presence of large amounts of polar ice. Although Antarctica became glaciated much earlier than 10 million years ago (see Chapter 1), the Arctic Ocean remained relatively ice free until several million years ago. Since about 800,000 years ago, this ocean has been perennially covered with sea ice.[53] This remains true in our own time, which is an interglacial period; we have all probably seen pictures of fur seals on the Arctic sea ice, for example. As for grounded ice, nearly 10 percent of the earth's land area is covered by ice—enough to cover the entire earth with about a 50-meter-high (164-foot-high) sheet of ice. Of course, the ice today is concentrated primarily in Antarctica and Greenland. But during glacial periods the ice cover was much more extensive compared to today. We can reexamine the most recent glacial expansion as an example of what a "typical" Pleistocene ice age was like.

The most recent glacial episode gradually gained intensity some time after 75,000 years ago, oscillated in severity several times over the next 50,000 years, peaked some 18,000 years ago, and ended about 10,000 years ago. At its height, ice sheets spread out from several centers to cover an estimated 45 million square kilometers (17.5 million square miles)—about 30 percent of the earth's present land area. In North America, ice spread out from the Hudson Bay region, burying most of eastern Canada, New England including New York, and much of the northern Midwest under a mile-high sheet. Another ice sheet spread from the Canadian Rockies over

---

*The Exxon sea level curve (labeled "short-term component" in Figure 1.2) somewhat challenges the assertion that the Pleistocene was the only era of rapid ice volume changes, although Pleistocene evidence is much more abundant.

western Canada and parts of Alaska, Washington, Idaho, and Montana. In Europe, an ice sheet centered in Scandinavia spread south to engulf Denmark, Scotland, most of Great Britain, and large parts of Germany, Poland, and the Soviet Union. A smaller ice cap centered on the Alps covered all of Switzerland and parts of Austria, Italy, and France. Parts of the Southern Hemisphere were glaciated as well: ice sheets developed over mountainous portions of Australia, New Zealand, and Argentina. Seemingly few high-latitude and mountain regions escaped extensive glaciation: even 5974-meter (19,600-foot) Mount Kilimanjaro in Africa and 4176-meter (13,700-foot) Mauna Loa in Hawaii were heavily glaciated, though CLIMAP members believe (see Figure 2.4a) mid-Pacific Ocean temperatures 18,000 BP were warmer than today. Sea ice also seems to have been more extensive than it is today, probably ranging as far south as lat. 40°N in the Atlantic. Icebergs were no doubt frequent off the coast of New England, England, and France. Today, sea ice ranges much closer to the poles. Around Antarctica, the extent of sea ice reaches from a March (autumn) minimum of about lat. 70°S to a September (spring) maximum of about lat. 55°S; in the north, sea ice always exists in the central Arctic Ocean, although in winter it increases its thickness and can range as far south as lat. 45°N to lat. 50°N along continental margins (see Chapter 4).

Of course, the earth wasn't totally encased in ice during the Pleistocene; there were nonglaciated regions too. In fact, more than three-quarters of the planet remained ice free. But the effects of extensive ice cover were felt well beyond the ice margins. These effects have been summarized nicely by paleoclimatologists John Imbrie and George Kukla.[54] In the Northern Hemisphere, just south of the glaciated regions, landscapes were vast treeless tundras, stretching thousands of kilometers in some places. The Rhône Valley, where some of the world's best wine grapes are grown today, was dry steppe. In other parts of Europe, short, cool summers permitted only hardier plants to grow, usually heather that hugged the earth. Herds of reindeer and mammoths grazed farther and farther south for food; and in some places the Stone Age hunters in Europe and Asia who followed these herds across the tundra could probably see the southern edge of the ice sheet.

In the ice-free regions in the Southern Hemisphere, large regions were also inhospitable. The interior of Australia was mostly arid, much as it is today. Huge sand dunes covered most of the central and southwestern regions of Australia. As in the Northern Hemisphere tundras, vegetation was relatively sparse.

While the data for South America and Africa are more scattered, they do point to a generally cooler and drier climate than today's. Mountain glaciers probably existed on some peaks in equatorial South and Central America, and of course in the southern Andes, as they do today, but more so. Northern Argentina was generally drier, with sparse grass and windblown dust. The dense tropical rain forests that exist today in the Venezuelan Orinoco basin, along the Amazon River, and in the African Congo basin were considerably smaller 18,000 years ago.

Temperatures in the tropical land regions were only a few degrees Celsius colder than today. But rainfall patterns were significantly different. The monsoon rains, which nurture agriculture for more than a billion people today in India and Africa, were weaker during the peak of the last ice age 18,000 years ago. Aridity was more extensive, along with the massive ice sheets. But even though it did rain and snow less on a global average, winter snowfall, which sustained the ice sheets, outpaced the summer snowmelt—at least during the thousands of years during which the ice sheets were building. Although on average deserts were much more extensive, there were a few notable exceptions, among them North Africa— which was generally wetter, as were regions of the central and southwestern United States—and some parts of southeast Australia and South Africa.

Coral reef terrace evidence demonstrates that sea levels altered from time to time (roughly every 20,000 years), suggesting associated warming or cooling climates. Warm periods are believed to correspond with higher sea levels since we assume there is less extensive glaciation during those times to lock up sea water. Hence, cooler climates are often associated with depressed sea levels. But is it possible that in a warm period part of a major ice sheet surging into the sea could create a pulse of raised sea level evidenced by one of those terraces found at Barbados or New Guinea? Because surges are complicated, relatively short-term events, it is not clear yet whether they are caused by—or even related to—climatic change. But a large surge would probably lead to climatic changes as well as at least temporary sea level rises. Therefore, we will look at the potential for rapid climatic events, perhaps related to surging of large continental glaciers. The evidence for these is hotly debated.

Indeed, the subject of the following section is so controversial that one well-informed prepublication reviewer of this book warned me that this topic is plagued by a "blizzard of popularizations and red herrings." Another commented "snowblitz is fun, but it is not the only theory and probably not even a very good one." But before we deal with it anyway, we will first describe a few examples of rapid mountain glacier movement, for which the evidence is far more conclusive.

Instant Glacierization:
The "Snowblitz" Theory

The possibility of rapid shifts from interglacial to glacial conditions is obviously of more than academic interest. The potential importance to societies of big climatic changes combines with the conflicting and incomplete nature of the factual record to generate considerable controversies among proponents and doubters of fast climatic change theories. Although the evidence cited by proponents is considerable, I believe it is not yet compelling. This is because of many still unresolved contradictions and missing pieces. A deeper look, though, is clearly warranted. We begin with a general discussion of glacial surges and conclude by presenting some of the evidence—pro and con—for the controversial snowblitz theory.

Glacial Surges

While rapid deglaciation of continental ice sheets has never been directly observed, scientists have been aware of mountain glacier surges since at least the beginning of this century. As we noted earlier, glaciers tend to deform and flow slowly under their own weight. Some mountain glaciers make what is called a *catastrophic advance* or *surge* of several kilometers within a few months, or at most within two or three years.[55] Then the glacier is relatively inactive for a few decades before surging again. While this is a rare occurrence, surges have been reported in many parts of the earth. A common element for surging glaciers is that the ice must be melting at its base.

In 1954, Italian geologist Ardito Desio described three tributary glaciers that joined in the Pakistani Kutiàh Valley and surged as one into the Stak Valley. The Kutiàh "is almost unknown," Desio wrote, "since even on the most detailed topographical map of the zone . . . it is shown without any name."[56]

The Pakistani government asked Desio to study the glacier. Authorities were alarmed when inhabitants of the Skardu district became "disturbed at the appearance of enormous masses of ice in their valley, and then terror-stricken by the continual advance of a glacier already covering a three-kilometer stretch in the Stak Valley, where there were many flourishing villages and cultivated fields." Village chiefs of the Stak Valley told Desio that from March 21 to June 11 1953, huge masses of ice flowed into the Kutiàh Valley, burying forests in their path. When Desio traveled to the glacier he found what is now recognized as a typical feature of surging glaciers. The glacial surface was "completely broken up by crevasses and ice pinnacles, making it very dangerous to cross." Desio reckoned that the glacier had moved 4.7 meters (15.4 feet) an hour, 113 meters (370 feet) a day. By September, the glacier had stopped.

A glacier prone to surging is inherently unstable—at least under certain circumstances; conditions at the glacial bed change in some way, allowing the ice to slide at much greater velocities than normal. There is much controversy over the exact causes of surges, but it is believed that *basal meltwater* plays an important part. When a glacier builds to a given height through snow accumulation, its weight creates severe pressure at the base. The glacier bottom ice, which melts from this pressure, provides meltwater that lubricates the junction between glacier and bedrock. Lubrication at the glacier base encourages further slipping, which in turn generates more heat and meltwater until ultimately the glacier is so unstable it surges. However, whether a valley glacier surges or not is a complicated function of several other factors as well. These factors include the angle of the slope on which it sits and the shape of the rock beneath a glacier, the so-called *basal roughness*. Because of these complicating factors, inferences from one glacier do not necessarily apply to another area, or even to another glacier in the same area.[57]

This caution applies especially to continental glaciers, which do not rest on mountain slopes and terminate in valleys. Is there any evidence that this type of glacier has surged? Cesare Emiliani and several colleagues at the University of Miami have hypothesized that 11,600 years ago, around the end of the last glacial age, the Laurentide ice sheet covering parts of North America deteriorated rapidly and surged into central Wisconsin.[58] From there, quick melting caused torrents of fresh water to pour down the Mississippi River and empty into the Gulf of Mexico, rapidly raising world sea levels. This event, Emiliani opines, coincides with the dates set by Plato in his dialogues *Timaeus* and *Critias* for the destruction of Atlantis by flooding. The account, according to Plato, was told to his ancestor Solon by Egyptian priests, who dated the deluge as occurring 9000 years before their time. Since Solon would have been alive in 560 B.C., this would have been 11,539 years ago.

Evidence for the surge comes from two sediment cores extracted from the northeastern Gulf of Mexico. Oxygen isotope ratios in fossil plankton suggested that the surface water there became notably fresh around 11,600 years ago—creating a so-called *meltwater spike* in the fossil record. After this time, the relative abundance of warm-loving forams increased. However, Glenn Jones and William Ruddiman at Lamont-Doherty showed that while one set of assumptions for sediment stirring could suggest the existence of dramatic meltwater spikes of Plato-flood proportions, other equally reasonable assumptions do not. Thus, the inference from deep sea cores of global meltwater spikes, they argue, could simply be an "artifact of invalid assumptions."[59] Arguments such as these still persist over inferences of any dramatic climatic events, and many skeptical geologists advise that this version of the Atlantis flood story be taken with many shovels of salt.

Ice Shelves and Sheets

A landed ice sheet is not influenced by mountain slope topography to surge. Continental glaciers, like Greenland or Antarctica, build up a dome of ice in the center, and the pressure created by the weight of the ice at the central dome forces the ice to flow outward. Ice either melts at the warm extremity of the glacier or "calves" into the sea as icebergs at the continental margins. And, as in mountain glaciers, the amount of horizontal movement depends on how much ice accumulates as well as on the ice's profile. Alex Wilson, a New Zealand geochemist, has theorized that the Antarctic ice sheet is a good candidate for a continental glacial surge.[60] Because of Laurentide evidence, Emiliani believes Wilson's theory should be taken seriously.

The Antarctic ice sheet is divided into two unequal parts that are different in character and history (see Figure 2.7). The East Antarctic ice sheet is mostly firmly secured on land. It is long established, having probably reached a very large size at least 15 million

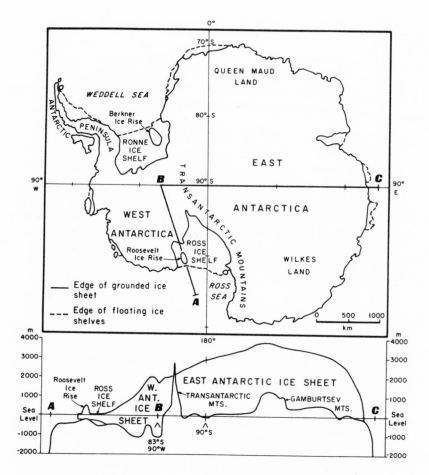

Figure 2.7

Two views of Antarctica and its ice sheets and shelves are shown. The bottom picture shows a profile along the line **A-B-C** seen in the top map. Notice the very different character between the largely continental East Antarctic ice sheet and the West Antarctic sheet, which ends with ice shelves stretching far out into the ocean. These are pinned on islands providing a buttressing effect for the ice on land. Much of the West Antarctic ice sheet is grounded below sea level, a fact which is related to many controversial theories suggesting that part of this glacier could disintegrate with a moderate climatic warming, thereby raising sea levels some 5 meters (16.4 feet). Other theories suggest that the East Antarctic ice could surge periodically, raising sea levels some 15 to 25 meters (49.2 to 82 feet). [Source: J. T. Hollin and R. G. Barry, 1980, Empirical and theoretical evidence concerning the response of the earth's ice and snow cover to a global temperature increase, Environment International 2: 437–444.]

years ago in the late Miocene after Antarctica separated considerably from South America. The West Antarctic ice sheet, on the other hand, is influenced by coastal mountain ranges. It is largely grounded below sea level, in part because the weight of the ice has depressed the continental margins. It is probably very much younger than the eastern half and is certainly much smaller. However, it has one interesting feature: ice shelves extend out into the southern oceans off West Antarctica. These shelves, many hundreds of meters thick, float on the oceans but are pinned on islands off the mainland. The East Antarctic ice dome contains enough water to raise sea level some 50 meters (164 feet), were it to melt, while the West Antarctic ice sheet would contribute only some 5 to 10 meters (16.4 to 32.8 feet). Unlike the primarily land-based East Antarctic ice sheet, support of the West Antarctic ice sheet is much more complicated. Its underwater grounded section is buttressed by the adjacent ice shelves that are pinned in spots to islands. Ice largely flows to the sea in *ice streams,* usually located between mountains. Hence, the relative stability of this complicated West Antarctic ice sheet has been frequently questioned. If the Ross and Filchner-Ronne ice shelves broke apart, perhaps from a climatic warming, the buttressing effect of the pinned ice shelves would be removed and large parts of the below-sea-level grounded ice sheet could, theoretically, surge along ice streams into the Weddell and Ross Seas, raising sea levels some 5 meters (16.4 feet).[61] This is a very important—and controversial—issue, because even 5 additional meters of sea level would be enough to inundate coastal areas worldwide, flooding land with values in excess of a trillion dollars. An East Antarctic surge, as hypothesized by Wilson, would be potentially even greater, perhaps causing a 15-meter (50-foot) or so sea level rise.

All of this would lead to quick planetary cooling, or *instantaneous glacierization,* suggests West German climatologist Hermann Flohn.[62] He cites at least five precedents for what he believes to have been very rapid coolings of about 5°C during the last 100,000 years alone. Each of these events took hold over a period of not more than a century. *Snowblitzes* (as they were dubbed by science writer Nigel Calder)[63] led either to a short-term glaciation, aborted within a few hundred years, or to a full glaciation lasting about 10,000 years.*
But, as with the great flood theory, many geologists and paleo-

---

*The physical connections among meltwater spikes, glacial surges, and rapid coolings could be as follows. A glacial surge would deposit large amounts of ice in the

climatologists—including me—remain skeptical of various subcomponents or even the entire snowblitz theory. But there is some intriguing evidence for such a phenomenon.

Evidence for a Snowblitz

Recall our discussion of sea level variations and Dansgaard's Greenland ice core. His results indicate one such startling "blip" of cold (actually, a blip of δO^{18}) occurring some 89,000 years ago (see detail in Figure 2.6). Flohn calls it the "most dramatic, short-lived cooling event . . . observed. Here the climate changed within 100 years ('almost instantaneously') from warmer than today into full glacial severity."

Was that cold snap—assuming the δO^{18} blip indeed was a cold snap—endemic to Greenland or was it felt worldwide? Although some nonglacier evidence suggests the latter, revised analyses by Dansgaard both changed the 89,000-ya date and seemed to make this spike seem less dramatic in a number of ice core records.[64] Others have argued that the Camp Century spike may be real, but is not caused by climatic change.[65] But the best evidence for rapid change comes from deep sea cores—even though the "snowblitz" might have come and gone too rapidly to be recorded clearly in most ocean sediments since, as we have seen, bioturbation tends to wipe out climatic details in ocean sediments that take place in time increments of less than thousands of years. Nevertheless, there are records that have been touted as substantiating evidence for the snowblitz—or at least a very rapid cooling.

In 1972, James P. Kennett of the University of Rhode Island and Paul Huddleston of the Georgia Department of Mines, Mining, and Geology looked at twenty-eight cores from the shallow waters of the western Gulf of Mexico.[66] At about 89,500 ya these cores show an abrupt faunal change that left a sediment layer bereft of warm-loving species. One interpretation, already discussed, is that a meltwater spike occurred, perhaps connected to a glacial surge. Another is a cooling episode that drove out these species in less than 350

---

oceans. This cools the surface water for three reasons: (1) the ice is cold and extracts heat from the water in order to melt; (2) the ice is white and reflects some solar energy back to space that otherwise would have been absorbed; and (3) the ice is fresh water, and as it melts it makes the oceanic surface less saline and thus more prone to freezing. These effects could lead to a rapid cooling of high-latitude oceanic areas, which might, in turn, decrease summer snowmelt on land thereby causing a rapid cooling (snowblitz) and perhaps result in the building of glaciers.

years. It took more than 1000 years before they recovered. (However, it is questionable whether these deep sea cores can be dated to an accuracy of even 1000 years or so.)

Pollen evidence also points to an abrupt cooling—although these data too are subject to differing interpretations. Dutch palynologist T. van der Hammen shows that about 90,000 years ago, thriving oak forests in Macedonia (northern Greece) and in the Netherlands were squelched within a millenium.[67] Though dates and details all vary, pollen evidence for rapid, large climatic shifts has also been reported in Germany and France.[68]

In 1980, geologist John Hollin, working at the University of Colorado, wrote an article in the journal *Nature* in which he argues that all this (and other) evidence for cooling and jumps in sea levels implied by proxy data "point to an East Antarctic ice surge at 95,000 BP."[69]* He cautions, however, that not all evidence has been gathered. The theory is based on "a very large quantity of data," Hollin adds, but "we need now more quality." Indeed, a year later another article appeared in *Science* arguing that a careful reexamination of Atlantic Ocean evidence for sea levels inferred from Bermuda does not support this 95,000-BP East Antarctica surge hypothesis.[70] The Bermuda data agrees, however, with Barbados and New Guinea reef terrace records to suggest a 5- to 10-meter (16.2- to 32.4- foot) higher sea level stand about 125,000 years ago compared to today's levels. This has been interpreted by yet others as evidence for a possible West Antarctic ice surge at this time: the maximum of the previous interglacial, the Eemian.[71] Temperatures and sea levels in the Eemian (around isotope stage 5 in Figure 2.3) appear to be comparable to or perhaps even a bit greater than those for our present interglacial, the Holocene.

Despite the unanswered issues, particularly regarding the duration, magnitude, and global synchroneity of various spikes or sea level jumps, a number of records do suggest the possibility that rapid coolings, meltwater bursts, or sea level increments may have occurred. Are these records reasonable proof of an instantaneous glacierization? The data certainly are intriguing; but they suggest events for which we have no clear explanation. Moreover, there are many other—quite possibly more plausible—explanations to be ex-

---

*He believes it was East (rather than West) Antarctic ice that surged then for several reasons. Most important of these is that sea level jumps of "about 16 meters" are evidenced in several places, which is too large to be explained by a West Antarctic surge, Hollin argues. His other reasons have to do with the sequence of various events.

plored before accepting the snowblitz as the cause of the sharp jumps in the proxy data—let alone proof of rapid climatic changes. Yet, while our knowledge of both rapid events or possible cause and effect mechanisms in the climatic system is crude, we cannot hope to estimate reliably our climatic future without carefully probing the past. As we have seen so far, paleoclimatologists, among many others, are doing just that. And despite some political objections, this research is likely to continue. If it does not, we could get caught by a dramatic climate fluctuation with little understanding of its nature and no warning of its advent.

The Digging Must Go On

In 1975, U.S. Senator William Proxmire of Wisconsin instituted his now infamous Golden Fleece Awards. He promised to cite each month his choice for the biggest waste of the taxpayers' money. In March of that year, the Senator lampooned the National Science Foundation for spending money on (among other programs) a study of the African climate during the last ice age. This study, he complained, cost the American people $112,000.[72] (The NSF has also spent $84,000 of taxpayers' money to try to find out why people fall in love—an expenditure that particularly raised the Senator's ire.)

But another look at such "waste" may be revealing. We saw in this chapter how studying the past might help us determine our climatic future. For example, scientists find that interglacial periods —such as the current one—typically last about 10,000 to 12,000 years. This is an important finding because it implies that, since our present interglacial has already lasted about 10,000 years, the earth could be due to slide down to the next ice age. Only by digging out the paleoclimatic evidence—in Africa and elsewhere—can scientists determine when and how interglacial periods ended. Then, they can develop and test more general theories of climatic change. This process is a working example of the use of the scientific method. The theories would then allow us to make estimates of the possible fate of the interglacial period in which we—and Senator Proxmire —are living. Moreover, the layers of the Pleistocene can also reveal climatic trends on even shorter time scales than thousands of years, yielding insights into the fluctuating climate during which civilizations have come and gone.

3 Climates of Civilization: The Holocene

In this chapter we will bring our discussion closer to modern times and look in more detail at the counterpart of an ice age: the warm interglacial or climatic optimum during which human civilizations began to flourish. We will also look at a cooler period, known as the *Little Ice Age*, when some civilizations began to stumble.

The Retreat of Ice

Once the last ice age ended, the earth did not become ice free. Ice still remains in high mountain ranges everywhere. Large regions of the Arctic and all of the Antarctic and the vast bulk of Greenland remain glaciated, and sea ice exists year-round in parts of the Arctic and Antarctic oceans.* Despite the lingering ice, we have already seen that the earth is now in an interglacial period.

By 12,000 years ago, ice had retreated in Europe to the northern end of the British Isles. However nearly all of Scandinavia, save southern Sweden and Denmark, was still covered. By 8000 years ago, as can be seen in Figure 3.1a, a rapid deglaciation occurred, and the so-called Fenno-Scandinavian Ice Sheet disappeared from Europe. In North America, on the other hand, remnants of the Laurentide Ice Sheet lingered in northeastern Canada until 6000 years ago; 12,000 years ago nearly all of Canada, the northern Great Lakes, upstate New York, and New England were still covered by ice (see Figure 3.1b).[1] Thus, the transition from the Pleistocene to the recent epoch—the Holocene interglacial—is generally set at 10,000 years ago, even though no such precise date can be seen in evidence like that shown in Figure 3.1.

Actually, this figure would be seriously misinterpreted if it were

*Antarctica now contains more than 90 percent of all the ice in the world.

taken to imply that the mile-high ice sheets melted in place in the fairly smooth time sequence shown. This is the classical interpretation, but more recently this notion of a smooth, in-place melting period for the European and North American ice sheets has been severely challenged.[2] The most daring of the alternative views is that of glaciologists George H. Denton and Terrence J. Hughes of the University of Maine at Orono. In a chapter they modestly subtitled "An Outrageous Hypothesis", Denton and Hughes assess a variety of proxy and theoretical lines of evidence and conclude that the great late Pleistocene ice sheets did not melt in place because of local climatic warming, but rather that most ice literally slid into the sea in a series of glacial surges along several ice streams that flowed out into the Arctic Ocean, the St. Lawrence Valley, Hudson Bay, Baffin Bay, and the North Atlantic.[3] During the ice-growth phase, great marine ice shelves extended into the Arctic and Atlantic, they suggest, and domes of ice built up over a number of continental areas of North America. Several lesser collapses and readvances also occurred during the last 10,000 or 20,000 years of the Pleistocene, these glaciologists believe. Indeed, some corroborating evidence for the Denton-Hughes theory was found by William Ruddiman and Andrew McIntyre in North Atlantic ocean sediment cores, suggesting that much of the North American deglaciation occurred between 13,000 and 16,000 years ago.[4]

Present-day marine-based ice shelves off Antarctica are, as mentioned in Chapter 2, implicated in controversial theories of rapid deglaciations or surges. Denton and Hughes note this and ask themselves why their hypothesized *Arctic Ice Sheet* disintegrated whereas the *Antarctic Ice Sheet*—and its marine ice shelves—are largely intact today. They argue:

> the major reason for this profound difference lies in the configuration of the components of these two ice sheets. The interior of the Arctic Ice Sheet was vulnerable to disintegration by calving bays [areas where icebergs break off into the sea] because it was composed of unstable ice shelves and marine domes and because the unstable ice shelf portions were subjected to melting by the North Atlantic Current. The Antarctic Ice Sheet remains largely intact because its huge interior consists of a stable terrestrial dome immune to disintegration mechanisms and because the large fringing ice shelves in West Antarctica have not been melted by warm ocean currents, which could not penetrate south of the Antarctic circumpolar current.[5]

93

RETREAT OF ICE (thousands of years ago)

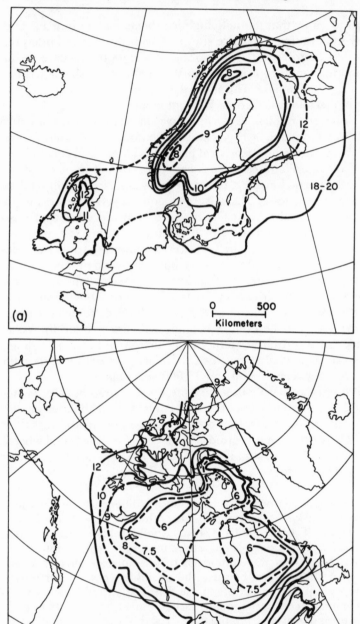

Figure 3.1

*As the last Ice Age ended and the (a)
Fenno-Scandinavian and (b)
Laurentide ice sheets melted, climatic
conditions generally moved toward their
interglacial states. By examining the
earliest dates of remains suggesting that
the ice sheets had gone, scientists have
reconstructed maps such as those shown
here. However, it would be misleading
to think that the ice sheets simply
melted in place following the progression
of time lines seen here. Large fractions
of the Pleistocene ice sheets, particularly
the North American one, could well*
*have melted in the oceans after having
been discharged more than 13,000
years ago as icebergs into the sea. Thus,
these maps could show simply when the
final remnants of snow and ice cover
melted on land. [Source: (a) J. I. S.
Zonneveld, 1973, Some notes on the
last deglaciation in northern Europe
compared with Canadian conditions,*
Arctic and Alpine Research 5:
*233–237; (b) R. A. Bryson, W. M.
Wendland, J. D. Ives, and J. T. Andrews,
1969, Radiocarbon isochrones on the disintegration of the Laurentide Ice Sheet,*
Arctic and Alpine Research 1:*1–14.]*

The Denton-Hughes theory gives us further reason to approach cautiously the interpretation of oxygen isotope ratio curves (see Figure 2.3) as sea level records. This is because the mechanism the Maine glaciologists invoke to get most ice off the land is calving of icebergs into the sea rather than melting in place on land, with the latter causing the fresh meltwater to flow into the sea. Sea level would rise as soon as either the meltwater or the ice chunks hit the oceans, but the O^{18}/O^{16} ratios in oceanic fossils would not respond as a global signal until the icebergs melted and the ocean waters mixed well. In addition, if ice shelves played an important role, then sea level reconstructions from deep sea cores would be even more difficult than they already are (recall our discussions of these diffi-culties in Chapter 2).

The main thing to emphasize here is that although the details and theories of both the coming and going of the ice are still sketchy —indeed seemingly growing more uncertain with the advent of some new hypotheses—there is clear evidence that large ice sheets such as those shown in Figure 3.1 existed in the late Pleistocene and that the European and North American ice sheets largely disap-peared over a period of some 10,000 years to usher in the Holocene. But for the more than 70 percent of the land area that was not glaciated, the transition was also felt: temperatures and precipita-tion levels altered markedly. We will look at what conditions were like 5000 to 10,000 years ago when civilizations began to stir and flourish, first reexamining Sarnthein's evidence for the climatic op-timum, the warm period known as the Altithermal or Hypsithermal.

Climate in Transition:
From Glacial to Interglacial Times

As the land glaciers calved or melted, sea levels in the post–ice age world increased. Land bridges between continents were overcome as the ocean rose some 100 meters or so.* As shown in Figure 2.5c, 6000 years ago there were relatively few dune-filled deserts in the world—that is, none as arid or widespread as today. Some active but minor dune field expansion appears to have occurred in areas such as northern Alaska, the Great Basin of North America, Canada, northern Minnesota, central Nebraska, and the Indian Thar desert. The Iranian and central south Australian deserts may have had more dune fields then. In Figure 2.5c the letter W indicates spots that were wetter than today. Some of these moist places are former desert sites of the last glacial period. Sarnthein's results are controversial in that his maps are labeled for specific paleodates. The dating is not that precise, and his maps really represent an *average* of conditions that occurred over several thousand years around each date. Dunes for the present date (Figure 2.5a), of course, are more accurate; they don't require proxies as the data are direct observations. As we mentioned in Chapter 2, each set of proxy data is not always synchronous with other sets, so the "freeze frames" we see in Figure 2.5 cannot represent conditions at precisely one time. In a general sense, however, the patterns of wet and dry can be corroborated, although studies of paleo–lake levels in Africa suggest periods of considerable wet-dry fluctuations in the mid-Holocene.[6]

Sarnthein says that his findings are evidence for reversing the classical geological concept that an arid climate generally accompanied warmth during the climatic optimum, and a wet climate accompanied the glacial maximum 18,000 years ago. Columbia University geologist Rhodes Fairbridge predicted in 1960 that the opposite would be found to be true. This issue is associated with the concept of moisture deficit. Increased surface wetness is not simply the result of having more rain, since precipitation is not the only factor creating moist conditions. For instance, moisture in soil depends upon what flows in and what flows out. You can get inflow from the sky (precipitation) or the land (increases in river or

---

*Geologists have found land plants and animals in what are now the ocean sediments of the Bering Straits. They call this former land area Beringia.

groundwater levels). These phenomena are typically associated with more rainfall, but not necessarily local—the moisture sources could be upstream. For example, the Nile Delta's habitability does not result from local rainfall, but from the downstream flooding of the Nile River caused by precipitation thousands of kilometers upstream.

Evaporation and runoff—the outflow—are also important wetness factors. Evaporation depends on such factors as solar radiation, temperature, windiness, relative humidity, plant cover, and surface roughness. Runoff in either a river or a stream is enhanced if vegetation cover is weak or the soil eroded. The latter allows more water to percolate through the ground as runoff into underground streams or reservoirs.

Despite all these complications, it is still true—particularly in the tropics and subtropics—that proxy evidence of paleoclimatic wetness usually means more rainfall locally even though we can't be sure in each case. We need to look further and get more information on what conditions were like at the time to try to estimate how important each of these factors were.[7]

Some corroboration for a wet Holocene comes from Hermann Flohn, who says that it is a "surprising but well established fact" that moist climates existed in the entire arid belt from Mauritania in northwest Africa to Rajasthan in India.[8] Even in the now extremely arid center of the Sahara, rivers flowed and nomads grazed their cattle on the grasslands. Today, this area of the Sahara receives a scant 5 millimeters (about one-fifth of an inch) of rainfall per year on average and is famous for its dunes (see Figure 2.5a). In order to support grazing animals on the scale it once did, Flohn suggests that the annual rainfall had to have been close to 300 or 400 millimeters (12 or 16 inches). Apparently, such precipitation levels were not restricted to the Sahara; the Thar desert in northwest India, which now receives an average annual rainfall of 250 millimeters (10 inches), reaped some 400 to 800 millimeters (16 to 32 inches) annually during a moist period from 10,500 to about 3800 years ago, according to Flohn.

How are these kinds of climatic inferences obtained? One research team, German scientists Mebus Geyh and Dieter Jäkel, looked in African soils for evidence of wet climates during this period.[9] Using radiocarbon dating, they determined the ages of clay and silt layers (which indicate more humid climates), and sand and gravel beds (which indicate drier climates). One of their conclusions is that the average wetness in Africa during the climatic optimum was much greater than at present or during the Pleistocene glaciation.

Six thousand years ago, in what is now Israel, the land was "more richly covered with vegetation than today," according to Tel Aviv University researcher Joseph Otterman.[10] He raises the question, "Are the changes in vegetation cover . . . due directly to [human activities] or to a climate change or both?" This is a fundamental problem. Was the climate the cause of the shift in human land use, or rather its effect? We will come back to this point later.

Despite the uncertainties and missing data, evidence is mounting to reveal the outlines of the climatic past in other parts of the world:*

- The west British Isles were warmed by 11,000 years ago, when there were few trees in now-green England. Robin Hood's Sherwood Forest was yet to grow.
- After 1000 years of warming, temperatures dropped sharply again and the climate cooled all over Europe for the next 600 to 700 years. Tundra stretched from northern England to the German plain. But at about 10,300 years ago, a sustained temperature rise marked the beginning of the postglacial period in Europe.
- Milder winters, warmer summers, the flourishing of pine and birch trees in England, and a return of oaks, elms, and hazels in Germany marked this warming trend.
- In North America the climatic optimum was slower in coming, perhaps due to the slower disappearance of the remnants of the Laurentide ice sheet. About 8500 years ago, there was a slight readvance that produced moraines visible today. Thereafter, from 8000 years ago, the spruce forest shifted north, keeping pace with the retreating ice margin. By 6500 years ago, the forest edge was north of its present position.

At this point we will look more closely at a climatic proxy to show climate in transition. The maps in Figure 3.2 show the distribution of pollen for two kinds of trees: spruce, which suggests colder climates, and oak, which indicates warmer climates.[12] In Figure 3.2g, a map of spruce pollen for 11,000 years before the present, note

---

*See especially Hubert Lamb's major work *Climate: Present, Past and Future,* Vol. 2, in which he details the evidence for this and other parts of climatic history.[11]

how much spruce there was in the northeastern United States. Today, as shown in Figure 3.2a, we have to look far to the north to find a similar percentage of this species in central Canada below Hudson Bay, where spruce forests stretch to the tundra. (We should mention that today deforestation as well as the warmed climate has a role in the disappearance of spruce.)

Oak trees now virtually stop growing at the U.S. border (see Figure 3.2b); this species is well adapted to the climate of the Midwest and Mid-Atlantic states. But as you can see in Figure 3.2h, 11,000 years ago, when ice still covered large amounts of Canada, only a much smaller percentage of oak grew. Its maximum concentration appears to have been in eastern North Carolina. Spruce pollen, as we noted, found its way far south of where it is today, well into the U.S. corn belt where oak now dominates (see Figures 3.2b and 3.2g).

Let's look at the warmer period 8000 years ago. A radical change occurred at that time, at least for oak. It had become a major species in the Mid-Atlantic states and the Midwest, as Figure 3.2f shows. Spruce pollen for that time period, depicted in Figure 3.2e, was no longer a major species, although a small percentage of it was following the retreating ice northward. We should note that the pollen evidence for climatic warming between 8000 and 4000 years ago does not automatically imply that all seasons in all areas warmed. Indeed, this fossil pollen evidence probably tells us more about trends in summer temperatures than for any of the other climatic variables. Figures 3.2c and 3.2d show that by 4000 years ago the Laurentide ice sheet had completely disappeared and the distribution of both spruce and oak pollen began evolving towards today's patterns.

Harvey Nichols of the University of Colorado has used fossil pollen remains to estimate temperature changes over the Holocene in northeastern Canada, finding July temperatures some 4°C (7.2°F) warmer about 5000 to 6000 years ago.[13] Temperatures in summer there dropped somewhat below today's levels for a few centuries about 2500 (and again 400) years ago, and were some 1°C (1.8°F) warmer about 800 to 1200 years ago.*

*More recent analyses of Canadian paleoclimate confirm that the Altithermal—a common name for the mid-Holocene—in this region *as a whole* took place roughly as Nichols notes, but that large space and time variations in summer temperature occurred during the mid-Holocene. (See Andrews, J. T., and Diaz, H. F., 1981, *Quaternary Research 16:*379–381.)

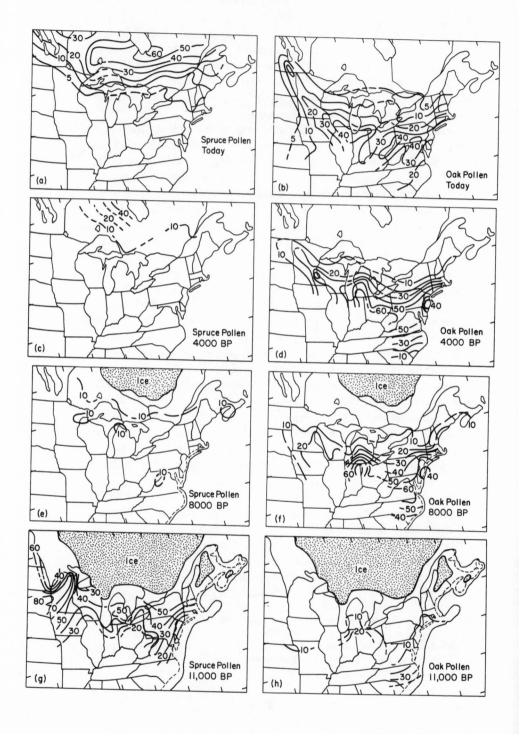

Figure 3.2

The relative fraction (in percent) of fossil pollen from various species of trees is shown on the maps. These pollen patterns can be correlated to climatic conditions. These maps show, for example, that at the end of the last Pleistocene Ice Age 11,000 years ago much of the northeastern United States was covered with spruce forests, which are found today in central Canada near Hudson Bay. As climatic conditions ameliorated the spruce "chased" the retreating ice sheet *northward into Canada, whereas more temperate- climate trees like oak moved outward from their refuge in the Carolinas into the middle Atlantic states and the midwest. Around 4000 years ago the distribution of these temperate-climate trees stabilized in what is roughly their present configuration. [Source: J. C. Bernabo and T. Webb III, 1977, Changing patterns in the Holocene pollen record of northeastern North America: A mapped summary, Quaternary Research 8:64–96.]*

In South America, paleoclimatologist Calvin Heusser examined the pollen remains of plants in the South Chilean Lake District, a region at about lat. 40°S that lies at the foot of the Andes Mountains. He found that the cold period tundra and grassland vegetation occupied the region until almost 10,000 years ago. Then forests slowly moved in, as temperatures and humidity rose, culminating in an extensive rain forest about 6500 years ago. Heusser estimates that midsummer temperatures in that rainforest were 1° to 2°C (1.8° to 3.6°F) warmer than today and about 10°C (18°F) warmer than during glacial times some 19,000 years ago. Heusser believes that this general "pattern of vegetation, climatic and glacial events in the Lake District seems to follow, in the main, schemes outlined in other parts of the Southern Hemisphere."[14]

China was probably warmer and wetter 5000 to 6000 years ago, as was northern Turkey. An abundant variety of eucalyptus trees flourished in southwestern Australia, where rainfall was above present levels from at least 6000 to 5000 years ago. But Australia then became increasingly dry, most notably around 3200 years ago, and continued dry for some centuries following. Between 500 B.C. and 500 A.D., wetness returned to much of Australia.

Growth of Civilizations

Hence, although there was considerable fluctuation, much evidence suggests that these shorter term, regional variations were superimposed on a fairly general Holocene pattern of typically increasing warmth and wetness compared to the late Pleistocene. How was this changing climate (and the alterations it implied for the landscape) affecting people? The generally benign climate that replaced the ice age coincided with the rise of civilizations; perhaps it even fostered their development. Climatologist Hubert Lamb cites cases of cultural development in which there are clear indications of more plentiful water supplies—a necessary ingredient for flourishing civilizations—in what are now relatively dry zones. We will give several examples of such growth, but, unlike some authors, we will make no claim that climate was the only—or even the dominant—factor in the growth of early civilizations in the Holocene. Methods of separating other factors influencing history are explored later on in this chapter. For now, we'll merely give some examples.

The Indus Valley civilization, for example, developed in what is today the Rajasthan (or Thar) Desert of India and Pakistan. Mohenjo-Daro and Harappa were its thriving centers, where cereals were grown during the Indus heyday around 4500 years ago. The Harappas grew wheat, barley, melons, sesame, and dates. Reid Bryson and Thomas Murray, in their book *Climates of Hunger,* say these ancient people may have been the first to cultivate cotton.[15] They populated areas where irrigation was not possible and not needed; the rainfall provided enough moisture for their crops. Around 3700 years ago, the civilization faltered and declined rapidly. The reasons, Bryson and Murray say, are not fully understood, but they believe a changing climate contributed significantly to the downfall: failing monsoon rains were partly to blame.

The Tarim basin of Sinkiang in central Asia apparently met with a similar fate. This basin was the site of the ancient Silk Route, and Lamb notes that it was once dotted with cities, settlements, and forests. The route was used by trading caravans between China and the West in Roman times. Today the area is mostly desert. (Interestingly, *tarim* means "agriculture" in Turkish; central Asia was an ancient homeland of Turkic tribes.)

The Chinese were already in their golden age by the time other civilizations were coming to their feet. Lamb suggests that the higher temperatures and humidity of the mid-Holocene may even have enhanced Chinese cultural development. Higher temperatures helped push the range of some flora farther north in China so that bamboo groves became much more widespread. Bamboo was the most important raw material; the young shoots provided food, while the more mature stems were used for construction, for making hats and other clothing, furniture, and musical instruments, and for writing on.

Among other civilizations that blossomed during the early Holocene were the Sumerians (ancestors of the Southern Iraqis), who established themselves in lower Mesopotamia some 7000 years ago. This culture originated city-states, clay tablets with writing, and the wheel, which helped improve agricultural methods. Their innovations also helped them accumulate food surpluses. Some settlements in the upper Euphrates river basin date back even further, to about 10,000 years ago.[16]

The Minoans in the Aegean region emerged around 4400 years ago. But by 3470 years ago this culture had declined. The explosion of the Aegean volcano Thera may have devastated it. The Egyptians, Romans, and Greeks also flourished in the Fertile Crescent, the cradle of western civilization. Meanwhile, Stone Age hunters elsewhere were using bows and arrows, domesticating animals, and building stone monuments to their gods. The first signs of agriculture in central and northern Europe appear several thousand years later than in the middle East, about 6000 years ago. Although there were more forested areas, people cut them down or burned them in order to cultivate the land. This primitive agricultural practice of *slash and burn* was an early human (as opposed to climatic) impact on the earth's surface. The technique is still used today; we will look at some of its climatic and other implications in Part II.

Farming and the use of grazing animals probably led to a robust human population increase during this time in Europe as well as in southwest Asia. There, the earliest beginnings of agriculture can be traced back even further, to about 11,000 years ago. Early forms of wheat and barley grew wild in Asia while goats, pigs, cattle, and sheep roamed. Hunters and gatherers in what is now the southwestern United States did not begin to sow the land until about 6000 years ago, when New Mexico and Arizona were more moist.

We have sampled very selectively a few examples of the transition from ice age to the Holocene climate and the coincidental expansions—and later decline—of many civilizations. The extent to which one can draw a cause-and-effect inference from such events, however, will be discussed later. The evidence gathered to reconstruct the climate for this period, when written records were not widespread, consists of proxies. In some cases, these proxies are similar to those we have examined before. Also, as before, the examples of Holocene proxies about to be presented are not intended as a balanced or complete survey of all important work, but rather as illustrative of the problems and prospects proxy studies offer for paleoclimatology or archeology of the Holocene.

Holocene Proxies

Moraines

Paleoclimatologists can determine the extent of now defunct glaciers (and hence past climate) even without being able to obtain cores from them. The nature of this glacial evidence lies in the moraines left behind; they fringe most alpine glaciers throughout the world. Scientists can date the moraines using radiocarbon techniques on the trees, peat, and other organic material found in them. As trees were overrun by advancing glaciers, they were swept up by the ice; when the ice melted, the wood became part of the remaining debris.

There were at least three noteworthy glacial readvances during the Holocene that peaked at about 5300, 2800, and 200 to 300 years ago, as seen in the lower part of Figure 3.3. These glacial expansions, which occurred about every 2500 years, each lasted at least several hundred years. Glacial contraction intervals lasted up to 1750 years. University of Maine and University of Stockholm geologists George Denton and Wibjörn Karlén have mapped and dated

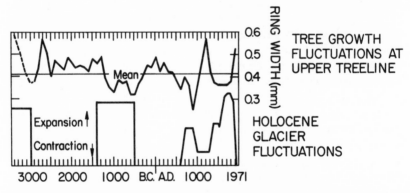

Figure 3.3

One of the best methods of reconstructing paleoclimatic conditions is to compare the proxy evidence from independent lines of evidence. This figure compares tree ring widths in the White Mountains of California against an analysis of mountain glacier expansions and contractions in the Holocene as inferred *from debris left behind from these events. [Source: V. C. LaMarche, Jr., 1978, Tree ring evidence from past climatic variability,* Nature 276:334–338; *and G. H. Denton and W. Karlén, 1973, Holocene climatic variations— their pattern and possible cause,* Quaternary Research 3:155–205.]

Holocene moraines in the Northern Hemisphere from Swedish Lapland to North America and Alaska.[17] They found that small mountain, or alpine, glaciers in these areas are relatively sensitive indicators of climatic fluctuations—especially high-frequency fluctuations (hundreds of years) superimposed on long-term trends (thousands of years).

Most small alpine glaciers outside of high polar latitudes react relatively quickly to climatic changes by growing or shrinking. Often, the lag time between the climatic shift and growth or decay of these small glaciers is measured in decades. Written records within the last 1000 years confirm that small glaciers can move substantially in such short periods of time. Many of these records written by inhabitants near western European mountain glaciers, for example, reflect the changes observed during the so-called Little Ice Age from about 1550 to 1850.

Pollen and the Prairie Peninsula

While the glaciers were moving, so were the tree lines. Extensive pollen surveys have been taken that track these shifts in northeastern North America. Such studies—which include the spruce and oak pollen maps (Figure 3.2) and the pollen talleys discussed earlier (Figure 2.2)—offer another proxy look at the Holocene.

In order to draw Figure 3.2, Bernabo and Webb compiled pollen data from sixty-two cores dug throughout northeastern North America, primarily by other scientists. Of three hundred plus pollen types identified and dated with radiocarbon techniques, thirteen were most abundant. Bernabo and Webb narrowed to five the major pollen groups they would use in their analysis: spruce, pine, oak, herbs, and a group known as BAFT—Betula (birch), Acer (maple), Fagus (beech), and Tsuga (hemlock). These five outnumber all others in the Holocene and can be used to define the extent of the boreal forest (which indicates the coldest regions of heavy forest growth), and the conifer-hardwood forest (which is more temperate), the deciduous forest (suggesting more humid temperate regions), and the prairie (indicative of drier temperate climates). For a complement to the oak and spruce counts shown in Figure 3.2, Bernabo and Webb mapped the movement of fossil herb pollen across the U.S. plains, large amounts of which generally indicate a semiarid prairie environment.[18] They found that from about 8000 to 4000 years ago—the Altithermal period—the prairie extended eastward across the Mississippi River into the humid cornbelt. The expanded arid zone has been called the "prairie peninsula" by some paleoclimatologists. If it recurred with a new climatic warming, then the consequences for agriculture as now practiced in the region could be serious.

Lamb has surveyed the pollen evidence for many parts of the world and notes many synchronous changes.[19] The timing and character of temperature changes in northern Canada west of Hudson Bay, for instance, match those in Europe, he reports. Likewise, northwestern North America and southern Chile exhibited correlated climate shifts. As we mentioned earlier in this chapter, birch and pine flourished from about 9000 to 8000 years ago in Europe, specifically Denmark, Poland, and Germany. Continued warmth brought birchwoods to England between 10,000 and 9000 years ago, and oaks, elms, lindens and hazel trees to Scandinavia and Germany.

Packrat Middens

Proxy evidence we have seen for climatic changes on land have ranged from beetles to pollen. Another somewhat unusual data source is the packrat. This animal lived during the early Holocene, when changes in its eating habits indicated vegetation shifts. As you might expect from their name, packrats store up many things; they accumulate refuse heaps of vegetation that they have gathered, eaten, and excreted. Hundreds of plants have been identified in their fossil junkpiles, called *middens,* many of which, in the southwestern United States, at least, have been found intact. The midden record compiled for this area by University of Arizona researchers confirms with radiocarbon dates an 11,000 years before the present (BP) boundary between the Pleistocene and the Holocene.[20] By examining the middens, these investigators found that at about 8000 years ago, woodlands began to disappear in what are now the Chihuahuan Desert in Texas, the Sonoran Desert in Arizona and California, and the Mojave Desert in Arizona, California, and Nevada. The evacuation of woodland species apparently took place over a relatively short period of time. This is indicative of the quick response that vegetation in the southwest had to Holocene climatic changes, compared to the slower responses of the central and eastern U.S. forests. The end of the early Holocene woodlands in these now warm deserts appears to have been a rapid, wide-spread, synchronous event about 8000 years ago, according to the researchers. As the woodland species migrated northward and to higher elevations, desert-adapted species increased and spread. In the Chihuahuan Desert, grasslands probably preceded the forma-tion of modern desert plant communities. A series of seven middens from Rocky Arroyo and Last Chance Canyon in New Mexico suggest that modern desert scrub communities arrived after 4000 years ago, just past the period of the climatic optimum.

Early Written Records: Chronicles, Tablets, and Oracle Bones

During the climate of the more recent period, we en-counter historical—that is, written—records. At times sketchy, usu-ally inconsistently recorded, and always seen through the often subjective eye of the observer, written accounts can nevertheless provide additional evidence about past climates. Among the earliest documentation are the writings found in ancient Chinese religious books. Translatable only by language experts (who are not usually interested in the scientific aspects of the records), these chronicles often offer cryptic mention of extraordinary meteorological and astronomical phenomena. Events such as floods, droughts, severe storms, or the appearance of comets were considered signs of God's displeasure with His son, the emperor. Thus, these events were considered worthy of record. The first chronicles of these climatic events were not published until around 300 B.C., when an anony-mous author engraved them on bamboo pieces bound with ropes. This *Bamboo Album* was recovered from the grave of King Shian of Wei, who died in 297 B.C. Two other books have been recovered and translated: the *Book of History*, written by Shih–Ma Chien (145–86 B.C.); and *Chronicles of the Han Dynasty*, written by Pan Ku (A.D. 32–92).[21]

Meteorological records are also found in China as inscriptions on animal bones and tortoise shells. Writing on these *oracle bones* of the Shang Dynasty (1751–1111 B.C.) was often in the form of ques-tions to God. An example: "Will the God give much rain in the eighth month?" Rain, snow, and drought were primary topics of Shang oracle bones; from this source one researcher has deduced that climate was warmer during that period than today.[22]

There are other records from Asia that can be helpful in reconstructing climate. In the Japanese Emperor's court yearly records were kept from the ninth century on the dates cherry trees blossomed. The flowering of these trees occasioned a celebration in Kyoto, the old capital of Japan. The dates also reveal whether the climate allowed springs to arrive early or late. Cold climate in the Far East was most marked in the twelfth century, when the average blossoming date was ten days later than the average during the last 1000 years. But this particular historical record is not entirely reliable as a climatic proxy; the celebration was sometimes ordered by the emperor arbitrarily. Hence, the date may not necessarily have coincided with the onset of spring as measured by the flowering of the trees, but rather with the date of the emperor's desire to see the blossoms.

Another type of record of the early historical period are the inscriptions on Babylonian tablets during two periods: 1800 to 1650 B.C., and 600 to 400 B.C. Ninety tablets dated to the latter period give an indirect indication of the time of the barley harvests.[23] Barley was used as currency in exchange for goods; the tablets detail who paid how much barley during what transaction. Interest rates, names of witnesses and the reigning king, and the date and place where the deal was made are all included on the tablets.

Tablets for the earlier Babylonian period (1800–1650 B.C.) reveal the harvest dates more directly; they include receipts for harvest work done on a certain day. Also recorded were receipts for advance payment for harvest work. Hence, researchers can compare the harvest dates of these two periods with each other and with those of the present. Providing there has been no significant change in the time barley varieties need to mature—that is, that uniformitarianism holds—these tablets suggest proxy climatic evidence for the early and late Babylonian times and today.

Israeli researchers Jehuda Neumann and R. Marcel Sigrist have deduced from the tablets that the harvest during the period from 1800 to 1650 B.C. began late in March or early in April; during the newer Babylonian period from 600 to 400 B.C., it began about one month later. It is known that today, in what was once central and northern Babylonia and is now Baghdad, harvest begins in the second half of April.

Neumann and Sigrist argue that these data imply that a climate colder than today's (and colder than the earlier Babylonian period) was responsible for the delayed harvest. The difference of a month between the ancient Babylonian dates seems too large to be accounted for by changes in the barley varieties cultivated. The colder period must have been wetter too, they reason, since in present-day Israel rainfall is closely associated with temperature: the larger amounts of rain occur on cold days. It is assumed that a similar relationship held true in ancient times. However, this assumption would hold true only if rainfall variations in ancient times were created by the *same* processes responsible for rainfall variations today—that is, only if climatic uniformitarianism holds for local causes of rainfall. Moreover, Israel and Mesopotamia are not in exactly the same place. Furthermore, there are the complications of calendar mismatches that confuse the precise dating of the harvest records, and the intervention of nonclimatic factors such as irrigation. Nevertheless, such records are of more than archaeological significance, even though caution is needed in their climatic interpretation.

Archaeological Remains

Archaeologists have been able to contribute to the store of knowledge about historical-era climate as well as prehistoric climate.[24] While their techniques are not designed to interpret evidence of past climatic change, they can use climatic fluctuations to explain events in the archaeological record. For instance, abandonment of a region once inhabited, sudden changes in population size, or introduction of new agricultural crops or techniques may be related to local environmental change and ultimately to climatic changes.

Archaeologists have been able to reconstruct a cultural history for most parts of the Holocene world. In an attempt to understand the three examples described on the following pages, archaeologists not only ask when and how they occurred, but why. Changing climate may be part of the answer, but by how much, we'll see, is difficult to pin down.

In the twenty-second century B.C., Egyptian tomb inscriptions refer to famine, depicting emaciated people. The inscriptions, carved within a few decades of 2150 B.C., refer to widespread disaster. Low water levels in the Nile and encroaching desert sands prevailed. Archaeologists have excavated many burial sites along the Nile dated to this period.[25]

Another dry region explored by archaeologists is southwestern Colorado. Rising abruptly from the floors of the Montezuma and Mancos valleys are tablelands with rugged sides, broken into many canyons. The cliffs of these canyons were turned into dwellings by the Anasazi Pueblo Indians, who first settled there about 1000 years ago. Overhanging rocks served as roofs for hundreds of ancient abandoned villages rediscovered by white men in December 1888.

The Pueblo Indians were probably peaceful people whose society was primarily agricultural. Archaeological remains suggest that around the year 1000 they were forced by decreased rainfall to turn from dry farming methods to irrigation methods. When the droughts worsened, maize grown had significantly smaller cobs. One theory from tree ring analyses suggested that a great drought between 1276 and 1289 caused abandonment of the Mesa Verde site. But as noted by University of Arizona dendroclimatologist Harold Fritts, it was "not as severe as droughts at other times," and thus climate must have been only one of the factors that led to abandonment of Mesa Verde.[26] Population greatly in excess of carrying capacity may have been another factor.

During the nineteenth century it was assumed that the North American High Arctic, which was then unoccupied, was too barren and climatically hostile to support human life.* But recent archaeological finds suggest that the area has been sporadically occupied for at least the past 4500 years.[27] It is believed that after about 4100 years ago the area was either abandoned or the population declined to the point where "the people become archaeologically invisible," according to Canadian archaeologist Robert McGhee. It is quite possible that the climate deteriorated so much that an increase in summer sea ice choked off the sea mammal population and ultimately the human population.

Subsequent occupations of the High Arctic were not as intense as the first. Eventually the Eskimos moved south along the west coast of Greenland, coming into contact with the Norse colonies. By 1600 the High Arctic appears to have been abandoned altogether. Again, the difficulty in separating climatic from other factors also applies to this example.

---

*This area includes the Canadian Arctic Archipelago lying to the north of Parry Channel, and the Pearyland region north of Greenland.

The Medieval Optimum

The benevolent climate that permitted expanded habitation of now harsh regions such as Greenland is widely believed to have been one of the warmest to have occurred since the early Holocene Climatic Optimum (or Altithermal) 5000 years earlier. In fact, it is referred to as the *Medieval Optimum,* having occurred during the Middle Ages from about 900 to 1200.[28] During this period a number of events appear correlated with warmer climate. These include the following:

- Oats and barley were regularly grown in Iceland, wheat in Norway, and hay in Greenland.
- The Viking colonists were able to settle in the most marginal and now inhospitable of their conquests, Greenland.
- Canadian forests were tens of kilometers north of their present limits.
- English vineyards regularly produced wine.
- Scottish agricultural settlements flourished in the highlands.
- Europe experienced locust plagues.

The Medieval Optimum has been called the Age of the Vikings. They did in fact prosper during this clement period. Bryson and Murray give an interesting account of the Vikings, whom we envision today as raiders and plunderers in breastplates and horned helmets.[29] The original Vikings were pirates; they plied the North Atlantic seas and terrorized northern Europe for three centuries, beginning around 800. Eventually Viking became equated with Norseman—that is, any Scandinavian from Norway, Sweden, or Denmark. These more peaceful people settled areas of Iceland and Greenland, helping them to escape the marauding Vikings.

In 960, the first settlers left Norway for Iceland led by Thorvald Asvaldsson who fled with his family from Norway after having murdered a man. Asvaldsson's son, Eric, later known as Eric the Red, launched a search for new land to settle after he was exiled from Iceland in 982 for murdering two men. Eric sailed west and found a hospitable area deep in a fjord on the southwestern coast, which he named Greenland in an effort to lure more tenants—an early example of a Heavenly Acres real estate swindle. Greenland was a misnomer because the country was rarely, if ever, very green. While Iceland had ample trees and tillable soil, Greenland was relatively harsh. Despite these drawbacks, settlers immigrated and raised vegetables, hay, and livestock. At one time as many as 280 farms were occupied by 3000 people.

Much of the information we have of Iceland and Greenland during the Medieval Optimum comes from the Viking Sagas, most of which were written during the twelfth and thirteenth centuries. These sagas recounted events in the lives of early settlers. The *Book of Settlements* gives especially detailed descriptions, including information on the sailing routes from Iceland and Norway to Greenland. They indicate that the route had to be altered as drift ice blocked Greenland's eastern coast. The sighting and recording of this ice can be used as a proxy thermometer of the temperature of this part of the North Atlantic. It is another indication that the climate began to cool again after the Medieval Optimum. Even in the best of times, the southwestern coast of Greenland could only support a modest colony.

Because of the ice hazard, ships detoured farther and farther south before they could swing back to reach the coastal settlements. Eventually the worsening climate prevented ships from sailing to Greenland.[30] In 1492, Pope Alexander VI reported from the church of Garda "situated at the ends of the Earth in Greenland" that "shipping is very infrequent because of the extensive freezing of the waters—no ship having put into shore, it is believed, for eighty years."[31] Cut off from outside contact, the people were finally isolated. Why they couldn't survive, when the Inuit native peoples could, is not yet clear, although the answer probably lies in cultural rather than climatic factors.[32]

When archaeologists found remnants of the Greenlanders' bones in the 1920s and 1930s, they concluded that the lack of nutrients and warmth caused a slow torturous death. The Norsemen's bones were crippled, their growth stunted and twisted. But these assumptions may have been wrong. Today, some researchers say that the bones had decalcified over time, deteriorating into a plastic substance called collagen.[33] In this condition, the remains twisted out of shape.

The cooling climate most likely did contribute to the Greenlanders' demise. It destroyed their ability to grow sufficient crops and inhibited the growth of trees from which they could have built ocean-going boats, which probably explains why they did not simply sail away when conditions worsened. Today, the site of Eric's settlement is largely barren tundra. Even though our century is warmer than many during the past millenium, fjords in that area are blocked by inland glaciers.

Plant roots that were found deep in the Greenland permafrost suggest that annual mean temperatures during the Norse heyday may have been 2° to 4°C (3.6 to 7.2°F) warmer than now.[34] Sea temperatures in the neighboring Atlantic, says Lamb, were probably raised by similar amounts. But there are other written records that bear evidence of this warm period.

In the eleventh century, William the Conqueror took a census of all the landowners and their possessions in his newly acquired kingdom—what is now England. The results, compiled in the *Domesday Book* in 1085, tally 38 thriving vineyards, besides those of the king. The wine was considered then to be on a par with French wines. Grapes were grown in England in York, Gloucestershire, and Herefordshire. This is regarded by Lamb as indicative of temperatures 1° to 2°C (1.8° to 3.6°F) higher than today.

Another type of written record pertains to the Medieval Optimum—the so-called Easter Tables.[35] Each year during the early Christian period, churchmen in Alexandria and Rome would calculate the date of Easter, which was a complex task. They were instructed to inform monasteries of the date by messenger. But as Christianity spread, this system became inadequate. In the early 500s, Dionysius Exiguus compiled tables that would allow monasteries to figure out the Easter date themselves. The tables were certified by the church and distributed. These Easter Tables had wide margins for ecclesiastics to scribble in notes, and the monks began to jot down interesting or unusual meteorological events during certain years. As this practice slowly caught on, comments with arrows pointing to the pertinent years soon covered the table. The monasteries exchanged copies of the annotated tables, and eventually the margin notes were transcribed onto separate sheets. Finally, independent annals were compiled by other authors. Bear in mind that the information filtered through several hands; like a rumor, it was probably altered somewhat. Wendy Bell and Astrid Ogilvie of the University of East Anglia, who documented the Easter Tables, report that the copying process did produce errors, especially in the transcription of dates, since the originals were often difficult to read and the copyists sometimes careless. Once the historical value of the tables was realized, analysts tried to corroborate their meteorological information, according to Bell and Ogilvie. But where sources were lacking they looked to legend. Although not attempting to draw general climatic conclusions from their study, Bell and Ogilvie do show that a number of previous inferences about the severity of some Medieval climatic periods can be challenged based on their work.

The Little Ice Age

As the Viking colonies died out, the English vineyards declined, North American boreal forests retreated, and Scottish farmers were driven to lower elevations in highlands.* The thirteenth and fourteenth centuries began a time of cooling. It was a prelude to the Little Ice Age—so called because in Europe as well as in many other parts of the world the extent of snow and ice on land and sea seems to have been as great or even greater than at any time since the end of the Pleistocene (see Figure 3.3). Various authors have dated the climax of the Little Ice Age at different times in different regions. Although very little evidence is available in the Southern Hemisphere to help verify that events such as the Little Ice Age were indeed global, a study of moraines in the southern Alps of New Zealand indicates glacial advances there began as early as the middle 1200s and continued through the mid-1800s—a period roughly coincident with the Little Ice Age in the Northern Hemisphere.[37] We do know that between 1500 and 1850 colder temperatures and advancing glaciers were common. The main phase of the Little Ice Age for most parts of the world has been considered 1550 to 1700, and in some places as late as 1850. Glaciers that advanced during this period are often believed to have been a result of longer and colder winters plus shorter and cooler summers, but this is not certain.

There are scores of written records that can be interpreted as pointing to a worsening climate during the sixteenth, seventeenth, and eighteenth centuries, which the Little Ice Age spanned, as well as some records from the thirteenth and fourteenth centuries. Diaries and weather journals are found throughout Europe. Monastic

---

*The downslope move of the Scottish farmers or the decline of English vineyards during the Little Ice Age were not wholly driven by climate, but also depended on a number of other social and economic factors as pointed out by English geographer Martin Parry.[36]

and manorial papers, chronicles, and other account books were written from Ireland to Russia; the records are so common that every season of any note from the year 1000 is discussed.

Hundreds of diaries were written in the seventeenth and eighteenth centuries, and many of the entries referred to weather events that directly affected the observers.[38] Among those who felt the impact of changing climate (and kept regular records of it) were the tax collectors. In seventeenth-century Europe, they saw the chilling climate as an erosion of their tax base: "In the village of La Roziere and Argentier seven houses were covered by glaciers, whose ravages continue and progress from one day to the next. . . . Because of all this ruin the tithe was greatly reduced."[39]

Some parallels to Little Ice Age hardships in Europe have been suggested for Latin America as well by historian Robert Claxton and climatologist Alan Hecht.[40]

Little Ice Age Proxies

Canal Freezes Another seventeenth-century record that reveals what weather and climate were like at times during the Little Ice Age is the bookkeeping on transportation of passengers and cargo through the Dutch canals. Built in the early 1600s to connect main cities of the Netherlands, the canals and the activity on them have been carefully monitored since 1633. For example, records exist on the number of barge trips during the winters from 1634 to 1682 in Haarlem and Amsterdam; the number of days that the Haarlem-Leiden canal was frozen from 1657 to 1757 and from 1814 to 1839; and temperatures at De Bilt from 1735 to 1757 and from 1814 to 1839. When winters were severe enough to keep the waterways frozen, movement ceased; the worst seasons stalled transportation for eighty to ninety days. During mild winters, the canals were hardly ever frozen.

Huug van den Dool and his colleagues at the Royal Netherlands Meteorological Institute in De Bilt state that because "the winter temperature varies very much from year to year, and because the long term average winter temperature is close to the freezing point of water, the range of days with a frozen canal varies extremely and can, therefore, be translated very well into an average winter temperature."[41] They found that "extremely cold winters" in the twentieth century have occurred only five times so far, whereas there were fourteen in the nineteenth century, twelve in the eighteenth century, and seventeen in the seventeenth century.

These results were obtained by means of *regression equations.* The Dutch scientists took advantage of the fact that their data from different series overlapped and they could relate, or "regress," one variable with another for these periods of overlapping. For instance, simultaneous data for temperature measurements and canal freeze days exist between 1735 and 1757 and between 1814 and 1839. From this, they related temperature to canal freezings to form relationship 1. There is also an overlap between 1657 and 1682 of the number of barge trips and the canal freeze days to form relationship 2. Although the only data van den Dool had for 1634 to 1656 was the number of winter barge trips, he and his colleagues could combine relationships 1 and 2 in order to predict winter temperatures as far back as winter in 1634; this, despite the lack of actual temperature data from 1634 to 1734.

Of course, the validity of their results depended on *social uniformitarianism.* Engineering projects that widened the canals, for instance, would have affected the variables, and hence the relationship between variables.* However, barring such changes, the regression equations can be used to estimate temperature even though thermometers were not used for part of the time. The principle is similar to that used in pollen assemblage or CLIMAP reconstructions of paleotemperatures, as described earlier.

Grape Harvests   The French were also meticulous bookkeepers when it came to documenting wine grape harvests. French viticulturists have recorded when their fruit was harvested since the 1500s. The warmer and sunnier the growing season (which extends roughly from March to October), the faster the grape will reach maturity. But if these months are cold and cloudy, ripening and harvesting are delayed and production decreases.

Emanuel LeRoy Ladurie, a noted French historian, has plotted these data and found, for instance, that from 1617 to 1650 wine harvests were frequently late, suggesting that there was an "outstanding cold episode."[42] This period, he says, was cold enough to build alpine glaciers in France, Italy, and Switzerland. By calibrating

---

*These complications probably did not occur in this case, according to de Vries, J., 1977, Histoire du climat et économie: des faits nouveaux une interpretation différante, *Annalés Economies Sociétés Civilisations 32:*198–227.

the overlapping records from the 1790s onward of Paris temperatures and wine harvest dates, the earlier part of the wine harvest record can be used to estimate temperatures from the late 1400s onward.

Historical Events and Climate: How Valid Are the Inferences?

Historians have recorded many other examples of events during the Little Ice Age that had a climate connection. Harsh winters at times influenced the outcome of battles.[43] Although individual historic events were undoubtedly influenced by individual extreme weather events, it is much more difficult to establish a connection between longer-term climatic anomalies and a significant change in the overall course of history.

Importance of Nonclimatic Factors

We said earlier that written reports of meteorological phenomena are often unreliable; typically, sagas were written long after the events they described. For example, the Easter Tables, some of which relied on folklore, passed from hand to hand, leading to errors. Dates of cherry blossoming and even wine harvests were at times decided arbitrarily—in Japan by edict and in France by a committee of experts that considered economic and social factors along with climate in deciding when to begin the harvest.

LeRoy Ladurie warns against taking a naive view that tries to connect climate too closely with human activities. He illustrates with a classic study done in 1955 by Gustav Utterström.[44] This Swedish historian published a paper entitled "Climatic Fluctuations and Population Problems in Early Modern History" in which he correlates deteriorating climate with economic decline in Europe during the fourteenth through seventeenth centuries. Utterström's findings and conclusions resemble others we have seen: he blames the decline of English vinegrowing in the fourteenth century after a peak in the thirteenth century, for instance, on a "climatic revolution" rather than calling it "a mere sign of an economic change," as does LeRoy Ladurie. A similar decline was reported in the "green book" of the monks who cared for vineyards at Saint Denis in France during the fourteenth century. But this decline was caused by increased labor costs that cut into their profits; the monks had told the abbot these problems, according to the *Livre Vert*. The reason labor became more expensive was that people were dying in plague epidemics and war—phenomena most likely not primarily climate related.

According to Utterström, the end of the fifteenth century and the first half of the sixteenth century were much more mild than the preceding period, but another cool period began that extended to the seventeenth century. He cites as evidence for this cooling trend dwindling Swedish grain harvests, the depopulation of Spain, and rigorous winters in England. LeRoy Ladurie points out that while Utterström's paper is filled with such "facts and data of all kinds," many of them do not necessarily implicate climatic change: decline of winegrowing or sheep rearing, the spread of wheat or cherry trees, or the changes in cereal trade can all be explained as easily, if not better, by economic changes.

For Utterström to prove his point that there were long periods of worsening climate that adversely affected Europe's economy, he would have had to use statistics, writes LeRoy Ladurie, to demonstrate that these bad years all resulted from more or less comparable meteorological conditions and that they occurred frequently enough during a certain period to be called a trend. If the researcher is unable to document such conclusions, he or she cannot justifiably use the fluctuations to argue that long-term climatic changes took place. "It is as if," LeRoy Ladurie says, "a historian or an economist were to try to demonstrate a lasting rise in prices by taking a few periodic peaks of a graph while taking no account of its general curve." A few exceptional winters during the sixteenth century are not sufficient proof that the whole century was a cold one.

In *The Genesis Strategy* I noted that "we need the average of many separate records to establish overall climatic trends reliably . . . A few examples of unusual weather do not necessarily imply a climatic change (just as five heads in a row do not necessarily indicate a loaded coin)."[45]

Utterström did cite the advance of glaciers in Europe during the Little Ice Age, and these data, LeRoy Ladurie concedes, are the most indicative of a long-term climatic change. But he believes that the chronology of this change is too vague, and the influence on human history too uncertain to "warrant such ambitious conclusions as [Utterström] draws from them." For each "climate-as-cause" explanation, there is a societal cause that is just as valid, according to LeRoy Ladurie; demographic trends, lack of currency, scarcity, and low productivity could all account for the "crises" in the seventeenth century.

Climatic Determinism

One extreme opposite view is that climate dominates human life; it was proposed by Yale University geographer Elsworth Huntington in the early 1900s.[46] His doctrine of *climatic determinism* even extended to an "explanation" of the differences between human races and their behavioral characteristics. His views have subsequently been branded as simplistic and even racist by many geographers and social scientists. For instance, Huntington claims that the "chief defect of the climate of the California coast is that it is too uniformly stimulating. Perhaps the constant activity which it incites may be a factor in causing nervous disorders." He goes on to say that the "people of California may perhaps be likened to horses which are urged to the limit so that some of them become unduly tired and break down." Referring to tropical regions, Huntington says:

> Day after day displays no appreciable variation from its predecessor. The uniformity of the climate seems to be more deadly than its heat. Such uniformity, perhaps as much as the high temperature and high humidity, may be one of the most potent causes of the physical debility which affects so many white men within the tropics, and which manifests itself in weaknesses such as drunkenness, immorality, anger, and laziness.[47]

Interactions Between Climate and History

Huntington's views neglect the complex interactions among environmental and social factors influencing history. They led to a backlash of social criticism, which perhaps overreacted by totally denying any significant component of climatic impact on human affairs. In reality, though, most case studies reveal that climate and society are so intertwined that it is difficult to separate the societal impact from the climate factor. In Part III we will examine some specific case studies in considerable detail to illustrate how the climate factor can be untangled—at least partially—from societal reactions to its change. But here we can reiterate that deductions about the cause and effect relationships between climate and human activities can be faulty; to be reliable, such deductions must be supported by statistical evidence of both climatic and societal change, as LeRoy Ladurie points out. The most reliable climatic statistics, of course, are obtained from meteorological instruments, not from diaries or monks' notebooks. However, we are forced to use such written accounts to reconstruct climate during the period before the advent of thermometers and barometers and the construction of networks of recording stations. Since we must turn to such subjective records, it is important to devise methods that will minimize misinterpretations. One such technique, called *content analysis,* attempts to quantify historical evidence to make it more "objective." One way of doing this is to count the frequency of some particular event in historical records. The number of references to unusually cold winters in the literature or chronicles of the Elizabethan period in England, for example, could be compiled and used to test the hypothesis that this was an unusually cold period. To facilitate the test, one could compare these to similar counts in French literature or chronicles. A. Catchpole and D. Moodie of the University of Manitoba have applied these methods to a number of climatic examples with considerable success.[48]

Scientists and historians at the University of East Anglia's Climatic Research Unit in Norwich, England have scrutinized historical climatology.[49] They note that general historians have developed techniques for evaluating the validity of their information. Such historians have a sense of which data are reliable and which are not. Historical climatologists could adapt such methods to their needs, according to Martin Ingram and his colleagues. Some of the steps they recommend for critically judging and using climatological records, as well as some of the pitfalls they suggest avoiding, can be briefly listed as follows:

- Consider the nature of the source—many narratives or chronicles were revised, making them exaggerated or inaccurate regarding dates or particular events.
- Building such a data base involves quantifying qualitative material such as historical records.
- Quantifying historical records involves interpreting them in terms of standard meteorological variables such as temperature or precipitation.

- Develop semiquantitative indices of possible climatic variations.
- Once an index is fabricated, the next step is to convert its data into meteorological variables such as temperature or precipitation.

We have seen some of the problems—and possible solutions—related to making climatic interpretations of historical records. But we have also offered earlier archaeological evidence of climatic events that, while not a written record, can still lead to biased inferences about human response to climate change—or even misinterpretation of what the climate actually was like. For instance, the cliff dwellers who abandoned their villages in the U.S. southwest are often thought to have been victims of a prolonged drought. Some evidence suggests this may be only part of the story. We mentioned that these people were probably peaceful; one of their few weapons uncovered by archaeologists was a simple stick, sharpened at one end. Archaeologist McGhee suggests that invasion by other, more warlike tribes could have pushed out the Pueblo Indians.[50] He cautions that "some cultural changes were likely a result of other forces: social, demographic, economic . . . you can rarely know that climate was the major influence."

McGhee also points out that the human response to environmental change often occurs over months, or even years. But archaeological events can usually be dated only to a precision of several decades and usually a century or more. Thus, archaeologists are usually capable of detecting only fragmentary chronological connections between environmental or climatic changes that might have caused human behavioral changes; cause and effect relations are difficult to prove.[51]

Corroborating the Historical Evidence with Proxies

Tree Rings and Sunspots

Coincidentally, one of the few precise dating methods available to archaeologists in the U.S. southwest turns out to be a principal biological proxy of climatic change: tree ring analysis. In 1917, Andrew Ellicott Douglass, an astronomer and tree ring specialist, was persuaded by Clark Wissler of the New York American Museum of Natural History to look at some wood fragments of a structural beam from prehistoric ruins in New Mexico in order to date them. Douglass had examined dozens of trees and their annual growth rings in Arizona around the turn of the century and was considered an expert in figuring out the ages of wood. He hadn't intended to specialize in that when he first came West from New England to the wild territory of Arizona. Originally, Douglass was trying to figure out how to extend the sunspot record into the past using tree rings, which, he reckoned, would record this solar phenomenon.

For centuries astronomers had observed the sun and recorded the appearance of the dark, splotchy sunspots, believing the sun was a constant and predictable star.* For example, more than a millennium before the telescope was invented, in *Metamorphoses* Ovid quoted Pythagoras as saying, "The great Sun is constant." Astronomers in Asia had recorded the larger sunspots with the naked eye since at least 1077; in the Western world the dark spots on the Sun were largely ignored until Galileo saw them through his telescope around 1611. There has been virtually continuous surveillance of sunspots since the middle of the seventeenth century.

In 1843, an amateur German astronomer, Heinrich Schwabe, surprised the professionals by announcing that the sunspots came and went in a ten-year cycle. Schwabe based this assertion on his graph of the average number of sunspots seen each year. Astronomers had apparently never bothered to plot these numbers, since they believed the sun was not cyclical, but unchanging. Later, other observers refined Schwabe's estimate to an average cycle length of 11.2 years, one that has been running fairly constantly since about 1700.

The Maunder/Eddy Minimum　　In 1893 E. Walter Maunder, the Superintendent of the London Royal Greenwich Observatory solar division, discovered some surprising evidence: in his search through old books and journals, he found that the sun had changed radically in recent times. The old accounts showed that for a period of seventy years, ending in about 1715, sunspot and other solar activity had all but ceased. Maunder found accounts that re-

---

*These relatively cooler regions of gas on the face of the sun are connected with disturbances in the solar magnetic field. The central, very dark portion of a sunspot is called the *umbra,* while the surrounding, less dark edge is referred to as the *penumbra.* This is surrounded by a very hot region called a *plage.*

corded the following: for thirty-two years not a single spot had been seen on the sun's northern hemisphere; for sixty-five years no more than one small group of spots had been seen at any one time; several decades had passed when not one spot could be found. Between 1645 and 1715 the total number of sunspots reported was less than what is seen in an average year today. This period of abnormally low sunspot activity came to be known as the *Maunder Minimum.* [52]

In 1894, and again in 1922, Maunder published a paper with the title "A Prolonged Sunspot Minimum." In these articles, which were mocked or ignored, Maunder pointed out that this unusual period could be used to test the hypotheses that there was a connection between the earth and the sun: he reasoned that if a normal eleven-year sunspot cycle could be detected in changes in the magnetic field of the earth or in the earth's weather, then a prolonged change in the sun's behavior should be reflected by major effects on earth. In 1893, the sunspot cycle was known to be associated with the appearance of the aurora—lights occurring in the earth's upper atmosphere and seen most often in the polar regions. Aurora lights are a direct result of protons and electrons bombarding the upper atmosphere at high speed. These particles are emitted by the sun and directed by the sun's magnetic field out into the solar system. They are known as the *solar wind.* These particles are also guided by the earth's magnetic field, which causes them to converge on the poles, thereby making auroras most prevalent in high latitudes.

Perhaps one of the reasons solar physicists and astronomers disregarded Maunder's conclusions was the nature of the early sunspot records. How reliable could they be? The quality of telescopes and the care with which astronomers watched for sunspots was in question. Also, no systematic, reliable set of records exists for much before the eighteenth century since no astronomical institution was recording daily observations of the sun. Rather, we have to depend on the diaries of individuals as they are intermittently uncovered. As with historical climate records, an independent source is needed for corroboration of these diaries. We now have an objective proxy that can help reconstruct the sunspot record: tree rings.

Trees incorporate carbon-14, among other elements, in their annual growth rings through photosynthesis of atmospheric carbon dioxide. This radioactive isotope is formed in the upper atmosphere when high-energy particles called galactic cosmic rays strike nitrogen atoms, knock out a proton, and create carbon-14 (C^{14}). Fluctuations in the number of these particles striking earth, which is regulated by the magnetic field at the earth's orbit, is related to the sun's activity. When the sun is very "active"—that is, when solar flares and sunspots occur more frequently on its face—its magnetic field extends and helps shield the earth from some of the cosmic rays by deflecting them. Hence, fewer cosmic rays hit the upper atmosphere and less C^{14} is formed. When the sun is less active, its magnetic field weakens and the earth gets a larger dose of rays, increasing the C^{14} content of the atmosphere. There are other influences that affect the tree ring record of carbon-14; for one thing it does not go directly from the upper atmosphere into the trees. The radiocarbon atoms diffuse slowly through the atmosphere; on the way some are absorbed and re-emitted by the oceans, while others are mixed and diluted with various carbon isotopes, including C^{14} formed in earlier and later years. Thus, when C^{14} atoms in atmospheric carbon dioxide finally do enter the tree, the amount reflects averaging processes carried out over several decades.[53] However, if trends in C^{14} production occurred over decades or longer, they would be recorded in tree rings.

Another factor has affected both the atmospheric concentration of C^{14} and the uptake of C^{14} by trees: burning of fossil fuels. Called the *Suess effect,* after its discoverer Hans Suess, a geochemist at the Scripps Institution of Oceanography, the basic trend since 1850 has been a sharp decrease in the atmospheric concentration of carbon-14. By combusting fossil fuels, we have liberated the carbon atoms that were fixed into hydrocarbons through photosynthesis hundreds of millions of years ago, as described in an earlier chapter.[54] Since the half-life of C^{14} is only 5870 years, there are virtually no carbon-14 atoms left in the fossil fuels. Consequently, by burning these C^{14}-free hydrocarbon fuels, humanity has injected into the atmosphere (and hence the biosphere) increasing numbers of C^{14}-poor carbon dioxide molecules. Dating trees (or anything else) by their C^{14} content is therefore virtually impossible for dates after 1850; the short half-life of this radioactive isotope also precludes using it as a dating technique for events that occurred more than about 40,000 years ago. Thus, tree rings are most useful as C^{14} proxies for times between the last glacial age and the beginning of the Industrial Age. Of course, with the advent of instrumental records, the need for this proxy during the more recent period (that is, after about 1850) has diminished greatly. (Incidentally, since 1945, in the era of atomic bomb testing, a new pulse of radioactive C^{14} has been put into the atmosphere. While further complicating the C^{14} technique for dating, it does allow scientists to trace this bomb radiocarbon as it moves through the oceans, revealing details about how oceanic waters mix.)

In 1958, the Dutch scientist Hessel DeVries observed that during the second half of the seventeenth century and the first part of the eighteenth century, C^{14} abundance in tree rings rose sharply, suggesting that the sun had been strangely inactive for a long time. DeVries' data were confirmed by tree ring evidence from around the world.[55] The Maunder Minimum coincides with the middle of the Little Ice Age, as solar astronomer John Eddy of the High Altitude Observatory (HAO) in Boulder, Colorado, noted in the mid-1970s. He cited climatic modeling evidence that global cold periods can be brought on by a decrease of no more than about 1 percent of the total solar radiation. Eddy asked whether the possible disappearance of sunspots and the accompanying distorted pattern of solar rotation could be indicators that solar radiation was slightly reduced.[56] More likely, he suggested, magnetic effects could be the cause of any solar-induced climatic changes, but he still cautioned that no reliable physical mechanism has been found yet to explain a connection between sunspots and climate. Incidentally, the Maunder Minimum implies that the modern period of solar activity is not necessarily "normal." Rather, according to Eddy, it seems that we are in a period of unusually high levels of solar activity. This could be significant for sun-climate connections, since we are currently in a warm climate period (discussed later on) that could be considered a recovery from the Little Ice Age.

Eddy acknowledges that the Maunder Minimum and the Little Ice Age could be unrelated, and merely coincidental. In this connection, some scientists suggest that if people continued the search for diaries and other evidence, these finds might reveal more sunspots than have been previously identified. For example, University of Maryland climatologist Helmut Landsberg has uncovered several additional European astronomical recordings suggesting that at least several sunspots had been observed on many occasions between 1678 and 1718. He also cites recent publication of additional evidence reporting some auroral sightings. Although none of these new findings suggest solar activity at today's levels, Landsberg argues that "considering the fact that all of these observations are additions to the major source of Eddy . . . and that most of them come from a limited European geographic area, the Sun cannot have been as quiet as described. There are undoubtedly other unexploited sources which might still add to the list."[57] Landsberg also argues that the coldest decades of the Little Ice Age were between 1600 and 1619 and between 1800 and 1819, not coincident with the Maunder/Eddy sunspot minimum (1650 to 1715). However, the data Landsberg used to reconstruct the Little Ice Age temperatures are widely scattered and, in my opinion, are hardly capable of providing a reliable estimate for *global* temperature reconstruction. The solar-climate interaction issue is still controversial.

The Twenty-Two-Year Drought Cycle   One other possible sun-climate connection—also closely related to tree rings —that has received some attention over the past several decades is the fairly coincidental occurrence of alternate sunspot cycle minima and drought in the U.S. High Plains. J. Murray Mitchell, Jr., an important climatologist at the National Oceanic and Atmospheric Administration, and Charles Stockton and David Meko, of the University of Arizona Tree Ring Laboratory, conducted a statistical analysis of tree rings looking for evidence of droughts.[58] These droughts seem to occur approximately every twenty-two years— that is, roughly every other eleven-year sunspot cycle; they have persisted since at least 1700, according to their study.

The cause of these apparent connections is not known. What solar mechanism would give rise to drought in a specific area on a specific continent and at a specific location? In order to understand better the seeming connection, Mitchell and his colleagues analyzed tree rings over most of the western half of the United States and found a tendency for summer droughts to occur every twenty to twenty-two years centered near or around every other minimum of the sunspot cycle. Still, even given this statistical evidence, the best we can say in all honesty is that the tendency for drought exists, although some parts of the western United States were wet during a drought cycle. Furthermore, of the droughts Mitchell and his colleagues found, all of which varied in intensity, timing and location, only about 25 percent corresponded closely with the twenty-two-year cycle. If directly connected, the next such round of droughts is due in the mid-1990s. However, Ronald Gilliland, a young solar physicist at the High Altitude Observatory in Boulder, Colorado, looked more closely at the whole question of solar-climate variations, and concluded that long-term cyclical variations in the size of the sun, the sunspot cycle, and the energy output of the sun might be found in the climatic record of the past century. These combined effects, he speculates cautiously, could cause the 1990s drought to be weak, but the 2010s one to be large.[59]

Varying solar activity cannot be the only—or perhaps even a major—cause for recurrent droughts in the United States, let alone elsewhere, although the statistical evidence for some solar connection is intriguing. While historians, solar physicists, and climatologists continue their research, tree rings, as Douglass suspected, can provide valuable bits of evidence to reveal any sun-weather connections. This science of *dendrochronology,* * which Douglass pioneered, would eventually aid climatologists in a different way—one less concerned with the variations of the sun.

Dendroclimatology We mentioned at the beginning of this section that Douglass was called on to date wood samples from a prehistoric ruin; he was qualified to do this by virtue of his fascination with, and knowledge about, tree rings.[60] Around 1901, Douglass had examined scores of tree rings in ponderosa pines near Flagstaff, Arizona, often going to lumbering camps and local sawmills to make crude rubbings from the tops of newly cut stumps.

In 1904, Douglass recognized a characteristic ring pattern in an old stump and boldly announced the year in which the tree had been cut down, much to the astonishment of the farmer who had felled the tree. By 1907 Douglass had scrutinized a considerable group of trees and their rings in Flagstaff and supposedly committed them all to memory. A few years later he was amazed to find virtually identical ring patterns of thick and thin rings in trees near Prescott, some 80 kilometers (50 miles) southwest of Flagstaff. Douglass had stumbled onto evidence that led to the principle of *cross dating*—matching rings from tree to tree in order to identify the exact year in which each ring was formed. This creates a time series, or chronology, of ring growth history.

The significance of dating tree rings for climatology, of course, is that the rings record how the tree responded to the climate during the year in which they formed. Douglass likened tree rings to the Morse telegraph code—the sequence of dots (narrow rings) and dashes (wider rings) convey a message about the life of the tree and

---

*This word for tree ring studies comes from the Greek *dendron* tree; *chronology,* of course, refers to time. Tree rings offer a yearly chronology of the tree's growth and its responses to environmental conditions. Climatic inferences from the size or chemical nature of tree rings fall into the field known as *dendroclimatology.*

the climate it encountered along the way. In the arid and sunny southwest, where it turns out that rainfall is the limiting climatic factor for growth of most trees, a narrow ring indicates that the tree had to withstand decreased precipitation that year and a wider ring suggests it benefited from increased precipitation. But reconstructing climate in this way is not quite that simple. For example, Douglass knew that trees have a storage capacity—he called it the *conservation term*—whereby they stock their roots with nutrients during wet years so that in dry years they won't be seriously deficient. Hence, a year with very dry climate might not be reflected in as thin a ring as might be expected. That is, the severity of dryness is not exactly proportional to ring width.

There are other complications that make the language of tree rings difficult to translate into climate. Among them are these factors: a tree's age and height can affect its ring widths; sometimes during a year of extreme climate a tree may not form a ring at all or may only partially form a ring; at other times false rings form, the result of a change in cell structure, so that the cell layer resembles a true annual ring; and different species respond differently to the same environmental conditions. Trees can be thought of as windows or filters through which a climatic input passes. The output is the ring width and its chemical composition (especially the amount of carbon isotopes). Different species pass different amounts of information through their windows at different times of the year.[61] During prolonged drought, some trees will weaken and die and fewer new trees will replace them. Consequently, after several decades each tree has more area from which to draw moisture and nutrients. This makes the rings widen again, but not because rainfall has increased. Interactions take place among internal conditions—growth regulators, enzymes, the amount of stored minerals, and water—and external conditions—temperature, precipitation, light and carbon dioxide available for photosynthesis, oxygen, and soil minerals. These interactions are complex and not well understood. Laboratory experiments on seedlings or relatively small plants grown under controlled conditions may not accurately reflect the ways in which larger trees interact with the actual environment. All of these complications, therefore, tend to make decoding the climate cipher difficult, particularly from a limited sample of tree rings.

Hence, many trees are needed to reconstruct climate reliably. A number of trees over a wide area must be used by dendroclimatologists to formulate a picture of what past climates were like. This is where cross dating enters the picture. Douglass used the technique by relying on his memory of tree ring patterns to compare and combine them. In this way he built a chronology of nearly 500 years. All he needed to know was the year for the outermost ring of a tree, which would have been the current year, and the occurrence of the same relative ring variations in many trees.* Using the overlapping lifespans of a number of trees, the tree ring record can be extended further into the past. The technique also allows for a continuity of the ring records, since it assures that one can accurately date each growth layer simply by counting backward from a known recent ring date.

Douglass used a mathematical expression to adjust the ring widths for varying environmental conditions and for the varying growth rate of trees whose rings are thicker in younger years. In this way he could obtain an average picture of past climate. Today, statistical techniques such as regression analysis have replaced Douglass' simpler procedures; graphic techniques afforded by computer analysis compile the information on many scores of rings.

Douglass' work is carried on today by a group of scientists at the University of Arizona Laboratory of Tree-Ring Research, of which he was the first director in 1938. Tree chronologies in the North American West have been extended back some 8200 years. Bristlecone pines, probably the oldest living things on earth (some are 4600 years old), have been cross-dated with other trees and dead members of their own species in mountains of southern California, thus supplying a very long proxy climate record. Among the other species of trees in the West that are useful to dendroclimatologists are the redwood, which can live 2000 years, ponderosa pine, limber pine, and the Douglas fir (named not for dendrochronologist Andrew Ellicott Douglass, but for a Scotsman who introduced the fir to England in 1827). Not only do chronologies of these trees record local precipitation, but scientists such as Harold Fritts and colleagues at the Tree Ring Laboratory have tried to infer from their rings maps of yearly averaged climatic patterns for North America over hundreds of past years.[62] One of their findings is that the mean

*We should mention that a tree needn't be cut down in order for its rings to be viewed—borers as small as 4 millimeters (0.16 inches) in diameter can extract cores from the tree trunk, much as with a biopsy sample taken from humans, leaving a relatively harmless wound. The bore hole is usually sealed to prevent diseases from entering.

winter temperature of the United States was a degree or so Celsius colder (except for an 0.4°C—0.7°F—warming of the intermountain basin area) between 1602 and 1900 than in the twentieth century. Summer temperatures everywhere in the United States were less than one degree different.

Another result of these tree ring reconstructions is the finding that it has been wetter in the central and western states (California was 15 percent wetter) and drier in the East, Midwest, and South this century as compared to the previous three hundred years. Also, all regions have had less annual departures from their long-term average in this century, implying that this measure of climatic variability has decreased in the warmer twentieth century. Enthusiasts of this technique of climatic reconstruction believe these emerging efforts should be extended to give an indication of past climate fluctuations in other parts of the world as well. Despite these impressive results, the technique should still be viewed as highly experimental and thus all inferences need to be compared against climatic reconstructions by other proxy means.

The ring widths of bristlecone pines in the lower altitudes of California's White Mountains are limited by low rainfall; at higher altitudes, however, growth is mainly influenced by temperatures. University of Arizona dendrochronologist Valmore LaMarche, Jr., has correlated the average ring width in temperature-sensitive pines over the past 5300 years with the expansion and contraction of mountain glaciers.[63] His data have been compared with that from glaciers by Denton and Karlén, whose work we discussed earlier. Figure 3.3 illustrates that periods for which rings indicate low summer temperatures seem to relate fairly well to periods in which glaciers grew and advanced. During the Little Ice Age the average growth rates for bristlecone pines at upper tree line dropped by half. Many trees succumbed to poor growing conditions and dendroclimatologists found tree trunks strewn on the ground at the site where core samples were taken. The Little Ice Age is represented in Figure 3.3 by a dip in tree ring growth and an expansion of glaciers.

The British, Europeans, and Soviets are also compiling tree ring chronologies. (They are able to take advantage of very old wooden structures—including medieval sidewalks—for their research.) Tree ring records in southern Germany have verified wine harvest dates that suggest cooler climate may have been widespread across Europe. Conversely, narrow rings during the even-numbered years between 1531 and 1540 correspond to early wine harvests, a sign of hot and rather dry conditions in the springs and especially the summers. LeRoy Ladurie refers to these alternating years of hot/dry and cool/damp growing seasons and their reflection in the tree ring record as the *sawtooth signature*. When this pattern was first detected by German dendrochronologists, they thought it was a fluke that occurred once every 5000 years. But the sawtooth formation has been encountered again in many old German timbers that were cut down after the period between 1530 and 1541. Cause and effect, however, are still not certain.

We have seen two examples of tree rings being used to corroborate historical records for the Little Ice Age period. Only by *corroboration among proxies* can we build confidence in such paleoclimatic reconstructions. Included in these proxies are *varves* and *stalagmites*, both of which are discussed below.

Varved Lakes

Varves—thin sediment layers that are laid down annually in some lakes—are much like tree rings in that they vary slightly in width and can be cross-dated. These underwater layers are unlike most ocean-bottom sediments in that they are much more distinct and form a year-by-year climate record that can be read, since they are not usually subject to bioturbation by bottom dwellers or disturbance by strong bottom currents. (Varves are also found in ancient rocks, but it is difficult to determine whether the layers are annual. In any case, the varves we will discuss are found under existing lakes.)

As with sea cores, it is the material that collects in varves that gives us clues to past climates. In Hell's Kitchen Lake, in north central Wisconsin, researchers have found pollen, charcoal, and seeds—remnants of past vegetation—that have been collecting in varve layers for 2000 years.[64] Extracting cores from lakes is basically the same as taking them from the sea floor; a metal tube is used for boring, but it is filled with a refrigerant to freeze the outer crust of the core. This prevents the laminated structure from being destroyed. The cores in the Hell's Kitchen study, which were about 2 meters (6.6 feet) long, are roughly equivalent to 3000 years of climatic history. The University of Wisconsin at Madison scientist who conducted this study, paleoecologist Albert Swain, divided this time span into six zones. Of interest to us now is zone 5—600 to 150 years ago. Swain found that in these layers there was an increased percentage of white pine and hemlock pollen and of yellow birch seeds. To him this suggests a return to moist conditions. Swain notes that this interval corresponds to the Little Ice Age when climate in this region was wetter. Swain and Chris Bernabo suggest that temperatures in the growing season for northeastern United States were about 1°C (1.8°F) colder during the Little Ice Age than today, and conditions "were relatively wet and snowy" at the coldest periods.[65]

Another varve-dated pollen study, this one conducted in Yellowstone Park, Wyoming, also gives proxy corroboration of earlier climate history.[66] A pollen sequence from Cub Creek suggests that from about 14,000 to 11,500 years ago, alpine vegetation prevailed on the Yellowstone Plateau. The vegetation then quickly shifted to spruce, fir, whitebark pine, and lodgepole pine, implying warmer climate. This trend, the researchers say, culminated in the Altithermal, which their varves date at 9000 to 4500 years ago in Yellowstone.

Stalagmites

Water-dissolved limestone dripping onto the floor of a cave builds stalagmites layer by layer. Reaching upward in a cave, these calcareous columns record O^{18}/O^{16} ratios, much like sea cores with fossil calcium carbonate remains in their layers. The water ultimately responsible for stalagmite growth originates in the oceans, which have a certain ratio of O^{18}/O^{16} at any given period of time. The O^{18}/O^{16} amount in rain water depends on this ratio in the sea where the evaporation took place and on the temperature of the evaporation and subsequent precipitation, as we saw in the last chapter. The relative amount of O^{18}/O^{16} incorporated into limestone depends on two factors: the O^{18}/O^{16} ratio in the water percolating down into the cave and the temperature of the cave itself; the latter is believed to be a close approximation of the mean annual surface temperature. By assuming that for periods of up to a few hundreds of years, the ratio of O^{18}/O^{16} in the water dripping down was constant, scientists can infer the effects of changing temperature on O^{18}/O^{16} of the limestone in the cave.

Researchers in New Zealand examined a stalagmite in a cave in Nelson, a small coastal town known as an artists' colony on the South Island.[67] The dating method used was C^{14} analysis; their aim was to compare the temperature record for England from 1100 to the New Zealand record. Meteorologically, they noted, these two locations are unrelated. The results suggest that the temperature curve for England and New Zealand are broadly similar. Hence, from this proxy it appears that the Little Ice Age was not just localized in Europe.[68]

Proxy Assemblages

None of these individual climate proxies—including the historical records—can give us the confidence that actual instrumental data can, although assemblages of proxies can certainly help. Certainly the historical evidence suggesting that the Little Ice Age occurred in Europe is bolstered and extended by proxy data such as the New Zealand cave or the California tree ring results. But the objectivity and precision of instrumental observations are needed both to establish comprehensive and reliable climatic histories and to formulate and verify hypotheses about the causes of weather and climate change. Although such instrumental records began in the seventeenth century, they did not become truly global in coverage until the advent of satellite monitoring in the 1960s.

PART II

THE CAUSES
OF
CLIMATE CHANGE

4. The Climate System and What Drives It

Ice layers, pollen grains, coral reef terraces, deep sea cores, traces of sand dune and forest movements, terminal moraines, the creep of lichen, archaeological findings of the waxing and waning of cultures, packrat leavings, and written accounts: all these bits of proxy evidence help us piece together the climate of the Holocene. The written records add a new dimension to the growing record of proxy testimony. But, as we found in Chapter 3, historical evidence is often sketchy, inconsistent, and subjective. Indeed, it always is an indirect—that is, a proxy—measure of climate.

What is needed, of course, is a more objective, direct, and quantitative measure of the weather. A basic step in the scientific method is to observe and record, and the more accurate and reliable the observation, the better the basis on which to build and confirm hypotheses. Hence, in order to obtain direct and consistent meteorological observations, standardized meteorological instruments are needed. Their invention, evolution, and use can be traced to seventeenth-century Italy.

The Evolution of Weather Instruments

Interestingly, it was not a scientist but a patron of science who first attempted to standardize the thermometer so that comparable observations could be made. The Grand Duke of Tuscany, Ferdinand II of the de' Medici family, instructed his master glass blower, Mariani, to manufacture dozens of thermometers that would all respond in kind to temperature changes.[1] At the end of 1654, Ferdinand sent these thermometers to observers in a number of Italian cities, including Milan and Bologna. He thus commis-

137

sioned the first known network of meteorological instruments. Ferdinand also had the foresight to retain Evangelista Torricelli as his official philosopher and mathematician.

In the 1640s, Torricelli was conducting experiments in an attempt to produce a vacuum in a tube filled with mercury. He knew that air had weight. "We live," he wrote, "submerged at the bottom of an ocean of elementary air." This was an apt analogy, as we shall see. The weight of the air pressed down on the mercury in the cistern, forcing it up into the tube, Torricelli believed. He observed that the mercury level in the tube changed from day to day, which indicated to him that the air pressing on the cistern of mercury was heavier at certain times and lighter at others.

Scholars of the time knew from observations (in Rome by the Cardinal Giovanni Carlo de' Medici, and throughout the network of ten stations around the country set up by Ferdinand II) that the mercury usually stood at its greatest height in good weather and at its lowest on the rainiest days. However, the reasons for this were not obvious to these scholars; they thought air was heaviest on rainy days when it is "most full of vapours and exhalations" and should therefore cause the mercury to rise.*

The Fellows of the Royal Society of England were also interested in the Torricellian tube. Sometime during the 1660s, Robert Boyle at Oxford appropriately labeled the instrument a *barometer,* which derives from the Greek words meaning "weight measure."

A variation on the barometer is the *aneroid barometer*—one containing no liquid. It was invented around 1700 by Gottfried Leibnitz, a German mathematician who discovered calculus independently of Newton. In 1698, Leibnitz wrote to his Swiss colleague Johann Bernoulli that he was considering making "a small closed bellows which would be compressed and dilated by itself as the

---

*Water vapor has a molecular weight of 18; it is actually lighter than dry air, which contains no water but rather a mixture of nitrogen, oxygen, argon, carbon dioxide, and other trace gases. These elements give dry air a combined average molecular weight of about 29. Thus, when there is a greater ratio of water vapor—that is, humidity—to dry air, a given volume of air is lighter. However, the major reason the mercury rises and falls is not the air's water vapor content per se, but rather the air's temperature and motions; these factors alter the number of air molecules in a column above the barometer. The fewer air molecules, the lower the air pressure. Hence, when seventeenth-century scholars observed high mercury levels on sunny days and low levels on rainy days it was because fair weather in Europe is typically accompanied by sinking air associated with higher pressure; foul weather generally comes along with rising air and lower pressure.

weight of the air increases or decreases."[2] In fact, *aneroid* means "without air"—that is, the bellows is in a vacuum. Leibnitz envisioned a portable barometer that could be put in a pocket much like a watch. "It is without mercury," he wrote, "whose [function] the bellows performs, which the weight of the air tries to compress against the resistance of the steel spring."[3] Unfortunately, no instrument maker at that time was capable of carrying out his ideas.

From these first crude instruments and scattered meteorological networks grew an increasingly complex array of instruments and instrument stations.[4] Only networks of weather records could provide the time and space coverage needed for the serious development of weather sciences. But it wasn't until the advent of satellites that scientists could obtain the global coverage that is needed to pursue modern atmospheric science.

We might consider satellites to be the ultimate in meteorological instrumentation. Their coverage is vast, their components sophisticated, and their measurements fairly precise. But ironically, the information obtained from satellites—on temperature, at least—is actually a return to proxy evidence! For example, satellites measure (or "sense" in the jargon of satellite meteorology) the amount of infrared, or radiant heat energy, emitted by the planet; they are not directly measuring temperature. Solar radiation reflected by the earth's atmosphere and surface is also measured with instruments. By gauging the distribution and amount of the emanating radiant energy, the sensors can provide data from which scientists use theories of radiative transfer to estimate the earth's temperature. While not yet perfected, such theories do produce good results in many applications. In any case, satellite data are essential to verify most theories that attempt to explain the behavior of the climatic system and its subcomponents. We turn next to the climatic subsystems that are probed by meteorological sensors.

Climatic Subsystems

The climatic system is composed of several interconnected subsystems: the atmosphere, oceans, cryosphere (ice and snow), lithosphere or solid surface (land and ocean floor), and biosphere (all of life, including humans and their technological baggage). It is in the atmospheric subsystem, of course, that we experience climate most directly. There, the constant redistribution of mass, momentum, and energy creates fluctuating weather and climate. In this section we give a brief overview of the various subsystems, focusing in more detail on the dynamics of specific subsystems in succeeding sections.

Changes in the atmosphere usually occur more quickly than variations in the other climatic subsystems. For example, temperature in the lower atmosphere can alter significantly from day to night or from one day to the next as compared to the more slowly changing ocean temperatures. Similarly, major ocean currents typically change speed or direction more slowly than the restless atmospheric winds.

Atmospheric composition can also change rapidly—for example, humidity today can be very different from humidity tomorrow. But such rapid changes do not occur for all atmospheric compounds or elements. Oxygen, for instance, changes extremely slowly over time; the atmospheric oxygen component evolved during hundreds of millions of years of volcanic outgassing, mineral oxidation, and biological evolution. This component is so stable that even if humanity burned all the trees on earth and all the fossil fuels in the ground, we would still be unable to change the oxygen content of the atmosphere by more than a small fraction.* The effect would be akin to lowering the amount of oxygen at sea level to that now encountered near the top of a Manhattan skyscraper. Hence, although it is often true that processes in the atmosphere occur more quickly than those in the other climatic subsystems, not every atmospheric variable abides by this fairly general rule, as the oxygen example suggests. A significant change in the level of carbon dioxide, a climatically more important atmospheric variable than oxygen, also occurs very slowly relative to short-term climatic variability.

To predict atmospheric changes occurring more slowly than over a few weeks or so, we must also predict how variables in the

---

*Calculations by atmospheric physicist and chemist James C. G. Walker suggest that if all fossil fuels were burned oxygen content would drop some 2 percent; and if, in addition, "we were to kill all the green plants . . . after a time on the order of 20 years . . . oxygen in the atmosphere would have decreased by less than one percent." Without photosynthesis to balance oxygen consumption by the weathering of rocks, however, oxygen would decline slowly if humanity were to kill all green plants. But, Walker notes, "the oxygen crisis . . . would, from man's point of view, occur in the very remote future . . . it would take approximately four million years for weathering to consume all of the oxygen in the atmosphere."[5]

oceans are changing simultaneously. The oceans, like the atmosphere, serve as a storehouse and factory for chemicals; they also store and distribute heat, momentum, and mass. Storing heat is one of the principal contributions of the oceans to the climate. Because of the oceans' large mass, they can store much more heat than the atmosphere. This capacity allows the oceans to "remember" past climatic conditions over a long period of time. For example, both the day-to-night and winter-to-summer temperature extremes at the center of continents can be several times greater than the extremes on coasts or islands, because the waters near the latter retain some of the heat of summer, slowly giving it back to the atmosphere in the winter. Thus, winter temperatures are much more moderate at coastal sites than at places at the same latitude but far away from the influence of heat-retaining oceans. Similarly, daytime temperatures are typically cooler near shore than inland in summer, and the nighttime temperature pattern is the reverse. Furthermore, to change appreciably the temperature of the upper few hundred meters of the oceans takes a decade or so; to warm or cool the abyssal depths of the oceans takes a century to a millenium. Oceans also redistribute heat through a variety of flows or currents, and heat transported this way can cause significant regional climatic differences.

The oceans not only interact with the atmosphere through heat storage and transport, but are also coupled to it chemically. The oceans are a major chemical reserve. They contain most of the water on earth as well as much of the carbon dioxide, oxides of nitrogen, sulfur compounds, and many other nutrients. Chemicals in gaseous form are constantly being transferred from the oceans and the atmosphere and vice versa in what are called *air/sea interactions.* In these interactions many times more total carbon dioxide is exchanged annually than is released into the atmosphere by the burning of fossil fuels or by deforestation.

Massive glaciers, which compose the bulk of the *cryosphere*—snow and ice components of the climatic system—are very slow to change relative to most variables in the atmosphere or oceans. Except for occasional glacial surges—a controversial issue, as we have seen— it typically takes ten thousand years or more for large glaciers to change their volume radically. But not all of the cryosphere is so sluggish. Snow cover, particularly in spring or fall, can disappear in a matter of hours. Sea ice, in the form of sheets a few meters thick or even icebergs a hundred meters thick, can be created or melted in a few months to a few tens of years. Regardless of time scale, snow and ice are very important parts of the climatic system. They make the surfaces they cover—such as blue water or brown land—much brighter and more reflective of sunlight; a snow- or ice-covered surface with its higher *albedo* (reflectivity) absorbs less sunlight than an open area. Since the amount of solar heat absorbed is the principal energy source driving the climate, a change in surface albedo is an important component of heating in the climate system.

Snow cover on land or ice cover on the sea changes considerably with season, and plays a large part in determining local seasonal extremes. On water, it is not so much the high albedo of the sea ice (or the snow cover on the floating ice) that matters, but the very presence of the ice itself that chills the local climate. As mentioned above, the vast heat-storing capacity of the oceans provides a memory of past summers' warmth, which is a major factor in keeping winter temperature extremes moderated. If sea ice is present, however, it physically cuts off direct contact between the air and the sea, thereby choking off most of the heat flow from the relatively warmer oceans to the colder air. The presence of sea ice, by isolating the air from the sea, is thermodynamically akin to having land rather than oceans as the lower boundary of the atmosphere. The air then behaves as though it were over land; its extreme ranges of temperature become much larger than if the air could "feel" the heat in the sea below the ice cover.

The thermal blanketing effect of sea ice has a cryospheric parallel on land: snow cover blankets the underlying soil. If you have ever gardened or farmed, you will probably have noticed that in winters where snow is present some plants survive the winter nicely beneath the snow cover. In the U.S. plains, for example, winter wheat crops in cold-winter states are usually better in years during which much snow covers the farm fields. There are several reasons for this. When the snow melts it slowly releases its water content to the soils. Slow release decreases runoff and minimizes the soil erosion that typically accompanies short, heavy bursts of rainfall. Although the snow itself is certainly cold, it has roughly enough heat capacity to "remember" the average temperature of the past few weeks. Thus, while retaining a below-freezing temperature, the bottom layer of the snow cover will be warmer than the few-hour-long, extremely low nighttime winter temperatures typically experienced in wheat-growing plains. The effect of the snow cover is analogous to the thermal-blanketing effect of sea ice, but in reverse. On land, the snow screens the plants from feeling the rapidly changing but often extreme air temperatures above. Without the protection of snow, winter kill is more likely.

There is another way snow cover can be beneficial to agriculture in plains regions. Persistent windiness is likely in winter. Fields covered by snow are less subject to wind erosion than open fields, particularly if the latter are plowed and unprotected by a dense vegetation cover. In 1976 and 1977, winter drought in the U.S. central plains led to serious episodes of wind erosion and dust storms when heavy plowing of agricultural land and unusually snow-free weather resulted in blowing soil.

The cryosphere, then, has an important impact on certain kinds of plants. It may be less apparent, though, that all of life taken together—the biosphere—is also an important contributor to the climate and is rightly considered a part of the climatic system.

Like the atmosphere and oceans, the biosphere is a major store-house and factory for producing or removing climatically significant chemicals. Plants transpire water vapor, produce such trace gases as N_2O, and consume CO_2 in order to photosynthesize carbohydrates. (If we include humans and their industrial and agricultural activities as part of this biological climatic subsystem, we can even say that carbon dioxide trends today are controlled principally by the biosphere.) Plants also emit hydrocarbon gases, which can be converted in the atmosphere into haze particles (which some believe are responsible for the "smoke" in the Smoky Mountains).[6] The biosphere can contribute to changes in atmospheric composition or land-surface characteristics on a variety of time scales. These range from a few hours for some hazes, through a season or so for some land albedo changes, to hundreds of millions of years for significant alterations of oxygen content.

We've already seen that on the longest time scales, continental drift is responsible for altering the amount and location of land masses and the volume of ocean basins. These external forces help to create climate, but are not themselves much altered by climate, so it seems that the earth's solid surface should be excluded from the interacting components of the climatic system. However, recall that the weight of big glaciers can depress land masses. In some instances such climatically induced changes to the earth's surface could, in turn, feed back and affect climate. For example, several theories of ice ages contend that the changing weight of ocean volumes and glaciers—both climatic effects—distorts the earth's

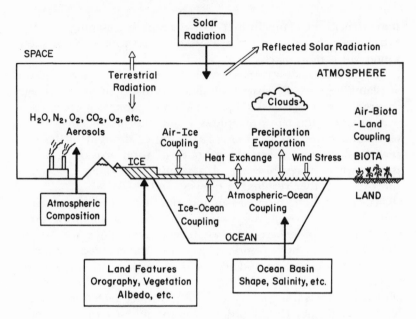

Figure 4.1

The climatic system of the earth consists of many interacting subsystems: the atmosphere, the oceans, the cryosphere (ice and snow), the biosphere (biota and their environment plus humans and their activities), the bottoms of the oceans, and some of the solid material below land and oceans. The interacting components of these subsystems are called the inter- nal *climate system, whereas those forces that drive the climate system, but are not an internal part of that system, are known as* external *forcing or* boundary conditions. *[Source: Modified after W. L. Gates, 1979, The physical basis of climate, in* Proceedings of the World Climate Conference *(Geneva: World Meteorological Organization), WMO 537, p. 114.]*

crust. This distortion, the theory goes, is enough to alter the shape of the ocean bottom, thereby changing the volume of warm water flowing into polar regions, and hence participating in climatic changes.[7] Thus, even the earth's solid surface—part of the lithosphere—can be considered one of the interactive components of the climate system, at least on time scales of thousands of years or more.*

Clearly, then, our definition of the climatic system is not fixed. Rather, the climatic system has a fluid definition—its extent de-

---

*And even the molten layer just below the solid upper earth is involved in climatic theories, since this viscous underlayer helps determine how the elastic solid earth above responds to the weight of oceans and glaciers.

pends on the time scale and climatic variables being considered (see Figure 4.1). With this perspective, we'll now explore the nature of each climatic subsystem in more depth.

The Atmosphere

Local air weight or pressure varies, both in time and from place to place. If a heavier column of air moves over a barometer it will push down harder on the mercury, making its column rise in order to balance exactly the weight of the air. Conversely, if a lighter column of air moves over the same barometer, the mercury will fall.

What causes the density and weight of air to change? Torricelli's remark that "we live submerged at the bottom of an ocean of air" is a very apt analogy for explaining this phenomenon. He was correct to say that air is much like a liquid, in that it follows the principles of fluid dynamics. *Fluid* is the generic term used by engineers and scientists to represent any continuous medium that flows. Under this definition, glass and ice are considered fluids since they flow, albeit very slowly relative to liquid water or gaseous air.

Air tends to flow from areas of high pressure to areas of low pressure. This is easily illustrated by blowing up a balloon and letting it go. The air inside the balloon, squeezed by the elastic membrane, has a higher pressure than the outside air; it will escape by flowing into the area of lower pressure outside when an opening is made in the balloon. In the atmosphere the creation of high- and low-pressure areas translates into weather. This process begins with the sun, the fundamental driving mechanism of the atmospheric machine.

The Troposphere

While it is difficult to define the exact top of the atmosphere, we can more easily discern a number of layers within it. These atmospheric layers are named according to their special characteristics. For example, the lowermost layer is the *troposphere*, a word that stems from the Greek word *tropos* meaning "turn or mix." In this bottom layer there is indeed much atmospheric motion—it is where most of our weather occurs. Above the equator, the troposphere extends upward about 18 kilometers (11 miles). The thickness of the troposphere diminishes away from the equator, and averages only about 8 kilometers (5 miles) of depth near the poles. Temperature averaged over the depth of the troposphere decreases moving away from the equator toward the poles. Temperature also generally decreases in the troposphere as one moves upward away from the earth's surface. The rate of decrease, which averages about 6°C per kilometer (3.6°F per 1000 feet), is known as the *temperature lapse rate*. (Exceptions to the decrease of temperature with height are known as *inversions*.)

The regions that divide characteristic layers of the atmosphere are labeled with the suffix "pause." Hence, the boundary between the troposphere and the next layer up—the stratosphere—is the *tropopause*.

The Stratosphere

The word *stratosphere* is an appropriate label for this next layer—the Greek translation is "smoothing out." The stratosphere, which extends from the top of the tropopause to some 50 kilometers (30 miles) above the earth, is relatively stable. It is stratified, with few clouds and relatively little vertical motion compared to the turbulent troposphere below. There are high winds in the stratosphere, but these blow primarily horizontally. This is why sunrises and sunsets on clear days around the world become more colorful only weeks after a volcanic eruption. Dust and other materials injected into the stratosphere by explosive volcanic blasts are quickly dispersed around the globe by the fast-moving horizontal winds. The dust, some of which persists for several years, then catches twilight sunbeams that cause the spectacular dawn and dusk glows. In the turbulent troposphere, most dust particles are eliminated in a few weeks or less by the weather. But in the stable stratosphere, materials injected—by nature or people—can last for years and spread worldwide before they are chemically altered or finally cross the tropopause and wash out.

The stratosphere is host to important chemical activity. Ozone, for instance, is produced primarily by the action of ultraviolet sunlight on oxygen molecules. Some of it is also destroyed in the stratosphere by the sunlight and by other trace gases serving as catalysts. These catalysts include water vapor, nitrogen oxides, and chlorine compound gases, some of which are added to the atmosphere by various human activities: flying aircraft at high altitudes;

exploding atomic bombs above ground; and releasing fluorocarbons originally used in refrigerators, air conditioners, or spray cans.

The temperature in the lowest few miles of the stratosphere averages about −57°C (−70°F); some 20 kilometers (12.5 miles) above the earth, temperature begins to increase rapidly with height, largely due to the ozone layer. Ozone absorbs much of the sun's ultraviolet radiation in the upper stratosphere (and some lesser amount of visible light is also absorbed by ozone). Because the air is not well mixed at these altitudes, the little solar energy that is absorbed (which only amounts to a few percent of the total solar input) can increase the temperature by some 50°C (90°F). About 40 kilometers (25 miles) above the earth's surface, ozone concentrations begin to decrease with height. At that region absorption of solar energy diminishes with height. At about 50 kilometers (30 miles) temperatures stop rising. Above this comes the stratopause, or top of the stratosphere. Above the stratosphere are several more layers, but we will not discuss these since they are very rarified and have little known influence on the climate at the earth's surface (although some controversial theories on the subject are debated). Also, they are well explained elsewhere, such as in Robert Kandel's *Earth and Cosmos*. [8]

The increase of temperature with height in the stratosphere causes this layer to be stratified. When cold air occurs under hot air, as it does in the stratosphere, the air is stable and very little vertical motion can be created. (We have all heard the dictum "hot air rises.") In the troposphere, on the other hand, warm air usually exists *below* cold air, which allows rising plumes of warm, moist air and creates vertical mixing—this, of course, results in weather. Thus temperature and pressure are not isolated elements, but act together to drive the winds.

While this discussion may give the impression that the atmosphere is a deep, thick "ocean of air," it is actually a thin envelope. In proportion to the earth, the *total* atmosphere has the approximate thickness of the skin of an orange; the troposphere is comparatively thinner than the skin of an apple.

Atmospheric Wind Systems

About one-billionth (10^{-9}) of the sun's total energy output is intercepted by the earth. Part of the intercepted radiation is immediately reflected back to space by clouds, the earth's surface, air molecules, and impurities in the air, which can either be natural or human generated. Among these are particles such as water droplets, dust, volcanic ash, industrial smoke, pollen, and sea salt spray, as well as gases such as water vapor and carbon dioxide. Satellites have shown that the earth's reflectivity (or albedo) returns about 30 percent of its received sun's energy to space; the remaining 70 percent is absorbed by the earth-atmosphere system, warming the planet.

Not all parts of the planet receive the same amount of *insolation* (*in*coming *sol*ar radi*ation*). The sun's rays strike the earth most vertically at the equator, since this region lies more directly perpendicular to the path of the rays. Hence, it is warmer there. The poles, where it is colder, receive only glancing solar rays. The atmospheric and oceanic fluid systems continually try to even out these temperature differences by redistributing the heat. One way this is accomplished is when warm tropical air rises and moves poleward while cooler air at the poles sinks and moves toward the equator.

The Hadley Cell   George Hadley, a British scientist, first proposed this theory of heat convection in 1735. He thought a current of air moved from the equator to the poles and back again. If the earth did not rotate, the flow might indeed behave like Hadley's proposed "cellular" structure. But the earth rotates, deflecting the air, causing drastic effects on the circulation. This deflection is known as the *Coriolis effect;* it forces air in the Northern Hemisphere to the right, and shunts air in the Southern Hemisphere to the left.[9] The earth's rotation prevents the equator-to-pole cells that Hadley envisioned from being a stable formation. The rotation causes deflection, which accounts in part for the large-scale wind belts—the doldrums, horse latitudes, trade winds, prevailing westerlies, and polar easterlies.

We mentioned that the greatest amount of heating takes place at the equator. This warm air, which is most directly under the sun, has slightly lower pressure near the surface than air in the zones to either side. Rising air is associated with this low pressure; it comes about as the higher-pressure air from both sides of the equator rushes in, meets, and rises. Equatorial thunderstorms are fueled by the moisture evaporated from the oceans and carried toward the equator by the trade winds. Sailing ships can get stalled because there is often no prevailing wind direction in the region of converging trades and rising air. That is how this equatorial zone, which

148

roughly circles the earth, got the name *doldrums*. Since the trade winds converge there, it is also called the *intertropical convergence* zone (ITCZ). The ITCZ is a major part of the thermal drive of the "heat engine" behind the weather.

As air rises in the doldrums, its pressure decreases and it cools by expansion. At the same time, the air is losing energy in the form of infrared radiation to space. Much of this lost radiation, which contributes to further cooling in the upper reaches of the ITCZ, comes from the tops of tall rain clouds. While cooling, the thunderclouds wring out their moisture as precipitation. Then, as Hadley envisioned, this dry, cooled air flows poleward. But it does not generally flow all the way to the poles. At about lat. 30° North and South, in the subtropics, the air sinks back to earth. The reasons for this sinking are complex, and there are still important unanswered questions about details of this phenomenon. Nevertheless, the basic pattern can be related to the effects of the earth's rotation, the buoyancy of air cooled by expansion, and radiation of energy to space.

The subtropical sinking is related to belts of high pressure. Also, the air is warmed by compression as it drops to the surface. Recall that the rising air is dried in the ITCZ where precipitation is squeezed out; thus little moisture is carried by upper air currents to the subtropics. This area of high pressure, called the *horse latitudes*, is marked by generally clear skies and calm winds. (Most of the great deserts exist under sinking, dry air in the subtropics, although a few are in the regions of subsiding air in the lee of great mountain chains such as in the United States and Argentina.) The term horse latitudes originated when sea captains, who frequently transported horses through this region, were forced to throw them overboard. Long periods of calm kept sailing ships from reaching shore, and the animals often died because of the heat and lack of food and fresh water.

As the high-pressure air in the horse latitudes subsides it flows back toward the equatorial zones to complete the circulation of what meteorologists call the *tropical Hadley cell* (see Figure 4.2). The Coriolis effect then comes into play: in the Northern Hemisphere these surface winds blow from the northeast; in the Southern Hemisphere they blow from the southeast.* These fairly steady winds, known as

*In meteorology, wind directions with the suffix *ly* always refer to where the wind is blowing *from*. For example, the Northern Hemisphere trade winds are "northeasterly."

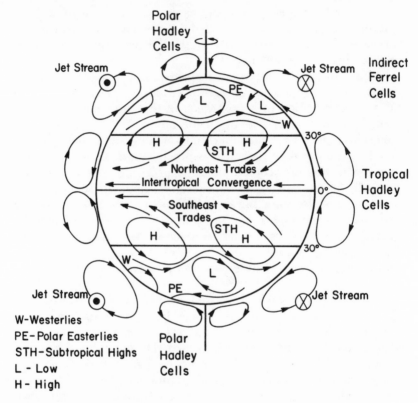

Figure 4.2

A number of major atmospheric circulation features are shown here in schematic form. The dots at the left-hand side of the figure labeled "Jet Stream" indicate air flow upwards, seemingly out of the page, whereas the cross through the circles representing the jet streams at the right-hand part of the figure represents flow into the page. In reality, the jet meanders across the middle to high latitudes in both hemispheres, with predominantly west to east winds. The highs and lows shown are primarily lower atmospheric features, extending up only a few kilometers into the atmosphere, whereas the Hadley cells, Ferrel cells, and jet streams can extend vertically as much as 10 to 20 kilometers (6.2 to 12.4 miles) through all of the troposphere and part of the stratosphere.

the trades, were probably "discovered" by such explorers as Columbus when they made their Atlantic crossings. Much earlier, they helped Polynesian explorers and settlers populate the Pacific. Later on, they fostered international trade by sailing ships.

The Jet Stream Coriolis forces also influence the high-altitude poleward flowing currents. These are deflected to the east (that is, they form "prevailing" westerly winds) in *both* hemispheres, since deflection of poleward air to the right in the Northern Hemisphere *and* to the left in the Southern Hemisphere causes high-altitude westerlies. These are shown in Figure 4.2 as *jet streams,* which are the core of circumpolar whorls of air or *vortices* in both hemispheres.

The jet stream was first widely recognized in World War II by pilots flying the U.S. B-29s that bombed Japan. Sometimes these bombers were buffeted by such strong headwinds that their progress was markedly impeded. Carl-Gustaf Rossby, a Swedish meteorologist, gave these winds their name. Like other circulation systems, the jet stream is caused by heating differences, in this case differences between the tropics and the poles. The temperature differences between these areas becomes more marked in the winter when the poles cool down relative to the equator. The result is a more vigorous tropical Hadley cell, along with an expanded, strengthened jet stream in the hemisphere experiencing winter.

Atmospheric Eddies and Waves

Cyclones There is considerable activity below and on the fringes of the jet stream. Most significant for surface weather are clockwise and counterclockwise rotating wind systems that occur near the surface and can extend several kilometers upward. If these lower atmospheric eddies reach high enough, they are steered by the jet stream. However, as pointed out later, eddies can occur at, alongside, or even above the jet stream—in fact some extend throughout the whole depth of the troposphere. When the eddies have a low-pressure center, they are called *cyclones;* * because of the Coriolis effect cyclones rotate counterclockwise in the Northern Hemisphere. When the center is composed of high-pressure air, eddies are called *anticyclones,* which rotate clockwise in the Northern Hemisphere. In the Southern Hemisphere the cyclones and anticyclones both rotate oppositely, but the associated weather type with high- and low-pressure centers is the same.

The discovery of the laws of thermodynamics during the 1840s and 1850s, according to meteorological historian Gisela Kutzbach,

*The word *cyclone* comes from the Greek *kyklon,* "coil of a snake."

151

led to a proliferation of attempts to develop a *thermal* theory of cyclones. This theory was based on the belief that cyclonic systems were driven by "thermodynamic processes associated with the ascent of warm air and condensation of water vapor."[10] Later on, in the beginning of this century, the thermal theory was extended to include *dynamical* processes such as fronts and jets.

The birth, growth, and decay of cyclones have been of special interest to the Norwegians. Their Atlantic coast is sometimes battered by highly changeable violent weather that accompanies these intense traveling systems. Around 1920, Vilhelm Bjerknes and his son Jakob described the life cycle of cyclones in unmistakably militaristic terms, perhaps a holdover from the experience of World War I. For example, one of their most important theories was that *fronts* of air advanced and retreated. It could be that because of the circumstances, these Norwegians (whose theories were borne out by networks of barometers and later by satellite pictures) were compelled to look for new ways to understand and forecast the weather. From 1914 to 1918 the Allied powers had cut off public weather reports and forecasts in an attempt to prevent the enemy from keeping posted on the weather.[11] Norway was neutral but was left without weather reports; hence, they were forced to create their own forecasting methods.

Vilhelm and Jakob Bjerknes postulated that cyclones are often born along a front—the boundary between relatively warm and cold masses of air. A *cold front* is one advancing toward warm air; a *warm front* is one moving toward relatively colder air. These masses of air are actually divided into four basic varieties that happen to be combinations of the four qualities that Aristotle distinguished—hot or warm (tropical), cold (polar), moist or humid (maritime), and dry (continental). Hence, according to geographic origin the four principal types of air masses are Polar Continental (cP), which is relatively cold and dry; Polar Maritime (mP), which is cold and moist; Tropical Continental (cT), which is warm and dry; and Tropical Maritime (mT), which is warm and moist.

Frequently two air masses, especially tropical and polar, meet and develop along a sharp boundary. The air masses may continue to flow side by side with no interaction. But for a variety of reasons, including the influence of topography and regional temperature differences, the warm and cold air masses can interact. Where opposing motions of the converging air masses occur, low-pressure centers or cyclones form. In this system in the Northern Hemisphere, cold air moves south and warm air moves north. The pole-ward-moving warm tropical air is typically less dense at the same altitude than the cold polar air, and thus the polar air undercuts the warm air and forces it upward. The weather that results from this growing and maturing cyclone is a broad system [up to 1000 kilometers (600 miles) or so] of upward-rising air. A wide band of cloudiness and precipitation precedes the warm front, and a narrower more intense band of precipitation lies ahead of and along the cold front.

Even as a cyclone grows, it sets the stage for its own eventual demise. As the winds around the rotating center grow strong, the cold front begins to overtake the warm front. The warm front becomes occluded, or shut off from the ground. The area initially occupied by the warm air is reduced as the cold mass spreads out along the ground and sinks. With the disappearance of the warm surface air, the cyclone fills with cold air, which gradually weakens its upward motion and cloud systems and raises its surface pressure. These various stages normally last about three to four days. The branch of meteorology that deals with air mass analysis is known as *synoptic meteorology*. In Bjerknes' day, this was the sole basis for forecasting fronts and their effects a few days ahead. But with the advent of new mathematical theories, computers, and satellites, the meteorologists' skill has been increased. Forecasts from six to ten days in advance are now possible because of these numerical weather prediction techniques, although their accuracy is typically well below that for shorter-period predictions by numerical or synoptic methods.

Rossby Waves Rossby was taught and inspired by Vilhelm Bjerknes at the Geophysical Institute in Bergen, Norway; he subsequently developed Bjerknes' ideas on using air masses for forecasting.

Using what Bjerknes had taught him, Rossby began to attack the problem of forecasting. The Bjerknes theory was based almost entirely on ground observations, but the air masses it described could reach to the top of the troposphere. Around 1930, Rossby reasoned that by studying air pressure, temperature, and other variables from a high altitude, meteorologists could obtain new information about the atmosphere's large-scale circulation. Rossby, then a meteorology professor at the Massachusetts Institute of Technology, hired a Cessna to make daily weather observations from the

East Boston Airport. (He later recognized the need to go much higher in order to encounter the important atmospheric motions. In line with Torricelli's surmise that we are submerged at the bottom of an ocean of air, Rossby said in a 1956 interview that, in terms of weather forecasting, we are like crabs on the ocean floor. We need, he said, a view from above.)

The radiosonde proved to be more efficient than Rossby's low-altitude plane in gathering data.* At first the upper-air weather appeared to be as chaotic as the ground weather. But Rossby saw a pattern emerge, made up of huge horizontal waves in the eastward drift of air around the earth. These so-called *long waves,* or *Rossby waves,* as they have become known, are elements of the circumpolar vortices discussed above. Because of their global scale, they are sometimes called *planetary waves* as well.

Generally four or five significant Rossby waves are undulating around the midlatitudes and polar regions in each hemisphere. As they shift positions, they guide the movements of cold and warm air masses that control the weather in the temperate zones. If the tip of a wave stretches too far equatorward or the speed of the winds is too fast, a large mass of polar air could well break away. Revolving counterclockwise (in the Northern Hemisphere) this cold *eddy* might drift off toward the tropics. In its place, warmer air can rush in, resulting in an exchange of warm and cold masses. These so-called *transient eddies* transport large amounts of heat from the tropics toward the poles. (The cyclones described earlier are also transient eddies, but typically occur lower in the troposphere.) The circumpolar vortex is not a purely circular current of air, but rather contains eddies or undulations because of the coincidence of two primary factors: the earth's rotation rate and the unequal heating of the earth from equator to poles. The latter factor, you will recall, gives rise to the westerly wind currents in the middle latitudes. The magnitude of the equator-to-pole temperature difference determines the jet stream's speed—typically several tens of meters per second (50 to 100 knots). This typical speed plus the effects of the other primary factor, the earth's rotation rate, allows Rossby waves and eddies to exist. The atmospheres of other bodies in our solar system, such as Venus, Jupiter, or the sun itself, have very different

---

*The radiosonde travels vertically through the atmosphere transmitting data on winds, temperatures, etc. as it changes altitude. It can either be dropped from a balloon or research plane, transmitting as it falls, or alternatively lifted by a weather balloon transmitting data as it rises.

circulation patterns from the earth because the rotation rates and heating patterns on these bodies are quite different from the earth.

Using an equation for the fluid flow of air on the rotating earth, Rossby was able to predict conditions for the onset of waviness in the circumpolar winds, thus explaining part of the shifting of the atmospheric waves. Because large-scale weather phenomena depend on this shifting, his equation made it theoretically possible to forecast evolving large-scale weather patterns by starting with the existing flow pattern—the so-called *initial condition*—and applying certain equations. His papers on the subject are considered a major breakthrough for the science of meteorology.[12] Rossby's achievements were so widely acknowledged that in December 1956 he found himself in an unusual place for a scientist—on the cover of *Time* magazine.*

Blocking   Regions on the poleward side of the circumpolar vortices usually experience cold weather, and those on the equator side warmer weather. Normally the loops and wiggles of the jet stream move several thousand kilometers per week, causing those living under them to experience alternating periods of warm, cool, wet, or dry weather. When the jet stream gets stuck, or blocked, then those under the resulting bulge (or *ridge*) tend to have prolonged periods of abnormally warm, dry weather; those under the blocked dip (or *trough*) tend to experience anomalously cool, wet weather.[13] (These terms, keep in mind, apply to waves that have high points—the crests or ridges—and low points—the troughs— in the Northern Hemisphere. In the Southern Hemisphere the physical processes and terminology apply, but the map needs to be drawn upside down for a ridge to bulge upward on the map.) Indeed, the last half of the 1970s, many meteorologists feel (intuitively, at least), was characterized by many such *blocking* patterns, with the summer of 1975 in Western Europe and the winter of 1976–77 in the United States now familiar examples. In the latter period, the circumpolar vortex in much of the Northern Hemisphere did not change its basic shape for months. The eastern half of the United States was plagued by punishingly cold weather under an extreme trough while the western half, under a strong ridge, was seized by abnormally warm and dry conditions resulting in a serious

---

*Rossby's picture—and the price "twenty cents"—both appeared on the cover of the December 17, 1956 issue of *Time*.

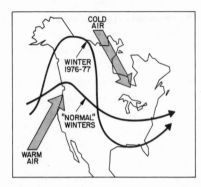

Figure 4.3

The jet stream normally loops and wiggles around the middle and high latitudes, typically taking the average position across North America in winter denoted on this schematic figure as "normal." The winter of 1976–77, however, was unusual in two respects. First the jet took the distorted pattern shown, plunging freezing temperatures as far south as Florida and bringing unusual warmth and drought conditions through the west. In addition, the distorted pattern remained in place— that is, was blocked—for much of the fall and winter season. This blocking event was marked by a long persistence of this unusual pattern rather than the normal progression of changing jet stream patterns, which causes normal week to week variability in midlatitude weather patterns.

drought. Figure 4.3 contrasts schematically a more normal jet stream pattern to the abnormal and persistent shape that caused the anomalous winter. Drought in Europe the previous summer was also connected to such blocking events.

Standing Waves Thus, it is not just the average latitude of the jet stream that makes one season deviate from its long-term normal. The regional distribution and time it takes for the troughs and ridges of the Rossby waves to evolve are also important. Regional abnormalities in the long-wave patterns are primarily responsible for the regional climatic anomalies that help determine whether a season is good or bad relative to the long-term climatic normals.* Although the long waves generally undulate over a period of a few days in which troughs and ridges are shifting their positions, they do favor certain locations over a long period. For example, in the Northern Hemisphere a ridge is more likely to be found in the eastern Atlantic and a trough over the western Atlantic. These preferred spots are determined by the distribution of continents and oceans; the long-term, preferred patterns are called *standing waves*. Heating differences between land and seas and high

*Although the term "normal" is commonly applied usage, "average" is a more apt description, since, as everybody knows, experiencing nonaverage weather is quite normal.

mountain ranges help to create the average patterns of standing waves. From season to season the standing waves change position and strength and help to transport heat and moisture between the tropics and the poles and the land and the sea. They are partly responsible for long-term climate being different at various places in the same latitude.

We can illustrate this phenomenon by looking at two widely separated islands: Madeira, a Portuguese island about 800 kilometers (500 miles) west of Africa roughly off the coast of Casablanca in the eastern Atlantic Ocean, and Bermuda, about 1600 kilometers (1000 miles) east of the United States off the coast from Charleston, South Carolina, in the western Atlantic. These places share approximately the same latitude—33°N and 32°N, respectively. But Madeira is much less stormy and receives less than half the rainfall of Bermuda. A major difference between these two islands is that the jet stream and its associated long waves are more likely to dip over Bermuda, pushing storms into it, and more liable to bulge out over Madeira, steering storms north of it. The detailed reasons the jet takes this course are debated, but it is likely to be largely due to the jet's interaction with the North American continent.

In the Southern Hemisphere the long waves behave somewhat differently, because they encounter different geographic conditions. For example, there is more ocean than land, which changes the standing-wave patterns relative to the Northern Hemisphere. Also, the existence of a topographically high continent at the South Pole (Antarctica) creates larger equator-to-pole surface temperature differences in the Southern Hemisphere than in the Northern Hemisphere. These geographic differences lead to a Southern Hemisphere jet stream that is relatively stronger, especially in the southern summer.

The Monsoons   A major regional phenomenon related to the land-sea geographic pattern is the monsoonal circulation. Earlier we mentioned the ITCZ, where the inflowing moist surface air of the trade winds converges. Despite the straight line representing the ITCZ in Fig. 4.2, it does not occur in such a fixed, rigid belt. In the Northern Hemisphere summer over central Africa and Asia, the low-pressure ITCZ bulges out of a zonal pattern (see Figure 4.4, July map). In this tropical area, the high solar heating induces low pressure on land, which results in the summer monsoon winds and rains that sustain food production on these heavily populated continents. The word *monsoon* means "season" in Arabic and refers to winds that blow fairly regularly and steadily at specific times of the year.* Aside from Africa and Asia, such summer monsoons also exist in January in the Southern Hemisphere in parts of Australia and South America.

In the summertime, the central Asian land area becomes heated more quickly than the ocean to the south. This is because the water of the ocean has a higher capacity for storing heat than the air or land surface. The warmed land surface causes air to rise, and a surface low-pressure area develops over Asia. The cooler, higher-pressure surface air over the Indian Ocean is thus unbalanced. Like the air trapped under high pressure inside a balloon with an open nozzle, air flows to the region of lower pressure—from sea to land in this case. Laden with moisture from the evaporation of sea water, southwesterly winds from the Arabian Sea, for example, pass over India and are forced up by the terrain as they approach the Tibetan Plateau (see July map in Figure 4.4). The rising moist air begins to condense and precipitate its high water content. In this way the summer monsoon leads to torrential rains in northern India from June to October. The winter monsoon is the reverse. Cold, dry, sinking air behind high pressure pours seaward from the colder interior of Asia and very little rain occurs (see January map in Figure 4.4). This pattern and timetable may vary over other parts of Asia, but the northern Indian example does typify the Asian monsoon.

The familiar summer breezes of day and night at the seashore are monsoons in microcosm. Instead of occurring seasonally, they occur diurnally—that is, daily. And instead of crossing continent-sized land masses, they affect only shoreline areas. The basic explanation for sea breezes, which occur mostly during the summer days, is the same as for the monsoon: differences in rates of temperature change between the land and the sea lead to pressure differences that lead to air movement. The air from the sea (being cooler, and higher in pressure during the day) flows in to replace warmer, drier, and lighter air rising from the solar-heated interior and shoreline. But at night a land breeze blows from the coastline to the sea when the sun has set, and the land area can radiate its heat away through

---

*Should the monsoons unexpectedly fail, as they often do, to provide regular rainfalls, then serious flooding and/or droughts causing food shortages can develop, as we discuss later on.

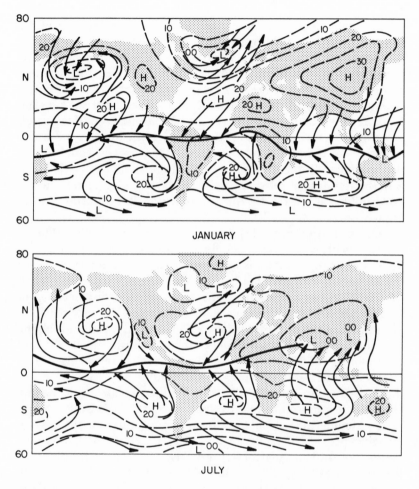

Figure 4.4

The geographic distribution of land and sea causes significant distortion of atmospheric circulation systems away from the purely latitudinal or zonal pattern so often shown on schematic figures. The solid dark line on this figure shows how the intertropical convergence zone (ITCZ) is distorted out of a zonal pattern because of the geographic effects of unequal heating of the land and sea. Typical patterns are shown for the extreme months of January and July. Surface features such as the Bermuda high and the Icelandic low can also be seen, as well as prevailing surface trade winds that converge to form the ITCZ. The numbers associated with high- and low-pressure systems are in units of millibars of sea level pressure above the 1000 millibar level typically found at that geographic place for the January or July season.

infrared radiation, thus cooling to temperatures below that of the sea and reversing the process of the daytime.

Our example of Bermuda and Madeira, mentioned earlier, is related to the monsoons. We said that Bermuda is stormier than Madeira—Hamilton, Bermuda, receives roughly 13 centimeters (about 5 inches) of rain in *each* of 12 months, whereas Funchal, Madeira, gets almost all of its rain, 70 *annual* centimeters (29 inches), in the winter season when the jet stream dips more frequently over the island. In the summer Madeira gets caught up in the sinking air of the descending arm of the Hadley cell—that is, it is in the spillover of subsiding air from the distorted ITCZ, a northward bulge caused by the African monsoon (see the July map in Figure 4.4).

This distortion in the ITCZ over Africa creates another climatic situation with which many people are familiar—that of the famed Riviera of Europe. There is little rainfall in the summertime along the Mediterranean Riviera because of sinking air that occurs when the ITCZ bulges far north over Africa, having been displaced out of a zonal pattern by the summer monsoon. When the air circulating in this part of the tropical Hadley cell finally sinks it extends all the way north to the resorts, well out of the latitudes normally thought of as subtropical. It is the northward displacement of sinking air that inhibits rainfall and encourages sunbathing. If Africa were not there, it is quite possible that the Mediterranean would have a climate much more like that of the east coast of the United States in the summertime, with traveling cyclones entering the region, bringing periods of rising air and rainfall. Thus, the geographic patterns of land and sea not only give rise to preferred locations for the tropical Hadley cell, but they also usually force the jet stream to stay north of the Mediterranean region. At the same latitude in North America (40°N), New York City is often directly under the jet; rainfall is then plentiful across much of North America at the same latitude. Subtropical sinking of the descending part of the Hadley cell is typically far to the south over the Gulf of Mexico, the Caribbean, and southern California, which is dry over most summers.

Walker Circulation
and the Southern Oscillation
Not only do geographic variations induce distortions that twist the ITCZ and the Hadley cell out of a purely zonal belt, but multiple Hadley like cells can develop at different longitudes at the same latitude. These

regional cells not only move air along lines running north to south —the classical motion—but also can have an important east-west component. Such winds along the equator are grouped into several cells (having an east-west flow as well as north-south). Together these cells are known as the *Walker circulation.* * The most interesting aspect of the Walker circulation is not the average pattern, but rather the fact that the winds undergo considerable changes every few years, what is known as the Southern Oscillation. This is accompanied by dramatic shifts in some regions of precipitation in the equatorial Pacific, as well as shifts in the pressure difference across this ocean. These significant changes also affect the sea surface temperature in the eastern tropical Pacific. This phenomena is having considerable impact on the development of long-range forecasting techniques, although a documented record of repeated success is still lacking. In 1982 and 1983 there was a major enhancement of the Southern Oscillation, which many analysts associated with the abnormally wet winter of 1982/83 in the United States.

Hence, we can see that regional climate and its changes arise from a very complicated mix of factors—incoming sunlight, barometric pressure, temperature, proximity to oceans, or topography. Later, when we examine how climate might be changed by, say, human pollution, we will need to take these factors—and others, such as tropical cyclones—into account.

Tropical Cyclones   Tropical cyclones are better known as hurricanes or typhoons. These phenomena are more than spectacular events—they are an important part of the long-term climate of some places. Much of Mexico and parts of Southeast Asia, for example, rely on the unscheduled passage of random hurricanes for their water supply. While precipitation from hurricanes is not reliable from one year to the next, they are significant bearers of precipitation when averaged over many decades.

In different parts of the world, powerful tropical cyclones are

*Walker, G. T., 1923, Indian Meteorological Department Memorandum 24, pp. 75–131, first outlined the hypothesis that pressure differences across the equatorial Pacific could create east-west circulation patterns that might prove helpful in long-range forecasting. Further development of Walker's ideas—in particular, a possible connection between variations in the Walker circulation patterns and equatorial Pacific Ocean surface temperatures and rainfalls—were given by Bjerknes, J., 1969, Atmospheric teleconnections from the equatorial Pacific, *Monthly Weather Review 97:* 163–172.[14]

known by different names: in the Caribbean they are called hurricanes, after Hunraken, the Mayan god of the winds; the ancient Greeks' word *typhons* meant both "monster" and "a wind containing a cloud"; in Australia they are called willy-willies; and in parts of China the storms are known as *t'ai fung,* meaning "a great wind." Much named, but little understood, these storms were described quite accurately by the seventeenth-century explorer William Dampier. His diaries give perhaps the earliest detailed accounts of how hurricanes and typhoons work.[15] After a severe typhoon off the coast of the Philippines in 1680, Dampier realized that his ship's position was nearly the same as when the storm had first hit. But he also knew that the ship had gone several hundred miles off course during the storm. Hence, he reasoned that "typhoons are a sort of vast whirlwind." This discovery of the storms' spiraling motion was a major first step in understanding them.

Eventually, a working theory of hurricanes began to form. In 1882, Lieutenant Colonel H. S. Palmer of Britain's Royal Engineers wrote an article for the Hong Kong Telegraph entitled "Typhoons of the Eastern Seas." Palmer said that the "affinity of typhoons for the sea which gives them birth is easily understood when we consider the enormous part that is played by the vapour of water in their internal economy. The absorption and condensation of immense volumes of vapour are necessary for the maintenance of a typhoon's existence and energy." Palmer was correct about the driving force behind a tropical cyclone's birth and development: the continuous supply of *latent heat* associated with their moisture-laden winds. (For an explanation of how latent heat is important to weather, see Chapter 5.) Part of this latent heat is transformed into the kinetic energy of the storm, which makes typical hurricanes so powerful that over their lifetimes they are estimated to release energy equivalent to 100,000 bombs of megaton strength.[16] Even at that magnitude, hurricanes do not have the highest winds. Tornadoes, while less than 1 percent of the size of hurricanes (which are typically several hundred kilometers across), can have much stronger winds in their vortex.

Hurricanes are the most violent storms usually experienced at sea. By international agreement, they are rated according to wind intensity. A *tropical depression* has winds up to 34 knots (39 miles, or 63 kilometers, per hour); a *tropical storm* is one with winds of 35 to 63 knots (40 to 72 miles, or 64 to 116 kilometers, per hour); and a full-scale hurricane reaches 64 knots (73 miles or 117.5 kilometers per hour) or higher. No one is exactly sure what causes the storms to form. For example, satellite pictures showed that Hurricane Anna in 1961 was found to have started as a weak cloud arrangement in the tropical Atlantic Ocean. How these clouds are concentrated into a storm when others are not is uncertain, but we do know that in order for cyclonic winds to develop, air currents near the ground —that is, the sea surface—must start to converge and spin by the Coriolis force. At the equator (and within a few hundred kilometers on either side of it) this twisting force is weak or nonexistent; hence hurricanes rarely form between lat. 5°N and lat. 5°S, although there are some exceptions.[17] We also know that nearly all hurricanes originate from weather disturbances such as monsoon depressions (weak, low-pressure cyclones), squall lines (a common and often severe type of rain system), and waves (winds that are organized in a wavelike pattern, with regions of clouds and heavy rain).

Generally, hurricanes do not form over water colder than 27°C (80°F). This relatively high sea surface temperature—typically present over the western parts of the oceans from August to October in the Northern Hemisphere and from January to March in the Southern Hemisphere—seems to be needed to heat the lower air that can initiate and sustain convection in the storm.

Among the nastiest surprises a hurricane holds for people is the *storm surge*. Since pressure at a hurricane center falls below that of the surrounding area, it raises sea level by sucking up the water into the storm's center, much like a gigantic straw. This effect, combined with winds that can reach 320 kilometers (200 miles) per hour, can temporarily raise sea levels by several meters, inundating coastal areas as the storm hits the coast. The catastrophic flooding that results typically takes more lives and ruins more property than any other aspect of the storm.

The paths hurricanes follow are determined by the prevailing winds, which typically make them drift in a variety of directions. When hurricanes drifting westward in tropical easterly winds move toward midlatitudes, they get caught by the westerlies and typically curve back on themselves. The storms tend to die out once they are over land or cold water, since they lose their warm, moist surface energy source. However, they do have a substantial influence on the climates of many hurricane-prone regions, particularly the rainfall statistics.

Other Mean Circulation Features

In addition to the north-south air flow in tropical Hadley cells, there are other north-south structures of mean meridional winds. One is the Polar Hadley Cell.

The Polar Hadley Cell Cold air at both poles forms a dome of high pressure; thus, another, smaller Hadley cell is created. This polar cell carries air between the relatively warm midlatitudes and the cold poles. Again, the earth's rotation causes these winds to deflect so that at the surface in the high latitudes of the Northern Hemisphere they blow on average from a northeasterly direction, and from a southeasterly direction in the Southern Hemisphere. These are the surface polar easterlies (see Figure 4.2).

The Ferrel Cell So far we have depicted a two-cell mean meridional circulation: the vigorous tropical Hadley cells with rising air near the equator and sinking air in the subtropics; and the weak polar Hadley cells with rising air in the high midlatitudes and sinking air near the poles. In between is a third circulation pattern —the Ferrel cell, so named for the nineteenth-century American meteorologist William Ferrel.[18]

Meteorologists call this pattern an "indirect" cell, since unlike the Hadley cells, which are primarily forced by temperature differences, Ferrel cells result from winds that move into, around, and out of the midlatitudes. These cells can be likened to a refrigerator in that they carry heat from a colder zone (in this case, higher latitudes) to a warmer one (the lower latitudes). This further enhances the differences between these regions. However, Ferrel cells are not nearly as vigorous as the tropical Hadley cells, and thus are a lesser feature of the general circulation.

Atmospheric Predictability

The Weather Predictability Limit One principal reason to study all these features of the atmospheric circulation is to predict atmospheric phenomena like tomorrow's weather or climatic anomalies next season in major world granaries. Weather forecasts usually begin with today's weather and extrapolate this *initial condition* forward in time. One issue of concern to meteorologists is how far forward we can go in time before the atmosphere essentially "forgets" all influences of today's weather. Put another way, is there a limit to long-range weather predictability?

For several decades meteorologists have been routinely producing so-called long-range weather forecasts. These are primarily short-range climate forecasts; they seldom attempt to give daily weather patterns, but rather predict regional anomalies of temperature and rainfall some months in advance. One reason no official weather service offers detailed daily weather forecasts for more than a week or so in advance is that most of the scientific community accepts a *predictability limit* as a constraint to weather forecasting. Weather is the instantaneous state of the atmosphere in space and time—a snapshot, as it were. Because the atmosphere is a fluid with turbulent motions generated by internal instabilities (such as those that produce transient eddies), it becomes impossible, in most circumstances, to predict accurately the daily details of atmospheric motions beyond a few weeks—regardless of how accurately today's weather is known. Despite the dubious claims of a few entrepreneurs who insist they have a secret formula for predicting daily weather years in advance—and who sell such forecasts to those faithful (or foolish) enough to believe them—there is abundant scientific evidence that daily weather is essentially unpredictable after a few weeks.[19]

A Climate Predictability Limit?   Why then do we talk about forecasting future climate changes decades or more beyond the weather predictability limit? The answer is simply that we are not referring to long-range weather predictions, but rather to long-range forecasts of climate: the averages of weather events over regions of space and blocks of time. There is no known predictability limit yet discovered to rule out some skillful prediction of *average* weather beyond a few weeks. Edward Lorenz of the Massachusetts Institute of Technology suggested once that an analogy to a pinball machine can be made to illustrate the predictability limit. If we knew precisely how hard the hammer would initially strike the ball, we would be able to predict fairly reliably the first pin it would hit. Knowing the spacings of the pins, we would probably be able to predict the second and maybe even the third hit. However, any dust in the ball's path or vibration in the room would cause the ball to deviate slightly from the forecasted path. So would any errors in estimating how hard the hammer first hit the ball. All of these initially small errors would be greatly magnified with each deflection of the ball from a pin. After only a few pins, these errors—called *perturbations* in the atmospheric analogy—would make more than the first few ball/pin encounters unpredictable. However, if we hit a hundred balls we would probably be able to get good statistics of the probability of a ball hitting any specific pin, even though the path of an individual roll would not be reliably predictable past the first few pins.

In this analogy the weather is the detailed path of each ball during each roll. The climate is the average of the paths of many balls over many rolls. Just because we can't predict the specific path of each ball past a few initial pin hits—no matter how well we know the initial speed of the ball—doesn't rule out a skillful statistical prediction of how many balls might be expected to hit the sixth pin in twenty rolls. If we tilted the machine and also understood how that tilt would deflect the average path of each roll, we could predict how the tilt might change the statistics of ball/pin encounters. Similarly, if we observed a large anomaly in sea surface temperature (SST) and understood how that SST anomaly distorted atmospheric patterns above it and far away from it, we would be able to predict the likelihood for anomalous climatic statistics in the future—at least that is our hope.

The Oceans

The development of the thermometer and the barometer provided the basis of description from which the science of meteorology has evolved. When networks of instrumental records of the atmosphere were compiled, complex phenomena such as mean circulation cells, long waves, hurricanes, or monsoons could be diagnosed and their causes at least partially understood. Although these phenomena are features of atmospheric circulation, we have seen that they are significantly influenced by the oceans. Hurricanes and monsoons are not the only examples of the oceans' important role in causing regional climates. We will now look more closely at the oceans and the part they play in the earth-atmosphere system.

First and foremost, the oceans store water. Most fresh water on earth originated as evaporated sea water that left its salts behind. This is why a sea such as the Mediterranean, where annual evaporation of fresh water exceeds annual rainfall, tends to be saltier than most of the rest of the oceans. The Dead Sea, a closed basin into which the Jordan River flows, is another example. This sea is called dead because its high salt content is lethal to most aquatic life. Because the Dead Sea is a closed basin, all the minerals carried into it by the Jordan River are left behind when water evaporates. Some of these minerals are "mined" through the isolation of Dead Sea waters in evaporation ponds that have been built to trap salts.

Similarly, river and groundwater runoff from continents to the oceans slowly alters the mineral and organic content of the oceans. At the same time, chemical transformations occur in sea water. Some minerals and organic compounds are incorporated into the bodies of sea life. These chemicals can be removed from the sea as creatures die or chemicals fall out and are deposited at the bottom as sediments. The distribution of chemicals in the oceans thus depends on a complicated, time-evolving, and regional set of processes such as evaporation, precipitation, chemical reactions, runoff, life, death, dissolution, and deposition. In our own time, with the introduction of hundreds of new man-made chemicals into the environment and the disruption of the cycles of hundreds of natural chemicals, man is, for better or (often) for worse, becoming a partner with nature in the biology and chemistry of the oceans.

The study of the physical and chemical processes in the oceans is part of the science of oceanography. Although closely connected to meteorology and climatology, oceanography evolved separately from its sister environmental sciences.[20] The oceans have long been regarded as a source of food, a means of transport, and a garbage dump for human refuse, but scientific interest in the oceans was minimal until Benjamin Franklin had the Gulf Stream mapped in 1769.

Ocean Currents

The Gulf Stream   One of the first oceanographic problems studied—the Gulf Stream—is also of considerable meteorological interest. This warm current, we now know, is what keeps northwestern European climates relatively moderate. Even though Scotland, Moscow, and Hudson Bay are all at about the same latitude, and thus get about the same amounts of incoming sunlight each year, temperatures in the British Isles are moderated by warming from the oceans. The currents of the Gulf Stream are significant to that moderation. But the Gulf Stream's importance for the climate of Europe was not always appreciated, even by some who may have known that a current flowed from North America across the Atlantic to the northeast.

Although some pre-Revolution American sailors were already aware of the Gulf Stream, it was not generally recognized until 1769, when Benjamin Franklin first had it charted. As the Deputy Postmaster General in London for the American colonies, Franklin was trying to figure out why mail packets took two weeks longer than the merchant ships to sail to North America. In October 1768, Timothy Folger, a Nantucket whaler, was visiting London. He told Franklin that many ship captains were ignorant of the Gulf Stream and frequently tried to sail against it. Folger knew of the "river in the sea" because of his experience in pursuing whales. The animals kept to the edges of the Gulf Stream and did not try to swim into it.

Folger sketched the Gulf Stream and Franklin had London cartographers print the map.[21] The British authorities reportedly snubbed the chart, apparently because they did not believe that an American fisherman could know more about ocean currents than they did. But Franklin's conception of the Gulf Stream was surprisingly accurate. He wrote that the Gulf Stream was probably generated in part by the trade winds. And Franklin made temperature measurements, saying that "it will appear from them, that the thermometer may be a useful instrument to the navigator, since currents coming from the northward into southern seas, will probably be found colder than the water of those seas, as the currents from southern seas into northern are found warmer."[22] The course and character of the Gulf Stream is difficult enough to measure with modern-day instruments, but Franklin's estimates have some impressive similarities to today's data.

Like all ocean currents, the Gulf Stream is driven by a combination of mechanical forces, thermal forces, and forces of chemical origin. The largest influence is the driving force of the winds, which carry momentum. Some of this momentum is imparted to the oceanic surface over which the winds blow. It might seem as though ocean currents should flow in the same direction as a prevailing wind. But the Coriolis force complicates this motion by deflecting ocean currents to the right of the wind direction in the Northern Hemisphere and to the left in the Southern Hemisphere. Were the Coriolis force the only factor, we might expect the Gulf Stream off the east coast of North America to flow south, not north, since the winds there are prevailing westerlies. That is, the waters driven from the west to the east by the winds should deflect to the right —south—rather than flow to the left—north—as Franklin had charted. This apparent dilemma is resolved when we look at the North Atlantic as a whole, not just at the western part, which contains the northward Gulf Stream flow. A map of North Atlantic currents does indeed show that most of the upper part of the ocean, particularly the eastern half of it, flows toward the south.

The southward flowing currents of cool Atlantic water encounter the trade winds as they pass off the west coast of Africa. Recall that the trades are northeasterly—they flow from the northeast to the southwest. Coriolis force deflects the trade-wind-driven ocean currents to the right—that is, to the west. In the subtropical latitudes these westward flowing waters bump into the American continents, which are the western boundary of the North Atlantic Ocean basin. This land mass forces much of these subtropical waters to turn northward. Considering their subtropical passage, it is not surprising—as Franklin surmised—that these waters are relatively warm as they pass off the North American coast and move toward the northeast, since they have earlier been in the Gulf of Mexico, the Caribbean Sea, or the tropical Atlantic.

Since it is most intense at the western margin of the ocean basin, oceanographers call the Gulf Stream a *western boundary current;* the same label is applied to the Kurishio Current in the North Pacific. We have seen that the Gulf Stream is driven by winds averaged over the entire ocean basin and not just by local winds. These averaged winds, combined with the physical shape of the ocean floor and the continental boundaries, result in this important oceanic feature.

Like the atmospheric jet stream, the Gulf Stream at any instant in time tends to be unstable. If over a year or two we took a short sequence of snapshots of the Gulf Stream off North America, we would see motion resembling a restless snake held near Florida by its tail—a thrashing and meandering current surrounded by rings or eddies of warm and cold water. Franklin's chart, however, depicts the Gulf Stream as a smooth, steady swatch across the North Atlantic; but we know now that this is not a very accurate depiction. Of course, if averaged over many years, the Gulf Stream flow would appear to be more like Franklin's image of a smoothly varying "river in the sea."

Unlike the eddies or whorls associated with the atmospheric jet stream—which are typically 1000 kilometers (620 miles) across and

169

last a week or so—the Gulf Stream eddies are usually ten to twenty times smaller and can maintain their identities for several months. The water inside an eddy can be a few degrees Celsius different from the surrounding sea, and nutrient concentrations or salinity can also be quite unlike the surrounding waters for many months. Thus, some well-adapted organisms can thrive inside such an eddy far removed from their usual environment. Science writer Susan West described these eddies metaphorically as "an aquarium for these organisms, maintaining the nutrient, temperature and salinity characteristics of the original water while moving through chemically and biologically foreign water."[23] Of course, as the eddy waters mix with the surrounding sea, they drop their biological cargo in often hostile environments. More important for climate, these eddies may be responsible for transporting significant amounts of heat and salt from one part of the ocean to another. In this way they could, like their atmospheric counterparts, be climatically significant.

Western boundary currents and their associated eddies are not the only mechanisms by which the oceans transport heat. They are part of clockwise (in the Northern Hemisphere) surface flows called *gyres*. In the middle of the North Atlantic and the North Pacific oceans, for example, are relatively warm pools of water that form the centers of the gyres. These pools are analogous to the subtropical high-pressure cells found in the atmosphere.

Deep Ocean Currents   In addition to the eddies and the gyres, both of which are primarily wind driven, there is another circulation pattern in the ocean, one that is primarily driven by thermal forces combined with those of chemical origin: the *thermal/haline circulation* or *mean meridional cell*.* When warm Gulf Stream water, for example, flows northward into the Norwegian Sea, it encounters cold air blowing from either the Arctic or Greenland. This water is relatively salty, in large part because the Mediterranean outflow through the Straits of Gibraltar dumps a fair amount of salty water into the North Atlantic. The saltiness determines at what temperature the surface water sinks, with salty water sinking at warmer temperatures than fresher water, since salt makes water of the same temperature more dense (recall the related discussion

---

*The chemical formula for salt, NaCl (sodium chloride), gives rise to the "haline" label, since chlorine is one of the elements called Halogens.

in Chapter 2). As salty water cools, it becomes less buoyant. In the high latitudes of the North Atlantic, the relatively salty water becomes heavy enough to sink when it has cooled to about 2°C (35.6°F). The sinking water in the Norwegian Sea hits the ocean bottom and spreads out horizontally. As explained in Chapter 2, the relatively less salty waters in the Antarctic region sink at about −2°C (28.4°F), and the two opposite hemispheric sources of so-called bottom waters combine to produce an average world bottom water temperature near 0°C (32°F). Freezing of salty oceanic waters typically occurs only when the temperature is cooled below −2°C (28.4°F).

Upwelling and the Thermal
Flywheel Effect Water cannot simply sink in one spot unless it rises in another. The cold waters that sank in polar seas rise in *upwelling zones,* mostly in the tropics, creating a net transport of heat. That is, the polar seas are cooled by the atmosphere and impart their heat to the air, and the tropical seas are heated from above and cooled by upwelling water from below.

The cooling of the poles (thermal-driven circulation), combined with the saltiness of the waters (haline-driven circulation), gives rise to this equator-to-pole transport of heat by the oceans into the atmosphere. This thermal/haline cell does its work in depth, that is, largely flowing in a plane perpendicular to the earth's surface, rather than circulating as gyres do, in a plane parallel to the surface. The gyres can transport water around the ocean basin in a complete cycle over perhaps a decade or so. But it is a very lengthy process for a parcel of water to travel from a polar sea down to the ocean bottom, upwell in the tropics, and then be returned to the poles. (Flows of very deep *bottom water* can also occur between different ocean basins or hemispheres, providing long-term energy flow links that connect far away regions.) Scientists have estimated the process of deep water turnover today takes on the order of 500 to 1000 years.[24] The vertical overturning of waters is very important to long-term climate, since it exposes the atmosphere to the vast mass of waters that constitute the large heat capacity of the deep oceans.[25] This *thermal flywheel* effect of the oceans on the atmosphere was already implied earlier in discussions of such climatic phenomena as the seasonal cycle of temperatures or monsoons. All these (and other) oceanic currents transport a great deal of heat, with important climatic consequences.[26]

Before ending our discussion of ocean currents, a few related —and climatically and economically important—phenomena are worth mentioning. Recall that the intertropical convergence zone (ITCZ) in the atmosphere is the place where the trade winds from each hemisphere collide, causing a storm belt and giving rise to the tropical Hadley cell (see Figures 4.2 and 4.4). These trade winds rub on the oceans, causing currents. As the Coriolis force deflects these surface currents—in the Northern Hemisphere towards the northwest and in the Southern Hemisphere towards the southwest—surface waters are pulling apart in *divergence zones.* Something must replace these diverging surface waters, so waters from below rise to fill the void. These rising waters are the upwelling waters just mentioned. As they are colder than most surface waters, upwelling is climatically significant. They are also typically more oxygen- and nutrient-rich than non-upwelling-zone surface waters, since plant life in the surface or *photic zone*—the surface layer in which penetrating sunlight drives marine plant photosynthesis—tends to deplete such nutrients as nitrates or phosphates. This nutrient depletion then limits further growth of marine plant and animal populations. This fact is of biological and economic significance, as upwelling zones tend to support prolific blooms of phytoplankton, which in turn are eaten by higher animals, and so up the food chain to schools of fish. Commercial fishing fleets thus search for upwelling.[27]

The ITCZ wind system is not the only source of divergence in the oceans. Another cause is the offshore winds, particularly off the west coasts of continents. Off California, for example, winds are often northerly; the Coriolis force then deflects the surface waters to the west, pulling them away from the continental margins. Cold, nutrient-rich waters then upwell to fill the void, giving rise to high biological productivity and the cool climate experienced along the California coast, particularly in the summer. Likewise, there are major so-called *coastal upwelling zones* off Peru and West Africa (see Figure 4.5). Every few years wind systems and ocean current and temperatures fluctuate and cause a weakening in coastal upwelling, particularly off Peru—an event known as *El Niño.* Weakened fisheries and an altered climate over the entire tropical Pacific region have been related to large El Niño events. When cool upwelling waters off Peru diminish, atmospheric winds, ocean currents, precipitation, and air and sea temperatures mutually adjust all the way to the Indian Ocean. This adjustment is not permanent, but it recurs from

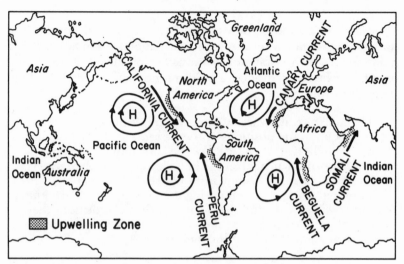

Figure 4.5

The interaction of surface winds and continental margins creates a number of upwelling zones around the world. Because nutrient-rich waters from below upwell in these zones, these cool coastal ocean areas are rich fishing grounds. However, fluctuations in atmospheric and oceanic circulation systems sometimes cause periodic shifts of these coastal upwelling zones, with potentially disastrous consequences to world protein availability and prices. [Source: J. D. Thompson, 1978, Ocean deserts and ocean oases, Climatic Change 1: 205–230.]

time to time. This multiyear vacillation is part of the phenomenon (described earlier) known as the Southern Oscillation. Some scientists believe it may be responsible for global weather anomalies thousands of kilometers away from the equatorial Pacific, where the Southern Oscillation occurs.[28]

Long-Range Forecasting from Sea Surface Temperature Anomalies

Because the oceans have a large heat capacity, they can retain anomalies in their surface temperatures for many months. As evaporation and heat exchanges with the atmosphere depend significantly on the sea surface temperature (SST), many scientists have hypothesized that knowledge of these persistent SST anomalies might provide some advanced warnings about anomalies in atmospheric conditions, both directly over the abnormal water as well as thousands of kilometers downstream. This is the basis for much of today's long-range forecasting, in which anomalies in atmospheric temperature or precipitation patterns are predicted up to several months or more in advance. The idea is not new; in 1891, Lt. John Pillsbury wrote:

> The moisture and varying temperature of the land depends largely upon the positions of the currents in the ocean, and it is thought that when we know the laws of the latter we will, with the aid of meteorology, be able to say to the farmers hundreds of miles distant from the sea, "You will have an abnormal amount of rain during the next summer", or "the winter will be cold and clear", and by these predictions they can plant a crop to suit the circumstances or provide an unusual amount of food for their stock.[29]

It is remarkable that today virtually the same words are often used to defend research grants or field programs aimed at improving long-range weather forecasts. In a 1978 article on the role of oceanic temperature anomalies in shaping climate, Scripps Institution of Oceanography scientist Tim Barnett referred to Pillsbury, saying, "After nearly 90 years, oceanographers and meteorologists are on the verge of testing Pillsbury's prophetic remarks."[30]

The most vigorous defender of this SST anomaly method of long-range climate anomaly forecasting is Jerome Namias. He was the method's chief practitioner in Washington, D.C., at the U.S. National Weather Service for several decades, and then left the civil service and moved to the Scripps Institution of Oceanography.[31] (His successor in Washington, Donald Gilman, uses a variety of techniques, including reference to SST anomalies, to produce the official Weather Service long-range forecasts each month.) Namias began his long-range forecasting work at Massachusetts Institute of Technology in the 1930s, working with the illustrious Carl Gustav Rossby. According to Alan Hecht, Director of the U.S. National Climate Program Office, the prime motivator of the effort at Massachusetts Institute of Technology to develop long-range forecasting techniques was the then Secretary of Agriculture, Henry Wallace.[32] In 1936, Wallace quipped: "They probably won't get anywhere. I have an idea that if AT&T were running this country, it would spend one million a year on long-range forecasting. We will probably spend $1,500."[33] Thus, the impetus for long-range forecasting came not so much from meteorologists, but from agriculturalists after the devastating droughts in 1934. Pillsbury had anticipated this demand forty years earlier. And forty years after Henry Wallace's try, the U.S. government once again demanded stepped up efforts at long-range forecasting, this time after a series of worldwide crop failures in the mid-1970s.[34]

In order to attempt to make forecasts a season ahead, Namias has looked at hundreds of charts of atmospheric anomalies in pressure, temperature, and precipitation and correlated them in different parts of the atmosphere. These correlations—so-called *teleconnections*—were then used to forecast long-range anomalies in climate. Namias looks, for example, at anomalies in Pacific Ocean SSTs from which he can construct corresponding anomalies in atmospheric variables directly over the unusual ocean temperature area—a fairly reliable and relatively uncontroversial part of the procedure. What is tricky is his next step. Knowing roughly how the atmosphere over the SST anomaly is distorted, he applies teleconnection charts to determine how atmospheric patterns might be distorted elsewhere. If all other factors that cause one month's climate to deviate from its long-term average were constant, then this procedure might produce fairly accurate forecasts. Unfortunately, other confounding factors have been cited as well: unusual coverage of sea ice, amounts of haze, changes in soil moisture from the long-term average, unusual wind or ocean current patterns in preceding months, wobbles in the earth's rotation about its axis, or even unusual solar activity.[35] All these factors have been proposed by various scientists and other prognosticators as plausible causes of unusual seasonal and regional climate. Perhaps this helps to explain why few such forecasts have more than minimal verified accuracy.[36]

The Signal-to-Noise Problem   There is yet another complication in making reliable long-range forecasts. Recall that we said individual weather systems were unpredictable for more than a few weeks' time. Since one month of climate is typically the average of only a few individual weather systems, one particularly unusual storm, for example, could dominate that month's climatic statistics. But individual events such as an unusual storm are not predictable very far into the future. Thus, the domination of a monthly average by a single, large, unpredictable weather event could swamp the predicted effect caused by, say, a Pacific Ocean SST anomaly. In other words, even if the SST and teleconnection procedure correctly predicted some downstream atmospheric anomaly in next season's climate, the forecasted anomaly would probably be of smaller magnitude than the anomaly in the climatic statistics caused by that one very unusual, unpredictable storm. Statisticians refer to this difficulty as a *signal-to-noise* problem, in which the climatic signal from SST anomaly effects is buried in the noise of a small number of unpredictable individual weather events.[37] There is no way around this problem, and it severely limits the potential average accuracy of climatic forecasts on the time scale of seasons. However, if we can identify some occasional mechanism that is likely to cause a very large distortion—that is, a very large signal—in expected atmospheric patterns, then much greater-than-average forecast skill might be possible.[38]

For the purpose of estimating the societal impacts of climatic anomalies, it is much more important to predict such infrequent but large departures from normal climate—like that shown in Figure 4.3—than it is to have some marginal amount of average accuracy on more frequent but smaller anomalies. When SST anomalies are either very large or occur in critical places, there is considerable hope that skillful forecasts warning of their significant atmospheric effects are possible for some regions. For example, computer simulations by Paul Julian and Robert Chervin of the U.S. National Center for Atmospheric Research reinforced the earlier suggestions of Walker and Bjerknes that one place to look for such critical SST anomalies in the Pacific Ocean is the tropical waters rather than North Pacific waters, where most previous North American climate anomaly forecasts were based. Julian and Chervin argued from simulated data that tropical events such as the Southern Oscillation could well be felt worldwide.[39] A subsequent study by Tim Barnett based on real data, not computer-generated simulations, confirmed the notion that tropical SST anomalies have greater influence on midlatitude climate than comparable anomalies in the North Pacific Ocean.[40] The massive El Niño event of 1982/1983 and the coincidence of major worldwide climatic anomalies has been pointed to by some as further proof of the hypothesized connection between tropical SST anomalies and unusual weather patterns. However, the simultaneous occurrence of a major volcanic eruption (El Chichon) spewing vast amounts of particles into the stratosphere has confused clear cause and effect inferences from either event.*

*See, for example, an editorial I wrote on this issue in the journal *Climatic Change* (Vol. 5, pp. 111–113, 1983).

Just how accurate season-ahead forecasts can ever be is still not clear, as such forecasting faces the two formidable obstacles: multiple causes and the signal-to-noise ratio barrier. Thus, even if the atmospheric consequences of SST anomalies—tropical or temperate—can be more firmly established, we may still be left with only marginal forecast skill. Remember too that the oceans are not the only likely cause of unusual atmospheric patterns. Ice, as we've said several times, plays an important role too. We turn now to the cryosphere, already identified as a major component of the climatic system.

The Cryosphere

As snow and ice have higher albedos than the land or water they cover, they help to maintain the cooling that is needed for their formation. They also contribute to the thermal blanketing described earlier—particularly over the oceans, where sea ice physically cuts off contact between air and sea, thereby dramatically reducing the thermal flywheel effect the oceans have on the atmosphere. Sea ice, then, is a major climatic component. We can look at the seasonal extremes of sea ice extent, both in the northern and southern polar seas, to get a feel for how rapidly floating pack ice can form or shrink.

Sea Ice

Figure 4.6a shows the seasonal average range of sea ice cover (shaded) in north polar seas, as well as the largest and smallest seasonal extent of ice in recent times. The relative isolation of the Arctic Ocean basin leads to virtually year-round coverage by pack ice over all but the margins of the Arctic Sea. In the winter the sea ice spreads to the entire Arctic Sea, the waters between Greenland and Baffin Island, Hudson Bay, the mouth of the St. Lawrence River, the Bering Straits, the Sea of Irkutsk, and the entire east coast of Greenland. In extreme years, northern winter sea ice extends to Iceland, as it apparently did routinely in Little Ice Age times. Some ice can form off Newfoundland and even the New England coast in maximum years, as the figure shows.

The area of sea ice in the Northern Hemisphere ranges between about 7 and 14 million square kilometers (2.7 to 5.4 million square

EXTENT OF SEA ICE

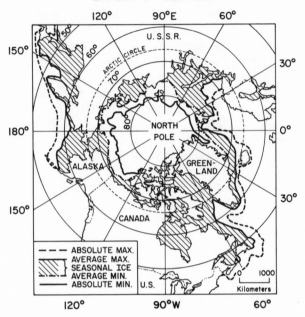

EXTENT OF SEA ICE

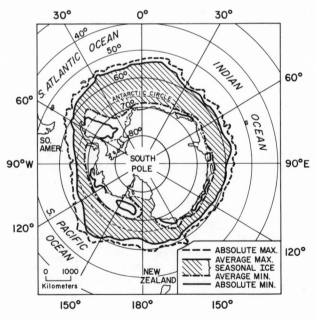

Figure 4.6

Sea ice is one of the most important and rapidly responding components of the climatic system. In the Northern Hemisphere, sea ice cover ranges from about 3 percent of the hemisphere in early autumn to a coverage of some 6 percent in spring. In the Southern Hemisphere, seasonal sea ice variations are much larger and more symmetrical, owing to the more zonally symmetric geography compared to the north polar regions. Early autumn sea ice covers only about 1 percent of the hemispheric surface area of the Southern Hemisphere, but in winter expands to perhaps 8 percent of that hemisphere. Sea ice chills the climate in two ways: (1) by blanketing the ocean thereby preventing large flows of heat into the atmosphere, particularly in winter time, and (2) by its high reflectivity, whereby sea ice significantly reduces the amount of solar energy absorbed relative to that which would be absorbed by open water. [Source: R. G. Barry, 1980, Meteorology and climatology of the seasonal sea ice zone, Cold Regions Science and Technology 2:*133–150.*]

miles). This means that in an average summer, sea ice covers about 3 percent of the hemisphere and in winter expands to some 6 percent. What Figure 4.6a doesn't show is that even in the middle of the Arctic Ocean, where ice cover is year round, the average thickness of pack ice in spring is several meters, but by fall it has thinned to a meter or so. If summer were a few months longer, or its temperatures were a few degrees warmer, it is possible that most of the pack ice would disappear by late summer. One other factor not apparent from the figure is that sea ice is not a static or fixed cap on the sea. Floating ice sheets break up into blocks or rafts that move with winds and ocean currents, opening cracks or *leads* between them. Researchers are investigating how leads can alter the exchange of heat or water vapor between the atmosphere and oceans, even in regions nearly covered by floating pack ice. Models of sea ice dynamics have been constructed and can simulate many of the seasonal changes in sea ice. However, scientists are still a long way from determining reliably the effect of climatic trends on the Arctic ice pack.[41]

If our ability to explain the seasonal behavior of sea ice in the Arctic region is tentative, then our knowledge of what happens in the Antarctic area must be called highly tentative. Figure 4.6b shows a seasonal pattern of ice extent that is generally much more zonally symmetrical than in the Northern Hemisphere. It also shows a much larger seasonal cycle of change in coverage than in the Arctic. Typical autumn ice coverage in the Antarctic is about 2.5 million square kilometers (about 1 million square miles), some 1 percent of the total hemispheric surface area, and only a third of the autumn sea ice area in the Arctic. In winter the southern ice pack typically expands to perhaps eight times the size of the summer coverage, something like 20 million square kilometers (7.7 million square miles), 8 percent of the hemispheric area.

Sea ice thicknesses in the southern oceans vary from autumn to spring, as in the Arctic. But the range of thickness change is usually smaller in the Antarctic: the pack ice thickness in late winter is typically a meter and by midsummer has shrunk to zero. The increase in solar heating that occurs in the spring is probably not great enough to explain the large areal extent of the seasonal melting of southern pack ice. Lamont-Doherty oceanographer Arnold Gordon has hypothesized that sea water salinity could be as important as solar heating in melting the ice.[42] When ice begins to form at the end of the summer season the surface waters become saltier, since ice rejects brine as it freezes. By winter's end the salt content of the waters below the meter-thick pack ice becomes sufficiently high to make this chilled, salty water dense enough to sink. This sinking water is then replaced by warmer, lighter water from below, which then works with the increases in solar heating of spring to melt rapidly the large quantity of sea ice. This mechanism, combined with wind-driven oceanic stirring, low precipitation rates, and seasonal solar heating, Gordon believes, provides enough heating to explain the large seasonal cycle in southern sea ice coverage.

The potential importance of salinity to sea ice extent in the southern polar seas is highlighted by a peculiar phenomenon recently observed from space.* Large areas of open water called *polynas* have been detected well inside the pack ice. Such polynas can migrate slowly, and can persist for the entire winter season or longer. Given the intense cooling of the sea surface that takes place in the frigid twenty-four-hour night of Antarctic winter, the only possible explanation for the failure of sea ice to form in polynas is

---

*The effect of changing salinity on sea ice formation is not only important in the Antarctic. For example, the diversion of northward flowing rivers in the Soviet Union for irrigation purposes would deprive the Arctic basin of a significant source of readily freezable fresh water. This has led to a longstanding series of speculations as to whether such a diversion project could inadvertently help to remove the Arctic Ocean pack ice. (See, for example, the discussion in Schneider, S. H. with L. Mesirow, 1976, *The Genesis Strategy: Climate and Global Survival* (Plenum: New York), pp. 206–208). More recently, computer simulations diminishing this possibility have been carried out by Semtner, A. J., Jr., 1984, The climatic response of the Arctic Ocean to Soviet river diversions, *Climatic Change* (in press).

vast vertical injections of heat from below, probably associated with vigorous overturning of waters that are cold and salty enough to sink below the surface before freezing.

Given the critical role of sea ice in climatic change, it is unfortunate that our knowledge of sea ice dynamics is so meager. In order to have much confidence in predictions of how the pack ice might respond to long-term climatic trends, we need more information on how the system works. Such knowledge is particularly relevant to human affairs when it comes to estimating possible climatic impacts from CO_2 increases or large-scale river diversions over the next few decades. Perhaps the safest statement is that, although detailed predictions are still tentative, it is clear that sea ice is a particularly sensitive element in the climatic system, probably subject to significant changes in response to certain kinds of small provocations.

Snow Cover

Snow cover is the other fast-changing component of the cryosphere. It has been monitored by a series of observations from space. For example, from the late 1960s to 1977, snow cover in the Northern Hemisphere increased from a little more than 20 million square kilometers (7.7 million square miles)—some 8 percent of the hemisphere—to a little more than 26 million square kilometers (10 million square miles)—over 10 percent of the hemisphere. From 1977 to the end of the decade there was a large decline.[43]

Although many in the U.S. Northeast might remember the very cold "winter of '77," those in the western half of North America probably recall warm, droughty conditions, with reduced mountain snowpacks and water rationing. Further analyses of satellite maps by U.S. National Environmental Satellite Service scientists Michael Matson and Donald Wiesnet showed that Eurasian rather than North American snow cover was unusually large in 1977.[44] Their studies show not only that one region may have much different snow cover anomalies than other regions, but even that in the same region coverage from one season to the next can fluctuate widely. For example, average Eurasian winter snow cover showed a large downward trend after 1978, whereas average spring snow cover there showed a moderate upward trend. Much like other climatic elements, season-to-season and year-to-year fluctuations in snow cover exhibit wide-ranging variability (or noise), which as yet seems uncorrelated to any apparent longer-term trends (or signal). Over longer periods, if seasonal snow cover doesn't fully melt in the summer, it builds up into ice fields and ultimately into large glaciers.[45] As we explained in Chapter 2, glaciers not only are governed by climate but can affect climate for tens of thousands of years: they can flow far from their points of origin and can alter atmospheric temperature and wind patterns simply by their height and albedo.

The Biosphere and Biogeochemical Cycles

We have been discussing the climate system, as intricate as it is, primarily as a physical entity made up of air, water, and ice. Climate also influences—and is influenced by—life on earth. Although many details are unknown, we do know that relatively fixed supplies of certain elements, or *nutrients*, which are essential to life, circulate in the environment. These materials are physically transported (via wind and water, for instance) to the places where they are needed, and by means of chemical transformation can become cast into forms taken up by life.

Nutrients move in so-called *biogeochemical cycles*, a term that describes the interaction of life, air, sea, land, and other chemicals.[46] One way climate makes its influence felt is by regulating the flow of materials through these cycles, in part through the vigor of the atmospheric circulation. In turn, the nutrients help determine the composition of the atmosphere, which determines the climate. Water vapor is one such material. When it collects to form clouds, more of the sun's rays are reflected back to space, thus altering the climate. Water vapor and clouds are also important elements in the greenhouse effect. But water is also one of the most important nutrients for sustaining life on earth.

The Hydrological and Sedimentary Cycles

At any one time, a vertical column throughout the depth of the atmosphere typically contains in vapor form only a few centimeters or so of liquid water, more than 100,000 times less water than there is in the oceans and ice caps. The amount of immediately accessible fresh water falling over the globe each year as precipitation is thus negligible by comparison to the water contained in the oceans. Yet this tiny fraction of precipitating fresh water—which is continually distilled and distributed by the hydrological cycle*—amounts to about 525,000 cubic kilometers (126,-000 cubic miles) of precipitation annually. This is enough to cover the earth's surface with about a meter of rainfall each year.[47]

The energy source for the circulations of the atmosphere and oceans is, of course, the sun, whose energy causes the water in oceans, lakes, and on land to evaporate or transpire and precipitate back to earth. How water is distributed—in what quantities and which places—largely determines which plants will grow where. Water is transferred to the air from the leaves of plants in a process called *transpiration.* This combined with evaporation from bodies of water and the soil is known as *evapotranspiration.* Evaporation of ocean water is about six times larger in magnitude on a global average than evapotranspiration on land, although evapotranspiration can be the principal local source of water vapor in the centers of continents.

The precipitation that results from the hydrological cycle interacts with the *sedimentary cycle.* Water helps shuttle materials from land to sea, where they may ultimately end up as sediments. In the relatively shorter term, the sedimentary cycle includes the processes of erosion, nutrient transport, and sediment formation for which water flows are mostly responsible. On the geologically longer term, the processes of sedimentation, uplift, sea floor spreading, and continental drift become important. Both the hydrological and sedimentary cycles are intertwined with the distribution of the stocks and flows of six important elements—hydrogen, carbon, oxygen, nitrogen, phosphorus, and sulfur—which are considered the *macronutrients.* These elements compose more than 95 percent of all living organisms. Appropriate quantities of them in proper balance and in the right places are required to sustain various forms of life. Although great stocks of all these nutrients exist in the earth's crust in various (but not always accessible) forms, at any one time the natural supply of these vital elements is fairly constant. Hence, they must be recycled for life to regenerate continuously.

---

*The *hydrological* cycle involves evaporation of water into the atmosphere, its precipitation back to the surface, runoff of surface and groundwater back to the oceans, and transport of water vapor in the atmosphere all about the globe. This nutrient cycle is powered by the net heating of the earth's surface, primarily from solar energy absorbed in the tropical and subtropical oceans.

The Nitrogen Cycle

Nitrogen is an important nutrient. It is also one of the most chemically complex, since it travels its cycle in many forms. Its primary form, nitrogen (N_2), makes up 78 percent of the atmosphere. Some of this gas is converted in the soils and waters to compounds containing ammonium (NH_4^+), nitrite (NO_2^-), or nitrate (NO_3^-) groups. This conversion is known as *nitrogen fixation,* which literally describes what happens. Nitrogen is fixed or attached to other chemical elements and a strong chemical bond between the nitrogen and other atoms is formed—a process also called *nitrification.* Nitrogen can be fixed abiologically by fires (including lightning) or biologically by special nitrogen-fixing organisms.

Fixed nitrogen resides in the air, soil, and water. Special bacteria —one type of which is called *Rhizobium*—take energy from plants to do their work: to fix nitrogen. They often live in nodules on the roots of legumes, members of the pea family such as alfalfa, beans, peas, and clover. Because these plants are able to fix nitrogen, they are often planted between crop seasons to replenish the supply depleted by non-nitrogen-fixing plants such as wheat, corn, and tomatoes. This natural fertilizer allows plants to incorporate appropriate forms of fixed nitrogen into their tissues by absorbing it in their roots. The plants then chemically transform it into amino acids and convert it into proteins.

Nitrogen, fixed as proteins, for example, into the bodies of living things, eventually returns via the nitrogen cycle to its original form of nitrogen gas in the air. This process starts when the plants containing the fixed nitrogen are either eaten or die. If they are eaten, most fixed nitrogen is returned to the environment as excreta from animals or as animal bodies when the animals die. These fixed nitrogen products (including dead, uneaten plants) encounter *denitrifying* bacteria that can undo the work done by the nitrogen-fixing bacteria. When the waste products are denitrified, their fixed nitrate is transformed in several steps back into nitrogen gas (N_2) for the most part, but also into lesser amounts of nitrous oxide (N_2O) (popularly known as laughing gas). Like water vapor and CO_2, N_2O is a "greenhouse gas" that can trap heat near the earth's surface. Over many years the nitrous oxide is transported by winds high into the atmosphere, where it is broken down by ultraviolet light. (Recall that we are shielded from most of these biologically harmful rays by the stratospheric ozone layer.) When nitrous oxide is so destroyed, other nitrogen oxide gases (NO_2 and NO) are created. Most interesting of all is that NO_2 and NO are believed to help control the amount of ozone.* Eventually, the NO_2 and NO are chemically transformed back either to N_2 or to nitrate or nitrite compounds, which get used by plants after they are washed by the rain back to the earth's surface.

To reiterate, all these processes are going on simultaneously in the *nitrogen cycle*—nitrification; the internal cycling of fixed nitrogen compounds among soil, water, plants, animals, and the air; and denitrification. At the same time some of the nitrogen forms in the air affect the transmission of radiant energy, which drives the climate. Thus, the nitrogen cycle represents the interconnectedness of climate, life, and the biogeochemical nutrient cycles.[48]

The Sulfur Cycle

Another example of a major biogeochemical cycle of significance to climate and life is the sulfur cycle. The nutrient sulfur plays an important part in the structure and function of proteins, thus influencing all life. While certain quantities and forms of sulfur can be toxic to plants or animals, others determine the acidity of rain water, surface water, and soil. This acidity controls the rates of processes such as denitrification.

Like nitrogen, sulfur can exist in many forms: as the gases sulfur dioxide (SO_2) or hydrogen sulfide (H_2S), or as the compound sulfurous acid (H_2SO_3), which, when exposed to sunlight, can change into caustic sulfuric acid (H_2SO_4). When sulfuric acid particles float in the air they contribute to the irritating smog that engulfs some industrial centers or cities where many sulfur-containing fuels are burned.

While large concentrations of sulfur in such forms can be dangerous to people's health, we do need certain safe levels of this nutrient. The sulfur cycle can be thought of as beginning with the gas SO_2 or the particles of sulfate ($SO_4^=$) compounds in the air. These compounds either fall out or are rained out of the atmosphere, contributing to the sulfur compounds in the surface environment. Some forms of sulfur are taken up by plants and incorporated into their tissues. Then, as with nitrogen, these organic sulfur

*The actual effects of nitrogen oxides in the stratosphere, whether from naturally produced N_2O or N_2O resulting from manufactured fertilizers, is still a controversial topic, as discussed in Chapter 7.

compounds are returned to land or water after the plants die or are consumed. Bacteria are important here too, since they can transform the organic sulfur to hydrogen sulfide gas (H_2S). The gas then re-enters the atmosphere, water, and soils, and continues the cycle.

Superimposed on these fast internal loops of the sulfur cycle are the extremely slow sedimentary-cycle processes of erosion, sedimentation, and uplift of rocks containing sulfur. In addition, sulfur compounds from volcanoes are intermittently injected into the atmosphere, and a continual stream of these compounds is produced from our industrial activities. When we burn fossil fuels, we release their sulfur content. These compounds mix with moisture in the atmosphere and form sulfuric acid, which in turn contributes to a serious environmental concern: acid rain. This complex topic is dealt with in summary form in Chapter 8.

Another climatic aspect of the sulfur cycle should be mentioned here. The sulfuric acid droplets of smog form a haze layer that modifies the atmospheric albedo and can thus alter the amount of solar energy absorbed by the climatic system (this is also discussed more extensively later). While many open questions remain, the sulfur cycle in general, and acid rain and smog issues in particular, are becoming major physical, biological, and social problems.

The Carbon Cycle

The biogeochemical cycle we believe to be of greatest interest to climatology is the carbon cycle. Carbon, we know, exists in trace amounts in the atmosphere as carbon dioxide (CO_2) and in this and other forms in larger amounts in the oceans and other bodies of water. Plants are able to use this carbon to form carbohydrates that build their tissues. They use solar energy, as you will recall, to combine CO_2 and water in the well-known photosynthesis process.* The carbon dioxide uptake speeds up during the spring and summer when increasing sunlight and warmer temperatures help plants take CO_2 out of the air at a faster rate.

Every year in the Northern Hemisphere the concentration of CO_2 in the air drops by about 3 percent from spring to fall; plants are taking up the carbon so they can grow. This annual inhalation of carbon involves tens of billions of tons of CO_2. In the Southern

---

*Some organisms that never "see" any sunlight are still able to convert inorganic CO_2 into organic hydrocarbons. They derive their energy from a chemical source, like H_2S, in a process known as chemosynthesis.

Hemisphere, where there are fewer plants, the exchange of CO_2 between the air and vegetation is only about one-third that in the Northern Hemisphere.

With the onset of fall and winter, temperatures drop and photosynthesis rates slow, since less solar energy is available to convert CO_2 to carbohydrates. Then the other part of the carbon cycle in plants dominates as respiration and the decay of dying plants proceeds faster than photosynthesis.

Of course, factors other than CO_2 are involved in the carbon cycle. CO_2 exchanges between air and the oceans are controlled by complex internal chemical processes in the oceans. The location and quantity of plant life on earth is another such factor. And, as we have seen, other nutrients such as water and nitrogen are required to sustain life. They interact with carbon and life in an interlocking set of biogeochemical cycles.[49] On geologic time scales, the great carbon reservoirs in sedimentary rocks are part of this biogeochemical cycling.

We mentioned that CO_2 is a trace gas in the earth's atmosphere. Though it constitutes only about 0.03 percent of the air, it has a substantial effect on the atmospheric heat balance. The climatic power of CO_2, as discussed earlier, lies in the fact that it tends to absorb infrared radiation, trapping some of the earth's heat in lower layers that normally escapes through the atmosphere to space. There are other trace gases in the atmosphere with strong greenhouse effects that could also increase in concentration. Notable among these is methane (CH_4)—produced by animals and as a human pollutant—and nitrous oxide, which might be increasing as a result of the rapid growth in the use of nitrogen fertilizers.

As explained in Chapter 1, the primordial CO_2 resulted from a combination of volcanic outgassing, the formation and weathering of rocks, the synthesis and decay of organic matter, and the chemical transformation of undecayed organic matter into fossil fuels, all of which took place over the aeons. But now humans are digging up those fossil fuels and releasing them at a much faster rate than they were made. Satisfying our energy and agricultural needs has probably contributed a 20 to 30 percent increase of airborne CO_2 since the Industrial Revolution. Most projections indicate about another 10 percent CO_2 increase by the year 2000 and perhaps as much as a 100 percent increase by the middle of the next century. (We will cover this controversial aspect of the carbon cycle in more detail in Chapter 8.)

If CO_2 increased that much, it could raise global mean surface temperatures by about 1°C (1.8°F) by the turn of the century and 2° to 3°C (3.6° to 5.4°F) by the late twenty-first century. These seemingly insignificant changes, as we saw in Chapters 2 and 3, approach the magnitude of the average global temperature changes from interglacial to glacial periods! Later on we'll talk more about some of the specific implications of such a possible carbon dioxide-induced warming. At this point it's important to remember that climate is a major determinant of what can grow where and of the rate at which nutrients cycle through life and the environment. Of equal importance is the fact that life affects albedo and atmospheric composition, both of which regulate the planetary energy balance, which in turn determines climate, completing the coevolutionary link between climate and life.

5 Planetary Energy Balance: The Power Behind the Climate System

The energy from the Sun is the principal power behind the climate. The various energy flows and storages in and between each of the climatic subsystems—the *planetary energy balance* —involve many components. Each of these items represents either input of radiant energy to the planet, its output from the planet, storage or release of heat within the climatic system, or transport of heat from one part of the climatic system to another. Taken together, these processes serve as the driving forces of the climatic system. The principal ones include:

- Solar heating (absorbed sunlight)
- Infrared cooling (the greenhouse effect)
- Latent heating (evaporation, condensation, melting, and freezing)
- Thermal energy storage (temperature changes)
- Atmospheric heat transport (winds)
- Oceanic heat transport (oceanic currents)

Each of these components is described below.

Radiation Balance

The overall energy available to drive all climatic processes on a planetary scale principally comes from the distribution of radiation arriving from space and leaving from the earth—the so-called *radiation balance.*

Solar Heating

The earth intercepts an extremely tiny fraction of the total energy continuously emitted by the sun. Of the roughly 380 trillion trillion (3.8×10^{26}) watts of power radiated by the thermonuclear reactors of our star, our planet intercepts less than one ten millionth of 1 percent (some 4.5×10^{-8} percent). Nevertheless, this amount is roughly 10,000 times greater than all the energy now consumed by humanity in all its domestic, industrial, and other pursuits.[1] Furthermore, the solar energy absorbed by the earth is about 100,000 times greater than the heat that comes up to the surface from its molten interior, called the *geothermal heat flux*. (Unlike solar heat, this upwelling heat is not evenly distributed around the earth. It surfaces everywhere, but most notably in hot spots like midoceanic ridges, volcanoes, and geysers.)

If all the energy of the sun intercepted by the earth averaged over a one-year period were divided uniformly across our planet's surface, it would amount to about 345 watts for every square meter of the earth at any one instant. Since an adult human being produces roughly 100 watts of metabolic energy from "burning" his or her food, this means the sun puts as much heat on average into the planet as if there were three to four people standing on every square meter of the earth.

The 345 watts per square meter or so of average solar power reaching the earth is called by climatologists the *earth-averaged solar constant*. The jargon is based on the long-standing assumption that the energy output from the sun has been constant. Indeed, in early philosophy and Renaissance religion, belief in the perfection and constancy of the sun was dogma. Galileo's infamous censure by the church was partly due to his observation of sunspots, blemishes whose discovery contradicted accepted teachings and thus cast doubt on other church dogma. Until recently, when satellites with carefully calibrated instruments could get above the blurring effect of the earth's atmosphere, sufficiently precise and reliable long-term measurements of the solar constant had not been possible. It was unknown to better than about 1 percent accuracy whether the sun was really constant over a period of a decade. Astrophysical theory suggests that on much longer time scales the sun has been steadily brightening—perhaps by some 25 percent over the past 4 billion years—and will continue to do so. Eventually, the theory goes, the sun's size and energy output will engulf the earth and other near planets. Long before this final earth catastrophe is scheduled—in some several billion years—the extra energy output from the sun will likely have boiled the oceans and fried all life on earth.

Despite the lack of long-term, precise measurements of the

total energy output of the sun or the solar constant, it has long been known that the sun's energy output is quite inconstant in some parts of the spectrum of solar radiant frequencies. The average surface temperature of the sun is about 5500°C (9900°F), and it emits radiation close to that of a similarly hot *black body*. Black body is a term used by physicists to describe a hypothetical object that gives off the maximum radiative energy output a body can emit for its temperature. As the temperature of a black body increases, its total radiant output increases with the fourth power of its absolute temperature.* A *grey body*, however, gives off radiant energy at some fixed percentage of the black body temperature. Most real substances, though, are neither black nor grey, but rather give off radiation that is some fraction of an equivalent black body, though a different fraction for each wavelength of emitted radiant energy.

A spectrum of radiant energy is emitted from every object with temperature greater than absolute zero. The amount of energy emitted at each frequency depends upon the temperature of the body and its physical characteristics. Hotter bodies emit more energy at high frequencies (short wavelengths), whereas colder bodies give off their lesser total amount of radiant energy mostly at low frequencies (long wavelengths). Although every object gives off some radiation at nearly every frequency, the amount actually radiated is infinitesimally small outside of a limited range of wavelengths determined by the body's temperature.†

The sun gives off its maximum radiant energy as light with wavelengths of about half a micrometer (a micrometer is one ten-thousandth of a centimeter or one-millionth of a meter).‡ The sun also gives off some short-wave, or *ultraviolet*, radiation, with wavelengths less than 0.3 micrometer. These rays tend to be harmful to biological tissues, and are mostly screened out by upper atmo-

---

*The *absolute temperature* is defined as the temperature measured from a reference temperature at which solid bodies emit no energy at all. This point is at −273.16°C or −453°F. Thus, at normal room temperature, we are at an absolute temperature of about 295K. (The "K" commemorates Lord Kelvin, the British scientist who clarified our understanding of radiation emission of heat.)

†This subject is discussed in more detail in most standard physics books. For a particularly clear treatment in the context of the climate, see Kandel, R. S., 1980, *Earth and Cosmos* (Oxford: Pergamon Press).

‡This (0.5 micrometer) is roughly the size of a typical small dust particle floating in the atmosphere.

spheric oxygen and the ozone layer in the stratosphere—one reason why life has flourished on earth over the past billion years despite the extreme sensitivity of many present life forms to ultraviolet radiation.

There is also some energy given off from the sun at very, very short wavelengths, such as those of X-rays, but the amount of energy at these high frequencies is so small it has no readily conceivable climatic influence. Most earth creatures see *daylight,* which is light with wavelengths between about 0.4 and 0.7 micrometer. This seems likely simply because our eyes have evolved to see the radiant frequencies that are energetically most abundant—those from the middle of the solar spectrum. But a significant fraction of solar energy falls at wavelengths longer than our eyes can see, so-called *infrared radiation* (*IR*). Most of the solar infrared radiant energy occurs in wavelengths of 1 to 5 micrometers. This is known as *near IR;* wavelengths longer than 5 and less than about 100 micrometers are known as *far IR.* There is almost no significant solar energy at far IR or at longer wavelengths such as microwaves or radiowaves.

As the spectrum of radiant solar energy impinges on the earth, some of it is absorbed, some of it is scattered, and some of it is directly transmitted to lower layers in the earth's atmosphere. The absorption, scattering, and transmission are selective, and do not occur uniformly with radiation frequency. Various molecules, particles, or surface features absorb, transmit, and reflect radiation with very different efficiencies at different wavelengths. For example, ozone, as already mentioned, absorbs most of the radiation of wavelengths below 0.3 micrometer. It also absorbs some of the visible and some far-IR frequencies. Carbon dioxide absorbs some of the near IR, but not very much. Water vapor absorbs quite a bit of the near IR.

All molecules tend to scatter radiation, and the character of the scattering depends on the wavelength of radiation relative to the size of the molecules or other particles in the atmosphere. The molecules that compose the gases of the earth's atmosphere are all very small relative to the wavelengths of most sunlight. For this reason, shorter-wavelength radiation is scattered more effectively than longer wavelengths through a process known as *Rayleigh scattering* (after the English physicist who studied it). The sky is blue simply because that Rayleigh scattering of sunlight by the many, many tiny molecules in the earth's atmosphere favors shorter wavelengths, such as blue light.

For the much larger particles (that is, particles larger than individual molecules) such as soil dust or sulfuric acid, which make up *atmospheric aerosols,* the scattering efficiency is more uniformly distributed across the visible wavelengths.* That is why a haze of particles or a cloud of droplets has a greyish-white appearance; sunlight is being scattered by these micrometer-sized aerosols in significant amounts for all visible frequencies. Some of the scattering from clouds and dust results in so-called *back scattering,* whereby a fraction of incoming solar radiant energy is scattered back—that is, reflected—to space. (The fraction of solar energy reflected back to space by the earth-atmosphere system is the planetary albedo. Earth satellites show this fraction to be about 30 percent for the entire earth-atmosphere system.[2])

Gases and particles in the earth's atmosphere tend to be fairly transparent to much of the solar radiant energy, allowing about half of the solar rays to pass through to the earth's surface. However, not all the sunlight reaching the surface passes directly through the atmosphere uninterrupted. Much of it—virtually all of it on a cloudy day—arrives as *diffuse radiation,* having been first scattered by atmospheric particles and molecules. About one-third of the total of the sun's radiant energy that reaches the earth eventually hits the surface without being scattered and about one-quarter reaches the surface as diffuse radiation. There, some 85 percent of the total amount is absorbed. Over dark surfaces such as the oceans, more than 90 percent of arriving radiation typically is absorbed; in the seas or very wet vegetated surfaces about 90 percent of this absorbed solar heat is used to evaporate water. Over the bright surfaces such as deserts and snow fields, 40 to 80 percent of the incoming solar radiation is reflected. Over deserts, for example, as little as 1 percent of the absorbed energy is used to evaporate water; the rest simply warms the surface.

To recap, a little less than a third of the sun's radiation that reaches the earth is reflected away, almost half is absorbed at the surface, and the remaining 20 percent or so is absorbed in the atmosphere by its gases and particles (see left-hand side of Figure 5.1). The principal energy-driving mechanism of the earth's climate is thus the absorption of solar energy by the molecules and particles of the atmosphere and the surface features of the earth.

---

*An *aerosol* is simply many particles—solid dust, liquid droplets, and so on—suspended in a gas.

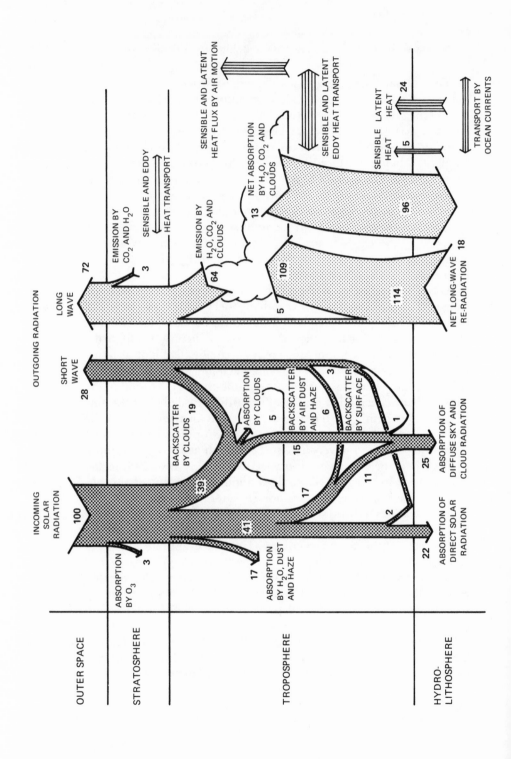

Figure 5.1

Solar heating of the earth-atmosphere system drives the climate. The left-hand side of the figure gives approximate— that is, accurate to perhaps 10 percent —percentages of the disposition of solar radiation coming into the earth-atmosphere system; the right-hand side indicates the approximate—also accurate to some 10 percent—amounts of terrestrial infrared (far IR) radiated back to space as well as the heat transported by air currents. The greenhouse effect occurs because infrared radiation is "trapped" near the earth's surface. Actually, it is the downward reradiation of IR that creates the greenhouse effect. This is represented on the figure by the broad downward-pointing arrow labeled as containing 96 units of energy. [Source: S. H. Schneider with L. Mesirow, 1976, The Genesis Strategy: Climate and Global Survival *(New York: Plenum Press), figure 25.]*

Infrared Radiation Cooling and the Greenhouse Effect

If the earth only absorbed radiation from the sun without giving an equal amount of heat back to space by some means, the planet would continue to warm up until the oceans boiled. We know the oceans are not boiling, and surface thermometers plus satellites have shown that the earth's temperature remains roughly constant from year to year. This near constancy requires that about as much radiant energy leave the planet each year in some form as is coming in. In other words, an equilibrium or energy balance has been established. The components of this energy balance are crucial to the climate.

All bodies with temperature, we've said, give off radiant energy. The earth gives off a total amount of radiant energy equivalent to that of a black body with a temperature of roughly 255K ($-18°C$, 0°F), although the amount of energy emitted by the planet to space at each frequency is typically quite different from the amount a 255K black body would emit. Only the total amounts are comparable. The wavelength that is in the maximum part of the spectrum of energy emission for a 255K black body is about 10 micrometers, in the middle of the far-IR frequencies. Nearly all the energy emitted by the earth's surface and its atmosphere falls in the far-IR wavelength range between 5 and 100 micrometers and is known as *terrestrial infrared radiation*. Although we can't see it, this terrestrial radiation emitted to space by the planet is nearly exactly balanced each year with the amount of absorbed solar radiation—the equilibrium referred to earlier that makes the earth's climate reasonably steady. If

195

the earth's albedo were somehow to drop, the darker planet would absorb more insolation and heat up. As it got hotter, more terrestrial IR would be emitted to space until eventually a new, but warmer, equilibrium would be established. Similarly, if the sun somehow gave off more energy, a warming process would ensue.

The mean global surface air temperature is about 14°C (287K, or 57°F). Earlier we said that the earth emitted radiation to space equivalent to a black body with a temperature of −18°C (255K, or 0°F), some 32°C (58°F) colder than the earth's average surface temperature. A satellite picks up radiation that appears to be emitted from an object some 32°C (58°F) colder than the earth's surface because of the celebrated *greenhouse effect.*

Although most of the earth's surface and thick clouds are reasonably close approximations to a black body, the atmospheric gases are not. When the nearly black body radiation emitted by the earth's surface travels upward into the atmosphere, it encounters air molecules and aerosol particles. Water vapor, carbon dioxide, methane, nitrogen dioxide, ozone, and many other trace gases in the earth's gaseous envelope tend to be highly selective—but often highly effective—absorbers of terrestrial infrared radiation. Furthermore, clouds absorb nearly all the infrared radiation that hits them, and then they reradiate energy almost like a black body at the temperature of the cloud surface (see the right-hand side of Figure 5.1). But since clouds occur high up in the atmosphere, they radiate to space as colder black bodies than the surface, thereby screening the warm surface radiation and replacing it with colder—less energetic—radiation from the tops of the clouds. Hence, the effect of the clouds and the gases in the atmosphere is to reduce by a large fraction the total infrared radiation that otherwise would have been emitted by the earth's surface to space. It also results in a large downward atmospheric emission of IR to the surface, as seen in Figure 5.1—114 units of radiation go up but 96 units (nearly 85 percent) are reradiated down to the surface from the clouds and greenhouse gases in the atmosphere.

The atmosphere is more opaque to terrestrial infrared radiation than it is to incoming solar radiation, simply because the physical properties of atmospheric molecules and particles tend on average to be more transparent to solar radiation wavelengths than to terrestrial radiation. These properties create the large surface heating that characterizes the greenhouse effect, by means of which the atmosphere allows a considerable fraction of solar radiation to penetrate to the earth's surface and then traps (more precisely, intercepts and reradiates) much of the upward terrestrial infrared radiation from the surface and lower atmosphere. The downward reradiation further enhances surface warming.

The term greenhouse effect arises from the classic analogy to a greenhouse, in which the glass allows the solar radiation in and traps much of the heat. However, the mechanisms are different, for in a greenhouse the glass primarily prevents convection currents of air from taking heat away from the interior. Greenhouse glass is not primarily keeping the enclosure warm by blocking or reradiating infrared radiation; rather, it is constraining the physical transport of heat by air motion. The atmosphere, like the glass walls, concentrates heat near the surface, but the term greenhouse effect applied to a planetary atmosphere refers solely to the role of the atmosphere in preventing some of the infrared radiation from escaping to space. Hence, some of the scientific community object to the use of the term greenhouse effect as applied to a planetary atmosphere. Despite the differences in mechanisms, the analogy is sufficiently apt —and is already so well entrenched—that we won't object to its popular use.

The most important greenhouse gas is water vapor, since it absorbs terrestrial radiation over most of the IR spectrum. But in the so-called *window for terrestrial radiation,* with wavelengths between about 8 and 12 micrometers, water vapor in small or even moderate amounts is relatively inefficient in absorbing and emitting infrared radiation. Indeed, much of the terrestrial infrared radiation emitted from the surface that escapes to space falls in this window. Carbon dioxide is another major greenhouse gas. Although it absorbs and reemits considerably less infrared radiation than water vapor, CO_2 is of intense interest because its concentration is increasing due to human activities. A major controversy exists over the extent to which our CO_2 emission will significantly enhance the greenhouse effect. Ozone, nitrogen oxides, sulfur oxides, some hydrocarbons, and even some man-made compounds like chlorofluorocarbons (such as Du Pont's Freon) are also greenhouse gases. The extent to which they are important to climate depends upon their atmospheric concentrations and the rates of change of those concentrations (discussed in Chapter 8).

The earth's temperature, then, is primarily determined by the planetary radiation balance, through which the absorbed portion of the incoming solar radiation is nearly exactly balanced over a year's time by the outgoing terrestrial infrared radiation emitted by the climatic system to space. As both of these quantities are determined by the properties of the atmosphere and the earth's surface, major climate theories that address changes in those properties have been constructed. Many of these remain plausible hypotheses of climatic change.

Heat Storage and Transport

The unequal heating of the earth-atmosphere system by the local radiative budget, we noted earlier, gives rise to energy flows and storages that create winds, ocean currents, rainfall, and temperature changes. First, we'll examine some heat storage processes.

Latent Heating

We have already seen that water vapor in the air is a major contributor to the greenhouse effect, as are the water droplets in clouds. The clouds themselves are a principal component of the earth's albedo, as are surface ice particles, since both are highly reflective of sunlight. Thus, water is a central element in the planetary radiation balance. Of course, most of the earth's surface is water, and most of the solar radiation received by the earth is absorbed at watery surfaces, especially in the tropical latitudes. One might thus expect that the tropical oceans would be warmer than other regions of the earth. However, the land masses in the tropics generally tend to have warmer, extreme temperatures, which may seem particularly surprising since oceans are darker and therefore absorb more solar radiation on average. But the surface of the tropical oceans is not generally warmer than the surface of tropical land regions because of their high heat capacity, mentioned before, and because of the latent heat of vaporization. Most of the radiation that is absorbed by the water surface is used not to raise the local temperature of the water, but rather to break the molecular bonds between the liquid water molecules and turn them into water vapor molecules.

Evaporation and Condensation   The process by which a liquid is transformed into a gas involves a considerable input of energy. An everyday experience illustrates this. Everyone knows that if high heat is applied to a tea kettle the water inside will warm up continuously until it reaches the boiling point. The temperature will then remain constant while the water boils out. This is because the energy that had been increasing the water temperature to the boiling point is now used exclusively to break the molecular bonds—which keep the water in liquid form—and to transform the water into vapor form. This latent heat of vaporization is extremely large; some 540 calories of heat are needed to boil only 1 gram of water.*

Let's suppose we have 100 grams (3.5 ounces) of pure water (a small juice glass full), which is in liquid form at the freezing point, 0°C (32°F). Since a calorie is defined as the amount of heat needed to raise 1 gram of liquid water by 1°C, it will take 100 calories of energy to heat each gram of that water to its boiling point (100°C at sea level). To evaporate that water as steam at 100°C (212°F) would take 540 percent more energy than it took to raise the water temperature all the way from 0° to 100°C. It took 10,000 calories (100 grams of water times 100°C temperature change) to raise our glass of liquid water from a freezing temperature to the boiling point. But the next 10,000 calories will not raise the temperature of the water even 1 degree; it will be needed to turn a small part (100/540) of the liquid water at 100°C to steam at 100°C. In other words, more than 80 percent (440/540) of the glass will still be filled with liquid water at 100°C.

The heat used to evaporate water overcomes the attractive forces between liquid water molecules. Thus, water vapor at 100°C contains more energy than an equivalent amount of liquid water at the same temperature. This additional stored energy is called *latent heat.* When the water vapor later cools and condenses back to water liquid, it gives back this latent heat at the point of condensation.

A dramatic way to prove to yourself the importance of latent heating is to put your hand briefly over a tea kettle's spout when the water boils. You will instantly feel it as the steam condenses on your hand. Compare that nasty—and potentially dangerous—feeling with that of putting your hand in a hot oven, even one where the air temperature is several hundred degrees higher than the temper-

---

*Calories are now an archaic unit of heat in physics. The preferred units are joules. One calorie is slightly more than 4 joules. We use the calorie here because it is familiar and convenient to our illustration.

ature of just-boiled steam. You will then appreciate the power of latent heating. The 100°C (212°F) steam, of course, burns your hand a great deal more in a second or two than the much hotter oven air. (Indeed, anyone familiar with the dry heat of a sauna knows that the addition of steam to the hot room dramatically increases the sensation of heating you feel.) The reason the cooler steam feels hotter than the warmer oven air is that the transfer of heat from dry air to hand versus steam to hand occurs at different rates, with steam having a higher rate. A major part of this difference is simply that the water vapor is condensing on your hand, giving up (to you) the 540 calories per gram of latent heat of vaporization that it took to evaporate the liquid water in the first place.

Precisely the same process occurs in the climatic system. As we said, more than 80 percent of the solar energy absorbed on average at the earth's surface is used to evaporate water. The remaining percentage of heat absorbed at the surface is used directly to maintain the temperature of that surface—so-called *sensible heating* (see right-hand side of Figure 5.1). Latent heating at the surface, you remember, is more than ten times that of the sensible heating for wet surfaces, but can be as little as one-fortieth or less of the sensible heating for very dry surfaces such as sandy deserts. Just feel how hot a dry piece of ground is in the noonday sun compared to a wet one and you'll appreciate how evaporation moderates the surface temperature. But the latent heat taken from the surface is not lost from the climatic system. Rather, it is transported upward into the atmosphere (see Figure 5.1). When the latent heat is later released in the clouds where condensation takes place, vast quantities of energy originally absorbed at the surface are deposited in the atmosphere. Recall that this is the mechanism that drives the tropical Hadley cell, as described in Chapter 4. It is also part of the greenhouse effect, since release of latent heat warms the atmosphere, which in turn radiates additional IR back down to the surface.

Evaporation and condensation are really transformations of energy from one form to another, and the physical transport of water vapor represents a significant transfer of stored energy in the form of latent heat; when the water vapor condenses it releases all the latent heat it had stored after its evaporation.

Melting and Freezing　　So far we've been talking about the transformation of liquid water to gaseous form and back again. That is not the only transformation involving water that occurs on earth. Freezing and melting are also important. Let's return to our 100-gram (3.5-ounce) glass of water. One hundred calories must be removed from that glass in order to cool the water from 1°C (33.8°F) to the 0°C (32°F) freezing point. But for freezing to occur, the molecular structure of liquid water must be transformed to the crystalline structure of ice. This involves a significant extraction of heat known as the *latent heat of fusion,* which requires 80 calories per gram. This means that we could cool our glass of water from 80°C (176°F) all the way down to the freezing point by extracting the same amount of energy as it takes to convert 0°C liquid water to 0°C ice. Conversely, if we add heat and warm a block of ice up to the freezing point, it will take an additional 80 calories of energy per gram of ice to break the lattice structure of the solid form and create liquid at the same freezing temperature. Thus, for liquid water vapor to be transformed into ice, extra heat is given off to the atmosphere or oceans. On the other hand, for snow or sea ice to be melted into liquid water, much of the heat needed will be used just in the conversion from solid phase before any increase in temperature above freezing can take place. To give you a rough idea of how much heat that is, consider this: if all the ice now in the Greenland and Antarctic glaciers were spread over the whole globe —a global 50-meter-thick ice cap—then melting all of it would require all the incident solar energy on earth for more than a year. And this would be true only if no heat in the form of terrestrial IR left the earth to space, which is, of course, an unreasonable assumption. Melting of a significant part of the big glaciers where they occur typically takes tens of thousands of years.*

Thermal Energy Storage

In one sense, latent heat of fusion or vaporization is heat storage, since large quantities of energy are taken in to transform liquid to vapor or ice to liquid water. When remaining in these phases, the latent heat is essentially stored for later release. Heat is also stored by any object in proportion to its temperature, mass, and a property known as its *specific heat.* Changing the temperature of a body is equivalent to changing its heat content or thermal energy storage. To do this requires the flow of heat to or from the body. We've already seen that the large mass of oceans provides a reser-

*Surges of ice sheets or their calving into the oceans can occur faster, as discussed in Chapter 2.

voir of heat so that coastal regions have much lower day-to-night and season-to-season temperature extremes than midcontinental regions. The buildup or release of stored heat tends to smooth out extreme variations of temperature in the climatic system that otherwise would occur from radiation variations.

Atmospheric Heat Transport

The atmosphere can transport heat in several forms. One is the direct flow of air by winds into a region at a different temperature. This is known as *sensible heat transport*. It is particularly important when winds are strong and are blowing from a region whose temperature is very different from that of the adjacent region. Another form of atmospheric heat transport is *latent heat transport*, which refers to wind currents carrying moist air. As mentioned earlier, when that moist air later condenses into precipitation, it releases the vast quantities of latent heat that were originally picked up at the point of evaporation. Latent heat transport towards the tropics takes place, you recall, through the trade winds, which pick up great amounts of water vapor while progressing over the oceans from the subtropics to the ITCZ.

Another form of atmospheric heat transport is known as *potential energy transport*. As the warm air rises in the tropics and gains altitude, it picks up potential energy. This process is analogous to raising an object off the ground and later dropping it. Potential energy is released as it falls, accelerating the object. Air that is lifted by surface heating can be transported horizontally and may later sink, such as occurs in the tropical Hadley cell. As the air sinks, heating occurs as gravitational or potential energy is released, helping to create the warm dry regions in the subtropics. A great amount of energy is exported from the tropics by this mechanism.[3]

Ocean Heat Transport

Ocean heat transport, we've already seen, is a significant factor in determining zonal and regional climates. Oceans can transport heat as horizontal mean currents or gyres, in the form of rings or eddies, or by sinking or upwelling currents. The latter are driven primarily by temperature and salinity differences from one part of the ocean to the next—the so-called *thermal/haline circulation*. At about lat. 30°N, some estimates suggest the oceans transport as much heat poleward as does the atmosphere.[4]

The Weather Machine

All the components of the planetary energy budget combine to determine the global and regional climates and their changes. The albedo and greenhouse properties of the climatic system, as we've seen, determine the planetary radiation balance, which, in turn, regulates the distribution of heating around the globe.[5] The important points to remember about this include:

- In the polar regions, infrared radiation to space vastly exceeds the amount of incoming solar radiation absorbed. In the tropics, on the other hand, incoming solar radiation is considerably larger than the infrared radiation emitted to space.
- The solar-heated tropics export much of their excess heating to the mid and high latitudes.
- Differential heating of the earth from latitude to latitude zone, or from land to sea, plays an important part in generating regional differences in temperature and barometric pressure. Currents of water and wind redistribute heat and chemical nutrients, modifying the climate and other environmental conditions that otherwise would have resulted from radiation energy balance effects alone.
- On the planetary average, absorbed solar radiation is nearly balanced from year to year by emitted infrared radiation, with any global inbalance leading to a change in heat storage—largely in the form of a temperature or ice volume change of the climatic system.

Any long-term change of planetary climate—on earth or any other planet—is related to a change in some (and perhaps all) components of the planetary energy balance, although heat storage, as we have noted, plays an important role in determining the rates of such a change. A short-term global climate anomaly or a longer-term climatic trend may be a result of changes in planetary radiation balance, although not necessarily. Changing the local character of the earth's surface or the composition of the atmosphere can alter the heating patterns of the climatic system. This can change the winds and ocean currents, causing different regional climatic changes, even though no significant net global changes may have occurred. Any regional climatic change could also be simply a local response to a global effect; such a change could as well be a much more complicated result of many regional changes of differing magnitudes and directions, with perhaps no net global change. It is also possible—indeed likely—that various global and regional energy budget changes can be occurring simultaneously, each from different causes. Some of the causes can be outside of the climatic system —such as a change on the sun—whereas others might be internal —such as the melting of a glacier.

The most difficult task facing climate theorists is to untangle the individual influences of many factors that can cause climatic changes on a variety of time and space scales. A principal tool for this task is the use of mathematical models of climate, which are discussed in the following chapter.

6 The Twin Earth: Computer Models of Weather and Climate

The mathematical model of climate is a principal tool for identifying the relative importance of many individual factors affecting climate. Thanks to the development of high-speed computers, such models have become basic devices in understanding and predicting the evolving climate.

Why Build a Model?

In 1628, the King of Sweden, Gustav Adolf of the House of Vasa, was anxious to step up ship construction. He wanted a large fleet of warships with which to attack Europe. At least one ship, named the *Vasa,* was built and launched in August of that year. Sixty-four bronze guns and a crew of 130 men were on board when the *Vasa* began her maiden voyage. Suddenly, before the *Vasa* left the harbor, a squall appeared and forced the ship to heel to port so far that water flooded in through the lower gunports. The list increased so quickly that the ship went down in the harbor with its sails up and its flags flying. Fifty men died.[1]

For more than 300 years the *Vasa* sat at the bottom of the Stockholm harbor in 100 feet of brackish Baltic water. She was raised in 1961 and found to be virtually intact, for the water's salinity was unfavorable for destructive marine boring clams to flourish. One of the marine archaeologists who helped excavate the Swedish warship was Anders Franzén. He wrote in 1962 that there was no evidence to suggest that the *Vasa* had been badly designed or improperly sailed. "It is reasonable to assume," Franzén says, "that the cause of the catastrophe was an incorrect division of the guns, ballast, and other heavy weights on board."[2]

Perhaps the *Vasa* would not have capsized and sunk if the engineers had thought to build a scale model of the ship and to test its stability in winds for different positioning of heavy guns. Such a model might have shown that the position of the guns would create what is called an unstable relationship between the ship's center of gravity and its center of buoyancy. Shipbuilding today depends not only on physical replicas of ships used as laboratory test models, but also on mathematical models of ships in which the shape and weight of the vessel are varied in equations stored in a computer memory bank. These models simulate the performance of the real ship on the high seas. Engineers and scientists build models—either mathematical or physical ones—primarily to perform tests that are either too dangerous or too expensive to perform with the real thing.

Basic Elements of Models

To build a model of any system means deciding beforehand what components of the system should be included. To build a model railroad, for instance, you must include the basic components such as tracks and then choose which cars to replicate —flat cars, tanker cars, passenger cars, or caboose. There are other features to consider, depending on how realistic a replica the model railroad is to be: for example, water towers, switches, signals, stations, towns, and mountains, among many others.

Likewise, to simulate the climate, a modeler needs to decide which components of the climatic system to include and which variables to involve. For example, if we choose to simulate the long-term sequence of glacials and interglacials, our model needs to include explicitly the effects of all the important interacting components of the climatic system operating over the past million years or so. In Chapter 4 we saw that, besides the atmosphere, these include the ice masses, upper and deep oceans, and the earth's crust. As you recall, even life influences the climate and thus must be included too; plants, for example, can affect the chemical composition of the air and seas as well as the brightness or water-cycling character of the land. These mutually interacting subsystems form part of the internal components of the model. On the other hand, if we are only interested in modeling very short-term weather events—say, over a single week—then our model can ignore any changes in the glaciers, deep oceans, land shapes, and forests, since their variables obviously change little over one week's time. For short-term weather, only the atmosphere itself needs to be part of the internal model's climatic system.

The slowly varying factors such as oceans or glaciers are said to be external to the internal part of the climatic system being modeled.[3] Modelers also refer to external factors as *boundary conditions,* since they form boundaries for the internal model components. These boundaries are not always physical ones, such as the oceans, which are at the bottom of the atmosphere, but can also be energy boundaries. An example is the solar radiation impinging on the earth. Solar radiation is often referred to by climatic modelers as a *boundary forcing function* of the model for two reasons: the energy output from the sun is not an interactive, internal component of the climatic system of the model; and the energy from the sun forces the climate toward a certain temperature distribution.

Sometimes we intend to predict the behavior of only one variable, ignoring its time variation and considering its very long-term mean value (that is, its *equilibrium* value). For instance, we could restrict a model to predict only a globally averaged temperature that never changes its value over time. This very simple model would consist of an internal part that, when averaged over all of the atmosphere, oceans, biosphere, and glaciers, would describe two characteristics: the average reflectivity of the earth and its average greenhouse properties. The boundary condition for such a model would be merely the incoming solar energy. Such a model is called *zero dimensional,* since it collapses the east-west, north-south, and vertical space dimensions of the actual world into one point that represents some global average of all earth-atmosphere system temperatures in all places. If our zero-dimensional model were expanded to resolve temperature either at latitude zones or at different heights in the atmosphere, then it would be a one-dimensional model. Further, if the model included temperatures at different longitudes (but only one height), then it would be two dimensional; if, in addition, it evaluated temperature at different heights in the atmosphere or depths in the oceans, then the model would be three dimensional. The *resolution* of a model refers to the number of dimensions included and to the amount of detail with which each dimension is explicitly treated.

Modelers speak of a hierarchy of models that ranges from simple earth-averaged, time-independent, temperature models up to high-resolution, three-dimensional, time-dependent models.[4] The latter explicitly include variables in the atmosphere, oceans, cryosphere, biosphere, and sometimes even in the lithosphere, since motions of the earth's crust, as we've shown, can vary as part of the internal climatic system. While three-dimensional, time-dependent models are more physically, chemically, and biologically comprehensive, they are also much more complicated and more expensive to construct and use. Choosing the optimum combination of factors is an intuitive art that trades off completeness and (the modelers hope) accuracy for tractability and economy. Such a trade-off between accuracy and economy is not scientific per se, but rather is a value judgment, based on the weighing of many factors. Making this judgment depends strongly on the problem the climate model is being designed to address.[5]

So far we have said little of a fourth dimension: time. Regardless of the spatial dimensionality of the model—one, two, or three dimensions—we can either omit or include the time variations as one of our variables. If we do include time, our so-called *time-dependent model* will then predict the evolution of, say, temperature. But in order to predict the evolution of a phenomenon, we must start with an initial condition. From there our model can build a future history of temperature.

To recap, in building climate models we need to decide on the climatic variables we wish to examine, the subcomponents of the climatic system to include in the interactive or internal part of the model, the degree of resolution we want, and whether or not to make the model time dependent. We must also specify our boundary-forcing factors and (for time-evolving models) the initial condition for each variable at each point that the variable is computed. This set of requirements is not unique to climatic modeling. Similar choices face people who model ships, the economy, or even human behavior.

Putting a Model Into a Computer

Clearly, the mathematical components of climate models are not tangible things, like plastic ladders or model firetrucks. Computers store climate models and, unlike toy chests, they don't store physical pieces. Rather, what computers store in their memory banks are instructions and data in the form of electrical energy, which, when properly organized by a computer program or code, represent the various components of a model. What follows is a very rough idea of how a modeler transforms ideas on models into mathematical statements and then into computer simulations of the real phenomenon under study—in our case, climate.

First, the components of the model and its resolution are chosen, as described earlier. Then, variables describing these elements are chosen and mathematical statements are written down to represent the interactions among climatic variables. We accept on faith that variables in the climatic system interact in accordance with basic physical laws of nature, including conservation of mass, momentum, and energy. The degree of resolution and physical comprehensiveness of our model determines how many and what kind of mathematical relationships must be written down in order to make our particular model a reasonable approximation of the known laws of nature. For very simple models, the mathematical equations that describe the behavior of the climatic variables can be solved exactly by any high school freshman who knows elementary algebra. However, most models are not this simple. As soon as the climatologist tries to include many climatic variables or more than one space dimension in a model, the complexity of the mathematics increases dramatically. In fact, it quickly becomes impossible to solve the equations exactly by any known techniques of higher mathematics. This is where the computer usually comes in.

Computers don't make better mathematicians than people. In fact, even the world's fastest machine is less sophisticated in mathematical logic than an advanced grade school child. Typically, computer solutions to most mathematical problems are only approximations to the exact solution. But the computer is billions of times faster than the fastest-thinking human being, rarely makes an error, has a vast memory, can rapidly transfer data in that memory, and can add, subtract, multiply, divide, and compare many numbers in millionths of a second or less. Therefore, in order to take advantage of these capabilities, people have devised special techniques to solve the complex mathematical equations with only the simple arithmetic and elementary logic that these electronic brains are capable of handling. Although such calculations are tedious, sometimes involving many billions of arithmetic operations or more, the speed and accuracy of modern high-speed computers are well suited to these dull but Herculean tasks. For example, to compute a few days of weather at each of about 40,000 points spaced around the world typically takes one hour of computer time on a modern fast machine.[6] Even a decade ago computers were too slow to accomplish a day's weather forecast at present accuracy in less than days' computing time.

Numerical Weather Prediction

A visionary British scientist, Lewis F. Richardson, tried to calculate weather without the aid of any electronic computers in the 1920s. In the preface of his 1922 book, *Weather Prediction by Numerical Process*, Richardson noted that forecasting—which by that time had already been carried on in London for many years—was made practical by one of the latest developments: Colonel E. Gold's *Index of Weather Maps*. [7]

These maps worked in the following manner: observing stations telegraphed the "elements of present weather" to the head Meteorological Office. These data were "set in their places upon a large scale map." The index then enabled the forecaster to find a number of previous maps that resembled the newly drawn one. The forecast, Richardson wrote, was based on the supposition that what the atmosphere did in the past it would do again—in short, atmospheric uniformitarianism. Hence, the history of the atmosphere was used as a "working model of its present self."

But Richardson noted that the approximate repetition did not hold true for very long. Three days in advance was then about the limit for forecasts in the British Isles. Richardson observed that a "particular disposition of stars, planets and satellites never occurs twice. Why then," he wrote, "should we expect a present weather map to be exactly represented in a catalogue of past weather?" The physicist proposed a scheme of weather prediction that resembled "the process by which the *Nautical Almanac* is produced, insofar as it is founded upon the differential equations, and not upon the partial recurrence of phenomena in their ensemble." (The *differential equations* to which Richardson referred are mathematical expressions of basic physical laws we mentioned earlier.)

Richardson acknowledged that his scheme was complicated, but, he noted, so is the atmosphere. He formulated a set of "computing forms" that could "assist anyone who wishes to make partial experimental forecasts from such incomplete observational data as are now available." Richardson knew that the forms were clumsy and hoped that they could be revised and simplified. "Perhaps some day in the dim future," he wrote in the 1920s, "it will be possible to advance the computations faster than the weather advances and at a cost less than the saving to mankind due to the information gained. But that is a dream." Today, of course, it is a reality.

Richardson was a scientist of great imagination. He fantasized a "forecast factory" in which his dream might materialize. His factory was quite an extravagant vision, as the following passage shows. (Bear in mind that when Richardson uses the word computer here he is referring to a *person* computing the solution to an equation at human speed, not an electronic circuit exchanging electrical impulses at the speed of light!)

> Imagine a large hall like a theatre, except that the circles and galleries go right round through the space usually occupied by the stage. The walls of this chamber are painted to form a map of the globe. The ceiling represents the north polar regions, England is in the gallery, the tropics in the upper circle, Australia on the dress circle and the Antarctic in the pit. A myriad of computers are at work upon the weather of the part of the map where each sits, but each computer attends only to one equation or part of an equation. The work of each region is coordinated by an official of higher rank. Numerous little "night signs" display the instantaneous values so that neighbouring computers can read them. Each number is thus displayed in three adjacent zones so as to maintain communication to the North and South on the map. From the floor of the pit a tall pillar rises to half the height of the hall. It carries a large pulpit on its top. In this sits the man in charge of the whole theatre; he is surrounded by several assistants and messengers. One of his duties is to maintain a uniform speed of progress in all parts of the globe. In this respect he is like the conductor of an orchestra in which the instruments are slide-rules and calculating machines. But instead of waving a baton he turns a beam of rosy light upon any region that is running ahead of the rest, and a beam of blue light upon those who are behindhand.
>
> Four senior clerks in the central pulpit are collecting the future weather as fast as it is being computed, and dispatching it by pneumatic carrier to a quiet room. There it will be coded and telephoned to the radio transmitting station.
>
> Messengers carry piles of used computing forms down to a storehouse in the cellar.
>
> In a neighbouring building there is a research department, where they invent improvements. But there is much experi-

menting on a small scale before any change is made in the complex routine of the computing theatre. In a basement an enthusiast is observing eddies in the liquid lining of a huge spinning bowl, but so far the arithmetic proves the better way. In another building are all the usual financial, correspondence and administrative offices. Outside are playing fields, houses, mountains and lakes, for it was thought that those who compute the weather should breathe of it freely.[8]

Richardson was pursuing his numerical methods of weather prediction at the same time Vilhelm Bjerknes was formulating his less quantitative air mass analyses. "Whereas Prof. Bjerknes mostly employs graphs," Richardson wrote, "I have thought it better to proceed by way of numerical tables. The reason for this is that a previous comparison of the two methods, in dealing with differential equations, had convinced me that the arithmetical procedure is the more exact and the more powerful in coping with otherwise awkward equations." Sadly, Richardson's attempts to forecast the weather by a much scaled down version of his forecast factory failed miserably—for reasons not understood until much later. More than four decades would pass before most modern weather services would replace largely graphical techniques of forecasting with more quantitative numerical methods of the kind Richardson envisioned. Dreams often come true, but many of them become reality only long after they have been dreamed—and the dreamer is gone.

Numerical Methods for Climate Models

The reason Richardson's attempt failed is that the mathematical techniques he used to fashion approximate solutions to his complex differential equations work only under carefully chosen conditions of which Richardson was unaware. He had not met these conditions. Decades later, after computers were well developed, mathematicians and scientists studied extensively the application of these various approximation techniques. Their research—spurred in large measure by pressures to solve complex differential equations found in nuclear physics—created a new discipline known as *numerical analysis*. The result has been formulations of *numerical methods* for solving approximately equations that were previously intractable. The approximation techniques affect the results of climate and other kinds of models by introducing errors in the solutions of the equations. To explain this problem we need to describe in more detail how these techniques work.

Equations for weather or climate models typically express the value of each climatic variable continuously over space and time. Approximation techniques usable on computers and attempted by Richardson don't generally do this. Consider temperature again as an example. Instead of solving an equation exactly for temperature everywhere, approximation techniques solve for temperature on a network, or *grid*, of points in space and at discrete times (called *time steps*). Temperatures that occur between the grid points or between the time steps are not explicitly resolved. This means that anything that happens between these discrete values cannot be explicitly predicted. Typically, in the most comprehensive global climate models the variables are estimated every few minutes on grids whose points are spaced a few hundred kilometers apart. Thus, one grid point value represents the average value of a variable over an area some ten thousand to several hundred thousand square kilometers—the whole state of Colorado, for example, or the southern half of England. As everyone knows, there is rarely a common value of temperature, or cloudiness, that occurs everywhere over such large areas at some instant. Therefore, model grid point variables only represent *averaged values.* If significant departures from the grid-scale average occur locally (such as near large lakes or in small mountain valleys), then model results may not be applicable to those places. Also, neglect of these small scales can cause errors at grid scale. Of course, we could use a very fine grid and very small time steps. Such a high-resolution model might permit more accurate local predictions, but it would entail many more calculations than low-resolution models. More calculations imply more computer time, which means a bigger budget to pay computer costs— typically hundreds to thousands of dollars per hour. To solve some problems, the price has to be paid.

The numerical approximation techniques, then, have been combined with the development of very fast, big-memory electronic computers, enabling weather and climate forecasters to turn to a *first-principles approach* that relies on highly detailed mathematical models of the climate systems to provide a basis for prediction. While these objective methods have largely replaced intuitive or subjective techniques of forecasting, we shall see that objective is not necessarily synonymous with accurate. Objectivity certainly is desirable, but accuracy is our goal.

The Problem of
Climatic Feedback Mechanisms

Approximations cause a number of problems. Earlier we noted that clouds, being very bright, reflect a large fraction of sunlight back to space, thereby helping control the earth's temperature. Thus, predicting the changing amount of cloudiness over time is essential to reliable climate simulation. But individual clouds are smaller than even the smallest area represented by the grid box of a climate or weather prediction model. A cloud is typically a few kilometers in size, not a few hundred—the size of many high-resolution model grids. Therefore, no global climate model available now (or likely to be available in the next few decades) can *explicitly* resolve individual clouds. These important climatic elements are therefore called *sub-grid-scale phenomena.* Yet, even though we cannot explicitly treat individual clouds, we can deal with them and their *effects* on the grid-scale climate. The method for doing so is known as *parameterization,* a contraction for "parametric representation." Instead of solving for sub-grid-scale details, which is impractical, we search for a relationship between climatic variables we do resolve (for example, those whose variations occur over larger areas than the grid size) and those we do not resolve. For instance, climatic modelers have examined years of data on the humidity of the atmosphere averaged over large areas and have related these values to cloudiness averaged over that area. It is typical to choose an area the size of a numerical model's grid—a few hundred kilometers. While it is not possible to find a perfect correspondence between these averaged variables, reasonably accurate relationships have been found in a wide variety of circumstances. These relationships require a few factors, or *parameters,* which are derived empirically from observed data, not computed from first principles. For example, to represent the average amount of cloudiness in each grid box we only need to give box-averaged values of temperature, winds, and humidity. The latter values are explicitly resolved in the models. Individual clouds, of course, are not resolved, but the effects of such parameterized clouds can be included objectively in the model through an empirical relationship between the amount of averaged clouds and other averaged variables. The big question is, are these empirical parameterizations accurate enough for the particular predictions being made with our model?

The most important parameterizations deal with processes called *feedback mechanisms.* This concept is well known outside of computer-modeling circles. The word feedback is common vernacular. For instance, you may ask a friend for feedback on a piece of work you are doing. Then you can, if you want, modify your project in response. As the term implies, information can be "fed back" to you that will possibly alter your behavior.

So it is in the climate system. Processes interact to modify the overall climatic state. One important feedback mechanism is easily visualized. Suppose a warm wind blows over a valley covered lightly with snow. The temperature will rise, of course, melting the snow cover and replacing a bright, highly reflective snow surface with a much darker, more sunlight-absorbing meadow. Thus, the temperature rise caused initially by the warm wind will be further enhanced by the *positive-feedback effect* on temperature of disappearing snow cover. Similarly, a cold snap that brings on a snow cover tends to reduce the amount of solar heat absorbed, subsequently thereby intensifying the cold. This interactive process is known to climatologists as the *snow-and-ice/albedo/temperature feedback mechanism.* Its destabilizing, positive-feedback effect is becoming well understood and has been incorporated into the parameterizations of most climatic models.[9]

Unfortunately, other potentially important feedback mechanisms are not usually as well understood. The most difficult one is so-called *cloud feedback.* Earlier we mentioned that clouds are highly reflective of solar radiation and that more cloudiness usually means less solar energy is absorbed by the earth. Let's construct a feedback process using this fact. A warm wind blows over a large lake. We know that warm, wet surfaces usually evaporate more water than cooler or drier surfaces. Thus, the warming lake puts more moisture into the air. Clouds form, blocking some sunlight from reaching the lake's surface, thereby cooling it back down a bit. This is a stabilizing, or *negative-feedback* example: the cloud formation, in response to initial surface warming, "feeds back" on that warming in a manner that inhibits large temperature changes.

In 1967, Syukuro Manabe and Richard Wetherald, climate modelers at NOAA's Geophysical Fluid Dynamics Laboratory in Princeton, New Jersey, published a paper, now considered a classic, on the response of the earth's average temperature to many given changes.[10] Among these changes were carbon dioxide content and the amount of cloud cover. Their findings suggested that clouds not only tend to cool the earth by reflecting sunlight away, but also warm the earth by enhancing the greenhouse effect. Thus, it isn't obvious that an increase of planetary albedo with increasing cloud cover will necessarily cool the planet, since the greenhouse effect compensates to some extent. The net effect cannot, as scientists like to say, be predicted by "hand waving"; rather, a careful calculation of both competing effects is needed. Manabe and Wetherald made a calculation in which they varied the amount of cloud cover at several fixed altitudes. They found that for globally averaged conditions the albedo effect was stronger than the greenhouse effect. That is, the extra reflection of sunlight from most clouds cools the earth more than the extra trapping of infrared radiation warms the earth. Thus, in 1967 it appeared that clouds were a negative-feedback mechanism, and that they could act as thermostats to help keep the earth's temperature fairly stable, even if disturbed by a pollutant such as CO_2.

However, five years later another paper (by Schneider) extending the work of Manabe and Wetherald, showed that increasing the *amount* of global cloud cover at fixed altitudes leads to a net cooling of the earth's surface. Clouds can, I argued, move up or down in the atmosphere without necessarily changing the amount of sky they cover.[11] Just increasing the height of cloud tops, my calculations showed, warms the earth by enhancing the greenhouse effect without necessarily altering the albedo. Similarly, decreasing cloud-top height weakens the greenhouse effect. Thus, clouds can enhance or oppose some climatic temperature trend already in progress, depending on the relative changes in their heights and amounts. Only a few percent change in cloud amounts or a few tenths of a kilometer change in cloud top heights can alter surface temperature about 1°C (1.8°F). It is conceivable then, that about a 10 percent sustained change in cloud cover or a 1-kilometer (1.6-mile) sustained change in cloud height could bring on or cancel an ice age!

The problem as of 1972 (and it remains as much a problem today) was not only what a given change in cloudiness would do to the climate, but how changes in cloudiness might interact with climatic trends and cause significant feedback effects.[12] The answer to

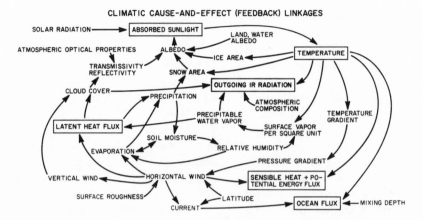

Figure 6.1

A number of interactive physical processes (or feedback mechanisms) that may need to be included in a climatic model, shown schematically. The visual image of complexity is representative of *that of the actual climatic system. [Source: Originally prepared by William D. Sellers for a workshop and modified in W. W. Kellogg and S. H. Schneider, 1974, Climate stabilization: For better or worse?* Science 186:*1163–1172.]*

this question is still unknown, and the issue never fails to provoke arguments whenever climatologists bring it up.

Figure 6.1 is a diagram of many of the feedback processes that are included in some climatic models. It gives a clear impression of the vast complexity of modeling the climate. The most difficult—and still controversial—issue is whether the net effect of all important feedback mechanisms can be sufficiently accounted for in climate models to allow their reliable use in predicting weather and climate. The answer depends on the questions we ask of our models.

Can We Verify Models?

If we ask a climate model to predict the average temperature differences between winter and summer, then we can verify its prediction, since abundant available data exist with which to compare the model results. Indeed, despite the uncertainties associated with climatic feedback mechanisms, models do very well in predicting the seasons. After all, it is possible that all the complex negative- and positive-feedback mechanisms so poorly understood individually might, taken together as in Figure 6.1, cancel each other out. If this were the case we could ignore most of them in our model and still get fairly accurate predictions. Looking at nature is one way to estimate the extent to which these feedback mechanisms would alter climatic predictions made with models that ignore them. For example, every year the amount of incoming solar energy varies by a large fraction from winter to summer. The amount of this variation, an external forcing for our model, is well known from astronomical considerations. The climatic response to this forcing —that is, the seasonal cycle of surface temperature—is also fairly well known from meteorological observations. What isn't so well known, of course, is *how* all the climatic feedback mechanisms combine to modify the climatic response to the seasonal march of the sun. However, the net effect of all these feedback factors can be approximated, at least implicitly, by simply answering the following question: How many degrees of surface-temperature change accompanies how many watts-per-square-meter energy change as the sun moves its position in the sky from season to season? Figure 6.2 is one example of how well a high-resolution, three-dimensional climatic model can do in simulating nature.

By using nature's "seasonal experiment," we can calibrate our climatic model's internal response to external forcings.[13] Then we can apply the calibrated model to a different problem for which nature has given us no such known natural experiments; CO_2 increase from human activities is one example. Unfortunately, the deep oceans and other slowly varying climatic subsystems do not participate significantly in the seasonal experiment, so a model that faithfully reproduces the seasonal climatic shifts is not verified for longer-term changes like CO_2 increases over decades.

As far as we now know, our fossil fuel burning and deforestation over the next century will probably increase atmospheric carbon dioxide to unprecedented levels in our geological epoch. There is no purely empirical basis for verifying the model predictions of how climate will respond to such an unprecedented external forcing. Since we have no twin earth with which to experiment, we must build a model instead to simulate both future and present climatic conditions. We can then compare a control experiment for present values of CO_2 to a model calculation in which CO_2 levels have been deliberately increased—a perturbation experiment. Efforts at determining the differences between the control and perturbed model results are called *sensitivity experiments,* since they are predictions of

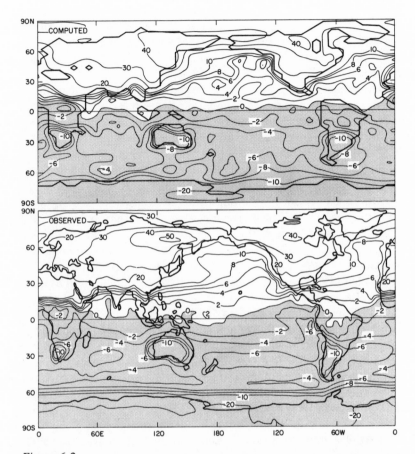

Figure 6.2

A three-dimensional climate model has been used to compute the winter to summer temperature extremes all over the globe. The model's performance can be verified against the observed data shown below. This verification exercise shows that the model quite impressively reproduces many of the features of the seasonal cycle. These seasonal tempera- *ture extremes are mostly larger than those occurring between ice ages and interglacials or for any plausible future carbon dioxide change. [Source: S. Manabe and R. J. Stouffer, 1980, Sensitivity of a global climate model to an increase of CO_2 concentration in the atmosphere,* Journal of Geophysical Research *85:5529–5554.]*

how sensitive the climate might be to a given change. But can we trust such predictions when there is no direct way to verify them—other than waiting for the real climate system to perform the experiment for us?

How can we have confidence in model predictions? At least three verification methods are used, and none by itself is sufficient.[14] First, we must check overall model-simulation skill against the real climate for today's conditions to see if the control experiment is reliable. The seasonal cycle is one good test, as we've seen in Figure 6.2. But even if the model does a good job in this test, there is no guarantee that the model will correctly predict long-term future climates unless the net effect of all the important causal factors of long-term climatic change are properly included. The seasonal-cycle test doesn't tell us how well the model simulates slow changes in ice cover or deep ocean temperatures, since these changes do not affect the seasonal cycle, though they do influence long-term trends.

A second method of verification is to test in isolation individual physical subcomponents of the model (such as its parameterizations) directly against real data. This still is no guarantee that the net effect of all interacting physical subcomponents has been properly treated. Third, some researchers express more confidence *a priori* in a model whose internal makeup includes more spatial resolution or physical detail, believing that "more is better." In some cases and for some problems this is true, but by no means for all.[15] The optimal level of complexity depends upon the problem we are trying to solve and the resources available to the task.

All three methods must constantly be used and reused as models evolve if we are to improve the credibility of their predictions. Perhaps the most perplexing question is whether we should ever consider our confidence in their forecasts sufficient reason to alter our present social policies—on CO_2-producing activities, for example. Viewed from this angle, the seemingly academic field of computer climate modeling becomes a fundamental tool for public policy.[16] If the public is totally ignorant of the nature, use, or validity of climatic (or many other kinds of) models, then public policy-making based on model results will be haphazard at best. In this case, the decision-making process tends to be dominated by a technically trained elite.

In *The Genesis Strategy* I put the issue this way:

> The processes at work in determining climatic change are simply not yet fully understood. Despite the uncertainty in

measurements and in theory, estimates must be given and difficult decisions may have to be made on the basis of the available knowledge. . . . In any case, efforts to develop better estimates and models of potential effects will be absolutely necessary to help us reduce the uncertainties in decision-making to a tolerable minimum. Improvement of the quality of these estimates is the responsibility that atmospheric scientists and their funding agencies owe to long-range planners, for the climatic effects of human activities are self-evidently the outer limits to growth. The real problem is: If we choose to wait for more certainty before actions are initiated, then can our models be improved in time to prevent an irreversible drift toward a future calamity? And how can we decide how much uncertainty is enough to prevent a policy action based on a climate model? This dilemma rests, metaphorically, in our need to gaze into a very dirty crystal ball; but the tough judgment to be made here is precisely how long we should clean the glass before acting on what we believe we see inside.[17]

Nothing has happened since I first wrote these lines that would have me substantially modify that statement, except perhaps to mention that the real climate is now a half-dozen years closer to a direct verification of model predictions of human impacts on climate.

7 The Causes of Climate Change

Our Cosmic Roots

With only a touch of poetic license it is fair to say that today's weather is the latest link in a 10- to 20-billion-year chain of cosmic events that stretches back to the big bang.[1] Most astrophysicists believe that the event referred to by this term created the universe—or at least was the most recent recreation in an endless cycle. Carl Sagan put it this way: "Big Bang may be the beginning of the universe, or it may be a discontinuity in which information about the earlier history of the universe was destroyed. But it is certainly the earliest event about which we have any record."[2] The cosmic debris from this cataclysm condensed into galaxies, stars, planets, moons, and smaller objects ranging from asteroids to cosmic dust clouds to the high-energy particles we call cosmic rays. Our galaxy, the Milky Way, with its billions of stars, is only one of billions of galaxies.

The lightest elements, such as hydrogen and helium, constitute most of the matter in the universe. Uranium, the heaviest natural element known, is much more rare—some dozen powers of ten less plentiful. Astrophysicists believe that the elements were created in stars by a number of processes in which protons, neutrons, and other elementary particles were collected, fused together, and later distributed around the universe as the ninety-two known natural elements. Oxygen and nitrogen in the earth's atmosphere, iron in our blood, and calcium in our bones are examples of these cosmic productions.

Current astrophysical theory tells us that the life cycle of stars provided the necessary forces to make the heavier elements out of the lighter ones. A star's death is often cataclysmic: a star either explodes as a gigantic *supernova* or expands rapidly into a *red giant* before collapsing into an intensely compact *white dwarf* and eventually becoming extinct.[3] As a result of such stellar paroxysms, clouds of interstellar dust containing a spectrum of chemical elements have been dispersed.

When compact enough, the matter in some clouds can condense further, forming new stars and planets like our sun and solar system. Long-lived radioactive elements, which are found in earth rocks, lunar materials, and meteorites, suggest that our solar system formed a little over 4.6 aeons ago (an *aeon* is commonly taken by cosmologists to represent a billion—10^9—years). The chemical elements left over as the debris of past cosmic events became the building blocks of the earth. Space scientist Robert Kandel, in his elegant yet simple book *Earth and Cosmos,* summarized our cosmic roots this way:

> The carbon and oxygen in our bodies were probably formed in the core of red giant stars, sometime during the first few billion years of our galaxy. The iron in our blood may well have been formed in the heart of a supernova, which took place before the solar system was formed some 4.7 billion years ago, perhaps as little as a million years before. The uranium which tempts us as an energy source also links us to such an explosion. Our Earth environment carries in it the history of the Galaxy.[4]

That we are "lumps of fallout from a star-sized hydrogen bomb" is "perhaps the strangest truth of all about our planet," wrote English chemist James Lovelock.[5]

The Evolution of Planetary Atmospheres

Since the solar system formed, the chemical makeup of planetary materials has undergone much transformation.* For example, radioactive decay changed the chemical state of the planets; it also generated heat in planetary interiors. This energy source powers the volcanic outgassing of so-called *juvenile volatiles,* gases that can accumulate in the atmosphere, be transformed chemically into different gases or nongaseous forms, and/or escape altogether from a planetary atmosphere.[6] (Geophysical theory tells us that the

---

*Some planets, such as Jupiter and Saturn, have atmospheric compositions closer to that of the sun, suggesting relatively fewer chemical changes have taken place on them over time than on planets like Mars or Earth, whose atmospheric compositions today differ radically from that of the sun.

heat of the earth's interior is also involved in the tectonic processes of sea floor spreading and continental drift.) Two factors determine the likelihood of a chemical element's escape from a planet: the speed of each molecule and the gravitational tug of the planet. The smaller planets, with less gravitational attraction, allow more elements to escape. Temperature, which governs the speed of particles in the atmosphere, also regulates the likelihood of escape; more materials are lost from a warm atmosphere with many fast-moving particles than from a colder one of similar composition. When they are at a common temperature, lighter elements in the atmosphere move at higher speeds than heavier elements. Thus, light gases such as hydrogen or helium can escape more easily to space than heavier ones such as nitrogen or xenon.

Processes external to a planet as well as internal ones determine the evolution of its atmosphere. For example, an energetic stream of particles called the *solar wind* constantly flows outward from the sun. Some theories of early atmospheric evolution rely on external catastrophes, such as nearby supernova explosions or very large solar flares that dramatically enhance the force of cosmic winds felt by the planets. These external events, some theorize, blew away some of the constituents of the primordial atmosphere.[7] Other external events, such as the accumulation over aeons of materials from striking meteors, also altered the surface composition of the planet —and thus its atmosphere too.

Thus, the present atmosphere of a planet depends on what chemicals it started out with, what compounds were added from or buried in the planet's interior, what materials escaped or were gathered from space, and what chemical transformations have taken place over the aeons. These, in turn, both depend on and influence the planet's climatic evolution.

The Early Evolution of the Earth's Climate

The rate of chemical reactions taking place among elements in the atmosphere, oceans, or crust depends upon the relative abundance and accessibility of various chemicals. And, as mentioned earlier, temperature can affect chemical reactions that determine the atmospheric composition. Temperature, in turn, is determined by a planet's distance from and orientation to the sun, the energy output of the sun, and properties of the atmosphere and planetary surface. (Recall from Chapter 5 the tremendous importance of water for the greenhouse properties and albedo of the earth; these in turn determine the radiation balance and temperature distribution of the atmospheres of planets.) For example, English scientists Ann Henderson-Sellers and A. J. Meadows have argued that the unique role of water on earth, as compared, say, to Mars' or Venus' present atmospheric composition, may well have created the equable climatic conditions that proved conducive to the formation and maintenance of life on earth.[8] The evolution of climate depends on the time rate of change of the surface albedo and the atmospheric composition, which in turn depend on—and influence—the climate. These factors influence each other's histories. Over time, changing albedo and composition, combined with outside forces such as solar radiation, contribute to the evolution of climate and to life—at least for the earth.

The Faint-Early-Sun Paradox   One of the most interesting questions encountered in the study of the early climatic history of the earth is how our planet could have been as warm as it seems to have been if, as most astrophysical theories suggest, the early sun was considerably *less* luminous 3 to 4 billion years ago than it is today.* Most estimates suggest that the sun emitted some 30 percent less radiant energy when life first formed on earth.[10] If in our own time the sun were somehow suddenly to drop its energy output by 30 percent, nearly all of our present climatic models

*The *solar constant* is the amount of solar energy impinging on the earth. It depends on the solar luminosity and the earth's orbit. The *solar luminosity* is the total radiant energy emitted from the sun. It is proportional to the square of the sun's diameter and the fourth power of its surface temperature. Astrophysical theory suggests that some 4 billion years ago the sun was smaller—the solar radius was some 8.5 percent smaller than today—and its temperature was perhaps 3 to 4 percent less than today. This implies that the solar constant was some 25 to 30 percent less 4 billion years ago than now. Although the sun will not get much hotter over the next 4 billion years, it will grow considerably in size, thereby becoming much more luminous. This theory of increasing solar luminosity has been called "the only firm theoretical prediction of the variation of the solar output" by Cambridge University astrophysicist Douglas Gough. The "rise is an unavoidable consequence of the increase in mean atomic weight of stellar material as nuclear reactions convert H to He," Gough explained, "provided textbook physics is correct"[9] This relative certainty in solar constant change is in contrast to an earlier speculation by Gough and Dilke (*Nature 240:* 262–294); in effect, they suggested, internal instabilities within the solar core could cause a few percent fluctuation in solar luminosity lasting a few million years and occurring every few hundred million years. These astrophysicists wondered whether these possible solar luminosity excursions could help explain some of the geologically prominent ice ages. Both astrophysically and climatologically, the issue remains speculative.

would tell us that the earth would soon be encased in ice—what climate modelers call a *runaway glaciation*. [11] Assuming the sun really was 30 percent or so less energetic at the dawn of the earth, how then did our planet escape such a permanent deep freeze?

Among the first to grapple with this paradox were Carl Sagan and George Mullen.[12] In 1972, they published a paper suggesting that despite a faint sun, the earth's surface missed a perpetual ice age because the greenhouse effect was enhanced. This warming, they postulated, resulted from relatively large concentrations of ammonia and methane—gases whose presence could also be implicated in the origin of organic molecules. However, ammonia has a relatively short residence time in the atmosphere, since it is broken down photochemically by sunlight. Further, there is no clear evidence suggesting that some source was pumping in ammonia as fast as it was probably being removed from the atmosphere. Hence, a number of critics challenged Sagan and Mullen's intriguing ammonia/greenhouse theory.[13] Recently, Sagan replied that "it is perfectly plausible that the outgassing rate of ammonia during the first few billion years of earth history kept pace with the photo dissociation rate," and could have created an enhanced greenhouse effect.[14] This issue is still a subject of debate.[15]

In the late 1970s, Tobias Owen and Robert Cess at the Stony Brook campus of the State University of New York, along with V. Ramanathan of the National Center for Atmospheric Research, showed that previously ignored radiative properties of carbon dioxide in high concentrations give this gas much greater greenhouse effect than that ascribed to it previously.[16] This fact, these authors claimed, combined with estimates of the rates at which CO_2 was outgassed by volcanic activity, explains the faint-early-sun paradox. They agreed with Sagan and Mullen that an enhanced greenhouse effect was the mechanism, but proposed CO_2 rather than ammonia as the principal greenhouse gas. Owen, Cess, and Ramanathan used the CO_2 concentrations estimated by astronomer Michael Hart, which held that the primordial atmospheric CO_2 content 4 billion years ago was up to 1000 times greater than today, dropping to perhaps 100 times today's values in the Archean Age, 3 billion years ago.*

---

*These high CO_2 concentrations assumed by Owen, Cess, and Ramanathan led to a calculated global mean surface temperature of 37°C (99°F) 4.25 billion years ago, even though they assumed that the solar constant was about 24 percent less than it is today. [Today's mean global surface air temperature you recall is about 14°C

Their conclusions that vast concentrations of primordial CO_2 solved the faint-early-sun paradox were challenged by researchers at NASA's Goddard Institute for Space Studies (GISS), who claimed that cloudiness-surface temperature feedback mechanism (see Chapter 6) effects could be "as important to the climate as changes in solar luminosity and atmospheric composition."[17] Unfortunately, there is no reliable—indeed hardly any—evidence as to what cloud cover may have been in the Hadean and Archean Ages over three billion years ago. Moreover, even if we accept their cloud feedback assumptions as truth, the NASA scientists' model predicted that global average surface temperatures for a 25 percent decrease in solar luminosity (but no CO_2 increase) would be near or below the freezing point of water. This was more than 20°C (36°F) colder than temperatures calculated for the assumptions of Owen, Cess, and Ramanathan. The principal difference between these two sets of scientists is, in essence, the minimum temperature each would allow to their models to produce and still have an "equable" climate. Only if one assumes that the cold globally-averaged surface temperatures produced by the NASA team's model would still have some above-freezing regions on earth can one call such a climate "equable enough" for early life to have held on.

Perhaps the real Archean Age earth maintained its equable climate because of multiple causes, negative cloudiness feedback being only one.* But it seems improbable that any set of internal climatic feedback mechanisms yet identified could have allowed a sufficiently equable earth climate 3 to 4 billion years ago to have existed in the face of greatly reduced solar luminosity without there having also been some enhanced levels of greenhouse gases—CO_2 now being the leading candidate.

Assuming CO_2 was many times more abundant 3 to 4 billion years ago, how did it drop to its present trace levels? Biologists are quick to point to photosynthesis as at least a partial explanation; as

---

(57°F).] For three billion years ago, when their assumed solar luminosity was "only" 17 percent below today's values, they still computed surface temperatures higher than today by some 5°C (9°F).

*In this connection Andrew Endal and Kenneth Schatten at NASA's Goddard Space Flight Center suggested that the lack of continents before 2.5 billion years ago "could have had a significant effect" on heat transport, allowing a solution to the faint-early-sun paradox without massive amounts of CO_2 (their article appeared in the *Journal of Geophysical Research* 87:7295–7302, 1982). Unfortunately, the model they used to back up their conclusions is too simple to lend much support.

life evolved and green plants emerged, they used up CO_2, some of which was later incorporated into the earth's crust as sedimentary rocks or hydrocarbons when dead organic matter was buried. But fossil remains suggest that life did not appear in prodigious numbers until only a half billion years or so ago, at the beginning of Phanerozoic time.* Moreover, only a small fraction of organic carbon is buried in sediments, most having been recycled, thereby giving back to the air and waters the CO_2 taken out during photosynthesis. There must have been other—probably inorganic— mechanisms active much earlier that could have removed CO_2 and maintained an equable climate over the first 4 billion years, during which early life evolved. Planetary surface temperatures much higher than 40° to 45°C (104° to 113°F) would destroy most life as we know it, and temperatures below freezing would be comparably devastating. Thus, as the sun warmed up over the aeons, CO_2 must have decreased in concentration.

Recently a clever calculation was offered to describe how planetary temperatures over the first few billion years may have been kept between the freeze and fry limits. Building on the well-known processes of weathering of rocks, James C. Walker and P. B. Hays of the Space Physics Research Laboratory at the University of Michigan along with then NCAR researcher James F. Kasting estimated the evolution of atmospheric carbon dioxide and water vapor that built up in the early atmosphere from volcanic outgassing.[18] The concentration reached sufficient amounts to produce a high enough surface temperature—even with a significantly less luminous sun— for water to flow in liquid form. In this way, silicate minerals in the earth's newly formed crust would have eroded quickly, and new carbonate sediments would have been formed using available CO_2. The rate at which CO_2 would have been consumed by this inorganic weathering process, the scientists postulate, would have been about equal to the rate of release of carbon dioxide by volcanoes. As the sun's thermonuclear engines gradually warmed over the aeons, the earth received more solar energy, and the climate heated up. The increased temperatures (and probably precipitation) hastened the continental weathering rate, removed more CO_2, reduced the greenhouse effect, and stabilized the surface temperature. Increased solar heating from a slowly growing sun, according to

---

*There may, of course, have been "prodigious numbers" of organisms before the Phanerozoic, but not the kind that are readily fossilized. For example, photosynthetic bacteria existed in the Archean but were rarely fossilized.

Walker, Hays, and Kasting, was balanced by the decreased CO_2-induced greenhouse effect. Aeons later, as life proliferated and oxygen built up, water vapor dominated CO_2 as the principal greenhouse gas on the earth—as it is today.*

However, to return to an explanation of Archean Age climate some 3.5 billion years ago, another problem for Walker's theory of CO_2 weathering rate and climate is: How could higher temperatures and more precipitation have increased runoff and weathering back then if, as Walker himself has written, the early Archean earth was largely a water-covered planet?[20] The operation of his temperature-precipitation-weathering-CO_2 feedback mechanism requires some land, for which there is no solid evidence before the mid-Archean about 3 billion years ago.

Like most efforts to reconstruct early earth history, these explanations of the faint-early-sun paradox are necessarily speculative. Regardless of the details, though, the processes discussed must work on earth to a considerable degree. And this set of processes is an excellent example of the complex internal feedback effects among the earth's climatic subcomponents, including the crustal materials, atmosphere, life, and oceans.

Climates of Early Life

Continuously Habitable Zones

In 1959, S. S. Huang defined a *habitable zone* as a region in space about a given star within which planetary temperatures would be neither too high nor too low for life to develop.[21] If somehow the earth were nudged out of its present orbit, the amount of solar heat we receive would, of course, be altered, since the earth-to-sun distance would change. Present climatic models typically suggest that if this change were more than a few percent or so in either direction, the temperature could become too hot or too cold to sustain most life as we know it. However, our climate's present-day sensitivity to changes in solar input is not necessarily

---

*In this connection Lovelock and M. Whitfield published a paper suggesting that over the next few hundred million years the weathering process could reduce CO_2 concentration to roughly half of its twentieth-century levels.[19] Such low CO_2 concentrations would spell the end for a large fraction of photosynthesizing plants alive today, signalling a major crisis for much of life on earth, Lovelock and Whitfield wrote.

the same as it would have been millions, let alone billions, of years ago when the atmospheric composition, land surface characteristics, and ocean volumes were radically different.[22] And the situation is even more complicated. We have already said that the sun (and probably most other similar stars that could have inhabited planets orbiting around them) has been growing over the aeons. All other factors being constant, as a star grows its habitable zone moves out away from it. However, a planet's climate must evolve over a long period of time within certain limits in order for life to develop. Michael Hart, now at Trinity University in San Antonio, Texas, noted that "for life to continue to exist on a planet, the shifting habitable zone about its Sun must continuously include the planet's orbit. The 'continuously habitable zone' which meets that requirement," he emphasized, "is far narrower than the habitable zone at any one time."[23]

Earth and Venus provide a ready example of how distance from the sun determines habitability. Venus, with its $450 + °C$ ($840 + °F$) surface temperatures and dense carbon-dioxide-laden atmosphere, orbits closer to the sun than earth. Planetary scientists Carl Sagan, Thomas Gold, and Andrew Ingersol were among the first to demonstrate this connection back in the 1960s.[24] They relied on arguments similar to those later used by Walker, Hays, and Kasting, based on Harold Urey's earlier suggestion that water, CO_2, temperature, and weathering were important factors in the evolution of a planet's composition and climate. These early studies were complemented in 1970 when space scientists S. Ichtiaque Rasool and Catheryn de Bergh published a paper on the theory of the evolution of planetary atmospheres.[25] These scientists suggested that the equable earth climate was a matter of astronomical luck—were the planet even 5 percent closer to the sun, they calculated, earth too would have had a Venus-like *runaway greenhouse*. Rasool and de Bergh reasoned that before any volcanic outgassing had occurred (which they assumed as comparable on both planets), the surface temperatures were determined solely by the albedo of each planet and its relative closeness to the sun. Having no solid reason to assume that the respective planetary albedos differed, Rasool and de Bergh surmised that the orbital distance from the sun is what determined the initial temperature of each planet before its atmospheres evolved.

On earth, they reasoned, volatiles such as CO_2 and water built up. Because earth was far enough away from the sun, it was also cold enough for most water vapor to condense into clouds and fall back to the surface as precipitation. (Indeed, the oldest rocks on earth—which formed nearly 4 billion years ago—do show evidence of sedimentary processes that suggest liquid water created the layering.) Such a "cold trap" kept the earth a watery planet. Water, in turn, leads to erosion, weathering, and the removal of CO_2 from the air and oceans to the rocks.

Venus, on the other hand, being 28 percent closer to the sun, started out a bit hotter than the earth—assuming the same initial albedo. As on earth, CO_2 and water built up in the Venusian atmosphere. But on the inner planet most of the water did not condense or precipitate back, as on earth. At high altitudes water molecules are broken down into hydrogen and oxygen by the sun's ultraviolet radiation. The light hydrogen atoms then escape to space, and are lost forever from the planet. Venus' warmer initial temperatures (compared to those of earth) prevented a "cold trap" from recycling water, Rasool and de Bergh argued. Thus, unlike earth—where most of the old outgassed carbon is now in the crust as sedimentary rocks and where water remains in the oceans and atmosphere—Venus lost its outgassed water and retained much of its carbon as CO_2 in its dense runaway greenhouse atmosphere.

Michael Hart tried to extrapolate these earth theories even further. He built an elaborate computer model incorporating many internal processes; his model made the standard assumption that the sun had become 30 percent more luminous over the past 4.5 billion years—an external process. In a series of clever and daring papers published in the scientific journal *Icarus,* Hart wrote down a simple equation (or parameterization, as explained in the preceding chapter) for each of a dozen or more major biogeochemical processes.[26]

Unfortunately, instead of concentrating on how dozens of reasonable variations to his assumptions could alter his overall conclusions—what climate modelers call *sensitivity analysis*—Hart chose instead to interpret the computed results virtually at face value. He argued his views vigorously in both scientific and popular circles, even appearing on U.S. national television advocating his position on "Walter Cronkite's Universe." Hart insisted that his calculations showed it was highly improbable that life could be found elsewhere in other solar systems because so few planets would exist in continuously habitable zones for long enough periods. By implication, then, it is foolish to spend large sums of public money searching for such extraterrestrial life. Ironically, at the time Hart first published his first paper in *Icarus* in 1978, the journal's editor was Carl Sagan, who believes strongly in the possibility of finding life elsewhere in the universe and the need to spend sufficient sums to search for it.[27]

It is not improper to try building models that simulate cosmic events, even those as complex and uncertain as the evolution of planetary atmospheres and their climates. Only by such bold efforts as Michael Hart's can we ever hope to figure out our climatic roots —or future. But scientists should minimize arguing publicly for unverified—or often unverifiable—model results, particularly when dealing with lay audiences, unless they make the effort to explain clearly and frequently the wide range of uncertainties accompanying the results. At this stage of scientific ignorance of our cosmological and climatic history, as Schneider and Thompson argued, "cosmic conclusions from climatic models" are rarely justifiable.[28]

The Coevolution of Climate and Life

One example of the incredibly complex mix of forces causing climatic changes is the coevolution of life and climate on earth during the past 4 billion years. We can assume that the weather machine has been operating continuously—although in different modes—since the planet's infancy, right through changing geological or biological eras. Volcanic outgassing and other processes helped create the primitive early atmosphere while surface features developed at the same time; these events determined the evolving albedo and greenhouse properties of the early earth. In ways not yet well understood, the basic chemical constituents of life (carbon, hydrogen, oxygen, and nitrogen) were somehow synthesized into primitive organic molecules from which early life forms evolved.* This probably occurred in the first half billion years of earth history in an atmosphere with practically no oxygen. The anaerobic bacteria developing at this early stage could not have survived in an oxygen-rich environment. They did thrive in the predominately water vapor and CO_2 atmosphere—with trace amounts of ammonia, methane, and other gases—that appears to have prevailed.[30]

---

*Many references are available on the synthesis of early proteins and on potential ways in which life began, ranging from those that suggest organic molecules were synthesized from lightning or ultraviolet light on earth to those that suggest the earth was impregnated with living material either deliberately or accidentally (a notion called panspermia) extraterrestrially.[29]

The ability of these early—or indeed any—organisms to survive depended on their finding the appropriate *ecological niche* in which the proper chemical and physical environment was available. Over the geologically long term, life contributes to the evolution of the environment, just as the changing environment shapes the formation or sustainability of organisms. For instance, green plants, when they use carbon dioxide to synthesize their tissues, release oxygen. Most biologists and atmospheric chemists who study the evolution of earth's atmosphere think that the large volume of oxygen present today is the result primarily of two processes occurring over aeons.[31] One is controlled by the rate at which oxygen is removed from the atmosphere and buried as oxide sediments such as iron oxide "red beds." The other is photosynthesis, a primary producer of oxygen.* (Lesser processes, like the breakup of water vapor or other molecules of hydrogenated oxygen atoms, are also involved in the oxygen balance.)

Stanford University population biologist and ecologist Paul R. Ehrlich coauthored a paper with biologist Peter Raven in 1965 that coined the term *coevolution.* It describes the process whereby the evolutionary paths of two or more species depend on their interactions.† Thus, despite perpetual debates over how life started and the precise mechanisms of its evolution, life and climate can be said to have coevolved; their mutual influence is well established over geological history. Figure 7.1 summarizes this relationship, using

---

*In a very complete review article about the importance of the sun to the earth, atmospheric scientist Robert E. Dickinson from the National Center for Atmospheric Research summarized what little is known about the appearance of oxygen: "The reason for the initial appearance of significant amounts of oxygen in the atmosphere about 2 billion years ago is not known, but is more likely due to oceanic mechanisms for loss of O_2 becoming less efficient rather than a rapid growth in the rate of photosynthesis. Perhaps the continental crust was by that time sufficiently oxidized that further deposition of oxygen into oceanic sediments could not keep up with photosynthetic production."[32]

†In this landmark paper Ehrlich and Raven comment that "One of the least understood aspects of population biology is community evolution—the evolutionary interactions found among different kinds of organisms where exchange of genetic information among the kinds is assumed to be minimal or absent . . . indeed, one group of organisms is all too often viewed as a kind of physical constant." In its place Ehrlich and Raven suggest: "One approach to what we would like to call co-evolution is the examination of patterns of interaction between two major groups of organisms with a close and evident ecological relationship, such as plants and herbivores."[33] Although originally applied to butterflies and their plant hosts, the concept of coevolution has now been extended to many evolving species.

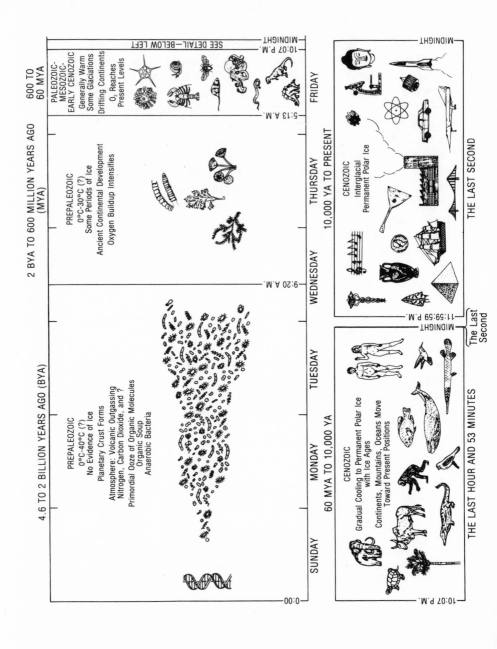

Figure 7.1

The six days of the coevolution of | *of a large diversity of species begins in*
climate and life are shown here schemati- | *the Phanerozoic era. All of art, science,*
cally. Although primitive life can be | *religion, and our cultural heritage are*
traced back to late Sunday, it is not | *crammed into the last second of the*
until early Friday that rapid evolution | *sixth day since the earth's formation.*

the now familiar device of compressing the 4.6 billion years of earth history into a metaphorical modern time unit.[34] In this figure we use a six-day week to provide perspective on the coevolution of climate and life from "creation" to today. Note that it takes until early Friday before life becomes diverse and abundant and oxygen attains something near its present levels.

The philosophical—perhaps theological—significance of this close interrelation between life and its environment struck James Lovelock and Boston University biologist Lynn Margulis. They labeled the complementary evolution of life and environment the *Gaia hypothesis*. (Gaia is the ancient Greek goddess of the earth.)[35] Modern science, Lovelock says, has "provided a new insight into the interactions between the living and the inorganic parts of the planet. From this has arisen the hypothesis, the model, in which the earth's living matter, air, oceans and land surface form a complex system which can be seen as a single organism and which has the capacity to keep our planet a fit place for life."[36] To Lovelock and Margulis, Gaia appears teleological (a philosophical term meaning purposeful). The implication is that somehow all of life is a directed organism that manages and evolves in its own environment while controlling its long-term destiny. To bolster the case, Lovelock cites the faint-early-sun paradox and the yet unexplained process of how early anoxic life, which apparently survived in an ammonia/methane environment, converted to the oxygen-loving forms adapted to today's physical and chemical conditions:

> The first appearance of oxygen in the air heralded an almost fatal catastrophe for early life. To have avoided by blind chance death from freezing or boiling, from starvation, acidity, or grave metabolic disturbance, and finally from poisoning, seems too much to ask; but if the early biosphere was already evolving into more than just a catalogue of species and was assuring the capacity for planetary control, our survival through these hazardous times is less difficult to comprehend.[37]

Regardless of whether you believe in a collective biological purpose behind environmental and biological evolution—or, further, take comfort from such a faith in "our survival through these hazardous times"—it is a profound realization that the physical, chemical, and biological subcomponents of the earth all interact and, whether by accident or design, mutually alter their collective destiny.*

The Phanerozoic Eon:
Climates of the Dinosaurs

Whether the coevolution of climate and life is purposefully self-directed may be an unanswerable question. Perhaps what we can determine is the specific combination of factors that have caused dramatic "recent" climates—that is, those since abundant oxygen and life appeared. Among these climatic episodes are the glaciation of the Carboniferous; the relatively ice-free Cretaceous climate, during which vast beds of fossil fuels were laid down in the earth and at the end of which dinosaurs mysteriously disappeared; the Pleistocene climates, when ice ages and interglacials fluctuated a few dozen times; the warm Holocene, in which civilization has flourished; the Little Ice Age; and the recent return to climatic warming in the twentieth century—a trend to levels that apparently have not occurred for many centuries. The next, and most important, question is simply: What will the dramatic climates of the future be?

Before we can predict future climates reliably, though, we have to be able to explain at least the major causes of the most extreme past climates. This is not such an easy task because of the vast number of variables involved. Climate is a multidimensional problem, as Figure 7.2 shows. Even with today's knowledge, we can barely provide details for many of the 900 (not counting the "Etc.") boxes in this three-dimensional climate matrix. Although not all 900 boxes are independent of each other (for example, ocean currents and upwelling are related), the number of independent climate dimensions is still formidable. However, we can use what information we do have on present and paleoclimates to fill in as many

*One possible interpretation of the Gaia hypothesis, attributed to Harvard University atmospheric chemist Michael McElroy, is that if humans perturb the environment too much it might maintain its stability by eliminating our ecological niche.

boxes as possible and to find causes for interactions among these many variables.

It took the first 4 billion years of earth history to set the stage for the Phanerozoic Eon: the past 570 million years, during which the majority of known species evolved in an oxygen-rich atmosphere. A legacy of fossils and fossil fuels attests to their presence; modern life forms are further evidence that these predecessors once inhabited the earth.

Although the geological record is filled with evidence of many local or short-term fluctuations, several more broadly based climatic changes stand out. Figure 1.1 shows them, including the unusual warmth of the Mesozoic, the gradual cooling of the earth during the last hundred million years, and three distinct periods of widespread glaciations: around 450 million years ago (mya), in the late Ordovician; about 260 mya, in the late Carboniferous/early Permian; and over the past 20 million years or so. Many causes of these episodes have been proposed. We'll encounter a number of them, along with some of those scientists who have argued for one explanation or another. Once again, our brief review of the possible causes of Phanerozoic climates is not offered as a comprehensive survey; rather, our purpose is to illustrate major issues with concrete examples and to show why hasty judgments on the validity of particular causes for certain climates are usually premature.

Effects of Paleogeography

In 1924, German earth scientists S. Köppen and Alfred Wegener made a clever speculation on the cause of the greatest Phanerozoic ice age.[38] If only the continents could have been rearranged some 260 mya, they mused, so that most of today's southern land masses might have clustered near the South Pole, then this ice age could be easily understood. This configuration, they believed, could explain the Permo-Carboniferous glaciations. Land existing near the poles is often cited as a cause of extended periods of glaciations, since land usually has a higher albedo and lower heat capacity than surrounding oceans, thus encouraging the accumulation of ice. Evidence uncovered since Wegener and Köppen's time for continental drift has led to paleogeographic reconstructions (see Figure 1.3) that do indeed vindicate their ideas, once thought fanciful.

Another theory invokes this idea that long-period glaciations are

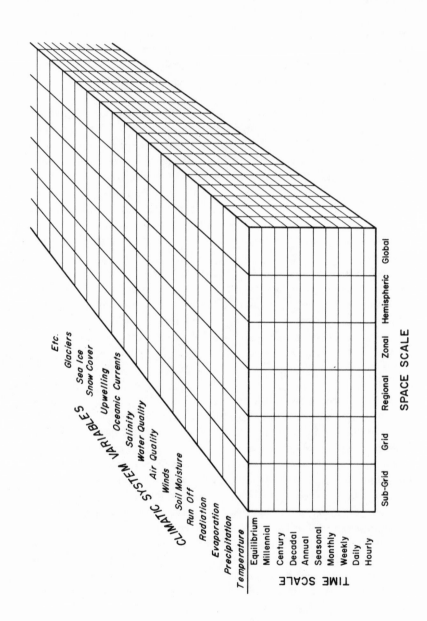

Figure 7.2

Before attempting to develop theories to explain the behavior of various climatic variables over time, it is necessary to define what those climatic variables are. Although temperature, precipitation, and winds are often spoken of synonymously with climate, the dimensionality *of climate is vastly larger, as the figure shows. Even though we cannot possibly fill in all 900 boxes, enough is already known about many of these climatic dimensions so that tentative—indeed often reliable—theories have been formulated to explain the behavior of at least a few of the climatic variables.*

related to changed paleogeography: periods of relative cold and lingering ice, it is postulated, occurred when there was simply more land area, especially when much of that land was at higher elevations where glaciers could be nurtured. Russian climatologist Mikhail Budyko has argued that glaciers could have formed and persisted on continents even at low latitudes if they were high enough above sea level. Once glaciers are in place, the high reflectivity of snow and ice tends to perpetuate them through the snow-and-ice/albedo/temperature feedback mechanism, as discussed in Chapter 6. This effect, Budyko believes, could sustain a glaciation even if the high-elevation land were later to sink back to sea level. Even if there were no continents near a pole, Budyko suggests that this mechanism would still cause "large stable glaciations at low latitudes," regardless of whether the poles were relatively ice free.[39]

A variation of the land/albedo effect was advocated by paleoclimatologists William Donn and David Shaw to explain the gradual cooling of global climate during the last two hundred million years.[40] By increasing the land area above a certain latitude, and by assuming that snow fell on this steadily increasing area, their model did indeed simulate the permanent polar glacial climate of our geological time. Unfortunately, more recent paleogeography reconstructions, like those in Figure 1.3, do not support the assumption that land area at high northern latitudes increased that much over the past 30 million years or so. Thus, as geologist and paleoclimatologist Eric Barron of the National Center for Atmospheric Research has argued, Donn and Shaw's assumption of automatic snow cover poleward of a given latitude, coupled with the changing high-latitude land areas they fed into the computer model, produced the present glacial era as a "built-in" result of their assumptions rather than as an internally generated, independent proof of the cause of permanent polar ice.[41] Clearly, other independent explanations must also be sought, even though the Donn and Shaw mechanism may well be at least a significant part of the explanation of the Cenozoic cooling trend.

Another frequently mentioned geography-related cause of ancient climatic changes is the varying shapes of ocean basins. The ocean bottom influences how heat is carried by the oceans from the tropics towards the poles. We have already discussed, in the context of Figure 1.3, how the separation of Antarctica from Australia and South America some 20 mya allowed the circumpolar Antarctic ocean current to form. The current isolated the now-frozen continent and prevented it from being directly warmed by poleward-flowing waters.

Effects of Radiation Balance Changes

The possible causes of Phanerozoic climatic changes mentioned so far involve shifts in continental positions and related modifications to atmospheric or oceanic flows. Another class of possible driving forces involves changes in the radiation balance of the earth-atmosphere system (see Chapter 5). These include variations in solar energy reaching the earth, atmospheric composition, or planetary albedo. Indeed, we have already cited the mystery of the faint-early-sun paradox, pointing out how changing albedo (or, more likely, greenhouse properties of the early earth atmosphere) could have maintained an equable climate over the first few aeons of earth history. Recall that basic physics applied to astrophysical theory suggests that the sun has been increasing its luminosity by some 6 to 9 percent every billion years. This slow rate of increase is unlikely to account for such relatively rapid glaciations as the Permo-Carboniferous episode, followed as it was by the very warm Mesozoic Era. Neither is it likely that the increase of a percentage point or less in solar energy output that astrophysical theory suggests may have occurred from the mid-Cretaceous to today could account for the gradual but large global cooling of the past 100 million years.*

---

*One classical explanation of how more solar radiation could increase glaciation was offered more than half a century ago by Sir George Simpson. He assumed that more heating caused such an increase in evaporation, precipitation, snow cover, and cloudiness so that the earth's albedo increased, causing a strong negative feedback effect to counteract—in fact, reverse—the heating of the planet. Simpson's papers on this subject have been summarized by C. E. P. Brooks.[42] However, if Simpson's feedback mechanism were operative, it would be very hard to explain the seasons, which do show significant, direct climatic responses to solar heating and cooling opposite to the direction implied by Simpson's reverse response mechanism.

The amount of solar energy reaching earth could have effectively been altered by another agent: interstellar dust and debris. Our planet passes through some relatively dense regions of cosmic dust associated with spiral arms of our galaxy, which could periodically (say, every hundred million years) alter the amount of solar radiation hitting earth, thus bringing on protracted ice ages.[43] However, W. H. McCrea at the University of British Columbia suspected that dust absorbed by the sun would increase the solar constant, and thus invoked Simpson's dubious inverse feedback mechanisms to explain glaciations. Moreover, the duration of each passage through such dusty space is probably measured in hundreds of thousands to millions of years—too long to explain the much shorter glacial/interglacial alternations of the recent Pleistocene. Perhaps this theory, or other periodic solar constant change theories on million-year time scales, is applicable to some of the earlier earth glaciations that lasted much longer, such as the Permo-Carboniferous period. It is doubtful, though, that passing through a relatively dusty arm of the galaxy or other solar constant fluctuations would have caused the fairly continuous temperature decrease shown in Fig. 1.1 from the mid-Cretaceous to our glacial times, let alone account for finer-scale fluctuations of global climate.

Terrestrial—as opposed to interstellar—dust figures heavily in another theory of glaciations. Scientists have long suspected that explosive volcanic eruptions cool the climate. Big volcanic blasts eject dust high enough into the atmosphere to penetrate the stratosphere, where these aerosols can reside as a dust veil for several years—a cloak that blocks sunlight. There have been times when volcanism was very active and presumably more dust was airborne. As the volcanic fallout of ash and lava rocks have been found in the layers of the geological record, it has become possible to make crude estimates of the relative amounts of volcanic activity—and its connection to a cooled climate.

M. I. Budyko and geochemist A. Ronov from the Soviet Academy of Sciences in Moscow have compiled an estimate of how the production of volcanic rocks varied over the Phanerozoic Era (see Figure 7.3).[44] Of course, not all volcanic rocks were produced by explosive volcanoes—that is, the kind that throw particles up into the stratosphere and that might be responsible for altering the climate. It is probably not unreasonable to assume, however, that more volcanic rocks may have meant more dust veils.

Also plotted in Figure 7.3 is an estimate of the CO_2 content of the atmosphere over the Phanerozoic. Note that the Russian scien-

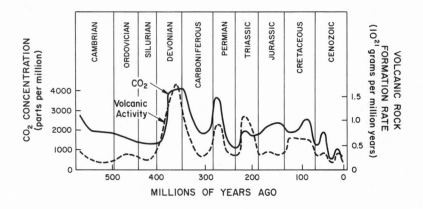

Figure 7.3

Reconstruction of possible levels of volcanic activity and atmospheric carbon dioxide concentrations over the Phanerozoic. These data are based on fossil remains of volcanic rocks and the carbonate content in sedimentary rocks; the latter is assumed to be proportional to atmospheric CO_2 at the time of formation of these sediments. Although these assumptions are highly speculative, these two curves are of considerable importance, and they could, if even partly correct, be a major part of the explanation of the varying climates of the Phanerozoic Eon. [Source: Redrawn from M. I. Budyko, 1977, Climatic Changes *(Washington: American Geophysical Union), p. 128.]*

tists believe that as recently as the mid-Cretaceous Period atmospheric CO_2 was roughly seven times its present levels! This conclusion has dramatic implications, not only for past climates, but for our immediate climatic future. Budyko explains that he and his colleagues constructed this plot by "using data on the carbon content in the sediments" over the last 570 mya, making "the natural approximation" that carbon content of the sediments is "directly proportional" to the CO_2 content of the air when the sediments were formed.[45]

This assumption, one geochemist told me, is "nonsense." The sediment mass versus time data are not nearly as good as Budyko and Ronov suggest, this critic said, and even worse, in their CO_2 concentration estimates they neglect a host of interacting chemical processes that both add and remove CO_2 to and from the environment.[46] Nevertheless, several scientists agree with Budyko and Ronov that CO_2 in the Phanerozoic could well have been many times higher than it is today, and suggest that research to improve the reliability of paleo-CO_2 concentration estimates should be a high scientific priority.[47]

In the American edition of his book *Climatic Changes,* published in 1977, academician Budyko characterizes the climatic conditions of the Mesozoic and Tertiary periods in this way: the mean temperature at the earth's surface, he says, was much higher than now, especially in high latitudes. Consequently, the temperature difference between the equator and the poles was smaller. The air temperature had a tendency to decrease over time, according to Budyko, especially in high latitudes. This tendency grew during the last half of the Tertiary Period, he claims.[48] So far, Budyko's description is close to others' paleoclimatic inferences.[49]

But these features, he goes on,

> were caused by changes in two climatic factors—the amount of carbon dioxide in the atmosphere and the elevation of the continents. The higher concentration of carbon dioxide provides for an increase of five degrees [Celsius] in the air temperature as compared with its present value. This temperature persisted through the Pliocene when, owing to a drop in the carbon dioxide concentration, the average temperature began to fall.

With little further elaboration or statements of uncertainty, the text concludes:

> The low level of continents facilitated the meridional heat exchange in the oceans, thus increasing the air temperature in middle and high latitudes.
> The heat exchange in the oceans was weakened by the elevation of the continents and led to a gradual temperature drop in middle and high latitudes. The rate of cooling was accelerated during the Pliocene when the thermal regime of the atmosphere appreciably changed under the influence of CO_2 concentration variation. This cooling was most pronounced in high latitudes and made the increase of polar glaciation possible.
> Although the thermal regime during the Mesozoic era and the Tertiary was in general highly stable due to the lack of large polar glaciation, nevertheless short-term temperature drops of the air and upper water level could occur. They were caused by the frequent occurrence of a series of explosive volcanic eruptions.[50]

And there his chapter abruptly ends.

243

While Budyko's insights and contributions to climatology are many and largely exemplary, we nonetheless must caution that explaining the causes of the climates of the last quarter of a billion years so flatly is simply premature. In an often-cited survey article, paleoclimatologist Samuel Savin ended more realistically, we believe, by expressing his hope that despite the large gaps in data and theory today, new evidence will be produced that will both improve our knowledge of the description of past climates and foster "a better understanding of the causes of those variations and the cause of large-scale formation of ice caps."[51]

Virtually all the causes of climatic change described so far in this chapter have been proposed by their authors in largely descriptive, qualitative terms—what some scientists pejoratively call "hand-waving." No major scientists claim (and neither does Budyko) that their climate theories of the Phanerozoic arise from carefully validated quantitative theories. And, as was true for Michael Hart's models of continuously habitable zones, when quantitative theories and models are used, they contain many speculative or unverified fundamental assumptions. To date, only a few quantitative climate-modeling studies of the late Phanerozoic have been performed, and these have been based on highly parameterized, fairly simple models or those laced with speculative assumptions.[52] To illustrate the method—and some of the pitfalls—we'll look at a recent example of such a modeling study for the mid-Cretaceous, a case with which I am personally quite familiar.

The Mid-Cretaceous Period:
A Geological and Climatic Optimum

The climate of the Cretaceous Period is of particular interest for several reasons. First, it is associated with relatively high organic content in the sediments of all the ocean basins. More than 50 percent of the known petroleum reserves exist in Cretaceous-age rocks; it has been estimated that 60 percent of that was laid down during the very warm mid-Cretaceous.[53] For economic reasons, at least, this is a time worth studying! Second, the mid-Cretaceous climate is most unlike today's glacial climates. Third, there is some data both on land and in ocean sediments with which to make meaningful comparisons between model results and observations. Oceanic evidence of what *pre*-Cretaceous conditions were like, however, is largely gone, because most of the ocean crust has been recycled by subduction since the mid-Mesozoic (see Chapter 1). Finally, sea levels were generally very much higher 100 mya (see Figure 1.2), and the ratio of land to sea on earth was smaller than it has been since (see Figure 1.3).

For all these reasons, Eric Barron, Starley Thompson, and I used an energy-balance climate model to catalog quantitatively some of the potential causes of the mid-Cretaceous climate.[54] But before any model was used, we needed to pull together as much proxy data as possible to get some quantitative idea of what the climate to be simulated by the model was actually like. Otherwise, the model results could never be validated. Eric Barron, then a geology graduate student at the University of Miami, culled all the evidence he could find relating to mid-Cretaceous climate. The data were fragmentary and often contradictory.[55] For instance, as noted in Chapter 2, the calcite shells secreted by certain forams have O^{18}/O^{16} ratios that vary with local temperature. Ocean temperatures can be estimated by assuming that there was no significant ice volume 100 mya, that chemical changes in the fossil remains were minimal (see Chapter 1) over the past 100 mya, and that now-extinct calcareous-shelled plankton (or other such calcium-carbonate-secreting organisms such as clams) incorporated O^{18}/O^{16} in the same proportions (with respect to temperature) 100 mya as do their modern counterparts. Unfortunately, Barron found that core samples from only a handful of ocean sites had been analyzed for mid-Cretaceous paleoclimatic reconstructions. Despite the uncertainties, all these still strongly suggested a warm climate.

Other evidence for extreme warmth 100 mya was available from paleontologists, primarily in the form of the fossilized remains of apparently tropical plants. This vegetation was found at very high paleolatitudes, and even at the continental margins of Antarctica. The classic geological interpretation of this evidence is that the Antarctica of 100 mya never experienced killing, freezing temperatures, even in the winter. But the massive ice sheet that now covers most of this continent conceals nearly all evidence on Antarctica dating from the mid-Cretaceous—or much later, for that matter— save a few areas at the continental margins. Thus, it is conceivable that, just as big mountain glaciers in New Zealand today end where lush, tropical plants begin, Cretaceous Period Antarctic glaciers ended at continental margins where warm-loving species could thrive, warmed sufficiently by penetrating ocean currents.

Since the proxy record was so paltry, Barron, Thompson, and I

245

knew that whatever model results we obtained could not be definitely rejected or validated. Cretaceous surface temperature (like any other climatic dimensions shown in Figure 7.2) was quite equivocal in details. Thus, Barron designed several possible latitudinal distributions of mid-Cretaceous surface temperatures consistent with the available data. In this way our model results could at least be tested against a plausible range of validating empirical data. The coldest of these profiles assumed the mean annual temperature at the poles was just at the freezing point, much cooler than the standard geological interpretation of the proxy evidence. The others had annual mean polar temperatures well above freezing.

The potential climatic forcing mechanism that is best documented from 100 mya to the present is paleogeographic conditions and this was the mechanism used to drive the model. Other plausible mechanisms—such as volcanic dust, CO_2, changes in solar energy output, or episodes of galactic dustiness, for example—are, quantitatively at least, more speculative. Therefore, recent estimates of paleogeographic conditions 100 mya were specified in the climate model as the principal forcing factor. As this simple model only had zonal resolution (see Chapter 6), all variables had to be broken down into latitudinal means, with important regional details being averaged. But even the zonal results raise interesting questions on what might have caused or contributed to this warm era.

Drawing on an earlier study by Thompson and Barron,[56] the three investigators computed a decrease in the albedo of the earth associated with the relative increase in oceanic area and the absence of ice cover. We found that these albedo changes, as large as they were, still couldn't warm up our climate model's surface temperature to even the coldest assumed 100-mya profile, especially at the poles. Moreover, the tropics heated up beyond today's temperature levels, a result that bothers many biologists who believe that, in order for life to have survived there, tropical surface temperatures could not have been more than a few degrees warmer than today. Further assumptions, such as internal cloudiness-feedback effects, helped improve the simulation but were still not enough to produce in the model even the coldest of the three plausible temperature profiles for 100 mya. Only by making the additional assumption that the atmosphere and oceans transported roughly twice the heat expected from the tropics toward the poles could the model simulate even the coldest of the mid-Cretaceous temperatures that Barron had constructed. This enhanced heat transport was needed not only

246

to warm the poles to the mean annual freezing point, but also to cool the tropics to temperatures near those of today. Such conditions are, we repeat, believed necessary for most species to have survived. Despite this seeming ability of the three investigators' climatic model to simulate successfully the coldest mid-Cretaceous temperature profile, the fact remains that there is no known method of reconstructing proxies for cloudiness or heat transport. Thus, the assumptions in our model about these factors needed for successful simulation results cannot be directly verified. The only thing the study by Barron, Thompson, and Schneider proved was that with a combination of known (and not wildly unreasonable) physical processes it is possible to simulate the coolest assumed mid-Cretaceous climate. Of course, the extent to which the assumptions needed to reach that achievement are correct is not yet clear.

In order to model an even warmer mid-Cretaceous than Barron's coolest one (extra warmth that many geologists still believe occurred), additional heat sources are needed. Clearly, if Budyko and Ronov's large estimate for CO_2 concentration then is even half right (see Figure 7.3), then it will be much easier to reproduce the equable mid-Cretaceous temperatures with climatic models driven by such a super CO_2 greenhouse effect. But CO_2 estimates for the Cretaceous are still quite uncertain. And at least one other interpretation—besides the obvious possibility that the model or our assumptions are faulty—is possible: that the classic geological reconstruction of the mid-Cretaceous temperature profiles, even the coldest one assumed by Barron, is still too warm. At the moment, this controversial issue is not resolved, primarily because the proxy data are too ambiguous and because the kinds of climate models needed to produce reliable calculations of cloudiness or heat transport have not yet been applied to the Cretaceous Period.

Transition to Permanent Ice: More Debate Over the Evidence

Nicholas Shackleton recently summarized a number of investigators' results—including some of his own—in which O^{18}/O^{16} ratios in surface- and bottom-dwelling fossil forams were plotted for the past 70 million years.[57] But because the O^{18}/O^{16} ratio in the remains of tropical surface-dwelling plankton stayed nearly unchanged back to about 40 mya, and because Shackleton assumed a decreasing ice volume from today back to about 30 mya, he was forced by these assumptions to conclude that between about 40 and 10 mya, tropical sea surface temperatures were actually colder than now, despite the strong evidence that global average temperatures were considerably warmer most of the time.

If, as Budyko believes, more CO_2 was the cause of the warmer early Cenozoic climates, then current models suggest it should also have produced warmer tropical sea surface temperatures 10 to 40 mya—unless, of course, something else intervened.[58] Possibly, that something else was a negative-feedback mechanism such as enhanced amounts of tropical clouds or lowered cloud height or even increased numbers of tropical cyclones.* In Chapter 6 we saw that one way to test such complex hypotheses quantitatively requires reliable, coupled, three-dimensional models of atmosphere and oceanic general circulation that contain the proper paleogeographic conditions. These are just becoming useful for such purposes.[60]

On the other hand, another interpretation of Shackleton's fossil O^{18}/O^{16} data is possible. Geologists Richard Poore and Robley Matthews suggest that it is reasonable to assume that tropical sea surface temperatures were constant over time in the Cenozoic and did not dip, as Shackleton proposed. "We contend," they wrote, that "our interpretation [that tropical sea surface temperatures remained constant] is a more valid approach to unraveling Earth history"—more valid, they believe, than one that assumes decreasing ice volume from now back to only 30 mya or so, and which then uses this assumption to calculate depressed tropical sea surface temperatures from the O^{18}/O^{16} fossil record.[61]

Which interpretation do we favor? It is probably clear to you by now that we believe not nearly enough evidence—either empirical or theoretical—exists to prove which, if either, interpretation is more likely. But as sketchy as things are, it is nonetheless very certain that the Mesozoic, culminating in the climatic optimum of

---

*Some authors feel that tropical cyclones—that is, hurricanes—could be enhanced sufficiently by extra evaporation from warming tropical ocean surface temperatures that their increased numbers might transport enough heat out of the tropical seas to prevent the sea surface from warming up very much despite any increased rates of heating, perhaps from increased CO_2.[59] As yet, there have been no quantitative confirmations of the hypothesis connecting increasing hurricane frequency with increasing heat export from the tropics, although it is certainly true that evaporation and hurricane frequency would, on average, increase markedly as tropical sea surface temperatures warmed. However, the extent to which such enhanced evaporation or hurricanes would limit sea surface temperature warming is still quantitatively uncertain.

248

the mid-Cretaceous, probably had the most benevolent climate and the most productive biota of all earth's past aeons—and quite possibly of its future aeons as well.

The Demise of the Dinosaurs:
A Biogeocosmic Catastrophe?

Whether caused by a single catastrophe or not, the end of the Mesozoic some 65 mya marks a mass global extinction. At this Cretaceous-Tertiary boundary, as geologists call it, all remaining dinosaurs and large animals perished; many other species, including oceanic dwellers from clams to plankton, died as well. Indeed, this great dying is so intriguing that the search for its cause has been a scientific—and pseudoscientific—fascination for decades. Very recently, though, an interdisciplinary team of scientists may have found at least part of the answer.

Explanations of the great dying have ranged from biological and evolutionary to astrophysical, climatological, and atmospheric. For instance, some have postulated that a CO_2 warming sterilized the male dinosaurs by overheating their testicles or impaired reproductive capacity of females by hyperthermia.[62] Cosmic catastrophes have been proposed: for example, the explosion of a near-enough supernova could have zapped earth creatures with its cosmic rays. Such an explosion would have had the additional effect of reducing the ozone layer and exposing plants and animals to damaging ultraviolet light.

The latest theory was born from the efforts of an interdisciplinary group of Berkeley, California, scientists headed by physicist Luis Alvarez and his geologist son Walter.[63] Like many of the most interesting discoveries in science, this group's hypothesis for the great dying emerged largely by serendipity, when the researchers were trying to figure out another problem. The geologist Alvarez was attempting to explain why unusually high concentrations of iridium, normally rare on earth, had been found in two places: the Appennines in northern Italy, where iridium levels were 30 times greater than expected, and near Copenhagen, where they were 160 times larger. The physicist Alvarez became interested in helping to find the causes of these anomalies. At first, the investigators believed that unaccountably slow sedimentation rates may have allowed the unusual element to concentrate at these two spots. But the evidence in the rocks suggested no unusual sedimentation rates.

Another possibility they considered was an influx of iridium from a supernova explosion, what Harvard biologist Stephen Jay Gould calls "that venerable old standby of cosmic theories."[64] But if a supernova had occurred, a relatively high concentration of a plutonium isotope should have been found as well.

What made the search so intriguing was the fact that the extra iridium occurred in layers of thin clay dated to the end of the Cretaceous—coincident with the great dying. Eventually these scientists hit upon the idea that a large object, like the 10-kilometer-wide asteroid (named Apollo) discovered in the 1930s, may have collided with the earth. Such objects, all of which are now called Apollo asteroids, contain a relatively high iridium level compared to the earth's crust. The scientists calculated that a big asteroid, if it hit a large body such as a planet, would vaporize on contact, taking with it a large chunk of the planetary crust. By computing the amount of iridium that would have been shot into the air as part of a giant cloud after impact, the scientists concluded that the northern Italy site had just about the right amount of extra iridium—if an Apollo asteroid had indeed struck the earth.

Needless to say, this theory made quite a splash in professional —and popular—scientific circles when it first appeared.* But like all dramatic and speculative hypotheses—the Antarctic glacial surge or the snowblitz theory mentioned in Chapter 2, for example—there are always nagging loose ends. First, the geological record is not yet so refined that the dates of dinosaur deaths can be proved to coincide exactly with the extinctions of phytoplankton in the oceans. Even if these events differed by the geologically infinitesimal amount of 100 to 1000 years, such a finding would debunk the Alvarez theory of a single cosmic catastrophe. Second, shortly after their results were published many criticized the fact that such a spectacular idea was announced with no impact crater yet identified and only two sites on earth as evidence.[68]

The Alvarez team has responded both politely and carefully to

*I first heard it presented in a lecture by Luis Alvarez at the January 1979 meeting of the American Association for the Advancement of Science in Houston, Texas. I commented from the floor that such a cloud could have climatic effects, particularly a sharp, but short-term climatic cooling on land, which may have contributed to the extinctions of species unable to withstand even a short period of freezing temperatures. The large heat capacity of the oceans, however, would probably have prevented any lasting direct climatic effects from the hypothesized dust cloud.[65] Calculations made by a NASA team later on reached similar conclusions.[66] A number of variants have been proposed by others.[67]

the first wave of criticisms and comments, stating that many details, particularly those dealing with the *agents* of extinction (for example, heat, cold, dark, or sunburn), are not yet well established. However, citing further evidence of enhanced iridium levels in the geological record, this time from halfway around the world in New Zealand, the Alvarez group somewhat confidently responded:

> We are prepared to abandon our "darkness hypothesis" when and if some other proposed killing mechanism is shown to fit the geological record better than it does. But we feel our major theoretical conclusion—that the worldwide boundary layer contains the remnants of a large asteroid that somehow triggered the extinction—now rests on a very solid experimental base.[69]

The mystery of the great dying isn't yet in the "solved" file, but we do have more clues now than ever before. For example, the work of a team of space scientists who examined in much more quantitative detail the nature of a giant dust cloud following a large impact supports the Alvarez theory.[70] On the other hand, whereas geochemists and geophysicists have been embracing the asteroid theory, paleontologists are becoming increasingly disenchanted with it. For example, a session at the 1982 American Association for the Advancement of Science was devoted to the asteroid/extinction hypothesis. It was reported in *Science* magazine by science writer Richard Kerr that University of California at Berkeley geologist Walter Alvarez "politely disagreed" with his paleontologist colleague William Clemens over the interpretation of some findings that "the dinosaurs of the Cretaceous period seem to have disappeared *before* the dust from the asteroid impact settled to the earth." While this may allow one to suspect the asteroid impact decimated life in the sea at the Cretaceous-Tertiary boundary, as far as dinosaurs are concerned the fossil evidence "argues strongly against the catastrophe hypothesis" Clemens reportedly said.[71] A bit of a compromise was suggested in an interview by University of Colorado geologist Erle Kauffman: "A supernova or the shock of a meteorite striking the Earth could have been the straw that broke the camel's back. But the actual fossil record shows no catastrophe. The fossil record shows a graded extinction for most organisms at the end of the Cretaceous period."[72] Then, just when it seemed the evidence for enhanced worldwide iridium levels was all pointing toward an extraterrestrial event, two scientists claimed that the excess iridium could have come from an enhanced period of explosive volcanic eruptions—also producing stratospheric dust clouds and a temporary climatic shock.[73] The jury is still out on what killed off the final dinosaurs.*

One final note on this biogeocosmic catastrophe theory. An ironic and very disturbing spinoff has arisen from the Apollo asteroid/extinction ideas. What if a big object is sighted heading our way? Could we do anything about it? While 10-kilometer asteroids are relatively rare, much smaller objects are not nearly so scarce. Meteor Crater in Arizona is a kilometer-sized remnant of such a small object that hit only 25,000 years ago.[74] This meteor certainly created no gigantic global dust veils, greenhouse effects, or ozone holes comparable to those hypothesized by the Alvarez team or their follow-up studies. But even if a piece of space junk only a few hundred meters across hit New York, London, Paris, Tokyo, Moscow, or Peking, the death toll could well be in the millions. Not surprisingly perhaps, a workshop has already been held in which one topic was whether such sighted objects could be diverted. One method might be to use the U.S. Space Shuttle loaded with nuclear bombs, to be delivered and then detonated at just the right moment. While some think this science-fiction-movie plot is technically possible, others argue that nuclear cargo on a spacecraft could violate international treaties intended to maintain space as a nuclear-free zone. In this connection, some of the very same people who worked on the asteroid/extinction problem applied their methods to another all too plausible disaster theory: the environmental effects from smoke and dust clouds that would be generated in the aftermath of a large-scale nuclear war (discussed in detail in Chapter 8).

Theories of the Ice Ages

There are many parallels between the theories explaining recent ice ages and those explaining the great dying. The possible causes offered for glacial/interglacial episodes of the Pleis-

---

*In a follow-up paper (1982, *Science 216:*886–888), the Alvarez team reports on yet another extinction event 34 million years ago in the Miocene. This "minor" mass dying also is coincident with an iridium-enriched layer. It also occured at the same time that some 1 to 10 billion tons of melted glass were deposited over a large part of the earth. An earth-meteor collision could, they hypothesized, explain all of these coincident events. Perhaps there is a terrestrial explanation as well?

tocene have also been as numerous as the biblical plagues. Some recent evidence, largely following after the CLIMAP effort discussed in Chapter 2, contains very promising leads for understanding paleoclimate. Here, we follow up on the largely descriptive material from Chapter 2 and concentrate on what mechanisms may have led to the ice age/interglacial cycles described there (see Figure 2.3). Despite major recent advances in the description and modeling of ice age climates, we still cannot explain definitely *why* the ice ages came and went. But there are many promising leads, and climatic sleuths may well be nearly ready to unmask the culprits.

Probably the most readable account of how classical ice age theories have evolved is John and Katherine Palmer Imbrie's book *Ice Ages: Solving the Mystery*, cited numerous times in Chapter 2. Although the authors advocate strongly the astronomical theory of ice ages, their book portrays vividly the vast array of conflicting opinions over the interpretation of ice age proxy records and the many explanations put forth for why the ice waxed and waned. As has been our custom in these pages, we will be highly selective in choosing a few leading explanations offered by a few individuals. Our goal once again is to illustrate some of the more widely recognized causal factors, and not to provide a balanced historical survey of all important ideas or contributors.

To begin, we will reexamine the primary climatic evidence—O^{18}/O^{16} ratios in oceanic cores, what most geologists believe is primarily an ice volume signal—from a new angle: what scientists and mathematicians call *spectral analysis*.

When examining a record evolving over time—that is, a *time series*—a scientist looks for a long-term average, a trend over the long-term, or fluctuations around the long-term average. Sometimes the fluctuations are cyclical or *periodic*—that is, they repeat themselves with a given frequency. The most obvious repetition period for many climatic variables is one year, the seasonal period. The *frequency* of the seasonal period is one cycle per year. However, other periodic repetitions can be discerned in the climatic record. For instance, over time scales of hundreds of thousands of years, 100,000-year cycles can be seen in O^{18}/O^{16} records, such as that shown in Figure 7.4. James Hays, John Imbrie, and Nicholas Shackleton found such cycles in the fossil O^{18}/O^{16} data in a number of oceanic cores. They also found a similar result in temperatures at the sea surface reconstructed from assemblages of fossils in the same deep sea cores. The relative strength of climatic variations

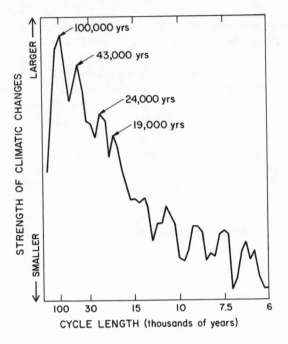

Figure 7.4

This curve shows the relative strength of climatic cycles versus the cycle length inferred from oxygen isotope ratios (O^{18}/O^{16}) in deep sea cores, which are assumed to be proportional to ice volume and thus a measure of glacial/interglacial states of the past million years. The principal feature of the curve is that it shows increasing strength with cycle length (what statisticians call redness) as well as several distinct peaks in which the strength of the climatic cycle is concentrated at certain periods. (For periods much shorter than 10,000 to 20,000 years the redness shown here has been disputed—see text.) Since the concentrations of climatic strength into these peaks coincide with some of the periods at which the earth's orbit varies, these results have been interpreted as strong evidence of a link between astronomical changes and the comings and goings of ice in the Pleistocene. [Source: J. D. Hays, J. Imbrie, and N. J. Shackleton, 1976, Variations in the earth's orbit: Pacemaker of the ice ages, Science 194:1121–1132.]

they found is plotted on Figure 7.4 against the cycle time of these variations.[75] This graph offers important clues on the causes of the ice age, since it shows that the variations of climate over the past half million years or so are not wholly random, but follow two distinct patterns: (1) between cycle lengths of a few thousand to 100,000 years, the generally downward-sloping line indicates that the strength of climatic fluctuations at each frequency increases with cycle length; and (2) discrete cycle lengths are seen as peaks at which larger fractions of past climatic variations are concentrated. This suggests that the actual climatic signal, such as that shown in Figure 2.3, is composed of some variations of all cycles of oscillation, but with significant concentrations around 19,000-, 24,000-, 43,000-, and 100,000-year periods.

Hays, Imbrie, and Shackleton were not the first to use spectral analysis to study past climatic behavior and its possible causes. In 1974, John Kutzbach and Reid Bryson at the University of Wisconsin analyzed many climatic records in this manner.[76] They concluded that most strength in climatic cycles occurs annually through the seasonal cycle. Kutzbach and Bryson found that the strength leveled off so that there was very little change in the strength or signal in climatic fluctuations (so-called *white noise*) for periods between 10 and 1000 years. Signal strength (in only one proxy record) then gradually increased up to periods of 10,000 years (a so-called *red spectrum*), after which Kutzbach and Bryson cut off this analysis for lack of data. In the same year Imbrie and Shackleton analyzed the O^{18}/O^{16} ratios in one deep sea core, finding a large increase in signal strength with cycle length up to 100,000-year periods.[77] (A *white noise spectrum* forebodes a lack of climatic predictability in the statistical sense, since it implies that each climatic fluctuation has no traceable memory of past fluctuations. On the other hand a red spectrum, where signal strength increases with increasing cycle length, implies a greater possibility of predictability, since this type of signal arises when different components of the climatic system have different response times, and some climatic subsystems are correlated to—and thus "remember"—past fluctuations in other subsystems.) The 1976 contribution by Hays, Imbrie, and Shackleton is important primarily because it refined the spectral analysis sufficiently to identify clearly the 19,000-, 24,000-, and 43,000-year peaks as well as to reconfirm the 100,000-year peak. (They also found a red spectrum, even for signal strengths with periods less than 10,000 years or so, a result that was later challenged as at least partially an artifact of the analysis.)

More recent analyses of longer cores suggest that the 100,000-year peak is dominant mostly over the past 900,000 years or less, but that a 400,000-year cycle becomes important over the past few million years.* Because of serious dating problems and some contradictions in the results from different long cores, these findings are still quite tentative. We will focus, therefore, on the more recent results for the past half million years (that is, the late Pleistocene), such as those shown in Figure 7.4.

Why should the climate system oscillate at the preferred frequencies shown in Figure 7.4, and why do the longer cycles generally contain more variation than the shorter cycles? The latter question is at least partially explained by what we have said so far about the relative response times of the climatic system's subcomponents. Two of the slowest-responding components, you recall, are the lithosphere (which, for example, can take many thousands of years to rebound after a glacier has melted) and the big glaciers themselves. Surges not withstanding, glacier building, flowing, and melting can take many tens of thousands of years. Bear in mind that Figure 7.4 was derived from O^{18}/O^{16} ratios in fossils—considered by many to be a record of ice volume (see Chapter 2). It is no surprise then, that the figure shows the largest-strength fluctuations in long-term climate as occurring over many tens of thousands of years, the time scales on which glaciers make significant changes. The detailed shape of the curve in Figure 7.4 for all periods shorter than about 10,000 to 20,000 years, however, is probably wrong. This is because of the confounding effects of sediment mixing by bottom dwellers (that is, bioturbation, as described in Chapter 2). If bioturbation were factored in, Figure 7.4 would very likely be much flatter (that is, not as red) for periods less than 20,000 years or so.[79]

Efforts at explaining the second feature of Figure 7.4, the concentration of climatic variations into a few peaks of distinct cycle length, generated a major controversy between two schools of thought. One school believed that the labeled peaks reflect the influence of the external astronomical forcings; the other school argued that the dominant peak at about 100,000 years is due to an

---

*Recent results using very long Deep Sea Drilling Project (DSDP) cores dating to 8 million years ago have been subjected to spectral analysis. Such studies suggest three dominant peaks at 43,000, 100,000, and about 400,000 years over the last two million years, but with only minor peaks every 43,000 and 100,000 years for cores dating back 5 to 8.5 million years ago. The 400,000-year peak is prominent throughout the record. Problems with dating and other cross checks of these results— attributed to Theodore Moore, Nicklas Pisias, and Dean Dunn—are described in a research news story by *Science* writer Richard Kerr.[78]

internal response involving the interactions of air, sea, land, life, and ice. Representatives of this second school do not necessarily dispute the astronomical forcing theory with regard to the lesser peaks at 19,000-, 24,000-, and 43,000-year cycle lengths, but they point to evidence that these lesser peaks contain *less than half* of the total strength of all climatic variations.[80] The astronomical theory has been around for a long time, as we will soon see. But first let's pursue further the basis for these different explanations.

Free and Forced Oscillations

It is somewhat of an oversimplification, but as we just said, the controversy over the cause of the dominant 100,000-year cycle in the late Pleistocene ice volume record of the past million years or so has been a debate between two sides: those who believe the cycle is a response of the climatic system to an outside forcing that undergoes a complete cycle each 100,000 years, and those who feel that it is an internal or so-called *free oscillation* of the climatic system that exists without a 100,000-year forcing. To clarify the difference we can compare the working of the climate system to the principles involved in a simple physics experiment. A weighted object is attached to a spring fixed on the ceiling. If something pushes briefly on the object to get it moving, it will bob or oscillate up and down, with each cycle of the oscillation taking roughly the same amount of time. This time period, characteristic of the mass/spring system, is known as its *natural frequency* or *period of free oscillation.* The frequency varies with the square root of the stiffness of the spring divided by the weight of the object. If the object is made heavier, it will oscillate more slowly, and if a stiffer spring is used the object will cycle up and down faster.

Picture next a more complicated system in which a heavy object is hung from the ceiling by a large spring, and a lighter object is hung from the heavier by a small spring. If one or both objects are given a push, the system can have several kinds of motion. For example, the light mass might bob up and down many times before the heavy mass completes even one cycle. Of course, the heavy object will slowly, but quite effectively, carry the faster-cycling lighter object up and down with it at a slower pace. Meanwhile, some energy is exchanged between the two objects, since they are connected physically by the smaller spring. This flow of energy between the masses allows additional modes of free oscillations,

257

including the simultaneous up and down movement of both objects. The comparison to climate comes in if we can think of the objects of different weights as subcomponents of the climate system. The lightest mass would be the fast-responding atmosphere; a slightly heavier mass, the upper oceans and sea ice. An even heavier mass or two would represent the deeper oceans or slowly varying parts of the biosphere, and the heaviest objects would be the lithosphere and big glaciers. The springs represent energy-flow mechanisms among various climatic subsystems. Of course, the real climate system is still more complicated because of friction on all physical motions, losses associated with all energy flows, and outside forcing from such influences as solar energy, volcanic dust veils, and carbon dioxide. In our multiple mass/spring analogy, forcings could be represented by imposing a variety of mechanical or electromagnetic pressures on one or more of the objects. The frequencies and distances over which the masses would move then become a complicated combination of the relative weights of the objects, the relative stiffness of the connecting springs, the amounts and kinds of frictional forces exerted on the weights, and the relative strengths and cycle times of the forcings compared to the free oscillation periods of the weights. As complicated as this seems, the complex motions of such masses can be replicated by laboratory experiments or computer models once we know the relative weights of the objects, frictional forces, energy loss rates, spring stiffnesses, and external forces.

If the forcing is strong enough and the system is not dominated too heavily by friction, then a vigorously pushed object will vibrate in close step with the predominant cycle of the external forcing. This would be a so-called *forced oscillation*. The seasonal cycle of temperature is an example; the annual solar forcing is so large that the one-year cycle time dominates the climate signal. After all, whereas an ice age/interglacial cycle involves some 5°C (9°F) variation every 100,000 years or so, the strength of the present annual cycle of surface air temperature in the Northern Hemisphere is about three times larger! In reality, any forced system with many different masses, varying springs, and complicated frictional tugs can oscillate at a variety of free and forced cycle times. In addition, if the friction or the springs have the added property of exerting forces that are not simply proportional to the movement of the objects, then the system can even oscillate at frequencies different from either its free modes or the periods of forcing—in a so-called nonlinear response.*

The climate machine is one of those sufficiently complicated and interactive systems that exhibits both linear and nonlinear characteristics. For example, the seasonal cycle can be viewed as a largely linear, forced oscillation; that is, the response will be roughly proportional to the strength of the forcing and near to the frequency of the forcing. The poles, for example, have a large annual temperature cycle caused by a large seasonal difference in incoming solar energy. The tropics, on the other hand, have small differences in seasonal solar energy input and small seasonal cycles of temperature. Since the strength of the response—the seasonal temperature change—varies in rough proportion to the forcing, this suggests linearity.[81] The seasonal cycle of temperature is forced, since the period of forcing is one year and so is the response. But because of the climate system's heat capacity, the response is delayed a few months relative to the forcing, particularly in or near the oceans. Hence, even though the least solar input occurs at the winter solstice, around December 21, the coldest months are January and February (in the Northern Hemisphere, of course); similarly, summer's warmest temperatures lag behind the summer solstice by a month or so.

An example of a probable free oscillation in the climatic system is the so-called *quasi-biennial oscillation.* Many important meteorological variables exhibit an oscillation with cycle times ranging between two and three years; these variables account for up to 10 percent or more of the variations in observed temperatures over a few decades —particularly in the tropics or high up in the atmosphere. "Springs" and "masses" in the climate system that account for this free oscillation are still not positively identified, but while the detailed causes are debated the temperature signal is detectable in many climatic records and has been used to make long-range fore-

---

*If an increment of some change altered the environmental state by a given amount, another identical increment would then alter the environment by a considerably different amount. This is what scientists call *nonlinear* behavior. If the response were *linear,* then equal incremental forcings would produce equal responses. The snow-blitz theory and glacial surge hypothesis discussed earlier are nonlinear. The response of organisms to environmental changes is, likewise, often nonlinear. Two aspirin tablets, for example, might cure your headache, but two dozen could well kill you.

casts. It is possible, however, that even the quasi-biennial oscillation is forced—if only we knew what natural external influence were doing the work. As yet, no one has found a plausible external forcing mechanism, but there are a number of candidates for internal mechanisms to explain the quasi-biennial oscillation.[82] We can see, then, that the climate is a complex mix of forced and free responses on a variety of scales. It is the climate theorist's quest to untangle the relative importance of each of these among the many causes and effects that might explain the climatic record.

Astronomical Theory of Ice Ages

In order to solve the ice age mystery, we need to ask what possible forcings could cause the major peaks that are apparent in Figure 7.4. At least for the three lesser peaks, the answer was partially anticipated in the nineteenth century by James Croll. He knew that small variations in the earth's orbit with cycle times of tens of thousands of years or so slightly adjust the earth-sun distance and orientation, periodically resulting in altered amounts of solar energy reaching the earth. He believed this was most important in winter. This alteration, Croll surmised, helped control the contraction or expansion of ice.[83]

But it took another half century before the astronomical theory of ice ages was more properly formulated, this time by a Serbian mathematician, Milutin Milankovitch. He first published his ideas in 1920, shortly after he was freed from an Austro-Hungarian jail as a prisoner of war.[84] Milankovitch carefully calculated the small changes in the earth's orbit caused by the gravitational tugs of other planets. These *orbital perturbations* then caused slight changes to the annual, latitudinal, and seasonal distributions of incoming solar radiation—changes that he calculated backwards in time over hundreds of thousands of years. When Wladimir Köppen, the German climatologist, read Milankovitch's 1920 book on these perturbations, he realized their potential climatic significance and began a correspondence. The result was modified and updated versions of the astronomical theory of ice ages.[85]

Milankovitch calculated how summer radiation in higher northern latitudes—where the ice age glaciers came and went—varied over the past half million years. He identified certain low points in summer radiation, which he correlated with several previous glacial ages in Europe. He spent the next forty years refining his theory.

We won't attempt to explain here the details of the orbital perturbations; that has been done in a number of other places.[86] Very briefly, though, there are three so-called *orbital elements* that vary nearly cyclically over time and that figure prominently in the astronomical theory. One is the obliquity (tilt) of the earth's axis. Introductory astronomy tells us that the spin axis of the earth is now tilted 23.5° from the plane of its orbit, and that this tilt is responsible for winter and summer. But most people have the impression that this 23.5° obliquity is immutable—after all, the Tropics of Cancer and Capricorn are permanently placed at 23.5° latitude in each hemisphere as the places of overhead noonday sun at the appropriate summer solstice. However, as with many laws once thought to be firm, a more refined analysis changes our notions. Milankovitch's calculations show that the earth's obliquity actually cycles between just over 22° to just under 24.5°, with a cycle time of about 41,000 years. More obliquity means more incoming solar radiation in the high latitudes of the summer hemisphere and less in winter. The opposite is true for less obliquity.

Basic astronomy also tells us that the earth orbits the sun not in a perfectly circular orbit, but rather in a slightly flattened one called an ellipse. This means that in some seasons earth is a few percent farther away from the sun than in other seasons. The amount of flattening is called the eccentricity, and varies somewhat irregularly with about a 100,000-year cycle time. However, the total annual amount of solar radiation received by the earth varies by no more than 0.25 percent because of this eccentricity change—hardly enough change on an annual basis to create an ice age based on any known internal feedback mechanisms.*

---

*There are at least two dissenters to these statements. Peter Fong, a physicist at Emory University in Atlanta, Georgia, built a zero-dimensional model that attempted to demonstrate that three-dimensional processes like latent heat of fusion released in the melting of polar glaciers (see Chapter 5) could create sufficient sensitivity of the climate system that even the small eccentricity effect on incoming solar radiation could explain the 100,000-year cycle found in paleoclimatic records. Despite some very critical referees' comments on Fong's assumption that his zero-dimensional model could replicate three-dimensional processes, I published his article anyway in the journal *Climatic Change* (which I edit) in order to spur debate on the 100,000-year cycle.[87] A second dissenter is C. Nicolis from the Institut d'Aeronomie Spatiale de Belgique in Brussels. Using an elegant mathematical climate model (see Chapter 6), she argued that random fluctuations in the planetary energy balance could, under certain assumptions, greatly amplify a small external force like the 100,000-year eccentricity cycle.[88] However, she used a very small value for oceanic mixed layer depth (see Chapter 4) and a large value for the size of the random fluctuations, assumptions that are both unrealistic and probably caused the amplification she found in her model.[89]

The third orbital element is known as the *precession of the equinoxes.* Today, the earth is closest to the sun during December, but the time of year of closest approach varies with an average period of about 22,000 years—actually two periods, 19,000 and 24,000 years. Hence, about 10,000 years from now the axis of the earth's orbit will have precessed (rotated) so that the earth will be closest to the sun in June. Thus, the Northern Hemisphere will receive proportionately more solar radiation in summer (and less in winter) than if there were no precession. This orbital element, combined with eccentricity and obliquity cycles, leads to significant changes in the latitudinal and seasonal amounts of incoming solar radiation—up to 10 percent or so in some seasons and latitudes. It is these variations that investigators have suggested could lead to ice coming and going.

A host of investigators have looked for statistical relationships between variations in orbital elements, incoming solar radiation, and Pleistocene climatic changes. Typically, they compare data from a figure such as Figure 2.3 with changes in incoming solar radiation during the summer season at high latitudes. The point is to see whether a match can be found between certain kinds of radiation changes and certain kinds of climates. It was Milankovitch who originally suggested this summer season/high-latitude connection, and indeed a number of matches have been found. Wallace Broecker, using sea level inferences from Barbados reef terraces (see Chapter 2), argued in the mid-1960s that coincidences between radiation changes and paleoclimatic data were so intriguing that "the Milankovitch hypothesis can no longer be considered just an interesting curiosity. It must be given serious attention."[90] Indeed, it has. But despite a number of suggestive correlations, nagging exceptions have emerged as well.[91]

Simply showing the correlation between two observed events can suggest a causal connection. But a verified theory or explanation must go beyond such correlations, which are really tantamount to circumstantial evidence. A verified theory must draw on fundamental physical laws and thus explain quantitatively the mechanisms by which changes in incoming radiation resulting from orbital variations create the complex climatic changes we call ice ages. Calculations have led to reconstructions of how much orbital elements have changed the incoming solar radiation over time.* Some

---

*There is even some question whether the mathematical techniques used to compute insolation perturbations from orbital element backwards over time allow much

simple climatic models driven by radiation changes inferred from such reconstructions have been run by various theorists, and nearly all these computer simulations are able to reproduce the lesser peaks seen in Figure 7.4—mostly as a linear response to the obliquity cycle. Typically, however, these models grossly underestimate the 100,000-year cycle that dominates the ice volume record. Thus these early simulations could not clearly reproduce the major feature of Pleistocene ice ages.[92]

Some 9000 years ago, the solar radiation hitting high Northern Hemisphere latitudes in June was up to 10 percent greater than that of either today or the height of the last ice age. This fact certainly suggests that the extra summer heating may have helped cause the end of the last ice age as well as the onset of the mid-Holocene climatic optimum.* But the increased summer heat at high northern latitudes is balanced by decreased heating at lower and Southern Hemisphere latitudes and during other seasons. If the suggestive correlations between summer insolation and glacial cycles are indeed cause and effect, then something must be operating in the climatic system that is highly sensitive to latitude- and seasonally dependent solar radiation changes. Most now believe that the "something" is ice, primarily through the snow-and-ice/albedo/temperature feedback mechanism explained earlier. If glaciers and the land below them are included, then a number of models have been able to reproduce a 100,000-year cycle.†

Glaciologist William Budd and several colleagues at the University of Melbourne, Australia, constructed a multidimensional model of North American ice sheets. They subjected their computed glaciers to orbit-induced variations of incoming solar radiation over the past hundred thousand years to see if there would be any significant ice sheet responses. Indeed, under a certain set of assumptions their model was able to reproduce ice sheets over North America

---

precision for reconstructed solar energy distribution over the earth beyond a half-million years (Buys, M. and Ghil, M., Milankovitch Symposium). If so, it would cast doubt on any astronomically driven, time-evolving climatic model simulations for dates much older than 0.5 to 1 million years ago.

*Indeed, John Kutzbach, has shown by a model result that the high obliquity and June perihelion which occurred in the early Holocene could explain some of the climatic warming during this period.[93]

†One of the first to argue for—and calculate—potentially important effects of ice sheets and their interaction with the lithosphere on glacial/interglacial cycles was glaciologist Johannes Weertman of Northwestern University, who for several decades has been interested in this problem.[94]

whose ice volume 20,000 years ago was enough to cause about an 80-meter sea level drop.[95] Their North American ice sheets were nearly gone some 40,000 and 80,000 years ago (times of high obliquity), and were widespread about 65,000 and 111,000 years ago. In other words, the regional glaciers of their model did indeed respond sensitively to the Milankovitch radiation change, as many of the theorists who used simpler models (without comparable calculations of glaciers) had surmised earlier. However, Budd's modeling results produced a predominant 40,000-year obliquity cycle rather than the big 100,000-year signal found in observations such as those summarized in Figure 7.4. To explain this discrepancy, Budd suggested that a complex interaction between Northern Hemisphere radiation and glacial changes was coupled with global sea level changes that caused the bigger Antarctic ice cap to ebb and flow, but not as rapidly as northern glaciers. Some 120,000 years ago ice sheets in the northern temperate latitudes began to grow, causing sea levels to drop. (Remember that the ocean water went into the glacier building.) As sea level subsided, the Antarctic ice cap was free to expand outward to a new shoreline. However, a rise in sea level from the melting of the North American ice sheets would not cause an immediate retreat of the bigger southern ice caps, at least "not until the bedrock is depressed," Budd argued.[96] The fact that it takes many thousands of years for the bedrock to rise and fall with increases or decreases of ice mass on top adds a big delay into the system that might help to explain the 100,000-year signal. "In this way," Budd hypothesized, "the ice sheets play the central role in a complex interaction of feedback between climate, sea level, and the ice cover."

However, as Budd readily admits in his writing, the Australians' glacial model is driven by an assumed relation between local amounts of solar radiation and local temperature. No internal feedback effects like snowfall, cloudiness, oceanic currents, or atmospheric wind-system changes are explicitly included. Moreover, the heating of any place on earth outside of North America is not explicitly accounted for either. Thus, despite the complex, multi-dimensional glacial dynamics of the Australians' ice sheet model, their overall climate model is not even based on the fundamental principle of global energy balance. To be sure, these glaciologists demonstrate the need to account for the complicated nature of three-dimensional glacial changes. But before confident statements can be made about the verification of the precise role of the Milankovitch mechanism, a coupling between the glacial models and more realistic climatic models is needed. Such work is slowly evolving, but several obstacles must be overcome. The first is the formidable size of computer resources needed to couple high-resolution glacier, ocean, and atmospheric submodels. Second, the problem of how to couple them is plagued by a number of sticky methodological problems. Finally, and not least, is the obstacle of cross-disciplinary communication. Traditionally glaciologists build glacier models, meteorologists work on atmospheric models, and so forth. It takes many years before modelers in the separate disciplines learn enough of each other's subject to communicate in sufficient depth to collaborate in a useful manner. Fortunately, in climatology this interdisciplinary integration process is well underway.[97] More is still needed.

To recap the modeling efforts to explain the ice age cycles, most models can reproduce the lesser 22,000- and 41,000-year Milankovitch peaks, but calculating enough of the 100,000-year signal with a global-energy-balanced model has been difficult. Even those models including regional glaciers generally have trouble reproducing a strong 100,000-year cycle. There is, we said, a Milankovitch forcing at 100,000 years. But no verified mechanism has yet been found to translate this very weak forcing into more than a small climatic signal. (Some promising leads will be discussed shortly.) However, simply because models cannot easily translate all Milankovitch cycles into matching climatic cycles doesn't disprove the theory. But neither does a coincidence of forcing and response periods over a few cycles guarantee cause and effect.

Internal and External
Compromise Theories   Some in the astronomical theory school simply believe that the modelers have not yet found the correct mechanism by means of which the 100,000-year eccentricity cycle forcing causes climatic change. However, another school believes that the observed 100,000-year cycle is not predominately a forced oscillation, but rather an internal mode of the complex climatic system. Vladimir Sergin, a Russian systems analyst from Vladivostock, and a number of his colleagues built a simple climate model coupling the climatic subsystems of air, sea, land, and ice.[98] Without any orbital forcing his model was able to reproduce glacial/interglacial-like cycles. The model worked essentially as follows. Starting at a warm time, the oceans would evaporate a great deal of moisture. At

high latitudes this moisture would fall as snow on the land, building up glaciers. It would take many tens of thousands of years before the glaciers would become so large that they would begin to flow toward lower latitudes. At this point their higher albedo would reflect enough sunlight back to space to cause the earth to cool, eventually cooling the oceans as well, thus plunging the planet into an ice age. However, this process contains the seeds of its own destruction, for as the oceans cool and become partially covered with ice, evaporation decreases greatly, starving the glaciers of snow and slowing their rate of growth. At the same time, the glaciers' massive size would cause the continental ice sheets to continue to slide into lower latitudes, according to Sergin's model. There, the more intense heat of the sun would melt them in place. Soon, the albedo of the planet would decrease, more solar energy would again be absorbed, the oceans would rewarm, evaporation would increase, and the cycle would then start all over again.

There is some empirical evidence to suggest that at least part of the mechanism of this internal free oscillation could be correct. For example, geologists and CLIMAP leaders Andrew McIntyre and William Ruddiman, of the Lamont-Doherty Geological Observatory, showed from sediment core analyses that the North Atlantic remained warm many thousands of years after ice volume began to build. This delay in cooling of the oceans, they suggested, may have provided the moisture source for storms to carry to the land the water needed to build the ice caps.[99] (These scientists, however, are strong believers in the astronomical forcing of glacial/interglacial cycles, an external cause theory.)

The real world, of course, is clearly more complicated than Vladimir Sergin's model, which treated each subcomponent of the climate system very simply and in highly parameterized ways (see Chapter 6). For example, a number of investigators have shown that the rate at which a glacier flows depends upon how much the land beneath it is depressed and its interaction with sea level changes—the mechanism Budd suggested to link the Antarctic ice sheet to the 100,000-year cycle. As you will recall from Chapter 3, Denton and Hughes suggested that the formation of an Arctic ice sheet was not so much a result of the transport of moisture to build glaciers on land as of the formation of thickening sea ice into ice shelves, which exist in the West Antarctic today. Also, they postulated that it was not so much the added warmth of the sun that melted most of the ice on land, but rather a surge that carried most of the ice into the warmer sea, where it eventually melted. Thus, we must still view as highly tentative climate-model results that are put forward to explain the sequence of glaciers and glacial meltings; the simulations we've discussed here are, like those for continuously habitable zones, highly simplified models compared to reality, and each is laced with speculative assumptions.*

To return to the debate on free versus forced oscillation in the dominant late Pleistocene 100,000-year cycle, it should be mentioned that some scientists have recently been trying to reconcile both these views. Recall that in discussing the mass/spring analogy we said that a nonlinear system could well have a response at a frequency different from its period of free oscillation or its forcing's frequency. Similarly, the large 100,000-year cycle could conceivably be a nonlinear response to shorter-period forcings, such as those of astronomical origin. The bedrock reaction time described by Budd is an example of a nonlinearity that could create such a response. In addition, since the bedrock would have sunk a kilometer or so after bearing a heavy glacier for ten thousand years or more, the top of that glacier would be lower down in the atmosphere than if no bedrock depression had occurred. This helps lead to rapid melting of mature glaciers once the radiation regime is again favorable to melting.

Simple energy-balanced climatic models have been constructed by Michael Ghil and several associates at the Courant Institute of Mathematical Sciences.[100] These are finely tuned models that can produce climatic oscillations at both Milankovitch frequencies and other periods. This is a demonstration of the plausibility of the idea of free oscillations as applied to ice ages. However, whether these results are an artifact of the fine-tuned model or a mimic of real world cause and effect is not yet established. For example, University of Toronto graduate student L. Danny Harvey and I showed that oscillations in one of these self-fluctuating models could be suppressed simply by altering the thermal inertia of the oceans to account more realistically for oceanic mixing.[101] A number of other investigators' work has recently lent credence to the idea that the 100,000-year cycle is a nonlinear property of the climatic system itself; for example, a response to predominately shorter-period orbital forcings. And some more recent results even suggest a mecha-

*Even worse, you may recall from the caveats on CLIMAP discussed in Chapter 2, is the potential uncertainty that Ruddiman and Mix, and then Covey and Schneider, found over the interpretation of δO^{18} as either ice volume or temperature.

nism to connect the weak eccentricity cycle forcing to the 100,000-year signal in the climatic record.* Nevertheless, as the Harvey/Schneider findings demonstrate, some of these conclusions can be radically altered by plausible changes in the internal model structure.

Many of the lines of evidence summarized here are leading candidates, but none are yet satisfactorily validated physical explanations of the dramatic late Pleistocene climatic variations seen on such graphs as Figures 2.3 or 7.4. Before any theory can be accepted as an explanation, we must be able to reproduce the time-evolving changes of many climate variables at many different places on earth. No one has yet built a convincing model capable of simulating the ice volume signal and the time-evolving response of regional surface temperatures, let alone other climatic variables such as precipitation. Indeed, it is not even clear yet that in order to explain the 100,000-year cycle all we need to find is the correct (nonlinear) internal mechanism through which the actual climatic system responds to the orbital forcings. It is quite possible that other factors, such as enhanced periods of volcanic activity, alterations of greenhouse gases such as carbon dioxide, or variations in solar energy could (along with astronomical forcing and perhaps climatic system nonlinear response) all work together to cause the record we have observed and called the ice age/interglacial oscillations of the Pleistocene.[103]

However, if you accept Milankovitch's notion that summer insolation in high northern latitudes is a likely forcing factor behind glacial/interglacial cycles, then it is an interesting experiment to use the laws of physics governing motions of planetary bodies to predict future perturbations in the earth's orbit.[104] Using the calculations

*At a recent meeting on Milankovitch and Climate, David Pollard, then of Oregon State University, showed that he could produce a large 100,000-year cycle based on several model assumptions. Moreover, he showed that it was partially forced externally by the eccentricity cycle. The combination of bedrock depression and so-called pro-glacial lakes left in the wake of melting glaciers could rapidly accelerate the melting phase of glaciers and help to create a 100,000 year cycle. In addition, when the eccentricity of the earth was high, he computed that it was less likely to have large glacial volume than when the eccentricity was low (and the earth had a more circular orbit). This is because at times of high eccentricity there would be a number of periods when the incoming solar radiation in the summer months in the high latitudes in the Northern Hemisphere will be very high, and thus it would be difficult for ice and snow to survive the heating season at these times; and it would be easier for snow cover to survive the summer melt season when the orbit was more circular.[102]

of Belgian scientist André Berger, John Imbrie and his physicist son John Z. Imbrie calculated that the present interglacial is already several thousand years past its optimum and on its way toward the next glacial age.[105] However, their forward extrapolation suggests that it will be some tens of thousands of years before we reach another ice age of a severity comparable to the one that peaked 18,000 years ago. Between now and then, the Imbries reckon, the earth will slide somewhat irregularly into the next deep freeze. Of course, this forecast admittedly assumed the original Milankovitch theory as the only important causal factor and put aside such additional imponderables as glacial surges, snowblitzes, and an industrial greenhouse effect occurring over the next century or so, let alone what else might happen during the next 50,000 years.

Climatic Changes Since Columbus

Global Temperature Trends and the Solar Connection

Christopher Columbus discovered the New World at just about the time the Little Ice Age began—a somewhat loosely defined period, you will recall from Chapter 3. One possible, but still disputed, cause of the Little Ice Age is the so-called Maunder minimum—the period of low sunspot activity from 1650 to 1700. Solar astronomer John Eddy suggested that this apparently unusual period in the sun's recent history might account for at least part of the Little Ice Age. Since the sun is the prime mover of the climate, it is really quite natural to propose that variations in sunspots and solar output might affect climate, photosynthesis, or other environmental processes. People have tried to correlate varying sunspots with all sorts of phenomena on earth, sometimes with amusing results. In 1939, Harvard University's Harlan True Stetson published a book entitled *Sunspots and Their Effects,* in which he collected examples of these efforts. Figure 7.5 shows two of these examples that imply a connection between sunspots and everything from cycles in the Dow Jones stockmarket average to the quality of wine vintages. (As we've never been fortunate enough to have tasted the 1929 vintage, we're not in a position to verify directly that this was indeed a very good year.) About eight years later Stetson wrote another book, in which he re-examined more critically the possible connections between solar cycles and human affairs.[106] Although it is easy to ridicule the "correlations" implied on Figure 7.5, the search for solar/terrestrial connections has become a serious and important scientific challenge.[107]

Probably the longest-running attempt to monitor the total radiant energy emitted from the sun—the so-called *solar constant*—was undertaken over a number of decades by Smithsonian Institution secretary and astronomer Charles Greeley Abbot.[108] As noted by science writer Kendrick Frazier in his lively and well-written book *Our Turbulent Sun,* Abbot's later writings offered "a charming mixture of hard science, personal reminiscence and zesty description." His results suggested that the solar constant may have gone up by as much as 1 percent while sunspots varied from very few to a moderate number. Where there was a very large number of sunspots, Abbot believed he found evidence that the solar constant decreased. However, his data contain considerable contamination, since his measurements were biased by the unavoidable problem of having to view the sun through the atmosphere, an interfering medium. The atmosphere can influence the amount and the spectrum of solar energy that is transmitted to the surface, but that influence was not very well known before the 1950s.

Two Russian scientists, Kirill Kondratyev and G. A. Nikolsky, attempted the same measurement that Abbot made, but they used stratospheric balloons as their observing platform in order to minimize the effects of the atmosphere.[109] They derived a similar, but even more startling, relationship between sunspots and solar constant. With meteorologist Clifford Mass, I attempted a calculation in 1975 to test whether the Kondratyev-Nikolsky formula was correct.[110] We found that the fifty-year Maunder/Eddy minimum would have been a time when global temperatures should have been about a degree or two colder than during more normally active sunspot periods. However, although the calculations could explain perhaps half the observed, long-term temperature variations, we found that by using sunspots and the Kondratyev-Nikolsky (or the Abbot) relationship alone, our model results still had some serious discrepancies with the few dozen available temperature records of the past few hundred years. (Other factors, such as volcanic dust, significantly improved our simulations, but that will be discussed later.)

When driven only by sunspot variations and an assumed solar constant-sunspot relationship, the Schneider-Mass climate model

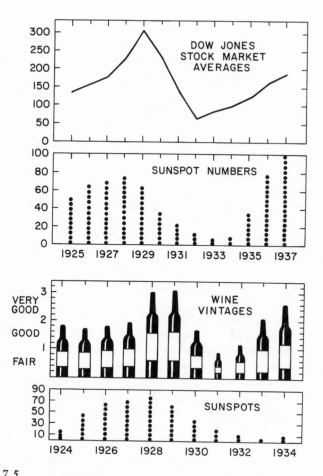

Figure 7.5

For many years people have attempted to correlate events on earth with variations in sunspot numbers. The variation of the Dow Jones stock market averages or the quality of wine vintages are just two such examples. Others include correlations with tree-ring width, storminess, and even major climatic events, like droughts. Although no reliable mechanism has ever been identified to connect sunspot activity with such earthly behavior, more careful research has been undertaken in recent years to examine the possibility that such fundamental changes on the sun could be related to events at the earth's surface. [Source: H. T. Stetson, 1939, Sunspots and Their Effects (New York: McGraw-Hill).]

could account for some of the major features of the climate record during the past few centuries. Nevertheless, Mass and I concluded it was unlikely that the Abbot or Kondratyev-Nikolsky formulas were valid relationships. The reasoning for this negative conclusion was very simple: it is well known that the sunspot cycle since about 1700 is very marked over an eleven-year period. If the solar constant varied by as much as 1 percent or more over this time then there should be a very strong eleven-year cycle evident in the historical temperature records—that is, if they are analyzed with the same kinds of spectral techniques discussed earlier. The temperatures should show concentrations of strength at periods of eleven years. A number of investigators, including Mass and Schneider in a subsequent paper, looked for such a so-called *eleven-year signal*.[111] They found little, and none nearly as globally extensive as would be required if the Kondratyev-Nikolsky or Abbot relationships were correct. Thus, either these relationships were incorrect or the climate model was a very poor replica of the actual climate's response to external forcing.

Subsequently, further analyses of Abbot's data by Douglas Hoyt at the National Center for Atmospheric Research showed that the data were not reliable enough to support the inference of the solar constant-sunspot relationship for the eleven-year cycle that had been suggested by Abbot.[112] Moreover, Kondratyev and Nikolsky re-examined their own data and concluded that changes in stratospheric transmission—from nuclear bomb testing and not solar constant variations, they believe—were more likely explanations of the relationship they observed. Thus they essentially retracted their earlier hypothesis of a connection between solar constant and sunspot variation.[113] However, all authors would likely agree that an idea suggested by John Eddy is worth considering: that the solar constant could vary slowly over decades, perhaps in proportion to the average number of sunspots over many eleven-year cycles.* If true, this idea would eliminate the problem of too much eleven-year signal cropping up in the computed temperatures while possibly retaining some needed features such as the Maunder minimum cooling or the early twentieth-century warming.

*Eddy made the suggestion nearly a decade ago, and still believes it is possible that long-term connections between sunspots, solar diameter, and solar constant could have occurred and might have influenced climate, although "there is as yet no direct, observational evidence for a longer-term secular change in [solar constant] that could be a strong force in climate."[114]

Douglas Hoyt pressed his studies of sunspot structure and climate even further. He noticed a remarkable correlation between the Northern Hemispheric temperature records of the past hundred years and a peculiar property of sunspots: their *umbral/penumbral ratio* (see Chapter 3). Hoyt found that "when the umbral/penumbral ratio is plotted adjacent to Northern Hemisphere surface temperature anomalies, the curves are very similar. Both increase to the mid-1930's and then decrease thereafter."[115]

But could this be another potentially spurious correlation like those in Figure 7.5? Hoyt admitted that "the high cross-correlation between the Northern Hemisphere temperature anomalies and the umbral/penumbral ratio may be a mathematical oddity without physical meaning." The importance to climatology and solar physics of understanding the total energy output from the sun and its possible variations has already motivated a number of interdisciplinary conferences.[116] More importantly, Eddy's stimulus and the studies it spurred has mobilized many in the solar physics community to consider this previously forgotten—and often taboo—subject as a priority topic for serious research.

Another possible observable solar change that might be connected with changes in the solar constant and the climate has been pursued by Ronald L. Gilliland, an astrophysicist at the National Center for Atmospheric Research. Gilliland, motivated by some suggestions and earlier work by his senior colleague John Eddy, carefully examined data on the diameter of the sun over the past few hundred years. The information suggested that the sun may actually shrink and expand over time. Moreover, it may have shrunk some 2 seconds of arc per century over the past few hundred years. Gilliland concluded that the solar diameter has oscillated with a 76-year and 11-year cyclical variation.[117] These cycles, he believes, could well be correlated with significant, but as yet unknown, variations in the solar constant.

To date, however, only a few years' worth of observations of the solar constant have been made from earth satellites. These observations suggest at most a few tenths of a percent change in solar constant with short-term changing sunspot numbers.

Richard Willson, at NASA's Jet Propulsion Laboratory in Pasadena, California, led a team that placed a solar constant instrument aboard the Solar Maximum Mission space craft, launched on February 14, 1980. Its results have been startling. Instead of finding a constant solar luminosity, which was dogma for some of the ancients, or one that primarily increased with sunspot numbers, as believed by Abbot, the satellite showed *drops* in luminosity of a tenth of a percent or two for several days when large groups of sunspots passed over the face of the sun.[118] A major question follows this finding: Where does the missing solar energy that is apparently blocked by the passage of sunspots over the solar face go? Does it leak out in a different place, later on or in the form of the emission of radiant energy at different wavelengths than is typically emitted from the sun? Questions such as these are of fundamental importance to both solar physics and climatology. Unhappily, they are still unresolved. But finally some real progress has been made in measuring that most fundamental physical entity: the energy radiated from the sun. Unfortunately, because these measurements have only been taken over a short period, we cannot rule out the possibility of longer-term, larger changes in solar constant accompanying more slowly varying changes on the sun.

Testing the Sun-Climate Connection
with Tuned Climate Models
Recognizing these uncertainties, Gilliland constructed a fairly simple model of twentieth-century earth's climate and tried to force it with five external factors: carbon dioxide, a 76-year solar cycle, a 22-year solar cycle, a 12.4-year solar cycle, and volcanic dust variations.[119] As noted by Schneider and Mass in their earlier study, Gilliland recognized that no verified quantitative relationships now exist that could tell us reliably how much each of these factors could change the radiation balance of the earth. Thus, the best one can do is to match observed temperatures of the past hundred years or so (see Figure 7.6) to those predicted by a climate model driven by these assumed external factors. Gilliland tuned the strength of each of these five external factors to get the best fit between model output and observed Northern Hemispheric surface air temperature data.* This semiempirical method suggested that each factor could contribute some

---

*"Tuning" simply means adjusting the numerical value of free parameters in the model in order to make the model prediction agree as well as possible—that is, obtain the best fit—with the observational data. A serious problem with this procedure can arise when a model contains many tunable parameters and the observational data set is of limited size. In this case even a good correspondence between model simulation results and observations is of little value in explaining climatic cause and effect since such extensive tuning simply builds the answer into the model; thus it loses its claim to be an objective, independent theory of climatic change.[120]

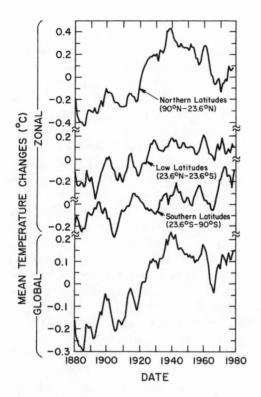

Figure 7.6

Observed surface air temperature trends for three latitude bands and the entire globe are shown for the 100-year period after 1880. The results are smoothed by filtering through the use of a five-year running mean averaging process to smooth out the noisy yearly fluctuations. Because many regions of the world—particularly the oceans—are not covered by thermometers during large parts of this record, these trends should be considered only as roughly representative of the true surface air temperature variations over the period. [Source: J. A. Hansen, D. Johnson, A. Lacis, S. Lebedeff, P. Lee, D. Rind, and G. Russell, 1981, Climate impact of increasing atmospheric carbon dioxide, Science 213:961.]

influence to the total temperature record. CO_2, volcanic dust, and the 76-year solar cycle (in the sun's diameter) produced the largest effects. Indeed, without the 76-year solar cycle, Gilliland could not reproduce very well the decrease in Northern Hemisphere temperatures seen after 1940.

Unfortunately, Gilliland's study, like that of Schneider and Mass and a number of other similarly tuned, semiempirical studies, all suffer from the same problem: too many plausible explanations can be invoked to explain only a few major trends in recent global temperature. For example, the global mean temperature record in Figure 7.6 really shows only two basic long-term events: about an 0.5°C (0.9°F) warming trend from the 1890s to the 1940s, followed by about an 0.3°C (0.54°F) cooling to 1970.* The warming could have been caused by a number of factors, such as increasing CO_2, increasing solar output through the 76-year cycle, or the relative absence of large volcanic eruptions and their dust veils between 1914 and 1950. It is not easy to distinguish the extent to which each of these possible—but overlapping—forcings contributed to that warming trend. Moreover, the thirty-year cooling in air temperatures after 1940 could also have been related to reduced solar luminosity associated with sunspot blocking, as just discussed, or to increases in dust from our industrial or agricultural activities. Reid Bryson, at the University of Wisconsin, has been a vociferous advocate of the theory that dust raised by humans, and not changes in solar constant from solar activity, helped produce the Northern Hemisphere surface air coolings after 1945. And he has produced tuned semiempirical models similar to those constructed by Gilliland and Schneider and Mass to "prove" it.[122] (We'll discuss this more in Chapter 8.)

None of these tuned, semiempirical model studies has yet yielded "statistically significant" results, in the language of statisticians, since the temperature records are not truly global in extent (in addition to being insufficiently long). The number of possible forcing mechanisms are too numerous and distinctions between surface, surface air, and ocean temperature trends are too ambiguous. Scientists are still unable to devise an unambiguous empirical test of which potential external forcing caused what response.[123] About the strongest statement one can make from the tuned, semiempirical models is that results such as Gilliland's "allow a self consistent explanation of the hemispheric temperature trends." However, such consistency is not formal verification.

*A more recent analysis by P. D. Jones at the University of East Anglia suggests a major rewarming over the 1970s and that 1981 was the warmest year for the Northern Hemisphere land areas since 1881, "the first year when some reliability can be accredited to a hemispheric average" [*Climatic Monitor 10* No. 5 (Norwich: University of East Anglia).] Other data sources are also available.[121]

Global Temperature Trends
and Volcanic Dust Veils

There is in Iceland a chain of mountains with lyrical names—Laki, Hekla, and Askja. They are underlain by a fissure in the earth's crust, a rift through which the planet's gases and molten rock come. In June 1783, Mount Laki belched sulfur-rich gases into the troposphere and stratosphere, casting a pall over Europe. The Parisian sun was dimmed and temperatures were believed to be colder than usual that winter. Benjamin Franklin, serving in France as an envoy, suggested there could be a connection between the three events. In May 1784, Franklin wrote of the summer of 1783 and the following winter:

> During several of the summer months of the year 1783, when the effect of the sun's rays to heat the earth in these northern regions should have been greatest, there existed a constant fog over all Europe, and great part of North America. This fog was of a permanent nature; it was dry, and the rays of the sun seemed to have little effect towards dissipating it, as they easily do a moist fog, arising from water. They were indeed rendered so faint in passing through it, that when collected in the focus of a burning glass, they would scarce kindle brown paper. Of course, their summer effect in heating the earth was exceedingly diminished.
> Hence the surface was early frozen.
> Hence the first snows remained on it unmelted, and received continual additions.
> Hence the air was more chilled, and the winds more severely cold.
> Hence perhaps the winter of 1783–4, was more severe, than any that had happed for many years.[124]

Franklin speculated on several possible causes of the "constant fog," including "the vast quantity of smoke" from volcanoes in Iceland, which "might be spread by various winds over the northern part of the world." Volcanologist Haraldur Sigurdsson at the University of Rhode Island recently commented that "the vast outpouring of volcanic gases . . . produced a bluish haze all over Iceland and led to destruction of most summer crops. The resulting famine caused the loss of 75% of all livestock in Iceland and the deaths of 24 percent of the Icelanders in the following years."[125] Reconstructed temperatures for the winter of 1784 in Europe and the northeastern United States were also reportedly several degrees colder than normal, as Franklin had already surmised from personal experience. However, the bulk of the fallout from Laki apparently was gone within six months of the eruption.

The Year Without a Summer   Although the effect of the Laki eruption may have been concentrated in the northern half of the Northern Hemisphere over a six-month period, the reach of Mount Tambora some thirty years later was apparently more global.[126] Over two days in April 1815, this Indonesian volcano ejected 100 to 200 cubic kilometers (24 to 48 cubic miles) of dust, ash, and lava, killing 10,000 people within a matter of hours. Eighty-two thousand more reportedly died from starvation when their crops were destroyed by Tambora's debris. The volcano's ash cloud was so dense that neighboring Madura, about 450 kilometers (280 miles) west, was in near darkness for three days. The dust veil shrouded the earth and created vivid "Turner sunsets" for at least a year—colorful sunsets like those immortalized in paintings by the British artist Joseph Mallord William Turner.

In England the following year, temperatures dropped 1.5° to 2.5°C (2.7° to 4.5°F). In eastern North America and in Western Europe, the summer of 1816 was reported in places to be 1° to 2.5°C (1.8° to 4.5°F) colder than the previous years; New Englanders complaining of untimely frosts called it "the year without a summer." It was, in fact, the coldest summer in New Haven during the whole period of record from 1780 to 1968. Henry and Elizabeth Stommel, who reviewed historical documents of the time, reported: "In New England the loss of most of the staple crop of Indian corn and the great reduction of the hay crop caused so much hardship on isolated subsistence farms that the year became enshrined in folklore as Eighteen Hundred and Froze to Death.' "[127]

Whether Tambora caused these events or was merely a component of them—or even a coincidence—is still debated. For example, even if the eruption caused a 3°C (5.4°F) drop in average summer temperatures at the latitudes of New England, this very large cooling still isn't enough by itself to create midsummer frosts. It would take many times that degree of cooling to drop July temperatures to freezing. However, if the jet stream coming across North America toward New England also dipped down unusually far south (as in Figure 4.3) at the same time the hemisphere cooled a few degrees, then the combination of the two factors could have created the few frosty days in the summer of 1816.* And even if these hypothesized simultaneous events did happen, it is still conjecture whether they were chance occurrences rather than a volcanic-dust-caused jet stream anomaly.† We need more than one eruption and potential climatic response to verify a volcanic dust climate connection.

Separating Volcanic from Other Effects on Climate   Tambora was followed many decades later by two other lesser volcanic eruptions that have also been linked to a hemispheric-scale climatic cooling of several tenths of a degree. In August 1883, another Indonesian volcano, Krakatoa, fired an estimated 20 cubic kilometers (4.8 cubic miles) of material into the upper reaches of the atmosphere. Thirty-six thousand people were killed, mostly by tidal waves set off by the explosion. More recently, Mount Agung in Bali erupted in the spring of 1963, throwing up 1 cubic kilometer (0.24 cubic miles) of debris. Fifteen hundred people died in hot mud flows and from glowing clouds of gases and hot ash that seared their lungs.‡ The 1980 eruption of Mount St. Helens in Washington state was a celebrated media event. But by comparison with the others cited, the Mount St. Helens blast was puny: it ejected perhaps less than 1 cubic kilometer (0.24 cubic miles) of dust and rocks, hardly enough to have a significant effect on the climate.[128]

It isn't so much the volume of total volcanic ejecta that is important for climatic impact, however. It is the volume of a certain kind of fine dust, particularly sulfate particles, injected high into the stratosphere where they can last several years that has most effect on climate. Volcanologists Michael Rampino and Stephen Self examined the three major eruptions (Tambora, Krakatoa, and Agung), concluding that although the volume of fine ash produced was in the ratio 150 to 20 to 1, respectively, for these three events, the ratio of climatically significant stratospheric sulfate particles was

---

*There has been some recent evidence suggesting just such a connection. See, for example, Schneider, S. H., 1983, Volcanic dust veils and climate: How clear is the connection? An editorial, *Climatic Change* 5:111–114.

†A similar, but less severely cool June in 1982 in New England was—too hastily I believe—attributed by some to the dust veil from El Chichon eruption in Mexico a few months earlier.

‡Geophysicists believe this South Pacific region produces so many volcanoes because it is the site of a major, active subduction zone; that is, the oceanic plate is being submerged beneath the continental plate, creating an arc-shaped fissure.

in the ratio 7.5 to 3 to 1.[129] The sulfate particles spread worldwide and interfered with the planetary radiation balance, which is the hypothesized mechanism for climatic influence of volcanic dust veils. These sulfate figures are directly measured data values for Agung in 1963, but only inferred from sulfate remains, for example, preserved in polar ice layers for the earlier two eruptions.[130] Theoretical calculations show that volcanic dust veils prevent some sunlight from reaching the lower atmosphere, heating the stratosphere but cooling the troposphere; they also enhance the greenhouse effect, warming the lower atmosphere.[131] These effects do not appear to be fully compensating, with the tropospheric cooling effect dominating the warmings. But these theoretical calculations need to be verified empirically before volcanic dust/climate hypotheses should be accepted.

Based primarily on eyewitness accounts of volcanic blasts and recordings of colorful sunsets and hazy skies a year or so after volcanoes, Hubert Lamb devised a *dust veil index* for the past few hundred years.[132] This index was used by Schneider and Mass to drive the volcanic forcing part of their climate model. Temperature changes produced by this mechanism in our model could explain about half the variations in temperature records over the past few hundred years. Unlike speculations on solar constant/solar property changes over decades, there is at least some hard data connecting volcanic dust veils in the stratosphere with decreases in radiant energy reaching the lower atmosphere. These data were initially obtained from the eruption of Mount Agung in 1963, and have been used to calibrate previous eruptions.

There are some independent data to verify Lamb's subjective dust veil index. Glaciologists, led by Claus Hammer from the University of Copenhagen, have looked at the acid content in ice cores over the past few thousand years and have reconstructed their own dust veil index.[133] Sulfur-related acids are connected to volcanoes because the sulfur oxides ejected into the stratosphere by certain large volcanic eruptions are converted into sulfuric acid, the principal component of climatically significant stratospheric dust veils. This index from the acid deposited in annual ice layers agrees fairly well with Lamb's more subjective, historical dust veil index.

The sulfate index was used by Gilliland in his effort to simulate Northern Hemispheric temperature trends. However, Northern and Southern Hemispheric acid records are different, suggesting that these ice core acid traces are biased toward local eruption events. J. Murray Mitchell, Jr., among many other scientists, has argued for years that large explosive volcanic eruptions are important for climate.[134] Unlike longer-term solar constant/solar activity relationships, volcanic dust veils in the stratosphere last up to a few years; their effects are short-lived, but should be detectable in past temperature records. Dust veils can cause bumps and wiggles occurring over a few years' time in the record (see Figure 7.6). Unfortunately, a number of major volcanic eruptions, such as Tambora in 1815, Krakatoa in 1883, and Agung in 1963—all of which were followed by a few years of large-scale cooling—occurred after cooling trends had already begun. This led one group of scientists to speculate, curiously, that cooling trends might initiate large volcanic eruptions![135]

Mass and Schneider recognized that many of the short-term cooling dips of the climatic record (shown in Figure 7.6, for example) for nonvolcanic years were roughly the same size as dips occurring near major volcanic eruption years. We concluded that one could not therefore automatically assume any single eruption created a subsequent temperature dip, since similar dips have taken place at times when no major eruptions had occurred.[136] In order to help distinguish volcanically induced dips from random, short-term cooling periods, Mass and Schneider used a technique known as *superposed epoch analysis* to combine a large number of volcanic eruptions with a large number of temperature dips that followed each eruption. This averaging or compositing process reduces the noise of interannual climatic fluctuations, and showed a fairly clear volcanic signal. The strength of the signal was a cooling of several tenths of a degree Celsius lasting a year or two following major eruptions.[137] Such cooling has been corroborated by the semiempirical modeling studies of Gilliland, Hansen, and others.[138]

The effects on global surface temperature changes of stratospheric dust veils seems to be fairly well established now from the many studies we've cited. As mentioned earlier, geological evidence like that shown in Figure 7.3 suggests possible connections between long periods of enormous and frequent volcanic eruptions and major paleoclimatic coolings. The magnitude of these prehistoric eruptions appears much greater than that of volcanoes of the past few centuries. Mount Toba, for instance, also in Indonesia, released an estimated 1000 to 2000 cubic kilometers (240 to 480 cubic miles) of debris 75,000 years ago, perhaps causing one of the snowblitz spikes in the pollen records of Europe mentioned in Chapter 2.[139]

In summary, then, external forcings, particularly volcanic eruptions, can be implicated in climatic trends of the past few centuries. Solar variability and carbon dioxide variations can also produce results in models that are consistent with some observations. But because of insufficient amounts of verifying data and the possibility of other causal mechanisms (in particular, volcanic dust veils), these CO_2 and solar effects cannot yet be said to have been conclusively detected in the climatic records.*

All the mechanisms discussed in this section so far are external forcings of the climatic system. What about the internal, or free, oscillations we discussed earlier in connection with the Pleistocene climatic record? Is it not possible that the record of the past few hundred years is nothing more than internal fluctuations of the climate system, with energy stored in deep oceans or glaciers being slowly absorbed or released? Moreover, why have so many studies so far stressed relationships between possible external factors and Northern Hemispheric surface air temperature records? What about the Southern Hemisphere? What about various regions around the world? Do they all go as the Northern Hemisphere goes?

From Global Temperatures to Regional Climates

There is an obvious explanation as to why so much attention is focused on the Northern Hemisphere's land-based surface air temperature records: this is where most of the thermometers have been and still are. Until the last few decades, there has been very little coverage in the middle of oceans, the tropics, or the Southern Hemisphere because of a lack of meteorological stations.[140] Recent worldwide cooperative efforts have significantly enhanced our knowledge of Southern Hemispheric climate, as have meteorological satellites, which do not discriminate between Northern and Southern Hemisphere data. Nevertheless, the Southern Hemisphere still has relatively poorer instrument coverage than the Northern, which makes it particularly difficult to reconstruct global climate trends of the past.

*As one example, Richard Willson's satellite data showed about an 0.1 percent decrease in solar constant averaged over an 18-month period in 1980 and 1981. He issued a press release that implicated this with a cold winter in the northeastern United States in 1982, a point contested by myself, John Eddy, and others (see Frazier, K., *Science News*, 21 May 1982, p. 294).

All is not hopeless, however, since many records do extend back over decades, and several even cover a century or two. These have been assembled into large-scale temperature trends. J. Murray Mitchell, Jr., was one of the first scientists to compute such long-term temperature trends. He published a paper in 1972 showing that the 0.5°C (0.9°F) average warming during the first half of this century was not a uniform trend across the whole Northern Hemisphere; a large fraction of the warming was concentrated in the high latitudes of the Northern Hemisphere, particularly in the winter months.[141] He also showed that a similar warming for the first half of the twentieth century was evident in the average of the few available Southern Hemisphere stations that he had analyzed. But Mitchell's study showed that after 1945 no clear southern cooling trend occurred, as it had for the northern half of the Northern Hemisphere. The average temperature of the southern stations he analyzed oscillated up and down by about a tenth of a degree during the 1950s and 1960s.

In 1976, University of Arizona scientists Paul Damon and Steven Kunen published a paper in *Science* entitled "Global Cooling?"[142] The question mark in their title was deliberate, since their analysis of Southern Hemisphere temperature records showed that the southern high-latitude stations actually showed a *warming* of 0.37°C (0.67°F) from the early 1960s to the early 1970s. In 1977, Harry Van Loon and Jill Williams at the National Center for Atmospheric Research re-examined the geographic distribution of warming and cooling trends for the Southern Hemisphere and concluded that the high southern latitudes—at least the parts where data were available—showed an average of 0.6°C (1.1°F) warming in winter and a 0.2°C (0.36°F) warming in summer from 1956 to 1972.[143] All analysts were plagued by a lack of data, though. As Damon and Kunen readily admitted, they had included in their analysis only fourteen stations with latitudes greater than 45°S, far too few to make very confident statements about Southern Hemisphere temperature trends. Nevertheless, they concluded cautiously that the cooling trend evident in the Northern Hemisphere from 1945 to about 1970 was by no means a global phenomenon, but rather one primarily concentrated in the northern latitudes.[144]

More recently, this conclusion was reinforced and updated by a team of NASA researchers in New York City at the Goddard Institute for Space Studies. James Hansen led the study, in which the investigators recomputed the temperature trends for various latitude bands of the earth, using essentially the same data sets as earlier investigators. They confirmed what earlier studies showed: not all latitude belts had temperature trends of comparable character as is apparent in Figure 7.6. The NASA team did, however, extend the record to the end of the 1970s. The data for this decade led to what Hansen's team called a "remarkable conclusion: That the global temperature is almost as high today as it was in 1940. The common misconception that the world is cooling is based on Northern Hemisphere experience to 1970."[145] The record was extended even further by T. M. L. Wigley, P. M. Kelly and P. D. Jones, who found 1981 to be the warmest year ever recorded by instruments for the Northern Hemisphere.[146]

Despite the seeming agreement among many reconstructions of zonal temperature trends for the past century, there are still some nagging uncertainties. For example, in the 1960s German scientist Horst Dronia argued that much of the Northern Hemispheric temperature data was gathered from thermometers located in urban areas of industrial countries, regions that have been heating up because of human activities over the past century (see the next chapter).[147] This, he argued, could lead to the false impression that the global average surface temperature had been warming. J. Murray Mitchell, Jr., who was aware of this problem, has claimed that his temperature records compensate to a considerable extent for this urban effect.[148] But the size of the urban effect and the adequacy of the compensation are issues still debated by climatologists. Damon and Kunen, in a later discussion of their Southern Hemisphere work, tested their data for an urban heating effect and found that five or eight cities with populations greater than 750,000 did show a significant warming trend of a few tenths of a degree over a number of years. Such a large warming trend was not evident over the same period in cities with populations below a quarter of a million or so. Since most of their high-latitude southern stations were not in cities with large populations, they tentatively decided that the warming in these areas was probably real and not a biased sample contaminated by urban heating effects.[149]

Another common argument over the representativeness of global or zonal temperature-trend charts is that the actual climate does not change in a smooth global or zonal manner. For example, we already saw in discussions of the unusual winter of 1977 in North America (see Figure 4.3) that persistent or "blocked" anomalies in the jet stream led to persistent or anomalous warming in the West and cooling in the East, with no large, uniform or continent-wide average temperature anomaly. Although the highly regional nature of climatic variations has been documented for a long time, one of the first quantitative techniques for representing regional climatic trends was developed in 1970 by John Kutzbach.[150] Subsequent investigators have been exploiting these techniques, known as *empirical orthogonal functions,* to the problem of seasonal climatic anomaly forecasts, as described in Chapter 4.

As an interesting example of the regional nature of temperature trends, Harry van Loon and Jeffery Rogers at the National Center for Atmospheric Research studied what they called "the seesaw in winter temperatures between Greenland and Northern Europe."[151] They found that since 1840, in more than 40 percent of the winter months when it was abnormally warm in northern Europe, it was simultaneously unusually cold in Greenland—or vice versa. These scientists attributed the seesaw in temperatures to changes in the types of atmospheric circulation patterns, rather than to long-term climatic trends caused by changes in, say, solar constant, volcanic dust, or other external factors.

However, the fact that large—even opposite—regional variations in temperature can occur within the same latitude zone does not rule out the possibility of a *net* warming or cooling averaged over that zone; nor does it rule out the possibility that any net zonal effect was caused by an external factor such as volcanic dust or solar constant change. After all, in only about 40 percent of the cases since 1840 did the seesaw occur. There are a number of examples in the past few hundred years of both Greenland and northern Europe having temperature anomalies in the same direction. Moreover, coherent trends in long-term records over wide areas are also well documented.[152] Such trends can occur simultaneously with nonzonal anomalies.

Nevertheless, despite the highly nonglobal, nonzonal nature of regional climatic trends, there are still net zonal and global average changes. For example, Williams and van Loon resolved the zonal averages of the available temperature trends between 1942 and 1972 into their seasonal components. They show that for summer, fall, and winter over this thirty-year period there is slight warming in the subtropics between lat. 15°N and lat. 25°N; for all the seasons there is a large cooling trend poleward of lat. 55°N. For three seasons there is moderate cooling between lat. 55°N and lat. 30°N, but for the winter season between lat. 45°N and lat. 55°N the average temperature trend is a slight warming.[153]

Semiempirical, tuned models, like those cited earlier of Bryson, Schneider and Mass, Gilliland, Oliver, and Hansen and his associates, among others, can only attempt to explain the global, and perhaps some of the zonal, temperature trends of the past century (or several centuries at most). This is because these models are driven by global-scale changes such as the solar constant, volcanic dust, and CO_2. Thus, they cannot possibly reproduce all the seasonal and regional variations that van Loon, Williams, and others have pointed to. These are probably associated with circulation changes, as van Loon often suggests. However, not yet clear is the extent to which these circulation changes themselves are partly driven by larger-scale temperature changes associated with external forcing. They also may be wholly internal—perhaps even random —fluctuations that would have occurred regardless of any changes to the energy output of the sun or other global-scale external causes.

Chance as a Cause
of Climatic Variations

The importance of random internal processes to long-term global climate trends is often proposed as an explanation of climatic fluctuations. MIT theoretical meteorologist Edward Lorenz raised this issue in the mid-1960s.[154] We can liken random forces in the climatic system to the random movements of particles in a liquid. Physicists have known for many years of a phenomenon called *Brownian motion.* If you examined microscopically a glass of water that contains suspended dust particles, you would see that, even in calm, undisturbed water, the particles move about aimlessly —they exhibit Brownian motion. This is because very small water molecules, whose masses are thousands and thousands of times smaller than the dust particles, travel at speeds sufficiently fast to bump or perturb the dust. The particle then jumps about in what physicists call *a random walk.* Because of the random nature of the water molecules banging on the dust particles they are as likely to "walk" in any one direction as any other. Over a sufficient period of time the larger particles will drift away from their point of origin, with all directions of drift being equally likely. Hence, a large number of particles will average no net motion, staying essentially at rest in a *statistical* sense, despite the fact that each bounces around or exhibits Brownian motion at any instant in time.

German oceanographer and climate theorist Klaus Hasselmann drew an analogy between the Brownian motion of individual parties and the behavior of the climatic system.[155] In his physical metaphor, the oceans are the large dust particles and the storm systems of the atmosphere are the high-speed, randomly perturbing water molecules. Hasselmann believes that such unpredictable weather disturbances (recall the discussion in Chapter 4) could be modeled as random fluctuations of the atmosphere imposed on the large heat capacity of the slowly responding oceans. He suggested that short-term fluctuations in the mean temperature of the planet (such as those shown in Figure 7.6) might be explained by this analogy. That is, random weather events disturbing the oceans could cause a few tenths of a degree warming or cooling fluctuations over a few years of time.

University of Maryland meteorologist Alan Robock later built a climate model incorporating both these random or *stochastic fluctuations* as well as external factors such as volcanic dust.[156] Despite the random fluctuations, which he believes account for much of the year-to-year fluctuation in Northern Hemispheric or global temperature records, Robock found from his model that volcanic dust can also significantly influence short-term climate change. His results, though, like the findings of Mass and Schneider, show that external influences must compete with the year-to-year internal fluctuations, which are inherently unpredictable. The big, hotly debated question is simply: To what extent are both short-term and longer term climatic variations traceable to external causes as opposed to internal causes (which are, presumably, largely unpredictable)?

Robock's climatic model assumed values for the strength of the atmospheric fluctuations instead of having explicit calculations for each individual storm system. Thus, it is possible that he overestimated the average strength of the year-to-year fluctuations resulting from random processes. We need to check this inference on more realistic climate models.[157] Very high-resolution, three-dimensional atmosphere-ocean models that compute individual storms explicitly have been run. One of these suggests that the effect of explicitly resolved atmospheric storms on ocean temperatures should cause random fluctuations from year-to-year of no more than about 0.1°C (0.18°F), not the variations of several tenths of a degree Celsius evidenced in records such as Figure 7.6 or obtained in Robock's model results.[158] At the moment, the relative influence of internal and external factors in creating both the long-term temperature trend evident in global temperature records as well as the year-to-year fluctuations remains an unanswered and controversial subject among climatologists. My intuitive suspicion from evidence now available is that these stochastic processes will turn out to be a minor component of global surface temperature changes on decade or longer time scales.

Semiempirical model results like those of Hansen and his coworkers have suggested that "much of the global climate variability on timescales of decades to centuries is deterministic" (that is, externally forced) and "the general agreement between modeled and observed temperature trends strongly suggests that CO_2 and volcanic aerosols are responsible for much of the global temperature variation in the past century."[159] Nevertheless, although I have considerable sympathy for this point of view, because of the yet unverified assumptions or missing observational data in all these studies the relative importance of internal and external factors, even for the global temperature record of the past few decades, is still not satisfactorily pinned down in my opinion. At least these recent results do show modeling to be consistent with observations, even though too few data are yet available to engender much statistical confidence in cause-and-effect inferences.

Sampling and Aliasing　　There is yet a third objection to records such as that shown in Figure 7.6. It has nothing to do with internal versus external arguments for the cause of climatic changes. Rather, it is purely a concern about the construction of charts that purport to represent zonal or global temperature trends based on a very irregular distribution of thermometers around the world. The problem is referred to by mathematicians as *aliasing,* which suggests that instead of being a representation of reality, the plotted graphs are an "alias" of reality. The notion is based on the following idea. We've mentioned several instances in which the regional surface air temperature trends have been both positive and negative within the same latitude zone, sometimes significantly exceeding the zonal average trend. If there were a densely spaced network of thermometers, uniformly distributed, devoid of urban influences, and sampling temperatures from both positive and negative regional anomalies, very little such aliasing would occur. By simply adding together all the many thermometers covering areas that warmed, cooled, or experienced no change, we would have an accurate representation of the true zonal or global *residual* (or net) temperature trend.

Unfortunately, thermometers tend to be bunched around industrialized population centers, especially for records more than fifty years old. Thus, it is clear that the straightforward average of all available thermometers provides a biased estimate of actual temperature trends over wide geographic areas. This kind of average is particularly biased against those places where very few thermometers have been present. For example, if no net zonal temperature change occurred but the positions of the troughs and ridges of the jet stream shifted so that by chance most thermometers registered anomalous cold and a few registered more than normal warmth, the average of all of those thermometers would give the false impression, or alias, of net zonal cooling. The reality would be only a shift of regional patterns. This mistake could also be referred to as a *spatial sampling error,* arising because our estimate of zonal temperature trend was taken from a limited sample of unevenly distributed thermometers. Our case is analogous to the problem that pollsters have in trying to learn the nation's opinion on some subject. Practical considerations limit them to a poll of only a few thousand people at most. If the people they poll are a truly random selection from all corners of the nation, it is likely that this limited sample will provide a fairly accurate reflection of the opinions of the national population. Of course, a residual or sampling error always remains because each and every person cannot be polled. In terms of climate, the best solution to the aliasing problem is to increase the coverage of fixed meteorological instruments and to augment these with nonlocal observations, such as satellite instruments or shipboard measurements.

Other Local Climatic Factors   In summary, we have seen that since the thermometer was invented only three centuries ago, the earth's surface air temperature has fluctuated by at most a degree or so Celsius over many decades, and by a few tenths of a degree or so from year to year. On a regional basis, changes can be much larger and need not be in the same direction as zonal or global long-term trends. Even in the twentieth century, where the greatest number of long-term observations is available, there are many remaining uncertainties: can the general warming of the planet to the mid-1940s, the cooling of the high northern latitudes to about 1970, or the rapid rewarming of the surface air during the 1970s be explained as the results of global-scale external factors such as volcanic dust veils, carbon dioxide, or solar constant changes? Can these changes be distinguished from regional-scale internal processes such as variations in atmospheric or oceanic circulation, the exchange of heat between such long-memory energy reservoirs as oceans or glaciers, or random processes generated by unpredictable atmospheric storms and their influence on the slowly responding oceans? And furthermore, any theory that attempts to explain temperature records averaged over the globe can never be perfectly verified, since the average of all thermometers is not exactly the same as the actual average temperature of the globe.

Sampling errors for precipitation records may be even more serious than for temperature. Climatologist Helmut Landsberg once quipped at a scientific conference that the ratio of rainfall falling on the earth to that trapped in rain gauges is a billion to one —what he dubbed the "Landsberg ratio."* With such a relatively small sample of measurements inherent in the present rain gauge network, errors in estimating precipitation can be large. This is particularly true for measurements of so-called *convective precipitation* —that is, thunderstorms—since these 10-kilometer (6.2-mile) or so wide cells of intense storminess have precipitation rates that vary greatly from one part of the storm to another. You've probably seen heavy rains uptown but light rain downtown, and none at the airport —where official records are kept—from the same thunderstorm.

We bring up this measurement problem here with respect to causes of variations simply to reiterate that before an investigator labors too hard to explain observed variations in some climatic variable over time or space, he or she needs to take great care to estimate the extent to which the record of variations reflects reality rather than sampling or other errors. To minimize sampling errors, a dense network of gauges, a large area of coverage, or long-term averages of each gauge's record must be used in computing precipitation statistics.

Figure 7.7 is an example of this, since it is a rainfall record for a large area (monsoon-dominated India) over a long period of time.[160] The most striking feature on the record is a short-term fluctuation with a strength of about 10 percent of the long-term average rainfall. This fluctuation occurs with an average cycle time of about 2.5 to 3 years (that is, the so-called quasi-biennial oscilla-

---

*It could be even larger, as the surface of the earth is 5×10^{14} square meters (193 million square miles); that is, a Landsberg ratio of only 1 billion implies that there could be as much as 400,000 square meters (5.4 million square feet) of rain gauges covering the world! Regardless of the best number for the actual ratio, Landsberg's underlying point is certainly valid.

tion mentioned earlier). Also noticeable in Figure 7.7 is higher average rainfall in the 1940 to 1960 period than for most earlier times. Reid Bryson has connected this wet period to the extra warmth of the high northern latitudes, a temperature anomaly he attributes to the relative absence of volcanic dust veils in the mid-twentieth century. Thus, Bryson suggests a global external forcing as a cause for this regional wet period. Should high-latitude cooling set in, as it did for nearly two decades after 1960, less monsoon rainfall would occur, Bryson has warned, with potentially drastic human consequences.[161]

The issue of whether global climatic trends are associated with regional climatic variations like monsoon rainfall failures, or, more generally, whether the level of interannual variability in the climatic system is connected to such trends, have been points of some heated dispute among some climatologists over the past decade. It is poignant because interannual variability is one of the principal causes of food production fluctuations, and thus the answer to this scientific question is of major social significance, as discussed later on. Bryson is perhaps the most prominent believer that trends control the variability, having written that "during cooler periods, our

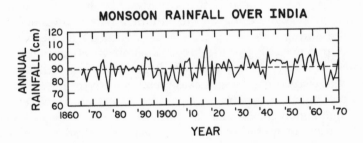

Figure 7.7

Rainfall over monsoon-dominated India is shown over a one-century period. Although local variations in rainfall can be quite large when compared to the large regional average shown, the figure does provide a large-scale representation of Indian monsoon rainfall over this century. Other than a few-decade period centered around 1900, rainfall for most of the twentieth century can be seen to have been both above "normal" and without any obvious trends. There is, however, a weak two- to three-year cycle that accounts for a small fraction of the variability in the record. *[Source: B. Parthasarathy and D. A. Mooley, 1978, Some features of a long homogeneous series of Indian summer rainfall,* Monthly Weather Review *106:771–781.]*

analysis of past climates indicates, there is greater variability in week-to-week, year-to-year weather."[162] Hubert Lamb, in some of his monographs, has also leaned towards this possibility.

On the other side, Harry van Loon has been strongly opposed to the idea that climatic variability can easily be linked with climatic trends. With Jill Williams, he constructed geographic maps of temperature means and standard deviations (a measure of variability) from the North Pole to Mexico in the North American region. These investigators found considerable regional and seasonal variations in trends of both means and variability of temperatures and precipitation, concluding that "there was no *single* relationship between means and variances." However, they went on to comment "there has been much speculation about whether year-to-year variability of climate elements is related to the temperature level, either in such a way that cooling at the surface of the polar regions causes high variability in temperate latitudes, or that cooling in general goes together with higher variability." Williams and van Loon note that "our investigation does not provide evidence for such a connection. Only in autumn did the correlation between mean temperature and variability of temperature show a bias toward negative values. During the rest of the year there was either no such bias or the correlation was more often positive than negative." Finally, these analysts suggest that "if there was an increase in variability in temperate latitudes during these decades, it would not then have been *caused* by the surface cooling in the Arctic which itself was caused by [a] circulation change."[163] In other words, van Loon and Williams believe that circulation changes cause temperature responses rather than the other way around, as suggested by Bryson. However, the van Loon and Williams analyses did not consider associations between Arctic temperature and monsoonal rainfall anomalies over India, which is one of Bryson's main points. Furthermore, whether circulation changes *cause* or are *caused by* temperature trends is still not clear from their analyses. Their assumed direction of cause and effect is no more proved than Bryson's. Van Loon and Williams have certainly proved association between temperature and circulation anomalies, but cause and effect still remains, as it were, a "chicken and egg" problem. It will take better theory to answer this question.

Other analysts also dispute the attribution of the rainfall anomalies shown in Figure 7.7 to global external causes such as changing dust veils. Instead, some argue for internal causes, such as unusual surface temperatures in the Arabian Sea.[164] We can see, then, that for precipitation variations, like temperature trends, there have been conflicting causal explanations based on internal versus external factors—to say nothing of the size of the sampling errors in the precipitation data.

Summary   We approach the twenty-first century with the uncomfortable knowledge that, despite some consistent, important new findings, our understanding of nature's role in causing climatic changes from the earth's beginning to now is still too unsatisfactory to provide more than a few reliable explanations and predictions. There are simply too many plausible explanations for most climatic events to convict any one of them beyond a reasonable doubt. To be sure, there is a great deal of circumstantial evidence pointing to volcanic dust veils and increasing greenhouse effect gases as the principal combined causes of twentieth-century climatic trends. But some other suspects—particularly internal causes—have still not been sufficiently well investigated to rule them out. We also know that humanity's ability to cause climatic change is growing rapidly to rival nature's, yet we carry on with business as usual in a state of considerable ignorance about the consequences. Thus, a question of basic social and economic importance is emerging from the seemingly academic debate among advocates of differing internal or external causes for climatic change: Will we be able to unravel the relative effects of man and nature in altering our climate before the climatic system itself performs the experiment, with all of us, our descendants, and the rest of life living in the laboratory?

8 The Human Connection

Left to her own devices, Nature will continue to nudge the earth toward the next ice age. The drop to colder temperatures appears to have begun some 5000 to 8000 years ago; fossil remains of various biota unearthed at different places suggest that climatic conditions then were milder than those found today. Temperatures, at least in summer, were frequently a degree or so warmer on average. At about that same time, against the backdrop of natural causes of climatic change that are only partially understood, came another ill-understood influence: people.

Evidence is mounting to suggest that through our industrial and agricultural activities we are inadvertently rivaling nature's ability to produce climatic changes. People are a relatively new force in shaping weather and climate, but some of our actions and the potential climatic consequences of our behavior are unprecedented, at least in recent climatic history. To estimate the potential climatic significance of our intervention, we need to compare the magnitude of human effects with natural influence locally, regionally, and globally.

Land Use

Since the dawn of civilization people have worked to use or modify the land to provide food or a more benevolent environment for themselves. But, since the land albedo and water cycling characteristics are important components of the surface energy balance, which helps determine the climate, alterations to the land can thus alter climate—at least locally. Whether the changes are significant depends on how rapidly and by how much the physical characteristics of the surface are altered. One example is the unnatural amassing of heat-retaining, nonevaporating stone and concrete in urban areas. As another example, when dark, vegetated areas like forests are denuded to make way for buildings or agriculture the result often is lighter, more highly reflective farm fields or cities. These alterations in the albedo and heat balance affect climate because they affect the absorption of solar energy. Deforestation also can alter the fraction of energy used to raise the temperature of the surface (so-called sensible heating) relative to the energy used to evaporate water (so-called latent heating, as described in Chapter 5). This proportion, the *Bowen's ratio,* is important in determining the temperature of the surface as well as the humidity and heating of the air above. If less water evaporates from some surface, it will usually be relatively hotter than a highly evaporating one; however, the total heating of the climatic system goes down if the albedo goes up.

Let's consider the effects of livestock grazing first. Joseph Otterman, a researcher from Tel Aviv University, has suggested that grazing has actually encouraged the growth of major deserts. In North Africa some 6000 years ago during the Altithermal period, climates wetter than today's encouraged plant growth (see Figure 2.5c). Otterman speculates that domestic animals may have been introduced in sufficient numbers to have trampled and overgrazed much of the Middle East, which might have been a significant factor in the ensuing desertification.[1] He argues that overgrazing might even have contributed significantly to the desertification of the formerly verdant Fertile Crescent over the past several thousand years. Similarly, overgrazing, along with the devastating droughts of the early 1970s, has been implicated in the human tragedy of Sahel in Africa, an issue we address in more detail in subsequent chapters.

Other researchers believe that people must bear even more responsibility for climatic change. Carl Sagan and two of his former students, Owen Toon and James Pollack (both with NASA at the Ames Research Center), examined the possible climatic impacts of humans since the domestication of fire, plants, and animals. They concluded that "the progression from hunter to farmer to technologist has increased the variety and pace more than the geographic extent of human impact on the environment. A number of regions of the earth have experienced significant climatic changes closely related in time to anthropogenic environmental changes" (see Table 8.1).[2] A major such anthropogenic change is the clearing of forests for agricultural purposes, an ancient activity now practiced with modern machinery in some countries.

Ferdinand Columbus wrote of this phenomenon in a biography of his father Christopher Columbus. This account describes the

Table 8.1 Human-Induced Changes in the Environment and Their Timing and Possible Consequences

Epoch	Some motives for environmental change	Some (largely) inadvertent environmental changes and examples of their timing
Hunting and gathering	Preparation of land	Deforestation of temperate regions (North America, Native American creation of grassland to about A.D. 1600; Eastern Europe, production of steppes—preclassical)
		Deforestation of tropical regions (Africa, production of savannas—since discovery of fire)
Agricultural	Expansion of farmland	Desertification (Sahara-Arabia region, beginning about 5000 B.C. to present; India, Pakistan, Sumeria, 2000 B.C. to A.D. 400; Peru, about A.D. 1200)
	Generation of energy	Deforestation of temperate regions (China, 2000 B.C. to A.D. 1950; Mediterranean Basin, 500 B.C. to A.D. 500; Western and Central Europe, A.D. 1000 to 1900; United States, A.D. 1800 to 1900)
		Deforestation of tropics (Africa, Indonesia, South America, since origin of agriculture)
Technological	Urbanization	Creation of urban heat islands
	Expansion of farmland	Concentration of surface and water pollutants
	Creation of artificial lakes	Alteration of hydrological cycle by farming and irrigation
	Production of synthetic chemicals	Destruction of soil by increased erosion
	Generation of energy	Alteration of composition of atmosphere (carbon dioxide, aerosols, smog)
	Production of raw materials	Destruction of natural plant and animal communities (desertification, deforestation, temperate and tropical regions—changes mainly after about 1800)

Source: C. Sagan, O. B. Toon, and J. B. Pollack, 1979, Anthropogenic albedo changes and the earth's climate, *Science 206:* 1363–1368.

explorer's 1494 departure for the Caribbean island of Jamaica:

> The sky, air, and climate were just the same as in other places; every afternoon there was a rain squall that lasted for about an hour. The admiral writes that he attributes this to the great forests of that land; he knew from experience that formerly this also occurred in the Canary, Madeira, and Azore Islands, but since the removal of forests that once covered those islands they do not have so much mist and rain as before.[3]

Reginald Newell at MIT was one of the first modern meteorologists to point out the important role of tropical forests in the global energy and water balances and the possible climatic alterations that might be induced if large-scale deforestation took place. Newell's work led to a controversy over possible global climatic effects from Amazon deforestation.[4] A variety of studies have shown that the inflowing moisture from the Atlantic Ocean to the Amazon region accounts for only about 50 percent of the observed precipitation, suggesting that at least half the rainfall in the basin is recycled water evaporated or transpired from the Amazon floor. Major alteration to evapotranspiration rates from deforestation would, therefore, lead to potentially serious and long-lasting reductions in the region's rainfall and perhaps even alterations to climatic patterns elsewhere on earth.[5]

Aside from altering water cycling and albedo, deforestation alters atmospheric composition. As we explained in an earlier chapter, the biosphere is a huge reservoir of carbon. When trees are cut down or burned, for example, the process liberates CO_2 and other gaseous and particulate pollutants. Just how much carbon dioxide has been added over the past few centuries through deforestation —and the potential effect of this addition—is controversial and speculative. We will return to these issues in a later section.

Whatever effects humans may have had on climate through particular land-use practices over the centuries have already been largely manifested in the present climate. However, population pressures coupled with modern land-clearing machinery could result in more rapidly occurring land-use changes in the future. In turn, the impacts of such changes would themselves be felt more quickly, requiring us to adapt more quickly with more far-reaching responses in order to minimize the negative effects.

The Urban Heat Island

We explained in Chapter 4 that the sun is the thermal driver of the weather machine. However, the sun is not the only immediate source of heat for the earth; human beings have been producing heat since cave-dwelling times. Simply by building a fire, a person can change the atmospheric conditions in the immediate vicinity. But one fire in a cave obviously is not enough to make a difference in the climate very far outside the shelter. If we took the cave dwellers and made them modern people, updated their heating sources to fossil fuel energy plants, multiplied their numbers into millions and their dwellings into hundreds of thousands of office buildings and homes, added energy-gulping factories, and then crammed all of this into a small area paved over with heat-retaining stone and concrete, the result would be a very definite impact: the so-called *urban heat island.* Most large urban centers today are several degrees Celsius warmer than the surrounding countryside, and their precipitation can be different too, not only in quality (it can be chemically polluted) but in quantity.

One cause of these effects is the additional heat generated around urban centers and released into the environment. This phenomenon is known as *thermal pollution.* Another cause is reduced evaporation related to the paving over of natural plants and soil. The extra heat of the city warms the local area and helps the air to rise, carrying with it surface-layer moisture. As the rising moist air cools it can condense, thereby releasing precipitation. This enhanced rainfall effect is most marked in the summertime, when natural heating of the surface by the sun's energy gets a boost from human-derived additions of energy. Higher levels of local rainfall and thunderstorms are fostered by such extra heating.[6]

Not surprisingly, this *anthropogenic* (human-made) urban heat island effect is most noticeable where human modifications of nature are most concentrated. For instance, the average amount of heat released in Manhattan actually exceeds the 160 or so watts of solar radiation typically absorbed per square meter averaged over a 24-hour period at the earth's surface.[7] No wonder suburban temperatures, especially at night, can be five or more degrees cooler than Times Square. Table 8.2, prepared in 1962 by climatologist Helmut Landsberg, compares urban environments with rural surroundings.[8] To this twenty-year-old list could be added decreases

298

in visibility and increases in toxic gases like carbon monoxide and sulfur dioxide.

Although we are capable of producing surface heating equivalent to a "sun on earth" in a few places, on a worldwide average basis the human contribution of heat is still only about 1/10,000 of the sun's absorbed heat. This total is not enough to cause detectable global climatic effects. Some studies, however, suggest that regional effects could be detectable.[9]

Evidence for such energy concentrations is visible from space.[10] On the eastern seaboard, for example, Boston, New York, and Washington, D.C., together appear as a single blur of lights—a megalopolis sometimes called *Bosnywash*. With increases in population and energy use in such megalopoli, the consequences for weather and climate could become regionally significant in areas even larger than this northeastern corridor.* It is conceivable that large *power parks*, if constructed to concentrate energy production in order to achieve "economies of scale," could create enough heat to generate severe storms—perhaps tornadoes.[11] Just how a larger region would be affected is unclear, but some researchers have made extrapolations that project international-scale effects.[12] The technical and legal—as well as ethical—questions raised by the prospect of local or downwind climatic effects from multi-*gigawatt* (that is, billion watt) power parks are largely unanswered.

Atmospheric Aerosols: Is Man or Nature the Bigger Polluter?

Urbanization is responsible for another type of pollution that can affect climate: *aerosols*. Aerosols, are simply particles suspended in a gas. These tiny particles range from droplets sprayed out of a can or nozzle to dust or smoke from agricultural activities, power plants, factories, or automobiles. Aerosols also come from natural sources such as plants (the biological kind) and volcanoes. Sea spray and windblown dust are other natural aerosols. Together, the natural aerosols are considered the *background supply*. Aerosols can "seed" the clouds—that is, encourage water to con-

---

*For example, Changnon (see note 6 above) has computed that the maximum percent increase in thunderstorm days goes up some 10 percent for each urban population increase of one million.

Table 8.2

Climatic Changes Produced by Cities

Element	Compared with rural environs
Temperature	
Annual mean	0.5° to 0.8°C (0.9° to 1.45°F) higher
Winter minima	1.1° to 1.7°C (1.98° to 3.06°F) higher
Relative humidity	
Annual mean	6% lower
Winter	2% lower
Summer	8% lower
Dust particles	10 times as many
Cloudiness	
Clouds	5% to 10% more
Fog, winter	100% more
Fog, summer	30% more
Radiation	
Total on horizontal surface	15% to 20% less
Ultraviolet, winter	30% less
Ultraviolet, summer	5% less
Wind speed	
Annual mean	20% to 30% less
Extreme gusts	10% to 20% less
Calms	5% to 20% more
Precipitation	
Amounts	5% to 10% more
Days with 0.5 cm (0.2 in.)	10% more

Source: H. E. Lansberg, 1962, City air—better or worse, in *Symposium: Air Over Cities* (Cincinnati, Ohio: U.S. Public Health Service, Taft Sanitary Engineering Center), Technical Report A62-5, p. 122.

dense on them within clouds, perhaps later to fall out as raindrops. If, through man-made *aerosol pollution,* too many extra particles reach the clouds, smaller raindrops can form, many too light to fall to the surface. Thus, depending on specific conditions, the release of extra particles can work with or against the release of extra heat in industrial areas in modifying precipitation amounts. Extra particles can also modify the brightness of clouds, an effect that potentially could have significant climatic consequences. However, our knowledge of this possible effect of aerosols is so limited that we are even uncertain of the direction of the changes they might create— warming or cooling—let alone the magnitude of the effect.[13]

During the 1980 U.S. presidential election campaign, Ronald Reagan said that trees were major polluters, thus implying that human pollution wasn't all that serious. Many challenged his views, although trees and other plant species do emit sulfur, nitrogen, and hydrocarbon compounds, some of which produce aerosols very similar to human pollutants. These emissions are greatly enhanced when vegetation burns. Often, their aerosol production is a result of an indirect process: the photochemical conversion of gases into particles in the atmosphere.[14] However, such "pollution" from undisturbed nature is relatively constant from year to year; it has already left its mark on the climate and environment as the so-called *background level* of aerosols. Anthropogenic aerosols, on the other hand, can rapidly alter background conditions, possibly creating serious impacts as the environment adjusts to their presence. Moreover, the concentration of such aerosols as sulfuric and nitric acid —often toxic to plants, animals, and humans—generated in heavily polluted areas vastly exceeds local natural background levels. Furthermore, from the point of view of ethics, the existing natural aerosols and their effects represent natural adaptations, whereas damages from human pollutants imply culpability and the likelihood of conflict between polluters and those hurt by pollution.[15] The fact that nature pollutes is no reason to discount the human contribution, particularly in the many places where that contribution is growing or already outstrips the natural one.

At one time anthropogenic aerosols were widely implicated in a cooling trend (see top of Figure 7.6), when a slight drop in average Northern Hemisphere surface air temperatures was observed from about 1940 to 1970.[16] This climatic event coincided with a period in which the level of human-produced aerosols apparently rose. However, the hypothesized role of aerosols in this cooling trend has

301

since been disputed for three reasons. First, whether human-caused aerosol concentrations continued to grow—at least in the United States—after pollution-control regulations were imposed in the 1960s is dubious.[17] Second, as explained in Chapter 7, a temperature decrease as small as the one from 1940 to 1970 in the Northern Hemisphere is a typical feature of long-term climate. A number of natural occurrences could account for such a drop—for instance, a decrease in the solar constant or an increase in the number of volcanic dust veils.

A third factor is that not all aerosols necessarily cool the climate. Particles of certain colors and in certain locations can *warm* the climate by absorbing extra sunlight or by increasing the greenhouse effect. Many aerosols (especially those of industrial origin that have soot attached) are darker than the surface over which they float, which means they absorb extra solar radiation. Such aerosols are largely a regional phenomenon because they rarely remain in the lower atmosphere more than a week or two before being washed out by rain or snow. Conversely, a plume of nonsoot dust that drifts over an ocean, forest, or vegetated field will probably be lighter in color than the underlying surface and will tend to reflect more of the sun's rays than normally would have been reflected. The lighter-colored aerosol would thus cause a net cooling of the surface and atmosphere taken together.* But if that same aerosol plume drifted over a bright snow field, it would be likely to absorb more solar heat than would otherwise be absorbed, causing a net warming.

In reality, matters are even more complicated, since dust from human activities is a highly mixed combination of light- and dark-colored particles. Moreover, such aerosol layers are primarily concentrated over regions where they are generated and stretch a few thousand kilometers downwind of continental areas in the industrialized or heavily grazed parts of the Northern Hemisphere. Indeed, these two features of human pollution have been invoked by some researchers to explain why the Northern Hemisphere has cooled slightly since the mid-1940s while the Southern Hemisphere has not.[19] Quite opposed to these views, William Kellogg has argued that the light-*absorbing* properties of industrial-origin aerosols will lower planetary albedo, causing a warming.[20] In this connection,

---

*Indeed, it has been argued that most natural—so-called background—aerosols do cool the climate, perhaps by as much as 3°C (5.4°F).[18] However, there is no cause to suspect any major recent changes in these background levels.

Ichtiaque Rasool and Schneider (in my first paper in the atmospheric sciences) calculated that increasing atmospheric aerosols would likely cool the earth's climate. This calculation was based on assumed optical properties for both natural and human-produced dust suggested from many observations available at that time.[21] However, even a year or so later, as new chemical observations of dust began to mount, I realized that "detailed knowledge of the intensity and location of sources and sinks of particulate matter as well as the geographic and vertical distribution of suspended atmospheric particles is still very unsatisfactory . . . better data for aerosol optical properties must [also] be obtained. . . . This suggests that monitoring programs be implemented at many locations on the globe in order to obtain long-term trends in both the concentration and optical properties of aerosols."[22]

In essence, these more "agnostic" views of the climatic effects —warming versus cooling—of human-created atmospheric aerosols are still, I believe, the only ones justifiable at this time. We simply do not have enough detailed measurements of the distribution and trends of human-produced dust—including dust from deforested or overgrazed lands—to allow definitive conclusions. Thus, although we can calculate the climatic effects of specific kinds of dust, we can only speculate on the extent to which the complex and uncertain mix of anthropogenic aerosols are changing global temperature trends. As I interpret it, the preponderance of present evidence suggests that anthropogenic aerosols are probably less likely than volcanic dust in the stratosphere or CO_2 to be a major long-term factor in the global heat balance.

Acid Rain

Industrial and automobile production of sulfur and nitrogen oxides, mostly from the burning of fossil fuels, produces much of the anthropogenic aerosols just discussed. These particles are often suspended nitric and sulfuric acid drops, which help to endow urban smog with its burning effects on our eyes and lungs and on some plants. Not surprisingly, there is evidence that the acidity of rainfall in and downwind of such industrial effluent areas or population centers has been increasing.[23]

The kind of pollution known as acid rain has been blamed for depleting nutrients from the soils of thousands of square kilometers in the northeastern United States, for poisoning hundreds of lakes in Scandinavia, making them uninhabitable for fish and other aquatic life, and for concentrating toxic metals in groundwater in Sweden.[24] Acid rain became better known after 1959, when a Norwegian fisheries inspector correlated the decline in local fish populations with the increasing acidity of the precipitation. Until the 1970s, acid rain was considered a European problem, but then lakes and rainfall in the northeastern United States were monitored, and scientists discovered their pH level was dropping.

The relative acidity and alkalinity of substances is rated on a *pH scale* (from the French *pouvoir hydrogène,* or hydrogen power), which ranges from 0 to 15. Neutral is 7, with lower pH values being more acidic and higher values being more alkaline. The scale is logarithmic—that is, each whole number increment represents a tenfold difference. At the low end of the scale are the most acidic substances, such as stomach acid (around 1), lemon juice (around 2), and vinegar (around 3). In the middle are milk (about 6.5), baking soda (8.2), and sea water (about 8.3). Ammonia, which is very alkaline, has a pH of about 12, and the antacid milk of magnesia is at about 10.5. Neutral distilled water has a pH in the middle at 7. Unpolluted precipitation theoretically should have a pH of 5.6; it is not neutral because atmospheric carbon dioxide dissolves in cloud droplets to form weak carbonic acid. Hence, even ordinary rain is slightly acidic, though it is not generally harmful, as most of life has evolved and adapted to such rain water.* Indeed, this slight acidity is central to the process of weathering and erosion of calcium carbonate and other rocks. However, it is not the pH of the raindrops per se that is most important to the viability of ecosystems, but rather the amount of acidifying chemicals that are carried to the surface waters and soils.†

It is known that too much acidity is unhealthy for aquatic life; entire fish populations have been wiped out in lakes in Canada and the eastern United States. In the Adirondacks the average rain acidity pH is about 4 to 4.5, some 10 to 40 times more acid than in "unacidified" rain with a pH of 5 to 5.6. Small mountain lakes in

---

*Actually, most rain in even very remote areas has a pH slightly below 5.6, probably because of natural background levels of sulphur and nitrogen oxides.

†When droplets or ice crystals carry acid to the earth's surface, this is known as *wet deposition.* When dry particles of sulfate or nitrate acids fall on the surface, this is called *dry deposition. Acid rain* really refers to the overall problem of acid deposition on the earth, and dry deposition is often the larger source.

locations such as these are particularly susceptible; they receive more rainfall and more acid, but they are also "unprotected." That is, the thin mountain soils lack the needed amount of alkaline substances such as calcium carbonate and magnesium carbonate to neutralize a continuous rain of acidity. This *buffering capacity* is generally larger in soils in the western United States than in the East, but such an endowment of buffering is not infinite.[25] Also, when sulfur compounds accumulate in snow covering lakes, the spring thaw can bring a short but devastating pulse of acidity.

High acidity threatens fish, frogs, and water bugs, but this is only part of the problem. On land, high acidity can kill some plant tissues, leach nutrients from the soil, and affect the ability of legumes to fix nitrogen. When the soils are too acid, more precipitation washes out more nutrients.

Whether acid rain can directly harm people is uncertain. Undoubtedly, the disruption of the biogeochemical cycles will eventually affect all of us. But so far no one has been able to prove that acid rain directly endangers human health. There may be long-term indirect health effects from, for example, the release of otherwise immobile toxic metals by acidity into groundwater and reservoirs. Moreover, it is known that acidified water tends to speed up the corrosion of pipes, as copper and lead have turned up in water supplies around the Adirondacks.

Pollution that causes acid rain—largely nitrogen and sulfur emissions from burning gasoline, coal, and oil—is transported over long distances in the atmosphere. Hence, industrial or populated areas are not the only ones afflicted with too much acid in the rain. Smokestacks hundreds of feet high are partly responsible. Originally, these extremely tall stacks were built to vent sulfur and nitrogen oxides from power plants higher into the air, thus preventing locally high levels of such toxic pollution. But ultimately the smokestacks only passed the problem along to others by creating national and even international pollution. Some European states have long been arguing about responsibility for export of acid to other countries, and more recently this issue has become a thorny one in relations between the United States and Canada.[26] What appears needed to minimize acidity from existing fixed sources are *scrubbers.* These devices trap most of the sulfur dioxide produced before it gets out of combustion—but at an economic cost, of course. Low-sulfur fuels would also help, but they are expensive and in diminishing supply. New industrial plants built to minimize emissions are the best long-term solution. Cars are also implicated, particularly in providing nitrogen oxides. The detailed chemistry of conversion of nitrogen or sulfur oxides to acid rain is still poorly understood. Because the technical details are so uncertain it is even more difficult to achieve a consensus on regulations and policies to deal with the acid rain problem than if we thoroughly understood the mechanisms involved and only had to deal with the political issues.

It is important to emphasize that a great many uncertainties remain over the relative contribution of human and natural chemicals to acid rain, the actual trends in acid rain, and the effects. These uncertainties are usually highlighted by the very people who are accused of causing much of the acid rain. For example, a major industrial state is Illinois, whose State Water Survey put out a brochure entitled *Acid Rain: What Do We Know?* (It was written by Elisabeth P. Siebel, a University of Illinois journalist working part-time at the Survey and Richard G. Semonien, the Survey's assistant chief.) The brochure is available from the Illinois Department of Energy and Natural Resources; it carries a May 1981 publication date. The Illinois brochure, while not denying the potential risks of acid rain, recites the litany of unknown factors, which taken together "precludes a firm conclusion" about either the causes or seriousness of acid rain. "So far, evidence coming out of Illinois has questioned the alleged trend of increasing acidity and has suggested that at least some instances of radical rain chemistry change may have natural, not man-made, causes." The brochure does not, however, suggest what the increased costs to either Illinois or downstream residents might be if the acid rain studies now underway prove the problem to be as bad or worse than presently suspected. Nor does the brochure discuss who would be responsible for the increased damages due to delays in regulating emissions that might occur while people study. Although the Illinois group translates uncertainty into a call for research, most environmental groups believe there is more than enough evidence already to warrant a strong regulatory response. For example, in a report dated January 1982 (Acid Rain-Research in the Intermountain West), the Environmental Defense Fund authors concluded that "in order to stop destruction of wildlife by acid rain . . . elected officials should support those existing limitations on emissions of sulfur and nitrogen oxides which have been set under the Clean Air Act" as well as to create "new legal authority" to "substantially reduce sulfur dioxide emissions by 1990." All parties, it seems, agree that more research on causes and impacts is essential, but disagree vehemently on when to act more forcefully.*

Carbon Dioxide: The Global Environmental Issue for the Twenty-First Century?

Although carbon dioxide is only a trace element in the atmosphere, it is a gas with strong infrared-absorbing properties. CO_2 constitutes just over 0.034 percent of the volume of the air, but its concentration is increasing, up some 9 percent in 1982 over the 1958 level, which was about 315 parts per million (ppm). In that year one of the most important atmospheric monitoring programs ever undertaken was begun high on the slopes of Mauna Loa on the island of Hawaii. About five years earlier a chemist named Charles David Keeling began postdoctoral work at the California Institute of Technology in Pasadena. He worked for geochemist Harrison Brown, who stimulated Keeling's interest in measuring CO_2. After several years of experimentation, the young Cal Tech chemist had developed highly accurate techniques for measuring CO_2. Oceanographer Roger Revelle of the Scripps Institution of Oceanography was also very interested in the CO_2-climate problem.[27] He brought Keeling to Scripps, after which their CO_2 monitoring program began, both at the South Pole and at the Weather Service's Mauna Loa Observatory (now run by the National Atmospheric and Ocean

*In this connection there is an excellent question and answer debate between environmentalist Michael Oppenheimer and atmospheric chemist Volker Mohnen over whether to act now against acid rain on p. 206 of the November 14, 1982 *New York Times*. Furthermore, a prestigious panel of scientists headed by Dr. Jack Calvert of the National Center for Atmospheric Research prepared a report on acid rain for the U.S. National Academy of Sciences (*Acid Deposition: Atmospheric Processes in Eastern North America*, 1983, National Research Council [Washington, D.C.: National Academy Press]). Although the report noted all the uncertainties over the acid rain problems and the difficulties these raised for policy, it did come out rather strongly in support of the notion that increased acidity in rainfall can be directly linked to sulfur emissions, particularly in the industrial parts of North America, a conclusion that most of the industries had been resisting.

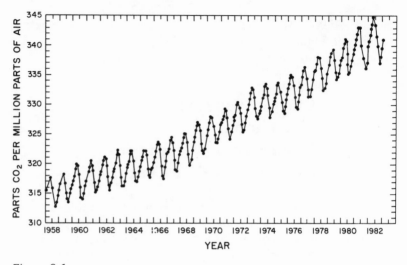

Figure 8.1

The observed trend of the concentration of atmospheric carbon dioxide (CO_2) as measured at Mauna Loa Observatory on the island of Hawaii. Each year CO_2 undergoes a cycle caused by the growth and decay of seasonal plants. Superimposed on this annual cycle is a long-term upward trend of some 9 percent over the 24-year period of record shown. The trend is widely believed to be the result of human activities, and it could cause significant global climatic warming if it continues. [Source: U.S. National Oceanic and Atmospheric Administration data, based initially on the work of C. D. Keeling at the Scripps Institution of Oceanography.]

Administration—NOAA). The results of the Hawaii measurements are given in Figure 8.1. (In the post-Sputnik year 1958 Revelle was one of the scientific leaders of the International Geophysical Year —a major research project whose public support flourished in response to the Soviets' technological success.)

Most climatologists believe that an increase in atmospheric CO_2 concentration will result in a general warming of the lower atmosphere. Most climate models simulating this warming indicate that a continued rise of CO_2 *at present rates* would cause average global temperatures to increase by about 1°C (1.8°F) some time after the turn of the next century, and by 2° to 3°C (3.6° to 5.4°F) by the middle to end of the twenty-first century. If sustained, these changes would exceed all known naturally caused temperature changes that have occurred in the past hundred thousand years.

CO$_2$ Sources and Sinks

Since the industrial revolution, fossil fuel burning has probably caused a 15 to 30 percent increase in airborne CO$_2$.* With the intensified use of coal, oil, and natural gas by both industrialized and Third World nations, some projections indicated a further 10 to 20 percent increase over present atmospheric CO$_2$ concentrations by the year 2000 and a 100 percent increase by the middle of the next century. But, as noted by Keeling, "to predict correctly future atmospheric CO$_2$ concentrations it is essential first to establish from past variations the factors which determine the fraction of CO$_2$ from combustion (industrial CO$_2$) which remains airborne"— the so-called *airborne fraction*. [28]

The Mauna Loa observations cited in Figure 8.1 suggest that the increase in atmospheric CO$_2$ concentration is roughly equivalent to half the CO$_2$ injected into the atmosphere from fossil fuel burning. The other, missing half has gone into some kinds of CO$_2$ sinks. This estimate is derived from a comparison of data on fossil fuel burning since 1958 and the Mauna Loa atmospheric CO$_2$ data.

As you will recall, plants give off carbon dioxide by respiration when alive and by decay after death. The seasons mark the cyclical nature of the biosphere, which affects the level of CO$_2$ in the atmosphere. In spring the so-called *seasonal biosphere* expands, taking up CO$_2$ faster than decay and respiration can give it back. In fall and winter, respiration and decay exceed photosynthesis, and CO$_2$ builds up again in the atmosphere. However, superimposed on these cyclical seasonal fluctuations is the long-term trend in CO$_2$ rise charted in Figure 8.1. Cutting down forests for fuel use or burning forests for land-clearing—activities that take place in many tropical areas—releases stored-up carbon from the trees into the atmosphere. Whether the net effect of biospheric destruction versus enhanced photosynthesis makes the biosphere a source or sink of CO$_2$ has become a topic of a growing debate. The primary uncer-

---

*The 15 percent increase assumes a preindustrial CO$_2$ concentration of 295 ppm and the 30 percent figure assumes a 260 ppm figure. By "preindustrial" is meant CO$_2$ levels about 1850. Preindustrial is really a poor word, since recent studies suggest that the value of CO$_2$ concentration over the nineteenth century alone has varied by many tens of parts per million. Therefore, it would be far better if people discussing pre-twentieth century levels of CO$_2$ specified a time series of CO$_2$ concentrations along with the dates they believe those concentrations occurred (see, for example, the editorial by Schneider, S. H., 1983, *Climatic Change 5*).

tainty can be traced to different opinions over estimates of globally averaged rates of deforestation and regrowth.

The Biosphere as Source or Sink:

Biologists versus Oceanographers   George Woodwell of the Marine Biological Laboratory in Woods Hole and several biologist colleagues estimated in 1978 that over the previous decade people had been denuding forests at the rate of about 1 to 2 percent per year.[29] They estimated the amount of carbon stored in these trees is roughly equal to that stored in the atmosphere (a little more than 700 billion metric tons). Thus, given this mass of stored carbon and this rate of burning, humans produced as much CO_2 by tampering with the biological reservoir as they did by burning fossil fuel (about 5 billion metric tons per year in 1980). If this were so, then much less than half of all the human-produced CO_2 was accounted for by the Mauna Loa measurements of atmospheric CO_2. In fact, only about 25 percent of the total injected anthropogenic CO_2 makes up the airborne fraction *if* the biospheric source was as large as the fossil fuel source of CO_2 since 1958. Hence, a full 75 percent of the CO_2 generated by man would have been taken up by a sink as yet unidentified. The biologists argued that the sink was probably the oceans.

Chemical oceanographers such as Wallace Broecker and Taro Takahashi at Lamont-Doherty did not agree with those biologists who view the oceans as the obvious sink. They argued that the oceans are incapable of absorbing the amount of CO_2 that would be released by biosphere destruction as large as Woodwell and colleagues estimated. Citing evidence obtained in what may seem to be a surprising way, Broecker and colleagues estimated the ocean uptake of CO_2 by tracing the oceans' absorption of radioactive fallout from the extensive nuclear bomb testing that took place in the early 1960s.[30] By examining profiles of the radioactive isotopes carbon-14 and tritium in the oceans in the early 1970s, they estimated the rate at which upper and lower oceanic waters mix. This mixing rate is a major factor in determining the rate at which atmospheric CO_2 can be taken up by the oceans.

The oceanographers also argued that deforestation rates are poorly known and that biologists who proposed the very large oceanic-sink theory based on 1 to 2 percent deforestation rates relied on only a few questionable reports from heavily deforested areas in order to estimate global values of biological origin CO_2.

These questionable reports then led to an overly high estimate. At times in the late 1970s the argument grew bitter.[31] The biologists countered that the oceanographers had overlooked the possibility of unknown sinks such as expanding midlatitude forests.[32]

However, a few years after the biologist-oceanographer controversy began, evidence suggested that the Woodwell-led biologists and the Broecker group of oceanographers were both at least partially right.* Wolfgang Seiler and Paul Crutzen, atmospheric chemists now at the Max Planck Institute for Chemistry in Mainz, West Germany, identified a potentially large missing sink: charcoal, the simplest form of carbon. A log or tree that is burned is not wholly consumed. Much of the wood remains as unburned matter and charcoal, carbon in its uncombined elemental form, C. Charcoal is relatively stable in the environment, and is not readily oxidized to CO_2. Thus, these researchers argued, one significant disagreement between the biologists' and the oceanographers' estimates of biospheric CO_2 injections might be accounted for by the charcoal sink. However, Seiler and Crutzen admitted that their data were poor. They tried to account for this by picking a range of values for factors such as forest regrowth in midlatitudes and tropical deforestation. Their range of estimates suggests that the biosphere could be either a source *or* a sink of up to 40 percent of the CO_2 produced annually by fossil fuels over the past decade or so.[34]

There are other ways to estimate the relative CO_2 contributions of the biosphere and fossil fuels besides the very difficult and expensive direct measurement of the rates of change in global biomass. Carbon-14 is virtually absent in fossil fuels, since the half life of C^{14} is about 5000 years and none is left when CO_2 is released by combustion. Indeed, the C^{14} to C^{12} ratio of the atmosphere has been dropping steadily since the industrial revolution, evidence that the atmospheric CO_2 reservoir is being filled with C^{14}-depleted fossil fuel products (this process is known as the *Suess effect* after its discoverer, Hans Suess of the Scripps Institution of Oceanography). But there is a stable carbon isotope C^{13} present in the air, and to a lesser extent in trees and fossil fuels. Trees discriminate against C^{13} during photosynthesis, so there is relatively less of it relative to C^{12} in

---

*And the biologists versus the oceanographers is not the only bitter conflict over the relative role of the biosphere in the CO_2 picture. Following a major report on deforestation by environmental consultant Norman Myers, the debate over the amount and implications of deforestation became even more acrid at times among disputing biologists.[33]

plants than in the air. Because of this *fractionation* of C^{13} relative to C^{12} in trees and fossil fuels and because of the Suess effect, it may be possible to reconstruct from a chronology of tree rings a history of fossil fuel versus biospheric injections of CO_2 over the past century or two. Minze Stuiver, a University of Washington geochemist, looked at the ratio of C^{13} to C^{12} and C^{14} to C^{12} in tree rings.[35] His results suggested that the extensive deforestation that took place during the nineteenth century in the midlatitudes could have increased atmospheric CO_2 by some 40 ppm.* However, Stuiver only examined C^{14} and C^{13} amounts in a handful of trees, and this very complex and uncertain technique requires the analysis of hundreds of samples. It will take many more tests to establish these results as valid.[36]

Other Factors Affecting the Biospheric Contribution

Another factor is the contribution of CO_2 from biospheric factors other than trees. Although the biggest living biotic reservoir of carbon is trees, they are not the largest biospheric pool of carbon. There is an estimated two to three times as much carbon in soil humus — derived from dead organic matter such as fallen leaves or dead roots or branches and tree trunks—than in living trees or in the atmosphere itself. When forests are cleared and the soil is exposed, it is likely that the rate increases at which humus oxidizes and releases CO_2. The rate can be increased by plowing for agriculture. On the other hand, CO_2 is sequestered when the stubble of dead crops is plowed back, thereby increasing dead organic soil matter. Further complicating the picture are chemical soil sterilizers, added to eliminate pests.† These chemicals also kill microorganisms and other organic recyclers, whose deaths permit a buildup of undecayed organic matter, thereby locking up carbon. Trying to estimate the magnitude of the humus contribution to atmospheric CO_2 is also difficult.[41]

---

*As this buildup phase of atmospheric CO_2 coincided with the end of the Little Ice Age, one might even argue that CO_2 increase from deforestation contributed to that ending.

†Other factors that affect the biospheric sink-or-source question are possible feedback mechanisms between CO_2-induced climatic changes and the biosphere. Environmental scientist Gordon MacDonald suggested that permafrost (permanently frozen ground below the tundra in subpolar regions) probably contains a large reservoir of organic matter.[37] If a warm climate thawed the permafrost, a vast amount of carbon-rich deposits would be exposed to potentially rapid oxidation, further enhancing CO_2 production.[38] Study on this aspect of the problem is just beginning; it is possible that the compound methane hydrate now locked in oceanic

**Carbon Cycle Models
and the Airborne Fraction**   To account quantitatively for the stocks and flows of carbon among atmospheric, biospheric, oceanic, and crustal reservoirs, scientists construct mathematical models of the carbon cycle. In order to project future CO_2
concentrations, these models start with some initial CO_2 concentration and a scenario of CO_2 injected into the atmosphere. Then, they
compute rates of CO_2 exchanges between air and sea, upper and
lower oceans, air and land plants, sea and marine plants, marine life,
oceanic sediments, soils, and so on. Inasmuch as each of these
exchanges is not reliably known, especially if the climate changes,
considerable uncertainty must accompany any carbon cycle model
results.[42]

Yet, despite all the uncertainties, CO_2 continues to build in the
atmosphere as if roughly half the injected fossil fuel carbon stayed
airborne. Groups of experts continue to project CO_2 increases
based on the assumption of "airborne fraction of the total emissions to be 40 to 55 percent."[43] Conflicting models and missing data
notwithstanding, it would be surprising if this mere educated guess
turns out to be more than 10 percent too high or too low over the
next several decades.*

---

sediments could release vast quantities of CO_2 should the oceans warm up by a few
degrees.[39] Another issue is the case for the so-called *negative greenhouse effect,* in which
increased blooms of algae induced by increased CO_2 would "muddy" the oceanic
surface waters, increase their albedo, and thereby *cool* the climate.[40] However, many
marine biologists consider this to be highly speculative, since CO_2 is not the principal limiting nutrient of most plankton blooms.
*Perhaps the best summary and the most consistent place to begin an in-depth study
of various debates over carbon cycle issues is W. C. Clark (ed.), *Carbon Dioxide
Review:1982* (New York: Oxford University Press). The first chapter by William
Clark and his associates at the Institute for Energy Analysis (IEA) in Oak Ridge,
Tennessee, collects into one place most of the significant references on many CO_2
issues, including carbon cycle modeling. The IEA authors note that major disagreements, like those between Broecker and Woodwell in the mid-1970s, have gradually
toned down, with Woodwell and colleagues suggesting in 1982 that biospheric
alterations by human activities would have been responsible for some 1.8 to 4.7
billion metric tons of CO_2 injected since 1970, well below the 20-billion-ton upper
limit estimate he and his colleagues made five years earlier. However, as the Clark
chapter notes, many researchers are beginning to agree that from about 1850 to
1950, the biospheric component of CO_2 injected was about 1 billion metric tons or
so per year, a rate greater than fossil fuel CO_2 emissions before World War II. This
means that either the airborne fraction has been considerably less than the 50
percent figure frequently cited, or the so-called "preindustrial" CO_2 concentration
in 1850 was below the 290 to 300 ppm level typically assumed. Clark and his
colleagues speculate (p. 16) that "the present airborne fraction is most likely near

Behavioral Assumptions
Underlying CO_2 Projections

The same meeting of experts that settled on an assumed airborne fraction of 40 to 55 percent used these numbers to project future atmospheric CO_2 concentrations: "the atmospheric CO_2 concentration in 2025 will be between 410 ppm and 490 ppm with a most likely value of 450 ppm."[45] Making such a projection takes more than assumptions about the workings of the carbon cycle that lead to an airborne fraction. It also takes assumptions about how much and what kinds of fossil fuels will be consumed far into the future.

Early Fossil
Energy Use Extrapolations

Anticipating future energy use or deforestation rates requires that we know how people will behave in the future—for example, what their energy appetite will be. Such behavioral assumptions are usually based on projections of growth rates and per capita levels of energy use and land use—that is, on how much and in what way we can be expected to alter the earth's surface and consume its fossil fuels based on past and present rates. Hence, the debate over future carbon dioxide levels and climate change is based on how we assume people will alter the natural carbon cycle in the future.

Ralph Rotty, a researcher at the Institute for Energy Analysis in Oak Ridge, Tennessee, has made several projections about future energy use, estimates he periodically revises. In 1974, Rotty's pie chart (see Figure 8.2a) indicated that the developed countries produced some 79 percent of the CO_2 released (note that the United States accounted for 27 percent of the total amount), while the developing nations and centrally planned Asia (that is, People's Republic of China) accounted for only 21 percent. He projected that by 2025, owing to assumed increasing populations and more eco-

---

0.4." While the IEA scientists are less willing to estimate a preindustrial CO_2 level, others are not. G. Stanhill of the Agricultural Research Organization in Bet Dagan, Israel, re-examined old French CO_2 measurements of the late nineteenth century and concluded cautiously that "an increase of approximately ten percent took place in the CO_2 concentration of the atmosphere during the final quarter of the nineteenth century," rising from about 280 ppm in 1877. More recent evidence from CO_2 in gas bubbles trapped in ice cores suggests an 1850 value of about 260 ppm.[44]

nomic power, the developing countries and China would dramatically increase their fossil fuel use to half the total CO_2 produced (see Figure 8.2b). (In subsequent projections Rotty first increased, then substantially reduced, these numbers.[46]) For these analyses Rotty assumed that up to 2025 the fraction of CO_2 that was airborne would be about 50 percent and that worldwide use of non-fossil-fuel-energy technologies such as nuclear or solar power would be small.

However, other authors have derived different estimates. In 1971, energy specialists Alvin Weinberg and R. P. Hammond projected an A.D. 2075 world of 10 billion people consuming at twice the present U.S. per capita energy consumption level—which is today five times greater than the world average level.[47] This scenario implies a staggering twenty-five-fold increase in world energy use over the present (compared to Rotty's three- to fourfold increase scenarios). And much of this energy and its associated pollution projected by Weinberg and his colleagues for 2075 would be produced by the populous Third World nations. Ten years later a very different view was emerging. For example, Robert Schware, at the National Center for Atmospheric Research, and Edward Friedman, of the MITRE Corporation, have calculated that for the developing nations to produce the lion's share of airborne CO_2—50 percent or more—by the middle of the next century, they would have to maintain an average energy growth rate of more than 6 percent while the developed nations held their growth at 2 percent. Schware and Friedman argue that although some developing nations have actually surpassed this growth rate in the past, the 6 percent level will be increasingly difficult to sustain, given the economic outlook for the next several decades.[48]

The Market Penetration Law Wild projections, like those for 20 to 30 times more energy than at present being used worldwide before the end of the next century, are often based on very optimistic assumptions of economic growth, technological progress, world cooperation, and environmental quality. While considerable fossil fuel resources are envisioned in such projections, this long-term energy-profligate future is seen as largely nuclear— a view now held by very few energy analysts, including most of those who made such bold projections a decade earlier. But regardless of how much total energy demand is projected to the end of the twenty-first century, for the next fifty years or so nearly all analysts believe that CO_2-producing fossil fuels will be the primary energy

315

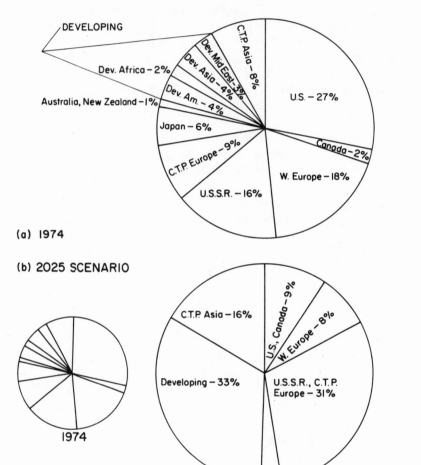

(a) 1974

(b) 2025 SCENARIO

DEVELOPING

C.T.P. Asia – 8%

Dev. Mid East – 3%

Dev. Asia – 4%

Dev. Africa – 2%

Dev. Am. – 4%

Australia, New Zealand – 1%

Japan – 6%

C.T.P. Europe – 9%

U.S.S.R. – 16%

U.S. – 27%

Canada – 2%

W. Europe – 18%

1974

C.T.P. Asia – 16%

U.S., Canada – 9%

W. Europe – 8%

Developing – 33%

U.S.S.R., C.T.P. Europe – 31%

Japan, Australia – 3%

2025

Figure 8.2

Carbon dioxide produced by the burning of fossil fuels is broken down by country or region for (a) 1974 and (b) a scenario for the year A.D. 2025. C.T.P. represents the words centrally planned (in other words, socialist) economies; Dev means developing countries. This projection by energy analyst Ralph Rotty was made in 1977, and the lower part of the figure shows that in his estimation at that time Third World countries (C.T.P. Asia and developing) would account for roughly half the fossil-fuel-produced CO_2 in 2025, whereas in 1974 they accounted for only 21 percent of the world total

production. These typical projections are based on behavioral assumptions regarding population and economic growth that have been challenged by many, including Rotty himself, since they were made in 1977. In the 2025 scenario the relative area of each "pie" for 1974 and 2025 is proportional to the amount of CO_2 produced, with the 2025 total being some four times greater than the 1974 total in Rotty's scenario. [Source: R. M. Rotty, 1978, The atmospheric CO_2 consequences of heavy dependence on coal, in Jill Williams (ed.), Carbon Dioxide, Climate and Society *(Oxford: Pergamon Press), p. 267.]*

source. One reason is a seeming economic law characteristic of energy system development over the past two hundred years. It is known as the *Market Penetration Law,* and it was first applied to the fossil-fuel-burning issue by the International Institute for Applied Systems Analysis analyst Cesare Marchetti.[49] The idea is simply that the economic lifetime of any single energy supply system (or any other industry or product for that matter) is long enough that it takes a characteristic time to replace that system, even after the advent of a new technology. For example, it took almost one hundred years for wood to lose 50 percent of its hold on the energy supply market to coal, which lost much of its share to oil over some fifty years, with natural gas then beginning some two decades later to displace much of oil's share of the market. If the market penetration time for a new energy source technology to replace 50 percent of existing ones is at least fifty years, then it will be very difficult to avoid a significant CO_2 buildup over the next fifty years by substituting new energy technologies—assuming of course that there are any supply sources practically capable of producing the amount of energy usually projected.[50]

Although the market penetration law seems to indicate that we must either act now or learn how to live with the pollutants from fossil fuel energy sources for at least the next fifty years, the situation is not necessarily inevitable. For instance, the very concept is entitled *market* penetration, which carries the implicit assumption of market economics. To be sure, market economics was the predominate system in operation over the past two centuries from which the data were gathered to arrive at the fifty- to one-hundred-year energy system market penetration time. But who can prove that market economics will govern all important future energy supply decisions? Strategic concerns, like minimizing nations' vulnerability to cartels such as OPEC, could intervene and lead to nonmarket interventions that totally override the energy supply system market penetration law over the next fifty years. Also, potential technological breakthroughs in both energy supply and demand technologies could well rapidly alter the picture. We do not doubt that fossil fuels will be a significant part of the energy supply picture for at least several more decades, but we do believe that willful actions by concerned nations can overwhelm any historically derived market penetration characteristics of world economic systems. A chief uncertainty in this context is whether nations will perceive the CO_2 problem as a threat sufficiently ominous to intervene in the normal market process to speed the phasing out of CO_2-producing fossil fuels. It is doubtful that this is likely to be a widespread occurrence, at least until people perceive some unmistakable and unpleasant signs of CO_2-induced effects.

The Carbon Wealth of Nations   Most resource estimates suggest that for us to create a serious CO_2 problem—say, a doubling of current atmospheric concentration—we will have to make a very substantial use of coal resources.* Can coal resources be exploited at the levels of energy growth projected by Rotty in Figure 8.2b? Jesse Ausubel, an economist then at the International Institute of Applied Systems Analysis in Austria, examined this question, focusing on the scale of development needed to fulfill the projected atmospheric CO_2 burden.[51] In the United States, for example, matching the Rotty projection might involve mining and burning 3 billion tons of coal each year—nearly five times the 1978 United States production, involving an enormous mining effort. Expanding the coal industry to this point could well be impossible owing to water, labor, transportation, or other environmental constraints (for example, acid rain) before CO_2 itself becomes an obviously limiting factor.

According to Ausubel, there is a second major reason to doubt the feasibility of a very high level of atmospheric carbon in the

*Important effects could occur at lesser amounts of CO_2 increase, but the ubiquitous "doubling" used by many scientists in CO_2 studies will suffice for the arguments in this section.

future: a global coal market, comparable to the current oil market, would have to develop. An overwhelming proportion of the world's coal supplies are concentrated in fewer than ten countries, and primarily in the USSR, the United States, and China. It is questionable whether these countries will be able to mine beyond their large domestic needs and muster substantial capacity for an export market. Moreover, potential coal customers might not like being dependent on these few energy giants (a future COPEC?) any more than most oil-importing countries today like their dependence on OPEC.

The very uneven distribution of carbon wealth can give us yet another perspective on Rotty's figure (Figure 8.2b). According to many present estimates, most less-developed countries (LDCs) have limited domestic supplies of carbon fuels (that is, too few to cause a doubling or more of CO_2). Thus, a scenario in which the LDCs are major emitters implies that these countries will also be major importers of foreign coal. Will these countries have enough exportable products to exchange for the amounts of coal to be used, according to the projections? Ausubel is understandably skeptical.

Whether coal will be available is not the only important factor in projecting future fossil fuel demand. Energy price is a major determinant. For example, if research and development of solar energy technologies continue to grow and bear results, the price of this renewable energy source will become increasingly competitive and the whole future energy supply picture will change. Coal could be priced out of the market.

The Efficiency Factor   According to Amory Lovins, what is more likely to curb future fossil fuel use—even in the developed countries with abundant resources—is the economic factor of price-induced efficiency. Lovins is an energy analyst who gained international attention by comparing so-called "hard" and "soft" alternative energy-supply options.[52] The viability of energy end use efficiency as a damper on CO_2 buildup has been argued by many, but perhaps most forcefully by Lovins. Along with colleagues L. Hunter Lovins, Florentine Krause, and Wilfrid Bach, Lovins conducted a highly detailed study whose very title suggests that the CO_2 problem need never reach its often-projected proportions: *Least-Cost Energy: Solving the CO_2 Problem.*[53] The Lovins team believes that the frequently forecast long-term CO_2 buildup can be virtually averted without draconian political measures or economic hardships. In fact, they argue that their path would also provide society with a positive economic benefit. This would occur simply by the cost-effective practice of price-induced energy end use efficiency; in a word: conservation. They offer a stinging critique of the energy use projections of an International Institute for Applied Systems Analysis study.[54] This widely cited (and also highly detailed) IIASA effort projects a many-fold increase in total world energy use over the next century—much of it fossil fuel based. (Such projections have been used by Rotty and others in CO_2 emission scenarios.) To such projections the Lovins team responds that "economically efficient energy investments will at least hold constant, and probably reduce the world rate of burning fossil fuel, starting immediately, even assuming rapid worldwide economic growth and complete industrialization of the developing countries."[55]

If, as *Least-Cost Energy* claims, conservation is already cost-effective relative to the development of new coal or nuclear power plants, then one might wonder why investment in such end use efficiency isn't catching on even faster. Lovins and his colleagues do face this question, and they come up with many explanations. One of the principal ones they cite is "substantial subsidies, in many subtle forms and often unevenly distributed, to make energy look cheaper than it really is." In the United States, for example, where at least some hard data on subsidies exist, Lovins and colleagues contend that current tax and price subsidies "total over $100 billion per year—enough to reduce the average energy price by over a third and nuclear electricity price by over half." If the government policies that create and maintain such hidden props behind the seeming economic advantage of the centralized hard energy systems were eliminated, the authors believe that cost-effective investments in efficient energy use by individual users would proliferate.* This would lead to an even more dramatic reduction in energy growth rates than the reduction that took place in the 1970s and would also lead to a low-climatic-risk energy future.

To examine how drastically energy use forecasts were scaled down over the 1970s, Lovins and his colleagues traced the evolution of his projections and those of his critics.[57] In 1970, Lovins estimated

---

*This point had, ironically, already been made by Alvin Weinberg, a long-time proponent of nuclear energy and a frequent critic of Lovins. In a 1979 conference paper, Weinberg wrote that the growth of nuclear energy was as rapid as it was "because it was subsidized—by the government in the form of support for R and D and demonstrations, by reactor vendors who in aggregate in the United States have lost perhaps one billion dollars on the reactor business."[56]

U.S. energy demand in 2000 would be some 166 percent over what was then being used. "Conventional wisdom" suggested energy demand in 2000 A.D. would be more than twice the 1970 energy use. But because of energy price increases, demand reduction, and improved end use efficiency that occurred during the 1970s, projections for future energy use decreased. In 1980, however, the traditionally bold projectors such as Exxon forecast U.S. energy use in 2000 to be only slightly above the present and well below Lovins's 1972 projection. Meanwhile, Lovins now projects the U.S. demand to be well *below* present usage. In essence, the Lovins team argues for decentralized, market-oriented, individual energy-related decisions as the preferred policy. Of course, their energy policy views reflect their values on how societies should be organized. Others, like some of the IIASA study authors, it is safe to assume, would challenge *Least-Cost Energy* on some factual and value grounds. For instance, in an otherwise generally favorable review of *Least-Cost Energy*, Jesse Ausubel nonetheless cautioned that:

> Different energy experts have different sets of facts, not only differing interpretations of the same facts, and the soft path people have a lot more facts than they used to. But they are certainly not the only facts in the analysis of the soft path. For example, around the same time as the publication of this book the National Research Council (1981) published a supplement to its report on *Energy for Rural Development: Renewable Resources and Alternative Technologies for Developing Countries*, and it contains decidedly less encouraging numbers and inferences. *Least-Cost Energy*, like all the other tracts in the energy wars, is said to be based on the "best available technical evidence," but to this reviewer it seemed that this often meant "best for making our case."[58]

We will not—indeed cannot—resolve here the wide differences in both facts and values among what Ausubel calls the warring "energy tribes."[59] But the graphs shown in Figure 8.3 demonstrate how their divergent projections of energy growth rates lead to radically different CO_2 futures. The figure emphasizes the basic importance of economic assumptions in projecting CO_2 increases. These radically divergent curves in Figure 8.3 reflect the gulf that separates the thinking of some of those projecting future energy demands of CO_2 buildup. A continuing debate is obviously in order to help clarify their differences.

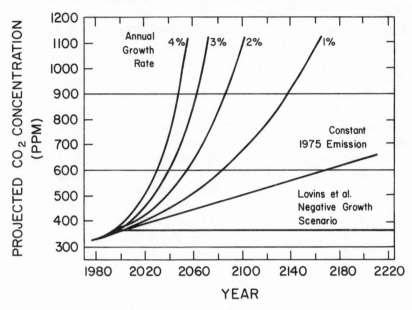

Figure 8.3

The extent to which CO_2-induced climatic change will prove significant in the future depends, of course, on the rate of injection of CO_2 into the atmosphere. This depends, in turn, on behavioral assumptions as to how much fossil fuel burning will take place. (This graph neglects biospheric effects.) Since the end of World War II, a world energy growth rate of about 5.3 percent occurred until the mid-1970s, the time of the OPEC price hikes. Rates have come down substantially since then. The figure shows projected CO_2 concentrations for different annual growth rates in fossil energy use, including the assumption that no increase in fossil energy use occurs (constant 1975 emission) and even a "negative growth scenario" in which energy growth after 1985 is assumed to be reduced by a fixed amount [0.2 terra watts (TW), which is about 2 percent of present demand] each year. [Source: A. B. Lovins, L. H. Lovins, F. Krause, and W. Bach, Least-Cost Energy: Solving the CO_2 Problem *(Andover: Brick House), p. 10.]*

But economic and engineering considerations are not the only uncertain behavioral assumptions underlying CO_2-increase projections. We need to consider still more factors in our estimates of future energy demands. A major one is food availability. If population pressures and poor agricultural development continue to create frequent food shortages in parts of the Third World—a likely prospect over the next several decades—then these countries will be forced to import food to alleviate hunger and malnutrition, as many already do. Since food imports come at the cost of precious foreign currency reserves, how will the poorest nations ever afford to import large quantities of both food and coal?* A breakthrough in food-producing techniques in the Third World or a dramatic reduction in population growth rates could alter this otherwise bleak prospect, but such developments are hardly guaranteed. In any case, it would be foolish to plan on them as certainties.

It is clear by now that the CO_2 problem is linked to the ways in which economics, energy production and end use technology, food production, and even international peace and cooperation will evolve into the twenty-first century and beyond. It is little wonder, then, that the long-term seriousness of the CO_2 question is an issue of hot debate. Ironically, when a group of experts at an international conference in 1978 was confronted by these staggering uncertainties, they simply stated that the best projection they could muster for the next twenty years or so was simply an extrapolation of the CO_2 increases recorded at Mauna Loa.[60] So far, they appear reasonable. But whether such extrapolations—which Lovins labeled as forecasts made "largely by the mechanical application of a straight edge to semilogarithmic graph paper"—will prove valid for much more than a decade or so remains to be seen. Still, some atmospheric researchers continue to repeat the early extrapolations.†
We hope that the major uncertainties inherent in CO_2 projections soon become common knowledge among atmospheric researchers, and that research to narrow these uncertainties in behavioral projections takes its place as an equal partner with parallel efforts by

---

*Computer simulation of future population, food, and economic trends with a so-called "world model" has been performed by Diana Liverman at the National Center for Atmospheric Research (Liverman, D., 1983, *The Use of a Simulation Model in Assessing the Impacts of Climate on the World Food System*, Ph.D. Thesis, Department of Geography, University of California, Los Angeles). Liverman found direct relationships among food and energy prices and imports and starvation deaths in the poorest Third World countries. Although the simulation skill of this model was deemed questionable, it seemed likely that the sensitivity of starvation rates in poor countries to both food and energy price and their availability is valid and important.

†The September 1981 (Vol. 1, No. 4) newsletter of the Australian Academy of Science, Educational Supplement on carbon dioxide is one such example. It was reporting on a statement prepared by Dr. G. B. Tucker for the Academy on CO_2 and climate. One paragraph in the newsletter states "It is now possible to say with some confidence that carbon dioxide levels would double their 1978 value, reaching about 680 ppm, sometime between 2030 and 2080 depending on net world energy strategies and fossil fuel conservation schemes adopted." Although some range of uncertainty is stated, it clearly is well inside the extreme ranges suggested as plausible by many energy analysts (see Figure 8.3).

natural scientists to elucidate the workings of the carbon cycle or the climatic system.*

Climatic Effects of CO_2 Increases

To begin our consideration of the projected effects of a CO_2 increase in the atmosphere, we restate the by now familiar facts that form the basis of the problem. CO_2 is part of the greenhouse effect, which warms the earth's surface. In the Altithermal, when climate—at least in summer—was probably a few degrees warmer, the prairie pushed eastward across the Mississippi River and deep into the Corn Belt. Clearly, this would pose a problem for agriculture today. This condition, you recall from Chapter 3, has been called the "prairie peninsula."

Warm-Earth Analogs

The aridity evidenced in fossil remains in the Sand Hills of Nebraska[61] or the Prairie Peninsula during the late Altithermal is by no means typical of global conditions at that time. As Sarnthein's dune maps (shown in Figure 2.5c) suggest, much of what is semiarid land today was wetter 6000 years ago. Wetter climate could improve agriculture in these regions—*provided* increased flooding or soil erosion potential were controlled.

The Altithermal Analog

Several years ago, climatologist William Kellogg of the National Center for Atmospheric Research recognized the potential importance of the Altithermal as a *warm-earth analog* in estimating any regional effects of future CO_2 increases.[62] He surveyed some of the paleoclimatic literature and compiled a much-cited map showing regions that he found to be wetter or drier in the Altithermal than at present. Kellogg's work prompted anthropologist and geographer Karl Butzer of the University of Chicago to re-examine proxy paleoclimatic evidence and

*See the recent U.S. National Academy of Sciences report (*Changing Climate: Report of the Carbon Dioxide Assessment Committee*, 1983, National Research Council [Washington, D.C.: National Academy Press]); in particular, see the review by Jesse Ausubel and William Nordhaus of previous CO_2 future projections; see also the new calculations by economists Nordhaus and colleague G. Yohe, which show the importance of different economic assumptions on future CO_2 projections.

construct his own map.[63] More recently, Kellogg combined these two maps onto a single figure showing areas of disagreement and agreement.[64] Kellogg's combined map appears here as Figure 8.4. Although the two researchers' reconstructions do not clearly agree over most of the world—perhaps not surprisingly, given the tentative climatic nature of proxy evidences, as seen in Chapter 4—they do basically agree on two points: drier central North American plains and wetter subtropics. Just because the Kellogg or Butzer maps agree on some climatic patterns for some regions, however, does not imply that these regions of agreement are necessarily representative of true Altithermal conditions. Indeed, in Chapter 3 we noted that the Altithermal was not a time of uniform warmth, but rather saw variable periods of climatic change in different phases. On the whole, though, summers do appear to have generally been warmer. But even if the Kellogg-Butzer maps are correct Altithermal reconstructions, they may not be valid analogs to CO_2-induced warmth, since the cause of the Altithermal was probably not more CO_2. And there is reason to believe that the cause was something else. John Kutzbach and Betty Otto-Bliesner of the University of Wisconsin developed a computer model that reproduced the summer warmth of the early Holocene with a very different mechanism.[65] Therefore, we cannot argue convincingly that a global warming of similar magnitude to Altithermal proxies induced by burning fossil fuels would result in regional climatic shifts similar to Figure 8.4—assuming, of course, we could know reliably what Altithermal seasonal and regional climatic patterns actually were.*

Warm-Year Analogs
in the Twentieth Century
The Altithermal is not the only empirical analogy for a warm earth. Several scientists have looked at a number of warm years in the past half-century, checking to see if any consistent or unusual patterns existed.[67]

Although there is considerable disagreement among the various patterns of wet and dry found by different scientists, the mid-North American dryness seems a principal common feature, as noted in a review paper by Kellogg.[68] However, three difficulties must be kept in mind. First, as Jill Williams pointed out, no globally uniform patterns emerge. "Even when the arctic area is warm, there are circulation changes such that large coherent anomalies occur else-

---

*I have given a detailed discussion of the reliability of Altithermal reconstruction and its utility as an analogy to CO_2 increases elsewhere.[66]

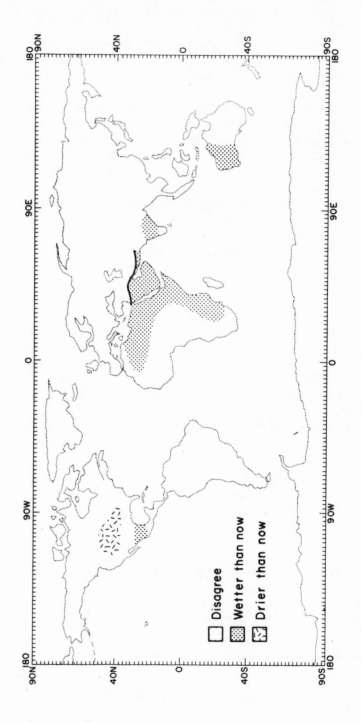

Disagree

Wetter than now

Drier than now

Figure 8.4

In the absence of direct evidence of how a CO_2-induced climatic warming might affect regional distribution of aridity or increased wetness, William Kellogg looked to the Altithermal, some 5000 to 9000 years ago, when (according to inferences made from a number of climatic proxies) summer temperatures were apparently a few degrees warmer than at present. While probably not caused by CO_2, the results he mapped could provide warm-earth analogies. Anthropologist Karl Butzer also produced such a map, and Kellogg combined onto another map (seen here) the areas of agreement and disagreement between these two Altithermal interpretations. Note that although the authors' reconstructions disagree over most of the land area, they do agree that there was increased dryness in central North America and increased wetness in parts of tropical and subtropical Africa, Asia, and Australia. Agreement between Kellogg and Butzer does not, of course, necessarily imply correctness, as there is a significant possibility that these maps could agree or disagree by chance. [Source: W. W. Kellogg and R. Schware, 1981, Climate Change and Society: Consequences of Increasing Atmospheric Carbon Dioxide *(Boulder: Westview Press), figure C.3.]*

where, with some regions warming and some cooling." Second, the causes of these sporadic warm years of our century are not CO_2 increases, since they are interleaved between cooler and normal years. Thus, a CO_2-induced warming will not necessarily result in similar seasonal or regional patterns of warmer, cooler, wetter, or drier climates, since CO_2 increase from human activities is an external forcing and individual warm years of the twentieth century could well be internally caused rather than externally forced.[69] Finally, there is some difficulty in establishing the statistical significance of these maps.[70]

"Reliable predictions of the potential impact of human activities on climate," Jill Williams wrote, "will only be made when a better understanding of the mechanisms of climatic change is achieved."[71] To help clarify such mechanisms, we can look at the most physically comprehensive climatic models, which include enough detail to resolve regional climatic variations in temperature or rainfall. Let's turn, then, to such climatic models and ask both what they predict and how well their predictions of CO_2-induced changes match with empirical analogs of a warmer earth.

Climate-Model Predictions

In Chapter 6 we noted that in the absence of direct evidence that past CO_2 concentrations were very different from today's levels, we have no choice but to use mathematical models to estimate potential effects of large future CO_2 increases. A hierarchy of models of varying complexity has been used by many different scientists to estimate the sensitivity of the climate to CO_2 increases, and most results for the overall global climatic effects of a CO_2 doubling tend to agree within about a 50 percent margin—except for a very few outliers, believed by most climate modelers to be based on faulty reasoning or unlikely assumptions as follows. (Nevertheless, the critics caused quite a flap for several years.)

The Idso Flap   The two best known public doubters are Reginald Newell at MIT and Sherwood Idso of the U.S. Department of Agriculture's Water Conservation Laboratory in Phoenix, Arizona.[72] Both attempted to derive empirical "response functions" through which they could scale how the climatic system responded to some known non-CO_2 forcing.* Whereas most "consensus models" predict a global temperature rise in steady state of some 1.5° to 4.0°C (2.7° to 7.2°F) for a fixed CO_2 doubling,[74] Idso in particular insists most vehemently that his "natural experiments" prove the consensus model CO_2 warming predictions to be an order of magnitude (that is, a factor of about 10) too high. However, like many inventors of perpetual motion machines, Idso has, I believe, faltered in his analyses of long-term, global climatic response to CO_2 by neglecting some categories of energy flows and storages. For example, in one of his "natural experiments" Idso compares the difference between incoming solar radiation from winter to summer (ΔQ) and winter to summer temperature difference (ΔT). Typically, ΔQ is about 200 watts per square meter and ΔT is about 20°C.[75] So far, Idso had been keeping to his claim to abide only by results "based upon detailed observation of the real world," and not to believe "the results of most current numerical models of the atmosphere," which, he says, when applied to "the CO_2 problem are grossly in error."[76] However, Idso then did what all self-confessed theoretical modelers do: he made assumptions—in effect, he built a model—about the relationships between the variables he had measured. In this case he formed the ratio $\Delta T/\Delta Q$ obtained from the United States seasonal "natural experiment." He next *assumed* that this value (about 0.1 degrees C temperature change per watt per square meter of radiant energy change) is a general property of

*The idea is a good one, but it is not new, of course, as direct verification of climate-model response to external forcing is a standard practice of most climate modelers.[73]

nature and applies to a different experiment, namely, the global, equilibrium surface temperature warming from a doubling of CO_2.* With this assumption his work necessarily became theoretical, not experimental, although Idso constantly claims it is the latter. It is wrong to assume that $\Delta T/\Delta Q$ obtained from the short-term (seasonal) temperature response of a limited region (the United States) can be applied directly to a long-term (equilibrium), global problem like CO_2 doubling.[77]

Indeed, most of the numerical modelers that Idso urges to "look to the 'living laboratory' " already do work hard to verify their models against natural experiments like the seasonal cycle —and with considerable success.[78] In fact, modelers can reproduce Idso's results in their models by using Idso's assumptions. This success in simulation of seasonal extremes by state-of-the-art models is one of the principal reasons that most modelers feel their models' CO_2 predictions are not simply unverifiable wild speculations. (For the global equilibrium problem most modelers get a value of $\Delta T/\Delta Q$ about five to ten times larger than Idso's estimates.)

To criticisms that he only looked at short-term local phenomena, Idso offered another "natural experiment": the global greenhouse effect. In a formal written criticism of one of V. Ramanathan's papers[79]—an article that showed why Newell underestimated the global temperature effects of CO_2 increase—Idso attempted to show how much planetary surface temperature change (ΔT) would occur if the earth's entire atmosphere were somehow removed. He assumed that the removal caused a change in radiative forcing (ΔQ), which he calculated (theoretically, of course). Once again, he obtained "an empirical response function" $\Delta T/\Delta Q$ some five to ten

---

*The seasonal U.S. estimate of $\Delta T/\Delta Q$ is much smaller than the long-term global value for two reasons: (1) Because it takes decades before the temperature can approach its equilibrium value and a seasonal period isn't nearly an equilibrium response; and (2) it neglects the very large input of energy connected with winds which blow from the oceans to the continents and back to the oceans again, transporting vast quantities of heat and connecting the atmosphere over the land to the large heat capacities of the ocean. Indeed, in the summer in central U.S., for example, the mean temperature does not change much over July and August, not because a radiative equilibrium has been reached, but rather because the extra solar radiative heating which should continuously drive summer temperatures upward as the summer progresses is balanced by an export of heat from the middle of continents associated with horizontal winds blowing from west to east, connecting the air over the land to the oceans.

times smaller than is typical for most "consensus models." Ramanathan discussed a draft version of his formal reply to Idso's comment with me. The draft showed that the reason Idso obtained such a low estimate for his response function this time was that he calculated an inappropriate ΔQ by looking only at the energy change at the earth's surface. Idso essentially ignored the total change in radiative heating of the entire earth-atmosphere system that would occur if somehow the entire atmosphere and its greenhouse chemicals were removed. With the more proper calculation of ΔQ by Ramanathan, this "experiment" also corroborated values of $\Delta T/\Delta Q$ typically obtained from numerical models. Several weeks later Ramanathan told me with some dismay that Idso withdrew his formal comment after seeing Ramanathan's written reply. I wasn't surprised, as exactly the same chain of events happened a few months earlier to Starley Thompson and myself when Idso withdrew a formal comment on one of our papers in *Nature*[80] after seeing our written reply.

It is clear by now that I don't view the conflict between Idso and most climatic modelers over estimates of global equilibrium surface temperature increase from CO_2 doubling as "just another one of those debates among experts." Unfortunately, science writer John Gribbin bestowed this status to the disagreement in his 1982 book *Future Weather and the Greenhouse Effect.* The law of the conservation of energy is no longer a valid subject for expert debate. Those who misapply it are simply wrong; there is no other side. In my opinion, it has been convincingly shown that the neglect of horizontal heat flow between land and sea, omission of heat storage in the air and oceans, and failure to account for *total* atmosphere/surface energy budget have caused Newell's and Idso's low estimates of global, equilibrium sensitivity to a doubling of CO_2.* If the consensus models are wrong, the reasons have yet to be found.

We do, however, agree with the critics that tentative model assumptions demand empirical verification, and that more verification exercises are needed to determine the extent to which the consensus models are indeed correct. However, such comparisons between models and observations must be properly applied. For every Ptolemy there eventually comes a Copernicus. But for every Copernicus there are probably a thousand claimants.

*Newell and Dopplick's work should be distinguished from that of Idso, since the former authors did explicitly state in their paper that they ignored certain atmospheric processes that could have caused them to obtain a different result from most models. Indeed, this explanation is correct.

Regional CO$_2$-Induced

Climatic Predictions   Most models with latitudinal
resolution suggest that the predicted 2°C (3.6°F) or so global surface
temperature increases for a doubling of CO$_2$ would not be distributed uniformly around the globe. Nor would the annual average
increase be the same from one season to the next. Because of the
snow-and-ice albedo/temperature feedback mechanism (see Chapter 6), for example, it is likely that any CO$_2$-induced temperature
increases would be higher in polar and subpolar latitudes. Some
models suggest increases up to five times larger in some higher
latitudes in the Northern Hemisphere where sea ice could melt. If
sea ice melted around or in the Arctic Sea, winter temperatures
would climb to near freezing (0°C), some 30°C (54°F) higher than at
present in late winter. On the other hand, except for the spectacular
(and speculative) possibility of triggering a collapse of the West
Antarctic Ice Sheet—and a subsequent 5-meter (16.4-foot) or so
rise in sea level—it is unlikely that enough snow or ice would melt
in Antarctica to amplify the global temperature rise at the South
Pole.

The reason to stress that parts of the polar or subpolar latitudes
might warm up several times more than tropical latitudes is not just
to point out the potential for long-term changes in ice amounts and
sea levels. If the polar areas warmed up on average more than the
equator, then the equator-to-pole temperature contrast would be
reduced. Recall from Chapters 4 and 5 that this temperature difference is a principal driving force behind the atmospheric and oceanic
circulation patterns, and thus a major determinant of local and
regional climates. Therefore, potentially more important than a
global temperature rise of a degree or two would be a change of a
few degrees in horizontal temperature differences, for the latter
could lead to significant alterations of accustomed patterns of rainfall, sunshine, soil moisture, and so on.

What do those models with high spatial resolution suggest about
possible regional changes in temperature or rainfall given a CO$_2$
increase? The most widely quoted results are from a series of gener-
al-circulation model simulations conducted by Syukuro Manabe and
his co-workers at the Geophysical Fluid Dynamics Laboratory
(GFDL) in Princeton.[81] In this CO$_2$-warmed computer world, rainfall
increases nearly everywhere, but so does evaporation. However, in
the midlatitudes on land, evaporation increases more than precipitation, thereby creating a summer "dry zone." This pattern makes

an interesting parallel to the Prairie Peninsula found in Altithermal proxy records and the composite warm-earth analogs. Also of interest is the generally increased wetness in the tropics and subtropics —another general Altithermal expectation. The extratropical dryness is not found in all seasons, however. In spring, for example, high latitudes are wetter in these model runs, primarily because snowmelt occurs earlier in the year with CO_2-induced warming.

Equilibrium Versus Transient Models Most climate modelers, at least until recently, did not use a time-evolving scenario of atmospheric CO_2 increases (like those in Figure 8.3) to force their models. Rather, they computed the equilibrium response of their models to a fixed CO_2 increase—typically a doubling of the 1958 value. A state-of-the-art estimate for the equilibrium, global surface temperature rise given a CO_2 doubling is, as mentioned earlier, in the range of about 1.5° to 4.0°C (2.7° to 7.2°F). This is as large or larger than most proxies suggest for average Altithermal warming as compared to today. This magnitude of warming at global level explains why many climatologists have suggested that a CO_2 buildup could lead to a climatic change of potentially unprecedented proportions since the end of the last Ice Age. Moreover, any such changes would be, at least on societal time scales, virtually irreversible, as it would likely take many centuries before most of the CO_2 could be removed by the oceans, even if all fossil fuel burning and deforestation activities were abruptly curtailed at some earlier point.

However, estimates of a global average temperature increase to a steady state CO_2 doubling are, like U.S. EPA automobile gas mileage ratings, not very useful except "for comparison." Reality will, of course, not see a sudden doubling of CO_2 snapped on one year and held fixed for all time. CO_2 will build up over time like one of the curves in Figure 8.3. The time-evolving response of the climatic system to such a time-evolving CO_2 increase is known as its *transient response*. Possible differences between equilibrium and transient responses lend considerable uncertainty to the utility of equilibrium-model predictions such as those of Manabe, Wetherald and Stouffer. Atmospheric scientist Starley L. Thompson and I have attempted to weigh the seriousness of deliberately neglecting the deep oceans in most models* and of using a fixed-CO_2 increase

---

*Modelers such as Manabe, Wetherald, and Stouffer are perfectly well aware that they neglected the very large oceanic heat storage capacity of the deep oceans in the simulations described earlier. The neglect was deliberate, in order to achieve

instead of a time-evolving scenario of CO_2 increase.[82] Thus, although albedo/temperature feedback processes in high latitudes eventually (that is, in equilibrium) may cause those regions to be warmed more than lower latitudes for a given CO_2 increase, midlatitudes or even some high-latitude regions would not necessarily warm up as fast as lower latitudes during the transition period towards the new equilibrium. In the transition, the larger thermal inertia of the deep high-latitude mixed layer could actually slow the temperature rise relative to tropical waters. Whether this factor causes a serious error in applying results such as those of Manabe and co-workers, Schneider and Thompson noted, depends on how rapidly the CO_2 concentration actually increases over time.* If CO_2 increases rapidly, as Rotty estimated in Figure 8.2, neglecting the transient would be more a serious error than if CO_2 increased more slowly, thereby making the result of an equilibrium computer model a closer approximation to the actual time-evolving change.

The behavioral assumptions underlying the CO_2 buildup rate in the atmosphere also partly dictate which climatic modeling assumptions are likely to be most valid. The implication here is that social science concerns must sometimes *precede* physical scientific investigation, an inversion of traditional research patterns. In this connection, we suggested earlier that a doubling of CO_2 may never occur, since a great increase in coal use may prove economically unfeasible or sufficiently undesirable. But since known reserves of gas and oil could still lead to a further 30 to 70 percent CO_2 increase over the next fifty years, it seems especially important that we de-emphasize the common practice of computing climatic responses to a fixed doubling or quadrupling of CO_2 and focus instead on a much more likely scenario: the transient climatic response to plausible evolving CO_2 concentrations over the next fifty years.

Still more factors complicate the simulation of time-evolving

---

a model response that is near to equilibrium in only a few tens of model-simulated years. If deep oceans were included, thousands of simulated years would have been needed to achieve steady state—a very expensive proposition, since the amount of computer time used in any model run is roughly proportional to how many simulated years are calculated. At $2000 per hour for computer time, a modeler is wary of multiyear simulations which typically require some several hours of computer time for each simulated year.

*Although some computer simulations suggest that neglect of the transient response may not be too serious an error,[83] other calculations have shown that it is simply too soon to know the extent to which neglect of realistic geography and oceanic mixing will permit meaningful transient results in the context of evolving CO_2 increases.[84]

climatic changes. Not only are the relative depths of the mixed layers of various parts of the oceans important, but the *rates* at which waters from below mix with upper layers also affect the warm-up rate of each part of the oceans, given any CO_2-increase scenario.[85] Thus, even if the current climate models were perfectly accurate in predicting the regional equilibrium climatic response to a given fixed CO_2 increase—such as a doubling—we cannot neglect the large thermal inertia of the deep oceans and the fact that CO_2 will increase smoothly over time. Temperature differences from place to place could well evolve very differently in transient models than the temperature differences predicted by equilibrium models and the Altithermal analogy. If so, these analogs or equilibrium calculations could be highly inaccurate predictors of regional patterns of climate change over the next several decades.

Verification of Climatic Model Predictions of CO_2 Effects

Of course, scientists are not totally ignorant of the possible climatic effects of increasing CO_2 or similar trends in other significant greenhouse gases such as fluorocarbons, ozone, or nitrogen oxides, which also could have potential influences on climate (as discussed a bit later). Don't forget that present climatic models can quite impressively simulate the temperature extremes of the seasons (see Figure 6.2), a much larger, much better understood climatic change than that posed by increases in CO_2 or other greenhouse gases. Such accurate model simulations of the seasons would be impossible if some unknown feedback mechanisms (short-term ones, at least) not represented in present models were dominant. This fact is often overlooked in discussions of the reliability of models for estimating CO_2 impacts on climate. For example, at the UN-sponsored World Climate Conference in Geneva in February 1979, the Director of the British Meteorological Office, Sir B. J. Mason, remarked to the audience that the atmosphere "is resilient," perhaps able to absorb the large changes predicted from models as a response to outside forcings (such as CO_2 increases).* He cited

---

*Dr. Mason made the same point a few years earlier in a July 30, 1977 article "Has the Weather Gone Mad?" in *New Republic Magazine* (July 30, 1977, p. 23): "The atmosphere is a robust system with a built-in capacity to counteract any perturbation . . . the atmosphere is wont to make fools of those who do not show proper respect for its complexity and resilience."

334

the case of hypothetical ozone depletion from several hundred supersonic transports (SSTs). In the early 1970s, crude chemical models of the stratosphere predicted that the proposed fleet of jets would cause about a 10 percent reduction in the ozone. However, as more data—mostly on chemical reaction rates—poured in, the models were refined; by 1979, when the conference was held, these updated models were predicting a slight ozone *increase* from the same SST fleet—"an expensive way to maintain the ozone layer," Mason quipped to the assembly. Perhaps, he strongly implied, as we learn more about the complex workings of the climatic system, other worries—such as CO_2 increases—will also disappear. A lively debate ensued. I commented from the floor that the same updated models that had diminished the predicted impacts of the hypothetical fleet of SSTs on ozone increased the predicted ozone reduction from fluorocarbons used as spray can propellants. My point was that "the sword of uncertainty cuts in both directions," and unknown processes or poorly treated feedback mechanisms are just as likely to increase state-of-the-art estimates as decrease them.[86] (Indeed, in the few years following the conference new findings once again led to ozone *decrease* predictions like those five to ten years earlier—see Figure 8.5.)

If the atmosphere were fully "resilient" to external forces, then there would be no winter or summer, just perpetual spring. Clearly, seasons do exist and clearly the climate does respond to external forcing. The issue for both policy and research is: *by how much* might the climate system respond given a particular forcing such as a scenario of CO_2 increase? Better climate observations, model experiments, and empirical verifications will do more to help to answer that question than speculations on the "resilience" of the climate in the face of external forces. Since the 1979 meeting a number of such important results have been obtained, many of which we've already discussed, and a number of which we'll discuss below.

Direct Verification: CO_2 Forcing and Climatic Response

The seasonal cycle provides a powerful, but *indirect* or *surrogate,* verification test for climatic models being used to predict the sensitivity of the climate system to CO_2 increases. Successful

335

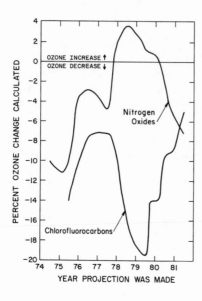

Figure 8.5

As an example of how complex, poorly understood processes can significantly alter the predictions of a climatic model regarding man-made environmental changes, we can consider the injection of nitrogen oxides or chlorofluorocarbons (CFCs) into the stratosphere, resulting from a hypothetical fleet of supersonic transports or certain emissions of spray can propellants, respectively. This graph shows the results of stratospheric ozone changes predicted by a series of models principally developed by atmospheric chemist Julius Chang from the Lawrence Livermore Laboratory to predict steady

state emissions of both nitrogen oxides and CFCs into the next century. It is not a graph of the amount of change of ozone over time, but rather a demonstration of how the model-predicted long-term changes in ozone varied over time as new discoveries (relating primarily to the rates of chemical reactions) became available to the modelers. Note that in the mid-1970s both CFCs and SSTs were predicted to reduce ozone something like 10 percent, but when new chemical information became available by 1979 SSTs appeared to have been likely producers of extra ozone, whereas CFCs became a serious ozone threat. Then, as more new chemistry again became available, the results came back to near where they were a decade earlier. The graph demonstrates that when human interventions in the climatic system are large enough to have potentially significant effects, then regardless of whether detailed predictions are possible, it is not at all unlikely that some effects may be large, although which ones will prove most important is often impossible to state in advance given the level of uncertainties involved. [Source: various reports from the Lawrence Livermore National Laboratory, University of California; for example, D. J. Weubbles, 1981, Chlorocarbon emission scenarios: Potential impact on stratospheric ozone, unpublished report of 30 pages.]

performance in this indirect test may be necessary before we have confidence in a model, but it is not sufficient, since CO_2 increase is a different forcing mechanism than seasonal solar forcing. We also need to subject our models to *direct* verification tests, such as the response of the climatic system in the past to historical variations in CO_2.

CO_2 Variations from the Ice Age
to the Climatic Optimum

In 1980 two groups—one in Grenoble, France, and another in Bern, Switzerland—published similar papers on what may yet prove to be among the most interesting recent discoveries dealing with CO_2.[87] The Swiss group, headed by geochemist Hans Oeschger, compared samples of ice cores taken at Camp Century in Greenland and Byrd Station in Antarctica. What they looked for were gas bubbles trapped deep in the ice, some of which was laid down in the Pleistocene. The scientists ground ice chunks in enclosed containers and tapped off the escaping gas for analysis. They (as did the Grenoble group) reported a remarkable finding: CO_2 amounts were tens of percent lower during the last ice age than at present. The Swiss laboratory measurements, however, suggested that during the middle and early Holocene CO_2 concentration was higher than today, by as much as 75 percent around 5000 years ago. The geochemists immediately recognized the potential climatic significance of this finding, and sought an explanation. They suggested two principal alternatives: the colder climates caused less CO_2 to be stored in the ice (and likewise warmer climates caused more CO_2 storage); or the actual atmospheric concentration of CO_2 was lower in the colder climate and higher in the warmer one. After further analysis, the investigators concluded that "the most probable explanation for the general trend—low values during glacial and higher values during post-glacial—is a corresponding change in atmospheric CO_2 content." However, they also cautioned that their analysis of the Greenland ice, which showed the high CO_2 peak in the mid-Holocene, differed from the analysis of Antarctic ice, in which CO_2 in the Holocene was never more than only slightly greater than at present, and probably was less. Thus, they admitted, "atmospheric CO_2 concentration during the climatic optimum was, therefore, not necessarily higher than the present one."[88] (Both ice cores implied a significantly lower CO_2 concentration—some 190 to 230 ppm—between 10,000 to 20,000 years ago than today's level of 340 ppm.)

But what if there were 40 percent less CO_2 in the Pleistocene and some 50 percent more CO_2 in the Altithermal? Thompson and Schneider argued in *Nature* that if the Greenland results of the Swiss group were right, present climatic models and paleotemperature reconstructions implied two things.[89] First, both the Pleistocene CO_2 minimum (about 12,000 years ago) and the possible Holocene CO_2 maximum (about 5000 years ago) occurred several thousand

337

years after the largest climatic extreme changes had already occurred. (Recall from Chapters 2 and 3 that by the time the Pleistocene ended about 10,000 years ago most ice was gone and temperatures were rapidly rising toward the Altithermal values in the early to mid-Holocene.) The fact that these reported CO_2 variations appeared to lag the temperature changes implies that CO_2 could not have initiated these climatic changes; rather, CO_2 may have amplified those trends already under way (still very important, if true). And second, if there really was a sharp peak concentration of CO_2 some 5000 years ago (with 75 percent more CO_2 than at present), then the climate record 5000 years ago should exhibit a sharp annual warming peak of some 1° to 2°C (1.8° to 3.6°F). Although 5000 years ago is still in the Altithermal in North America, and the Altithermal has been cited by some to have been a degree or two warmer globally than at present, the paleotemperature evidence certainly doesn't suggest a sharp, annually and globally averaged prominent warm peak 5000 years ago. Probably only the summer temperatures were significantly warmer, as suggested by John Kutzbach, with winter termperatures perhaps a bit colder.

But the Swiss team had warned that their very early results could be wrong and that much reconfirmation is needed before the quantitative reconstruction of paleo-CO_2 levels can be reliable. Indeed, reanalysis by the Bern group reconfirmed the Pleistocene CO_2 minimum, but placed it around 15,000 years ago, not 10,000 to 12,000 years ago. They also concluded that drilling fluid contamination of the Greenland samples may have accounted for the very high CO_2 levels originally suggested for the Altithermal. They still found some evidence for the possibility of slightly higher CO_2 concentrations than at present between 5000 and 10,000 years ago.[90] These refined—but still tentative—results eliminate some of the difficulties we mentioned in interpreting the first set of findings, but nevertheless raise many interesting issues. (They also point out the danger of accepting spectacular new results right after they appear.) For instance, the 20 to 30 percent or so variation between Pleistocene CO_2 minimum and Holocene CO_2 levels reported in the refined analysis by the Swiss team (or the Antarctic results of the French group) translates into about a degree Celsius (or less) of temperature change across the Pleistocene-Holocene boundary. This is quite a bit less than the 3° to 5°C (5.4° to 9°F) change cited often as the ice age to interglacial global average surface air temperature difference. But since many climatic models cannot easily reproduce this large difference (see Chapter 7), an extra degree or so push from a 30 percent CO_2 variation certainly would be helpful in explaining the magnitude of the temperature change. But perhaps more fundamental is the question: Why should CO_2 concentration go down in an ice age and rise at—or after—its termination?

Wallace Broecker tried to hypothesize how CO_2 could change with—perhaps even slightly behind—long-term climate trends.[91] First, he noted that oceanic biological productivity, as indicated by the rates at which dead organisms built up into oceanic sediments, depends on the amount of available nutrients for plankton growth —particularly phosphorus compounds. Next he noted that high sedimentation rates take nutrients like phosphorus out of the surface waters and deposit them below, either in deep waters or on the ocean floor. Thus, he suggested, it is possible that phosphorus is pulled out of the upper oceanic layers during the transition from glacial to interglacial times, leading to reduced biological productivity in upper waters, less photosynthesis, and thus more CO_2 as the Holocene began. He reasoned that the cycle started when sea levels dropped after glaciers somehow began to build on land. The exposed coastal shelves could then have eroded, sending a nutrient-rich runoff into the oceans. Biological productivity then increased, ocean chemistry altered, and the net effect was pulling CO_2 out of the surface waters and the air, thereby further cooling the climate during the ice age. Then, for reasons not yet satisfactorily understood (see Chapters 3 and 7), the glaciers began to disintegrate and sea levels rose, covering the continental shelves once more,[92] reducing the runoff of nutrients, increasing the sediment buildup, dropping the phosphorus availability to surface plankton, cutting total biological productivity, and allowing CO_2 to build up again, enhancing the warmth of the early Holocene.

About the same time Wolfgang Berger at the Scripps Institution of Oceanography began to think about this problem. He came up with a similar mechanism, what he termed "the coral reef hypothesis."[93] Centering on the Pleistocene-Holocene transition, Berger hypothesized that the sea level rise coincided with a buildup of carbonate deposits (for example, coral reefs) along the newly reestablished continental shelf sea areas. Ocean chemical reactions that combine calcium and bicarbonate groups in sea water into carbonate deposits (that is, $CaCO_3$) also produce CO_2 as a by-product of the reaction. Some of this extra CO_2 then makes its way to the air, causing the CO_2 increase found in the air bubbles in the ice cores.

These clever hypotheses are, of course, still tentative.[94] Clearly, as we explained above and in the preceding chapter, some factors other than CO_2 were at work in the basic glacial cycles. And an explanation of why the world apparently cooled slightly after the end of the Altithermal, even though sea levels are roughly the same now as they were 5000 years ago, is also not yet completely nailed down—although a decrease in the obliquity and shift in the perihelion of the earth's orbit since 9000 years ago is a prime candidate, as we've noted.

Past CO_2 variations are at least consistent with the direction of proxy temperature changes: some 30 percent less CO_2 in the late Pleistocene glacial times and perhaps as much or slightly more CO_2 than at present in the early to mid-Holocene climatic optimum. (The preindustrial levels in ice cores for samples about 1850 are around 260 ppm, though.) Although this consistency could be taken as a direct test of the CO_2 greenhouse theory, it is not conclusive either way for two reasons. First, there is still considerable uncertainty in this technique, which is the only available way to estimate what CO_2 concentrations existed over the past few tens of thousands of years. Second, we are certain that other mechanisms, both within and external to the climatic system, were also operating. It is not yet possible to separate these simultaneously operating forces from the CO_2 effect. Hence, a definitive direct test of the CO_2-greenhouse warming estimates from climatic models cannot yet be made over these Pleistocene time scales.

CO_2 and Climatic Changes
Since the Industrial Revolution
What of the past hundred years, a period for which we have considerably more knowledge of how climate varied than for the Pleistocene? This century is a time in which the very slowly changing orbital forcing, at least, can have played no significant part in observed climatic trends. As mentioned earlier, we have very little reliable evidence of what CO_2 concentration was before 1958. Various estimates, we've noted, place the so-called *preindustrial* CO_2 concentration between about 260 and 295 parts per million, with many recent results suggesting it was closer to the smaller figure. (In 1982, CO_2 in the air averaged about 340 ppm.) As explained earlier, this implies an increase of some 15 to 30 percent in the concentration of atmospheric CO_2 over the past century. If the consensus climatic models are roughly correct, this translates into a global warming of as little as a few tenths and as much as a degree Celsius from 1880 to 1980. The middle of this range is consistent with the observed global surface air warming shown in Figure 7.6. Does this finally constitute

proof of a direct verification test of climatic models' predictions for CO_2-induced temperature rise? Although some believe this is strong proof, we feel it is simply too soon to officially proclaim "detection."

As discussed earlier, any global temperature signal much smaller than 0.5°C (0.9°F) would be hard to detect reliably with less than a decade or two of data, since each year the natural temperature can vary globally by several tenths of a degree. A simple analogy may help to make the signal-to-noise problem clearer. If one builds a sand castle on the seashore and it is wiped out by a particularly strong wave, does this mean the tide is coming in? We cannot know from just one wave. Quite a few waves would have to be observed and their positions on the beach noted and compared to the average positions of hundreds of waves before a trend could be established: that is, the tide is rising. The one wave that washed away the sand creation could well have been just a natural fluctuation in the strength of the waves. It may have been part of the ocean's "noise" and not necessarily a component of the "signal" heralding the changing tide as the cause of the wipeout. The more encroaching waves that are observed, however, the better the chances that their average reach is part of the signal, that is, the rising tide.

A number of climatic modeling studies based on semiempirical methods, as described in Chapter 7, have shown that recent climatic trends in surface air temperature are not inconsistent with model predictions of CO_2 warming. But the warming is still too small to provide a satisfactory signal-to-noise ratio, in part because there are still too many plausible competing explanations of recent global temperature trends. If these mechanisms are unknown or quantitatively questionable, then we must consider all climatic variations other than our hypothesized CO_2-induced changes as "noise." This then creates a high noise level against which any suspected CO_2-induced climatic trend must be compared. This signal-to-noise approach was used by V. Ramanathan and Roland Madden, at the National Center for Atmospheric Research, who said in early 1980 that we may well have to wait until 2000 or beyond to detect an unambiguous CO_2 signal above the natural background noise of the climate. However, as pointed out in a paper by T. M. L. Wigley and P. D. Jones, the Madden-Ramanathan results only applied at lat. 65 °N, and noise levels are usually much smaller in lower latitudes, particularly in summer.[95] Thus, it would be better, they suggested, to look at temperature trends there than at lat. 65°N, even though climatic models like those of Manabe and co-workers suggest that

341

the equilibrium climatic response to a fixed CO_2 doubling is higher at 65°N than at lower latitudes.

To test the models' prediction that high-latitude CO_2-induced signals may be large, George Kukla and Joyce Gavin at Lamont-Doherty looked at sea ice records over the past several decades. Although finding no significant trends in the Northern Hemisphere, they found from satellite pictures a decrease in Antarctic summer pack ice of some 2.5 million square kilometers (1 million square miles) from 1973 to 1980—about 50 percent of the average coverage. Navy atlases and whaling ship reports dating back some forty years were then consulted. From these it appeared that the ice pack in the 1930s was heavier than in the 1970s. Again, these results were claimed to be consistent with observed warming trends, which in turn are consistent with increasing CO_2. But, as Kukla and Gavin properly noted, whether the changes they observed were natural fluctuations or CO_2-related is not known, and any possible "cause-and-effect relation cannot yet be established."[96]

All of these attempts to look for regions on earth where a CO_2-induced signal might be more easily detected than in other regions —a so-called *precursor indicator*—suffer from a common problem: each is attempting to detect a signal derived from an equilibrium climatic model driven by a fixed, large CO_2 increase. Earlier we saw that CO_2 is building up steadily over time, which could give rise to a transient CO_2-induced climatic response of very different character from that inferred from equilibrium climatic models.[97] Although the temperature trends shown in Figure 7.6 calculated by NASA scientists correlate well with other independent studies by Jones and his colleagues at the University of East Anglia and several Russian scientists, all of these suffer from the same problem: the temperature trends are primarily measures of surface air temperatures in Northern Hemisphere continental regions—where most of the thermometers are. Some attempts to compile useful global ocean surface temperature trends from decades of ship passages were made by the Australian atmospheric physicist Garth Paltridge and S. Woodruff of the U.S. National Atmospheric and Oceanic Administration in Boulder, Colorado. Paltridge and Woodruff found that the large warming from 1910 to 1940 and the smaller cooling trend from 1940 to 1970 in Northern Hemisphere surface air records (like those in Figure 7.6) were paralleled in their ocean surface temperature plots, but that the oceans lagged behind the largely continental air temperature stations by a decade or two— somewhat close to what one would expect to happen given the large thermal inertia of the oceans. Paltridge and Woodruff relied on a historical data set that compiled so-called "bucket temperatures"—the temperatures of buckets of ocean water hauled out of the seas and recorded by sailors on ships for over a century.[98] Both the geographic coverage and reliability of this record are not of the caliber that climatologists would hope for.

For example, C. Folland of the British Meteorological Office showed that a gradual switch from bucket to engine intake temperatures accounts for about a third of the magnitude of the SST temperature trends computed by Paltridge and Woodruff; the ten-to twenty-year lag, however, was not removed by Folland's correction.[99] But it is a valuable record, nonetheless, which clearly demonstrates that trends in surface water temperatures, surface air temperatures over water, and surface air temperatures over land can all be distinct and different climatic variables. Unfortunately, it will take many years—probably decades—before sufficient data are gathered from the oceans to check whether our models are faithfully simulating reality for this climatic subsystem. For all these reasons, one of the greatest uncertainties in climatic model predictions is simulating reliably the time-evolving *regional* distribution of climatic changes from some CO_2-increase scenario.[100] The most reliable single measure of CO_2-induced climatic change may thus still be the variable that first called attention to the problem: a global surface air temperature increase.* If the current crop of climate models is

---

*One global measure of climatic change that we have not yet discussed in the CO_2 context is sea level rise. Sea levels can change locally because of tectonic activity or isostatic rebound (see Chapter 2) or because of true eustatic (that is, global) ocean water volume changes. Because of the noneustatic features, local sea level variation trends have little global meaning. But averages all over the world or at selected places where local effects are small can be indicative of global trends in ocean volume. A warming of the oceans will raise sea levels even if there is *no* change in global ice volume. This is because warmer water physically expands, thereby raising sea levels. Measurements from tide gauges in many parts of the world have been compiled by scientists at the NASA Goddard Institute for Space Studies.[101] They suggest a trend in sea level rise of about 10 centimeters (4 inches) per century from 1880 to 1980, results that "represent weak indirect evidence for a net melting of the continental ice sheets." A different study of polar ice volume was undertaken by NOAA scientists Robert Etkins and Edward Epstein. They concluded that the rotation speed of the earth dropped slightly over the last forty years, mostly because of melting polar ice. Also by calculating the thermal expansion of sea water that would accompany the observed global surface temperature rise of the twentieth century, they too concluded that it alone was not enough to explain all of the increase. "Significant discharges of polar ice must also be occurring", they wrote, and their rotation rate arguments were given as added indirect evidence.[102] All this, these various authors presume, is at least consistent with the twentieth-

right, the signal-to-noise ratio of global temperature from CO_2 should become much larger by the end of the century. And if the climatic noise level can be reduced by the technique of subtracting out climatic effects from other known—or believed known—natural forcing factors like volcanic dust or solar variations, then detection of a believable CO_2 signal to climatic noise ratio will come even sooner.

The uncertainties given here are why many different time-evolving scenarios of CO_2 increase are needed as forcing mechanisms to be applied to a hierarchy of climatic models. No one such study should be considered a "prediction," but rather each can be viewed as a plausible scenario of an alternative CO_2-induced climatic future. Over time, as more data become available, some scenarios can be ruled more probable and others just ruled out. These more probable scenarios can then be used as a basis for asking the socially important question: "So what if CO_2-induced climatic change occurs?"[104]

Other Human Activities That Could Alter Future Climate

The Combined Greenhouse Effect of Trace Gases

It is also possible that trends in other human activities could work with or against the CO_2-greenhouse effect, further confusing the reliable detection of a CO_2 signal over the next few decades. Table 8.3 lists some of the possibilities. Already some of these entries have become important in theories of past climatic changes, and some have been used along with CO_2 to explain recent temperature trends, like the 0.15°C (0.27°F) or so warming of the globe from 1971 to 1981 shown in Figure 7.6. For example, it has been known for many years that trace gases like methane or nitrous oxide could enhance the greenhouse effect, but their climatic effects have been considered small since their concentrations in the atmosphere are so much less than the two principal gases, water vapor and carbon dioxide. However, in 1975 V. Ramanathan noted that

---

century warming trend and the CO_2 buildup. However, care is needed to be certain that the observed temperatures used are sea water, not surface air trends. For this and other reasons it is not yet certain the extent to which cause and effect should be inferred.[103]

chlorofluorocarbons (CFCs)—used as spray can propellants or re-frigerants—could do more than interfere with processes responsible for stratospheric ozone. Despite their relatively trace amounts in the atmosphere (measured in units of fractions of parts per billion as compared to hundreds of parts per million for CO_2), use of CFC had been growing very rapidly. In addition, they have a very strong greenhouse effect, even in relatively small amounts. Ramanathan calculated that they could be responsible for a global warming of several tenths of a degree Celsius by the end of the century.[105] CFCs are not the only gases (other than CO_2) released by human activities with a growing potential to augment any CO_2 greenhouse effect. Nitrous oxide (N_2O) is a by-product of fossil fuel burning and denitrification (see Chapter 4) and may increase significantly as a result of both fossil fuel use and (especially) the growing use of nitrogen fertilizers.* Methane (CH_4) also may be increasing, due to human activities that increase the numbers of livestock or rates of deforestation; its cycling in nature is complex and very much related to biological activity.[106] Moreover, the ozone changes themselves can cause large temperature changes (see Table 8.3).

Hermann Flohn recognized that these trace greenhouse gases, each associated with human activities causing their concentrations to be altered, could, taken together, add a significant increment to a CO_2-induced warming. Flohn calls the combination of these trace greenhouse gases plus CO_2 the *virtual CO_2 concentration* of the atmosphere.[107]

Earlier we mentioned that a team of scientists from NASA's Goddard Institute for Space Studies (GISS) in New York City attempted to match the temperature records of the past century (see Figure 7.6) to a climate-model-generated temperature based on assumed CO_2, solar, and volcanic forcings. Despite the problems with signal-to-noise ratio or surface air versus surface water temperatures just mentioned, the NASA scientists obtained results that were at least broadly consistent with theoretical expectations. Several months after publishing their first study, the GISS group released another calculation, this time stressing the combined greenhouse effect of

---

*N_2O is also implicated in stratospheric ozone chemistry, but its potential impacts on ozone are still quite speculative. Indeed, this entire question of the climatic effects of variations in trace gases is one of great potential importance, but is punctuated by great uncertainties. For an authoritative review, see the *Report of the Meeting of Experts on Potential Climatic Effects of Ozone and Other Minor Trace Gases* (Boulder, Colorado, 13–17 September 1982), WMO Global Ozone Research and Monitoring Project, Report No. 14 (Geneva: World Meteorological Organization).

Table 8.3 Summary of Principal Human Activities That Can Influence Climate

Activity	Climatic effect	Scale and importance of the effect
Release of carbon dioxide by burning fossil fuels	Increases the atmospheric absorption and emission of terrestrial infrared radiation (greenhouse effect), resulting in warming of lower atmosphere and cooling of the stratosphere.	Global: potentially a major influence on climate and biological activity.
Release of chlorofluoromethanes, nitrous oxide, carbon tetrachloride, carbon disulfide, etc.	Similar climatic effect as that of carbon dioxide since these, too, are infrared-absorbing and fairly chemically stable trace gases.	Global: potentially significant influence on climate.
Release of particles (aerosols) from industrial and agricultural practices	These sunlight scattering and absorbing particles probably decrease albedo over land, causing a warming and could increase albedo over water causing a cooling; they also change stability of lower atmosphere; net climatic effects still speculative.	Largely regional, since aerosols have an average lifetime of only a few days, but similar regional effects in different parts of the world could have nonnegligible net global effects; stability increase may suppress convective rainfall, but particles could affect cloud properties with more far-reaching effects.
Release of aerosols that act as condensation and freezing nuclei	Influences growth of cloud droplets and ice crystals; may affect amount of precipitation or albedo of clouds in either direction.	Local (at most) regional influences on quantity and quality of precipitation, but unknown and potentially important change to earth's heat balance if cloud albedo is altered.
Release of heat (thermal pollution)	Warms the lower atmosphere directly.	Locally important now; could become significant regionally; could modify large-scale circulation.

Upward transport of chlorofluoromethanes and nitrous oxide into the stratosphere	Photochemical reaction of their dissociation products probably reduces stratospheric ozone.	Global but uncertain influence on climate: less total stratospheric ozone allows more solar radiation to reach the surface but compensates by reducing greenhouse effect as well; however, if ozone concentration decreases at high altitudes, but increases comparably at lower altitudes, this would lead to potentially very large surface warming; could cause significant biological effects from increased exposure to ultraviolet radiation if total column amount of ozone decreases.
Release of trace gases (e.g., nitrogen oxides, carbon monoxide, or methane) that increase tropospheric ozone by photochemical reactions	Large atmospheric heating occurs from tropospheric ozone, which enhances both solar and greenhouse heating of lower atmosphere.	Local to regional at present, but could become a significant global climatic warming if large-scale fossil fuel use leads to combustion products that significantly increase tropospheric ozone levels; contact with ozone also harms some plants and people.
Patterns of land use, e.g., urbanization, agriculture, overgrazing, deforestation, etc.	Changes surface albedo and evapotranspiration and causes aerosols.	Largely regional: net global climatic importance still speculative.
Release of radioactive Krypton-85 from nuclear reactors and fuel reprocessing plants	Increases conductivity of lower atmosphere, with possible implications for earth's electric field and precipitation from convective clouds.	Global: importance of influence is highly speculative.
Large-scale nuclear war.	Could lead to very large injections of soot and dust causing transient cooling lasting from weeks to months, depending on the nature of the exchange and on how many fires were started.	Could be global, but initially in mid-latitudes of Northern Hemisphere. Darkness from dust and smoke could wipe out photosynthesis for weeks with severe effects on both natural and agricultural ecosystems of both combatant and non-combatant nations. Transient freezing outbreaks could eliminate most warm season crops in mid-latitudes or be devastating to any vegetation in tropics or subtropics.

increasing CO_2, CFCs, N_2O, and CH_4 over the decade of the 1970s.[108]

Interestingly, the computed global equilibrium warming from CH_4, N_2O, and CFCs combined was 0.1°C (0.18°F), nearly as large as the 0.14°C (0.25°F) warming computed from the CO_2 increase alone during this decade. However, the NASA scientists recognized that the thermal inertia of the climatic system would restrain any climatic response to this greenhouse heating. They estimated that the transient effect of oceanic heat capacity would reduce the combined CO_2 plus other trace gases warming for the period between 1970 and 1980 by about half the equilibrium value. Thus, they predicted that there should have been about a 0.1°C (0.18°F) warming from all such greenhouse gases during the 1970s. Indeed, there appears to have been such a warming (as seen earlier in Figure 7.6c). But warmings of 0.1°C per decade are not at all uncommon in past temperature records. Thus, this coincidence between observed data and model calculation may simply have been chance, not a cause-and-effect relationship. However, their estimate for climatic response to increasing greenhouse gases over the decade of the 1980s is larger still, about 0.2° to 0.3°C (0.36° to 0.54°F)— perhaps twice the decadal average noise level. This prospect prompted the NASA scientists to offer a rather bold prediction: "Global warming due to increased abundance of infrared absorbing gases can be expected to exceed natural variability in the 1980s."[109] This statement led Thompson and Schneider to comment that if the NASA scientists "are right, then *this* decade, not the often-cited year 2000, is when a clear warming signal is due. Verification of model predictions by the real atmosphere, of course, takes time; these recent results strongly suggest that the time is closer at hand than previously believed."[110]

But all predictions of future climatic response to greenhouse gases have to contend with the possibility of unexpected climatic forcings from nature—volcanic dust veils, for example—or human activities. One dramatic possibility for human alteration of the climatic system is a massive disruption of atmospheric composition from a large-scale nuclear war.

Nuclear Winter: Climatic Effects of a Large-Scale Nuclear War

It seems absurd, perhaps, to worry about climatic (or other environmental) consequences in the aftermath of a large-scale nuclear exchange between superpowers, given the self-evident initial holocaust the war would bring. There are, however, several reasons to look beyond the initial blast and radiation effects that could kill up to a billion people or so immediately or within a few weeks. First, what climate changes might the targeted nations' survivors face? Second, what environmental side effects would the three billion or so noncombatants be forced to accept? Third, and not least, there are still those who, in their warped military logic, believe a large-scale nuclear war is winnable. Perhaps knowledge of the potential climatic aftermath of such an exchange might convince even the most narrow-minded of tacticians on either side that winning is an absurd concept.

In the early 1960s, the controversial futurist Herman Kahn shocked many with his book *Thinking About The Unthinkable* and other writings on the survivability of a nuclear exchange.[111] Unfortunately, at first his works were more criticized for being written rather than for what they said (that a nuclear war is easily survivable). Later on Kahn's basic conclusions were severely challenged. For example, environmentalists Paul Ehrlich, Anne Ehrlich, and John Holdren said that the "it wouldn't be so bad" tone implicit in Kahn's writings was a result of analyses that were "hopelessly flawed by—among other things—the author's ignorance of ecology."[112] A U.S. National Academy of Sciences study published in 1968 did address more explicitly environmental aspects of a postnuclear world, pointing out, for instance, the possibility of lingering fires,* although with relatively uncertain ecological consequences.[113] Subsequently, a much expanded Academy study was released in 1975 that brought out a new postwar environmental threat: a stratospheric ozone depletion of perhaps 50 percent or more for up to several years could follow a 5000- to 10,000-megaton war. The "Atmospheric Effects" group, in which Schneider participated, noted that dust kicked up from the numerous blasts could be roughly equivalent to a volume of ejecta like that from Krakatoa—some 10 million to 100 million tons. This implied a worldwide cooling of a degree or so for a year or two—much larger in the Northern Hemisphere, the probable venue of the hypothesized holocaust. The estimate was based on the assumption that "a significant fraction of the bombs may be detonated as air bursts."[114] However, if the exchange were designed to knock out hardened missile sites then fewer air bursts would occur. Moreover, the report notes, surface bursts would pro-

---

*The possibility of mass fires following a nuclear attack was discussed even earlier by A. Broido, *Bulletin of the Atomic Scientists* 16:409–413, 1960.

duce more dust than air bursts and "an 'optimal subsurface burst' yields about a ten times higher estimate" for dust injected than a surface burst. In other words, the estimates of stratospheric dust from a 5000- to 10,000-megaton nuclear exchange could be ten or more times greater than assumed in the 1975 study, depending on the yield and number of weapons and on where the bombs were detonated.

Ironically, the most controversial aspect of the report was not its contents nor even its very being—which is what caused such a stir when Herman Kahn first unearthed his "unthinkable" thinking. Rather, the letter of transmittal published in the front of the report from then NAS president Phillip Handler contained the most unfortunate phrase that "the principal findings of this report are encouraging" since they suggested that after all "interim effects subside, much of the planet will appear to have recovered."[115]

Aside from the furor over Handler's "encouraging" letter, serious substantive shortcomings were soon pointed out. For example, the NAS committee members were not permitted to make any "social assumptions," for example, how elimination of trade in fertilizer, medicine, or other products of the combatant industrial nations would affect the well-being of dependent, less-industrialized noncombatants.[116] Ehrlich, Ehrlich, and Holdren also challenged the NAS document, not only for Handler's questionable language, but because it virtually ignored the prospect of large-scale fires following the thermonuclear fireballs. "Huge fire storms" could be created, they wrote, fueled by depots of combustible materials and, especially in a dry summer, forested regions.[117]

Five years later Paul Crutzen and John Birks re-examined the question of what the atmosphere might be like after a nuclear war.[118] Their conclusions on stratospheric ozone depletion were a little less severe than the NAS study; but Crutzen and Birks went beyond the earlier work in two important ways. First, they considered lower atmospheric effects, concluding, for instance, that injected hydrocarbons and nitrogen oxides could create "severe smog conditions" for months in the Northern Hemisphere, with blue sky giving way to a dimmer brown and yellow heavens. Second, and most important, they too believed that large-scale forest and chemical fires could well burn for many weeks, perhaps months.* The tropospheric aerosols generated from such continuous injections of

---

*Crutzen, you may recall, became an expert on chemical emissions from fires when working on the carbon cycle issue several years earlier. Thus, he was a logical choice for building a quantitative theory of fire effects.

combustion products into the atmosphere would produce staggering environmental effects. Thus, we consider the Crutzen-Birks contribution to this grizzly set of assessments as a quantum leap more horrible than what has already been projected. What they concluded is that for at least several weeks following the initial fireballs, fires from chemical, industrial, urban, and forest areas would cause smoke clouds so thick that much of the Northern Hemisphere surface would be virtually blacked out. In essence, there could be a month or so of extended twilight—a scaled-down version of the Alvarez earth-asteroid collision theory, whose dark, dusty aftermath may have sent a significant fraction of all extant species into extinction.* Aside from yet uncertain climatic consequences of their scenario, the Crutzen-Birks estimates suggest that photosynthesis in most of the Northern Hemisphere could not proceed for a month or two. Such a pall would deprive both survivors and noncombatants of much of their immediate food needs; it would also likely wreak considerable long-term damage to many food-producing environmental systems. (However, the reduced carrying capacity of the post–World War III world might or might not be further limiting, since the postwar food needs of a depleted world population would be much less than now.) And after the dust cleared, photochemical reactions would then proceed to create dangerous levels of ozone near the earth's surface for another several months.

Carl Sagan, along with Richard Turco, Owen Toon, Thomas Ackerman, and James Pollack—the same basic team that calculated climatic effects of the hypothesized Cretaceous-ending asteroid cloud—modified their Cretaceous extinction study to simulate the effects of large-scale smoke and dust clouds from a hypothesized nuclear war. Their battle scenarios included the use of enough large bombs to create a devastating pulse of stratospheric dust and tropospheric smoke. After a few weeks light would be drastically reduced and land surface temperatures could drop by 10° to 30°C (18° to 54°F) for many months, they calculated.[119] This could be especially disastrous if the war occurred in late winter, with cool temperatures already present and spring buds about to take advantage of the normal increasing hours of daylight.

Other war scenarios are also possible. The recent tendency of

*The hypothesized Cretaceous extinction dust cloud would have been both global and longer-lasting, as it was supposed to have been a stratospheric cloud (see Chapter 7), whereas the Northern Hemisphere smoke aerosol proposed by Crutzen and Birks would be largely tropospheric.

the superpowers to build larger numbers of more accurate missiles has also decreased the likelihood that these missiles would carry large multi-megaton warheads.[120] Only the large warheads are capable of generating massive stratospheric injections of dust. Both large and small bombs could start fires, but a scenario of many small explosions is more likely to create extensive smoke plumes in the lower atmosphere than an exchange of fewer, bigger warheads. If there is no overlying layer of stratospheric dust and dense smoke clouds were confined to the first few kilometers of the atmosphere (not a very likely scenario), this smoke would absorb most of the sunlight near the surface. Such smoky sky areas would lead to significant transient heating of vast areas of the lower atmosphere.[121]

One of the curiosities about the climatic effects of smoke is that since smoke particles are relatively black they collectively tend to absorb more sunlight than they reflect, thereby warming the earth-atmosphere system. How then can we talk about a "nuclear winter?" The reason the surface could cool even though the overall atmosphere heats is simply that the heating can be confined to layers of the atmosphere well above the surface. By analogy, the atmospheric heating due to ozone presently causes stratospheric temperatures to rise by nearly 100°C as one rises from 10 to 40 kilometers (6 to 25 miles) up. In essence, what the addition of post–nuclear war dust and smoke in the middle and upper troposphere could do is bring the stratosphere lower down—to a few kilometers above the surface. This would cause a warmer atmosphere but a colder surface. Moreover, such a radical change in the temperature structure of the atmosphere would set off very different flow patterns. Such dynamic feedback processes would both mix the dust and the radioactivity in ways that are not now easily predictable.

The TTAPS Team   It is against this background of growing concern that a meeting of major importance took place in Cambridge, Massachusetts in April 1983. Under the general leadership of Carl Sagan, and with the guidance of Paul Ehrlich, John Holdren, Peter Raven, Walter Roberts, George Woodwell, myself, and some others, two back-to-back workshops were held as part of the five-day Conference on Long-Term Worldwide Biological Consequences of a Nuclear War. The first meeting was attended mostly by physical scientists, and was under the chairmanship of Sagan. Its purpose was to dissect a lengthy report by Richard Turco, Owen Toon, Thomas Ackerman, James Pollack, and Carl Sagan— later to be referred to as the TTAPS Team report. Taking the lead from Crutzen and Birks' quantitative reaffirmation of the postwar fire problem, the TTAPS Team postulated large dust injections into the stratosphere from nuclear blasts and smoke injections into the lower and upper troposphere from subsequent vegetation, chemical, and urban fires. These aerosols would absorb enough sunlight in the atmosphere to drop temperatures at the earth's surface radically as well as reduce light levels at the ground to a small fraction of normal for periods ranging anywhere from a week to several months. The second meeting was predominantly for biologists, and was held under the chairmanship of Missouri Botanical Garden director Peter Raven—who, along with Paul Ehrlich, coined the term coevolution. The biologists were to assess the biological consequences of the findings from the first meeting.

Several physical science groups did their best to find flaws in the TTAPS analysis. For example, Curt Covey, Starley Thompson, and I, among others at the National Center for Atmospheric Research (NCAR), worked hard to see if any neglected factors could make the large surface cooling effects disappear—not to negate the work of the TTAPS team, but rather to insure the credibility of the results. By clinging to the limits of possibility, we at NCAR could argue that the neglect of cloud feedback effects (see Chapter 6) or the possibility that missing dynamical or infrared radiative effects combined might lead to a surface warming. This opposite effect could occur if the soot remained very low in the atmosphere or if the lower atmosphere were well mixed. But this *boundary layer soot* scenario certainly could not negate the much more likely possibility that dust in the stratosphere or soot mixed vertically into the upper troposphere would dominate, producing both temperature decreases and darkening at the surface like those calculated by the TTAPS team— and by us for these same assumptions. Our principal criticism—one reflected by many others at the physical scientists' meeting and one prominently admitted in the TTAPS report in several places—was that the TTAPS scientists had used a simple, one-dimensional model of the climate that ignored seasonal effects, cloud feedback, and the effects of atmospheric winds. The latter could smooth out somewhat the radical temperature differences predicted by the TTAPS model for the response of the air over the oceans versus that over the lands. In the TTAPS model the ocean temperatures would decrease only a degree or so, whereas the land temperatures could decrease anywhere from 20° to 40°C (36° to 72°F). Covey and Schneider, using a very simple model, calculated that winds blowing from the high heat capacity oceans could ameliorate the continental

353

temperature drops by perhaps as much as half, close to what James Pollock of TTAPS had himself guessed.

However, as discussions continued, it became clearer that whenever someone argued that one process neglected by the TTAPS analysis might ameliorate their dramatic results for one variable, the neglect of this process might also make another variable worse. For example, Jerry Mahlman from the Geophysical Fluid Dynamics Laboratory at Princeton suggested that intense cooling of the continental surfaces following such a war-generated aerosol might lead to an analogous situation to the winter monsoon in Asia, whereby high altitude air would sink over the land. This would result in a net heat transport from the air over the oceans to the air over land. This heat transport could reduce somewhat the average continental values of cooling predicted by the TTAPS model—which neglected such dynamical effects. However, as I speculated to the group, sinking air over land could then mean that although average temperature drops might be reduced relative to the TTAPS calculations, cold air outbreaks along coasts and even into the subtropics might also occur. Biologist Ehrlich then said that it isn't the mean temperature decrease over land that is of principal concern, but rather whether even a few days of subfreezing temperatures could follow from a blob of cold air moving away from the chilled continental interiors toward the warmer coastal or subtropical areas. Such cold air outbreaks over India, the Caribbean, or Northern Hemisphere tropics could be absolutely devastating to a large range of biota in those regions, since most plants and animals outside of mid-latitude ecosystems do not have inherent defenses against even short-period outbreaks of subfreezing temperatures.

People associated with the U.S. Defense establishment working in laboratories like the Los Alamos National Laboratory in New Mexico were present. Some tried hard to argue that a 10,000-megaton war envisioned in the "baseline" case in the TTAPS report was unrealistically large. The TTAPS scientists responded by showing that much lesser nuclear exchanges of a few thousand megaton scale could produce nearly as devastating climatic results. This is because an attack on a thousand cities or a thousand silos could still produce enough smoke and dust to obscure the light levels and drop the temperatures nearly as much as for the larger war case. Moreover, a number of participants pointed out that the TTAPS groups may have underestimated the potential area that might burn by as much as several times. TTAPS may also have assumed that the soot would wash out of the atmosphere much too quickly, because the soot removal rates TTAPS used in their calculations assumed atmospheric conditions as they are today, rather than the perturbed atmospheric conditions following a nuclear war. Heating of the atmosphere a few kilometers up could well reduce rainfall rates and therefore prolong the time it takes for soot to wash out of the skies. (This delay would, however, lower the exposure of people to radioactive fallout.)

Another difficulty pointed out at the Cambridge meeting was the possibility that the smoke and dust may not spread uniformly around the hemisphere but rather circle for only a few weeks in patchy blobs. The patchiness problem, some argued, would seriously reduce the severity of longer-term environmental effects, for light would be able to penetrate intermittently after a few days of darkness, thereby averting the photosynthetic death of most plants. Also, some critics argued, warm solar rays could be felt by the surface in between the patchy smoke passages, perhaps eliminating much of the deep freeze calculated by TTAPS based on continuous, non-patchy aerosol assumptions.

The conference attendees all agreed that much uncertainty still remained over the magnitude of the fire and dust injection scenarios and that the effects of dynamic feedbacks induced by dramatic changes in the temperature structure of the atmosphere could significantly modify the TTAPS results. Nevertheless, these uncertainties would not necessarily reduce the seriousness of the calculated effects. For example, the strong heating in the middle of the atmosphere due to the absorption of sunlight by dust and soot could well set up temporary circulation cells that could transport much of that soot into the tropics and the Southern Hemisphere. While at first glance that might seem to dilute the seriousness of the effect in the Northern Hemisphere, it would thus drag the Southern Hemisphere into the nuclear winter. Under worst-case (but still plausible) assumptions, there would be enough dust and smoke to go all around the world, dropping global temperatures and light levels to lethal values for most plants and animals for perhaps as long as several months. Indeed, as Carl Sagan pointed out, dust storms on Mars have proceeded in just such a manner: localized clouds in one hemisphere caused sufficient disturbance to the atmospheric absorption of solar radiation that winds were induced that propagated the dust rapidly around the planet. The Martian atmosphere got hotter, but the surface cooled. Were a similar event to occur following a large-scale nuclear war, then much of life on earth would be gravely threatened, the biologists cautioned. Even if a first-strike

355

agressor achieved every desired military objective by a preemptive strike, the smoke, dust, ice, and darkness could make any such victory short-lived.

These results of the physical scientists' meeting (putting aside the worst case) were then transmitted to the biologists' meeting two days later. Not surprisingly, most of those in attendance concluded that a Northern Hemisphere land temperature drop of 10° or 20°C and a reduction in light levels to 1 percent or less of normal for a week to a month would cause severe damage to much of the biosphere. Although it was deemed uncertain whether massive extinctions would occur, the productivity of both natural and agro-ecosystems would be reduced severely for at least a year or two following the war, even though the skies would clear and the temperatures return to near normal within a few months. Quite simply, one participant remarked, few food plants then growing would survive such a holocaust, and even the capacity to replant and replow could be severely damaged for many years to come. John Harte of Berkeley calculated that most fresh water lakes, as well as water supplies, could freeze over and would take several months to melt. Severe residual ecological damage would also be caused. For example, coastal fisheries would cease to be useful as food supplies for the survivors, because they would be disrupted by the washout of radioactivity and toxic chemicals. Coastal survivors could face the choice between starvation or eating radioactive shellfish.

Noncombatant nations in the tropics would be severely affected, most participants felt, even if the interhemispheric exchange of smoke postulated in the worst case did not take place. Much of the food productivity in Third World countries today is derived from the transfer of chemical and other technological aids from the developed world. If the latter countries were destroyed, then perhaps as much as half the food-delivering capacity of noncombatant nations could be severely reduced in the years following such a war, probably leading to the starvation—to say nothing of civil unrest—of perhaps half of the inhabitants in these mostly Third World nations. This holocaust could occur if the tropical countries or those in the Southern Hemisphere were lucky enough to be relatively untouched by loss of light or freezing temperature caused by the Northern Hemisphere dust clouds (of course, if enough tropical or Southern Hemisphere sites are targeted, then dust and smoke clouds could be generated there regardless of any interhemispheric transport by winds.)

To the statement of skeptics that many uncertainties remain, conference chairman Sagan noted that we have no choice but to rely on models and theoretical assessments, for after all this is an experiment that can be performed once, at most. To arguments that we should not stress worst-case assumptions but rather "more probable" nuclear war scenarios, I argued that all we need demonstrate was a plausible chance that environmental consequences could wipe out most of the agriculture in the Northern Hemisphere and a large fraction of that in the Southern Hemisphere in the year or so after the war to have made clear the point that any nuclear planning in the absence of these possibilities is sheer madness. One Harvard University psychologist reminded the group that rational behavior from national leaders cannot be expected in the stress conditions of nuclear war. John Holdren of Berkeley then commented that what amazed him was that anybody who had seriously contemplated the acceptability of losses implied by direct blast and radiation effects (which could be as high as a billion people) could be considered rational, and would probably be unmotivated by the further recognition that perhaps four billion people could be threatened by the longer-term climatic effects.

After leaving the Cambridge meeting I recall being disturbed by the remarks of some of the participants about the slight impact our discussions would probably have on military planners. Several people had commented that the TTAPS war scenarios and models were simply too unsophisticated to provide enough credibility to motivate military planners to alter their thinking; in particular, these simple models neglected dynamic feedback processes which could radically alter their predictions. Thus, to back up the simple model results, it seemed imperative to make an early attempt at simulation of the climatic effects of large amounts of smoke generated in the wake of a potential nuclear war with a fully three-dimensional atmospheric general circulation model (see Chapter 6). Since just such a model already existed at NCAR, I resolved to join with several colleagues in an attempt to make the necessary modifications to the existing model. We faced a short first deadline, since the U.S. National Academy of Sciences had convened yet another panel to re-examine the long-term atmospheric consequences of nuclear war, initially motivated by the Crutzen and Birks contribution. This latest study group, headed by George Carrier of Harvard University was planning a summer working session to write a document on the issue. Thus, the NCAR group had to produce its preliminary results in less than three months if it was to contribute to this National Academy Study.

357

The general circulation model then at NCAR, known as the Community Climate Model (CCM), had just been emerging from several years of development. Although not documented and tested to the extent one would desire, we turned to it nonetheless, using a research version of the CCM given to us by Robert Chervin, who had modified it to include a calculation of the seasonal cycle. We needed to modify the radiative transfer part of the computer program, originally written by V. Ramanathan. Curt Covey, Starley Thompson, and I undertook these modifications, with considerable consulting help from Ramanathan, Chervin, and radiative transfer experts Jeffrey Kiehl and V. Ramaswamy. In two months' time we could modify the CCM radiation program only to include the effects of a hypothetical tropospheric soot cloud, an aerosol which absorbs 100 percent of all sunlight and scatters none. (Real smoke is roughly half-absorbing and half-scattering.) Time forced us to neglect the effects of dust or light scattering properties of real smoke. Despite a number of nagging technical problems, we were able to make a series of half a dozen simulations or runs with the CCM to simulate atmospheric effects on the time frame of a few weeks after the injection of a relatively plausible nuclear war-induced soot injection —one with a so-called *absorption optical depth* of about 3. Our results can be summarized as follows:

- Intense heating of the middle troposphere begins right after soot injection, and is so extensive that after several days the atmospheric winds make radical departures from their present state. Therefore, any inference about transport or removal of soot based upon present atmospheric conditions will be invalid after a few days.
- The CCM also predicted that nearly all clouds more than a few kilometers up in the atmosphere would be eliminated in a matter of a few days. This occurred because the soot-induced heating of the mid-troposphere both stabilized the atmosphere, preventing the penetration of moisture from below, and increased the temperature without increasing the moisture content, thereby decreasing the relative humidity of the mid-troposphere. The model also suggested that there would be a significant increase in the relative humidity of the lowest kilometer or so of the atmosphere, leading to considerable increase of low level clouds (and probably fogs) a few days after the soot injection.

- There is a significant difference in the climatic perturbations following soot injection in January versus July. If the soot is narrowly confined to a belt between latitude 30 and 70 degrees in the Northern Hemisphere, then the January simulation shows considerably less aftereffects than a July simulation. Perhaps this is obvious, for in January there is relatively little mid-latitude incoming solar radiation. Even if all of it were absorbed in the middle of the atmosphere in the soot layer, this extra heating is much less of a serious perturbation than in July, when the incoming amounts of solar energy are much larger. Nevertheless, even the January mid-latitude soot layer caused significant drops in surface land temperatures to well below their already near freezing or below freezing values.

- For the July case, heating at the southern edge of the soot layer was so intense that it created a large rising motion which would probably transport mid-latitude soot upward and Equatorward, as Sagan and others had suspected at the Cambridge meeting. These southward moving upper atmospheric winds could send streamers of soot some 5–20 kilometers overhead deep into tropical latitudes (and even to the Southern Hemisphere), dragging these places into the environmental aftermath of their northern neighbors' nightmare. Even in January, once soot gets high enough or far enough south to absorb large amounts of sunlight, it could create dynamic feedback mechanisms that could enhance its own spreading, as in the Martian analogy.

- At the Cambridge meeting Jerry Mahlman speculated that the surface cooling of central Asia from overhead soot might lead to conditions, even in the summertime, similar to present-day winter, that is, sinking air over central Asia with surface outflow southward toward the Indian Ocean. Indeed, our simulation for mid-latitude soot injection in July tentatively confirmed some of his suspicions. It also raised another potential major problem: along with the reversed wind flow was a drastic reduction of the summer Asian monsoon rainfall—which would probably mean a major reduction of food production in South Asia, even if the smoke and dust never drifted over that subtropical region.

- The most spectacular surprise from our calculations occurred when we first looked at surface temperature maps over land, only a few model-simulated days after the soot was injected. We discovered that temperatures at quite a few land areas had already dropped below freezing—even in the tropics when we

359

allowed soot to penetrate that far in one of our scenarios. (In this connection, recall my speculation of Cambridge that a switch from summer to winter Asian monsoon winds with the cooling of central Asia might lead to cold air outbreaks in the nearby subtropics. Early examination of the CCM results did not apparently confirm this mechanism for cold air outbreaks in the subtropics, but suggested nonetheless that quick freezing was indeed a very real possibility.) At first this quick freeze seemed counter-intuitive, since some simpler climate models suggest that it should take several weeks to achieve such freezing. These models often treat the atmosphere and surface as a whole, whereas the CCM separates the surface from the air and subdivides the air in many layers. Therefore, the three-dimensional dynamical model was simply reflecting the obvious fact that day to night temperature differences over land presently range from between about 5 to 20°C (9–36°F). Twenty-four hours of overhead soot is analogous to two consecutive nights; and 48 hours is four consecutive dayless nights. If temperatures continued to drop at rates like 5–20°C per 12 hours, then it wouldn't take too many "days" of perpetual night to create freezing temperatures over most land areas in the world. (Of course, one can't defend this extrapolation as valid, but must instead rely on models to estimate the longer-term rates of temperature drop.)

Perhaps we shouldn't have needed a three-dimensional dynamical model at all to have drawn the last conclusion: that even a patchy distribution of soot—with patches that could be a thousand kilometers across—thick enough to absorb most sunlight overhead could still be sufficient to drop virtually any place on earth temporarily below freezing in a matter of a few days. This could be true even if that patch of soot moved on on a few days and fairly normal sunlight returned. This spectacular inference made us realize that perhaps no place on earth could necessarily feel itself immune from temporary severe environmental aftereffects of large scale nuclear war. Patchiness was no longer a way out, as some proposed at the Cambridge meeting.

Thompson, Covey, and I presented these preliminary results to a sub-panel—including most TTAPS members—of the National Academy study in Stanford, California in July 1983 for consideration by the entire Academy group several weeks later. Thompson represented the NCAR group at this latter workshop at Flagstaff,

Arizona in August. That report is expected to mention the potential seriousness of this quick freeze scenario, whereby only a few days of overhead soot could lead to near-the-ground freezing. On the other hand, the Academy report also notes that increases in ground fog could be very substantial, perhaps retarding the quick freeze cooling effect somewhat relative to that calculated in the NCAR CCM.[121] Moreover, although the Academy report is expected to reduce emphasis on upper atmospheric dust and soot scenarios that were so prominent in the TTAPS report, it will reaffirm the likely possibility of tropospheric smoke associated with urban fires and, to a lesser extent, forest fires. Despite this toning down of some of the Crutzen and Birks or TTAPS assumptions, the Academy study will conclude, nonetheless, that even a "modest war" with these conservative assumptions could still lead to major long-term climatic and other environmental consequences, of the same type suggested by Ehrlich, Ehrlich, and Holdren, refined by Crutzen and Birks, and calculated by the TTAPS team, NCAR researchers, and others.

The principal inadequacy of the efforts so far is that no one has attempted to build an *interactive* model in which dust and smoke are initially injected and these aerosols can then modify the heating and therefore the wind structure of the atmosphere. In turn, the smoke would be transported and removed by that modified wind structure, thereby feeding back on the atmospheric heating patterns and once again modifying the wind. Presumably, until such a calculation has been made and shows comparably serious results to modeling studies so far, doubts will linger over the credibility of the details of nearly all calculations now available. However, these doubts cannot destroy the high plausibility of the existing calculations. No present rational planning can ignore them.

The hope of many of us who attended the meetings was simply that, since most people either didn't know of or refused to think about these issues, perhaps by bringing these findings to public attention as credibly as we could we might spark the kind of expanded public debate needed to convince political leaders to agree to meaningful reductions in the numbers and megatonnage of nuclear weapons. It can now be shown quite credibly that nuclear war poses more than a threat to millions of individual humans, but to humanity as a whole. Moreover, none of this deals with the release of radiation from destroyed nuclear power plants, epidemics, or toxic chemicals produced by industrial fires, nor the possible escape of deadly radioactive, chemical, or biological agents stockpiled in many countries. To expect anything but a small fraction of humanity to survive and recover from all these combined effects will take more than a few shovels of dirt over our makeshift bomb shelters.*

One of the absurdities of the civil defense fallacy is that somehow a Northern Hemisphere nation could survive the environmental effects of the war even though this might mean the possible destruction of most food crops and standing plant life for perhaps a year or more. After all, it could be argued, there would still be enough grain in the elevators in the U.S. Plains, for example, to feed most of the present population for a year or more (let alone the postwar population, reduced by blast and immediate radiation effects). What such simple thinking neglects is the fact that transportation and economic infrastructure would also be smashed by a full-scale attack, as would social structure. It is a mighty dangerous gamble to believe that there would be sufficient ability, both technical and political, to get the grain from the elevators that were still standing to the dispersed and dazed masses living in places up to thousands of miles away.†

Regardless of many unassessable details, it seems quite possible that the climatic and other environmental changes—to say nothing of social or political disruptions—in the aftermath of a large-scale nuclear war could well be more devastating to humanity as a whole than the blasts themselves. In light of all these mind-boggling but real possibilities, we would be appalled to learn that any government official who continues to believe in a winnable large-scale nuclear war could remain in a position of responsibility in any sane nation on earth. Perhaps most disquieting of all is the fact that people with such warped values are both responsible for strategic planning and are at the same time protected from public censure by the legal cloak of secrecy.

The Dependence of Climate on Life

Regardless of how life on earth actually began, it seems clear that its earliest development was almost totally depen-

---

*In this connection, T. K. Jones, a U.S. official in charge of civil defense planning, reportedly told journalist Robert Scheer (*With Enough Shovels*, New York: Random House, 1982) that "If there are enough shovels to go around, everybody is going to make it. . . . It's the dirt that does it."

†See also, Jonathan Schell's *The Fate of the Earth*, 1982 (New York: Knopf).

dent on the environment, with little influence in the other direction. However, as life spread its physical and chemical presence about the land, seas, and air, the environment was both controlling life and being controlled by the biosphere. Indeed, earlier we borrowed from evolutionary biologists the concept of coevolution and applied it to the interdependent changes that life and the climate have undergone over the aeons. Since humanity is certainly part of life, and if we allow our technology and social organization to be included as well, then it seems safe to say that this generation of humans is rapidly altering some of the conditions under which life and climate have coevolved. We are—largely inadvertently—tipping the balance away from the prehistorical one of our dependence on climate towards the opposite condition. Indeed, unless the human juggernaut is derailed by some dramatic cataclysm such as the nuclear exchange just discussed, life will become a prime force for climatic change in the next millenium. Even with all uncertainties openly acknowledged, at the very least it is appropriate to repeat what, in this context, was termed "the bottom line" in *The Primordial Bond:* "we are insulting our environment at a faster rate than we are understanding it."[122] One of the principal such "insults" from a climatic point of view is the buildup of carbon dioxide and other trace gases. CO_2 is, perhaps, the most important single past, present, and future component affecting the coevolution of climate and life.

Summary of the CO_2 Connection

Carbon dioxide has been of significant importance to climate from the earth's planetary beginnings. Our galactic inheritance some 4.6 billion years ago included heat from the sun that was perhaps 25 to 30 percent less energetic than today, as well as a collection of elements that condensed into the earth, including carbon and oxygen. As the earth's planetary crust cooled and hardened, hot gases from the interior were ejected, and carbon dioxide surely was one of the important ones. Its content in the primordial atmosphere has been estimated by some to have been many, many times greater than today, and indeed this is one of the principal explanations of how the earth's climate could have been warm enough for liquid water to have flowed and life to have evolved from the organic soup that brewed some four billion years ago. This "super greenhouse effect" may have helped preserve the early habitability of the planet we inherit today. Then, as life evolved, the solar output increased and photosynthetic organisms used the carbon dioxide to create their tissues.

CO_2 was also intimately connected with the weathering cycles that maintain mineral abundance on earth. Fossil fuels were laid down over a several-hundred-million-year period during the recent Phanerazoic Eon of abundant life—the past 600 million years or so. The richest fossil fuel deposits occurred mostly at times when proxy evidence suggests the earth was considerably warmer and possibly much more CO_2-rich than it is today. As the era of permanent polar ice descended over the past two million years, some evidence suggests that CO_2 levels dropped by severalfold relative to those in the times of the dinosaurs. Gas bubbles trapped in ancient ice in great glaciers on Greenland and Antarctica suggest that during the end of the last great ice age between 10,000 and 20,000 years ago, CO_2 levels were reduced by one-third relative to today, near to the lower limit for successful photosynthesis in many green plants. Then, CO_2 concentrations became nearly as large (or perhaps even slightly larger) than today, during the early to mid-Holocene, the warm era known as the climatic optimum. Finally, as humanity burns the buried organic matter from past geologic periods (or the forests of today) in order to power the engines and economies of modern society, we are reinjecting at an incredibly accelerated pace this legacy of fossil carbon. It is dumped into the atmosphere at a much faster rate than it can be absorbed by the oceans or biosphere. CO_2 buildup in the next few decades to centuries could well be one of the principal controlling factors of the future climate.

In a metaphorical sense, carbon dioxide plays the role of a suspended cable of a great bridge of coevolution, starting at the earth's dawn, crossing the present, and leading into the future. CO_2 not only spans periods of geologic time, but joins together both climate and life on earth in all eras.

Should CO_2 and other trace greenhouse gases continue to increase as many project, then a global temperature rise seems virtually certain. This in itself is not necessarily bad, as anyone suffering through unduly harsh winters or ice-clogged ports might suspect. However, melting ice could raise sea levels, although the timing for such events is problematic.[123] Also, a few degrees extra summer warmth in scorched places like sub-Saharan Africa, to say nothing of exacerbated July swelter in Washington, D.C.; Houston, Texas; or Phoenix, Arizona would certainly present no boon to humanity.

Although global surface temperature rise is a fundamental indicator that the CO_2-greenhouse theory is valid—and most preliminary indications to date suggest that indeed such projected rising temperatures are not inconsistent with observations over the past hundred years—what is far more important for humanity is how CO_2-induced climatic effects will be distributed around the globe. Changes to regional climates, such as those suggested in the CO_2-climate scenarios discussed earlier, almost certainly indicate that some parts of the world would be adversely affected, others virtually unaffected, whereas yet others would perhaps be improved. Moreover, if large amounts of CO_2 once produced vegetation prolific enough to support dinosaurs and build up fossil fuel deposits 100 million years ago, it might also be true that CO_2 increases would likewise raise plant productivity in the future. Indeed a number of agronomists have welcomed the prospect of CO_2 increases from this point of view.[124] However, it is not just the plants we like that would grow more effectively if CO_2 increases, but weeds and plants that harbor pests or disease-bearing insects could also be aided. Indeed, it is not even clear that the part of the plant we wish to harvest would increase relative to the parts we are less interested in (the so-called *harvest index*). For example, we would want fruits to grow faster, not just the leaves.

The study of CO_2's possible effects is an exciting part of climatological research. Perhaps the most pressing question, though, is whether our knowledge will have increased enough by the end of this century—when the climatic effects of CO_2 from human activities are presently predicted to grow unambiguously larger than natural fluctuations in the climate. As of now, it still appears probable that the climatic system itself will conduct "the great geophysical experiment"—verifying the validity of our present climatic theories of increasing trace gases and CO_2—before a consensus of climatologists offers a definitive statement. Such an increase in CO_2 is almost certain to have climatic, biospheric, and human significance. But the extent to which this is good or bad—and for whom—is not obvious from the mere fact that environmental and economic life will be altered by changes in CO_2 and climate. Thus, before one can declare the "CO_2 problem" a crisis, we must proceed with the very obvious next step and ask, simply: So what if CO_2 increases? So what if the climate changes?

PART III

WEATHER PERMITTING: CLIMATE AND HUMAN AFFAIRS

9 Food, Water, Health, and Climate

Climate and Society

It's easy to credit or blame the weather for many of society's ups and downs, such as a bumper harvest or a famine following drought. And certainly the elements are often partly to blame. But viewing weather and climate as controlling such events dismisses the role of other influences: a society's economic infrastructure, level of technological sophistication, political responsiveness, or long-term planning vision, among other factors. Such nonclimatic variables must be taken into account when we try to assess the impact of weather, climate, and climatic change on human affairs.

It is true that when it comes to food production, water supplies, and human health, adverse weather and climate can play a major role and take a heavy toll. In this sense climate is a short-term *hazard*. Sudden drought is a common example of a short-term climatic hazard; being unprepared for drought exacerbates the problem. An abnormally hard winter is another typical climatic hazard.

Of course, climate is not only a hazard. It has another persona too: it can be a *resource* to be exploited to improve the quality of human life. The warm and humid summer conditions in the U.S. corn belt, for example, have made this region a principal granary for much of the world. While no one expects the yearly climate there to be constant, matching precisely the average climatic year,* society does expect the climate to be stable enough over time to allow sensible long-term investments in agricultural lands, equipment, and irrigation systems.

But, of course, the climate has changed and will continue to do so regardless of our expectations or recent experiences. In that sense, climate takes on another meaning for society: as an evolving,

---

*The word "average" is often erroneously replaced by the word "normal." It is abnormal to have the statistically average weather at any one time.

long-term *trend*. Because a trend implies a change, these changes could alter the distribution of the climatic resources we are accustomed to, including the location, severity, and frequency of such climatic hazards as drought and extreme cold or heat. These, in turn, could lead to a change in the preferred geographical patterns of forests, grain belts, and watersheds.

We cannot overlook the fact that society is changing at the same time that our environment is changing. Growing human populations and rising affluence combine to create demand for consumer goods and services, especially food, water, and energy. This demand will almost certainly continue to increase for several decades, at least. Simultaneously, the burden of many kinds of atmospheric pollution will likely continue to grow—a burden that is already implicated in a century-long trend of climatic change.

Increasing energy use and the economic development it affords is virtually universally desired, since it usually means improving most peoples' well-being. As we will discuss in Chapter 11, there are major disagreements over the specific ways in which the quality of life can be improved; but nearly everyone seeks to have sustainable levels of the essential components of food, water, health, and energy. In this chapter we discuss the first three of these components and how they are influenced by climate and climatic change. The fourth, energy, is given special attention in Chapter 10. The reason for the separation is that human use of energy can also influence climate considerably—as well as being influenced by it. Earlier we saw that society now has the capability to alter the climate for better or for worse with, for example, the carbon dioxide emitted from some agricultural and industrial activities.

How well people can cope with impending climatic changes of any cause depends on how quickly they occur relative to how quickly we can adapt to new conditions. The last three chapters of this book focus on examples of climatic impacts on society and on how people perceive the impact of climate on human affairs. It is this perception that will lead us to take action—if and when we are ready or able.

In discussing the principal aspects of climate, climatic change, and its impact on humans in these pages, we have been sampling knowledge from geology, biology, agronomy, chemistry, physics, engineering, glaciology, geography, oceanography, history, anthropology, psychology, economics, sociology, political science, and of course meteorology and climatology. Such a broad interdisciplinary inquiry is not unique to problems of climate change or of climatic impact assessments. Many other sociotechnical problems require integrating information from such diverse sets of disciplines. Such problems include toxic waste disposal, nuclear safety, arms control, food and drug safety, the ethics and safety of new medical techniques, and even the control of inflation. These are but a few examples of real problems that compel society to make policy judgments even when we do not have enough scientific information (sometimes it seems we never have enough) to satisfy individual specialists that the components of the problem within their field are well understood. What information we do have must be used to formulate public policy to deal with such problems, both present and potential. To do nothing should be a choice made by design, not by ignorant accident. Chapter 11 summarizes some specific policy areas, general conclusions, and principles for dealing with climatic change. It also focuses on the conceptual framework that people use to assess any possible anticipatory responses to potential problems. These biases, often more than the issues themselves, dictate what will be done to mitigate potential hazards or to take better advantage of new opportunities.

We are not the first to be concerned about climate, climatic change, and human affairs. Even the U.S. Congress, not always the most forward looking of parliamentary bodies, nonetheless recognized the long-term need to improve and use climatic information by passing (virtually without opposition) the National Climate Program Act in 1978.* The legislation called for concerted national efforts in climatic research, data collection, and applications. Other nations have also recognized the need to improve knowledge of climate and its impacts, including a worldwide international effort led by UN agencies.†

The discussion in Part III is not a comprehensive treatment of the growing field of climatic impact assessment,‡ nor is it intended as a balanced history of thought on the role of climate in human affairs. Rather, we aim to use selected specific examples to illustrate some urgent policy issues and the critical need to integrate our understanding of the physical climate system and the biosphere with many social variables.

*U.S. National Climate Program Act., PL 95-367, September 17, 1978.
†*Proceedings of the World Climate Conference,* WMO No. 537, 1979 (Geneva: World Meteorological Organization).
‡For such a review, see Kates, R. W. (ed.), 1983, *Improving the Science of Climatic Impact Assessment* (New York: Wiley), in press.

Climate and Food

Climate plays a major direct role in global survival through its powerful influence on the long-term geographic patterns and year-to-year productivity of food systems. In some circumstances that influence appears pervasive, as climatic determinists would expect. But a careful examination of case studies involving climatic shocks to food systems will show that society often has as much if not more influence.

Environmental Stress in Subsistence Cultures

Societies with fairly simple social and economic structure have long had to deal with environmental stress. University of California at Berkeley anthropologist Elizabeth Colson has studied several such groups, hoping to find the common responses they have used to adapt to such adversity. One group she studied was the Makah people, hunters of the Pacific Northwest coast.

From ancestral accounts, it seems the Makah knew that the abundance of sea mammals, fish, and birds in the Cape Flattery waters varied. To cushion themselves against changes in their harvest they exploited a number of different sea and land plants and animals. As a result, the disappearance of one or more species "did not leave them vulnerable or force them into sudden experimentation or improvisation."[1] The fifty-year disappearance of the fur seal during the eighteenth century, for instance, was not a catastrophe for the Makah because they had diversified. But later, with the advent of lucrative markets for fur seals, they ignored the lessons of their ancestors and became economically dependent on the animals. When fur seals became scarce again at the end of the nineteenth century, the Makah suffered the consequences of opting for such economic "progress"; they had become less resilient to environmental stresses.

As a result of this and other studies, the anthropologist lists five devices that self-reliant peoples use to decrease their vulnerability to environmental stresses:

1. Diversification of activities, rather than specialization or reliance on a few plants or animals;

2. Storage of foodstuffs;

3. Storage and transmission of information on what we can call famine foods;

4. Conversion of surplus food into durable valuables that could be stored and traded for food in an emergency;

5. Cultivation of social relationships to allow the tapping of food resources of other regions.

According to Colson, the extent to which societies ignore these devices determines how they become vulnerable to damage from climatic causes.

The Irish Potato Famine

The Irish potato famine of 1845–50 has become a classic in the literature of environmental disasters. Cool, damp weather contributed to potato blight in nineteenth-century Ireland. The result was drastically reduced potato harvests, which contributed to millions of deaths and forced migrations that reduced the Irish population by nearly half. The story has an age-old double moral: if a population grows too large, food demands will outstrip food supplies; if people depend on a monoculture for their food, they risk devastation if that single subsistence crop is affected by climatic stress or disease.

The lessons of this famine do not seem quite so straightforward, however, when the Irish experience is compared with a similar potato blight that occurred at the same time in the Netherlands. Both countries suffered considerably between 1845 and 1850. But, as economic historian Joel Mokyr has shown, during this period in the Netherlands fewer people suffered: excess deaths* and decreases in births (compared with a precrisis year) were some fifteen times *less* severe in the Netherlands than in Ireland.[2] Moreover, forced migration from Holland after 1850 was a trickle compared to the flood from Ireland. Nevertheless, Holland did sustain heavy losses, at least by today's standards. Mokyr estimates that the number of famine-caused casualties in the Netherlands was about 126,000. At the same time, Belgium was also enduring harvest failures. Yet the increase in the death rate in Belgium was far below that of the Netherlands.

Why did these three countries differ in their vulnerability to short-term food production stresses? Joel Mokyr attributes the variations in resilience primarily to the different levels of industrialization and of economic diversification in these countries. According

---

Excess deaths are those above normal expectations. They occur during a time when certain events (such as a food crisis) are believed to have created more than the usual number of deaths.

to Mokyr, the western countries that modernized their economies during the first half of the nineteenth century, in this case represented by Belgium and (slightly less so) by Holland, were able to withstand much better these environmentally induced commodity scarcities. They avoided the ordeal that Ireland had to undergo in the 1840s. Once industrialization had become firmly established, such *subsistence crises* gradually disappeared.

Agricultural commercialization came along with industrialization in these then developing countries. This meant that more produce was sold in the market and more people were buying their food than growing it. Such development implies that fewer people were living a hand-to-mouth life; more had the money to purchase food, especially when local harvests failed because of climatic or other causes. For this food trade to take place, an economic and political infrastructure for marketing, storage, and transport had to have developed. Such an infrastructure evolved with industrial and economic growth and the political will to encourage it. But in Ireland, burdened with colonial rule, there was much less infrastructure and economic diversity.

Unfortunately, we can only speculate about the comparative yield losses in Ireland, Holland, and Belgium. Thus, our evaluation of the relative importance of environmental versus economic and political factors can only be a qualitative one. Nevertheless, it seems reasonable to conclude that economic and social factors contributed significantly to the vastly different levels of damage from the potato blight experienced in these three countries.

The Sahelian Drought

A more modern example of a climate-related disaster took place in the Sudano-Sahel region of North Central Africa, just to the south of the Sahara Desert. Nearly everyone agrees that during the early 1970s in the sub-Saharan region of Africa, there were two predominant events: rainfall for several years running was generally well below long-term averages; and famine occurred along with considerable losses of livestock and crops. While most analysts of the Sahelian crisis believe that these two events were cause and effect, respectively, this view is increasingly being challenged. A number of conflicting interpretations of the Sahelian drought cloud the general view of what should have been done to offset its effects—and what might currently be done as a matter of policy to prevent people from suffering in the future as a result of climatic variations.

Climatic Trend as Cause   One theory, propounded by Reid Bryson, is that the suffering followed drought caused by a cooling trend in the Northern Hemisphere, creating a "Sahelian effect"—shifts in the monsoon rains in the Sahelian part of Africa and the northern parts of India.[3] If this theory is right, and such a Sahelian effect continues to suppress the monsoon rains in inhabited areas, deserts will spread southward and hundreds of thousands or more will die—or be forced to migrate—in succeeding decades. His is a controversial position, particularly since he attributes part of that cooling to atmospheric aerosols generated from industrial and agricultural activities of countries mostly outside of the Sahel. The inherently divisive nature of potentially human-induced climatic modification is obvious from this example, regardless of whether the assumed modifications were perceived, rather than proved, as true.

Climatic Fluctuations as Cause   Other researchers contend that droughts in the Sahel are a regular, hazardous feature of the climate, and not part of an evolving trend. The 1970s event, they say, was much like previous extremes.[4] University of Maryland climatologist Helmut Landsberg suggests that the recurrence of drought was "an entirely foreseeable event, if not precisely predictable on a time scale as to when it would strike."[5] Both this view of climate as a hazard and Bryson's view of climate as a trend suggest that populations of humans and animals were too high to be sustained in bad climate years.

**Inappropriate Technology and
Foreign Aid as the Culprits**   Political scientist Michael Glantz of the National Center for Atmospheric Research stresses another aspect of the problem. He says that western countries intervened with an inappropriate technology that exacerbated the drought's impact. Foreign aid financed the digging of wells, or boreholes, which upset the well-established nomadic way of life that was well adapted to periodic droughts.[6] While these wells provided a short-term solution to the perennial problem of water shortage in the Sahel, they encouraged nomads to increase their herd's size beyond the long-term carrying capacity of the land and to stay in

375

areas close to the wells. As a consequence, the herds overgrazed these areas and depleted and trampled the available vegetative cover.

Social Structure as Cause   Still others believe the roots of the Sahelian crisis to be even more deeply imbedded in social factors. In their book *Food First,* Frances Moore Lappé and Joseph Collins argue that the governments that took over after independence in the Sahelian countries forced peasants to grow cotton for French export markets, even though the soil of this region was ill suited to yearly cotton growing.[7] Over the centuries Sahelians had developed a way of coping with periodic drought. Farmers traditionally rotated millet and legumes to replenish soil nutrients—and to nourish themselves. But the continual planting of cotton depleted the soil, forcing further expansion of cotton cropping and locking up land and other resources that would otherwise have been used for farming and grazing. Thus, in this view, modern technological, social, economic, and political influences actually *increased* the vulnerability of subsistence farmers and nomads to climate stress. Only by overthrowing "elites" who "put profits ahead of people" will the harm of periodic bad years be alleviated, they believe. In a similar vein, Argentinian meteorologist and social critic Rolando Garcia led a major study on the Sahel events and published his controversial views in a book with the title *Nature Pleads Not Guilty.* He decries "the official view"—malevolent nature, overpopulation, and indigenous mismanagement—of the Sahelian catastrophe, and instead argues that it was a "structural problem, the unavoidable consequence of a *system*" that combines the "prevailing international economic order," plus the "international division of labor," the application of "comparative advantages" plus the "prevailing ideas on international aid."[8] He suggests "structural adaptations" to prevent recurrence of catastrophes (based on reduction of the influence of market economics), redefinition of the value of "productivity" (to de-emphasize output and encourage resilience), and reformulation of productive organization to aid in agricultural work.

The Technology and
Free Market Incentive View   Another interpretation, however, forwards the opposite view: that the only way to avoid chronic food shortages and to build food-growing capacity is to give farmers a bigger stake in a growing economy through

greater cash sales. Producers need an incentive to purchase necessary technologies—such as fertilizers—in order to increase production, according to food analysts Sterling Wortman and Ralph Cummings.[9] Access to markets and the profit motive, they argue, would
encourage farmers to grow more food—whether cash or subsistence crops. More food and production, of course, are the best
means of preventing famine.

Summary The example of the Sahelian disaster
shows that climate is only one element of societal vulnerability to
climatic stresses. While nearly all analysts would concede this point,
the differing emphasis placed on environmental, social, and political
factors often stems more from the differing ideological viewpoints
of the analysts than disagreements over the events themselves. Missing, incorrect, or distorted facts have been piled on top of the
conceptual differences, providing even further cause for disagreement over interpretation of cause and effect.

To put the climatic factor in meeting world food needs into
better perspective, we turn next to the U.S. Plains, the principal
food-exporting region of the world.

The Weather/Technology Debate:
The Case of the U.S. Plains

The percentage of world oil exports dominated by
OPEC is dwarfed by the portion of the world grain trade controlled
by the United States. It was this fact that led some members of
recent Administrations to revive the early 1970s views of former
Secretary of Agriculture Earl Butz that the United States should use
its food as a "weapon" to influence potential purchasers. It may be
helpful to look beneath the political rhetoric to determine how the
United States became such a major grain exporter and how stable
the high agricultural production of the United States has been—or
might continue to be—over time.

From 1958 to 1973, the weather in the U.S. Plains was excep-
tionally good for agriculture. High U.S. productivity and growing
world food demands after shortfalls in the USSR and India in 1972
led the federal government to encourage the country's farmers to
plant all available land. The hope was to achieve bumper crops that
could be sold to the burgeoning markets abroad. Secretary Earl
Butz was so confident in the continued success of this scheme that
the landbank program (originally established as a soil-conservation

377

and price-stabilizing measure after the 1930s Dust Bowl) was curtailed. Under the landbank program, the government had paid farmers not to plow on selected lands. Even though a significant portion of U.S. croplands had been set aside, huge North American surpluses of grain grew in the 1960s and early 1970s; but there were too few paying customers to buy these surpluses and farmers complained of a glut on the market. Thus, the government bought the surplus grain, storing it for food emergencies or using it for food aid under Public Law 480—the so-called Food for Peace bill. In the mid-1960s PL 480 food had helped India stave off a major famine following poor growing-season weather (see Figure 7.7).

Several agrometeorologists then said that unusually benign weather in the United States in the fifteen years before 1973 helped to boost crop yields and reduce variability in the yields from year to year. United States Department of Agriculture (USDA) experts claimed that it was technological advances in agriculture, not climatic conditions, that were responsible for the bumper harvests. These modern practices, the experts believed, made U.S. food production nearly impervious to weather variations. Thus, the USDA declared that food reserves as a hedge against such potentially hazardous fluctuations were largely unnecessary—and also held down farm income needed to encourage full production. A heated exchange ensued on the relative roles of weather and technology in determining crop-yield variabilities.

James McQuigg, one of the skeptical agrometeorologists, headed a team of scientists in Columbia, Missouri, to study this question. In 1974 they issued a report claiming that the chance of experiencing another fifteen consecutive years of comparably good weather was about "one in 10,000."[10] Both McQuigg and his colleague Louis Thompson, Dean of Agriculture at Iowa State University, became embroiled with the USDA in a major controversy during the mid-1970s. The debate was over the relative contribution of technological advances and good weather conditions to the high yields and the low-yield variability experienced between 1958 and 1973.[11] Understanding the debate requires a close look at several interrelated issues. These include how yield variability in one nation is coupled with trade to other nations; how climatic variability is distributed around the world; crop-climate timetables, or phenology; the cultural practices of farmers; soils and their protection; and, of course, data on how crops have performed over the past few decades in the face of technological change and climatic fluctuations.

378

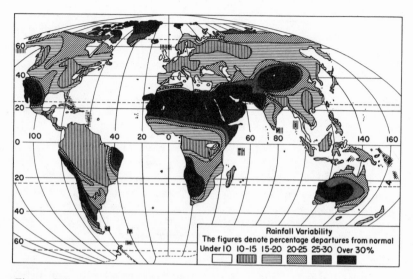

Rainfall Variability
The figures denote percentage departures from normal
Under 10   10-15   15-20   20-25   25-30   Over 30%

Figure 9.1

Annual rainfall divided by long-term average precipitation is one useful statistical measure of climatic variability. This rainfall variability measure tends to be highest in places where there is either very little annual average precipitation or where most of the annual rainfall occurs in a few storms or over a short season. [Source: S. Pettersson, 1969, Introduction to Meteorology, *3d ed. (New York: McGraw-Hill), p. 275.]*

Climatic Variability

Figure 9.1 shows the likelihood of one kind of climatic variation—a departure from "normal" annual amounts of rainfall—in different regions. In assessing the suitability of a region for certain crops, a farmer needs to know not only the long-term average precipitation rate, but also the severity of typical short-term variations. The latter variations are often more important to agricultural producers than long-term averages, since crops are usually chosen to match mean conditions.

To discuss climatic variability coherently requires defining it, and that's not easy. It can mean the difference between one year and a long-term average, or it can mean the differences between successive years. To illustrate the confusion that can arise from using the concept of climatic variability, consider Figure 9.2, an idealized weather record covering twelve years in a hypothetical growing region. The weather in the first four years can be characterized as a *downward trend;* years 5 through 8 constitute a period of *high*

379

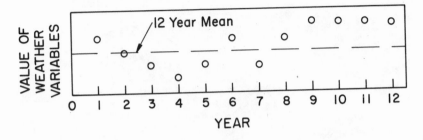

Figure 9.2

Schematic diagram of a time series of
an annually averaged weather variable
over twelve hypothetical years. See the
text for discussion of the concepts of
downward trend, high variability, and

low variability. Confusion about the
application of these terms often leads to
difficulty in defining or interpreting
climatic variability and its application
to food production.

variability; and years 9 through 12, one of *low variability.* But if we
use as our measure of variability how much *each* of the twelve years
differs from the twelve-year mean (represented by the dashed line),
then each of years 9 through 12 is actually more variable than any
of years 0 through 8. The reason is that years 9 through 12 have
values *farther* away from the twelve-year average than do the individual years from 0 to 8.

Clearly, two interpretations of variability are possible here: the
term can refer to the difference between a yearly value and the
long-term mean, or it can refer to the difference in the values of the
variable *between successive years.* In the case of Figure 9.2, years 9
through 12 are clearly less variable than earlier years in the interpretation based on successive years, and the opposite is true for the
other interpretation. Furthermore, even where the definition of
variability is consistent, one climatic variable, such as monthly temperature, could be increasing in variability while another, such as
rainfall, is decreasing. The debate among climatologists as to
whether or not climatic variability has been increasing has often
grown bitter, and frequently the conflict centers on implicit definitions and arbitrary choices of variables rather than on differing
interpretations of the implications.* We shall see in this chapter that
despite the debate over definitions of variability, clear signs of the
effects on U.S. yields of climatic variability emerge from the data.

*Canadian climatologist and geographer F. Kenneth Hare gave several examples and
wrote of his exasperation over this confusion: "this litany of conflicting views can
be continued to the point of tedium," he said, and we agree.[12]

Phenology:

The Crop-Climate Timetable

Conflicting definitions and analyses of climatic variability represent only one of several factors that cloud the weather/technology debate. Another is the complex influence of weather on crop physiology.

To explain a crop's response to its climatic environment we begin with a brief introduction to *phenology,* the study of the growth stages of plants (mentioned briefly in connection with dendrochronology in Chapter 3). Rice, for example, has three basic phenological states—vegetative, reproductive, and ripening.[13] During the early part of the vegetative phase, young plants develop, usually after the early sprouts have been transplanted. The number of shoots that sprout depends on the weather, soil type, soil moisture, nutrients, competing plants, and the distance between plants. The shoots are especially sensitive to light and temperature during their one- to two-month growing period. But this sensitivity decreases during the subsequent three-week reproductive phase. During its final phase—ripening—the grain becomes fully developed, typically over one month, depending on the temperature. Thus, rice yields are not a simple function of temperature or light averaged over the whole growing period. Rather, yields depend considerably on *when* during the growing period environmental variations occur. People can and do intervene in the phenological cycle—by irrigation, for instance—and this further alters the response of plants to climatic fluctuations.

Figure 9.3 shows a general phenology of crop production, and includes several categories that are not part of plant physiology but depend on the cultural practices of the farmer, such as fallowing and harvesting. Cultural practices, especially, when tuned to the phenology cycle, can enhance plant yields. For example, irrigating spring wheat in the northern Great Plains with 1 inch of water generally improves yields, especially if the water is added in the middle of the growing cycle.* However, if the water is added near harvest time, yields will be reduced.[14]

---

*This example has implications for the CO_2-increase results of the Manabe, Wetherald, and Stouffer climate models discussed in the previous chapter. If early snowmelt from CO_2 heating increased soil moisture in the spring, but extra evaporation led to more dryness in summer, the effects could be quite detrimental for crops planted in the spring, such as corn or spring wheat. But this scenario could be beneficial to winter wheat, since more spring moisture and early summer dryness at harvest time would probably increase yields.

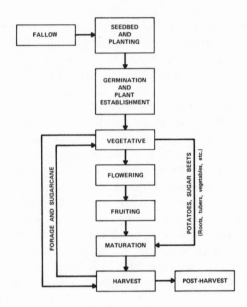

Figure 9.3

Generalized scheme of crop production events, including the phenological stages of plant development as well as several categories controllable by the farmer (for example, fallow and harvest date). [Source: Committee on Climate and Weather Fluctuations and Agricultural Production, 1976, Climate and Food: Climate Fluctuation and U.S. Agricultural Production *(Washington, D.C.: National Academy of Sciences), p. 92.]*

The severe heat wave in the south central United States in the summer of 1980 serves as another good example of how phenological stages for various crops interact differently with climatic anomalies. This hot spell began in Texas in late spring and spread into the south central states in midsummer. Crops planted in the spring, most notably corn and soybeans, suffered considerably. In the affected states, yields of these crops typically dropped by tens of percentage points or more below long-term averages. On the other hand, winter wheat, which is harvested in the spring in the south central states, thrived. Above-normal temperatures and dryness actually improve wheat when these conditions occur in the ripening and harvesting phases of the crop's phenological development. The phenological stages of corn and soybeans, on the other hand, were mismatched to the anomalous heat of 1980.* Clearly, the relationship between climate and food production is not a simple one, and types of crops—as well as species of livestock or marine animals—must be considered individually. Few general statements such as "drought is bad for yields" apply to all food-producing activities.

Cultural Practices of Growers   Farmers can time a number of agricultural practices to match the phenological states of specific crops. Irrigation is used extensively—and its use is growing rapidly—to prod the development of rice, especially in Asia. Irrigation is also popular for crops grown in semiarid parts of North America and the USSR. The addition of nitrogen and other fertilizers is another common agricultural practice. Though some strains actually decrease in yield as fertilizer applications increase, most strains respond favorably to it.[15] Agriculturalists have been searching for and geneticists have been working to create crop strains that respond consistently well to heavy doses of fertilizer.

At first glance, the selection and cultivation of a single strain that responds well to fertilizer may appear to be an ideal technique for improving productivity. However, this method has its own problem. Modern agricultural sciences and associated technology—often labeled the "Green Revolution"—have certainly increased productivity, but they have frequently done so by simplifying existing agroecosystems—that is, by planting relatively few genetic varieties of high-yielding species, matched to the cultural practices of the farmer and to normal weather. Among the obvious effects of simplification is the vulnerability that comes from loss of species diversity. A simplified, nondiversified agroecosystem can be vulnerable to the attack of a single pest. Thus, farmers who plant large single-strain crops have to ward off the pests that could decimate these "monocultures" by using chemical pesticides, herbicides, and other environmentally harmful methods of control. An example of this vulnerability is the considerable losses in yields suffered in the United States in 1969 and 1970 as a result of the Southern Corn leaf blight. This disease affected most of the high-yielding corn plants

*Again in 1983, a year of anomalous heat in the U.S. corn belt and southeast in mid-summer, winter wheat harvests were generally excellent but corn and soybean production was damaged.

sharing a common genetic origin planted at the time; owing to the lack of genetic diversity, fewer plants were present that might have been resistant to the blight. The U.S. national corn yield dropped by 10 to 20 percent in those years, despite otherwise favorable weather. After that disaster, seed stocks of varieties that could resist this blight were developed. The difficulty lies in anticipating such problems. Clearly, then, enhancing food production involves more than simply matching a high-yielding strain with prevailing climatic conditions.[16]

Soils Soil condition is another major ingredient in food production related to climate.[17] Soil must store water and nutrients in the quantity and quality appropriate to the plant and provide a hospitable environment for a variety of natural recyclers —bacteria, insects, worms, and some larger animals. Far from being just a substance to prop up the plants, soil is a complex mixture of mineral compounds, organic compounds, living organisms, air, and water. Its composition varies over time and in response to geologic, climatic, vegetative, and anthropogenic factors. Plants and some animals take nutrients from the soil and return them when they either excrete waste or die. People add nutrients (and other chemicals) by planting and fertilizing and extract nutrients from the soil by harvesting. Organic matter in soil can also be altered by human activities.

At least three layers called *horizons* exist in most soils. A soil's fertility depends primarily on the composition of its top zone, called the A-horizon, where many forms of chemical compounds containing nutrients can be *leached,* or dissolved in water. In a rainy climate, the top layer of soil typically contains fewer soil nutrients because of leaching. The rainfall in a region determines how fast leaching occurs and thus influences how nutrient-rich the soils will be. Growers must be cognizant of these factors if their productivity is to be large and their soil losses small.

By now it should be obvious that many interacting elements contribute to food productivity, which is why it is so difficult to make simple statements of how weather changes affect crops. To help untangle weather from other factors, we will try another approach and concentrate next on food production fluctuations during the fifteen years of favorable climate in the United States. This survey will help to determine whether Butz or his detractors were closer to the truth in the weather technology debate.

U.S. Grain Trends in
the Technological Period
During the homesteading era of the late 1800s, growers were generally successful. Good weather encouraged the settlers, and "rainfall follows the plow" was a popular line on railroad posters advertising the lure of the Plains. But drought in the 1890s shattered the illusion and drove out many settlers. This pattern of boom-and-bust farming recurred several times, with good weather and high production years followed by drought years, economic ruin, and disastrous soil erosion.[18] The most severe and intensive drought and soil degradation occurred in the 1930s in an area that became known as the Dust Bowl, where average wheat and corn yields plunged by 50 to as much as 75 percent and millions of tons of valuable topsoil were lost. The economic depression of the 1930s was worsened by this climatic depression.

The country learned painful lessons from this experience. As a result, the government established the U.S. Soil Conservation Service to help farmers protect the soil; geneticists later developed new crop strains that were better adapted to regional climates; and irrigation and chemical fertilizer were made available to take advantage of the new strains and to aid production. As a result, the productivity of the U.S. Plains has increased 200 to 300 percent since the 1930s.

Productivity—that is, yield per unit area—has expanded, primarily due to increased energy inputs used to power technologies such as field machines, irrigation pumps, and agrochemicals. Thus, more crops have been harvested per acre. There has also been more total *production* (average yield per harvested area multiplied by total harvested area). Similarly, for most grains, the variability of yield from year to year as a percentage of long-term mean yield has decreased —that is, the amount of year-to-year yield variability has decreased over time relative to the average yield. But during the decades of technological advances, the absolute or total amount of yield variability has increased for most crops in the United States.* In other

---

*Consider an example. Corn yields in the first half of the twentieth century fluctuated by some 10 bushels per acre from year to year, with average yields of about 30 bushels per acre. The *relative variability* was thus about 30 percent. In the 1970s, however, average yields were some 90 bushels per acre, but year-to-year *absolute variability* in yields was typically 15 bushels per acre. Thus, absolute variability increased some 50 percent in this example (from 10 to 15 bushels per acre), while relative variability decreased by 50 percent (from about one-third to one-sixth).

words, the relative variability (year-to-year variability as a percent-age of long-term average yield) has usually decreased for a crop in recent years, whereas its absolute variability (year-to-year yield vari-ability by itself) has on the whole increased.[19]

This is the heart of the debate, for the next step is to distinguish the role of climate from the role of technological advances in both average yield and yield variability trends during the 1960s and 1970s. Some relevant USDA statistics are represented graphically in Figure 9.4.[20] Figure 9.4 shows that the year-to-year fluctuations in yields of total U.S. grains were fairly low before 1973. (We can draw this conclusion from Figure 9.4c because the plotted data before 1974 closely follow the upward-sloping trend line, with very little scatter.) During 1969 and 1970, total grain production dropped (see Figure 9.4a). Two reasons for the dip in production are that the amount of area harvested declined (Figure 9.4b), and the corn blight attacked a large portion of genetically similar hybrid strains, thereby slashing corn yields substantially. Total grain yield (see Figure 9.4c) increased close to the trend line until 1973, and the yield then dropped in 1974, staying well below the trend line until 1978. In 1974 bad weather was a major factor in the corn belt— simultaneously too wet for early planting, too hot and dry for pro-ductive flowering, and too cold for anticipated late harvesting. Each weather event occurred at the worst time in the phenological cycles of corn crops in the Midwest. Earl Butz referred to this 1974 anom-aly pattern as a "triple whammy."

It's clear from Figure 9.4 that after 1973 variability of grain yield and production both increased markedly, just as McQuigg and Thompson had forewarned. Significant increases in the harvested area (Figure 9.4b) were necessary merely to maintain total produc-tion close to the trend line, despite the loss of yield below trend between 1974 and 1978 (see the shaded area in Figure 9.4c). The increase in harvested area—which totaled some 25 percent from 1972 to 1976—was largely the result of returning fallowed land to production. These areas typically were fallowed because they had lower production potential or a greater likelihood of suffering ero-sion than those left under the plow in 1971. Hence, at least part of the lower-than-trend yields seen in Figure 9.4c resulted from the federal government encouraging farmers to recultivate relatively inferior land; another consequence of that government policy was increased soil erosion. In connection with the latter issue, Univer-sity of Nebraska agrometeorologist Norman Rosenberg remarked

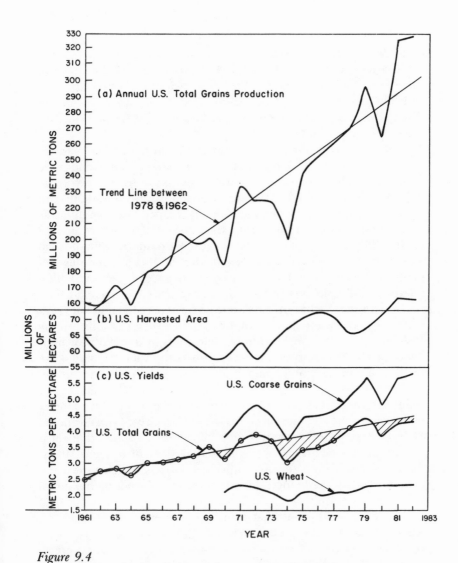

Figure 9.4

Grain production harvested area, and yields in the United States from 1961 through 1982. (Preliminary estimates suggest that U.S. production of coarse grains in 1983 will be nearly cut in half by a combination of summer heat and planted-area reductions encouraged by a government program.) Note that yields of total grains showed relatively little departure from the long-term trend line before 1973, but that the variability seemed to have increased after 1973. [Data from U.S. Department of Agriculture, **World Grain Situation and Outlook: Foreign Agricultural Circular** *(Washington, D.C.: Government Printing Office), FG-26-82, August 1982.]*

that "despite the proven beneficial effects of windbreaks planted in the Great Plains during the drought years of the 1930s, many of them are now being removed", because "windbreaks may interfere with the mechanical operation of the large center-pivot sprinkling systems that are revolutionizing irrigation in the Great Plains region."[21]

Without doubt, then, technology has been the prime factor in increasing grain-yield trends. But the debate has continued into the 1980s over whether technology was responsible for the favorable decrease in the United States and Canada during the 1960s and 1970s of relative yield variability—that is, year-to-year variability as a percentage of long-term average yield. As noted earlier, compared to the 1930s, 1940s, and 1950s, when most modern technological aids such as fertilizer, chemical pesticides, herbicides, and new genetic varieties were not widely used (if they were even available), relative yield variability in the last twenty years has declined.[22]

Geographer Richard Warrick and some of his colleagues at Clark University have argued that although relative yield variability in the 1970s went down compared to the bad years in the 1930s or mid-1950s, agrotechnology is not necessarily responsible.[23] Only if the weather anomalies in the mid-1970s were as bad as those in the 1930s or 1950s could modern farming practices take credit for the reduced impact of climatic stress on yields. They compiled an index of the severity of summer droughts in the U.S. Great Plains from the early 1930s to late 1970s, shown in Figure 9.5. It shows that since the era of modern farming methods took hold in the mid-1950s, there has not been a set of weather years bad enough to test the hypothesis that technological methods have reduced the fractional variations of grain yield.

Based on yield losses that actually occurred in the mid-1970s, the scientists at Clark attempted to extrapolate the yield losses that *might* have occurred had the weather in the 1970s been as severe as in the 1930s or 1950s. They concluded tentatively that even relative yield variability would have been about as bad in the 1970s as in those earlier periods if weather had been the same as back then. Absolute yield variability—already larger than before—would have gone up substantially more. Thus, the assumption that the North American breadbasket could maintain stable yearly productivity should the climatic dice roll a few years like the 1930s or mid-1950s is still a dangerous gamble. Now, however, the stakes are higher: hundreds of millions of people depend on the stability of the region's harvests. Because of world grain trade, the weather gamble

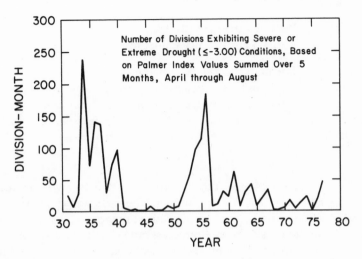

Figure 9.5

U.S. Great Plains drought area, 1931–1977. This figure is based on the work of Richard Warrick and his colleagues at Clark University, who divided the U.S. Great Plains into sixty-four climatic divisions and analyzed the number of divisions exhibiting severe or extreme drought for five months (April through August) of each year. Their measure of drought is the Palmer Drought Index, which suggests extreme or severe drought for values lower than −3. The units of the graph are division-months, that is, the number of divisions and months of each year in which the Palmer Index was less than −3. Note the extreme intensity and widespread nature of the droughts of the 1930s and, to a lesser extent, 1950s, but the relatively mild droughtiness in the Great Plains in the summers of the 1970s. [Source: R. A. Warrick, 1980, Drought in the Great Plains: A case study of research on climate and society in the U.S.A., in J. Ausubel and A. K. Biswas (eds.), Climatic Constraints and Human Activities (Oxford: Pergamon Press), pp. 93–123.]

in the Great Plains is no longer the local farmers' alone, but the world's.

Who was right in the great weather/technology debate—Agriculture Secretary Butz or his agrometeorological critics? At least regarding the United States, McQuigg and Thompson were justified in their outspoken concerns: farmers in highest-grain-production states had experienced a long lucky streak of good growing weather, and when more average climate finally reappeared, yields tumbled well below trend levels for several years while grain prices spiraled. Really unfavorable weather, like that of the mid-1930s, has yet to recur in the United States; thus, we can only speculate as to what would happen.

World Food Security, Food Trade, and Climate

Through the 1960s, world food production outpaced population growth, and many began to believe that the technologies responsible for the so-called "Green Revolution" had once and for all ended the threat of Malthusian disaster.[24] However, 1972 badly shook the confidence of the optimists that technology had finally solved the problem of world hunger.

1972: A Bad Year Nineteen seventy-two was not a good year for Bordeaux wines. Indeed, this year was characterized by worldwide climatic, economic, and human setbacks: serious droughts in the USSR, India, Southeast Asia, Australia, Latin America, and the Sahelian region of Africa; devastation of the protein-rich Peruvian anchovy fishery; depletions of the grain supplies in many major food-producing areas; soaring food prices everywhere; and resulting famines that eventually killed or debilitated tens of millions of people. In India and Bangladesh alone, a million or more excess deaths have been attributed to this bad-weather year.[25] Coming on the heels of a number of good harvest years, the bad weather of 1972 made some scientists and a host of writers wonder whether a turning point had been reached that put adverse climatic variations on the rise.[26]

A close look at the 1972 collapse of Peru's anchovy fishery is now warranted, since it is a good example of climate becoming hazardous to food production and an excellent reminder that the oceans are a significant part of the climatic system. In 1972 the temperature of Peru's coastal waters rose by several degrees. El Niño, a recurring phenomenon associated with the Southern Oscillation, is blamed for disrupting the upwelling process that brings cool, deep ocean waters to the surface. Accompanying the increase in water temperature was a weakening of the upwelling of oxygen and nutrient-rich waters from below. The warmer, nutrient-poorer water caused plankton booms to decrease and the anchovies, higher up the food chain, either swam off, failed to spawn, or died. The anchovy was once considered an inexhaustible source of protein; in 1970, Peru's anchovy catch reached a record high of 12.5 million metric tons. But within three years the catch had plummeted to less than 2 million metric tons.[27] After a brief recovery to about 4 million metric tons, the catch dropped off even further by 1977 to less than 1 million metric tons. (Considerable debate surrounds the question of whether climatic hazards or overfishing were principally responsible for this damage.)[28]

This major fishery has shown few signs of recovery, and some wonder if it ever will. Peru's experience echoes the disappearance of California's sardine fishery, related in John Steinbeck's *Cannery Row*. If the Peruvian anchovy follows suit, nearly 20 percent of the yield of fish protein from the ocean will have been lost, a serious nutritional blow.

The combined effects of shortfalls in the Soviet, Indian, African, and Peruvian food production led to a 3 percent drop in grain production in 1972, the first such worldwide production setback in many years. Prices spiraled and death rates climbed. At the same time, climatologists became embroiled in public controversy over the role of climate in these events, and the likelihood that climate-induced troubles would increase.

The Food Crises
of the Mid-1970s
Except in 1974, world grain consumption rose steadily after 1966 (see Figure 9.6d). Total grain yields also dropped about 4.5 percent in 1974 from the 1973 yields (see Figure 9.6c). These yield figures (as well as those shown in Figure 9.4c) are based on harvested rather than planted area. Harvested area is always smaller than planted area, especially in climatic stress years, when the percent of land planted but not harvested increases. This is because bad weather or pests make harvesting either fruitless or too expensive to undertake in the damaged crop area. Thus, crop yields per planted area are always lower than yields per harvested area, especially in bad years. However, farmers' production costs—as well as the environmental impacts of chemicals and soil erosion from badly managed fields—are usually more closely tied to the number of land units *planted* rather than harvested. The yields per harvested areas that are typically quoted by most statistical services [including the U.S. Department of Agriculture (USDA) and the United Nations' Food and Agriculture Organization (FAO)] really overestimate actual crop productivity as seen from the perspective of the person planting or investing in agriculture.

Since harvested area was up only about 0.4 percent in 1974 over 1973 (see Figure 9.6b) and yields dropped significantly (see Figure 9.6c), worldwide production in 1974 was set back by some 4 percent —about 51 million metric tons (see Figure 9.6a). In addition, the unbroken upward trend in world grain trade broke in 1974—the

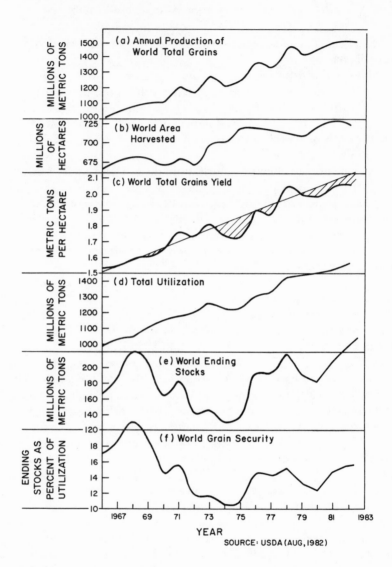

SOURCE: USDA (AUG, 1982)

Figure 9.6

Data for production, harvested area, grain yields, utilization, ending stocks, and grain security for total world grain production between 1966 and 1982. Note the apparent increase in year-to-year variability of world total grain yields (part c) after 1972, in rough agree- *ment with results for the United States seen earlier in Figure 9.4c. [Data from U.S. Department of Agriculture,* **World Grain Situation and Outlook: Foreign Agricultural Circular** *(Washington, D.C.: Government Printing Office), FG-26-82, August 1982.]*

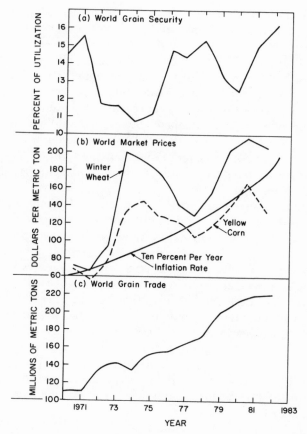

Figure 9.7

World grain security, world market prices for winter wheat and yellow corn, and world grain trade, 1970–1982. Note the obvious inverse relationship between market prices and world grain security, reaffirming the classical market principle that increase in supply (relatively more grain storage) coincides with decreasing prices, and vice versa. However, the price trends do go up steadily over this period, and the 10 percent per year inflation rate curve in part (b) illustrates this inflationary effect. Note that with the exception of 1974, world grain trade increased steadily, showing no significant relationship with fluctuating world grain prices. This violation of classic economics doctrine for supply, price, and demand is probably rooted in the increasing demand for feed grains by affluent nations willing to pay virtually any price to maintain meat-eating habits. [Data from U.S. Department of Agriculture, World Grain Situation and Outlook: Foreign Agricultural Circular *(Washington, D.C.: Government Printing Office), FG-26-82, August 1982.]*

only such trade decline over a previous year since 1968. This set-back in production, yield, and trade occurred at a time when food stocks were about the lowest in decades: the USDA estimated that at the end of 1974 stocks had dropped to 134 million metric tons, the lowest in this sixteen-year record (see Figure 9.6e). Because of increasing world population and the affluent countries' demand for feed grains, these reserve stocks represented a significantly smaller percentage of world grain demands than they would have ten years earlier. The worldwide grain shortfall, in conjunction with the U.S. policy (and that of other major grain-exporting countries as well) of liquidating government-held stocks, forced world grain security to a new low (see Figure 9.6f).

It is interesting to compare the world prices of grains (see Figure 9.7b) with the index of world food security (see Figure 9.7a). An obvious inverse relationship exists, as one would expect from classical market economic theory, since prices go up when supplies dwindle and vice versa. But a very different picture emerges in Figure 9.7c, which shows that (aside from the exceptional year 1974) world grain trade has increased steadily regardless of price! The reason for such seeming noneconomic (that is, unresponsive to price) behavior is that the principal purchasers of grains are not the cash-poor, food-needy developing countries, but rather the more affluent developed countries (capitalist and socialist alike). The rich, who have considerable elasticity in their purchasing power, are willing to cope with food-price fluctuations while still maintaining their dietary standards.

Figure 9.8 shows world grain trade for 1977 through 1981 for wheat and flour (usually consumed directly by humans), coarse grains (usually fed to animals), and (only for 1979 through 1981) rice (also directly eaten by people). The number in parentheses atop each bar graph represents trade as a percentage of total world production of that commodity. It is obvious that the rice trade represents a miniscule fraction of total rice production compared to trade of the other commodities, even though total world rice production in 1980 was about 87 percent of wheat and 52 percent of coarse grain production. This relatively small rice trade simply reflects the fact that most rice is directly consumed near where it is grown, largely as a staple in the diets of Third World countries. Also clear from Figure 9.8 is that the United States and Canada control more than half the world's grain exports and that their grip on exportable coarse grains is even greater.

The economic and political significance of the overall trade

394

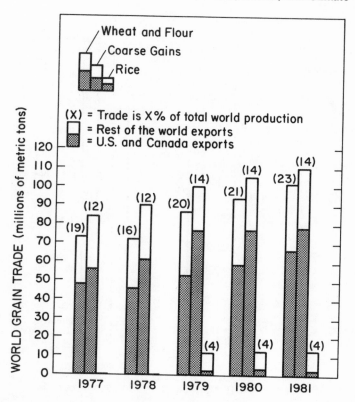

Figure 9.8

World grain trade in wheat, coarse grains (mostly fed to animals), and rice (except for 1977 and 1978), subdivided into U.S. and Canadian exports (the shaded fractions of the bars) and the rest of the world. The numbers in parentheses above each bar represent the percentage that trade represents of total world production. Note that wheat and *coarse grain trade has been an increasing percentage of production, but rice trade has been a steady, low 4 percent of world production. [Data from U.S. Department of Agriculture,* World Grain Situation and Outlook: Foreign Agricultural Circular *(Washington, D.C.: Government Printing Office), FG-26-82, August 1982.]*

figures is easier to see in Figure 9.9, which expands the wheat and coarse grain data for 1980 into principal exporting and importing countries. The dominance of the exports by the United States, Canada, and a few other developed countries is once again apparent, but the grain import story is also quite revealing. Whereas Western Europe is a net exporter of wheat, it is a large net importer of feed grains. This simply reflects the demand in Europe (both East and

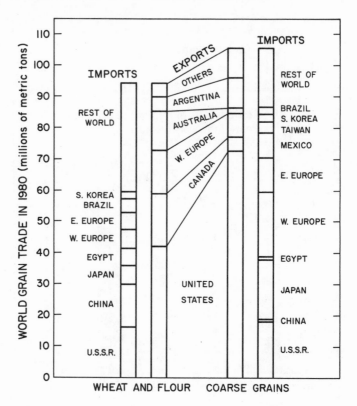

Figure 9.9

World grain trade in wheat and flour versus coarse grains for 1980, broken down into the principal importing and exporting regions. The very large contribution of the United States, particularly to trade in coarse grains, is clear from the bars labeled exports, as is the large import of feed grains to affluent nations like the USSR, Japan, Western Europe, and so on. [Data from U.S. Department of Agriculture, World Grain Situation and Outlook: Foreign Agricultural Circular (Washington, D.C.: Government Printing Office), FG-26-82, August 1982.]

West—including the USSR) for grain-fed animals, notwithstanding the cost. China, on the other hand, is a significant importer of wheat but buys only a negligible amount of coarse grains. The Chinese have other priorities for their precious foreign exchange resources than purchases of feed grains. Japan, on the other hand, was the single largest importing nation for coarse grains in 1980, perhaps not surprising in view of Japan's reputedly abundant hard currency and lack of suitable geographic endowment for growing feed grains. Data such as these clearly reveal that the effects of climatic variations

396

on food production are felt well beyond the location of weather anomalies, and that the distribution of impacts is hard to predict in advance given the complex consuming, trading, and producing patterns of various nations.

We have already discussed the consequences of the combination of events that caused food security problems in the mid-1970s. It might be easy to blame poor weather alone for periods of falling yields, rising food prices, decreasing food supplies, and some expanded famine conditions, but it is apparent that other factors are involved: population size, dietary standards, economic well-being, purchasing power, and the political climate controlling access to food supplies. Trading, pricing, agricultural investments, land tenure, food reserves, and food distribution policies of many countries also figure in. It was the *interaction* of all of these social factors with environmental conditions and farmers' cultural practices that created the food crisis of the mid-1970s.

Although a number of good-weather years returned to most of the world near the end of the decade, 1979 saw bad harvests in India; 1980 was hot and dry in the central United States, which led to low yields in summer crops (see Figure 9.4c). The USSR also had disappointing harvests. Thus, at the beginning of the 1980s the world had about the same level of grain security as it did entering the 1970s—about 14 percent. Although this level dropped by an additional percentage point the next year, it recovered somewhat by 1982. Figure 9.7a shows in quantitative terms how a relatively "safe" margin of food security was quickly eroded in the mid-1970s and again in 1980; in more emotionally tangible terms, the images of old and young victims of food price rises and famines of the mid-1970s are still vivid and poignant. They remind us of the risks of low food security and high volatility in grain stocks and prices. These memories must not be forgotten.*

*As this book was going to press in the summer of 1983, the headlines were again warning of major heat and drought related damage to U.S. corn crops. The opening sentence of a Page 1 story by William Robbins in the Sunday August 21, 1983 *New York Times* reported on the developing situation: "with a swiftness that has shocked both farmers and economists, the nation's burdensome corn surplus has apparently been all but wiped away by a severe drought and a costly government program." One wonders why anyone should be shocked, since this basic scenario is a virtual replay of events less than a decade old. What is shocking is that some farmers and government officials never seem to remember the past. In the August 15, 1983 U.S. Department of Agriculture *Foreign Agriculture Circular* (FG-23-83) the USDA estimated that because of the new government program which pays farmers surplus grains roughly equivalent to acreage they agree to withhold from production (called

Because of the complexity of food-climate interactions, policies for dealing with potential climatic hazards, trends, or resources cannot be formulated in isolation, ignoring other important aspects of the food system. On the other hand, the lesson of the yield and price fluctuations of the 1970s is that climate cannot—as it so often has been in past analyses—be assumed as constant in food policy making, even if the elements are only one component. To put the climate factor in the perspective of world development, we will next touch in some detail on some of the primary factors that affect our ability to meet world food needs. An in-depth treatment of this critical subject for human survival takes volumes.[29] Nevertheless, we hope that the following brief summary will at least point out some of the complexity of food systems.

Meeting World Food Needs for the Year 2000 and Beyond

In developed countries (DCs), the threat of peacetime subsistence crises is long past; but in less developed nations (LDCs) where famine and malnutrition are still problems, there is considerable debate over how best to develop in order to meet basic human needs. Whatever one's political, social, economic, or climatic theory, most people would agree that an essential step toward this goal is decreasing the chances of food crises by increasing food production. This means that productivity must be increased—something that Japan, for instance, has done. Over time, Japan's rice yields have increased (compared to recent yields in other countries) with new innovations in farming, modern technologies, and structural reforms such as farm credit systems or rice price supports.[30]

Of course, increasing agricultural productivity (that is, *agricultural intensification*) to meet world food needs is more complicated

---

the Payment In Kind Program—PIK), harvested area in the U.S. for the coarse grains will drop from over 43 million hectares in 1982 to an estimated 33 million hectares in 1983. This 23 percent drop in crop area caused by the government's PIK program came at the same time the 1983 heat wave struck the corn belt. By mid-summer the USDA estimated about a 25 percent drop in coarse grain yields for 1983 relative to 1982. The combined effects of reduced crop area and bad weather are expected to drop coarse grain production to a little under 140 million metric tons, a reduction of nearly half compared to 1982. Stocks of coarse grains, the USDA predicts, are also expected to drop by about two thirds by the 1984 season. This situation has some uncomfortable parallels with that just before the food crisis of the early to mid-1970s.

than simply making use of technological innovations. As we saw above, food production depends on many elements, both natural and anthropogenic. Hence, increasing yields of crops, livestock, or fish will require an integrated approach that considers all these interacting factors. In the next few pages we will look at some of the possible ways agricultural production can be intensified and try to explain some of the problems farmers face in deciding how to use limited resources when contending with a mix of climatic, technological, and social factors.

Plow More Land   Seemingly, the most obvious way to increase the amount of food is to plant more area. Of course, this requires more arable land. The physical requirements for cultivable land include sufficient temperature and precipitation, adequate soil, and workable topography—that is, relatively flat land as opposed to mountainous or very rocky terrain. People have adapted agriculture to such steep areas by terracing the land—that is, carving steps out of the mountainside on which to grow crops—but often this leads to erosion and other problems.

A definition of arable land cannot be very precise when it must make use of words such as sufficient, adequate, and workable. Because the definition is flexible, estimates of potentially arable land are also wide-ranging: some recent estimates range from 2425 million to 3419 million hectares.[31] This is roughly two to three times greater than the amount of land presently cultivated. In 1975 the UN Food and Agricultural Organization estimated that there were 1473 million hectares under cultivation; in 1965 the U.S. President's Science Advisory Committee (PSAC) estimated 1388 million plowed hectares.[32] These figures are less than half the potentially arable land estimates just given. Yet the potential for opening new lands for cultivation is lower than these statistics seem to indicate. For instance, much of the so-called potentially arable land in Australia and Africa is in very arid regions that would require developing irrigation systems for productive crops. Moreover, vast areas of humid tropical forest lands in Africa and especially South America are called arable but quite possibly will never be used to grow food: there are formidable ecological and economic constraints to such development, including infections from tsetse flies or the risk of waterborne diseases such as schistosomiasis.[33]

It might appear from these estimates that expanding arable land alone could increase world food production two or three times. If this is multiplied by the number of times it is theoretically possible to increase yields of presently available crops (two- to four-fold), then theoretically five to ten times the current world population of four and a half billion people could (apparently) be supported. Indeed, these numbers are often cited by those who claim that there is no population problem and that the world's carrying capacity for humans could be 20 billion to 40 billion people.[34] However, for a number of reasons it is highly unlikely that we could safely expand sustainable food production to maintain world population at this level. The relatively poor condition of soils that are often labeled as arable but are in fact quite marginal for sustained food productivity is one such reason.[35] The well-developed areas of Asia, Europe, the USSR, and North America have already cultivated one-half to seven-eighths of their estimated potentially arable land; Africa, Australia, and South America, on the other hand, have barely tapped their estimated arable land resources; hence, the label less-developed is clearly appropriate. But it is primarily in these countries that ecological constraints will cause the most problems for expansion of farming.

Aside from the environmental problems, there are also economic constraints to cultivating more land. In the developed regions of the world mentioned above, the best agricultural land is already being cultivated. According to environmental specialists Paul R. Ehrlich, Anne H. Ehrlich, and John P. Holdren, it is simply not economically feasible to try growing food on intractable land classified as arable but suffering from various defects: lack of nutrients, subject to erosion, rocky terrain, or short growing season, among others. "Neither subsistence nor commercial farmers are stupid; they farm first where food can be produced from the smallest investments of labor and money (this is the definition of the best land)," these authors write.[36]

Ehrlich, Ehrlich, and Holdren make what they call a conservative estimate of how much it would cost to develop new lands: their figure is $1000 (1975 U.S. dollars) per hectare. If each such hectare could support four people, then an annual $20 billion investment is needed merely to keep up with a current world population growth rate of 75 million more people per year. They point out that as more marginal land is brought under cultivation, the quality of the land will go down and the amount of money needed to grow crops will go up. These economic concerns have been echoed by many other analysts as well.[37]

Irrigation   Irrigation is used for different reasons in different places: for example, to maintain high yields in dry years; to grow crops where they can't be grown otherwise; or to grow particularly water-intensive crops. It's not surprising that in countries like the United States and the Netherlands, where precipitation is often reliable enough for sustained runs of good crops, irrigation is used only on a small percentage of the land. In China and Japan, where precipitation can be plentiful but where large areas are devoted to water-intensive rice crops, irrigation is crucial to maintain —let alone increase—productivity. In Tanzania, where rainfall is often absent for many months at a time, irrigation would need to be an integral part of any plans for intensified agriculture. But an irrigation project can cost billions of dollars.[38] Although this seems small—at least compared to world armament expenditures, which are many hundreds of billions annually—such costs preclude most Third World countries from developing substantial irrigation systems with their own resources. It has been pointed out many times that not only will irrigation systems be expensive to construct, but they will be increasingly expensive to operate due to high energy costs.[39] Sometimes, making irrigation more energy efficient with such methods as drip irrigation also makes it less environmentally sound by salinating soil. Victor Kovda, an eminent Soviet soil scientist, calls salinization the "main scourge of irrigated agriculture."[40] Millions of hectares of soil have been polluted when lack of proper drainage resulted in either salinization and alkalinization or waterlogging. Furthermore, these damaged soils tend to become compact and crop yields are further reduced. With few exceptions, he says, irrigation systems today are built and used almost exactly as they were in ancient Egypt and Babylon. Hence, in the attempt to increase agricultural productivity through irrigation, great care is needed to ensure that such long-term, virtually irreversible (on human time scales) environmental damage is minimized, lest the long-term productivity of the earth's agricultural regions be reduced.*

Another type of environmental problem associated with irrigation is its effect on water quality. Runoff from agriculture frequently contains dissolved organic matter, soil nutrients, or pesticides and

---

*Techniques that do minimal ecological damage to agro-ecosystems come under the rubric of "eco-farming."[41] To some, it is as much a way of life as a farming practice, particularly if these techniques employ many farm workers rather than machines. To others, it is more ideology than agricultural or economic necessity.

herbicides that may damage water quality downstream. If water becomes poor in quality, a significant portion of upstream runoff may not be diverted to agricultural uses downstream, unless some inexpensive recycling technologies become available to improve and maintain downstream water quality. (Indeed, the United States and Mexico have negotiated a treaty whereby the United States is obligated to keep Colorado River water above a certain standard of quality. To do this by energy-intensive desalinization techniques is expensive.)

Water quality degradation from surface contamination not only affects surface runoff downstream, but also groundwater supplies. Inasmuch as groundwater is being used increasingly for agricultural intensification, and as a hedge against individual dry years in places like the California central valley or the U.S. Plains, it is critical to sustain both water supplies and quality.

Another uncertainty over the future role of irrigation in meeting world food needs is the problem of competing users of water supplies. In the U.S. West, for example, scarce resources are coveted by industrial and urban users as well as farmers. Typically, the cities and industries can—and will—pay more for water than agricultural users, setting up knotty policy and priority problems. This will be examined further in a later section.

Another insidious side effect of irrigation, at least in many developing countries, is the potential for spreading waterborne diseases. Millions of people and animals in the tropical and semitropical regions of the world have suffered from schistosomiasis, liver fluke infections, and malaria, all of which flourish in wet environments.[42] While these diseases are not new, they have been introduced into previously uncontaminated areas by irrigation systems.

Despite the environmental, health, and economic problems of irrigation, expanding its use is usually essential if food production is to be intensified and world food needs are to be met. As we can see, then, achieving that balance between irrigation costs and benefits will take careful, far-sighted management and large capital investments in many specific cases. Quick-fix solutions to specific irrigation needs—or more generally to meeting world food needs—will almost always fail to deliver sustainable results.

Fertilizers Fertilization, either by natural or artificial means, is essential to high-yielding agriculture designed to meet world food needs. In Chapter 4 we said that large quantities of fixed nitrogen can build up to damaging levels in soils or run off into groundwaters, lakes, streams, or oceans. Fertilization is the principal way to increase the fixed nitrogen (or other nutrient) pools needed to improve crop yields. But these man-made additions of fertilizers also cause local and global environmental problems because they represent a significant alteration of the natural nitrogen or other nutrient cycles.[43] However, here we will concern ourselves primarily with the food-producing role of fertilizer rather than its role as a pollutant.

Simply blanketing a field with chemicals will not ensure bumper crops. The fertilizers need to be used selectively; that is, they must be matched to the crop and cultural practices of each specific application. We noted earlier that some crop strains actually can decrease in yield as fertilizer applications increase. But most crops do respond to increased use of fertilizers, even though they approach some diminishing return at higher levels of fertilizer use. Farmers have to weigh the environmental and economic costs of fertilization, which are tied to the high amounts of fossil fuel energy required for manufacturing, against the benefits of increased yield.[44] Of course, the marginal economic return from higher yields will depend on food prices. Because of these complications it is uncertain to what extent fertilizer applications will increase production further in fields that are already heavily fertilized. In this connection, the dramatic yield increases after 1950 in industrialized countries—which were proportional to fertilizer use—may not continue much longer on already intensively fertilized farms. In the LDCs, on the other hand, where fertilization levels are lower and food needs more urgent, it seems likely that increased fertilization levels will materialize regardless of the marginal return issue.

Energy and Fertilizer   Approximately 15 percent of all the energy used in the United States is devoted to producing, distributing, processing, and consuming food, but most of that energy is not expended on the farm.[45] In 1970, almost 40 percent of it was used to process, package, and transport the food. Thirty-five percent was used primarily for refrigeration and cooking in homes and businesses. Only 25 percent, still a very large amount of energy cost to food producers, went toward manufacturing fertilizers, pesticides, farm machinery, fuel, and electricity for irrigation pumps.[46] A decade later that same energy cost several times more. However, the ecological as well as economic cost of obtaining fertilizers could be reduced. David Pimentel at Cornell University has calculated that intercropping nitrogen-fixing plants with grain crops may be a less expensive way to obtain fixed nitrogen in the soils.[47] He recommends serious consideration of the use of such "green manure," or use of human or livestock wastes directly. (Of course, such wastes must be treated to prevent transmission of diseases and parasites.) Treated sewage water and sludge is used successfully as fertilizer in many countries including the United Kingdom, Australia, Germany, and parts of the United States.[48] However, in other countries burning dung directly as a low-energy fuel is a current practice in many rural villages, where children can be seen foraging behind animals in search of cowpies. This is not only a less efficient way to extract energy from wastes, it also diminishes much of the fertilizer potential as well.*

Pesticides   Another technique of agricultural intensification is pest control by chemicals. We need not recount here the fundamental environmental problems caused by residues of long-lived herbicides or chemical pesticides. These ecological risks were first brought to public attention in 1962 by Rachel Carson's *Silent Spring;* a comprehensive update has been provided by Ehrlich, Ehrlich, and Holdren in Chapter 10 of their book *Ecoscience.* The burgeoning use of pesticides has sprung from the perceived need to protect high-yielding agromonocultures, which, as we have said, can be susceptible to a single attack of pests. (Just how much marginal return in the form of higher yields really does arise from heavy uses of pesticides is a controversial issue.)[51] Since the early widespread use of very long-lived pesticides such as DDT, a number of more rapidly degrading chemicals have been developed; malathion, for

---

*Biogasification is a promising method for more efficient recovering and recycling of nutrients (as well as obtaining high energy hydrocarbon fuels) from manure, human sewage, and other organic wastes. In this process organic matter is broken down by bacteria to produce methane gas and carbon dioxide. The methane has a high energy content and if the carbon dioxide is removed—which can be done with known technology—nearly pure methane with an even higher energy content can be produced. This fuel, already suitable for cooking, heating, and electricity generation, can also be used in adapted farm machinery. Nutrients in the "waste" material that remain behind after biogasification are a major bonus. These nutrients form a compact residue that is actually more useful as a fertilizer than the original material. The process is one that seems especially appropriate economically and environmentally for many rural villages in Asia, Africa, and Latin America.[49] Biogas is not the same as gasohol, which is produced by mixing gasoline with alcohol made from fermentation of agricultural products like corn in the United States or sugar cane in Brazil.[50] This technology is more controversial than biogas since it can be both energy inefficient and wasteful of food supplies—depending on how the gasohol is produced.

example, was used in 1981 for the celebrated aerial spraying in California against the Mediterranean fruit fly. Even such short-lived pesticides or herbicides can have serious unwanted side effects when they kill helpful microbes, insects, animals, or plants. And without careful handling, such chemicals pose potential health hazards to humans. For these reasons, some growers have used biocontrols—for example, certain insects or animals that are natural enemies of suspected harmful pests. Other strategies include crop rotation or multiple cropping schemes that disrupt the life cycles of some pests. In this way, farmers can achieve the benefits of some pest control without having to risk the economic costs or other dangers of chemical pesticides. But muiltiple cropping usually requires human, rather than mechanical, maintenance. This is an economic constraint in developed-country agribusiness; but it is often appropriate, if not necessary, in subsistence-farming communities. However, even in high-technology, intensive agricultural regions conflicts tend to arise when the immediate costs of crops lost to uncontrolled pests exceed the immediate price of pesticides—as in the 1981 medfly controversy in California. This is because large-scale farming, which is capital-intensive, is based on current economic practices designed to maximize short-term return on capital investment. These practices tend to put little value on the hard-to-quantify health risks of pesticides or the long-term ecological benefits of minimizing the applications of chemical controls.*

Losing Ground:
The Tragedy of Soil Erosion   Meeting world food needs in the future will require maintaining adequate soils for high future productivity. Soil erosion, detrimental to long-term food productivity, occurs widely, but most seriously in regions where very intense precipitation falls on sloping surfaces that have been cleared of their protective forest or other vegetative cover. The foothills of the Himalayas and the plowed rolling lands exposed to wind and water in parts of the United States are examples of such

---

*In the Third World, growers also worry about another problem that pesticides can't always deal with: loss of food during storage. Some studies suggest that rodents alone eat enough food every year to feed hundreds of millions of people. In tropical developing countries, for example, 20 percent or more of all crops are estimated to be lost in storage.[52] This compares to only about 9 percent losses in the United States. Some local areas in developing nations in the tropics lose up to 50 percent due to insects, birds, rodents, or diseases that attack poorly stored harvests. Nearly half of all food grown is lost at some stage to pests.

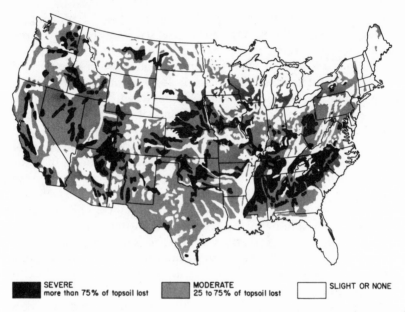

| | SEVERE more than 75% of topsoil lost | | MODERATE 25 to 75% of topsoil lost | | SLIGHT OR NONE |

Figure 9.10

Soil erosion in the United States. This figure shows that more than half the country has been affected by moderate to severe erosion. Perhaps one-third of all croplands have already been lost. Erosion tends to be most severe in areas frequently under the plow, exposed to strong dry winds, subject to periods of intense precipitation, and/or including many steep slopes. [Source: Committee on Climate and Weather Fluctuations in Agricultural Production, 1976, Climate and Food (Washington, D.C.: National Academy of Sciences), p. 45; based on U.S. Department of Agriculture data.]

regions. Every year, nearly 30 tons of soil per hectare erode away on typical U.S. agricultural lands.[53] When this rate of erosion is compared to the natural rate of soil formation, which on average is many times slower, the seriousness of the problem becomes evident. In the United States, more than 75 percent of the topsoil in a disturbingly large fraction of farming areas has already been lost to erosion (see Figure 9.10). If this continues, U.S. agriculture will deservedly lose its label as a renewable resource in a matter of decades.

Soil erosion in other countries is often even worse. Table 9.1 shows soil erosion rates for various land forms and crop types in the humid tropics, where intense rainfall can cause much higher erosion rates (especially on slopes) than in midlatitude regions like the

United States. If we take 30 tons per hectare as a typical annual rate of soil loss for cultivated lands (including the United States), then soil depth shrinks about 1.6 millimeters (0.06 inches) per year.* It has been aptly stated by former Worldwatch Institute writer Erik Eckholm that "losing ground" is perhaps our most serious long-term environmental problem.[54]

One response to growing food demand is to increase the area planted. This was a primary policy of grain-exporting countries for much of the 1970s. Unfortunately, pressure to grow more food year after year has led to some serious long-term problems. In drought years the percentage of acres planted but not harvested increases.[55] This is because it has been uneconomic—and in some cases agriculturally impossible—to harvest drought-damaged crops. Moreover, there is a correlation between an increasing fraction of unharvested area and soil losses. Pressure to plant "to the fence posts"—and even to remove the fence posts to bring in every additional inch of the land—has put many marginal fields back under the plow; these are often most vulnerable to wind and water erosion. Soil erosion is not just an environmental tragedy, but a long-term economic problem, since lost soil ultimately reduces the productivity of the land.†

One of the long-range dangers resulting from the short-range pressures to produce and sell more food is that in major food-growing places we are mining today's soils at the risk of tomorrow's productivity. Carefully timed irrigation can help to reduce the damage, but it can be expensive and must follow sound environmental practices that minimize salinization, waterlogging, and further erosion of the soils.

*Consider this hypothetical example. Assume soil losses in the U.S. Plains have been at the rate of 1.6 millimeters (0.06 inches) per year over the past 100 years of intensive farming in this region. This means that some 16 centimeters (6 inches) of topsoil have already been lost. If topsoil loss continues at this rate, the U.S. Plains may have only another hundred years or so before much of the topsoil is gone. Soil typically regenerates at a much slower rate than it is lost in these exposed agricultural areas. Figure 9.10 shows that in large regions of the United States the topsoil is already depleted by 50 to 75 percent, an alarming statistic. This is consistent with our hypothetical calculation.

†A team of Minnesota agricultural researchers examined the soil erosion-productivity issue quantitatively in their state, concluding that while the problem is serious, its severity varies greatly according to geographic conditions. It is not so much the total tonnage of soil eroded that affects crop productivity, they argue, but rather loss of economically "irreplaceable inputs" such as "water storage capacity, depth, and subsoil acidity."[56]

Table 9.1 Annual Rates of Soil Erosion
by Land Form and Vegetative Cover Type and in the Humid Tropics

Land form and vegetative cover type	Annual rate of erosion Millimeters	Metric tons per hectare
Almost flat		
Cotton	4.00	80
Annual field crops	1.60	32
Pasture, dense	0.10–0.50	2–10
Pasture, open	1.00–10.00	20–200
Undulating, moderate slope		
Natural forest tree plantation (teak)	0.01–0.50	0.2–10
Wide spacing, mixed understorey	0.10–0.50	2–10
Dense, no understorey	1.00–8.00	20–160
Moderate to steep slope		
Natural forest	0.50–2.00	10–40
Shifting cultivation during cropping years	30.00–60.00	600–1200

Source: J. J. Burgos, 1979, Renewable resources and agriculture in Latin America in relation to the stability of climate, in *Proceedings of the World Climate Conference* (Geneva: World Meteorological Organization), WMO-No. 537, p. 536.

Should Soils Be Owned
or Just Managed?

As we have just said, great care must be taken to minimize environmental damage as we pursue agricultural intensification in order to get higher food yields for growing world demands. Maintaining the productive potential of the world's agroecosystems is probably one of the most critical requirements for future populations. Sustaining our productive potential in the future raises a basic ethical and political question: should anyone have the right to claim ownership of the soils, or are the soils a global commons to be protected for all future inhabitants even though they might be maintained temporarily by the stewardship of a few? In one view, the present owners of the land should be entitled to use it and benefit from its bounty *as long as they protect the land's productive capacity.* Others believe that farmers—or businesses—who legally own the land should be permitted to do anything to the land, if necessary, in pursuit of an economic or any other gain. People who adhere to the latter view—which is the dominant economic ethic in market systems today—primarily grow food for marketing. They have a strong immediate economic incentive to squeeze as much productivity out of the land as possible. However, we have seen the long-term problems associated with such an ethic. Conservation techniques, while beneficial both ecologically and economically in the long run, can be expensive—and often unprofitable in the short term. A group of Cornell researchers and students noted that when "there is a reduction of four bushels per acre in yield per inch of top soil lost, and that about twenty tons of top soil per acre are lost annually in corn production, then the annual per-acre reduction in yield (from land with an initial top soil depth of 12 inches or less) would be about one-half bushel of corn (worth about $1.50). When per-acre costs of corn production are estimated at $190, the $1.50 represents an annual loss of less than 1 percent, a negligible amount for a single year. The total of cumulative effects of soil erosion on crop productivity are, however, considerable."[57]

Bottom-line thinking in our economically rational society whose goal is to maximize return on investment carries a low value in the long term, particularly when capital is scarce, interest rates are high, and there is uncertainty of long-term effects. Agribusiness in the developed world has grown quite large, and today's farmer is often a business executive more responsible to his or her board of directors for this year's profits than to society for the next generation's productive capacity. "The next generation doesn't pay the fuel, seed, water, or machinery bills," we've heard farmers lament. Indeed, farmers must face the realities of market economics: fluctuating prices, high interest rates, and banks threatening foreclosure if loans aren't repaid on schedule. However, if producers must deplete the soil or the groundwater to squeeze out enough production in order to survive financially for another year, essentially treating these environmental resources as depletable, nonrenewable economic commodities, then it may be time to re-examine the premises underlying such business practices.

Perhaps in the interest of long-term productivity, farm lands should be viewed as national parks and the present stewards—the farmers—should be expected to maintain the productive potential of the land. As techniques to do this can be expensive, perhaps society, which benefits, should pay any financial losses associated with conservation measures needed to insure sustainable agriculture. We suggest this even at the risk of an added layer of bureaucracy or perceived loss of property rights, although such risks can be controlled. Added layers of bureaucracy may not even be necessary; soil depletion taxes or soil conservation tax credits are obvious examples of convenient and precedented instruments to provide incentives to ensure future soil quality and quantity.

Creating national soil parks out of our farmlands may seem a radical step for so-called free market nations, particularly since there are less draconian measures available like grants, special loans, fines, and so on. But unless something more is done to protect soils, we predict that in a matter of decades soil preservation will become a major item on the political agenda for long-term survival in both market and planned economy countries. In any case, the soil protection issue clearly demonstrates that food production issues have a strong ethical component.

Ethical Considerations in Meeting World Food Needs

We shouldn't become so preoccupied about future prospects that we forget to deal with the present food situation. Wealthier countries must grapple with the question of whether they should help poorer nations directly by giving food, food technology (such as new crop strains), or financial aid to help purchase food or equipment such as tractors or irrigation systems. Less developed countries must decide whether they should spurn such outside help and stress self-reliance, as China did during its Cultural Revolution. Poorer countries could thereby gain greater control over their fate by decreasing their dependence on the rich. On the other hand, by refusing aid the needy might lose some opportunities to intensify production or accelerate the timetable for achieving self-reliance. And apart from food aid issues, food trade too raises a similar question about the trade-offs between short-term relief and long-term dependence on outside sources for areas not self-sufficient in food production. Part of the problem the less developed nations face in picking an approach to improve their own agricultural output and food security is choosing between small-scale technology and labor-intensive techniques or larger-scale technology and capital-intensive techniques, such as using crop duster planes or tractors. Of course, the backdrop for all of these questions is political control of the food-producing and food-distributing mechanisms, the sustainability of food supply systems, and the maintenance of long-term environmental quality. As we have seen, intensifying food production in the short term for a growing population by certain methods could have alarming long-term consequences. These trade-offs must constantly be made in the face of the continuing Malthusian question: Can food production keep pace with population growth rates? And for any country where the answer is no, then trade, aid, or increasing death rates are inevitable. In discussing this question, we will review food production and population trends over the two decades between 1955 and 1975, comparing the developed countries (DCs) and less developed countries (LDCs).

The Malthusian Situation   Although the percentage increase in *total* food production for both DCs and LDCs is similar over the past few decades, the per capita production is much less in the LDCs. There, population growth has almost kept pace with production, whereas in the DCs, production has significantly exceeded population growth. Although population and food production have kept up with one another when averaged over *all* the less developed nations, Figure 9.11 shows considerable differences in this Malthusian statistic among various LDC regions. For example, East Asia has gained in per capita food production, while Africa has faltered. East Asia's success is largely due to rapidly increasing crop yields and a relatively low population growth rate compared to other regions. Africa's plight can be accounted for to a considerable extent by its high population growth rates—among the largest in the LDCs, as can be noted in Table 9.2. Equally troublesome, grain yields have increased little since the early 1960s in Africa, primarily because their use of common intensification techniques, particularly chemical fertilizers, to boost production has been relatively meager. Where per capita food production falls over time, people who cannot easily afford to import food are bound to suffer from malnutrition; they are forced to use scarce foreign exchange reserves—if they have any—to buy food on the world market. Ironically, in some instances LDCs actually export food or other agricultural products—so-called cash crops—to developed nations in order to garner foreign exchange; this can lead to insufficient production of subsistence crops and starvation in some areas where food is shipped out for cash instead of being available to the population.* (This criticism was brought out earlier in the discussion of the Sahelian drought disaster.) Moreover, the foreign exchange so

---

*One example is called the "Hamburger Connection" by Norman Myers, referring to the beef exports from Latin America to the United States to support fast food hamburger chains.[58] Myers, however, was more concerned with the destruction of Central American forests for the purpose of creating pastures to graze animals that would be exported to the U.S.

earned is not necessarily spent on improving long-term agricultural development or for emergency food imports to minimize malnutrition in a bad-weather year. Rather, precious foreign currencies are all too often used to buy high-technology gadgets, particularly military hardware.

Food Aid, Food Trade, and Food Consumption   Who are the chief food buyers and sellers? Earlier we noted that Canada, the United States, and Australia accounted for about three-fourths of the wheat exports in 1980 (see Figure 9.9). Europe (East and West), the USSR,

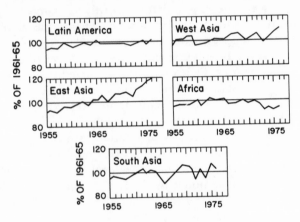

Figure 9.11

Trends in food production per capita for selected regions comprised of less-developed countries. Although overall food production was ahead of population growth in the less-developed countries, it can be seen here that such average conditions do not necessarily reflect local or regional status. For example, during the twenty-one-year period from 1955 to 1976 this statistic showed virtually no improvement in Latin America or South Asia, whereas East Asia showed dramatic increase in food production per capita while Africa as a whole showed dangerous signs of losing the Malthusian race. If such data are broken down further into countries, and even states within countries, what emerges is the recognition that averages over large regions tell very little about the food production versus population status of localities, with many parts of the Third World showing significant progress, and others falling further behind with the specter of repeated famine in food-stress years increasing all the time. [Source: S. Wortman and R. W. Cummings, Jr., To Feed This World: The Challenge and the Strategy (Baltimore: Johns Hopkins Press), compiled from U.S. Department of Agriculture data.]

Table 9.2 World Population Data by Region, Mid-1982 Estimates, and with Projections to the Year 2000

Region	No. of countries	Population (millions) 1982	Population (millions) 2000[a]	Annual growth rate (%)[b]	Doubling time (yrs.)[c]
Africa					
Northern	6	117	190	3.1	22
Western	16	150	265	3.0	23
Eastern	17	141	246	3.0	23
Middle	9	56	90	2.6	27
Southern	5	34	55	2.5	28
Total	53	498	846	2.9	24
Asia					
Southwest	16	106	171	2.7	26
Middle South	9	988	1396	2.2	32
Southeast	11	374	519	2.2	32
East	8	1204	1441	1.4	50
Total	44	2672	3527	1.9	37
Americas					
North	2	256	286	0.7	95
Middle	8	95	142	2.6	26
Caribbean	16	30	41	1.8	38
South					
Tropical	9	209	313	2.4	28
Temperate	3	43	53	1.5	45
Total	38	633	835	1.7	41
Europe	27	488	511	0.4	187
U.S.S.R.	1	270	302	0.8	88
Oceania	8	24	30	1.3	55
World					
More Developed		1152	1248	0.6	116
Less Developed		3434	4835	2.1	33
Total		4586	6083	1.7	40

Source: Population Reference Bureau, 1982 World Population Data Sheet, Washington, D.C., 1982.
[a]Projection to year 2000 based on assumed projections in population growth rates "actually anticipated under a reasonable set of assumptions regarding future birth and death rates", made by Population Reference Bureau.
[b]Based on population changes during the late 1970s.
[c]Assuming that present growth rate continues over the doubling period.

Japan, China, and Brazil imported about 60 percent of the wheat sold on the world market. Of the total amount of coarse grains—primarily used for animal feed—the United States exported about three-fourths in 1980 (see Figure 9.9); about 95 percent of this amount of feed grains went to Japan, the USSR, and Europe (East and West). All told, in 1980 coarse grains (which have become the largest grain trade commodity because of imports by wealthy countries for livestock feed) comprised about half of total world grain production and half of total world grain trade. Rice, on the other hand, as seen in Figure 9.8, is one of the smaller food trade commodities. In 1980 rice production was some twenty times larger than rice trade, according to USDA statistics; it is a staple crop in LDCs, where most grains are produced and consumed locally. Twenty percent of coarse grains, on the other hand, are traded.

There was a dramatic drop in U.S. shipments in the form of food aid and concessional sales after the world food crisis in 1972 (from more than 15,000 million tons in the early 1960s to less than 3500 million tons in 1973).[59] But food *trade* has skyrocketed (see Figure 9.7c), particularly in the form of coarse grain shipments. In other words, while food sold on concessionary terms or given as aid for *direct* consumption by humans has dropped or remained reasonably stable, sales of feed grain have risen dramatically—an export of grain for indirect consumption by people. The indirect consumption of grain—after it is converted to food energy through livestock—is extremely inefficient. That is, only about a tenth of the energy content of grains fed to animals is retained by their bodies and is thereby available to human consumers. Most of the rest is either belched, excreted, or used to maintain the animals' metabolic needs.[60] Protein intake per capita in DCs is typically two to three times greater than in LDCs. Animal proteins in the developed countries' diets largely account for this difference.[61]

We don't mean to oppose any role for livestock in meeting world food needs. On the contrary, in some climates or geographic conditions livestock that forage are the principal economically viable agricultural product. Moreover, livestock constitutes a huge hidden grain reserve in the sense that if there were a global food emergency, both the livestock and their intended feed grains could be consumed directly by people. However, economics and politics make this option unlikely, since most food emergencies typically occur in countries with few grain or livestock reserves.

Many poorer countries cannot afford—or do not choose—to buy enough grains in the world marketplace to prevent malnutrition by direct consumption, even in times of domestic shortfalls, which are often climatically induced. Balance-of-payments deficits, debts, credit policies, and other economic factors affect their ability or desire to purchase food grains—let alone develop a taste for grain-fed animals.

If a country is not self-sufficient in food production, then, of course, imports must be obtained to prevent famine. Such food transfers can be in the form of hard currency purchases by nations like Japan or the USSR, as concessional sales, or as outright donations from private or governmental donors, as occurred often in the Sahel in the 1970s. However, a number of analysts have opposed such food transfers in principle, often for very different reasons. One rationale is that food transfers for recipient nations create a dangerous dependence that allows suppliers to gain undue political control over the recipients. This view was active policy in China during the Cultural Revolution years, when contacts with outside nations were strongly discouraged on the ideological grounds of self-reliance. A radically different reason to oppose food transfers has been expressed by those who believe that any nation not self-sufficient in food production is overpopulated and that food transfers merely prop up an unsustainable situation. Examples of such views of food trade are taken up next.

Food Triage   There are some who even question whether food aid is ethical. In a classic and controversial 1967 book entitled *Famine-1975!*, William and Paul Paddock suggested somewhat prophetically that by the mid-1970s, chronic food shortages in some LDCs would overwhelm the capacities of even the grain-rich countries for providing sufficient aid.* Those developing nations whose population growth rates exceeded their capacity for food production were singled out. The Paddocks recommended that a food policy analogous to the medical use of *triage*—the World War I battlefield policy—be adopted. Here is the way it worked in wartime. The wounded were divided into three groups: the hopelessly injured, for whom treatment was unlikely to do any good; the superficially wounded, who despite pain could wait to receive treatment; and the seriously wounded, for whom treatment was most likely to be effective. This system was designed to save the largest number of people, given too few doctors and too many patients.

*Although famine certainly increased in the mid-1970s' food crises, it was the unwillingness rather than inability of grain-rich countries that helped sustain that food crisis in some LDCs.

The Paddocks believe that world food shortages will reach such proportions that those requesting food aid will either have to be helped or turned away, depending on how desperate they are or how much it is deemed they could—or should—be helped.

For example, the Paddocks suggested in their book that countries like India, with cumbersome bureaucracies and high population growth rates, cannot be saved and therefore food should not be "wasted" on them.* An oil-rich but food-poor country like Libya probably has enough resources to buy their food in emergencies, so aid need not be sent them. On the other hand, a country like Pakistan, which the Paddocks believed showed promise of self-sufficiency in the long run, should be given food aid in crises.

Is such a policy unethical? It was condemned as such by many people. But the Paddocks believed it was a moral alternative, since the triage is designed to save the maximum number of people with limited food aid available.[62]

However, their battlefield analogy to the world food situation breaks down when we realize that *there is no worldwide shortage of grain* (especially if we include feed grains as potentially consumable by people); there are only regional and local shortages. The food-rich are the "triage officers" with their surpluses. Changes in dietary standards or more uniform per capita distribution of existing food could prevent chronic malnutrition or periodic famines—at least for a decade or two more—after which unconstrained population growth probably would outstrip food production, even on a worldwide average basis. Thus, unlike battlefield triage, a policy of food triage today would not save the maximum number of lives possible, unless one accepts the present systems of food ownership and distribution as a given that is beyond negotiation. But the latter is a political caveat, not a moral imperative.

Lifeboat Ethics   While the triage concept may seem a harsh or even immoral view of reality, ecologist Garrett Hardin's well known doctrine of "lifeboat ethics" is even tougher.[63] Like the Paddocks, Hardin believes that food aid just tends to discourage the efforts of many less developed countries to increase their own pro-

---

*Although India's population growth remains high in a number of states and their increasing food production is not yet safely ahead of the population growth, their emergency planning helped greatly in 1980, when poor monsoon rains caused production shortfalls. India's grain reserve policies set up after the painful food crises of 1972 and 1974 were successful in staving off comparable famine conditions in 1980.

416

duction and to lower their birth rates. Hence, he agrees that offering food aid today will create a less supportable, larger population in the future. The crises that have only been delayed would then cause even more people to suffer famine. If food aid were withdrawn today, Hardin suggests, food-deficient nations would have more of an incentive to solve their problems—and future populations would be relatively smaller and better off in the end. Hardin likens the world and its food problem to a sinking ship: richer nations have managed to get safely into the lifeboats, filling nearly all the seats. The people from poorer nations are splashing about in the sea, desperately trying to climb aboard. In this metaphor, there are more people in the sea than empty seats in the boat, so that any attempt to allow all of them on board would only cause the lifeboat to sink, drowning everybody. (The metaphor has also been applied to the problem of Latin American immigration to the United States.)

Hardin also opposes the idea of an international "food bank," even to help nations through periods of climate-caused food shortages. He argues that those who tend to make the "withdrawals" are often beset by chronic shortages anyway, rendering them unable to make deposits back into the bank. Like the Paddocks' triage analogy to food policy, Hardin's lifeboat metaphor generated a storm of protests calling it both unethical and likely to create international conflicts.

Global Survival Compromise　Has the world food situation become so critical that either the Paddocks' or Hardin's analogies apply? Schneider stated in *The Genesis Strategy* in 1975 that "the implicit and crucial assumption invoked by these metaphors is that the Earth has already reached or surpassed its carrying capacity."[64] But the latter has not been established as accepted scientific fact, despite strong pronouncements both pro and con from well-qualified experts. Nobody really knows scientifically just how large the carrying capacity of the earth is now or could be in the twenty-first century. When arguing the ethical issue of food aid, we need to scrutinize the earth's limits and recognize that although limits do exist, they are not fixed but rather are dependent on a variety of social, economic, industrial, and agricultural practices. Given the uncertainty of what these practices will be, the triage and lifeboat metaphors do not necessarily apply to the real world. I proposed a "global survival compromise," an alternative policy that would offer short-term emergency aid and longer-term technological assistance and capital investment from the wealthier nations. This assistance would be *"coupled to and contingent on mutually agreeable plans* between the donor and recipient nations to bring about self-sufficiency for the recipients as rapidly as possible but within a fixed time, after which aid would be unnecessary and not forthcoming."[65] I acknowledged that this could be most costly for developed countries and that developing countries will have to make many painful changes —some of which may not work—in order to find the best routes toward self-sufficiency. Eventually, I conceded, the alternatives might boil down to triage or lifeboat ethics unless there are "spectacular and unforeseen technological or demographic breakthroughs that would place food supplies comfortably ahead of food needs." But it seems preferable to work to prevent *both* present and future carrying-capacity catastrophes, even at some risk of enhancing potential long-term problems. This is preferable to accepting such catastrophes as inevitable, thereby practicing triage or lifeboat ethics before it is certain that these analogies do—or will—apply.

This principle of compromise seems to us a more ethical course to steer between an indefinite commitment to outright blanket food or food technology transfers to nations not yet self-sufficient and an immediate, total abandonment of the undernourished, especially in bad-weather years. In any case, a diversity of national and international efforts to increase sustainable food production and to lower population growth rates as fast as possible are urgently needed— elements of a similar food and development strategy that scientist and humanist Walter Orr Roberts labeled "pragmatic humanism."[66]

Food-Climate Policy Actions

There is little doubt that making policy related to food-climate interactions will involve technical uncertainty and ethical controversy. Nevertheless, certain obvious actions suggest themselves. We continue this chapter with an exploration of these necessary, if minimal, precautions against climatic hazards.

Food Reserves   Short-term, climate-induced fluctuations in food production typically average several percent from year to year worldwide, and many tens of percent regionally. To compensate for the hazard implicit in these fluctuations, regional food stocks and distribution systems are needed as a hedge against shortfalls. Thus, a high priority on a world food policy agenda should be to identify regional food needs and work out the mechanisms for establishing and distributing the reserves should food emergencies arise. Such mechanisms might include the slaughter of some livestock and transfer of feed grains to direct human consumption. Deciding the terms of access to reserves is a major political component of maintaining food security. It is complicated by the fact that most reserves and surpluses are held by those not likely to face food crises and disinclined to turn their bounty over to the truly needy, who have least control over food resources.

As another step towards minimizing climatic hazards, nations need to disseminate weather and climate information in a comprehensible form to food producers, consumers, and the governmental and nongovernmental bodies concerned with food production fluctuations. The World Climate Programme, an international collaboration administered by the World Meteorological Organization and other UN agencies, already lists this step on its international agenda.[67]

However, many hundreds of millions of people, particularly peasant farmers in LDCs, don't look towards elaborate international or even national mechanisms to provide them and their families with credible advice or food security. Rather, they rely principally on themselves. Storing a part of this year's production to tide over until next year's harvest is an age-old practice. Adding extra provisions against the precedented possibility that next year might also be bad is similarly venerable. UN food policy analyst Pierre Spitz has studied the pressures that influence peasant farmers in India in their decisions on how much food to put aside in the process called *self-provisioning*.[68] Spitz describes two sets of forces tugging these self-provisioning farmers in opposite directions: one to keep as much of the food they had grown as possible (the *forces of retention*) and one to release it (the *forces of extraction*). Many factors combine to favor retention: the fear of lower production and consequent food shortages from future bad weather, concern over future price increases for necessary inputs such as fertilizer, low prevailing prices for farm products, the hope of future price increases, and the possibility of higher rent and taxes. On the other hand, there are considerations that tend to pressure farm families either to seek outside jobs or to sell a larger fraction of each year's harvest to raise cash: the prospect of a future drop in market prices for food (for example, through unusually good weather and oversupply), an immediate increase in rent requiring quick cash, and a rise in the costs of nonfood necessities. Weather fluctuations combine with non-weather-related price fluctuations to compound the difficulty of deciding how to self-provision for each year.

Spitz points out that not all producers in LDCs face the same kinds of dilemmas when weather causes production fluctuations. Large landholders [so-called category (a) producers] who typically produce a big surplus are usually able to survive most production anomalies without catastrophe. But the same is certainly not the case, Spitz asserts, for the "vast majority of poor peasants" in LDCs [so-called category (b) producers]. These people are unable to produce enough food to feed their families over an average year and must somehow supplement their insufficient production either by purchasing food with cash earned from other labors or by using food from their remaining stocks, if any.[69]

The impact of a bad year on these different categories of producers is quite opposite, Spitz writes:

> A decline in output, following a drought, for example, forces them into debt to category (a) producers, to whom they sell their labour power at a lower wage rate, and to whom they sell what they still possess, including their means of production, at knock down prices; it also obliges them to mortgage their land and, eventually, to sell it. The shocks repeatedly inflicted by climatic variability thus accentuate the long-term tendency for the polarization of these two groups of producers and for elimination of the weakest, who are driven into the cities.[70]

In this scenario a bad year for the peasant farmers is a windfall for large producers, who can increase their own landholdings at rock-bottom prices.

To minimize this polarization, Spitz suggests, the government must intervene with aid immediately after the harvest, since "it is too late when land has been mortgaged and tools sold in the period preceding the next harvest: the situation cannot be rectified by soup kitchens, the distribution of food, relief works, nor even by loans." Thus, Spitz's suggestion is that the solution to this food-climate problem is primarily social and political: "agrarian reform aimed at a more equitable distribution of land" and a "redistribution of economic and political power."[71] Of course, his solutions, like those mentioned earlier in connection with the Sahel region in Africa, stem from a particular conceptual view of the underlying causes of the problem. But ideological viewpoints aside, the Spitz scenario strongly suggests that reserve stocks and distribution systems as a means of food security need to be examined at both local and more centralized levels to determine just how much security they really provide—and for whom.

Let's step back from the issue of local-scale self-provisioning for a moment and take a broader view of world food security in the face of year-to-year climatic variability. Figure 9.7 shows that when grain stocks dip below about 15 percent of utilization, local scarcities, worldwide price jumps, and sporadic famines were more likely to occur. This suggests that a *minimum world level of accessible grain stocks near 15 percent of global utilization needs to be maintained as a hedge against year-to-year production fluctuations.* Of course, as we have already seen, access to this buffer for those who need it in emergencies is limited by social and economic factors. This inability to use reserves as a hedge for such people is the chief obstacle to achieving a workable world food security system, whatever the global level of stocks may be, since such stocks in the hands of private owners often makes them of little use to the needy.

Minimizing Climatic Risks

for Producers   While food reserves and distribution systems are primarily security measures for consumers, the financial risks to producers must also be minimized. Farmers in both DCs and LDCs need fertilizers, seeds, labor, and other appropriate technologies, all of which cost money. Often, farmers borrow money and then must pay it back from the money they earn by selling crops. Typically, debts must be repaid on a fixed credit cycle regardless of how the annual crop turns out. A few bad-weather years can create such severe financial risks to producers (including the ultimate risk of losing the land) that as a "climate defensive" strategy they restrict their investments to production materials such as parts for irrigation systems or fertilizer. Not only does this strategy tend to lower overall production in the short run, it also limits the development of the infrastructure necessary to encourage long-term productivity increases. Thus, it is important to ensure that the short-term financial risks of potentially bad weather do not unduly inhibit the producer investments needed to maintain or increase production.[72] Crop insurance is one way to accomplish this. But more creative solutions are necessary as well, such as farm loans with flexible repayment terms, analogous perhaps to floating-interest-rate mortgages. Thus, in a good production and marketing year producers might pay creditors larger-than-average payments, whereas in lean years payments would be reduced. In this way the burden of adverse climate anomalies on food production and prices would be shared in the general economy, rather than being concentrated wholly on the producer. The concept is akin to the pooling of risk practiced in the insurance industry.

Clearly, specific solutions as well as the relative roles of private and public institutions will have to be tailored to local environmental and political conditions. Nevertheless, there is a general worldwide need to combine public and private investments at all levels to maintain food security and to protect producers. Developing such measures is an urgent matter for local, national, and international policy makers. It is our hope that along with food reserve policies for the benefit of consumers, producers too will be protected by policy makers against climatic hazards.*

Diversity and Security   As we have hinted already, another important strategy to combat food shortages is maintaining diversity—for example, planting a variety of different crops in different places and at different times. Particularly in warmer climates where more than one crop can be planted each year, multiple cropping can both raise yields and offer some measure of natural pest resistance. Diversification also minimizes the vulnerability of a whole cropping system to an adverse climatic anomaly. Moreover, this approach usually requires labor-intensive management, important for employment in many poor nations. As mentioned earlier, in the U.S. south-central states the impact of heat and drought in the summer of 1980 was somewhat mitigated by the diversity of planted crops, since winter wheat benefitted although corn and soybean yields were reduced.

Weatherproofing Crops   Building food security systems, providing crop insurance, and developing flexible credit schemes for producers are examples of social protection measures designed to minimize the negative impacts of bad weather. Planting a diverse mix of crop strains to minimize weather- or pest-induced crop failure is an example of a biological protection measure. Technical protection measures make up a third category. Technical mea-

*Despite my various writings over the past decade on food reserves and food security issues, I now realize that I did not properly appreciate the importance of this point until a conference on food-climate issues held in Berlin in 1980. Maintaining *both* consumer and producer protection against year-to-year climate anomalies was one of the very few points upon which both developed and developing country representatives—comprised of market and nonmarket advocates—could agree.[73]

sures include installing irrigation systems to overcome drought, blowers or heaters to combat frost, windbreaks to minimize evaporation or wind erosion, and even enclosures to isolate plants or fish from natural elements.*

Norman Rosenberg noted that the most efficient weather-proofing technique is simply "proper selection of the land and climate in which the crop can be grown with minimal weather risk."[75] There are, of course, a number of other more modern techniques of weatherproofing that can be effective protections against bad-weather effects. (Rosenberg details a number of these, which include increased capture of precipitation, runoff, or snowmelt; minimum tillage to reduce evaporation from soil and its erosion; various mulching practices; windbreaks; irrigation scheduling optimized to crop growth stages; reflectants applied to soil or plants to minimize leaf overheating; antitranspirant materials to cut leaf evaporation rates; and even modification to plant architecture by a number of means, including breeding of strains designed to take advantage of a particular set of climatic resources.) Despite the growing arsenal of technical weatherproofing fixes, including new kinds of crops such as salt-tolerant *halophytes,* which are potentially growable in desertlike areas near sea water, or even synthetic foods, the major stumbling blocks to the success of the more innovative measures are more social than technical.[76] Rosenberg cautioned: "Adaptive research is needed and markets for such crops must be developed before a major conversion can be expected."[77] Although new ideas and products could well have unforeseen promise in the distant future, it seems obvious that the more well-known solutions to meeting world food needs that we have reviewed here could work —if only there were sufficient will to implement them.

Render Unto Weather . . .

It is obvious that actions for meeting world food needs are both immensely complex and controversial. We've barely outlined the basics. Climate, we've seen, plays a major role both as a resource and as a hazard. While climate is an important component of food production and security, we have also seen that it cannot be viewed (or blamed for disaster) in isolation. The case studies of the Irish and Dutch potato blights have showed that social, political, and

---

*The potential for high yields in controlled environments is good, but indoor climate control systems are problematic, and economic constraints on such "exotic" food production methods remain to be worked out.[74]

economic factors combined with environmental stresses to produce negative fluctuations in yields and create significantly different societal impacts. In an editorial "Render Unto Weather . . ." printed in the journal *Climatic Change,* political scientist Michael Glantz summarized the situation this way:

> It is extremely important to distinguish between direct adverse effects of weather events which could not have been prevented, and other adverse weather-related effects which, in fact, have their origins in political, economic, and social policies. This distinction will make it possible for society to place the blame for the severity of an impact of a particular weather phenomenon where it actually belongs—on the weather event or on society. This distinction also makes it possible to minimize such adverse effects by more adequately matching solutions to the correctly identified problems.[78]

To approach the food-climate problem from any single perspective is almost guaranteed to fail to produce workable solutions. Only an integrated, interdisciplinary attack on the many facets of each region's short- and long-term food needs—combined with mechanisms that give people access to the food—has any hope of success. Some approaches may succeed and others fail. But what is certain is that we must not allow a recurrence of the food-climate crises of the 1970s simply because we failed to do what we already know could help to prevent them.

Climate and Water

Besides the air itself, there are few weather elements more precious than fresh water. As a component of climatic resources, it is basic to both food production and energy use. We are utterly dependent on fresh water supplies and their continued renewal.

Despite all the increasing—and we believe very real—concerns often expressed about a growing worldwide "water crisis,"* there is enough fresh water on earth in each year's rainfall to meet most projections of human needs for many decades to come.[79] How is it, then, that a looming water crisis is very plausible while at the same time fresh water on earth is so plentiful? The answer is simply that the places where rain and snow fall are not necessarily the same

*For example, the February 23, 1981 issue of *Newsweek* had a cover story on the water crisis.

places where water is needed or can be stored in adequate amounts. This mismatch suggests that water needs to be transferred from regions of high supply to regions of high demand—once the water has been impounded, of course. However, such transfers are not easily accomplished. For instance, water storage and diversion projects take many years to plan and build, and they can incur very large environmental, social, and economic costs. In addition, political or legal barriers such as national boundaries, outdated compacts, or water access laws seriously complicate the problem.

The variability of local climate over time presents another difficulty in meeting regional water needs (see Figures 7.7 and 9.1).

The Colorado River

The Colorado River provides a good example of how water supplies can change—from acts of God or man.* Figure 9.12, a reconstructed hydrograph, depicts the annual runoff from the Colorado River in millions of acre feet flowing past Lee Ferry, Arizona, the dividing point between the Upper Basin states (Colorado, Wyoming, and Utah) and the Lower Basin states (Nevada, Arizona, and California). The graph is reconstructed from tree ring proxies (see Chapter 3). By calibrating tree rings formed after the turn of the century with measured river runoff after that time, specialists at the University of Arizona Tree Ring Laboratory were able to decipher what the river's runoff was for times before any direct measurements of runoff or rainfall were made.[81] The upper record ("unfiltered") in Figure 9.12 shows the estimates of the highly fluctuating annual runoff; the lower ("filtered") shows an effective running average over ten-year periods. The latter averaging illustrates how reservoir capacity along the river can smooth out the otherwise extreme water variability due to the swings of climate from year to year.

The period between about 1900 and 1925 is particularly interesting for climate watchers. The runoff then was some 15 million to 16 million acre feet. However, the overall long-term (and more

*In 1537, when the Spaniard Francisco de Ulloa first discovered the mouth of the Colorado, a fierce tidal current and river flow made him fear for the safety of his ship. Nevertheless, de Ulloa sailed some 100 kilometers upstream to where the Colorado meets the Gila River from Arizona. But, as UCLA hydrologist/engineer John Dracup noted, "Today, Colorado River diversions have caused the river to disappear before reaching the Sea of Cortez. Therefore, such a journey is no longer a possibility."[80]

recent) average is closer to 13 million acre feet. In 1922, the Colorado River Compact was formulated based on the statistics from only a few previous decades. In that agreement, the Upper Basin states were required to release a fair share of water to the Lower Basin states. This share was set at 7.5 million acre feet, roughly half of what seemed to be the river's annual 15 million to 16 million acre feet runoff. We know now that this high level was a fluke; 1900 to 1925 was an unusually wet period in the Colorado basin.

Today, the Upper Basin states are beginning to develop water-dependent economies primarily due to expanded energy development and growing urban centers. However, Colorado, Wyoming, and Utah will soon find themselves at a disadvantage; in order to abide by the Compact, they will have to provide a high *fixed amount* of water regardless of annual supply, rather than a *fixed percentage* of available water. If the Compact is not renegotiated and based on actual yearly precipitation and runoff, the Upper Basin states may soon run into a serious long-term water crisis regardless of how many reservoirs they build to deal with year-to-year climatic fluctuations.

Dracup noted that "any major basin-wide drought could have significant and damaging effects on the Upper Basin" because of the Compact. Suppose that the ten-year low flow period from 1584 to 1593 (see Figure 9.12) recurred, with a mean runoff at Lee Ferry of about 9.7 million acre feet. Assuming an Upper Basin storage capacity of 31 million acre feet—that is, full reservoirs—when the drought hit, the Compact requirements would leave the Upper Basin with a mere 4.6 million acre feet annually averaged over each of the ten years Dracup calculated.[82] This is well below the 7.5 million acre feet that they owe to the Lower Basin states. This scenario implies that the Colorado River Compact leaves the Upper Basin very vulnerable to negative climatic anomalies or trends.

Whether one believes it is necessary to renegotiate the terms of the Compact, develop other new water sources or reservoirs, encourage conservation, or reconsider the seniority system to water rights,* one point is clear: the Colorado River states must examine the long-term and (we believe) serious implications of a potential

---

*The seniority system is one in which "senior" users—those whose ancestors first claimed the water—get their water needs fulfilled first and users with "junior rights" get what's left. This archaic system in much of the U.S. West provides little incentive for those near the top of the priority list to conserve or use water more efficiently.[83]

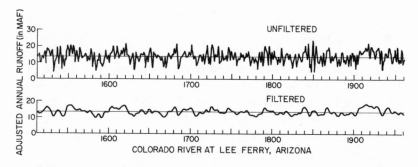

Figure 9.12

Runoff from the Colorado River in millions of acre feet (MAF) over the past four and a half centuries, estimated from an analysis of tree rings in the Colorado River Basin. The unfiltered record shows estimates of yearly runoff. The filtered line is from the same data, but with fluctuations occurring on shorter than ten-year time scales removed. Only the last seventy years or so of this proxy record coincide with actual measurements of runoff, which are used to calibrate the tree ring estimates from 1500 to 1900. [Source: C. W. Stockton, 1977, Interpretation of past climatic variability from paleoenvironmental indicators, in Panel on Water and Climate of the Geophysics Study Committee, Climate, Climatic Change and Water Supply (Washington, D.C.: National Academy of Sciences), pp. 34–45.]

water supply and demand crunch. Moreover, it is important that solutions to the problems of the Upper Colorado Basin are not considered in isolation from overall western (and even national) water policy issues. Most of these questions involve long-term public policy problems, which we will discuss further later on.

The Winter of '81:
When Connecticut Almost Ran Dry

The winter of 1981 brought considerable local water supply problems to the U.S. East Coast, a region where precipitation is usually much more reliable than in the West. However, despite the unusual extent of drought in the East, many local water districts had more than sufficient supplies for their needs, but would not or could not help adjacent areas with shorter supplies because the mechanical transfer of water, even over short distances, could not be easily accomplished.[84] Inadequate pipes or ditches, or economic, legal, or political constraints often prevent much needed water trade. In view of the high cost of building water transfer

427

projects and the relative infrequency of droughts, perhaps many East Coast localities or water districts feel the investment (or the drought risks) are not worth the costs of going ahead with such projects. However, when viewed from a regional or national perspective, having adequate mechanisms to share needed water among local regions of varying supplies does seem a worthwhile problem to address, even in the humid East.

The Ogallala Aquifer

Much of the central U.S. Plains overlies a vast underground reservoir whose water is being pumped to the surface at a rapid rate. The dark spots visible from overflights of this region are caused by center-pivot irrigation systems, often fed from underground water supplies.[85] The Ogallala aquifer, a vast underground reservoir that stretches from South Dakota to north Texas, has been dropping because the rate of its recharge in many parts of this semiarid area is now considerably less than the rate at which it is being used up. In some areas the water level is now so low that it is uneconomical, at today's energy costs, to pump it all the way up to the surface. According to a U.S. National Academy of Sciences study, there is a danger that in the next few decades an increasing fraction of farmland now irrigated from the aquifer might have to be cultivated through dry land farming, thus becoming considerably less productive and more vulnerable to climatic hazards.[86]

Mining of groundwater and soils could well reduce the productive potential of future farms at a time when sustained high productivity will be needed most, as most future world population and economic growth demand more and more food and water. This risk could be further exacerbated if CO_2-induced warming (see Chapter 8) materializes and leads—as some evidence suggests—to increased summer dryness in the U.S. Plains. We may be prematurely using up the very irrigation source that will be needed to help us adapt to a new and potentially drier central Plains.

Recognizing Climatic Fluctuations in Long-Term Water Planning

Society can certainly counter water shortfalls by networking or by increasing reservoir capacity. But such water projects require long-term planning based on guessing at future demographic and economic changes. Even though climatic fluctuations and trends will affect future water supply, human behavior is what primarily sets long-term water demand. Often it is much more difficult to forecast the latter than to put bounds on the former. We should also point out that water shortage or abundance is based on neither absolute supply nor absolute demand per se, but rather on the difference between supply and demand. Thus, it is necessary to build simultaneous scenarios of both supply and demand in order to assess the likelihood of shortages. While we certainly agree that society needs to maintain safe levels of reservoir capacity, there are environmental, social, economic, and other costs associated with such large water projects. The trade-offs involved in weighing costs and benefits require making tough choices. For example, if we are willing to invest in water projects for the express purpose of increasing reservoir capacity to mitigate precedented climatic fluctuations, then we are committed in principle to accomplish this goal. However, in practice, a problem often arises. In a region such as the Colorado River Basin, population and water user demand is growing rapidly. A project to provide a certain projected population with adequate water supplies may take ten or twenty years to complete. By that time demand may well have increased so much that the extra reservoir capacity originally designed to protect a smaller projected population against the hazard of fluctuating weather would be used instead to provide more water annually to increasing numbers of users. Thus, should a subsequent drought occur, even more people would be at risk of shortage than if no project had been built.[87]

This is one of the most difficult questions of water planning: estimating—or regulating—long-term increases in the number of annual water users. Whether this calls for national land use planning, vigorous regional zoning on a watershed scale, or even a constitutional amendment dealing with limits on the rates of regional population shifts, it is a question whose answer has no clear consensus. Nevertheless, if some of the present higher-growth-rate development plans in semiarid regions are to be realized without severe future water crises, we must find a formula to allocate limited water supplies to various conflicting users: urban, industrial (particularly energy development in the U.S. West), and agricultural. If no such allocation scheme can be negotiated, then unrealistic growth expectations must be scaled down.

Climate and Health

Direct Effects

Climatic conditions can directly affect health. Every winter newscasters relate cases of indigent elderly people freezing to death because their heat was faulty or shut off by the landlord or power company. Likewise, excessive heat kills the vulnerable when they are unable to escape the worst of summer. Thousands of heat-induced diseases and many deaths, mostly among the poor who were unable to afford air conditioning, and billions of dollars in damages were attributed to the extreme heat in the U.S. Southwest in the summer of 1980 and again in 1983 in the Midwest.[88]

But we need not cite only the extreme cases to demonstrate the direct effects of weather on health. The seasonal cycle of temperature in midlatitudes has a high correlation with many diseases and also affects the death rates for people who are not economically disadvantaged. In New York City, for example, mean daily mortality in the winter time averages some 240 people, dropping to below 190 average deaths each day in August.[89] This climate-health relationship is not an isolated case; similar seasonal patterns are observed elsewhere.

One very interesting case is the change in Japanese infant mortality rates from pneumonia and bronchitis between 1951 and 1972. There is a very large seasonal cycle of mortality in the early part of the record, with winter peak death rates some five to seven times higher than summer rates.[90] Such strong, direct climatic influence on human well-being is the kind of example that Ellsworth Huntington might have used in support of his theory of climatic determinism (see the discussion in Chapter 3). However, although the seasonal effect is not completely diminished over time, both the average death rate and winter peaks in mortality declined drastically from 1950 to 1970. Even the most ardent climatic determinist probably wouldn't be foolish enough to infer from such data that winters in Japan became much less severe over these two decades, thereby lowering the mortality rate. Obviously, other factors are involved. Improvements in sanitation and health care, combined with better living conditions and higher economic levels in postwar Japan considerably reduced the vulnerability of infants to winter's cold. Winters did not change much, nor did babies' resistance to these diseases. What changed, of course, was the *vulnerability* of this group to climatic variation. Once they could afford it, people chose to invest in resilience to climatic variation. Simply stated, *climatic impacts on society have as much to do with society as with climate.*

Indirect Effects

The epidemic zone for yellow fever in Africa extends from about lat. 15°N to lat. 15°S. This virus infection of primate species is transferred to humans by a mosquito, *Aëdes aegypti.* The primary reason that the yellow fever epidemic zone is largely confined to tropical zones is that the virus needs high temperatures (above 24°C, or 75°F) to thrive in the mosquito.[91] If CO_2 or other trace greenhouse gases warmed the earth and broadened the area of the tropical regions, then this disease vector would also expand its thrust. A similar situation exists for malaria. Such indirect health effects of climatic changes could be more important than the more obvious direct effects.

Possible Health Effects of a CO_2-Induced Warming

Wolf Weihe of the University Hospital, Zurich, commented on possible direct and indirect health aspects of a long-term CO_2-induced warming at the World Climate Conference in Geneva in 1979:

> The human adaptive responses would be to provide protection against the heat or to migrate to higher latitudes with their cooler, more favourable climatic conditions during the hot season. Since the highest population density already exists in this warm moderate zone, crowding and competition for room could be anticipated with such a migration. The possibilities for man to cope with considerably higher temperatures are small. He will have to look for more suitable climatic conditions where he can develop and can produce the food for his subsistence. In addition to the changing conditions for man the vectors for communicable diseases would follow the climatic changes and introduce diseases into areas that were hitherto disease-free.[92]

The probability of five consecutive above-100°F July days in Dallas, Texas, for example, is now about 38 percent. If more CO_2

431

increased the mean July temperature by, say, 3°F, then the probability of such a health-threatening heat wave could increase to some 68 percent.

Connections Among Climate, Water, Energy, and Food

In order to assess future water demand in the U.S. Plains, for example, we must also assess future world food demand and the likelihood that U.S. exports of grain will continue at high levels. If world food demand grows more rapidly than supplies, then reserves will fall and food prices will climb. Expectation of greater return will stimulate investment in hedges against climatic variability like irrigation systems. As food security diminishes, though, malnutrition and famine would depend more and more on yearly weather fluctuations that cause the year-to-year fluctuations in world food production. If food reserves are high and prices drop precipitously after a string of good years, then producers are hurt, investments in production infrastructure are reduced, and longer-term productivity is threatened. This problem is only exacerbated when energy prices rise, since energy is so basic to irrigation, transport, or the manufacture of chemical fertilizer. As we have argued several times, there is a need to smooth out such yearly yield as well as price fluctuations. Irrigation is one way to minimize climatic hazards, and the demand for irrigation water is likely to continue to increase. The amount of increase, we have seen, will depend on future population size, dietary standards, trade policies, food reserves, commodity prices, energy prices, water prices, interest rates, the availability of capital, political commitment to agriculture, environmental protection and, of course, the climate.

We will now focus on only one aspect of these issues: the effects of long-term climatic trends. It may take a decade or two to plan, finance, and build mechanisms to provide adequate water for the coming generation; but present calculations of future needs are usually based on the assumption that there will be no long-term changes in climate, only precedented, short-term fluctuations. If in twenty years it becomes clear that significantly decreased average precipitation or increased evaporation might occur in some regions —as in Kellogg's or Manabe's CO_2 scenarios, described in Chapter 8, for the U.S. Plains—it will then be too late to be prepared unless present water supply planning recognizes that the climate of the future could well be significantly different from today's, and we respond now by building larger margins of safety in either supply or demand requirements to meet that contingency.

Even with the many uncertainties plainly admitted, climatologists still know enough now to state responsibly that significant changes in climatic trends are possible—perhaps even likely—but that the regional details cannot be given at present with anything but intuitive probabilities. This suggests that *increased flexibility in water supply planning is needed to enhance our ability to cope with plausible climatic trends.*[93]

It remains to be seen to what extent such flexibility can be achieved without large-scale governmental intervention. Ideological battles over free (i.e., haphazard) versus planned regional population growth, environmental protection versus economic development, or the ownership and uses of water, particularly in the U.S. Plains and the West, are likely to continue into the foreseeable future.*

The need for flexibility in long-term planning not only applies to the question of water supplies, but also to the need for accelerated development of alternative energy supply systems. The greater the available alternatives or standby capacity, the less painful it would be to shift rapidly among various supply options, if necessary. Such shifts may be seen as necessary if we obtain more proof that a CO_2-induced warming is too risky or costly, or if a political consensus on how to deal with the energy crisis were to emerge. The bottom line can be stated simply: we should be careful not to get overly dependent on a single energy supply system or a single limited source of water in a region, particularly if the source is nonrenewable or the supply projections are based on average sunlight, wind, evaporation, and precipitation records, especially those spanning mere human memory. Moreover, it is comparably risky to have all future supply planning based on any single scenario

---

*For example, the June issue of *Science 81* (published in Washington, D.C.) refers to the problem of water in the West as one "of crisis proportion." This led to a somewhat angry response from a group of high plains water users, whose publication *The Cross Section* (a monthly publication of the High Plains Underground Conservancy District No. 1, 2930 Avenue Q, Lubbock, Texas 79405, June 1981) quotes this article in a story with the headline "Yanks takin' pot shot at the waterin' hole." "It is NOT a problem of crisis proportion," the *Cross Section* reported; "it sure has been a tough job teachin' those Yanks to shoot straight. . . . We're NOT drying up and blowing away."

433

for future demand—of energy or water. Rather, planning should be based on the differing costs and consequences of different policies, given a *set of scenarios* that span the range of plausible future climatic, economic, and demographic trends. As we improve our ability to forecast the economy, demography, or the climate, preferred scenarios can be identified, probabilities assigned to each, and plans altered to meet changing conditions or projections.* Since flexibility—particularly too much of it—can be expensive, it is important to be as quantitative as possible in estimates of future fluctuations and trends in supply and demand.

Much research is underway to identify the causes of natural climatic variations, for example, so that both interannual and longer-term changes can be predicted. And since economic and other social trends also need to be forecast to perform climatic impact assessments, it is imperative that social science join the natural sciences in these studies. Indeed, if anything is to be learned from our examples about climatic impacts on society, it is that society is as important as climate in determining our vulnerability to the elements.

Energy is the economic cornerstone of most societies. Its relation to climate is our next concern.

---

*In an attempt to estimate the probabilities of some CO_2-induced climatic change scenarios, I joined with colleagues Linda Mearns and Richard Katz in calculations of how increased mean temperatures might affect the probabilities of crop- or health-damaging summer heat waves. Society probably feels climatic changes more through changing frequencies of extreme weather than changes in mean conditions, as in the 1980 and 1983 summer heat extremes and their impacts on corn yields and death rates for elderly poor people. As an example, we calculated that, at present, the chances for five consecutive corn-yield reducing July days above 95°F in Des Moines, Iowa, are about one year in seventeen years. This helps explain why Iowa is a leading corn-producing state. However, if July mean temperature increased by 3°F (and there were no changes in the daily variability above the mean), then our calculations increased the probability of a run of such devastating heat about one year in five years. This could markedly change the economics of the Corn Belt.

10 Energy and Climate

Climatic Hazards to Energy Use

Of the various energy production sources, the ones most directly influenced by climate are those tied to the sun, the wind, and the rain. We are referring, of course, to solar power, wind power, and hydropower. If it's cloudy, those dependent on solar collectors must rely on backup systems or their storage capacity; if the day is calm, windmills cease cranking; and if there is a drought, reservoirs will be low and hydropower will produce less wattage. On these grounds, critics of such renewable sources of energy claim that large backup systems are needed.[1] But one must not forget that climate will rarely deal a triple blow of too many clouds, no wind, and little precipitation. For example, 1977 was a bad year for hydropower and windpower in western North America because of the unusual jet stream pattern and the accompanying drought (see Figure 4.3). But warm weather and drought in the U.S. West in 1977 meant it would probably have been a good year for solar power—had collectors been in widespread use—to take advantage of this positive weather anomaly. We shouldn't view weather anomalies that affect energy supply systems in isolation; rather, we need to correlate the impacts of such anomalies on different renewable energy sources. It is likely that considerable cancellations will occur that could balance out negative and positive climatic fluctuations, making them a less serious obstacle to renewable energy production technologies than is often claimed. Although climatic fluctuations do indeed influence the reliability of each of the weather-dependent renewable systems, it is foolish to argue against such alternative sources solely out of fear that anomalous climatic periods would adversely affect all renewable sources simultaneously.

There are other obvious ways in which climate influences energy use: summer heat waves generate more electrical demand for air conditioning; winter cold snaps mean people will need more heating fuel. In 1977, during the bitter winter in eastern North America, many industrial plants in Ohio, for example, were forced to shut

435

down owing to insufficient stocks of fuel to meet the needs of all consumers. Residences received priority. However, this direct climatic impact on human affairs in the energy sector was as much a problem of insufficient fuel supply and storage as of bad weather. It was, of course, people who chose how much fuel to store for winter—the less stored, the lower the costs of storage but the bigger the price of anomalous cold. The gamble was costly indeed. Thus it was human will—and not just adverse climatic strength—that caused human institutions to become temporarily so vulnerable to extreme climatic conditions.

The biggest potential climate-energy interaction, however, is not the hazard short-term climate extremes pose for energy use, but rather the possible influence of energy use on climatic trends. This is not only a problem for the future. That is, if the prevalent *perception* of the potential risks of large power parks, acid rain, or CO_2-induced climatic changes were that these hazards should be avoided, then this could markedly alter our perception of what constitutes the best set of energy supply systems. Because switching energy technologies can take many decades and trillions of dollars, this is a potentially major issue.

Interactions Between Climate and Energy Use

The case studies in Chapter 9 illustrated why it can be very difficult to develop cost-efficient, sustainable supply systems. Climate, as we have said, is only one of many factors to be considered in planning for such systems. Just as we noted that food and water are interrelated, so are food, water, and energy all components of the two most important topics on the world's political agenda: the problem of social and economic development, and the prevention of nuclear war. While sustainable yearly levels of food production require a steady water supply, for example, reliable irrigation usually requires a stable energy source. Expanding food production requires both physical and economic resources; energy availability is often the underpinning of such resources. Especially in Third World countries, some increased energy use is essential to improving standards of living, especially to increase food production capacity. A nation does not need to opt for the Western model of energy-intensive, machine-oriented farming to benefit greatly from some products—like fertilizers—that require large amounts of energy. Of course, the question of which are the best pathways to development and a better standard of living is subject to considerable debate. When gauging various energy options that might afford a better standard of living, the long-term connection to climate should be weighed along with a host of other risks and benefits. The CO_2 case is a concrete example of such a long-term connection.

In Chapter 9 we mentioned that a CO_2-induced warming could cause an increase in the severity and frequency of extreme heat waves. This could cause severe health stress to those too weak or poor to avoid the extreme heat; and it could change summer crops, perhaps leading to billions of dollars worth of losses. In light of this possibility, what should society do to avoid such a catastrophe—even if scientists do not yet have enough information for reliable forecasts of such distant events or their consequences? Deciding on a course of action—including no action—means that some value judgments will have to be made to balance the potential risks and benefits of alternative plausible outcomes. In order to do this, we must understand in some detail the basic issues that form the general problem of risk analysis, which we will discuss later in this chapter.

Climatic Impact Assessment: The CO_2 Case

Assessing the relative merits of various options for energy production is very difficult, especially since billions of lives and trillions of dollars are involved. What is needed for rational decision making is a detailed *impact assessment* to weigh the potential costs and benefits of each specific energy system against other risks. Robert Chen and I made one such study of the hypothetical advent of a sea level rise from a CO_2-induced warming which leads to a deglaciation of West Antarctica. It is a useful example of the issues involved in risk/benefit assessment.

The CO_2 Increase and
Coastal Flooding Scenario
Some economists argue that if a sea level rise of several meters occurred over, say, a century or two, then the risk associated with increased fossil fuel burning would be more manageable. Perhaps the risk would even be acceptable, some say, because cities these days are largely rebuilt anyway on the time scale of a century.[2] But suppose the climatic warming and induced sea level rise were to occur more abruptly? A rapid flooding—that is, over a few decades—would cause immediate and unavoidable losses of property. However, assuming, as most glaci-

437

ologists do, that such a rapid sea level rise is not imminent, there would still be some people—those who live on coasts—who would eventually suffer disproportionately.* Thus, this minority would be at higher risk. However, the benefits from fossil fuel use fall more uniformly across society, to inlanders and coastal dwellers alike. Fairness—we could call it *redistributive justice*—would dictate that, at a minimum, the minority of losers be compensated for their losses by the majority of winners.

The loss of any area also would likely place population pressures on other parts of a country, possibly altering long-term food needs. This is especially true in low-lying areas such as Holland or Bangladesh, where a 5-meter (16-foot) sea level rise would destroy a large portion of the existing agricultural land.

One possible way of compensating losers is to adopt global "no-fault climate disaster insurance." This was originally proposed in 1974 by Kellogg and Schneider as a way of coping with the adverse side effects of intentional weather or climate modification.[3] Their idea was based on this assumption: those proposing a modification would certainly believe that the immediate benefits of their modification scheme would outweigh the long-term risks. Hence, that group should be willing to compensate those who lose a favored climate (based on comparisons with past statistics) as a result of the modification program. But because we are still so ignorant about the working of the atmospheric system, we could easily find honest experts who could testify that the weather modification did (or did not) cause the loss of a favored climate. Hence, compensation would have to be made even if the injured party failed to prove beyond a reasonable doubt that the modification project (rather than natural climatic fluctuations or other unrelated factors) caused the loss of a favored climate.

The concept of no-fault climate insurance could also be applied to inadvertent climate modification, like the CO_2-(or other greenhouse gas) induced sea level rise. If such a disaster were perceived as an "act of God," most people would tend not to blame anyone and would likely take their losses philosophically and rebuild elsewhere. But if a flooding of coastal areas could be seen as an "act of man" due to the burning of fossil fuels, then the group most affected might well insist that someone be accountable and restitution be paid.[4] Should we force posterity to adapt to the risks of an

*Even if there were no West Antarctic ice sheet collapse, as noted in Chapter 8, sea level could still rise up to a meter or so over the next century as a result of thermal expansion of CO_2-warmed sea water and melting of mountain glaciers.

altered climate, whatever they may be, so that people today benefit from CO_2-producing activities? This intergenerational equity problem hits us squarely now, even if potentially serious CO_2 effects are the next century's problem. Nevertheless, virtually nothing has been done about our increasing use of fossil fuels. Why?

In view of the possible negative consequences of a large carbon dioxide buildup in the future, why don't people act to prevent it—or at least agree to set up some mechanisms to compensate losers? There are at least five reasons for hesitation and inaction:

1. Not many people know much about the potential impacts of a CO_2 buildup.

2. There is still considerable technical uncertainty as to the likelihood, distribution, timing, and magnitude of these impacts.

3. It is difficult to identify clearly the expected winners and losers.*

4. There are few mechanisms for resolving conflicts between perceived winners and losers.

5. We are uncertain how to value the future against the present.

This last point is crucial. Even if we did know what CO_2 increases will do to future climate and could specify in detail the economic and other ramifications, we would still need to know more before we could incorporate this economic externality into today's economic planning. In order to do so, we would need to identify some rate at which different activities or commodities in the future should be discounted or valued. In the case of CO_2 and coastal flooding, discounting the future makes it appear more expensive to mitigate carbon dioxide impacts now than it is to wait and pay for damages later. But damages in the future are not of zero concern today, even economically. How much is it worth today to invest in measures that might prevent a worldwide flooding catastrophe of some 5 meters in 150 years? By extrapolating the Schneider-Chen figures for U.S. losses to world scale, we can assume for illustrative purposes that global property losses might be about 2.5×10^{12} (two and a half trillion 1971 dollars—ten times the estimated value of U.S. losses). If we discount the future at 7 percent per year (the interest payment you might expect from a bank), this represents a doubling time for investments—neglecting inflation—of roughly ten years. Therefore, a dollar invested at 7 percent interest per year today would

---

*There would likely be some winners, for any climatic change increases or decreases yields of different kinds of crops as well as alters the regional distribution of crops.[5] In addition, direct CO_2 fertilization of crops will increase most yields, a clear benefit to many farmers.[6] However, such fertilization will also benefit weeds and hosts to pests, clearly not a benefit. The net effects are, naturally, still quite speculative.

double its value fifteen times in the next 150 years and, ignoring inflation, would be worth about \$30,000 ($2^{15} = 32,768$).*

To prevent today the loss of a dollar in 150 years (at 7 percent per year discounting), we might be willing to spend only about 1/30,000 ($\frac{1}{2}^{15}$) of a dollar today. Thus, a coastal inundation that costs $\$2.5 \times 10^{12}$ in 150 years is only worth about \$75 million today. Seventy-five million dollars is hundreds of times less than the economic value of fossil-fuel-related industries or the potential agricultural income from deforested lands. Thus, many people today would not consider it economically rational to spend much more than \$75 million now to prevent a two and one-half trillion dollar catastrophe 150 years in the future, even if it were certain to occur (which it is not).

On the other hand, if the inundation were to occur in only twenty years, its discounted cost would be (discounting again at 7 percent per year) \$600 billion, a loss sufficiently serious to warrant immediate, dramatic action. Again, uncertainties in the likelihood or timing of sea level rises and the economic and ethical difficulty involved in picking a discount rate complicate our attempt to make a meaningful, quantitative impact assessment. But regardless of the discount (or even markup) rate used to evaluate the present worth of the future, one thing remains clear: if we discount at high rates, it further diminishes the likelihood that this generation will invest heavily now to hedge against potential CO_2-induced losses in the future. The same can be said for spending on nuclear waste disposal or investing present capital to make energy use more efficient.

Integrated Scenario Analysis   Since the future is essentially unpredictable in other than broad generalizations, the best way to examine the potential impacts of CO_2 increases is probably to develop scenarios of CO_2 increases that are consistent with other scenarios of economic, population, agricultural, technological, and other interrelated nonclimatic factors. Such *integrated scenario analysis* was endorsed by several CO_2 assessment groups as a promising method for pursuing climatic impact assessments related to the CO_2 problem.[8] One international meeting report noted:

> A useful framework for study of economic and social impacts might be the development of comprehensive and internally

---

*Of course, we can't ignore inflation in any real calculation. If the late 1970s and early 1980s are any guide, the 7 percent interest we assume for a bank implies a zero real discount rate, since all the interest income would be eaten up by inflation. In this case the present real value of future losses should not be discounted.[7]

consistent scenarios of possible future socio-economic development, energy and land use patterns, CO_2 levels, climate and the implications for agriculture and other economic sectors.

The function of scenario analysis is not to attempt to predict the future: the future is unknown and probably unpredictable. Instead, scenario analysis is a tool that may help us to choose appropriate policies by making possible the exploration of the implications of alternative actions. Development and discussion of these scenarios by international and interdisciplinary expert teams might be an important mechanism for building a consensus on the major scientific and policy issues in the global community of physical and social scientists.[9]

It is important to get on with this job.

Policy Options to Deal
with CO_2 Increases
Certain policy options are available to us now. Schneider and Chen described several of them as follows:[10]

- *Do nothing.* A passive policy is usually favored by those who are either unaware of the issues, totally befuddled by the uncertainties, or have a vested interest in maintaining the status quo. It also has been referred to as the *adaptation strategy.*[11]
- *Study more.* It's not a bad idea to learn more in an effort to narrow the uncertainties and put the trillion-dollar decisions on a firmer factual basis. But we shouldn't allow ourselves to believe that study itself is without risk. Implicit in this option is the idea that we still have time to do research—ten more years or so, without risks. This figure is typically suggested for the CO_2 problem.[12] However, while we were compiling the data needed to confirm or annul the predictions of our tentative climate models, or analyzing the consequences of plausible integrated scenarios, CO_2 (and other trace gases) would be accumulating in the system. By choosing this option alone, we would commit future generations to an even larger dose of carbon dioxide or other trace gases and their impacts than if we acted now to limit CO_2-producing activities.
- *Build resilience.* A more active response than research alone would be to act to minimize our vulnerability to climatic changes. If doing nothing is the adaptation strategy, then building resilience could be called the *anticipatory adaptation strategy.*

441

To summarize specific suggestions from earlier chapters, anticipatory adaptation might mean increasing efforts to develop food security systems and widely adapted varieties of seed stocks, conserving soils to preserve higher productivity, and perhaps even developing international environmental compensation mechanisms to repay those who lose—or believe they have lost—a favored climate. Other policy options in this category include developing techniques for reducing energy demand, expanding the research and development of non-fossil-fuel energy sources, conserving water supplies, and developing reservoir and flood control systems. To this list of options to build resilience economist Lester Lave has added "a strong economy with high scientific and engineering capabilities, a well educated population, and a more flexible, resilient capital stock."[13] All such anticipatory strategies are the kind of actions we should consider in any event regardless of whether there are to be significant CO_2-induced environmental changes. Ensuring continued high levels of food production capability, renewable energy availability, and water control is obviously important regardless of the increased rates of CO_2 and other trace greenhouse gases. In this sense, public responses to the advent or prospect of CO_2 increases have many tie-ins with policies dealing with other environmental and societal problems.[14]

· *Reduce the CO_2 burden.* Making an effort to turn around the CO_2 increase stemming from fossil fuel use is, of course, the most active policy response. One way of limiting fossil fuel use is through conservation—by imposing cuts in energy services and/or encouraging more efficient use with no cuts in service, the last being vastly preferable. Another important element of this option is to accelerate development of some mix of alternative, non-fossil-fuel energy sources—solar, nuclear, wind, geothermal, biomass, and hydroelectric power, for example. In addition, once CO_2 concentrations reached some critical threshold level, we would attempt to control worldwide emissions by reversing the rate of deforestation, instituting reforestation programs, and formulating a "law of the air" that would allow each nation certain polluting rights.[15] One could even go so far as instituting climate-control schemes to counteract possible CO_2 effects.[16] Yale University economist William Nordhaus has pointed out that the worldwide economic consequences of imposing limits on the CO_2 buildup need not be devastating.[17]

The CO$_2$ Pyramid   The various components of the carbon dioxide problem can be visualized as an inverted pyramid.* At the base are behavioral factors: the injection of CO$_2$ into the atmosphere by human activities. Next comes the carbon cycle response: how nature will distribute the added carbon. The next level consists of the climate's reaction to the CO$_2$ increases. Impacts on the environment and society come next, followed by our own adaptive strategies (that is, policy responses).

It is unlikely that scientists will reach a consensus before the end of this century on the probable impacts of a CO$_2$ increase during the next 100 years. By then it will probably be too late to avoid the environmental and societal effects of a clearly detectable climatic change, since such a detectable change from increasing greenhouse gases is due over the next ten years or so. Whether to face that change without any anticipatory responses is not, as we have said repeatedly, a strictly scientific question, but rather a multifaceted value choice. Personally, we favor vigorous, immediate policy actions in the "build resilience" category just discussed. We would like to see a *strategic* (as opposed to market-driven) response to the prospect of climatic change. A strategic response might mean immediate government-supported efforts at developing alternative renewable energy sources coupled with strong, cost-effective conservation efforts.† Not only would such a program to develop

---

*An illustration and discussion of this concept can be found in S. H. Schneider, 1981, Carbon dioxide and climate: Research on potential environmental and societal impacts, in *Carbon Dioxide and Climate: The Greenhouse Effect*, Hearing before Subcommittee on Natural Resources, Agriculture Research and Environment and the Subcommittee on Investigations and Oversight of the Committee on Science and Technology, U.S. House of Representatives, 97th Congress (Washington, D.C.: U.S. Government Printing Office), pp. 31–39.

†What about nuclear energy, one of the renewable energy sources (at least in breeder or fusion forms)? Although not a major CO$_2$ threat, nuclear energy presents a number of basic serious difficulties. First, the uncertainties involved in assessing the risk of a nuclear reactor meltdown disaster (popularly known as the China Syndrome) are formidable and the societal consequences now largely inestimable (like those of CO$_2$ increases). Second, like fossil fuel energy sources, nuclear power "exports its externalities," to use the language of the impact assessors. Fossil fuels export their emissions from the place where they are burned to the regional and global atmosphere; nuclear power exports the consequences of its radioactive waste products, accidents, sabbotage, or damage in war from the present time to dozens of generations in the future. The uncertainties in estimates of risks of both the fossil and nuclear "hard technologies," as Amory Lovins has called them, are basically inestimable.[18] For example, in one celebrated and controversial study (WASH-1400) a group of nuclear engineers and scientists rated the probability of a nuclear reactor

443

alternative, renewable energy systems help reduce many nations' long-term dependence on uncertain supplies of oil, but it would also buy some time for evaluating and reacting to real and predicted impacts of airborne carbon dioxide and other trace greenhouse gases as our knowledge base expands.

Risk Analysis

Because energy is so critical to development, it would be absurd to argue that anyone's energy policy should be based solely on potential risks to climate, such as those we discussed in Chapter 8. Nor should these potential risks be completely ignored, as is too often the common practice. As we said earlier, climatic risks should be weighed along with a host of other risks and benefits of different energy supply systems (such as nuclear, solar, and wind energy). In order to do this, we must understand in some detail the basic issues that form the general problem of *risk analysis*. This will provide a perspective from which climatic and other factors of development can be compared. Without such a perspective on risk/benefit trade-offs for different development strategies, choosing the pathways for development becomes a random exercise at best, or an ideological charade at worst.

Safety Versus Risk   Many times people use the words *risk* and *safety* improperly, believing that if something is safe it carries no risk, or if something has a risk associated with it, it is not safe. Few actions can be taken without some risk. Hence, making decisions requires first identifying the risks associated with various options, pinpointing the benefits, and then weighing both to decide whether the risk is worth taking. Often, one makes this personal value judgment in the face of considerable uncertainty.

When measuring risk, we measure (or more likely estimate) the likelihood *and* the degree of harm; this is a scientific, technical assessment, although often an imperfect one. But when we weigh

---

meltdown as typically less than one in twenty thousand per reactor per year. Then, after the Three Mile Island accident, nuclear risk experts rated the chances 10 to 20 times higher.[19] Quite simply, if the probabilities of a nuclear mishap are essentially inestimable, then at least we can try to minimize the potential consequences. Risk, we'll explore shortly, is defined as probability times consequence. To minimize the consequences of a nuclear accident, for example, we could simply place no nuclear facilities near populated areas. In summary, a strong argument emerges for conservation and the increased use of other renewable technologies that involve less far-reaching risks and inherent uncertainties than nuclear or fossil fuel supply technologies.

safety, as in the expression "safe enough," there is a value judgment implied as to the acceptability of risk—assuming that the risks are scientifically known. Simply, judging safety is a personal value choice, whereas assessing risk is primarily a technical job. Setting safety standards for some activity depends on the technical assessment of risks, but these factual assessments must be weighed against each judge's perception of the benefits from that activity in comparison to the risks. Out of such judgments come standards of what is safe; that is, what risks are judged acceptable in light of the benefits of some action. What really complicates judging safety are the large uncertainties that often accompany risk assessments, uncertainties punctuated by vocal technical disagreements among risk analyst experts. These can even make the technical analysis of risk—that is, the probability of some occurrence multiplied by the consequences of that occurrence—a personal value choice, but here the choice involves deciding which set of conflicting experts' numbers to believe.[20]

Risks can vary in duration, imminence, location, severity, and other aspects. For instance, risks such as genetic mutations or global climatic changes can be protracted, occurring over generations. Some risks are immediate (such as automobile accidents) or delayed (such as cancers that appear decades after exposure to harmful radiation or chemicals). Some risks, such as urban heat islands that concentrate thermal releases, affect only small areas. Others spread worldwide, such as carbon dioxide emissions. And risks can range from minor accidents to health irritants, serious injuries, death, or even irreversible changes in world sea level.

Marginal Risks and Benefits   A basic concept of risk analysis is *marginal risks and benefits*—that is, the incremental risks and benefits that would accrue from an incremental (or marginal) change in, say, present levels of energy use. A typical argument of those in favor of technological growth goes like this: Where would we be if our ancestors living before the industrial revolution worried so much about the risks of industrialization and economic growth that they decided not to embark on two centuries of technological innovations? Many modern people would think back to those days of widespread disease and poverty and reason that most of us are better off for such progress having been made. The risks, such defenders of technological growth believe, clearly were justified in light of the benefits of industrial progress. Despite the environmental and social ills of modern society—many a direct outgrowth of the

445

industrial and economic boom—we too are personally inclined to reject the romantic notion of the superiority of the "good old days." Of course, this is our value judgment. But to believe that we are better off today than a century or two ago is not to agree automatically that we would be better off tomorrow by taking another incremental or marginal step towards more of the same kinds of industrial growth. Our present levels of energy use, for example, have undoubtedly made modern life healthier and wealthier than the lives of most people who used relatively little energy around 1780. However, given our high standard of living in the Western countries, it does not necessarily follow that another increase in energy use over present levels will make us healthier and wealthier—let alone happier. In fact, more energy of some kinds can actually degrade our health, wealth, and independence—witness our nervousness about dependence on foreign oil or radioactive releases from nuclear plants.

A simple extrapolation of the policies that delivered us from the "good old days" is not an adequate means of assessing the next steps we need to take. Remember this analogy: Two aspirins can cure your headache, but a whole bottle at once can kill you. In other words, the marginal benefits of more and more of a good thing may well be less than the marginal risks of the next added increment above present levels of consumption. Some polemicists might accuse those of us who are deeply concerned about the risks of more energy growth as favoring a return to the horse-and-buggy days. We are not arguing for a dismantling of all twentieth-century technology! But what we do believe in is the need to re-examine at the margin the costs of progress. We need to determine whether each next bit of so-called progress is worth the potential risks given available or forseeable options and our present economic status.

For instance, an already affluent urban society might not benefit enough economically from the addition of one more air-polluting power plant to warrant the risks of greater heart or lung damage to local inhabitants. On the other hand, a city in a less developed country might well increase its inhabitants' average standard of living considerably by adding another power plant. The resulting economic progress could, if wisely spent, lead to widespread improvements in nutrition and medical care. These marginal benefits would probably exceed the marginal risks of extra heart or lung disease in the opinions of most people living in a less developed country. Hence, a society's current social and economic status helps determine whether it is likely to value the same marginal benefit more or less than the same marginal risk of some venture, at least where energy use is concerned.

Energy benefits often rise rapidly at first with increasing energy use, but then level off despite the continuing increase.[21] This is similar to the concept of diminishing returns in economics: greatest benefits from energy come first, and the harder-to-obtain benefits take relatively more energy and come later. If this is the case, as it may well be at least for the wealthy nations, another increment of energy should produce less benefit today than that same increment produced a century ago. But then, too, there tends to be relatively little risk associated with low uses of energy, and far greater risks associated with larger energy usage. (This, of course, assumes the energy is produced from the same source.) Each society, then, has to decide whether in its value system the marginal risks outweigh, or are outweighed by, the marginal benefits of a small increase in energy—or any other action. This is the foundation of making public policy; inevitably, trade-offs are involved.[22]

Measuring Risks There are several other complications involved in trying to balance risks and benefits. For example, can risks and benefits be measured in the same units? How can different types of risks—such as the risk of disabling injury and the risk of death—be compared? Consider the question of how many days of lost work from an injury are equivalent to a death. It is relatively easy to value in dollars the cost of a minor injury that causes a worker to miss one day of work. Let's say the value is $50 per worker-day lost. If 10,000 workers lost an average of one day each year as a result of minor accidents associated with, say, one energy system, then this total yearly risk would be expected to cost 10,000 × $50 = $500,000. An average working lifetime is about 10,000 days. Should we equate the risk of 10,000 workers losing one day each at $50 per day lost to an equal risk of one worker losing 10,000 days of work—that is, his life? Both risks cost the same in these dollar terms, but some people would value the one lost life much higher than the 10,000 minor injuries; others might hold the opposite view. Which job is "safer"? Both options involve personal value judgments about the nonmonetary value of each job risk. Inevitably, it boils down to the simple—yet most difficult—question: what is the value of a human life? In the United States, a life is typically worth a few tens to a few hundreds of thousands of dollars; at least that is close to what governments are willing to spend per life saved, for example, to improve highway safety, according to

447

some estimates.[23] Few political leaders or government officials are willing to endorse publicly any dollar figure for a human life, despite the fact that their actions to restrict spending on public safety projects implicitly assign such a monetary equivalent. Sometimes you may think you "feel like a million dollars," but it is rare for a society to spend that much to protect an individual against routine hazards.

Externalities and Inequities:
The Problem of Redistributive Justice   Another problem arises when we recognize that not all the benefits accrue to the same people who are exposed to the risks of energy use. For instance, those who live close to smokestacks may be exposed to disproportionate health risks compared to those who live farther away. Both groups may benefit to the same extent from the power generated, but one group is in greater danger of experiencing the associated risks. Hence, the distribution of risks and benefits is inequitable in such a situation, and we may need to devise some just means of compensation to reduce these inequities.* However, such compensatory mechanisms are neither automatic nor uncontroversial. The reason lies in current economic practices.

A characteristic of most economic systems—market-oriented or centrally planned—is that they often allow limited special interests—public or private—to degrade common property without penalty. Your automobile, for example, pollutes the air, but you may not be required to pay for the harmful effects to others from that pollution except perhaps with your own degraded health when you breathe automobile pollution. In the jargon of economists, the term for this loophole in the economic system is *externality;* it describes the cost (or sometimes benefit) of some economic activity to parties not directly involved in—that is, external to—that economic activity.[24] We mentioned the example of people living near a smokestack and being subjected to greater health risks than others. The resultant medical costs to these people are usually external to the economic considerations of the polluters, unless environmental regulations for emissions are enforced. Just as utilities may be forced to control or pay for their pollution (that is, internalizing to some extent the external costs previously foisted on outsiders), countries that produce air

---

*Some may argue that the marketplace provides that compensation, since living near a smokestack probably means a lower rent than living farther away. Even if it were so, the rent differential is unlikely to be based on an evaluation of potential health costs to those who live near the stack.

pollution—particularly acid rain—are being increasingly pressured by their neighbors to curb their activities or pay compensation.[25]

But what should we do when the externalities of our activities don't hurt us or even our neighbors today, but might hurt future generations? This issue is called the *intergenerational equity* problem by risk analysts. For instance, a generation that chooses to dispose of radioactive wastes by cheap, unproved methods externalizes the risk by committing the next several hundred generations to live with it, while the benefits of cheap disposal fall to us. This question is intimately tied to economic methods via the discount rate.

Discounting the Future   One reason for externalizing many risks is that most people act—economically, at least—as if they consider the present to be worth more than the future. As discussed earlier with regard to CO_2 risks or soil erosion, such a philosophy heavily discounts the future. This is not necessarily an unethical or wholly selfish societal behavior, since most of us cannot be sure what the future will bring, whereas the present is more clearly defined and tangible. We also assume the future will be richer, in part because of our investments today. If so, then perhaps people later will be better able to pay the costs of the risks we transfer to the future by our present actions. In a sense, discounting could be viewed as building future wealth while at the same time borrowing from that buildup in the form of a legacy of risks like pollution, for which future generations will have to pay the costs of cleanup or adaptation—presumably out of their increased wealth.

On an individual basis, we must already place some value on the future or we wouldn't pay for education or health insurance, nor would we raise children or preserve wilderness areas; these actions will garner benefits primarily in the future. However, when the future is far off and the risks uncertain but the present is at hand and benefits clear-cut, most people think—and act—with today in mind. Particularly in hard times, an argument like "it is better in the long run" usually goes by the boards. But living for the moment can cause enormous long-term problems. Soil erosion, as we have seen, is a good example. The short-term view of squeezing as much productivity out of the current soil as possible without regard to its degradation could be devastating in the long term. The fact that there will be more people in the future and a greater need for food suggests that perhaps we should value the soil (and the future) by marking up its future price instead of marking it down.

449

It is not always irrational to discount the future, though. Consider the case of a suspected carcinogen; let's say some present food additive or drug could cause a certain number of cancers in the future. There are at least two options: one could spend money now to find a substitute for the cancer-causing product, and thereby eliminate the marginal cancer risk even though it will be felt largely in the future. This has, in fact, been required by the so-called Delaney Amendment in the United States.[26] Alternatively, the dollars spent on finding a noncarcinogenic substitute could be invested in medical research instead, perhaps eliminating cancer altogether. In this sense it seems rational to discount the future risk of a marginal increase in cancer in the hopes that a cancer cure would be found in time. But suppose that hoped-for cure doesn't materialize? The immediate benefits of not spending extra money on substitutes leads to virtually certain incremental cancer costs later on. That is the kind of gamble that accompanies uncertain risk/benefit analyses. Clearly, there is no simple, rational, scientific way to place a price tag on the future versus the present. And what seems rational to one set of people may not be considered rational by others, particularly since the risk estimates themselves are often very uncertain, as are present estimates of the risks of future alternatives.

This sort of intergenerational value judgment, like that involved in deciding what can be regarded as safe, should reflect the opinions of people armed with as much information as possible—that is, the best available estimates (or, more typically, range of estimates) of the risks and benefits. It is the role of science to narrow the uncertainties by trying to fill in the gaps of information on the distribution, magnitude, and timing of the risks and benefits of each activity. In this way the probability of costs and benefits and their potential consequences can be made clearer—at least to those who are willing to seek and absorb this information. Individual values can then be applied to the political and ethical issues inherent in judging safety: that is, agreeing on what activities or levels of risk are acceptable.

Risk Perception   Personal as well as public policy decisions on the acceptability of an activity are based more on people's perception of the risks than on the actual risks involved, which may not even be known to experts.[27] For instance, risks that are easy to remember, cause death instead of just injuries, take many lives at one place and one time, or have other dreaded or unusual consequences are often the ones we overestimate relative to actual statistical probabilities. Risks that are new or unfamiliar are often feared more than those that have been around for some time. Some risks are symbols; abhorrence of nuclear weapons, for instance, leads some people to oppose nuclear power regardless of the actual risks of the latter. The ability to identify the victims of some risks is also important in the perception of risks. For instance, society might be willing to spend large sums of money to compensate known victims of an auto accident, but unwilling to spend nearly as much per person on routine highway maintenance to prevent "statistical" accidents from occurring to a larger number of yet unidentified travelers. An important goal of the developing field of risk analysis is to illuminate meaningful comparisons of different risks so that peoples' perceptions of them can at least be based on the best available information. The many unknowns, however, make the emerging science of risk analysis a very tentative policy-making tool. A similar statement could be made about cost benefit analysis, an economic cousin to risk analysis.[28]

In the 1970s, the U.S. Department of Energy (and its predecessors) funded a multimillion-dollar National Research Council study to analyze nearly every facet of energy. The Committee on Nuclear and Alternative Energy Systems (CONAES) was divided into panels, on one of which—The Risk and Impact Panel—one of us served. This panel examined the comparative risks of various energy systems in every stage of their use, from production to consumption. Tables 10.1, 10.2, 10.3, and 10.4 indicate the vast complexity and difficulty of comparing different types of risks associated with different energy systems.[29] The entries do not give quantitative probabilities, costs, or benefits, which need to be compared and weighed for each of these enumerated classes of risks in order to make rational decisions on how much and which types of energy systems to use and develop. Part of the reason is that it is now impossible to provide more than crude estimates of the probabilities, costs, and benefits of most of the activities that give rise to these entries. The difficult question is what to do while we wait for the experts to fill in more of the blanks.

Balancing Benefits and Risks: The PQLI

We have stressed here the risk side of fossil fuels, mostly with respect to a related CO_2 increase. What about benefits of fossil fuel use, though, particularly to developing countries that are trying to improve their economic status?

451

Table 10.1 Some Health Risks from Energy Generation and End Use

Stage of the fuel cycle	Nuclear	Fossil fuels Coal	Oil	Gas	Hydroelectric	Geothermal	Solar
Extraction	Lung cancer Accidental deaths and injuries	Accidental deaths and injuries Lung disease Water contaminants	Accidental deaths and injuries	Accidental deaths and injuries	Accidents in construction	Accidents in construction	Accidents in construction and equipment shipping Toxic by-products of construction materials
Processing	Cancer and mutation from tailings	Lung disease	Lung disease				
Transportation	Theft Accidents	Accidents	Accidents	Death or injury from explosion	Accidents from dam failures	Possible toxic effects from emissions (H_2S)	Possible toxic effects (e.g., from metals) Accidents
Generation	Cancer and mutation Accidents Sabotage	Bronchitis and exacerbation of chronic disease Possible risk of cancer and mutation Water contaminants Acute respiratory disease, increased mortality Annoyance reactions Altered physiological functions					
Transmission	Accidents; possible ozone and electromagnetic radiation changes						
Waste disposal	Cancer and mutation	Cancer, lung disease, mutation				Unknown	
End use	Deaths and injuries from automobile and other transportation; accidents from other sources; electrocution; fires; accidents from solar rooftop maintenance						

Source: Schneider, S. H., 1979. Comparative risk assessment of energy systems, Energy 4: 919–931, based on unpublished data from the CONAES Risk/Impact Panel.

Table 10.2 Some Environmental Risks from Energy Generation and End Use

Stage of the fuel cycle	Nuclear	Fossil fuels			Hydroelectric	Geothermal	Solar
		Coal	Oil	Gas			
Extraction	Scarred land	Scarred land, Damaged and decreased water supplies, Subsidence, Excess rubble	Water pollution from seepage and spills, Subsidence	Subsidence			
Processing	Mine tailings	Effluents, Water shortage	Air and water pollution		Loss of rivers, Silting, Estuarine imbalance, Water loss	Subsidence, Brine discharge, Thermal effects, H_2S, Water pollution, Water shortage	Local temperature effects, Land use, Water shortage, Loss of shade
Transportation		Coal dust	Pollution and wildlife harm from spills				
Generation	Thermal effects, Water shortage	Acid rain, water pollution particles					
		Climate changes from CO_2; thermal effects; watershortages; NO_x effects					
Transmission	Damage to wildlife, forests, and aesthetics from transmission lines						
Waste disposal	Radioactivity	Excess rubble, Trace metals				Pollution	
End use	Ecological damage from high energy use (photochemical smog)						

Source: Schneider, S. H.. 1979. Comparative risk assessment of energy systems. Energy 4: 919–931. based on unpublished data from the CONAES Risk/Impact Panel.

Table 10.3 Some Sociopolitical Risks from Electric Energy Generation and End Use

ELECTRIC

Stage of the fuel cycle	Nuclear	Solar thermal	Hydroelectric	Fossil electric				Geothermal
				Coal	Oil	Gas		
Extraction	Land-use impacts withdrawal from other uses legal impacts land rights; access aesthetic	Land use impacts aesthetic legal impacts boomtowns Siting impacts	Aesthetic (loss of free-flowing rivers)* Boomtown effects* Siting conflicts* Land use† Risks of accidents/ sabotage*	Same as nuclear* (more widespread) Boomtown effects* Water shortages* Reclamation costs* Regional/local inequities	Spill impacts* aesthetic recreational	Foreign policy impacts* (wars, embargoes) Land subsidence		Siting, land use impacts Land subsidence Noise
Processing	Safeguards* civil liberties diversion				Refinery siting* Tank farm siting			
Transportation	Safeguards civil liberties diversion			Accidents		Pipeline and liquified natural gas tankers: availability and safety conflicts		

		Siting impacts				
Generation	Safeguards* civil liberties diversion Siting fiscal impacts institutional impacts Risk of accidents*				Regional equity disputes (mine site vs remote conversion* Infrastructure investment	
Transmission					Land use and aesthetic impacts; power lines System vulnerability	Capital intensity of control technologies*
Waste disposal	Opposition to siting* Long-term care/intergenerational impacts					
End use						
Whole-system risks	Arms proliferation* Political conflicts over safety, economics, equity (local, national, international)* Federal preemption Second-order health impacts		Local political conflicts Equity impacts Federal preemption	Second-order health impacts Conflicts over safety, economics, equity Intergenerational impacts (e.g., CO_2 effects on climate)		
	Inflated demand from inefficient energy utilization; greatest dissociation of costs and benefits; regional disputes*				Capital requirements; inflated demand from inefficient energy utilization; greatest dissociation of costs and benefits; regional disputes; CO_2 and climate control*	

*Particularly important risk

Source. Schneider, S. H.. 1979. Comparative risk assessment of energy systems, Energy 4: 919–931, based on unpublished data from the CONAES Risk/Impact Panel.

Table 10.4 Some Sociopolitical Risks from Nonelectric Energy Generation and End Use

NONELECTRIC

Stage of the fuel cycle	Fossil direct use			Solar heating and cooling	Conservation
	Coal	Oil	Gas		
Extraction	Same as fossil electric*			Legal impacts sun rights Land use impacts scattering*	Capital costs materials redesign of industrial processes* Institutional impact* Curtailment allocation (equity) problems* Lifestyle impacts* First-cost equity impacts Civil liberties Second-order health risks
Processing		Same as fossil electric			
Transportation		Traffic generation			
Generation		Same as fossil electric		High initial costs Operation and maintenance risks	
Transmission				Governmental interventions	
Waste disposal	Capital intensity of control technologies†				
End use		Transportation impacts*			
Whole-system risks	Second-order health impacts* Regional disputes Allocation problems Intergenerational impacts (e.g. CO₂ effects on climate)			Backup requirements* Regional imbalances	

*Particularly important risk

Source: Schneider, S. H., 1979. Comparative risk assessment of energy systems, Energy 4: 919–931, based on unpublished data from the CONAES Risk/Impact Panel.

Energy and Standard of Living We often associate a high standard of living in a country (typically measured by economists as per capita gross national product or GNP) with a high per capita rate of energy consumption. It is true that the per capita energy use is higher in the well-to-do countries than in poor ones. But in the United States and Canada, per capita energy use is much greater than in other equally or more affluent nations. The United States accounts for more than 10 kilowatts per capita, whereas Sweden uses 5 to 6 kilowatts per capita and Switzerland uses less than two-thirds the amount of energy per capita consumed by the United States.* Both Sweden and Switzerland, however, have higher living standards than the United States as measured by GNP per capita![31]

Why doesn't the formula "more energy equals more GNP" necessarily apply to Sweden and Switzerland? For one thing, the Swedish are much more energy-efficient than Americans; they conserve energy in housing and industry, use smaller cars, have better mass transit, and use waste heat more efficiently. The result, according to the Berkeley, California energy analysts Lee Schipper and A. Lichtenberg, is a significant savings of the total energy used.[32] Switzerland is similarly advanced in conservation techniques. For example, their garbage-recycling scheme for fuel ranks as one of the world's most sophisticated systems, at least twenty years ahead of the United States and the Soviet Union.[33] For the United States and Canada at least, an increase in energy use is unlikely to be a cost-effective, efficient method to increase GNP—and is certainly not likely to reduce pollution and dependence on OPEC. It has been shown in study after study that energy conservation and other means of increasing productivity of energy end usage through efficiency and innovation will be more cost-effective.[34] They also buy time, as we've already pointed out, to develop cheaper and safer renewable energy systems and to study more definitively the nature of a range of energy system risks, which are now highly uncertain. In poorer countries, however, more total energy use would likely have very different cost/benefit ratios than for developed rich countries.

---

*To be fair, it should be pointed out that the structure of the Swiss economy is such that about one-third of Switzerland's energy is imported in the form of goods and services (so-called gray energy).[30] In addition, fluctuating monetary exchange rates complicate comparisons of standards of living between such nations as the United States and Switzerland. Nevertheless, even with these considerations accounted for, Switzerland still uses much less energy per capita than the United States for a comparable standard of living.

457

The Demographic Transition   Nevertheless, in the grossest sense, as is evident from energy use and GNP data, for very poor nations more energy—or at least more energy services—would still bring valuable marginal returns in terms of GNP growth. If such growth were channeled into basic human services such as increased food production, refrigeration, and the medical care so desperately needed to bring down the death rate, the net effect would probably be an improvement in the quality of life for most people. But would reducing the death rate and improving the physical quality of life in LDCs also bring down the birth rates? A birth rate decrease is necessary if the world population size is eventually to stabilize—an essential precondition to a sustainable future.*

An improvement in the GNP could well have just such an effect in poor countries. If parents could be assured that their offspring had a chance of surviving early childhood, they might not be driven so hard to have many children as insurance against a high mortality rate.[36] This notion is a basic tenet of a theory of population proposed by demographers in the first half of this century.[37] They observed the birth and death rates both in Western Europe and in other countries that industrialized during the nineteenth century. According to their hypothesis, population growth rate automatically decreases a generation or two after per capita income rises, largely through industrial development that improves living conditions, alters the economy, and reduces economic incentives for having large families. Countries that have achieved this so-called *demographic transition* include the United States, Japan, the USSR, Canada, Australia, New Zealand, and most European nations. In all these nations the per capita GNP figures are above several thousand dollars and per capita energy use levels are well above the global average of 2 kilowatts per capita.† Since developed countries prospered—in large part through increased fossil fuel use—and reduced

---

*Population size affects the CO_2/energy dilemma, since total CO_2 (or other) pollution is equal to the product of these terms: (the per capita use of energy) $\times$ (the CO_2 produced per unit energy) $\times$ (population size). This general equation has been denoted "the population multiplier" by Ehrlich, Ehrlich, and Holdren.[35]

†To get a feeling for the magnitude of 2 kilowatts (that is, 2000 watts) per capita we can consider a few examples. Twenty 100-watt bulbs or three hand-held hairdryers or one electric oven or fifteen medium-sized refrigerators, operating continuously, each represent about 2 kilowatts of energy use. Delivering this energy to your house, however, takes several hundred percent more energy at the power plant, most of which ends up as waste heat injected into the environment. The United States averages some five times more than the world average of 2 kilowatts per capita, whereas some LDCs use several times less than the world average.

458

their population growth rates without special coercion, some argue that developing nations in Africa, Asia, and Latin America should be entitled to limit their population growth rates noncoercively by becoming similarly wealthy and industrialized.

This theory of population, derived from past experiences in developed countries, may not be valid for today's developing nations. Critics point out that big industry in most LDCs employs and benefits just a small fraction of the population, creating a two-tiered system in which the majority of the people are left untouched by modernization.[38] This unequal distribution of access to food, clothing, adequate shelter, education, employment, and health care is most marked in rural areas, where a majority of the populations of poor nations live. The countryside is also where population growth rates are high. Ehrlich, Ehrlich, and Holdren argue that demographic transition occurred in the developed countries only after the fruits of income growth reached the masses, which took centuries of industrial and social development. They believe that there just isn't time anymore to wait for the economic benefits of industrialization, managed by elites in LDCs, to trickle down to the masses.[39] By the time this occurs many decades of dangerously high population growth will have elapsed. In the meantime, more industrial effluents will have been injected into the environment.

Average GNP Per Capita: A Questionable
Measure of Individual Well-Being   Merely increasing GNP per capita by some marginal increment in LDCs is no guarantee that birth rates will automatically fall, as predicted by the demographic transition theory. A glance at Figure 10.1 shows that there is no discernible pattern to birth rates and GNP for per capita GNP levels below $1000. Above $2500 GNP per capita—not shown in the figure—there is a strong correlation, but the prospect of raising most countries listed in Figure 10.1 to this income level in less than several generations appears, politically at least, virtually nil. Part of the lack of correlation in Figure 10.1 between decreasing birth rate and increasing GNP per capita is related to the use of a nationwide average GNP as the principal measure of individual well-being. The distribution of wealth within a nation is at least as important a measure of well-being as average GNP per capita. Recognizing that measuring standard of living and birth rate solely by nationwide average of per capita GNP was unsatisfactory, economist Morris D. Morris developed the *Physical Quality of Life Index (PQLI)* while at the Overseas Development Council.[40] This index

459

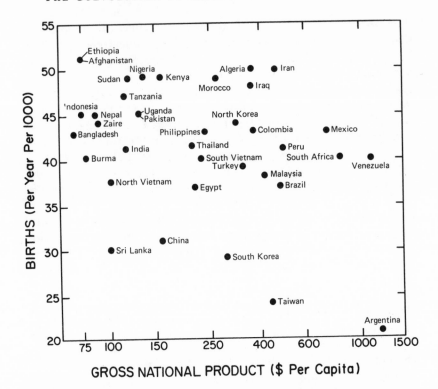

Figure 10.1
Birth rate plotted against gross national product (GNP) per capita for nations with per capita GNP less than $1500. Although there is a slight downward trend in the data, it is very difficult to argue from such data that an increase in GNP in any nation would necessarily result in decrease in birth rates [Source: P. Demeny, 1974, The populations of underdeveloped countries, Scientific American, September, pp. 149–159.]

measures a country's success in meeting three basic human requirements for the physical well-being of its population: infant mortality, life expectancy, and literacy. Life expectancy and infant mortality are good measures of nutrition, public health, income, and general environment; literacy is both a gauge of well-being and a skill important to economic development. Even though the data in different nations for these three indicators are uneven in quality, Morris says they are easily available and express basically "unethnocentric objectives." Making improvements in these three categories is a fairly universal goal, he says, and the indicators shouldn't make any assumptions about special cultural patterns. Also, Morris notes, these factors are *results*, not inputs. Because these results reflect

460

fairly universal objectives, Morris believes they are appropriate indicators by which to compare the basic quality of life among countries.

There are limitations to the applicability of the PQLI. For instance, the data are not broken down by sex and there is no indicator for illness. The PQLI does not attempt to quantify other characteristics associated with quality of life such as justice, political freedom, or happiness. It does not fine-tune subcultural definitions of the quality of life. But it does give a much more composite picture of physical quality of life than the aggregate economic GNP alone. Countries are assigned a PQLI number in the following manner. For the life expectancy index, for example, the highest figure (seventy-five years) achieved by any country in 1973 (chosen as the year of best performance overall since World War II) was Sweden, valued at 100. The worst figure (twenty-eight years) occurred in Guinea Bissau in 1950 (the year of poorest performance), and was rated 1. A composite index is calculated by averaging the three components of the index, each having equal weight.*

To what extent is PQLI related to GNP? You might think that a country's PQLI rating goes up as the per capita income increases, since theoretically more economic resources could be channeled into bettering nutrition, public health, and education. This turns out to be true only for the very rich and the very poor. The relationship between PQLI and per capita GNP is apparently much more complicated between the extremes of rich and poor; it depends on a combination of economic and cultural circumstances.

PQLI, Well-Being,
and Birth Rates   Figure 10.2, drawn by Harrison Brown (when he was at the East-West Center of the University of Hawaii) from Morris' work, illustrates the complexities of the relationship between PQLI and per capita GNP. There are five major cultural fields depicted here; two other fields describe the industrial countries. At one end of the range are the African nations south of the Sahara. The most wealthy of those nations in the Black Africa grouping in Figure 10.2 have per capita GNP figures around $500, and the poorest below $100. But PQLI remains low, between 10 and 30. Here, large differences (up to 500 percent!) in the per capita GNP are *not* reflected proportionately in the PQLI. At the other end of the spectrum (see the upper right corner of Figure 10.2) the PQLI

---

*The equal weighting of these three factors is an arbitrary choice that needs to be re-examined in future refined calculations of *PQLI.*

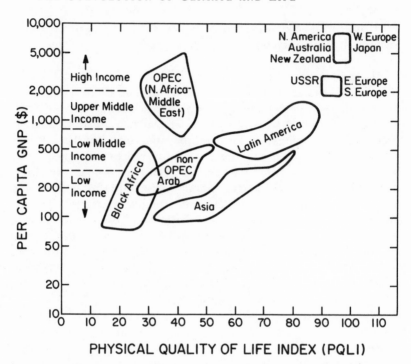

Figure 10.2

Gross National Product (GNP) per capita plotted against Physical Quality of Life Index (PQLI) for various

cultural fields. See text for explanation. [Source: H. Brown, 1977, Relating the PQLI to other factors, International Development Review *19:36–37.]*

is strongly correlated with GNP in the industrialized countries. The non-OPEC Arab countries, Asia, and the Latin American countries are put in separate groups in which the PQLI is also related to some extent to the per capita GNP. That is, the fields slope toward the upper right. In other words, in these groups higher GNP tends—with some exceptions—to be correlated with greater PQLI. But in all of these groups, for a given per capita GNP number, the PQLI is greater in Asia. This is important; for any given per capita income the PQLIs of Asian countries are higher than in other parts of the world. This could well be because income distribution in Asia is generally more equitable than in other parts of the developing world. Regardless of the reasons, it does show that GNP alone is not necessarily the best—or sometimes even a valid—measure of quality of life. This is especially so in the fifth cultural group, made up of the OPEC nations of North Africa and the Middle East, which obvi-

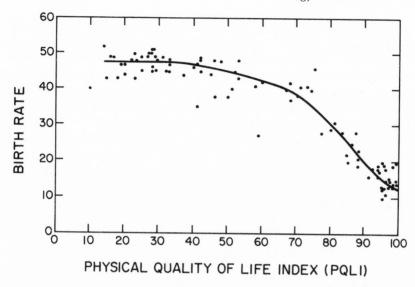

PHYSICAL QUALITY OF LIFE INDEX (PQLI)

Figure 10.3

Birth rate (per year per thousand) versus Physical Quality of Life Index (PQLI), showing the strikingly good fit between these two variables. The result suggests that increases in economic well-being in developing countries must be spread at the economic bottom of the society, not concentrated merely among the elite and allowed to "trickle down" if population growth rates are to be reduced by a demographic transition. *[Source: H. Brown, 1977, Relating the PQLI to other factors,* International Development Review 19:36–37.]

ously have very high national income levels from oil revenues. Yet the range of the PQLI values in these nations is similar to that of the non-OPEC Arab world! Brown attributes this to the lack of widespread distribution of oil revenue in OPEC countries, where high income concentrated in the hands of a few has had minor impact on the quality of life of the masses. That these cultural clusters do not overlap much suggests development policies may need to be tailored to the need of specific regions. Fundamentally, though, they show that average income nationwide is not a reliable measure of national well-being.

Figure 10.3 suggests that there is a fairly good correlation between birth rate and PQLI. Compare the cluster of points (for individual nations) in Figure 10.3 around the solid line to the wide scatter in Figure 10.1. This result suggests that if a demographic transition is to work *quickly* in reducing LDC birth rates without major draconian measures, then development strategies must concentrate on bringing up the PQLI, not just raising overall national

GNP. Even if birth rates in all LDCs somehow miraculously dropped soon to the point where each couple merely replaced themselves (as now appears to be the case for China), world population would still nearly double over the next fifty to seventy-five years. This problem, known as the *momentum of population growth*, occurs because of the age distribution now prevalent in the Third World. That is, a high proportion of people in LDCs today are below childbearing age. Even if they eventually only replace themselves, population size will still not level off for several generations. Thus the problem would be greatly compounded if we waited for the benefits of GNP growth enjoyed by a few to trickle down to the masses and thus lead toward an eventual demographic transition.

In the developed countries, where the age distribution is not heavily weighted toward children, it is no longer necessary to raise the standard of living in order to bring down birth rates.* Moreover, these countries clearly have high standards of energy use, high PQLI, and high levels of CO_2 emissions. However, it must be conceded that for the poor of the world, at least in the short run, more energy —and certainly more energy services—can mean a better quality of life. If energy use—even fossil fuel based—can be focused on providing services that improve health care, education, and nutrition for the bulk of the people in less-developed nations, then we would personally endorse its increase in LDCs as a worthwhile gamble *despite* the environmental risks of more CO_2. But it is essential, we believe, that all such risks taken for the sake of economic development in LDCs help bring about some rapid form of demographic transition—that is, a sharp decrease in population growth rates— for, as population or affluence grows, so usually does pollution. In other words, we would be willing to accept a little additional pollution now if it meant that ultimately the world population would stabilize sooner and thus future pollution levels would be lower for any per capita standard of consumption. A stable population is, of course, an essential component of a sustainable future.

*In order to achieve zero population growth (ZPG), even if a nation has achieved replacement fertility levels—that is, each couple has two children—it is necessary to wait for an equilibrium to be established between birth and death rates. If replacement fertility is suddenly attained, there will still be a larger proportion of the population concentrated in younger people who haven't had their children yet. To reach ZPG in a hurry it would be necessary for several generations of parents to reproduce less than two children per couple, at least until equilibrium was reestablished for some fixed population size.[41] Below-replacement fertility has become policy in China, largely because the Chinese recognized the problem of the momentum of population growth.

If the policy choice were to accept the risks of more fossil fuel use in order to improve PQLI and reduce birth rates in LDCs, any plan with that end would have to be implemented quickly (over decades). Then reasonable, sustainable levels of per capita energy consumption might be obtained in these countries before world population becomes so large that the atmospheric concentration of CO_2 (and other pollutants) would become high enough possibly to cause major disruptions to health, food production, water supplies, or an irreversible sea level rise. The urgency of this problem underscores just how intimately connected the CO_2-climate problem is with global economic development strategies. Of course, accepting this trade-off of a little more CO_2 growth now (and for several decades more) for stable concentrations later on suggests that we must have in mind some long-range target figures for both a stable population size and per capita energy use. Policy makers should try to agree on such long-range targets *before* we gamble that it is worth the risk to increase pollution now in order to achieve the improved quality of life necessary to a population size that is sustainable (and achieved without famines or draconian coercion). We can't realistically be optimistic that a round of global negotiations on such targets will begin soon, but the dialog should begin now.

The Global Survival Compromise

The issues described in this chapter have much in common with the food issue explored earlier. We saw that intensified agriculture can increase food production and help prevent shortages and famine, thereby improving the quality of life for many. But we also saw that intensified agriculture can have its negative side: soil erosion, disruption of biogeochemical cycles, and increased levels of toxic wastes, all results that jeopardize human beings and other parts of nature. A common trade-off we have endorsed in food production strategies, as in energy use planning, is rapid development in the present, even at the risk of exacerbating some future environmental problems. What are the possible consequences if we refuse to accept a few of the long-term environmental risks inherent in efforts to increase food and energy production? Social, economic, and perhaps, ultimately, military dangers loom large if we do not narrow the huge gap between the world's rich and poor. Certainly political turmoil or terrorism cannot help the rich enjoy an improving quality of life, regardless of what their economic indicators read. Moreover, anything that increases the probability of

465

nuclear war is also a very great threat to the environment, for as we saw in Chapter 8, the climate and other environmental variables could be seriously disturbed for long periods in the aftermath of a nuclear exchange, lowering the carrying capacity of the planet by a large fraction. And the ethical issues associated with prolonged inequity among nations are equally pressing—or should be.

One suggestion of a principle that might help steer a hopeful course through these uncertain risks and benefits of development is the global survival compromise, mentioned earlier in our food policy discussions. It was suggested that richer nations should contribute vastly increased sums to aid poorer nations with their development projects, provided such aid were used to improve the quality of life for the bulk of the poor and that population growth rates dropped rapidly as a result. It is a compromise simply because both sides are called upon to sacrifice for the long-term common good. The compromise also applies in the context of energy. In *The Genesis Strategy* I argued

> it must be emphasized that any strategy to create a solution to the world predicament must begin immediately and be rapidly implemented (that is, in a generation or two). As stressed repeatedly here, large-scale technological solutions to problems of underdevelopment and overpopulation are inherently risky, and they grow in risk as they increase in size. Nevertheless, a few such risks are *now* worth considering since the social, economic and, ultimately, military dangers of a widening gulf in the material living standards between rich and poor could well prove greater than the present or near-future environmental risks from carefully chosen technological solutions, provided a stable world equilibrium is reached rapidly. Should such an equilibrium not be achieved before world population grows hopelessly past the potential (long-term) carrying capacity—which admittedly it *may* already have—then our big technological "solution" will only subject vast populations to even more hazardous dependencies and bring us ever nearer [catastrophe].[42]

The potential for climatic change resulting from human activities essentially sets up a time frame within which fossil-fuel-based economic and population growth must be brought under control. At the same time it is urgent, we believe, to raise per capita living standards in LDCs *and* to lower population growth rates as fast as possible. To ignore the urgency of the potential social and climatic consequences of such unconstrained growth is to risk either a widening gap between rich and poor, with very low living standards for angry, impoverished billions or catastrophic environmental disruption for whomever inherits the long-term legacy of our shortsightedness. "We have not inherited the Earth from our fathers," wrote Lester Brown on the cover of his book *Building A Sustainable Society;* rather, "we are borrowing it from our children."[43]

If a global survival compromise can help to bring up the quality of life and bring down birth rates in LDCs for a relatively small increase in CO_2, acid rain, and other fossil fuel effluents, then the benefits of a lower, stable population size as soon as possible are, we believe, greater than the risks from a few tens of percent more pollution during the transition. The issues related to trade-offs between the environment and economic development raised in this chapter are vastly more urgent for human well-being, we're sure, than whether or not to impose automobile import tariffs, build B-1 bombers, reform government overregulation, expand oil depletion allowances, or monitor the Nielsen ratings of the TV networks' programs. Perhaps one day soon some major world developments will jolt the political consciousness of those who still cling to the old priorities. We can only hope that by then the most ominous of current trends won't have become irreversible.

11 Society Permitting: The Future of Climate and Life

We are now ready to collect and distill some general conclusions from our examples of environmental and social interactions. Some of these conclusions and general principles will not seem particularly novel; many are relatively simple and age-old. Yet again and again societies have been slow to adopt such well-known principles. The result is often crisis management: a situation must deteriorate to an obvious predicament before people wake up and act. Much of the societal damage that is wrought by climatic hazards, for example, can often be prevented, and it usually does not require great foresight or even great forecasts. If only society would hedge its bets by anticipating the consequences of plausible changes, we could substantially reduce the adverse impacts of fluctuating climate or weather.

It is often said that, weather permitting, society can avoid the next food crisis. To be sure, we've seen that weather plays an important role in food security. But we do not have to be slavishly dependent on the constancy of the weather to prevent famine. In the end, creating a sustainable future will depend on *society permitting* the implementation of polices that recognize and deal with climatic risks and opportunities. And even more importantly, we must also deal with two very pressing global problems: economic development and population control.

Of course, whatever actions various subgroups of society take will have to allow for fundamental ecological constraints such as climatic hazards. But implementing policies to create sustainable development, we believe, will depend primarily on whether society can alter the political philosophies behind a number of current economic practices.

468

Some General Conclusions and Principles for Living with Climatic Change

Three distinct and interrelated perceptions of the role of climate in human affairs have been traced throughout Part III of this book: climate as a short-term hazard; climate as a stable resource; and climate as an evolving trend. The following principles are listed in roughly this sequence.* However, many of these points are interrelated.

- *Beware of generalizing from short-term records.* Because climatic fluctuations can occur over many time scales, estimates of the likelihood or severity of climatic extremes should be based on as long a term as possible. As the Colorado River case showed, relying on records only a few decades long can lead to serious policy mistakes. This case also emphasized that when there is only a short record of direct instrumental observations, it should be supplemented with as many cross-checked proxy records as possible. Then, from the longest possible data set, actuarial analyses of all sorts of climatic risks can be performed and suitable policy hedges can be devised.
- *Build diversity to provide stability.* Maintaining diverse food, water, and energy sources is obviously a good hedge against large fluctuations in each year's supply. This principle is particularly applicable at national levels, where a diverse supply mix guards against catastrophe should a single source of some commodity become temporarily threatened. Where climatic or human labor resources permit, planting appropriately matched multiple crops in the same fields is a prime example of how to reduce the likelihood of a climatic or pest-caused hazard from wiping out much of the expected production. Most home gardeners already employ the multiple cropping technique, although it is not widely practiced by large-scale agribusiness in most developed countries or by large-scale farmers in developing countries. Short-term economic factors often prompt agriculture on a large scale. Farmers are encouraged to plant monocultures

---

*We will omit details and references in this list of general conclusions and principles. Please see Chapters 8, 9, and 10 for details of specific examples and citations to background references.

469

sustained by (often toxic) chemicals and harvested by machine-intensive labor. However, the problems this creates could be mitigated significantly and rapidly at a national scale without pressing individual farmers to adopt multiple cropping if many different kinds of monocultures were planted in different farm fields in the same region or nation; this practice can help a country weather a bad year, even though individual farmers may face a higher climatic risk by not planting multiple crops in their own fields. Indeed, this practice helped the United States get reasonable total production despite the summer heat that damaged summer crops in 1980 and 1983.

- *Improve genetic resources.* Developing and testing a number of genetic varieties that can deal with a range of climatic, nutritional, or other conditions is an important component of crop diversity, which is essential to sustainable food production. Breeding and stockpiling many varieties is also a hedge against climatic trends. A wider variety of crops to choose from obviously makes it easier to adapt to—or even take advantage of—a new set of climatic resources.

- *Match agricultural practices to crop-climate timetables.* Phenology, the science of the sequence of biological growth stages, suggests that producers can increase production with minimal amounts of irrigation water, fertilizers, or pest controls by carefully timing their applications to match evolving crop and climatic conditions. This practice is not only a more cost-efficient use of these materials, but also reduces serious environmental side effects that often arise from less efficient farming practices.

- *Maintain adequate storage.* Whether it be food, water, or energy, maintaining sufficient reserves *and* distribution systems to see us through some degree of climate-induced risk is time-worn wisdom. However, such a "genesis strategy" to protect consumers against nature's variations must also be designed so that producers are not discouraged from making the investments needed to maintain and develop production capacity.

- *Match credit and climate cycles.* The threat of climatic variability often causes underinvestment in food production inputs such as fertilizer. This climate-defensive behavior is simply a way for food producers faced with fixed debt repayments to hedge against foreclosure should yields or prices fluctuate wildly in anomalous climatic years. Just as we need food security to protect consumers against negative climatic anomalies, so must producers be protected from sudden yield losses or price drops. Often, the cycles for repaying loans to a farmer's creditors are fixed, regardless of how the crops or related prices turn out each year. By matching repayment to production variations caused by climatic anomalies, the consequences of such fluctuations—good and bad—could be shifted from the producers alone to a larger part of society. Such a pooling of risks and benefits would likely lead to increases in farmers' long-term investments in production capacity. This in turn would not only reduce the magnitude of food shortages due to short-term climatic hazards, but also could increase the long-term productivity so essential to meeting world food needs.

- *Charge the true costs: internalize the externalities.* If, for example, producers who indiscriminately overuse chemicals to increase production and profits were charged for the actual or some plausible estimate of the potential costs of environmental or health damages to others (so-called externalities), then such producers would be encouraged to be more prudent in their practices. Similarly, if the potential costs of CO_2-induced climatic changes or acid rain damages were part of today's cost of doing business that produces such emissions, then the economics of acid- or CO_2-producing activities would likely be altered. The result would probably be reduced emissions—and smaller potential consequences from such emissions. In the same vein, if hidden government subsidies—for example, to certain energy supply systems—were openly figured into the price of that commodity, there would be incentives to employ less subsidized alternative systems; and more cost-efficient production and end uses would increase. In most Western countries, for example, some producers and politicians invoke philosophical arguments against government regulation of businesses in favor of a free market approach. But many of these ideologs conveniently forget that in a truly free market producers would be required to internalize their externalities as well as to pay the costs of what are now public subsidies to their businesses.

- *Develop alternative energy supply options.* Just as we need to increase the genetic base of crop varieties, we also need to develop and test alternative energy supply systems. With a better-developed mix of options we can more easily switch among them, should it become necessary, with less likelihood of major economic or strategic disruptions. Society may be pressed to shift from fossil

471

fuel use, for example, should we gain firmer proof of CO_2-induced climatic changes and associated negative consequences. Avoiding reliance on too few energy systems or on those of questionable safety is of overriding strategic importance. A vigorous research and development program to speed along promising alternatives, regardless of present "market signals," seems a high priority for national security planning. We must maintain flexibility in providing future energy systems as more knowledge of the costs, benefits, and strategic risks of each option becomes available.

· *Improve end use efficiency.* Conservation is one of the best ways to buy time to develop economically and environmentally attractive energy systems and to minimize environmental disruptions from present systems. It also makes good economic sense if the same service can be obtained with more efficient use of energy. Insulating your house is one obvious way this can be done. The more we invest in efficiency, the less we'll have to invest in unneeded supply and the more options we will have to deal with whatever problems crop up in the future. Buying time in this way permits a more thorough scientific assessment of the risks and benefits of many endeavors, particularly acid- or CO_2-producing activities.

· *Maintain future productive potential.* It is certainly true that increased individual or national wealth can ease adaptation to many kinds of future stresses. But if that present wealth is bought at the price of seriously degrading the environment—topsoil, groundwater, air quality, or the climate itself—then the future costs of replacing such environmental services could easily exceed the benefits. This issue always presents a difficult value trade-off, particularly since specific cases of risk and benefit assessments are typically clouded by a high degree of technical uncertainty. However, hedging strategies, like a number of the principles described above, can reduce long-term environmental risks of increased production without necessarily creating unacceptable economic hardships in the interim.

· *Maintain a diversity of political and economic ties.* It is unlikely that all countries will suffer simultaneously from the same shortages, particularly if the shortages are climate induced. Trade is a principal means of compensating for regional imbalances caused by regional climatic anomalies. Trade is not only important to mitigate short-term, local climatic hazards, but can also permit exchange of commodities with places where average climatic resources are optimal for production of different goods. However, even in good weather such an optimal strategy imposes strategic risks. To minimize dependence on a single outside source for a strategic commodity, local or regional stockpiles could be built to weather a few years of bad relations with a trading partner. Moreover, agreements could be made with as many nations as possible to trade for the same commodity, minimizing the risk of cutoff from a single supplier. A long history of many trading relationships could ease difficulties should evolving long-term trends (from CO_2, for example) alter climatic resources. Finally, good international rapport among nations will be absolutely necessary to solve global commons problems such as CO_2 buildup, acid rain, or stratospheric ozone modification.

- *Take a broad view.* Transferring climatic information to users involves an array of specialties. Climatology, we've seen in these pages, is an integrating discipline, drawing information from the physical, biological, and social sciences. Despite the essential need to have specialized knowledge from each of these disciplines, climatology cannot be usefully applied unless the contributions from these diverse fields are individually understood and placed in the broad context of real problems. Like many other modern sociotechnological problems, learning to live with climate is an interdisciplinary business that demands *both* refinement and integration of specialized knowledge.

- *Reduce the inventory of nuclear arms.* We conclude our list of principles and conclusions with one that might seem out of place in a book on climate and life. But, as we saw in the "Nuclear Winter" section in Chapter 8, the dust and smoke clouds that could persist for weeks following a large-scale nuclear war could both shut off light for photosynthesis and drop temperatures to sub-freezing levels lethal to most species of plants and animals on earth. The loss of life from the nuclear winter scenarios could well exceed that of direct blast and radioactivity effects. It would be a cruel irony if in only six or so real days the "highest" life form created climatic conditions harsh enough to snuff out many of the forms of life on earth—living things that share our time at the end of the 4.6 billion years that comprised our six metaphorical days of the coevolution of climate and life.

473

Interdependence, Specialization, and Vulnerability

While most of these conclusions and principles are neither new nor exclusively confined to climatic applications, we believe they are so basic to creating a sustainable future that it has been worthwhile to condense and recapitulate them—and to press for their implementation. If there is a common thread among all these interdependent conclusions and principles, it surely must be the urgency of making the necessary efforts to hedge our bets and pool our risks through a diversity of individual and collective mechanisms. As anthropologist Elizabeth Colson learned from the repeated experiences of self-reliant cultures on different continents, "Those who have a variety of skills are more likely to find a niche or niches in which to survive the hard times, than those who have become highly specialized in a narrow range of skills."[1]

If this is so, then why is our postindustrial society, made up as it is of so many well-paid specialists, seemingly *less* vulnerable to droughts or floods than poorer countries with large percentages of self-reliant people? If we compare two similar incidents, one in an industrialized nation and the other in a less developed country, we may see the reason. When a Bay of Bengal cyclone struck Bangladesh in November 1970, some 250,000 people (and an equal number of cattle) were killed, and some $63 million in crops were lost.[2] By comparison, when Hurricane Agnes struck the panhandle of Florida and cut a path to New England in June 1972, about 120 people died, but property damage exceeded $3.5 billion and a quarter of a million people had to be evacuated, many in flood-prone parts of Pennsylvania. In a pioneering study of natural hazards, geographers Ian Burton, Robert Kates, and Gilbert White note that industrialized countries seem to suffer greater absolute damages, at least monetarily, than poorer nations. But in human terms, the death tolls and misery are usually far greater in the LDCs—2000 times as many people died in the Bangladesh storm compared to the losses in the United States from Hurricane Agnes. Moreover, they note, "to be poor as a nation or a person is to be particularly vulnerable. . . . Inequity was not randomly distributed. It was not mere chance that the burden fell most heavily on the landless laborer of Bangladesh or the old retiree of Wilkes-Barre."[3]

Assessing the whole range of factors that differentiate the vulnerability of different groups to different stresses is a complex and controversial matter. The growing field of hazards research has developed quite a literature of case studies and hypotheses in an attempt to find the answers.[4] Our purpose here is to point out that even seemingly straightforward wisdom, such as maintaining diversity, has different interpretations in specific situations. To cite an example at hand, one of us is specialized as a scientist, and the other as a journalist. It is likely that most readers of this book are specialists of one form or the other, as well. But all of us taken together in an industrialized country like the United States make up a vast diversity of skills and economic activities compared to most poorer societies. Thus, while each specialist may be at some considerable personal economic risk should demand for his or her particular skills drop off, our society as a whole is more wealthy than societies in which each person must provide everything for himself. As a result of our collective and diverse specializations we have also been much less physically vulnerable to natural hazards. (We may, however, become more vulnerable to societal hazards, as discussed shortly.) In this sense, people living in industrialized nations are more diverse economically than those living in most LDCs even though most people in industrialized nations (as individuals) are more specialized than self-providing farmers in LDCs. Therefore, the extent to which it is wise for us to embrace the principle of maintaining diversity depends in part on who is included in the "us" group. Even this most basic principle must be applied carefully in specific applications to be sure its intent is not lost.

Risks of Interdependence

Of course, there is a price we (both as individuals and as members of postindustrial society) pay for the wealth generated by our collective economic pluralism and the diminished personal risks we face from natural hazards. This price takes several forms.

For example, if we as a society allow ourselves to become dependent on a single (or diminishing) source for such commodities as imported oil, imported food, water, or irreplaceable topsoil, then the advantages of our economic pluralism can become diminished by a dangerous collective dependence on such commodities. Obviously, few of us in industrialized countries are individually food, water, or energy self-reliant; our "good life" depends on cooperation—that is, we require political stability to receive the goods we need to survive. One reaction to this disquieting dependence is seen

475

in the recent upsurge of survivalists. The stereotypical survivalist retreats to remote mountain areas and practices basic survival skills —including violent combat—in anticipation of imminent societal collapse. To us, it is a more effective strategy to work to *prevent* such a breakdown by dealing with the most probable causes. These include inequitable sharing of societies' benefits or overreliance on unreliable lines of supply of essential goods and services. A strategy for survival that attempts to build resilience at many levels of society seems much more efficacious than hiding in a private fortress to ward off—probably unsuccessfully anyway—the hungry hoards escaping from the turmoil of starving cities and suburbs in the wake of societal collapse. Some elements of this strategy have been suggested earlier.

A second price of our collective pursuit of wealth has been the advent of large-scale environmental disruptions such as increasing CO_2 concentrations, acid rain, and soil erosion. This external cost of doing business, as we've argued several times, must be internalized if we are to live under a fair set of economic rules.

A third price is that we have become collectively tied by food trade to natural climatic fluctuations everywhere, even those that might occur on another continent. As noted by Schneider and atmospheric scientist Richard Temkin:

> Many people now depend for their food upon the continuous productivity of only a few world granaries; these food production and distribution systems are, in turn, sensitive to relatively small variations in regional climate. In essence, societal vulnerability to climatic variations has been transformed from the pre-technological condition of high-frequency, low-amplitude risk to the present situation of low-frequency, high-amplitude risk. That is, most local adverse weather situations can be smoothed out by food transfers; but the less probable *simultaneous disruption* * of growing conditions in only three or four major granaries could threaten the survival of perhaps half a billion people.[6]

Interdependency is not necessarily bad, however. But to mitigate the risk of simultaneous disruptions we must respond actively

---

*A group of agrometeorologists in Columbia, Missouri attempted to estimate some such probabilities of simultaneous disruptions.[5] For example, there is about an 8 percent chance of a simultaneous reduction of at least 10 percent in wheat yields in the United States and the USSR in any one year. Longer runs of simultaneous reductions have not yet occurred, but would be much more devastating.

476

by setting up food security schemes commensurate with regional food needs, indigenous production, and interdependent trading.

Another risk of the postindustrial brand of economic progress is measured in different units: the increasing complexity of society threatens our very ability to comprehend what is going on around us and, by implication, how to deal with it. In *The Primordial Bond,* Schneider and Lynne Morton recalled H. G. Wells' well-traveled insight, "Human history becomes more and more a race between education and catastrophe."[7] The authors then commented that "if people don't expend the effort to keep up with what's happening, or what could happen, and if they don't keep in touch with their feelings and values about these events, catastrophe seems likely to be the winner." Following up an informal suggestion from Paul Ehrlich, Schneider and Morton called for a "social tithe: We should consider giving ten percent of our free time to the task of keeping abreast of central issues, or in some other way helping society to function. Being informed is a necessity for successful democracy."[8] (Keeping informed on a wide variety of issues is also a way to restore some diversity to our otherwise highly specialized individual work lives.) U.S. President Woodrow Wilson was concerned about another aspect of the problem of complexity and democracy seventy years ago: "What I fear is a government of experts. . . . What are we for if we are to be scientifically taken care of by a small number of gentlemen who are the only men who understand the job? Because if we do not understand the job, then we are not a free people."[9]

But what has societal complexity and its relationship to democracy to do with the weather? We hope we've convinced you that, at least indirectly, the weather has quite a bit to do with societal vulnerability to shortfalls in food, water, and energy supplies. These vulnerabilities, in turn, are related to complexity and maintaining a vital democracy. The climatic connection becomes clearer when—because of special interests' pressure or average citizens' indifference or ignorance—societies permit food security margins to become so small that price instability and even famines can result from precedented climate fluctuations. Moreover, classic, market-oriented economic practices that do not internalize externalities or protect common property can lead to the erosion of soil, exclusion of pollution-caused health problems from the cost of doing business, or underreaction to the possible consequences of long-term climatic changes from worldwide industrial and land-use activities.

477

And because these issues are complex, we must make a considerable effort to understand related probabilities and consequences. From such knowledge we can then choose through the democratic process how to allocate resources to mitigate climatic hazards or to achieve any other societal goal. Society largely determines the societal consequences of weather variations.

Free Markets and Economic Growth: The American Ideology

How is it that so many governments ignore some of the fundamental principles summarized earlier and thus make their people more vulnerable to the elements than need be? In large part the answer lies in current economic practices. Without attempting a survey of all relevant economic philosophy, it is probably worthwhile to explore a few of the major related arguments. In his famous text *Economics,* used since 1948 by most students in introductory economics courses, MIT economist Paul Samuelson recounted that Adam Smith, in his classical *Wealth of Nations,* was

> thrilled by the recognition of an order in the economic system. Smith proclaimed the principle of the "invisible hand"; each individual pursuing only his own selfish good was led, as if by an invisible hand, to achieve the best good of all, so that any interference with free competition by government was almost certainly to be injurious.[10]

Despite the strong rejection of such a free market philosophy within Marxist countries, all nations tend to act as if they are pursuing their own selfish good when it comes to international trade. Any rhetoric about other nations' use of monopolistic capital or their unfair internal distribution of resources always seems hollow in the face of the behavior of nearly all nations in striking trading deals. Grain is one good example. When the USSR buys large quantities of grains from producers such as the United States or Argentina to support the Russians' taste for meat, the worldwide price of grain is thereby raised. As a result, less grain can be obtained on the world market by the LDCs that need it most and have limited purchasing power compared to the industrialized countries—capitalist or communist. In bad growing years, like the early and mid-1970s, such

478

grain trading among the developed countries was almost certainly life-threatening to some of those living at the margins of survival in some LDCs. The continued pressure of spiraling grain costs from bad weather, rich nations' trading patterns, and the OPEC oil price hike (which sent fertilizer prices skyward in 1974) undoubtedly combined to help cause the millions of excess deaths in several LDCs mentioned earlier.

Despite the frequent claim in most capitalist nations that they have evolved to the point that "ours is a mixed system of government and private enterprise," as Samuelson states it,[11] most business people and many politicians, particularly in the United States, still cling passionately to the Adam Smith type of free market philosophy. David Vogel, professor of business administration of the University of California at Berkeley, and Leonard Silk, economist and *New York Times* business correspondent, critically examined this view in their book *Ethics and Profits.* They recounted Alexis de Tocqueville's observation a century and a half ago that the "deepest American ideology" is " 'the philosophy of self-interest.' "[12] But "by clinging to an outmoded ideology," Silk and Vogel caution,

> American businessmen and their political representatives are trying to impose solutions that not only fail, but also impede more effective means of dealing with national and international problems, such as inflation and unemployment, poverty and the maldistribution of income, the decay of cities, environmental deterioration, the shortage of food and other vital resources and the energy crisis. It is this failure to solve crucial problems . . . which is really undermining the legitimacy of corporations and threatening their autonomy.[13]

Silk and Vogel do not recommend abandoning altogether this classic American ideology. Rather, they suggest that Western economies "redefine the relationship of the corporation to the commonweal" in order to "lead to a better reconciliation of private objectives and public goals."[14]

The American ideology—and its counterparts abroad—has had harsher critics. One of the most influential was a former industrialist who for twenty years was head of planning at the British Coal Board. Economist E. F. Schumacher became a counterculture hero when he published *Small Is Beautiful: Economics As If People Mattered.* In it, he rejects the goals of our classical economic system:

We shrink back from the truth if we believe that the destructive forces of the modern world can be "brought under control" simply by mobilising more resources—of wealth, education, and research—to fight pollution, to preserve wildlife, to discover new sources of energy, and to arrive at more effective agreements on peaceful coexistence. Needless to say, wealth, education, research, and many other things are needed for any civilization, but what is most needed today is a revision of the ends which these means are meant to serve. And this implies, above all else, the development of a lifestyle which accords to material things their proper, legitimate place, which is secondary and not primary.[15]

His solution to economic development, particularly in the Third World, was not to abandon technology, but to scale it down toward "intermediate technologies." After Schumacher's death, this concept was popularly altered to "appropriate technology."[16]

A more vociferous critic of modern industrial economic goals is the American economist Herman Daly. He takes on squarely the principal goal of most businesses and their governmental allies: economic growth itself. The first line of Chapter 1 of his book *Steady-State Economics* lays out his challenge: "The theme of this book is that a steady-state economy is a necessary and desirable future state of affairs and that its attainment requires quite major changes in values, as well as radical, but nonrevolutionary, institutional reforms."[17]

Daly goes on to say that we need to learn that the axiom "enough is best" is much more sound than "more is better." The underlying philosophy that growth and more growth is necessary must be replaced with a more "moral solution," Daly writes. But he concedes that overturning the "paradigm of growth" will be no easy task. It is, he says, the most universally accepted goal in the world. Growth appeals to capitalists, communists, fascists, and socialists as a basis of national power; it is an alternative to "sharing as a means of combating poverty." Daly adds that "if we are serious about helping the poor, we shall have to face up to the moral issue of redistribution and stop sweeping it under the rug of aggregate growth."[18]

In his always witty, sometimes brilliant, and often polemical critique, Daly essentially blames economic growth values for problems ranging from environmental degradation to social injustice to the threat of nuclear war. His substitute value system is "the steadystate paradigm," which he defines as follows: "What is held constant is capital stock in the broadest physical sense of the term, including capital goods, the total inventory of consumer goods and the population of human bodies."[19] Although Daly admits that a steady-state economy is far from a sufficient answer to all human problems, he says at least it offers the "alternative of stability on the material plane" while freeing us "for growth in those infinite moral and spiritual dimensions."[20]

While such sentiments are appealing to a growing number of economically comfortable people fed up with problems like pollution or military actions designed to protect overseas business ventures, Daly's disciples are few, particularly in the developing countries. Many people in LDCs still lack basic amenities; and as we saw from the Physical Quality of Life Index (PQLI) statistics in Chapter 10, economic growth can help improve their quality of life—provided the fruits of growth are well distributed and not merely concentrated at the top, only to trickle down to the disadvantaged at a rate the upper-income classes choose. Also, for steady-state economics to provide a fixed per capita "inventory of consumer goods" requires a fixed population size, an unlikely prospect in most LDCs for at least several more generations, even if draconian measures were implemented now. Without economic growth in LDCs—or an equivalent transfer of wealth from developed countries—during the transition to a steady-state population, the poor will only get relatively poorer. (Recall from Chapter 9 how Japanese postwar economic recovery and growth led to a dramatic drop in infant mortality rates.) On the other hand, unless the world moves rapidly toward a sustainable economy—which ultimately may be a steady-state economy—pollution, the arms race, and other societal problems rightly decried by critics of present economic values will eventually become globally catastrophic. (Of course, this long view ignores the potential dangers along the way.)

The problem of working for a sustainable future then is twofold:

- To identify, and then to agree, on fixed resource use and population size limits (even if they are only working targets for a hypothetical steady-state world).
- To negotiate a transition strategy to try to achieve these goals without huge inequities or high risk of environmental or other catastrophes along the way. The global survival compromise discussed in earlier chapters is one example of such a transition strategy.

Economic Versus Strategic Thinking: Philosophy for a Sustainable Future

We've used the word "strategic" often, and frequently in contrast to "economic" thinking. The American College Dictionary includes the following among its definitions of the word strategy: "skillful management in . . . attaining an *end*" (our italics). We italicize *end* precisely because the critics of traditional economic values we've cited have disparaged the goals of current economic thinking, in particular the self-interest motivation of free market philosophy and the growth orientation of nearly everyone. Their critiques are challenges on value issues rather than technical ones, although much technical material is both cited and relevant.*

A personal experience of mine may make this point clearer. Several years ago I met with the top management of a major U.S. food company. I raised the issues of soil erosion and CO_2 concentrations and challenged the executives to show how their economic philosophy of fast growth and free enterprise could solve such issues. One manager expressed concern for these problems but said he would be fired after complaints from his stockholders if, for example, he placed priority on the consequences of future soil erosion ahead of their dividends for next year. A dialog ensued, somewhat like the following:

"How do you measure your success?" I asked.

"By the growth of the corporation," he quickly replied, with many heads nodding around the room.

"Why is that?" I wondered out loud to quizzical faces.

"That's the purpose of business," one executive suggested, "it's always been that way." The others appeared to agree—or said nothing.

"I always thought the principal social value of business was to improve the overall quality of life," I replied, "and that growth is,

---

*Of course, some economic critics also decry the tendency to overuse modern methods. Herman Daly is one. He wrote: "Economics began as a branch of moral philosophy, and the ethical content was at least as important as the analytic content up through the writings of Alfred Marshal. From then on, the structure of economic theory became more and more top-heavy with analysis. Layer upon layer of abstruse mathematical models were erected higher and higher above the shallow concrete foundation of fact. . . . Only by returning to its moral and biophysical foundations and shoring them up will economic thinking be able to avoid a permanent commitment to misplaced concreteness and crackpot rigor."[21]

under some circumstances, only a *means* to that good end. But what do we do when more growth no longer provides a clear consensus that it will bring improvement in the quality of life for most people? Have we lost sight of the original end for enterprise and gradually replaced it with a nineteenth-century means?" At that point the coffee came, served in bone china cups neatly placed on silver trays; the discussion drifted to other more immediate matters.

Of Means and Ends

In these pages we've followed a crooked path that has touched on many topics dealing with the coevolution of climate and life. In Chapter 8 we argued that this coevolutionary path, over 4 billion years old, is now at a point where humans are on the verge of overwhelming in a few decades (or a few weeks if there were a nuclear war of major proportions) what nature has constructed over eons—the elaborate and evolving balance between organic and inorganic forces that control climate and the environment. In this chapter we've suggested that current technologies and economic practices and a philosophy of individual—or national—self-interest have brought us to this rapid coevolutionary departure. Moreover, if our principal goal is to create a sustainable future relatively free from hunger or environmental vulnerability, then we believe the prevailing public philosophy needs some basic alteration; we need to adjust the balance between economic and strategic thinking. In his book *The Public Philosophy,* Walter Lippmann wrote in 1955 about the need for leaders to "assert a public interest against private inclination and against what is easy and popular. If they are to do their duty, they must often swim against the tides of private feeling."[22] Such courage is even more essential today to deal with the growing power of political action committees at a domestic level or commodity-controlling cartels internationally.

As diverse and seemingly unrelated as many of the subjects we've discussed might appear, there have been several connecting threads. Carbon dioxide, for example, was present at—or shortly after—the earth's creation. It appears to have played a principal role in the evolution of climate and life. At present, CO_2 is a potentially significant component of the challenge to the classical economic paradigm of individuals pursuing their perceived self-interest. This philosophy encourages resource use that increases CO_2 and other pollutants that may substantially alter future climate and well-being. We've also seen that when individuals or nations pursue their own self-interests they can markedly influence how climatic variations affect world food security, water supplies, or reserves of topsoil. To mitigate some of the negative consequences, we've argued, requires a strategy—a goal—in relation to which individual and collective actions can be chosen. That primary goal, we believe, should be to create a sustainable future world. If, instead, the strategy is to pursue the maximum short-term return on individual or group investments, then it is unlikely that we would soon realize our primary goal; it is also unlikely that we would minimize the negative impacts of climatic fluctuations over time. But not all people can agree on basic goals, which helps to explain the frequently divergent strategies of various analysts.* Perhaps, then, it is practical to agree to pursue a *mixed set of goals.* One of these might be to preserve strategic commodities such as topsoil or the present distribution of rainfall in the U.S. Plains; and another might be reward for productive individual enterprise. To achieve a mixed set of goals we will need to employ a mixed set of means. That is, we will need to make the growth paradigm and return-on-investment criteria that are dominant today more compatible with the other important goal: long-term sustainability. Specific programs to accomplish this mixed set of ends will tax our abilities to manage and to compromise, and may represent some changes that some will view as radical and dangerous. But stepping up our pursuit of strategic goals is not as radical a departure from current economic practices and political ideology as it may seem to some. Even officials of the Reagan Administration, probably the most die-hard political defenders of the American ideology of free enterprise and pursuit of self-interest to come along since the early days of the 1930s Depression, have used noneconomic means to pursue one of their most cherished strategic

---

*In this connection one could cite the *New York Times Book Review* of September 13, 1981. It contained pieces on two diametrically opposing views of future economic development; and both were favorably reviewed! University of Illinois Professor of Economics and Business Administration Julian Simon touts the classical economists' line that innovation and free market economic incentives will be the best hedge against future disaster. He argues for, among other things, greater population growth, since more people ("the ultimate resource") produce more wealth. This cornucopian vision is strongly challenged by the iconoclastic economist and futurist Hazel Henderson, who, in the words of the *Times* reviewer, "chides the economists for their fixation on rigid unrealistic categories, in particular ones that define the world as a set of cash transactions and money flows." The differing strategies that each author recommends are largely rooted in their different goals. Indeed, this pair is typical of many "optimist versus pessimist" debates over the future outlook for humanity.[23]

goals: a strong national defense. It is not cost/benefit analyses or return-on-investment calculations that motivate such a desire to spend hundreds of billions on a military machine; rather, it is strategic thinking. To be sure, once a decision to build a new bomber, for example, is made on strategic grounds, economic means are employed to define the tactics to obtain that strategic goal.

We need to convince those who already rely on strategic (rather than economic) arguments to justify the investment of untold billions of dollars for weapons to protect themselves from theoretical threats posed by hypothetical enemies to extend their own logic to other categories of strategic threats to our security: ozone reduction, acid rain, eroding topsoil, fluctuating food security, a permanently altered climate, or a nuclear winter scenario. It would be possible, then, to mobilize resources needed to address some of these problems of sustainability within the existing conceptual frameworks of nearly all societies, including those advocating the free market philosophy.

"We Have Met the Enemy"

If we so choose, the caveat "weather permitting" that circumscribes so many of our plans could be weighted less heavily. It is not so much the weather that will permit us to get through the next ten years without major famines, for example (although it is essential to know the bounds of climatic influences in order to make cost-effective investments in building resilience against them). Rather, it is societies and the way they set up their food security systems to deal with fluctuating climate and the resulting impacts that constitute the most critical factor.

In a sense, those of us who make a living studying the probability of climatic variations in order to estimate climatic impacts on people are largely in business because society, more than nature, has been permitting unnecessary adverse effects to occur. Bad weather is not a legitimate excuse for bad management that fails to build in safeguards against plausible environmental change. Likewise, scientists' ignorance of the precise consequences of CO_2 or other pollutant buildups is no excuse for politicians' complete inaction, a policy that guarantees no hedging against plausible adverse effects. If more people demanded it of their leaders, policies could be implemented that might once again return the weather to its old status as a topic for small talk. In the meantime, remember that in order to minimize climatic hazards, be prepared for possible trends, or maximize the opportunities for using present or future climatic resources, informed citizens must actively participate in shaping policy decisions.

Keep informed, keep involved, and keep at it. Individual efforts can help to create a sustainable future, if only enough of us would articulate the goal and then work to achieve it.

Notes

1. Climate Before Man

1. Strahler, A. N., 1963, *The Earth Sciences* (New York: Harper & Row), pp. 411–412.
2. Kummel, B., 1970, *History of the Earth: An Introduction to Historical Geology* (San Francisco: Freeman), p. 12.
3. Some authors have argued that the Phanerozoic, a time of abundant life, really should have begun a hundred million years earlier, about 670 million years ago and should include a period known as the Ediacarian, since there is considerable evidence for the existence of soft-bodied multi-cellular creatures during this period. For example, see Cloud, P., and Glaessner, M., 1982, *Science 217:*783–792.
4. McDougall, I., Allsopp, H. L., and Chamalaun, F. H., 1966, Isotopic dating of the newer volcanics of Victoria, Australia, and geomagnetic polarity epochs, *Journal of Geophysical Research 71:*6107–6118, especially 6112–6115.
5. Reid, G., et al., 1976, Influence of ancient solar proton events on the evolution of life, *Nature 259:*177–179.
6. Carslaw, H. S., and Jaeger, J. C., 1959, *Conduction of Heat in Solids,* 2d ed. (Oxford: Oxford Clarendon Press), pp. 85–87.
7. Damon, P. E., 1977, Solar induced variations of energetic particles at one AU, in White, O. R. (ed.), *The Solar Output and Its Variation* (Boulder: Colorado Associated University Press), pp. 429–448. This article is a good review of the use and problems of C^{14} dating for climatic events of the last several thousand years.
8. Andrews, J. T., and Miller, G. H., 1980, Dating quaternary deposits more than 10,000 years old, in Cullingford, P. A., Davidson, D. A., and Levin, J. (eds.), *Timescales in Geomorphology* (New York: Wiley Interscience).
9. Walker, J. C. G., 1982, Climatic factors on the Archean Earth, *Paleogeography, Paleoclimatology, Paleoecology 40:*1–11. See also Lowe, D. R., 1980, Archean Sedimentation, *Annual Reviews of Earth and Planetary Sciences 8:*145–167.
10. Margulis, L., and Lovelock, J.E., 1981, Atmospheres and evolution, in Billingham, J. (ed.), *Life in the Universe* (Cambridge, Mass.: MIT Press), pp. 79–100.

11. Frakes, L. A., 1979, *Climates Through Geologic Time* (Amsterdam: Elsevier).
12. Valentine, J. W., 1978 (September), The evolution of multicellular plants and animals, *Scientific American 239:* 140–158.
13. *Scientific American* 1978:*239,* September issue. This entire issue, which is devoted to evolution, serves as a good survey of the topic.
14. Strahler, A. N., 1971, *The Earth Sciences,* 2d ed. (New York: Harper & Row), pp. 522–523.
15. Hallam, A., 1977, Secular changes in marine inundation of USSR and North America through the Phanerozoic, *Nature 269:* 769–772. Hays, J. D., and Pitman, W. C. III, 1973, Lithospheric plate motion, sea-level changes, and climatic and ecological consequences, *Nature 246:* 18–22. Hays, J. D., 1977, Climatic change and the possible influence of variations of solar input, in White, O. R. (ed.), *The Solar Output and Its Variation* (Boulder: Colorado Associated University Press), pp. 73–90.
16. Frakes, *Climates Through Geologic Time,* pp. 208–210.
17. Vail, P. R., Mitchum, R. M., Jr., and Thompson, S. III, 1977, Seismic stratigraphy and global changes of sea level, Part 4: Global cycles of relative changes of sea level, in Payton, C. (ed.), *Seismic Stratigraphy— Applications to Hydrocarbon Exploration,* American Association of Petroleum Geologists Mem. *26:* 83–97.
18. Frakes, *Climates Through Geologic Time,* p. 211.
19. Kerr, R. A., 1980, Changing global sea levels as a geologic index, *Science 209:* 483–486.
20. Kerr, R. A., 1982, New evidence fuels Antarctic debate, *Science 216:* 973–974.
21. Budyko, M. I., 1977, *Climatic Changes* (Washington, D. C.: American Geophysical Union), p. 128. This has been translated from a 1974 Russian edition.
22. Barron, E. J., 1983, Climate models: A frontier in petroleum exploration, *Weatherwise 36:* 230-232.
23. See, for example, Bird, J. M., and Isacks, B. (eds.), 1972, *Plate Tectonics* (Washington, D.C.: American Geophysical Union). This volume is a compilation of papers written over the past two decades on plate tectonics—the theory of why continents drift. Included is a bibliography of over 900 pages. For a more popular treatment, see Calder, Nigel, 1972, *The Restless Earth* (New York: Viking Press).
24. Barron, E. J., Harrison, C. G. A., Sloan, J. L. II, and Hay, W. W., 1981, Paleogeography, 180 million years ago to the present, *Eclogae Geologicae Helvetiae 74* No. 2:443–470.
25. Köppen, A., and Wegener, A., 1924, *Die Klimat der Geologischen Vorzeite* (Berlin: Borntraeger). These scientists were the first to hypothesize climatic effects from this theory, decades before volumes of evidence supporting the existence of continental drift were obtained with modern methods.

26. Imbrie, J., and Imbrie, K. P., 1979, *Ice Ages: Solving The Mystery* (Short Hills, N. J.: Enslow).

27. See, for example, Pichon, X. L., 1968, Sea floor spreading and continental drift, *Journal of Geophysical Research 73* No. 12:3661–3697.

28. Gould, S. J., 1982, Darwinism and the expansion of evolutionary theory, *Science 216:*380–387. See also the cover story on Stephen Jay Gould in the March 19, 1982 issue of *Newsweek.* An interesting debate on evolutionary mechanisms can be found in Schopf, T. J. M., and A. Hoffman, 1982, Punctuated equilibrium and the fossil record, *Science 219:*438–439 and the reply by Gould pp. 439–440.

29. Wilson, J. T., 1965, A new class of faults and their bearing on continental drift, *Nature 207:*343–347.

30. Denton, G. H., Armstrong, R. L., and Stuiver, M., 1971, The late Cenozoic glacial history of Antarctica in Turekian, Karl K. (ed.), *Late Cenozoic Glacial Ages* (New Haven and London: Yale University Press), pp. 267–306.

31. Kennett, J. P., 1977, Cenozoic evolution of Antarctic glaciation, the circum-Antarctic Ocean, and their impact on global paleo-oceanography, *Journal of Geophysical Research 82:*3843–3860.

32. Ibid., p. 3845.

33. Kaneps, G., 1979, Gulf Stream: Velocity fluctuations during the late Cenozoic, *Science 204:*297–301.

2. The Coming of Ice: The Pleistocene

1. This anecdote (p. 42) and many others are found in the insightful and readable book: Imbrie, J., and Imbrie, K. P., 1979, *Ice Ages: Solving The Mystery* (Short Hills, N.J.: Enslow).

2. Agassiz, as quoted by Imbrie and Imbrie, p. 33.

3. One of the best books on the physics of glaciers is Paterson, W. S. B., 1981, *The Physics of Glaciers,* 2d ed. (Elmsford, N.Y.: Pergamon Press).

4. Walcott, R. I., 1972, Past sea levels, eustasy and deformation of the earth, *Quaternary Research 2:*1–14; and Chappell, J., 1974, Late Quaternary glacio- and hydro-isostasy on a layered earth, *Quaternary Research 4:* 405–428, were early attempts to describe in quantitative terms the extent and timescales for uplift and depression of the earth's crust to changes in ice or water loading.

5. This was widely accepted by 1960, as summarized by Fairbridge, R. W., 1961, Eustatic changes in sea level, in Ahrens, L. H., (ed.), *Physics and Chemistry of the Earth 4* (New York and London: Pergamon Press), pp. 99–185.

6. For a review article on coral reefs see Goreau, T. F., Goreau, N. I.,

and Goreau, T. J., 1979, Corals and coral reefs, *Scientific American 241:* 124–136.

7. Because of impurities and other complications, "thorium-230 dating of coral can be a tricky business," commented R. K. Matthews, in The sea level record of the structure of an ice age: discussion (abstract), *Sixth Biennial Meeting of the American Quaternary Association* (Orono, Maine: University of Maine), 18–20 August, 1980, p. 132.

8. Bloom, A. L., Broecker, W. S., Chappell, J. M. A., Matthews, R. K., and Mesolella, K. J., 1974, Quaternary sea level fluctuations on a tectonic coast: New [230]Th/[234]U dates from the Huon Peninsula, New Guinea, *Quaternary Research 4:*191.

9. Plafker, O., 1972, Alaskan earthquake of 1964 and Chilean earthquake of 1960: Implications for arc tectonics, *Journal of Geophysical Research 77:*901–925.

10. Bloom, A. L., 1980, The sea level record of the structure of an ice age (abstract), in *Sixth Biennial Meeting,* p. 29.

11. Broecker, W. S., Thurber, D. L., Goddard, J., Ku, T.-L., Matthews, R. K., Mesolella, K. J., 1968, Milankovitch hypothesis supported by precise dating of coral reef and deep-sea sediments, *Science 159:*297–300. Later evidence using different techniques for dating the terraces yielded similar results: Fairbanks, R. G., and Matthews, R. K., 1978, The marine oxygen isotope record in Pleistocene coral, Barbados, West Indies, *Quaternary Research 10:*181–196.

12. Broecker et al., Milankovitch hypothesis, p. 299.

13. Bloom et al., Quaternary sea level, p. 185.

14. Harmon, R. S., Land, L. S., Mitterer, R. M., Garrett, P., Schwarcz, H. P. and Larson, G. J., 1981, Bermuda sea level during the last interglacial, *Nature 289:*481–483.

15. For a review of isotopic temperature methods for ancient paleoclimates and references to the classical literature see Savin, S. M., 1977, The history of the earth's surface temperature during the past 100 million years, in *Annual Reviews of Earth and Planetary Sciences 5:*323. A very useful review of stable isotope methods of paleoclimatic reconstruction over more recent time scales is given in Gray, J., 1981, The use of stable-isotope data in climate reconstruction, in Wigley, T. M. L., Ingram, M. J. and Farmer, G. (eds.), *Climate and History: Studies in Past Climates and Their Impact on Man* (Cambridge: Cambridge University Press), pp. 53–81.

16. Dansgaard, W., Johnsen, S. J., Clausen, H. B., and Gundestrup, N., 1973, *Stable Isotope Glaciology* (Copenhagen: C. A. Reitzels Forlag).

17. The difficulty of misinterpreting δO^{18} as ice volume when temperature effects are also important has been reiterated recently by Mix, A. C., and Ruddiman, W. F., 1981, The nonlinear relationship between ice volume and δO^{18}: Implications for the spectral signature of ice volume (abstract), *Geological Society of America 94th Annual Meeting,*

Abstracts With Programs, p. 512. See also Covey, C., and Schneider, S. H., 1984, Models for reconstructing temperature and ice volume from oxygen isotope data, in Imbrie, J., and Berger, A. (eds.), *Milankovitch and Climate Change* (Amsterdam: Elsevier), in press.

18. Berger, W. H., and Gardner, J. V., 1975, On the determination of Pleistocene temperatures from planktonic foraminifera, *Journal of Foraminiferal Research 5:*102–113.

19. Fairbridge, R. W., Eustatic changes in sea level, p. 125.

20. Yapp, C. J., and Epstein, S., 1982, Climatic significance of the hydrogen isotope ratios in tree cellulose, *Nature 297:*636–639.

21. See, for example, Price, P. W., 1975, *Insect Ecology* (New York, London, Sydney, and Toronto: Wiley) for a detailed discussion of factors controlling insect population sizes.

22. Coope, G. R., 1977, Fossil coleopteran assemblages as sensitive indicators of climatic changes during the Devensian (Last) cold stage, in *Proceedings of the Philosophical Transactions of the Royal Society of London B 280:*313–340.

23. Ibid., p. 328.

24. Webb, T. III, 1979, paper presented at Climate and History Meeting, sponsored by *Journal of Interdisciplinary History.* A revised version of this paper has been published in the *Journal of Interdisciplinary History 10* No. 4:749–772.

25. Kukla, G. J., and Koci, A., 1972, End of the last interglacial in the Loess Record, *Quaternary Research 2:*374–383. See also Imbrie and Imbrie, *Ice Ages,* pp. 153–156.

26. Imbrie and Imbrie, *Ice Ages,* p. 123.

27. Hays, J. D., 1977, Climatic change and the possible influence of variation in solar input, in White, O. R., (ed.), *The Solar Output and Its Variation* (Boulder, Colo.: Colorado Associated University Press), p. 78. Although this was written in the context of paleoclimatic reconstruction over the past 100 to 200 million years (before which most oceanic floor has been recycled), it also applies to the Pleistocene as well.

28. Perry, J. S., personal communication.

29. Berger, W. H., and Heath, G. R., 1968, Vertical mixing in pelagic sediments, *Journal of Marine Research 26:*134–143. See also Peng, T. H., Broecker, W. S., Kipphut, G., and Shackleton, N., 1977, Benthic mixing in deep sea cores as determined by ^{14}C dating and its implications regarding climate stratigraphy and the fate of fossil fuel CO_2, in Andersen, N. R., and Malahoff, A. (eds.), *The Fate of Fossil Fuel CO_2 in the Oceans* (New York and London: Plenum Press), pp. 355–373; and Paul, Allen Z., 1977, The effect of benthic biological processes on the CO_2 carbonate system, in *The Fate of Fossil Fuel CO_2 in the Oceans,* pp. 345–354; these papers come from the Proceedings of a symposium conducted by the Ocean Science and Technology Division of the Office of Naval Research on the Fate of Fossil Fuel CO_2

in the Oceans held at the University of Hawaii, Honolulu, January 16–20, 1976.

30. Broecker, W. S., and Van Donk, J., 1970, Insolation changes, ice volumes, and the O^{18} record in deep-sea cores, *Reviews of Geophysics and Space Physics 8:*169–198.

31. See the discussion in Imbrie and Imbrie, *Ice Ages,* chapter 11.

32. Emiliani, C., 1955, Pleistocene temperatures, *Journal of Geology 63:* 538–578.

33. Imbrie and Imbrie, *Ice Ages,* 137–139.

34. Yapp, C. J., and Epstein, S., 1977, Climatic implications of D/H ratios of meteoric water over North America (9500–22,000 BP) as inferred from ancient wood-cellulose C-H hydrogen, *Earth and Planetary Science Letters 34:*333–350.

35. See, for example, Dansgaard, W., and Tauber, H., 1969, Glacier oxygen-18 and Pleistocene ocean temperatures, *Science 166:*499–502.

36. Imbrie and Imbrie, *Ice Ages,* p. 162.

37. Shackleton, N. J., and Opdyke, N. D., 1973, Oxygen isotopes and paleomagnetic stratigraphy of equatorial Pacific core V28–238: Oxygen isotope temperatures and ice volumes on a 10^5 and 10^6 year scale, *Quaternary Research 3:*39–55.

38. CLIMAP Project Members (Andrew McIntyre, Leader), 1981, Sea surface temperature anomaly maps for August and February in the modern and last glacial maximum, Geological Society of America map and chart series M–36, maps 5A and 5B. The principal members of CLIMAP include A. McIntyre, T. C. Moore, B. Andersen, W. Balsam, A. Bé, C. Brunner, J. Colley, T. Crowley, G. Denton, J. Gardner, K. Greitzenauer, J. D. Hays, W. Hutson, J. Imbrie, G. Irving, T. Kellogg, J. Kennett, N. Kipp, G. Kukla, H. Kukla, J. Lozano, B. Luz, S. Mangion, R. K. Matthews, P. Mayewski, B. Molfino, D. Ninkovich, N. Opdyke, W. Press, J. Robertson, W. F. Ruddiman, H. Sachs, T. Saito, N. Shackleton, H. Thierstein, and P. Thompson.

39. Imbrie and Imbrie, *Ice Ages,* p. 164.

40. Corliss, B. H., 1982, Linkage of North Atlantic and Southern Ocean deep-water circulation during glacial intervals, *Nature 298:*458–460.

41. Broecker, W. S., 1978, The cause of glacial to interglacial climatic change, in *Evolution of Planetary Atmospheres and Climatology of the Earth* (Toulouse, France: Centre National d'études Spatiales), pp. 165–190. See also the more recent discussion of the floating ice hypothesis by Williams, D. F., Moore, W. S., and Fillon, R. H., 1981, Role of glacial Arctic Ocean ice sheets in Pleistocene oxygen isotope and sea level records, *Earth and Planetary Science Letters 56:*157–166. See also a similar calculation of −2°C change in glacial bottom-water temperature by Keigwin, L. D., 1982, An Arctic Ocean ice sheet in the Pleistocene? *Nature 296:*808–809.

42. Mix and Ruddiman, The Non-Linear Relationship.

43. Covey and Schneider, Isotopic composition of snow.
44. Peterson, G. M., Webb, T. III, Kutzbach, J. E., van der Hammen, T., Wijmstra, T. A., Street, F. A., 1979, The continental record of environmental conditions at 18,000 yr BP: An initial evaluation, *Quaternary Research 12:*47–82.
45. Lancaster, I. N., 1979, Evidence for a widespread late Pleistocene humid period in the Kalahari, *Nature 279:*145–146.
46. For an example of the complexity of such reconstructions, see the calculation of Kutzbach, J. E., 1980, Estimates of past climate at Paleo Lake Chad, North Africa based on a hydrological and energy-balance model, *Quaternary Research 14:*210–223.
47. For a brief discussion of the scientific method see Schneider, S. H., and Morton, L., 1981, *The Primordial Bond: Exploring Connections Between Man and Nature Through the Humanities and Sciences* (New York: Plenum), chapter 6.
48. Sarnthein, M., 1978, Sand deserts during glacial maximum and climatic optimum, *Nature 272:*43–46.
49. For an expanded discussion and an extensive bibliography on African paleoclimate see Nicholson, S. E., and Flohn, H., 1980, African environmental and climatic changes and the general atmospheric circulation in late Pleistocene and Holocene, *Climatic Change 2:*313–348.
50. Dansgaard, W., Johnsen, S. J., Clausen, H. B., Langway, C. C. Jr., 1971, Climatic record revealed by the camp century ice core, in Turekian, R. (ed.), *Late Cenozoic Glacial Ages* (New Haven and London: Yale University Press), pp. 37–56. For a more recent discussion, see Dansgaard, W., 1981, Paleo-climatic studies on ice cores, in Berger, A. (ed.), *Climatic Variations and Variabilities* (Dordrecht: Reidel), pp. 193–206.
51. Nye, J. F., 1959, The motion of ice sheets and glaciers, *Journal of Glaciology 3:*493.
52. Dansgaard, W., Clausen, H. B., Gundestrup, N., Hammer, C. U., Johnsen, S. F., Kristinsdottir, P. M., and Reeh, N., 1982, A new Greenland deep ice core, *Science 218:*1273–1277.
53. Herman, Y., and Hopkins, D. M., 1980, Arctic oceanic climate in late Cenozoic time, *Science 209:*557–562.
54. For example see Kukla, G. J., 1976, Around the Ice Age world, *Natural History 85:*56–61; and Imbrie and Imbrie, *Ice Ages.*
55. Paterson, W. S. B., 1969, *The Physics of Glaciers* (Oxford: Pergamon Press), p. 135.
56. Desio, A., 1954, An exceptional glacier advance in the Karakoram-Ladakh region, *Journal of Glaciology 2:*383–385.
57. Paterson, *The Physics of Glaciers,* p. 228.
58. Emiliani, C., Gartner, S., Lidz, B., Eldridge, K., Elvey, D. K., Huang, T.-C., Stipp, J. J., and Swanson, M. F., 1975, Paleoclimatological analysis of late quaternary cores from the northeastern Gulf of Mex-

493

ico, *Science 189:*1083–1088. For a series of criticisms of this paper, see the September 24, 1976 issue of *Science,* p. 1268. See also Emiliani, C., 1980, Ice sheets and ice melts, *Natural History 89:*82–91.

59. Jones, G. A., and Ruddiman, W. F., 1982, Assessing the global meltwater spike, *Quaternary Research 17:*148–172.
60. Wilson, A. T., 1965, Origin of the ice ages: An ice shelf theory for Pleistocene glaciation, *Nature 201:*147–149.
61. Mercer, J. H., 1978, West Antarctic ice sheet and CO_2 greenhouse effect: A threat of disaster, *Nature 271:*321–325.
62. Flohn, H., 1974, Background of a geophysical model of the initiation of the next glaciation, *Quaternary Research 4:*385–404; reprinted in Gribbin, J. (ed.), 1978, *Climatic Change* (Cambridge: Cambridge University Press) pp. 249–265.
63. Calder, N., 1975, *The Weather Machine* (New York: Viking Press).
64. Duplessy, J. C., Labeyrie, J., Lalou, C., and Nguyen, H. V., 1971, La mesure des variations climatiques continentales application à la période comprise entre 130,000 et 90,000 ans B.P., *Quaternary Research 1:* 162–174; and Dansgaard et al., A new Greenland deep ice core.
65. Hughes, T. J., 1975, Do oxygen isotope data from deep core holes reveal dike-sill convection in polar ice sheets? In *Isotopes and Impurities in Snow and Ice,* Grenoble Symposium, pp. 336–340.
66. Kennett, J. P., and Huddleston, P., 1972, Abrupt climatic change at 90,000 yr BP: Faunal evidence from Gulf of Mexico cores, *Quaternary Research 2:*384–395.
67. van der Hammen, T., Wijmstra, T. A., and Zagwijn, W. H., 1971, The floral record of the late Cenozoic of Europe, in Turekian (ed.), *Late Cenozoic Glacial Ages,* pp. 319–424.
68. Müller, H., 1979, Climatic changes during the last three interglacials, in Bach, W., Panakrath, J., Kellogg, W. (eds.), *Man's Impact on Climate,* Developments in Atmospheric Science 10 (Amsterdam: Elsevier), pp. 29–41; and Woillard, G. M., 1978, Grande Pile peat bog: A continuous pollen record for the last 140,000 years, *Quaternary Research 9:* 1–21. A more recent report (but also containing rapid climatic shifts) is Woillard, G. M., and Mook, W. G., 1982, Carbon–14 dates at Grande Pile: Correlation of land sea chronologies, *Science 215:*159–161.
69. Hollin, J. T., 1980, Climate and sea level in isotope stage 5: An East Antarctic surge at 95,000 BP? *Nature 283:*629–633.
70. Harmon, R. S., Land, L. S., Mitterer, R. M., Garrett, P., Schwarcz, H. P., and Larson, G. J., 1981, Bermuda sea level during the last interglacial, *Nature 289:*481–483.
71. Aharon, P., Chappell, J., and Compston, W., 1980, Stable isotope and sea-level data from New Guinea supports Antarctic ice-surge theory of ice ages, *Nature 283:*649–651.
72. Office of U.S. Senator William Proxmire, press release dated Tuesday, March 11, 1975.

494

3. The Climate of Civilization: The Holocene

1. Zonneveld, J. I. S., 1973, Some notes on the last deglaciation in northern Europe compared with Canadian conditions, *Arctic and Alpine Research 5:*233–237; and Bryson, R. A., Wendland, W. M., Ives, J. D., and Andrews, J. T., 1969, Radicarbon isochrones on the disintegration of the Laurentide Ice Sheet, *Arctic and Alpine Research 1:*1–14.

2. The notion that glaciers grew in place and were of "highland origin" fed by moisture carried by the winds was championed by Flint, R. F., 1943, Growth of North American ice sheet during the Wisconsin age, *Geological Society of America Bulletin 54:*325–362; and was expanded in Flint's well-known book *Glacial and Quaternary Geology* (New York: Wiley, 1971). The extreme complexity of both glacier formation and destruction in North America and the ways in which evidence for this complexity challenged the classical interpretation have been presented by three University of Colorado glaciologists and paleoclimatologists: Ives, J. D., Andrews, J. T., and Barry, R. G., 1975, Growth and decay of the Laurentide Ice Sheet and comparisons with Fenno-Scandinavia, *Journal Naturwissenschaften 62:*118–125.

3. Denton, G. H., and Hughes, T., 1981, *The Last Great Ice Sheets* (New York: Wiley Interscience), chapter 8.

4. Ruddiman, W. F., and McIntyre, A., 1981, The mode and mechanism of the last deglaciation: Oceanic evidence, *Quaternary Research 16:* 125–134. See also: Kerr, R. A., 1983, An early glacial two-step?, *Science 221;* 143–144, for a review of a recent meeting on the timing of the last deglaciation.

5. Denton and Hughes, *The Last Great Ice Sheets,* p. 463.

6. Butzer, K. W., Isaac, G. L., Richardson, J. L., and Washbourn-Kamau, C., 1972, Radiocarbon dating of East African lake levels, *Science 175:* 1069–1076.

7. Another approach is to use mathematical models to reconstruct paleo–lake level, such as done by Kutzbach, J. E., 1980, Estimates of past climate at Paleo Lake Chad, North Africa based on a hydrological and energy-balance model, *Quaternary Research 14:*210–223.

8. Flohn, H., 1979, Can climate history repeat itself? Possible climatic warming and the case of paleoclimatic warm phases, in Bach, W., Pankrath, J., Kellogg, W. W. (eds.), *Man's Impact on Climate* (Amsterdam: Elsevier), pp. 15–28.

9. Geyh, M., and Jäkel, D., 1974, Late glacial and Holocene climatic history of the Sahara desert derived from a statistical assay of C[14] dates, *Paleogeography, Paleoclimatology, Paleoecology 15:*205–208.

10. Otterman, J., 1977, Anthropogenic impact on the albedo of the earth, *Climatic Change 1:*137–156.

11. Lamb, H., 1977, *Climate: Present, Past and Future,* Vol. 2 (London: Methuen).

12. Bernabo, J. C., and Webb, T. III, 1977, Changing patterns in the Holocene pollen record of northeastern North America: A mapped summary, *Quaternary Research 8:*64–96.
13. Nichols, H., 1975, Palynological and paleoclimatic study of the late Quaternary displacement of the boreal forest-tundra ecotone in Keewatin and Mackenzie, N. W. T., Canada, *Occasional Paper No. 15,* Institute of Arctic and Alpine Research, University of Colorado, Boulder, Colorado, p. 67; Nichols, H., 1974, Arctic North American paleoecology: The recent history of vegetation and climate deduced from pollen analysis, in Ives, J. D., and Barry, R. G., (eds.), *Arctic and Alpine Environments,* (London: Methuen) pp. 660–667.
14. Heusser, C. J., 1974, Vegetation and the climate of the southern Chilean lake district during and since the last interglaciation, *Quaternary Research 4:*313.
15. Bryson, R., and Murray, T., 1977, *Climates of Hunger: Mankind and the World's Changing Weather* (Madison: University of Wisconsin Press). See also McGhee, R., 1981, Archaeological evidence for climatic change during the last 5,000 years, in Wigley, T. M. L., Ingram, M. J., Farmer, G. (eds.), *Climate and History: Studies in Past Climates and Their Impacts on Man* (Cambridge: Cambridge University Press), pp. 162–178.
16. Moore, A. M. T., 1979, A pre-Neolithic farmers' village on the Euphrates, *Scientific American 241* (August issue):62–70.
17. Denton, G. H., and Karlén, W., 1973, Holocene climatic variations—their pattern and possible cause, *Quaternary Research 3:*155–205. A useful review of how glaciers can be used for climatic reconstruction is given in Porter, S. C., 1981, Glaciological evidence of Holocene climatic change, in Wigley et al. (eds.), *Climate and History,* pp. 82–110.
18. Bernabo and Webb, Changing patterns in the Holocene.
19. Lamb, *Climate: Present, Past and Future,* pp. 80–81.
20. van Devender, T. R., and Spaulding, W. G., 1979, Development of vegetation and climate in the southwestern United States, *Science* 204:701–710.
21. Wang, P.-K., 1979, Meteorological records from ancient chronicles of China, *Bulletin of the American Meteorological Society 60:*313–318. See also Wang, P.-K., 1980, On the relationship between winter thunder and the climatic change in China in the past 2200 years, *Climatic Change 3:*37–46.
22. Wittfogel, K. A., 1940, Meteorological records from Divination inscriptions of Shang, *The Geographical Review 30:*110–113.
23. Neumann, J., and Sigrist, R., 1978, Harvest dates in ancient Mesopotamia as possible indicators of climatic variations, *Climatic Change 1:* 238–252.
24. Robert McGhee's paper "Archaeological Evidence for Climatic Change during the Past 5000 Years" discusses this issue and gives several references.

25. Ibid., p. 167.

26. Fritts, H. C., 1970, *Tree Rings and Climate* (New York: Academic Press), pp. 405–407. Fritts' interest in multiple causes of the decline of the canyon-dwelling Indians would certainly be supported by a more recent study: Betancourt, J. L., and van Devender, T. R., 1982, Holocene vegetation in Chaco Canyon, New Mexico, *Science* 214:656–658. These authors, using plant remains in packrat middens concluded: "Middle and late Holocene vegetation in the canyon was pinyon-juniper woodland up until Anasazi occupation between 1000 and 800 years ago. Instead of climate, Anasazi fuel needs may explain the drastic reduction of pinyon and juniper after 1230 years ago. The lack of pinyon-juniper recovery over the past millenium has implications for contemporary forest and range ecology."

27. McGhee, Archaeological evidence, pp. 170–175.

28. Lamb, H. H., 1965, The early medieval warm epoch and its sequel, *Paleogeography, Paleoclimatology, Paleoecology 1:*13–37.

29. Bryson and Murray, *Climates of Hunger,* p. 49, pp. 66–67. For a more in-depth discussion of the interactions between climatic and social factors in the Greenland case, see McGovern, T. H., 1981, The economics of extinction in Norse Greenland, in Wigley et al. (eds.), *Climate and History,* pp. 404–433.

30. Bryson and Murray, *Climates of Hunger,* p. 70–71.

31. Lamb, *Climate: Past, Present and Future,* p. 6

32. McGovern, T. H., 1981, The economics of extinction in Norse Greenland, in Wigley et al., *Climate and History,* pp. 404–433.

33. Personal communication to Randi Londer from Thomas McGovern, 1980.

34. Lamb, The early medieval warm epoch, p. 16.

35. Bell, W. T., and Ogilvie, A. E. J., 1978, Weather compilations as a source of data for the reconstruction of European climate during the medieval period, *Climatic Change 1:*331–348.

36. Parry, M. L., 1978, *Climatic Change, Agriculture and Settlement* (Folkestone, England: William Dawson and Sons).

37. Barry, R. G., 1978, Climatic fluctuations during the periods of historical and instrumental record, in Pittock, A. B., Frakes, L. A., Jenssen, D., Peterson, J. A., and Zillman, J. W. (eds.), *Climatic Change and Variability: A Southern Perspective* (London: Cambridge University Press), p. 158.

38. For example, see Lawrence, E. N., 1972, The earliest known journal of the weather, *Weather 27:*494–501.

39. Bryson and Murray, *Climates of Hunger,* p. 73.

40. Claxton, R. H., and Hecht, A. D., Climatic and human history in Europe and Latin America: An opportunity for comparative study, *Climatic Change 1:*195–203.

41. van den Dool, H. M., Krijnen, H. J., and Schuurmans, C. J. E., 1978,

Average winter temperatures at De Bilt (The Netherlands): 1634–1977, *Climatic Change 1:*319–330.

42. LeRoy Ladurie, E., and Baulant, M., 1980, Grape harvests from the fifteenth through the nineteenth centuries, *Journal of Interdisciplinary History 10:*839–849.

43. Neumann, J., 1978, Great historical events that were significantly affected by the weather: 3, the cold winter of 1657–58, the Swedish army crosses Denmark's frozen sea areas, *Bulletin of the American Meteorological Society 59:*1432–1437. See also Lindgren, S., and Neumann, J., 1982, Crossings of ice-bound sea surfaces in history, *Climatic Change 4:*71–97.

44. LeRoy Ladurie, E., 1971, *Times of Feast Times of Famine: A History of Climate Since the Year 1000,* translated by B. Bray (Garden City, N. J.: Doubleday). This book is a revised, English language edition of *Histoire du Climat Depuis l'An Mil* (Paris, 1967). See his first chapter, especially pages 7–22, for a complete discussion of Utterström's study.

45. Schneider, S. H., with Mesirow, L. E., 1976, *The Genesis Strategy: Climate and Global Survival* (New York: Plenum, p. 91. Paperback edition —New York: Delta, 1977, p. 91).

46. Ellsworth Huntington's book *Civilization and Climate* was published by Yale University Press in 1915, 1922, and 1925. The last edition was reprinted (revised and enlarged) in 1971 by Shoestring Press, Hamden, Conn.

47. Ibid., p. 227.

48. For example, see Moodie, D. W., and Catchpole, A. J. W., 1976, Valid climatological data from historical sources by content analysis, *Science 2* (July):51–53; or Catchpole, A. J. W., and Moodie, D. W., 1978, Archives and the environmental scientist, *Archivaria* No. 6:113–136.

49. Ingram, M. J., Underhill, D. J., and Wigley, T. M. L., 1978, Historical climatology, *Nature 276:*329–334; see also Ingram, M. J., and Underhill, D. J., 1979, The use of documentary sources for the study of past climates, in University of East Anglia Review Papers, 59–90. A number of authors discuss this question in Wigley et al. (eds.), *Climate and History.*

50. McGhee, Archeological evidence, p. 170.

51. Dahlin, B. H., 1983, Climate and prehistory on the Yucatan Peninsula, *Climatic Change 5:*245–263, is another example.

52. Eddy, J. A., 1977, The case of the missing sunspots, *Scientific American 236:*80–92.

53. Fritts, H. C., 1976, *Tree Rings and Climate* (London: Academic Press). This book gives an excellent overview of the complexities involved in interpreting all sorts of tree ring-derived variables. A recent review of the C-14/sunspot connection is given by Stuiver, M., and Quay, P. D., 1980, Changes in atmospheric carbon-14 attributed to a variable sun, *Science 207:*11–19; and some possible connections between climate

and carbon isotope concentration in tree rings are given by Fraser, P. J. B., Francey, R. J., and Pearman, G. I., 1978, Stable carbon isotopes in tree rings as climatic indicators. In Robinson, B. W. (ed.), *Stable Isotopes in the Earth Sciences, DSIR Bulletin 220:* 67–73, New Zealand Department of Scientific and Industrial Research, Wellington, New Zealand.

54. For example, see the classic paper by Revelle, R. and Suess, H. E., 1957, Carbon dioxide exchange between atmosphere and ocean and the question of an increase of atmospheric CO_2 during the past decades, *Tellus 9*:18–27.

55. Eddy, Missing sunspots, p. 85.

56. A highly readable, popular account of these solar phenomena and possible terrestrial connections is given in Frazier, K., 1981, *Our Turbulent Sun* (Englewood Cliffs, N. J.: Prentice Hall).

57. Landsberg, H. E., 1980, Variable solar emissions, the "Maunder Minimum" and climatic temperature fluctuations, *Archiv für Meteorologie Geophysik und Bioklimatologie* Ser. B, *28:* 181–191. Eddy has countered [Eddy, J. A., 1983, The Maunder minimum: A reappraisal, *Solar Physics 87*] that "the historical sunspots found by Landsberg are almost entirely duplicates of spots included in prior analyses" and that the "drop in solar activity during the Maunder Minimum" is "unequivocal."

58. Mitchell, J. M. Jr., Stockton, C. W., and Meko, D. M., 1979, Evidence of a 22-year rhythm of drought in the western U.S. related to the Hale solar cycle since the 17th century, in McCormack, B. M., and Seliga, T. A. (eds.), *Solar-Terrestrial Influences on Weather and Climate* (Dordrecht, Holland: D. Reidel), pp. 125–143.

59. Gilliland, R. L., 1982, Solar, volcanic, and CO_2 forcing of recent climatic changes, *Climatic Change 4:* 111–131.

60. Bannister, B., 1965, Andrew Ellicott Douglass, in *Year Book of the American Philosophical Society*, pp. 121–125.

61. Fritts, *Tree Rings and Climate*, is one of the best sources for details of dendroclimatology.

62. Fritts, H. C., Lofgren, G. R., and Gordon, G. A., 1979, Past climate reconstructed from tree rings, in Rotberg, R. I., and Rabb, T. K. (eds.), *Climate and History*, (Princeton: Princeton University Press), pp. 193–213.

63. LaMarche, V. C. Jr., 1978, Tree-ring evidence of past climatic variability, *Nature 276:* 334–338.

64. Swain, A. M., 1978, Environmental changes during the past 2000 years in North-Central Wisconsin: Analysis of pollen, charcoal, and seeds from varved lake sediments, *Quaternary Research 10:* 55–68.

65. Bernabo, J. C., and Swain, A., 1980, Reconstructed temperatures, precipitation and snowfall patterns for Michigan and New York based on two 2000-year long pollen records, in *International Palynological Conference Abstracts*, Cambridge, England.

66. Waddington, J. C. B., and Wright, H. E. Jr., 1974, Late Quaternary vegetational changes on the east side of Yellowstone Park, Wyoming, *Quaternary Research 4:*175–184.
67. Wilson, A. T., Hendy, C. H., and Reynolds, R. F., 1979, Short term climate change and New Zealand temperatures during the last millennium, *Nature 279:*315–317.
68. For one interpretation of Little Ice Age proxies for oceanic conditions in the northeast Atlantic sector see Lamb, H. H., 1979, Climatic variation and changes in the wind and ocean circulation: The Little Ice Age in the northeast Atlantic, *Quaternary Research 11:*1–20.

4. The Climatic System and What Drives It

1. Middleton, W. E. K., and Spilhaus, A. F., 1953, *Invention of the Meteorological Instruments* (Toronto: University of Toronto Press), p. 54.
2. Frisinger, H. H., 1977, *The History of Meteorology: to 1880* (New York: Science History Publications), Historical Monograph Series, American Meteorological Society, p. 76.
3. Ibid., p. 77.
4. For a review of weather network beginnings in England see Manley, G., 1974, Central England temperatures: Monthly means 1659–1973, *Quarterly Journal of the Royal Meteorological Society 100:*389–405; for a historical review of the development of weather networks in the U.S. see: Landsberg, H. E., 1964, Early stages of climatology in the United States, *Bulletin of the American Meteorological Society 45:*268–275.
5. Walker, J. C. G., 1977, *Evolution of the Atmosphere* (New York: Macmillan), pp. 101–102.
6. Went, F. W., 1960, Organic matter in the atmosphere, *Proceedings of the National Academy of Sciences 46:*212.
7. One classical ice age theory dealing with flow of water into and out of the Arctic basin as a function of ocean bottom shape influences is described in Ewing, M., and Donn, W. C., 1958, A theory of ice ages, II, *Science 127:*1159–1162. Another theory more directly related to ocean bottom shape change has been proposed in Vigdorchik, M. E., 1981, Isolation of the Arctic from the global ocean during glaciations, in Allison, I. (ed.), *Sea Level, Ice, and Climate Change,* IAHS Publication No. 131 (Wallingford, Oxfordshire, U.K.: International Association of Hydrological Sciences), pp. 303–322. Different versions of the glacier-land interaction theories, which we will explore in Chapter 7, are part of the most recent ice age causal models.
8. Kandel, R. S., 1980, *Earth and Cosmos* (Oxford: Pergamon Press).
9. One of the best sources for description of the atmospheric circulation, including a summary of historical development of modern ideas dating back to Hadley, is Lorenz, E. N., 1967, *The Nature and Theory*

of the General Circulation of the Atmosphere (Geneva: World Meteorological Organization).

10. Kutzbach, G., 1979, *The Thermal Theory of Cyclones: A History of Meteorological Thought in the Nineteenth Century* (Boston: American Meteorological Society), p. 1.

11. Forrester, I. H., 1961, *1001 Questions Answered About the Weather* (New York: Dodd, Mead and Company), p. 348.

12. For a modern review of Rossby's contributions in the context of dynamic meteorology, see, for example, Holton, J. R., 1979, *An Introduction to Dynamic Meteorology* (New York: Academic Press).

13. Dole, R. M., 1978, The objective representation of blocking patterns, in *The General Circulation: Theory, Modeling and Observations* (Boulder: National Center for Atmospheric Research).

14. For a more modern review of the entire issue of the Southern Oscillation and additional references, see Newell, R. E., 1979, Climate and the ocean, *American Scientist 67* (July-August):405–416.

15. Moyer, R., 1980, Eye to eye with the great wind, *Science 80, 1* No. 7:60–65.

16. Donn, W., 1975, *Meteorology*, 4th ed. (New York: McGraw-Hill), p. 338.

17. Riehl, H., 1978, *Introduction to the Atmosphere*, 3d ed. (New York: McGraw-Hill), p. 218.

18. Lorenz, *The Nature and Theory of the General Circulation of the Atmosphere.*

19. A discussion of and references on the weather predictability limit are provided in Lorenz, E. N., 1975, Climate Predictability, in *The Physical Basis of Climate and Climate Modeling*, GARP Publication Series No. 16 (Geneva: World Meteorological Organization), pp. 132–136.

20. Long, E. John (ed.), 1964, *Ocean Sciences* (Annapolis: United States Naval Institute).

21. Richardson, P. L., 1980, Benjamin Franklin and Timothy Folger's first printed chart of the Gulf Stream, *Science 207:*643–645.

22. Gordon, B. L. (ed.), 1970, *Man and the Sea* (Garden City, N.J.: The Natural History Press), pp. 32–35.

23. West, S., 1980, Ring around the Gulf Stream, *Science News 118* No. 21:331.

24. Broecker, W. S., 1979, A revised estimate for the radiocarbon age of North Atlantic deep water, *Journal of Geophysical Research 84:*3218–3226.

25. The large heat capacity of the oceans, the "thermal flywheel," is not only important to the regional climatic response to seasonal solar forcing, but also governs the response of the climatic system to volcanic dust injections, CO_2 changes, and so on. See Thompson, S. L., and Schneider, S. H., 1979, A seasonal zonal energy balance climate model with an interactive lower layer, *Journal of Geophysical Research 84:* 2401–2414; Schneider, S. H., and Thompson, S. L., 1981, Atmospheric CO_2 and climate: Importance of the transient response, *Journal of Geophysical Research 86:*3135–3147; and Manabe, S., and

Stouffer, R. J., 1980, Sensitivity of a global climate model to an increase of CO_2-concentration in the atmosphere, *Journal of Geophysical Research 85:*5529.

26. For a discussion of energy flows in the oceans, see Bryan, K., 1978, The ocean heat balance, *Oceanus 21:*19–26.

27. A number of articles discuss upwelling/fishing issues in Glantz, M. H., and Thompson, J. D. (eds.), 1981, *Resource Management and Environmental Uncertainty: Lessons from Coastal Upwelling Fisheries* (New York: Wiley Interscience).

28. For a review see Newell, Climate and the oceans; see also Kerr, R. A., 1983, Fading El Niño broadening scientists' view, *Science 221:*940–941, and Rasmusson, E. M., and Hall, J. M., 1983, El Niño, *Weatherwise 36:*166–175.

29. Pillsbury is quoted in Barnett, T. P., 1978, Ocean temperatures: Precursors of climate change? *Oceanus 21* No. 4:27.

30. Ibid., p. 27.

31. For an overview of Namias' work and a list of references, see Namias, J., and Cayan, D., 1981, Large-scale air-sea interactions and short-period climatic fluctuations, *Science 214:*869–876.

32. Hecht, A. D., 1983, Drought in the Great Plains: History of societal response, *Journal of Climate and Applied Meteorology 22:*51–56.

33. Wallace was quoted in the *New York Times,* February 6, 1936.

34. A U.S. National Climate Program was established by Congress (Public Law 95–367) in part to improve skill in long-range forecasting.

35. For one example, see Bryson, R. A., and Starr, T. B., 1977, Chandler tides in the atmosphere, *Journal of the Atmospheric Sciences 34:*1975–1986.

36. See, for example, Bettge, T. W., Baumheffner, D. P., and Chervin, R. M., 1981, On the verification of seasonal climate forecasts, *Bulletin of the American Meteorological Society 62:*1654–1665.

37. See, for example, Leith, C. E., 1973, The standard error of time-average estimates of climatic means, *Journal of Applied Meteorology 12:*1066–1069; and Chervin, R. M., Gates, W. L., and Schneider, S. H., 1974, The effect of time averaging on the noise level of climatological statistics generated by atmospheric general circulation models, *Journal of the Atmospheric Sciences 31:*2216–2219.

38. One such mechanism would be a very large SST abnormality, termed a "super anomaly" in Chervin, R. M., Washington, W. M., and Schneider, S. H., 1976, Testing the statistical significance of the response of the NCAR general circulation model to North Pacific Ocean surface temperature anomalies, *Journal of the Atmospheric Sciences 33:*413–423. Another technique is to search for particularly sensitive forcing mechanisms of climatic change.

39. Julian, P. R., and Chervin, R. M., 1978, A study of the Southern Oscillation and Walker circulation phenomenon, *Monthly Weather Review 106:*1433–1451.

40. Barnett, T. P., 1981, Statistical prediction of North American air temperatures from Pacific predictors, *Monthly Weather Review* 109: 1021–1041.
41. Semtner, A. J. Jr., 1984, On modelling the seasonal thermodynamic cycle of sea ice in studies of climatic change, *Climatic Change* (in press).
42. Gordon, A. L., 1981, Seasonality of southern ocean sea ice, *Journal of Geophysical Research 86:*4193–4197.
43. Matson, M., and Wiesnet, D. R., 1981, New data base for climate studies, *Nature 289:*451–456, figure 8.
44. Ibid.; compare their figure 4 to figure 6.
45. See the EBM group report in Imbrie, J., and Berger, A. (eds.), in press, *Milankovitch and Climate Change* (Amsterdam: Elsevier), which suggested that one key to the ice age interglacial cycles of the Pleistocene is the extent to which midcontinental winter snows melted in the summer.
46. For a general reference on biogeochemical cycles, see Stumm, W. (ed.), 1977, *Global Chemical Cycles and Their Alterations by Man* (Berlin: Dahlem Konferenzen); and Bolin, B. (ed.), 1981, *Carbon Cycle Modeling*, SCOPE 16 (New York: Wiley).
47. Lindh, G., 1979, Water and food production, in Biswas, M. R., and Biswas, A. K., (eds.), *Food, Climate and Man* (New York: Wiley), figure 3-1 on p. 54.
48. For a fuller discussion, see also chapter 7 of Schneider, S. H., and Morton, L., 1981, *The Primordial Bond: Exploring Connections Between Man and Nature Through the Humanities and Sciences* (New York: Plenum).
49. Ibid., figure 7-11.

5. Planetary Energy Balance: The Power Behind the Climatic System

1. Schneider, S. H., and Dennett, R. D., 1975, Climatic barriers to long-term energy growth, *Ambio 4:*65–74.
2. Report of the Study of Man's Impact on Climate (SMIC), 1971, *Inadvertent Climate Modification* (Cambridge, Mass.: Massachusetts Institute of Technology).
3. Lorenz, E. N., 1967, *The Nature and Theory of the General Circulation of the Atmosphere* (Geneva: World Meterological Organization).
4. Oort, A. H., and Vonder Haar, T. H., 1976, On the observed annual cycle in the ocean-atmosphere heat balance over the Northern Hemisphere, *Journal of Physical Oceanography 6:*781–800.
5. For a discussion of techniques and requirements for observing various components of the planetary energy balance, see Chapter 6 of *The Physical Basis of Climate and Climate Modeling*, Report of the Interna-

tional Study Conference, Stockholm, 29 July–10 August, 1974, (Geneva: World Meteorological Organization, April 1975) GARP Publication Series No. 16.

6. The Twin Earth: Computer Models of Weather and Climate

1. Franzén, Anders, 1962, *VASA: The Brief Story of a Swedish Warship from 1628* (Stockholm: Banniers Norstedts).
2. Ibid.
3. An early discussion of the internal/external climatic subsystems can be found in Leith, C. E., 1975, The design of a statistical-dynamical climate model and statistical constraints on the predictability of climate, Appendix 2.2 in *The Physical Basis of Climate and Climate Modeling*, Report of the International Study Conference in Stockholm, 29 July–10 August, 1974, GARP Publication Series No. 16 (Geneva: World Meteorological Organization, April 1975), pp. 137–151. A more expanded discussion is offered by Gates, W. L., 1981, The climate system and its portrayal by climate models: A review of basic principles, in Berger, A. (ed.), *Climatic Variations and Variability: Facts and Theories* (Dordrecht: D. Reidel), pp. 3–19.
4. Schneider, S. H., and Dickinson, R. E., 1974, Climate modeling, *Review of Geophysics and Space Physics 12:*447–493.
5. Schneider, S. H., 1979, Verification of parameterizations in climate modeling, in *Report of the JOC Study Conference on Climate Models: Performance, Intercomparison and Sensitivity Studies* (Geneva: World Meteorological Organization, October 1979), pp. 728–751; and Bergman, K., Hecht, A., and Schneider, S. H., 1981, Climate models, *Physics Today 34:*44–51.
6. Private communication, R. M. Chervin.
7. Richardson, Lewis F., 1922, *Weather Prediction by Numerical Process* (Cambridge: Cambridge University Press). See also Thompson, P. D., 1961, *Numerical Weather Analysis and Prediction* (New York: Macmillan).
8. Richardson, *Weather Prediction*, pp. 219–220.
9. North, G. R., 1975, Theory of energy-balance climate models, *Journal of Atmospheric Sciences 32:*2033–2043, is one example.
10. Manabe, S., and Wetherald, R. T., 1967, Thermal equilibrium of the atmosphere with a given distribution of relative humidity, *Journal on the Atmospheric Sciences 24:*241–259.
11. Schneider, S. H., 1972, Cloudiness as a global climate feedback mechanism: The effects of radiation balance and surface temperature of variations in cloudiness, *Journal of the Atmospheric Sciences 29:*1413–1422.
12. See, for example, Schneider, S. H., Washington, W. M., and Chervin,

R. M., 1978, Cloudiness as a climatic feedback mechanism: Effects on cloud amounts of prescribed global and regional surface temperature changes in the NCAR GCM, *Journal of the Atmospheric Sciences 35:* 2207–2221; and Cess, R. D., 1976, Climate change: An appraisal of atmospheric feedback mechanisms employing zonal climatology, *Journal of the Atmospheric Sciences 33:* 1831–1843. For more up-to-date discussions see also, Thompson, S. L., 1979, Development of a seasonally verified planetary albedo parameterization for zonal energy balance climate models, in *Report of the JOC Study Conference on Climate Models.*

13. For examples of the use of seasonal cycles to verify models' performances, see Thompson, S. L., and Schneider, S. H., 1979, A seasonal zonal energy balance climate model with an interactive lower layer, *Journal of Geophysical Research 84:* 2401–2414; Schneider, S. H., and Thompson, S. L., 1980, Cosmic conclusions from climatic models: Can they be justified? *Icarus 41:* 456–469; Warren, S. G., and Schneider, S. H., 1979, Seasonal simulation as a test for uncertainties in the parameterizations of a Budyko-Sellers zonal climate model, *Journal of the Atmospheric Sciences 36:* 1377–1391; and Manabe, S., and Stouffer, R. J., 1980, Sensitivity of a global climate model to an increase of CO_2 concentration in the atmosphere, *Journal of Geophysical Research 85:* 5529. An earlier relevant work is Sellers, W. D., 1973, A new global climatic model, *Journal of the Atmospheric Sciences 12:* 241–254. A very early suggestion to use the seasonal cycle to verify the sensitivity performance of climate models was made in Climate modification, in *Report of the Study of Man's Impact on Climate* (SMIC) (Cambridge, Mass.: MIT Press, 1971), p. 145.

14. Schneider, Verification of parameterizations in climate modeling.

15. Ibid.

16. For example, see the July 30, 1979 testimony before the U.S. Senate, Committee on Governmental Affairs (Senator Abraham Ribicoff, Chairman), *Carbon Dioxide Accumulation in the Atmosphere, Synthetic Fuels and Energy Policy, A Symposium* (Washington, D.C.: U.S. Government Printing Office). In a subsequent hearing in 1981 Tennessee Congressman Albort Gore, Jr. commented, "Many of our witnesses today are from the academic environment. But the greenhouse effect is not merely an academic question. The paths we take today I hope will help us determine whether we have disasters or merely manageable problems in our future." This appeared on page 5 of *Carbon Dioxide and Climate: The Greenhouse Effect,* Hearing before the Subcommittee on Natural Resources, Agriculture Research and Environment and the Subcommittee on Investigations and Oversight of the Committee on Science and Technology, U.S. House of Representatives, 97th Congress (Washington, D.C.: U.S. Government Printing Office, 31 July, 1981).

17. Schneider, S. H., with Mesirow, L. E., 1976, *The Genesis Strategy: Climate and Global Survival* (New York: Plenum), p. 149.

7. The Causes of Climatic Change

1. For a recent review of knowledge of the big bang, see Chaisson, E. J., 1981, Three eras of cosmic evolution, in Billingham, J. (ed.), *Life in the Universe* (Cambridge, Mass.: MIT Press), pp. 1–16. See also the discussion by Waldrop, M. M., 1983, The new inflationary universe, *Science 219:*375–377, for a journalistic review of more recent theories on the origin of the big bang.
2. Sagan, C., 1977, *The Dragons of Eden* (New York: Ballantine), p. 13. See also Sagan, C., 1980, *Cosmos* (New York: Random House).
3. An early—and readable—popular account is given by Jastrow, Robert, 1967, *Red Giants and White Dwarfs* (New York: Harper & Row). Later editions are available, as well as two subsequent works in a trilogy of which *Red Giants* is the first volume.
4. Kandel, R. S., 1980, *Earth and Cosmos* (Oxford: Pergamon Press), p. 40.
5. Lovelock, J. E., 1979, *Gaia: A New Look at Life on Earth* (Oxford: Oxford University Press), pp. 15–16.
6. Walker, J. C. G., 1977, *Evolution of the Atmosphere* (New York: Macmillan). This text is one of the best recent sources for detailed discussions of many aspects of this subject.
7. A discussion of this and other issues of planetary evolution can be found in Owen, T., 1978, The origins and early histories of planetary atmospheres, in *Évolution des Atmosphères Planétaires et Climatologie de la Terre* (Toulouse: Centre National d'Etudes Spatiales), pp. 1–10.
8. Henderson-Sellers, A., and Meadows, A. J., 1977, Surface temperatures of early earth, *Nature 270:*589–591; see also their discussion in 1978, The atmospheric composition and the surface temperature of the early earth, *Évolution des Atmosphères Planétaires,* pp. 25–29.
9. Gough, D. O., 1977, Theoretical predictions of variations in the solar output, in *The Solar Output and Its Variation,* O. R. White (ed.), (Boulder: Colorado Associated University Press), pp. 451–474; see especially pp. 467–468.
10. For example, see Gough, D. O., 1977, Theoretical predictions of variations in the solar output. See also Newman, M. J., and Rood, R. T., 1977, Implications of solar evolution for the earth's early atmosphere, *Science 198:*1035–1037. One of the earliest suggestions that varying solar luminosity could be involved in great glaciations of geologic history was contained in Opik, E. J., 1958, Climate and the changing sun, *Scientific American 198:*85–92.
11. For example, see Warren, S. G., and Schneider, S. H., 1979, Seasonal simulation as a test for uncertainties in the parameterizations of a Budyko-Sellers zonal climate model, *Journal of the Atmospheric Sciences 36:*1377–1391.

12. Sagan, C., and Mullen, G., 1972, Earth and Mars: Evolution of atmospheres and temperatures, *Science 177:*52–56.
13. Among these critics are Kuhn, W. R., and Atreya, S. K., 1979, Ammonia photolysis and the greenhouse effect in the primordial atmosphere of the earth, *Icarus 37:*207–213. Additional discussions can be found in Owen, The origins and early histories, and Henderson-Sellers and Meadows, Surface temperatures of early earth; the latter believe that the albedo of the earth was much lower because of decreased cloudiness, thereby solving the faint-early-sun paradox without an ammonia/methane enhanced greenhouse effect.
14. Sagan, C., 1982, private letter to Stephen H. Schneider.
15. Walker, *Evolution of the Atmosphere,* p. 217.
16. Owen, T., Cess, R. D., and Ramanathan, V., 1979, Enhanced CO_2 greenhouse to compensate for reduced solar luminosity on early earth, *Nature* 277:640–641.
17. Rossow, W. B., Henderson-Sellers, A., and Weinreich, S. K., 1982, Cloud feedback—A stabilizing effect for the early Earth?, *Science 217:* 1245–1246. Also see Henderson-Sellers, A., and Cogley, J. G., 1982, The earth's early hydrosphere, *Nature 298:*832–835.
18. Walker, J. C. G., Hays, P. B., and Kasting, J. F., 1981, A negative feedback mechanism for the long-term stabilization of earth's surface temperature, *Journal of Geophysical Research 86:*9776–9782. Incidentally, a very similar theory was proposed informally in the late 1970s by Robert E. Dickinson.
19. Lovelock, J. E., and Whitfeld, M., 1982, Life span of the biosphere, *Nature 296:*561–563.
20. Goldberg, E. D. (ed.), 1982, *Atmospheric Chemistry* (Dahlem Konferenzen, Berlin, Heidelberg, New York: Springer-Verlag), pp. 189–198.
21. Huang, S. S., 1959, Occurrence of life in the universe, *American Scientist 47:*397–402.
22. Schneider, S. H., and Thompson, S. L., 1980, Cosmic conclusions from climatic models: Can they be justified? *Icarus 41:*436–469. This article discusses the potential changes over the aeons in the sensitivity of the earth's climate to external forces.
23. Hart, M. H., 1978, The evolution of the atmosphere of the earth, *Icarus 33:*23–39. The quoted passage is on p. 37.
24. Sagan, C., 1960, The radiation balance of Venus, California Institute of Technology, Jet Propulsion Laboratory Technical Report No. 32–34, September 15, 1960; Gold, T., 1964, Outgassing processes on the moon and Venus, in Brancazio, P. J. and Cameron, A. G. W. (eds.), *The Origin and Evolution of Atmospheres and Oceans* (New York: Wiley), pp. 249–265; and Ingersoll, A. P., 1969, The runaway greenhouse: The history of water on Venus, *Journal of the Atmospheric Sciences 26:* 1191–1198.
25. Rasool, S. I., and de Bergh, C., 1970, The runaway greenhouse and

the accumulation of CO_2 in the Venus atmosphere, *Nature 226:* 1037–1039.

26. Hart, The evolution of the atmosphere of the earth; Hart, M. H., 1979, Habitable zones about main sequence stars, *Icarus 37:* 351–357; and Hart, M. H., 1982, The effect of a planet's size on the evolution of its atmosphere, in Gott, P. F., and Riherd, P. S. (eds.), *Proceedings of the Southwest Regional Conference for Astronomy and Astrophysics,* Vol. VII, pp. 111–126.

27. For criticism of Hart's views on life in the universe, see Newman, W. I., and Sagan, C., 1981, Galactic civilizations: Population dynamics and interstellar diffusion, *Icarus 46:* 298–327. For criticisms of Sagan's views of extraterrestrial life see the April 1981 issue of *Physics Today,* especially F. J. Tipler, Extraterrestrial intelligent beings do not exist. (The last word in this debate is, of course, not in!)

28. Some criticisms of the Hart model can be found in Schneider, S. H., and Thompson, S. L., 1980, Cosmic conclusions from climatic models: Can they be justified?, *Icarus 41:* 456–469; Owen et al., Enhanced CO_2 greenhouse; and Kasting, J. F., 1979, Evolution and oxygen and ozone in the earth's atmosphere, Ph.D. dissertation (Ann Arbor: University of Michigan).

29. A number of articles on early life are found in Billingham (ed.), *Life in the Universe.* (In particular see the papers in this volume by Sherwood Chang and by Lynn Margulis and James Lovelock.) See also *Scientific American 239,* No. 3 (September 1978), which is devoted to evolution (see in particular the articles by Francisco Ayala, Richard Dickerson, J. William Schopf, and James Valentine); also of some direct interest is Ponnamperuma, C. (ed.), 1981, *Comets and the Origin of Life* (Dordrecht: Reidel).

30. Walker, *Evolution of the Atmosphere,* pp. 211–212, goes over a number of arguments as to what gases were released from volcanoes and may have been significant in the very early atmosphere.

31. For example, Kasting, J. F., and Walker, J. C. G., 1981, Limits on oxygen concentration in the prebiological atmosphere and the rate of abiotic fixation of nitrogen, *Journal of Geophysical Research 86:* 1147–1158.

32. Dickinson R. E., 1983, Effects of solar electromagnetic radiation on the terrestrial environment, in *Physics of the Sun,* Space Science Monograph (Chicago: University of Chicago Press) (in press).

33. Ehrlich, P. R., and Raven, P. H., 1965, Butterflies and plants: A study in co-evolution, *Evolution 18:* 586–608.

34. Perhaps the most well-known time compression is Carl Sagan's "cosmic calendar" presented in his Pulitzer-Prize-winning *The Dragons of Eden.*

35. Lovelock, J. E., and Margulis, L., 1973, Atmospheric homeostasis by and for the biosphere: The Gaia hypothesis, *Tellus 26:* 2. See Lovelock's more recent book *Gaia;* see also the discussion in Chapter 7 of

Schneider, S. H., and Morton, L., 1981, *The Primordial Bond: Exploring Connections Between Man and Nature Through the Humanities and Sciences* (New York: Plenum).

36. Lovelock, *Gaia*, p. vii.
37. Ibid., pp. 31–32.
38. Köppen, A., and Wegener, A., 1924, *Die Klimate der geologischen Vorzeit* (Berlin: Borntraeger).
39. Budyko, M. I., 1977, *Climatic Changes* (Washington: American Geophysical Union), p. 127. This is translated from the Russian version: Budyko, M. I., 1974, *Izmeneniya Klimata* (Leningrad: Gidrometeoizdat).
40. Donn, W. L., and Shaw, D. M., 1977, Model of climate evolution based on continental drift and polar wandering, *Geological Society of America Bulletin 88:* 390–396.
41. Barron, E. J., in press, Climate models: Applications for the Pre-Pleistocene, in Hecht, A. (ed.), *Paleoclimate Analysis and Modeling* (New York: Wiley). You can see Barron's reasoning by studying his drawings, which show that land area north of lat. 70°N changed very little from 100 million years ago to present. This is according to paleoclimatic reconstructions and albedo inferences of Barron, E. J., Sloan, J. L. II, and Harrison, C. G. A., 1980, Potential significance of land-sea distribution and surface albedo variations as a climatic forcing factor: 180 m.y. to the present, *Paleogeography, Paleoclimatology, Paleoecology 30:* 17–40. Another suggestion that albedo change associated with increasing land fraction could have caused the trend toward glaciation over the Cenozoic is found in Cogley, J. G., 1979, Albedo contrast and glaciation due to continental drift, *Nature 279:* 712–713.
42. Brooks, C. E. P., 1970, *Climate Through the Ages*, 2d ed. (New York: Dover), pp. 91–94. This book was first published in 1926 and revised in 1949.
43. McCrea, W. H., 1975, Ice ages and the Galaxy, *Nature 255:* 607–609. For a larger discussion of the probability and magnitude of solar system encounters with interstellar dust and their possible effect on the solar wind and other solar properties, see Talbot, R. J. Jr., and Newman, M. J, 1977, Encounters between stars and dense interstellar clouds, *Astrophysical Journal Supplement Series 34:* 295–308.
44. Budyko, M. I., and Ronov, A. B., 1980, Chemical evolution of the atmosphere in the Phanerozoic, *Geochemistry International 1979, 16:* 1–9. The data also appear in Budyko, *Climatic Changes*, p. 128.
45. Budyko, *Climatic Changes*, p. 115; and Budyko and Ronov, Chemical evolution of the atmosphere, p. 4.
46. As an example of the complex interacting chemical processes that must be accounted for before paleo–CO_2 levels can be reliably calculated see Garrels, R. M., and Lerman, A., 1981, Phanerozoic cycles of sedimentary carbon and sulfur, *Proceedings of the U.S. National Academy of Sciences 78:* 4652–4656.

47. More recently, a team of scientists concluded that CO_2 in the mid-Cretaceous was something like five to seven hundred percent greater than at present, but their conclusions are based on entirely different reasoning than Budyko and Ronov's, and the closeness in their estimates is apparently a coincidence; see Berner, R. A., Lasaga, A. C., and Garrels, R. M., in press, The carbonate-silicate geochemical cycle and its effect on atmospheric carbon dioxide over the past 100 million years.
48. Budyko, *Climatic Changes*, p. 131.
49. For example, see Frakes, L. A., 1979. *Climates Throughout Geologic Time* (Amsterdam: Elsevier); or Savin, S. M., 1977, The history of the earth's surface temperature during the past 100 million years, *Annual Reviews of Earth and Planetary Sciences 5:*319–355.
50. Budyko, *Climatic Changes*, p. 131.
51. Savin, The history of the earth's surface temperature, p. 350.
52. Among these are Donn and Shaw, Model of climate evolution; Barron, E. J., Thompson, S. L., and Schneider, S. H., 1981, An ice-free Cretaceous? Results from climate model simulations, *Science 212:* 501–508; and Barron, E. J., and Washington, W. M., 1982, The atmospheric circulation during warm geologic periods: Is the equator to pole surface temperature gradient the controlling factor?, *Geology 10:* 633–636.
53. Irving, E., North, F. K., and Couillard, R., 1974, Oil, climate and tectonics, *Canadian Journal of Earth Sciences 11:*1–17.
54. Barron et al., An ice-free Cretaceous? pp. 501–508.
55. Barron, E. J., 1983, A warm, equable Cretaceous: The nature of the problem, *Earth Science Reviews 19:*305–338 gives more details on the nature of the paleo–proxy evidence used in Cretaceous temperature reconstructions; see also Note 51 above.
56. Thompson, S. L., and Barron, E. J., 1981, Comparison of Cretaceous and present earth albedos: Implications for the causes of paleoclimates, *Journal of Geology 89:*143–167.
57. Shackleton, N. J., 1978, Evolution of the earth's climate during the Tertiary era, in *Évolution des Atmosphères Planétaires*, pp. 49–58.
58. Barron et al., An ice-free Cretaceous. See also Petersen, W. H., 1978, A steady thermo-haline convection, Ph.D. Thesis, University of Miami; see also Kraus, E. B., Petersen, W. H., and Rooth, C. G., 1978, The thermal evolution of the ocean, in *Évolution des Atmosphères*, pp. 201–211.
59. Newell, R. D., Navato, A. R., and Hsiung, J., 1978, Long-term global sea surface temperature fluctuations and their possible influence on atmospheric CO_2 concentrations, *Journal of Pure and Applied Geophysics 116:*351–371. See also Adam, D. P., 1975, The tropical cyclone as a global climate stabilizing mechanism, *Geology* (November):625–626.
60. Barron and Washington, The atmospheric circulation; see also Barron in A. Hecht, *Paleoclimate Analysis and Modeling;* see also Schneider,

S. H., Barron, E. J. and Thompson, S. L., Effect of ocean surface temperatures on mid-continent winter freezing for Cretaceous paleogeography, Paper presented at the Chapman Conference on Natural Variations in Carbon Dioxide and the Carbon Cycle, Tarpon Springs, Florida, January 1984.

61. Matthews, R. K., and Poore, R. Z., 1980, Tertiary, $\delta^{18}O$ record and glacio-eustatic sea-level fluctuations, *Geology 8:*501–504.

62. McLean, D. M., 1981, Size factor in the late Pleistocene mammalian extinctions, *American Journal of Science 281:*1144–1152; see also McLean, D. M., 1978, A terminal Mesozoic "greenhouse": Lessons from the past, *Science 201:*401–406. For an additional view, see Harvey, P. H., and Slatkin, M., 1982, Some like it hot: Temperature-determined sex, *Nature 296:*807–808.

63. Alvarez, L. W., Alvarez, W., Asaro, F., and Michel, H. V., 1980, Extraterrestrial cause for the Cretaceous-Tertiary extinction, *Science 208:*1095–1108.

64. Gould, S. J., 1980, The belt of an asteroid, *Natural History 89:*26–33. See also Reid, G. C., and Isaksen, I. S., Holzer, T. E., and Crutzen, P. J., 1976, Influence of ancient solar-proton events on the evolution of life, *Nature 259:*177–179.

65. Examples of climate model experiments suggesting that such a short-term shock to the climatic system would not result in permanent climatic change can be found in Schneider, S. H., and Gal-Chen, T., 1973, Numerical experiments in climate stability, *Journal of Geophysical Research 78:*6182–6194; and Schneider and Thompson, Atmospheric CO_2 and climate.

66. Pollack, J. B., Toon, O. B., Ackerman, T. P., McKay, C. P. and Turco, R. P., 1983, Environmental effects of an impact-generated dust cloud: Implications for the Cretaceous-Tertiary extinctions, *Science 219:*287–289.

67. Emiliani, C., Kraus, E. B., and Shoemaker, E. M., 1981, Sudden death at the end of the Mesozoic, *Earth and Planetary Science Letters 55:*317–334; Hsü, K. J. et al., 1982, Mass mortality and its environmental and evolutionary consequences, *Science 216:*249–256; Kasting, J. F., 1982, Depletion of stratospheric ozone by asteroid or cometary impact (unpublished manuscript). Others have suggested acid rain or poisoning from chemicals in the wake of the collision as causes of the extinctions.

68. For example, a series of letters appeared in the issue of *Science* for February 13, 1981 contesting the Alvarez hypothesis. In particular, see Kent, D. V., 1981, Asteroid extinction hypothesis, *Science 211:*648; Reid, G. C., 1981, *Science 211:*253.

69. Alvarez, L. W., Alvarez, W., Asaro, F. Michel, H. V., 1981, Asteroid extinction hypothesis, *Science 211:*654–656. (This is the response by Alvarez et al. to the various letters of criticism cited in Note 68 above.)

70. Pollack et al., Environmental effects. For further support of the Al-

varez theory, see also O'Keefe, J. D., and Ahrens, T. J., 1982, Impact mechanics of the Cretaceous-Tertiary extinction bolide, *Nature 298:* 123–127.

71. Kerr, R. A., 1982, Extinctions: Iridium and who went where, *Science 215:*389.

72. Kauffman was interviewed by Janet Wiscombe in the *Boulder Sunday Camera,* January 17, 1982, p. 17.

73. Rampino, M. R., and Reynolds, R. C., 1983, Clay mineralogy of the Cretaceous-Tertiary boundary clay, *Science 219:*495–498. See also Officer, C. B., and Drake, C. L., 1983, The Cretaceous-Tertiary transition, *Science 219:*1383–1390.

74. A nice pictorial essay on the Alvarez team's work and such earth-meteor collision issues appeared in the PBS network series Nova in 1981. The program is entitled "The Asteroid and the Dinosaur." A transcript is available from WGBH-TV, Boston.

75. Hays, J. D., Imbrie, J., and Shackleton, N. J., 1976, Variations in the earth's orbit: Pacemaker of the ice ages, *Science 194:*1121–1132.

76. Kutzbach, J. E., and Bryson, R. A., 1974, Variance spectrum of Holocene climatic fluctuations in the North Atlantic sector, *Journal of the Atmospheric Sciences 31:*1958–1973.

77. Imbrie, J., and Shackleton, N. J., 1974, Climatic periodicities documented by power spectra of the oxygen isotope record in equatorial Pacific deep-sea core V28–38, cited as "in preparation" in Appendix A of United States Committee for the Global Atmospheric Research Program, 1975, *Understanding Climatic Change: A Program for Action* (Washington, D.C.: U.S. National Academy of Sciences). See this reference for a discussion of spectral analysis, white noise, and red spectra applied to paleoclimatology.

78. Kerr, R. A., 1981, Milankovitch climate cycles: Old and unsteady, *Science 213:*1095–1096. See also Pisias, N. G., and Moore, T. C., 1981, The evolution of Pleistocene climate: A time series approach, *Earth and Planetary Science Letters 52:*450–458.

79. A bioturbation distortion to climatic spectra from deep sea cores was first calculated in Goreau, T. F., 1980, Frequency sensitivity of the deep-sea climatic record, *Nature 287:*620–622. The distortion to the now famous Hays, Imbrie, and Shackleton result was then estimated in Dalfes, H. N., Schneider, S. H., and Thompson, S. L., 1983, Effects of bioturbation on climatic spectra inferred from deep sea cores, in Imbrie, J., and Berger, A. (eds.), *Milankovitch and Climate Change* (Amsterdam: Elsevier) in press.

80. For example, Kominz, N. M. A., and Pisias, N. G., 1979, Pleistocene climate: Deterministic or stochastic?, *Science 204:*171–173, suggests that as little as 25 percent of the signal strength is concentrated in the lesser peaks, with the rest occurring at the 100,000-year frequency

and all the other cycle lengths in between the three lesser peaks. However, see also Imbrie's later work enhancing the astronomical theory in Berger et al. (eds.), *Milankovitch and Climate.*

81. Thompson, S. L., and Schneider, S. H., 1979, A seasonal zonal energy balance climate model with an interactive lower layer, *Journal of Geophysical Research 84:*2401–2414; and Cess, R. D., and Goldenberg, S. D., 1981, The effect of ocean heat capacity upon global warming due to increasing atmospheric carbon dioxide, *Journal of Geophysical Research 86:*498–502 discuss a number of aspects of the seasonal response of the climate to solar forcing. See also North, G. R., and Coakley, J. A., 1979, Differences between seasonal and mean annual energy balance model calculations of climate and climate sensitivity, *Journal of the Atmospheric Sciences 36:* 1189–1204.

82. The quasi-biennial oscillation is strongest in the upper atmosphere. A number of theories attempting to explain this have recently been refined and updated by Hamilton, K., 1981, The vertical structure of the quasi-biennial oscillation: Observations and theory, *Atmosphere-Ocean 19:*236–250.

83. Imbrie and Imbrie, in *Ice Ages,* Chapter 6, review Croll's ideas and those of some critics who pointed out important flaws in his arguments.

84. Milankovitch, M., 1920, *Théorie Mathématique des Phénomènes Thermiques Produits per la Radiation Solaire* (Paris: Gauthier Villars).

85. This relationship and the publications from Milankovitch that follow his 1920 work are discussed in detail in Chapter 8 of Imbrie and Imbrie, *Ice Ages.*

86. For example, see Imbrie and Imbrie, *Ice Ages,* or Hays, J., 1979, *Our Changing Climate* (New York: Atheneum). See also Berger, A. L., 1981, The astronomical theory of paleoclimates, in A. L. Berger (ed.), *Climatic Variations and Variability: Facts and Theories* (Dordrecht: Reidel), pp. 501–525; and Vernekar, A. D., 1972, Long-period global variations of incoming solar radiation, *Meteorological Monographs 12* (Boston: American Meteorological Society).

87. Fong, P., 1982, Latent heat of melting and its importance for glaciation cycles, *Climatic Change 4:*199–206.

88. Nicolis, C., 1982, Stochastic aspects of climatic transitions—Response to a periodic forcing, *Tellus 34:*1–9.

89. Wiin-Nielsen, A., 1983, Comments on simple climate models with periodic and stochastic forcing, *Tellus 35A:*332–335.

90. Broecker's remarks came from a symposium on the causes of climatic change held in Boulder, Colorado, in August 1965, published three years later as Broecker, W. S., 1968, In defense of the astronomical theory of glaciation, *Meteorological Monographs 8* (Boston: American Meteorological Society), pp. 139–141. Incidentally, Broecker attrib-

utes much of the resurgence of interest in the Milankovitch hypothesis to a 1955 paper by Cesare Emiliani.

91. John Imbrie and his son John Z. Imbrie discuss several correlations (and some difficulties) between orbital element variations and climatic responses, and even propose a fairly simple model that connects variations in solar radiation as suggested by Milankovitch with glacial/interglacial cycles in Imbrie, J., and Imbrie, J. Z., 1980, Modeling the climatic response to orbital variations, *Science 207:*943–953. A later attempt to match solar radiation variations associated with orbital elements and climatic fluctuations in different periods was attempted by Kukla, G., Berger, A., Lotti, R., and Brown, J., 1981, Orbital signature of interglacials, *Nature 290:*295–300. In both of these cases the authors concluded that the associations they found explain many of the observed climatic variations, but that not all observations matched up as well as they would like for their theory to be watertight. Moreover, the 100,000-year cycle does not hold over the whole Pleistocene—see Kerr, Milankovitch climate cycles.

92. Among these early models are Shaw, D. M., and Donn, W. L., 1966, Milankovitch radiation variations: A quantitative evaluation, *Science 162:*1270–1272; Suarez, M. J., and Held, I. M., 1976, Modeling climatic response to orbital parameter variations, *Nature 263:*46–47; Suarez, M. J., and Held, I. M., 1979, The sensitivity of an energy balance climate model to variations in the orbital parameters, *Journal of Geophysical Research 84:*4825–4836; Pollard, D., 1978, An investigation of the astronomical theory of the ice ages using a simple climate/ice sheet model, *Nature 272:*233–235; Schneider, S. H., and Thompson, S. L., 1979, Ice ages and orbital variations: Some simple theory and modeling, *Quaternary Research 12:*188–203; Pollard, D., Ingersoll, A. P., and Lockwood, J. G., 1980, Response of a zonal climate/ice sheet model to the orbital perturbations during the quaternary ice ages, *Tellus 32:*301–319; and North, G., and Coakley, J., 1979, Differences between seasonal and mean annual energy balance model calculations of climate and climate sensitivity, *Journal of the Atmospheric Sciences 36:*1189–1204.

93. Kutzbach, J. E., 1981, Monsoon climate of the early Holocene: Climate experiment with the earth's orbital parameter for 9000 years ago, *Science 214:*59–61.

94. See in particular Weertman, J., 1976, Milankovitch solar radiation variations and ice age ice sheet sizes, *Nature 261:*17–20.

95. Budd, W. F., 1979, The importance of ice sheets in long term changes of climate and sea level, in Ian Allison (ed.), *Sea Level, Ice and Climatic Change,* International Association of Hydrological Sciences (IAHS), Publication No. 131, publication available from the IAHS, 2000 Florida Ave., N.W., Washington, D.C. 20009.

96. Ibid., p. 459. See also Oerlemans, J., 1982, A model of the Antarctic ice sheet, *Nature 297:*550–553.

97. A major step in this direction was the Symposium on Ice and Climate Modeling, Northwestern University, Evanston, Illinois, 27 June–1 July 1983. See *Annals of Glaciology 5,* 1983, International Glaciological Society, Cambridge, England.

98. Sergin, V. Ya., 1979, Numerical modeling of the glaciers-ocean-atmosphere global system, *Journal of Geophysical Research 84:*3191–3204. This paper, published in an American journal, is a condensation of Sergin and his colleagues' work dating back over more than a decade. Another scientist who felt that time lags in the temperature changes on land and sea could be responsible for Ice Age interglacial cycles without necessarily having any changes in solar radiation is U.S. Geological Survey geologist David Adam. His hypothesis is given in Adam, D. P., 1975, Ice ages and the thermal equilibrium of the earth, II, *Quaternary Research 5:*161–171. Another self-sustained set of oscillations for a hypothesized land/sea ice system was found in a model built by Saltzman, B., Sutera, A., and Evenson, A., 1981, Structural stochastic stability of a simple auto-oscillatory climatic feedback system, *Journal of the Atmospheric Sciences 38:*494–503. However, this model has roughly 1000-year-period oscillations and is based upon the interaction of atmosphere/ocean/sea ice rather than glaciers, which explains its relatively rapid period of fluctuation compared to Sergin's model or that of other internal oscillator models with big glaciers.

99. McIntyre, A., Ruddiman, W. F., and Durazzi, J. T., 1979, The role of the North Atlantic Ocean in rapid glacial growth, in *Évolution des Atmosphères.* See also Ruddiman, W. F., and McIntyre, A., 1981, Oceanic mechanisms for amplification of the 23,000-year ice-volume cycle, *Science 212:*617–627, which builds on a long series of papers by these authors on this issue and presents some interesting speculations on possible physical processes involved in glacier formation, decay, ocean temperatures, and insolation variations.

100. Ghil, M., 1981, Internal climatic mechanisms participating in glaciation cycles, in Berger (ed.), *Climatic Variations,* pp. 539–557. This summarizes a long series of studies conducted by Ghil and colleagues E. Kallèn, C. Crafoord, H. Le Treut, and K. Bhattacharya.

101. Harvey, L. D. D., and Schneider, S. H., 1983, Sensitivity of internally-generated climate oscillations to ocean model formulation, in Berger et al. (eds.), *Milankovitch and Climate.*

102. See the article by Pollard in Imbrie et al. (eds.), *Milankovitch and Climate Change;* see also Report of the Energy Balance Modeling Working Group in this volume. Among those scientists building models of the earth's climate including atmosphere-ocean, glacier, and bedrock depression effects that show 100,000-year response to shorter-period orbital forcings are Oerlemans, J., 1982, Glacial cycles and ice-sheet modelling, *Climatic Change 4:*353–374; Pollard, D., 1982, A simple ice sheet model yields realistic 100 kyr glacial cycles,

Nature 296: 334–338; and Birchfield, G. E., Weertman, J., and Lunde, A. T., 1981, A paleoclimate model of Northern Hemisphere ice sheets, *Quaternary Research 15:* 126–142. As noted by the latter authors, "the model prediction lends support to the hypothesis that the non-linearity of the ice-sheet physics is responsible for the 100,000-yr periodicity in the geological record of the late Pleistocene."

103. Bray, J. R., 1976, Volcanic triggering of glaciation, *Nature 260:* 414–415; Neftel, A., Oeschger, H. Schwander, J., Stouffer, B., and Zumbrunn, R., 1982, Ice core sample measurements give atmospheric CO_2 content during the past 40,000 yr., *Nature 295:* 220–223 (the alteration of greenhouse gases such as carbon dioxide is discussed in depth in Chapter 8); and Schneider and Thompson, 1979, Ice ages and orbital variations.

104. Berger, *Climatic Variations and Variability.*

105. Imbrie, J., and Imbrie, J. Z., 1980, Modeling the climatic response to orbital variations, *Science 207:* 943–953.

106. Stetson, H. T., 1947, *Sunspots in Action* (New York: The Ronald Press), pp. 200–203.

107. Three recent edited volumes attest to the resurgence of serious scientific interest in solar/terrestrial connections: White, O. R. (ed.), 1977, *The Solar Output and Its Variation* (Boulder: Colorado Associated University Press); McCormac, B. M., and Seliga, T. A. (eds.), 1979, *Solar-Terrestrial Influences on Weather and Climate* (Boston: Reidel); and R. Kandel (President, Scientific Committee), 1980, *Soleil et Climat* (Toulouse, France: Centre National d'Etudes Spatial).

108. One of Abbot's many publications is Abbot, C. G., 1929, *The Sun and the Welfare of Man* (Washington, D.C.: Smithsonian Institution). A very well-written popular account of the history of solar constant measurements and their interpretations for earth phenomena is given in Frazier, K., 1982, *Our Turbulent Sun* (Englewood Cliffs, N.J.: Prentice Hall).

109. Kondratyev, K. Ya, and Nikolsky, G. A., 1970, Solar radiation and solar activity, *Quarterly Journal of the Royal Meteorological Society 96:* 509–522.

110. Schneider, S. H., and Mass, C., 1975, Volcanic dust, sunspots and temperature trends, *Science 190:* 744–746.

111. Mass, C., and Schneider, S. H., 1977, Statistical evidence on the influence of sunspots and volcanic dust on long-term temperature records, *Journal of the Atmospheric Sciences 34:* 1995–2004; see also Gerety, E. J., Wallace, J. M., and Zerets, C. S., 1977, Sunspots, geomagnetic indices and the weather: The prognostic value of any connections, *Journal of the Atmospheric Sciences 34:* 673–678; and Currie, R. G., 1981, Solar cycle signal in air temperature in North America: Amplitude, gradient, phase and distribution, *Journal of the Atmospheric Sciences 38:* 808–818.

112. Hoyt, D. V., 1979, The Smithsonian Astrophysical Observatory solar constant program, *Reviews of Geophysics and Space Physics 17:*427–458.

113. Kondratyev, K. Ya., and Nikolsky, G. A., 1982, The solar constant and climate, manuscript submitted to *Climatic Change,* now being revised.

114. See Eddy, J. A., 1982, The solar constant and surface temperature, in Reck, R. A., and Hummel, J. R. (eds.), in *Interpretation of Climate and Photochemical Models, Ozone and Temperature Measurements* (New York: American Institute of Physics). See also Sofia, S., O'Keefe, J., Lesh, J. R., and Endal, A. S., 1979, Solar constant: Constraints on possible variations derived from solar diameter measurements, *Science 204:* 1306–1308; these authors are more skeptical of the earth/solar diameter calculations.

115. Hoyt, D. V., 1979, Variations in sunspot structure and climate, *Climatic Change 2:*79–92.

116. The proceedings of three such meetings with interests in variable solar output were given in Note 107. See also *Weather and Climate Responses to Solar Variations,* (B. M. McCormac, ed.), 1983 (Boulder: Colorado Associated University Press).

117. John Eddy, with mathematician Aran A. Boornazian, using observations at both the Greenwich Observatory in England and the Naval Observatory in the United States, resurrected a 125-year-old suggestion that the sun may be shrinking. The history of their involvement is well described by Kendrick Frazier (*Our Turbulent Sun,* pp. 74–83), and has subsequently been analyzed in more depth in Gilliland, R. L., 1980, Solar luminosity variations, *Nature 286:*838–839; and Gilliland, R. L., 1981, Solar radius variations over the past 265 years, *The Astrophysical Journal 248:*1144–1155.

118. Willson, R. C., Gulkis, S., Janssen, M., Hudson, H. S., and Chapman, G. A., 1981, Observations of solar irradiance variability, *Science 211:* 700–702. See also Willson, R. C., 1982, Solar irradiance variations and solar activity, *Journal of Geophysical Research 87:*4319–4326; Eddy, The solar constant and surface temperature; and the discussion in Frazier, *Our Turbulent Sun,* Chapter 7.

119. Gilliland, R. L., 1982, Solar, volcanic and CO_2 forcing of recent climatic changes, *Climatic Change 4:*111–131.

120. Harvey, L. D. D. and Schneider, S. H., 1984, Transient climate response to external forcing on 10^0–10^3 year time scales Part I: Experiments with globally averaged, coupled, atmosphere and ocean energy balance models, submitted to *Journal of Geophysical Research* discusses the problems of tuning simple models and other techniques to use them for more valid inferences.

121. Jones, P. D., Wigley, T. M. L., and Kelly, P. M., 1981, Variations in surface air temperatures: Part 1, Northern Hemisphere, 1881–1980, *Monthly Weather Review 110:*59–70; Borzenkova, I. I., Vinnikov, K. Ya., Spirina, L. P., and Stekhnovskiy, D. I., 1976, Change in air tempera-

ture in the Northern Hemisphere during the period 1881–1975, *Meteorologiya i Gidrologiya 1976* (7):27–35 (in Russian; translation available from U.K. Meteorological Office); Paltridge, G., and Woodruff, S., 1981, Changes in global surface temperature from 1880 to 1977 derived from historical records of sea surface temperature, *Monthly Weather Review 109:* 2427–2434; and Folland, C. and Kates, F., 1983, Changes in decadally averaged sea surface temperature over the world 1861–1980, in Imbrie et al. (eds.), *Milankovitch and Climate.*

122. Bryson, R. A., and Dittberner, G. J., 1976, A non-equilibrium model of hemispheric mean surface temperature, *Journal of the Atmospheric Sciences 33:* 2094–2106.

123. Thompson, S. L., and Schneider, S. H., 1982, Carbon dioxide and climate: Has a signal been observed yet?, *Nature 295:* 645–646. See also Harvey, L. D. D., and Schneider, S. H., 1984, Transient climate response to external forcing on 10^0–10^3 year time scales Part II: Sensitivity experiments with a seasonal, hemispherically averaged coupled atmosphere, land and ocean energy balance model, submitted to *Journal of Geophysical Research;* and for an updated and expanded semi-empirical study, see Gilliland, R. L., Schneider, S. H. and Harvey, L. D. D., 1984, Volcanic CO_2 and solar forcing of Northern and Southern Hemisphere surface air temperatures, submitted to *Nature.* This study found more evidence for the plausibility of a 76-year solar constant cycle, volcanic dust forcing, and CO_2 influences—where CO_2 forcing is at the low end of most model studies, about $+1.5°C$ warming for a doubling of CO_2.

124. Franklin's observations were taken from a letter entitled "Meteorological Imaginations and Conjectures" that was written in May 1784 and read before a scientific audience six months later. It is reproduced in an article about the Laki eruption by Sigurdsson, H., 1982, Volcanic pollution and climate: The 1783 Laki eruption, *EOS* (August 10, 1982):601–602.

125. Ibid., p. 601.

126. An interesting account of the massive eruption of Mount Tambora in Indonesia and its possible climatic and social consequences is given by Stommel, H., and Stommel, E., 1979, The year without a summer, *Scientific American 240* No. 6:176–186.

127. Ibid., p. 176.

128. Robock, A., 1981, The Mount St. Helens volcanic eruption of 18 May 1980: Minimal climatic effect, *Science 212:* 1383–1384.

129. For a thorough discussion of the relationship between volcanic eruptions, their ejecta, stratospheric dust veils, and potential climatic changes, see Rampino, M. R., and Self, S., 1982, Historic eruptions of Tambora (1815), Krakatau (1883), and Agung (1963), their stratospheric aerosols and climatic impact, *Quaternary Research 18:* 127–143.

130. Hammer, C. U., Clausen, H. B., and Dansgaard, W., 1980, Greenland

ice sheet evidence of post-glacial vulcanism and its climatic impact, *Nature 288:*230–235.

131. Among those investigators who have found a theoretical connection between volcanic dust veils and small global climatic cooling are Pollack, J. B., Toon, O. B., Sagan, C., Summers, A., Baldwin, B., and Van Camp, W., 1976, Volcanic explosions and climatic change: A theoretical assessment, *Journal of Geophysical Research 81:*1071–1083; Coakley, J. A., Jr., and Grams, G. W., 1976, Relative influence of visible and infrared optical properties of a stratospheric aerosol layer on the global climate, *Journal of Applied Meteorology 15:*679–691; and Harshvardhan, and Cess, R. D., 1976, Stratospheric aerosols: Effect upon atmospheric temperature and global climate, *Tellus 28:*1–10.

132. Lamb, H. H., 1970, Volcanic dust in the atmosphere; with its chronology and assessment of its meteorological significance, *Philosophical Transactions of the Royal Society of London A266:*425–533; see especially Table 7 (a).

133. Hammer et al., Greenland ice sheet evidence; see also Goldberg, E. D. (ed.), 1982, *Atmospheric Chemistry* (Dahlem Konferenzen, Berlin, Heidelberg, New York: Springer-Verlag).

134. For example, see Mitchell, J. M. Jr., 1973, A reassessment of atmospheric pollution as a cause of long-term changes of global temperature, in Singer, S. F. (ed.), *Global Effects of Environmental Pollution,* 2d ed. (Dordrecht: Reidel).

135. Rampino, M. R., Self, S., and Fairbridge, R. W., 1979, Can rapid climatic change cause volcanic eruptions? *Science 206:*826–829.

136. A similar point had been made earlier by Helmut Landsberg for the case of the "summer that never came" following the Mt. Tambora eruption; see Landsberg, H. E., and Albert, J. M., 1974, The summer of 1816 and vulcanism, *Weatherwise 27:*63–66.

137. Mass, C., and Schneider, S. H., 1977, Influence of sunspots and volcanic dust on long-term temperature records inferred by statistical investigations, *Journal of the Atmospheric Sciences 34* No. 12:1995–2004. See also a followup study: Taylor, B. L., Gal-Chen, T., and Schneider, S. H., 1980, Volcanic eruptions and long-term temperature records: An empirical search for cause and effect, *Quarterly Journal of the Royal Meteorological Society 106:*175–199.

138. Hansen, J. E., Wang, W. C., and Lacis, A. A., 1978, Mt. Agung eruption provides test of a global climatic perturbation, *Science 199:*1065–1068; Oliver, R. C., 1976, On the response of hemispheric mean temperature to stratospheric dust: An empirical approach, *Journal of Applied Meteorology 15:*933–950; Bryson, R. A., and Goodman, B. M., 1980, Volcanic activity and climatic changes, *Science 207:*1041–1044; and Robock, A., 1979, The "Little Ice Age": Northern Hemisphere average observations and model calculations, *Science 206:*1402–1404.

139. Rampino, M. R., private communication to Randi Londer contained the Mt. Toba data.

140. One of the first studies to use expanded surface air temperature coverage in the oceans is Chen, R. S., 1982, *Combined Land/Sea Surface Air Temperature Trends, 1949–1972*, M.S. Thesis, Department of Meteorology, Massachusetts Institute of Technology. However, Chen's results for surface air temperature trends over oceans are not yet reconciled with the few studies of the ocean surface temperatures themselves.

141. Mitchell, J. M. Jr., 1972, The natural breakdown of the present interglacial and its possible intervention by human activities, *Quaternary Research 2:*436–445.

142. Damon, D. E., and Kunen, S. M., 1976, Global cooling? *Science 193:* 447–453.

143. van Loon, H., and Williams, J., 1977, The connection between trends of mean temperature and circulation at the surface: Part IV. Comparison of the surface changes in the Northern Hemisphere with the upper air and the Antarctic in winter, *Monthly Weather Review 105:* 636–647.

144. Damon, P. E., and Kunen, S. M., 1978, Reply to "Letter concerning the paper 'Global cooling?' " *Climatic Change 1:*387–389.

145. Hansen, J. A., Johnson, D., Lacis, A., Lebedeff, S., Lee, P., Rind, D., and Russell, G., 1981, Climate impact of increasing atmospheric carbon dioxide, *Science 213:*957–966. The quotation in the text appeared on page 961.

146. Jones, P. D., and Wigley, T. M. L., 1980, Northern Hemisphere temperatures, 1881–1979, *Climate Monitor 9:*43. See also subsequent issues of *Climate Monitor,* the house publication of the Climatic Research Unit of the University of East Anglia, Norwich, England; also see Jones, P. D., Wigley, T. M. L., Kelly, P. M., 1982, Variations in surface air temperatures: Part I, Northern Hemisphere, 1881–1980, *Monthly Weather Review 110:*59–70.

147. Dronia, H., 1967, Der stadteinflub auf den welfweiten temperaturtrend, *Meteorologische Abhandlungen 74,* 65pp.

148. Mitchell, J. M., Jr., 1967, Climatic variation (instrumental), in Fairbridge, R. W. (ed.), *The Encyclopedia of Atmospheric Sciences and Astrogeology* (New York: Reinhold), pp. 211–213.

149. Damon and Kunen, Global cooling? p. 387.

150. Kutzbach, J. E., 1970, Large-scale features of monthly mean Northern Hemisphere anomaly maps of sea-level pressure, *Monthly Weather Review 98:*708–716.

151. van Loon, H., and Rogers, J. C., 1978, The seesaw in winter temperatures between Greenland and northern Europe, Part I: General description, *Monthly Weather Review 106:*296–310.

152. Chen, *Combined Land/Sea Surface Air Temperature Trends.*

153. Williams, J., and van Loon, H., 1976, The connection between trends of mean temperature circulation at the surface, Part III: Spring and autumn, *Monthly Weather Review 104:*1591–1596.

154. Lorenz, E. N., 1968, Climatic determinism, *Causes of Climatic Change, Meteorological Monographs 8:* 1–3; and Lorenz, E. N., 1975, Climatic predictability, in *The Physical Basis of Climate and Climatic Modelling,* GARP Publication Series No. 16 (Geneva: World Meteorological Organization), pp. 132–136.

155. Hasselmann, K., 1976, Stochastic climate models, *Tellus 28:* 473–485; a more recent expanded discussion on what has come to be called "stochastic climate models" is given in Hasselmann, K., 1981, Construction and verification of stochastic climate models, in Berger (ed.), *Climatic Variations,* pp. 481–497.

156. Robock, A., 1978, Internally and externally caused climate change, *Journal of the Atmospheric Sciences 35:* 1111–1122.

157. Dalfes, H. N., Schneider, S. H., and Thompson, S. L., 1983, Numerical experiments with a stochastic zonal climate model, *Journal of the Atmospheric Sciences 40:* 1648–1658. These authors make this point and discuss other problems with stochastic climate models.

158. For example, Manabe, S., and Stouffer, R. J., 1980, Sensitivity of a global climate model to an increase of CO_2-concentration in the atmosphere, *Journal of Geophysical Research 85:* 5529.

159. Hansen et al., Climate impact, p. 964.

160. The Parthasararthy and Mooley figure for Indian monsoon rainfall was obtained from Hare, F. K., 1979, Climatic variation and variability: empirical evidence from meteorological and other sources, in *Proceedings of the World Climate Conference* (Geneva: World Meteorological Organization), WMO No. 537, pp. 51–87.

161. Bryson, R. A., and Murray, T. J., 1977, *Climates of Hunger* (Madison: University of Wisconsin Press), p. 152.

162. Bryson and Murray, *Climates of Hunger,* p. 155.

163. van Loon, H., and Williams, J., 1978, The association between mean temperature and interannual variability, *Monthly Weather Review 106:* 1017.

164. Shukla, J., 1975, Effect of Arabian sea-surface temperature anomaly on Indian summer monsoon: A numerical experiment with the GFDL model, *Journal of the Atmospheric Sciences 32:* 503–511.

8. The Human Connection

1. Otterman, J., 1977, Anthropogenic impact on the albedo of the earth, *Climatic Change 1:* 137–155.

2. Sagan, C., Toon, O. B., and Pollack, J. B., 1979, Anthropogenic albedo changes and the earth's climate, *Science 206:* 1363–1368.

3. Colon, F., *The Life of Christopher Columbus by His Son Ferdinand,* translated and annotated by B. Keen (New Brunswick: Rutgers University Press), pp. 142–143.

4. Newell, R. E., 1971, The Amazon forest and atmospheric general circulation, in Matthews, W. H., Kellogg, W. W., and Robinson, G. D. (eds.), *Man's Impact on the Climate* (Cambridge, Mass.: MIT Press), pp. 457–459. A more recent discussion of the potential climatic effects of deforestation is given in Dickinson, R. E., 1981, Effects of tropical deforestation on climate, in *Blowing in the Wind: Deforestation and Long-range Implications, Studies in Third World Societies 14:*411–441.

5. Discussion of Amazon basin water cycling and observations of Amazon water budgets can be found in Salati, E., Dall'Olio, A., Matsui, E., and Gat, J. R., 1979, Recycling of water in the Amazon basin: An isotopic study, *Water Resources Research 15:*1250–1258. See also Shukla, J., and Mintz, Y., 1982, Influence of land surface evapotranspiration on the earth's climate, *Science 215:*1498–1501; these researchers used a computer model to show that summer rainfall is dependent on previous seasons' storage of moisture in the soils.

6. Changnon, S. A. Jr., 1979, Rainfall changes in summer caused by St. Louis, *Science 205:*402–404. See also Changnon, S. A. Jr., 1979, What to do about urban-generated weather and climate changes? *APA Journal*, January: 36–47; "APA" stands for the American Planning Association, headquartered in Washington, D.C.

7. Report of the Study of Man's Impact on Climate (SMIC), 1971, *Inadvertent Climate Modification* (Cambridge: MIT Press), p. 58.

8. Landsberg, H. E., 1962, City Air—Better or Worse, in *Symposium: Air Over Cities,* U.S. Public Health Service, Taft Sanitary Engineering Center, Cincinnati, Ohio, Technical Report A62-5, p. 122.

9. For example, see Schneider, S. H., and Dennett, R. D., 1975, Climatic barriers to long-term energy growth, *Ambio 4:*56–74; see also Llewellyn, R. A., and Washington, W. M., 1977, Regional and global aspects, in *Energy and Climate,* Report of the Geophysics Study Committee, (Washington, D.C.: National Academy of Sciences), pp. 106–188; and Bhumralkar, C. M., and Williams, J., 1982, *Atmospheric Effects of Waste Heat Discharges* (New York: Marcel Dekker).

10. For night photos and a brief description of the low light sensor images of the United States taken from the defense meteorological satellite program see Brandli, H. W., 1978, The night eye in the sky, *Photogrametric Engineering and Remote Sensing 44,* No. 4:503–505; see also Brandli, H. W., 1981, Turn down the Lights, America!, *Bulletin of the American Meteorological Society 62* No. 2:238–239.

11. See the discussion and references in Schneider and Dennett, Climatic barriers.

12. Williams, J., Häfele, W., and Sassin, W., 1979, Energy and climate: A review with emphasis on global interactions, in *Proceedings of the World Climate Conference,* WMO-No. 537 (Geneva: World Meteorological Organization), pp. 267–289.

13. SMIC Report, *Inadvertent Climate Modification,* Chapter 8. Very little

research since this 1971 volume has been forthcoming, and the issue remains speculative. However, a few studies under limited assumptions suggest that aerosols in clouds could increase cloud albedo, thus cooling the climate. For references and a brief discussion see Report of the Meeting of JSC Experts on Aerosols and Climate (Geneva, 27–30 October 1980), World Meteorological Organization.

14. Several chapters in the following volume discuss aerosols in some detail, including photochemical conversion of gases to particles: Rasool, S. I. (ed.), 1973, *Chemistry in the Lower Atmosphere* (New York: Plenum); see especially Chapters 1–3. For a list of more recent references and discussions related to photochemical production of atmospheric aerosols, in particular the effect of fires creating haze and smog layers, see Crutzen, P. J., and Birks, J. W., 1982, The atmosphere after a nuclear war: Twilight at noon, *Ambio 11:*114–125.

15. Although written in the context of weather modification, a comprehensive discussion of legal principles involved in interstate pollution conflicts is given in Weiss, E. B., 1978, International liability for weather modification, *Climatic Change 1:*267–290.

16. SMIC Report, *Inadvertent Climate Modification,* Chapter 8.

17. Although trends in anthropogenic aerosol concentrations seem to have been largely upward to about the mid-1960s (see Note 7, above), in the past several decades many measures of urban air pollution seem to show decreases, perhaps indicating the effectiveness of air pollution control devices. See Council on Environmental Quality, 1981, *Environmental Trends* (Washington, D. C.: U.S. Government Printing Office). Although the *weight* of aerosol suspended particulate matter appears to have been going down recently, at least in the United States, it is not weight, but rather the *number* of particles, that is most important for climate, as noted by Schneider, S. H., and Kellogg, W. W., 1973, The chemical basis for climate change, in Rasool (ed.), *Chemistry of the Lower Atmosphere,* pp. 203–249.

18. Coakley, J. A., Jr., Cess, R. D., and Yurevich, F. B., 1983, The effect of tropospheric aerosols on the earth's radiation budget: A parameterization for climate models, *Journal of the Atmospheric Sciences 40:* 116–138.

19. Reid Bryson is a chief proponent of this Northern-Hemisphere-only aerosol cooling theory as described in Bryson, R. A., and Murray, T. J., 1977, *Climates of Hunger* (Madison: University of Wisconsin Press), pp. 151–152.

20. A strong presentation of the idea that the net effect of anthropogenic aerosols is largely a regional warming is found in Kellogg, W. W., 1980, Aerosols and climate, in Bach, W., Pankrath, J., and Williams, J. (eds.), *Interactions of Energy and Climate* (Dordrecht: Reidel), pp. 281–296.

21. Rasool, S. I. and Schneider, S. H., 1971, Atmospheric carbon dioxide

and aerosols: effects of large increases on global climate, *Science, 173:* 138–141; see also Rasool, S. I., and Schneider, S. H., 1972, Aerosol concentrations: Effect on planetary temperatures, *Science 175:*96.

22. Schneider, S. H., 1974, Atmospheric particles and climate: The impact of man's activities, in Willums, J. O. (ed.), *Experientia Supplementa* (Basel: Birkhauser Verlag), pp. 10–25.

23. Brimblecombe, P., and Stedman, D. H., 1982, Historical evidence for a dramatic increase in the nitrate component of acid rain, *Nature 298:* 460–462. See also Oppenheimer, M., 1983, The relationship of sulfur emissions to sulfate in precipitation, *Atmospheric Environment 17:*451–460.

24. For a review article of the problem of acid rain see Likens, G. E., Wright, R. F., Galloway, J. N., and Butler, G. J., 1979, Acid rain, *Scientific American 241* No. 4:43–51.

25. Lewis, W. M., Jr., 1982, Changes in pH and buffering capacity of lakes in the Colorado Rockies, *Limnology and Oceanography 27:*167–172.

26. A beautifully illustrated short pamphlet on the problem of acid rain has been produced by the Canadian government: *Downwind: the Acid Rain Story,* Environment Canada, Minister of Supply and Services Canada, 1981, En 56-56/1981e. For further information contact Information Directorate, Environment Canada, Ottawa, Ontario K1A 0H3.

27. Revelle, R., and Suess, H. E., 1957, Carbon dioxide exchange between the atmosphere and ocean, and the question of an increase in atmospheric CO_2 during the past decades, *Tellus 9:*18–27. This is one of the classic papers on CO_2.

28. Keeling, C. D., 1973, The carbon dioxide cycle: Reservoir models to depict the exchange of atmospheric carbon dioxide with the oceans and land plants, in Rasool (ed.), *Chemistry of the Lower Atmosphere,* pp. 251–329; the quote is from page 252. In his chapter Keeling gives a short history of early carbon cycle source and sink work by Roger Revelle, Hans Suess, Bert Bolin, Wallace Broecker, and other scientists.

29. Woodwell, G. M., 1978, The carbon dioxide question, *Scientific American 238* No. 1:34–43; Woodwell, G. M., Whittaker, R. H., Reiners, W. A., Likens, G. E., Delwiche, C. C., and Botkin, D. B., 1978, The biota and the world carbon budget, *Science 199:*141–146. Other biologists were making independent assessments at that time, all of which suggest that significant CO_2 input from deforestation or natural forest fires has been occurring. See Adams, J. A. S., Montovani, M. S. M., and Lundel, L. L., 1977, Wood versus fossil fuel as a source of excess carbon dioxide in the atmosphere: A preliminary report, *Science 196:* 54–56; and Wong, C. S. 1978, Atmospheric input of carbon dioxide from burning wood, *Science 200:*197–200.

30. Broecker, W. M., Takahashi, T., Simpson, H. J., and Peng, P.-H.,

1979, Fate of fossil fuel carbon dioxide in the global carbon budget, *Science 206:*409–418.

31. A particularly bitter exchange between Broecker and Woodwell took place at a meeting sponsored by the Department of Energy in Miami in 1977. Articles by both these scientists appear in the conference proceedings: Elliott, W. P., and Machta, L. (eds.), Carbon Dioxide Effects Research and Assessment Program, Workshop on the Global Effects of Carbon Dioxide from Fossil Fuels, Miami Beach, FL., March 7–11, 1977, U.S. Department of Energy CONF 770385, DOE 001, Washington, D.C.

32. One interesting example of a possible sink for about one billion metric tons of carbon per year (one-fifth the 1980 fossil-fuel-injected amount) has been suggested by a University of Hawaii researcher who related CO_2 removal rates to the burial of certain kinds of submerged plants such as sea grasses and microalgae, termed marine *macrophytes:* Smith, W. V., 1981, Marine macrophytes as a global carbon sink, *Science 211:*838–840; another set of biological arguments, this time dealing with carbon metabolism, production, and exchange along coastal shelf food webs, could provide another significant, but reasonably small, sink of global carbon: Walsh, J. J., Rowe, G. T., Iverson, R. L., and McRoy, C. P., 1981, Biological export of shelf carbon is a sink of the global CO_2 cycle, *Nature 291:*196–201.

33. Myers, N., 1980, *Conversion of Tropical Moist Forests,* A Report to the Committee on Research Priorities in Tropical Biology of the National Research Council (Washington, D.C.: National Academy of Sciences). Myers' Academy study, in the words of an international group of experts [Meeting of Experts, *On the Assessment of the Role of CO_2 on Climate Variations and Their Impact,* Villache 1980, (Geneva: World Meteorological Organization, January 1981), p. 12], "expands the scope of tropical forest conversion studies from 13 to 22 countries, but relies fundamentally upon the same statistical bases, and appears to be flawed for purposes of CO_2 budgeting by ambiguous definition and the use of the term 'conversion,' by having ignored forest regrowth in cut-overs and in shifting cultivation areas." These issues led to a rather bitter attack by biologists Lugo, A., and Brown, S., 1980, *Are Tropical Forests Endangered Ecosystems?* Institute of Tropical Forestry, Rio Piedras, Puerto Rico and Center for Wetlands, University of Florida, Gainesville. Given the unusually strong attack and subsequent unpublished response from Norman Myers, one might expect that Lugo and Brown estimated net carbon release from deforestation to be many times less than that from Myers. Surprisingly, at a seminar held at the National Center for Atmospheric Research by Sandra Brown, the atmospheric scientists present found that the biologists' arguments were more over methodological issues and style than deforestation rate numbers, with these different scien-

tists less than a factor of two apart; they were probably no more than a few tens of percent different in their estimates of deforestation rates.

34. Seiler, W., and Crutzen, P. J., 1980, Estimates of gross and net fluxes of carbon between the biosphere and the atmosphere from biomass burning, *Climatic Change 2:*207–247.

35. Stuiver, M., 1978, Atmospheric carbon dioxide and carbon reservoir changes, *Science 199:*253–270.

36. Such a cautionary note was sounded by Meeting of Experts, *Role of CO_2 on Climate Variations,* p. 16. See also Stuiver, M., 1982, The history of the atmosphere as recorded by carbon isotopes, in Goldberg, E. D. (ed.), *Atmospheric Chemistry,* (Dahlem Konferenzen, Berlin, Heidelberg, New York: Springer-Verlag), pp. 159–179.

37. MacDonald, G. J., 1980, Climate effects of trace constituents of the atmosphere, a paper presented at the Third International Conference on the Environment, Paris, December 11, 1980.

38. Carbon Dioxide Effects Research and Assessment Program, Environmental and Societal Consequences of a Possible CO_2-Induced Climate Change: Influence of Short-Term Climate Fluctuations on Permafrost Terrain, Volume II, Part 3, DOE 013 (Washington, D.C.: U.S. Department of Energy.)

39. Bell, P. R., 1982, Methane hydrate and the carbon dioxide question, in Clark, W. C. (ed.), *Carbon Dioxide Review 1982* (New York: Oxford Press), pp. 401–406.

40. Siemerling, R., 1978, The negative greenhouse effect of carbon dioxide, in MacDonald, G. J., and Roberts, W. O. (co-chairpersons), *The Consequences of a Hypothetical World Climate Scenario Based on an Assumed Global Warming Due to Carbon Dioxide,* A Symposium and Workshop held at the Aspen Institute for Humanistic Studies, Aspen, Colorado, 8–14 October 1978.

41. A team of nine scientists (including George Woodwell) attempt to estimate soil oxidation rates in the chapter by B. Moore et al. in Bolin, B. (ed.), 1981, *Carbon Cycle Modeling* (New York: Wiley), pp. 365–385, SCOPE 16. This article suggests a range of net biospheric CO_2 emission in 1970 between 2.2 to 4.7 billion metric tons (fossil fuel CO_2 injection being in between these numbers in 1970).

42. Indeed, most carbon cycle modelers do include strong cautions for unsuspecting readers to avoid "over-interpretation" of their results. Examples of such carbon cycle models include: Siegenthaler, U., and Oeschger, H., 1978, Predicting future atmospheric carbon dioxide levels, *Science 199:*388–395; Kohlmaier, G. H., 1981, Possible self-consistent paths of the terrestrial biota/humus/atmosphere system in response to man's impact, *Radiation and Environmental Biophysics 19:* 67-78; and Viecelli, J. A., Ellsaesser, H. W., and Burt, J. E., 1981, A carbon cycle model with latitude dependence. *Climatic Change 3:*281–302.

43. Meeting of Experts, *Role of CO₂ on Climate Variations,* p. 15.

44. Stanhill, G., 1982, The Montsouris series of carbon dioxide concentration measurements, 1877–1910, *Climatic Change 4:*221–237; Wigley, T. M. L., 1983, The pre-industrial CO_2 level, *Climatic Change 5;* see also a number of articles on CO_2 trapped in gas bubbles and ice cores in *Annals of Glaciology 5* 1983, (Cambridge: International Glaciological Society), in press.

45. Meeting of Experts, *Role of CO₂ on Climate Variations,* p. 15.

46. A subsequent projection by Rotty suggests that the Third World contribution will be even greater than 50 percent, with CTP Asia some 19 percent and other developing countries some 40 percent of world total CO_2 production in 2025: see Rotty, R. M., 1979, Energy demand and global climate change, in Bach, Pankrath, and Kellogg (eds.), *Man's Impact on Climate,* pp. 269–283. He then reduced the Third World projection in Rotty, R. M., and Marland, G., 1980, Constraints on fossil fuel use, in Bach, W., Pankrath, J., and Williams, J. (eds.), *Interactions of Energy and Climate* (Dordrecht: Reidel), pp. 191–212. This projection assumes that in 2025 the Third World will account for only 41 percent of CO_2 production and that the whole world will be consuming roughly 27 terra watts (TW) of primary energy (1 TW $= 10^{12}$ watts). For comparison the present world consumption of energy is about 8.2 TW, and in Rotty's earlier analyses he assumed an energy demand scenario of about 32 TW for A.D. 2025, with the Third World's share being 50 percent or more.

47. Weinberg, A. N., and Hammond, R. P., 1972, Global effects of increased use of energy, in *Peaceful Uses of Atomic Energy,* Proceedings of the Fourth International Conference on the Peaceful Uses of Atomic Energy, jointly sponsored by the United Nations and the International Atomic Energy Agency (IAEA) Vienna, Vol. 1.

48. Schware, R., and Friedman, E. J., 1981, Climate debate heats up, *Bulletin of the Atomic Scientists 37* No. 10:31–33.

49. Marchetti, C., 1975, Primary energy substitution model: On the interaction between energy and society, *Chemical, Economic and Engineering Review 7* No. 8:9.

50. Laurmann, J. A., 1979, Market penetration characteristics for energy production and atmospheric carbon dioxide growth, *Science 205:*896–898.

51. Ausubel, J. H., 1980, *Climatic Change and the Carbon Wealth of Nations,* International Institute for Applied Systems Analysis, Working Paper WP-80-75, Laxenburg. Ausubel argues that a CO_2 doubling may be far off, if it ever comes, because it is difficult to mine, transport, and burn coal on such a large scale. Of course, he does not take into account the (probably remote) possibility of finding vast nonfossil sources of natural gas, such as that proposed in the interesting but highly speculative article Gold, T., and Soter, S., 1980, The deep-earth-gas hypothesis, *Scientific American 242* No. 6:154–161.

52. The article Lovins, A. B., 1976, Energy strategy: the road not taken, *Foreign Affairs* October, which coined the phrase "soft energy paths," and his followup book Lovins, A. B., 1977, *Soft Energy Paths: Toward A Durable Peace* (Cambridge, Mass.: Ballinger), stirred up an international debate of conflicting facts and values over energy, past and future. An interesting followup to the debate was published by Friends of the Earth, in which letters and articles of Lovins' critics are published along with his responses. It makes lively reading: Amory Lovins and His Critics, 1979, *The Energy Controversy: Soft Path Questions and Answers,* Hugh Nash (ed.) (San Francisco: Friends of the Earth).

53. Lovins, A. B., Lovins, L. H., Krause, F., and Bach, W., 1981, *Least-Cost Energy: Solving the CO_2 Problem* (Andover: Brick House).

54. Häfele, W., 1981, *Energy in a Finite World,* Vols. 1 and 2 (Cambridge, Mass.: Ballinger).

55. Lovins et al., *Least-Cost Energy,* p. 12.

56. Weinberg, A. M., 1979, Are the alternative energy strategies achievable? *Energy 4:*941–951; the quote is on p. 950.

57. Lovins et al., *Least-Cost Energy,* p. 73.

58. Ausubel, J., 1982, Book review of *Least-Cost Energy: Solving the CO_2 Problem, Climatic Change 4:*313–317.

59. Lovins, A. B., and Lovins, L. H., 1983, Reply to J. Ausubel, *Climatic Change 5:*105–108 contains the Lovins' response, in which they claim it is not their estimates that are faulty, but "the lack of information" on the part of potential energy conservation investors as to what are the most efficient investments in efficiency. "Remember," they say, "we never said that a low-climatic-risk, least-cost energy strategy is easy; only that it is possible, and easier than dealing with the climatic and other consequences of high-energy, economically inefficient futures" (p. 106).

60. Williams, J., 1978, *Carbon Dioxide, Climate and Society* (Oxford: Pergamon Press), p. 303.

61. Schultz, C. B., and Frye, J. C. (eds.), 1968, *Loess and Related Eolian Deposits of the World* (Lincoln: University of Nebraska Press); in particular see Chapter 8 by C. B. Schultz and Chapter 9 by A. L. Lugn.

62. Kellogg, W. W., 1977, *Effects of Human Activities on Global Climate* (Geneva: World Meteorological Organization), WMO Technical Note 156, WMO No. 486.

63. Butzer, K. W., 1980, Adaptation to global environmental change, *The Professional Geographer 32* No. 3:269–278.

64. Kellogg, W. W., and Schware, R., 1981, *Climate Change and Society: Consequences of Increasing Atmospheric Carbon Dioxide* (Boulder: Westview Press), Figure C.3.

65. Kutzbach, J. E., and Otto-Bliesner, B. L., 1982, The sensitivity of the African-Asian monsoonal climate to orbital parameter changes for 9000 years B.P. in a low-resolution general circulation model, *Journal of the Atmospheric Sciences 39:*1177–1188.

66. Schneider, S. H., 1984, On the empirical verification of model-predicted CO_2-induced climatic effects, in Hansen, J., and Takahashi, T. (eds.), *Climate Processes: Sensitivity to Irradiance and CO_2* (Washington, D.C.: American Geophysical Union), in press.
67. Williams, J., 1979, Anomalies in rainfall during warm Arctic seasons as a guide to the formulation of climate scenarios, *Climatic Change 2:* 249–266; Wigley, T. M. L., Jones, P. D., and Kelly, P. M., 1979, Scenarios for a warm, high CO_2 world, *Nature 283:* 17–21; and Pittock, B., and Salinger, J., 1982, Towards regional scenarios for a CO_2-warmed earth, *Climatic Change 4:* 23–40. See also Jäger, J. and Kellogg, W. W., 1983, Anomalies in temperature and rainfall during warm arctic seasons, *Climatic Change 5:* 39–60. Incidentally, Jill Williams and Jill Jäger are the same person.
68. Kellogg, W. W., 1982, Precipitation trends on a warmer earth, in Reck, R. A., and Hummel, J. R., (eds.) *Interpretation of Climate and Photochemical Models, Ozone and Temperature Measurements* (New York: American Institute of Physics), pp. 35–46.
69. Lorenz, E. N., 1979, Forced and free variations of weather and climate, *Journal of the Atmospheric Sciences 36:* 1367–1376.
70. Livezey, R. E., and Chen, W. Y., 1983, Statistical field significance and its determination by Monte Carlo techniques, *Monthly Weather Review 111:* 46–59.
71. Williams, Anomalies in rainfall, p. 265.
72. For example, see Newell, R., and Dopplick, T. G., 1979, Questions concerning the possible influence of anthropogenic CO_2 on atmospheric temperature, *Journal of Applied Meteorology 18:* 822–825; and Idso, S. B., 1980, The climatological significance of a doubling of earth's carbon dioxide concentration, *Science 207:* 1462–1463
73. For a discussion of empirical verification of climate models' sensitivity to external forcing see Chapter 6 of the present volume; or Schneider, S. H., 1979, Verification of parameterizations in climate modeling, in *Report of the JOC Study Conference on Climate Models: Performance, Intercomparison and Sensitivity Studies* (Geneva: World Meteorological Organization, October 1979), pp. 728–751; or Schneider, S. H., and Thompson, S. L., 1980, Cosmic conclusions from climatic models: Can they be justified? *Icarus 41:* 456–469; or Manabe, S., and Stouffer, R. J., 1980, Sensitivity of a global climate model to an increase of CO_2 concentration in the atmosphere, *Journal of Geophysical Research 85:* 5529–5554.
74. Ad Hoc Study Group, 1979, *Carbon Dioxide and Climate: A Scientific Assessment* (Washington, D.C.: National Academy of Sciences).
75. Idso, S. B., 1982, An empirical evaluation of earth's surface air temperature response to an increase in atmospheric carbon dioxide concentration, in Reck and Hummel (eds.), *Interpretation of Climate and Photochemical Models.*
76. Ibid., p. 133.

77. Ramanathan, V., 1981, The role of ocean-atmosphere interactions in the CO_2 climate problem, *Journal of the Atmospheric Sciences 38:*918–930; Schneider, S. H., Kellogg, W. W., and Ramanathan, V., 1980, Carbon dioxide and climate, *Science 210:*6; and Report of the CO_2/Climate Review Panel of the Joint Climate Board/Committee on Atmospheric Sciences, Climate Research Committee 1982, *Carbon Dioxide and Climate: A Second Assessment* (Washington, D.C.: National Academy of Sciences).

78. For example, see Note 73, or the earlier discussion accompanying Figure 6.2.

79. Ramanathan, The role of ocean-atmosphere interactions.

80. Thompson, S. L., and Schneider, S. H., 1981, Carbon dioxide and climate: Ice and ocean, *Nature 290:*9–10.

81. Manabe, S., Wetherald, R. T., and Stouffer, R. J., 1981, Summer dryness due to an increase of atmospheric concentration, *Climatic Change 3:*347–386.

82. Schneider, S. H., and Thompson, S. L., 1981, Atmospheric CO_2 and climate: Importance of the transient response, *Journal of Geophysical Research 86:*3135–3147.

83. Bryan, K., Comro, F. G., Manabe, S., and Spelman, M. J., 1982, Transient climate response to increasing atmospheric carbon dioxide, *Science 215:*56–58.

84. Thompson, S. L., and Schneider, S. H., 1982, CO_2 and climate: The importance of realistic geography in estimating the transient response, *Science 217:*1031–1033; and Hoffert, M. I., Callegari, A. J., and Hsieh, C.-T., 1980, The role of deep sea heat storage in the secular response to climatic forcing, *Journal of Geophysical Research 85:*6667–6679.

85. Thompson, S. L., and Schneider, S. H., 1979, A seasonal zonal energy balance climate model with an interactive lower layer, *Journal of Geophysical Research 84:*2401–2414; National Academy of Sciences, "Carbon Dioxide and Climate: A Second Assessment"; Harvey, L. D., and Schneider, S. H., 1984, Transient climate response to external forcing on 10^0–10^3 year time scales Part I: Experiments with globally averaged, coupled, atmosphere and ocean energy balance models, submitted to *Journal of Geophysical Research* and also Schneider and Harvey, Transient climate response to external forcing, Part II: Sensitivity experiments with a seasonal, hemispherically averaged coupled atmosphere, land and ocean energy balance model.

86. I made the same point a few years earlier in Schneider, S. H., with Mesirow, L., 1976, *The Genesis Strategy: Climate and Global Survival* (New York: Plenum), p. 196. Incidentally, a nice review of the state-of-the-art as of 1981 for the possibility of ozone depletion from chlorofluorocarbon emissions is contained in *Environmental Assessment of Ozone Layer: Depletion and Its Impact as of November 1980*, Bulletin No.

6, United Nations Environment Program, Nairobi, Kenya, January 1981.

87. Respectively, Delmas, R. J., Ascencio, J.-M., and Legrand, M., 1980, Polar ice evidence that atmospheric CO_2 20,000 yr BP was 50% of present, *Nature 284:*155–157; and Berner, W., Oeschger, H., and Stauffer, B., 1980, Information on the CO_2 cycle from ice core studies, *Radiocarbon 22:*227–235.

88. Berner, Oescher, and Stauffer, Information on the CO_2 cycle, pp. 231–232.

89. Thompson, S. L., and Schneider, S. H., 1981, Carbon dioxide and climate: ice and ocean, *Nature 290:*9–10.

90. Neftel, A., Oeschger, H., Schwander, J., Stauffer, B., and Zumbrunn, R., 1982, Ice core sample measurements give atmospheric content during the past 40,000 yr., *Nature 295:*220–223. See also articles by various members of the Swiss and French research groups in *Annals of Glaciology 5* 1983 (Cambridge: International Glaciological Society) in press, for more recent results.

91. Broecker, W. S., 1981, Glacial to interglacial changes in ocean and atmosphere chemistry, in Berger, A. (ed.), *Climatic Variations and Variability: Facts and Theories* (Dordrecht: Reidel), pp. 111–121.

92. Ruddiman, W. F., and McIntyre, A., 1981, The North Atlantic Ocean during the last deglaciation, *Paleogeography, Paleoclimatology, Paleoecology 35:*145–214. This gives some examples of how glacial meltwater may have seriously decreased biological productivity, at least in the North Atlantic, during various deglacial phases between 10,000 and 20,000 years ago.

93. Berger, W. H., 1982, Increase of carbon dioxide during deglaciation: The coral reef hypothesis, *Naturwissenschaften 69:*87–88.

94. For instance, Michael McElroy of Harvard University argued that the nutrient nigrogen could be just as important as phosphorus in regulating biological productivity/CO_2 levels driving glacial/interglacial transitions. He goes beyond Broecker's or Berger's theories, though, suggesting that perhaps it was the extra CO_2, not some other factor like orbital elements, that ended the ice age. This is highly speculative.

95. Madden, R. A., and Ramanathan, V., 1980, Detecting climate change due to increasing carbon dioxide, *Science 209:*763–768. Wigley, T. M. L., and Jones, P. D., 1981, Detecting CO_2-induced climatic change, *Nature 292:*205–208.

96. Kukla, G., and Gavin, J., 1981, Summer ice and carbon dioxide, *Science 214:*497–503.

97. Schneider, S. H., and Thompson, S. L., 1981, Atmospheric CO_2 and climate: Importance of the transient response, *Journal of Geophysical Research 86:*3135–3147; Cess, R. D., and Goldenberg, S. D., 1981, The effect of ocean heat capacity upon global warming due to increas-

ing atmospheric carbon dioxide, *Journal of Geophysical Research 85:*498.

98. Paltridge, G., and Woodruff, S., 1981, Changes in global suface temperature from 1880 to 1977 derived from historical records of sea surface temperature, *Monthly Weather Review 109*:2427–2434.

99. Folland, C., and Kates, F., 1983, Changes in decadally averaged sea surface temperature over the world 1861–1980, in Imbrie, J., Berger, A., (eds.), in press, *Milankovitch and Climate Change.*

100. See Thompson and Schneider, CO_2 and climate: The importance of realistic geography. See also the semi-empirical modeling of Gilliland, Harvey, and Schneider (Gilliland, R. L., Schneider, S. H. and Harvey, L. D. D., 1984, Volcanic CO_2 and solar forcing of Northern and Southern Hemisphere surface air temperatures, submitted to *Nature*) which breaks down atmospheric temperatures over land and oceans as well as ocean surface temperatures and compares the land temperatures in the model to those of observations. These results suggest that over the past century the magnitude of CO_2 doubling most consistent with the observed record is in the range $1.5°C \pm 0.3$ °C—at the lower end of the "consensus model" range (see Note 74), but still an order of magnitude larger than Idso's "semi-empirical" estimates. See also the discussion in a recent U.S. National Academy of Sciences report *(Changing Climate: Report of the Carbon Dioxide Assessment Committee).*

101. Gornitz, V., Lebedeff, S., and Hansen, J., 1982, Global sea level trend in the past century, *Science 215:*1161–1164.

102. Etkins, R., and Epstein, E. S., 1982, The rise of global mean sea level as an indication of climate change, *Science 215:*287–289.

103. Barnett, T. P., Recent changes in sea level and their possible causes, *Climatic Change 5:*15–38 discusses the sea level issues; and Harvey, L. D. D., and Schneider, S. H., Sensitivity of transient climate response to ocean model formulation, Part II, questions the issue of surface water versus surface air temperature trends.

104. This question is discussed extensively in Schneider, S. H., 1981, Carbon dioxide and climate: The greenhouse effect, testimony before the Subcommittee on Natural Resources, Agriculture Research and Environment and the Subcommittee on Investigations and Oversight of the Committee on Science and Technology, U.S. House of Representatives, 97th Congress (Washington, D.C.: U.S. Government Printing Office), pp. 31–59; Schneider, S. H., 1982, Climatic impact assessment in the CO_2 context, in *Carbon Dioxide Reviews 1982* (Oak Ridge: Institute for Energy Analysis), pp. 50–53. See also the discussion by W. Nordhaus and G. Yohe and by T. Schelling in National Research Council, *Changing Climate.*

105. Ramanathan, V., 1975, Greenhouse effect due to chlorofluorocarbons: Climate implications. *Science 190:*50–52.

106. Zimmerman, P. R., Greenberg, J. P., Wandiga, S. O., and Crutzen, P.

J., 1982, Termites: A potentially large source of atmospheric methane, carbon dioxide, and molecular hydrogen, *Science 218:*563–565; and Goldberg, E. D., *Atmospheric Chemistry.*

107. Flohn, H., 1980, *Possible Climatic Consequences of a Man-Made Global Warming* (Laxenburg: International Institute for Applied Systems Analysis), p. 57.

108. Lacis, A., Hansen, J., Lee, P., Mitchell, P. T., and Lebedeff, F., 1981, Greenhouse effect of trace gases, 1970–1980, *Geophysical Research Letters 8* No. 10:1035–1038.

109. Ibid., p. 1037.

110. Thompson and Schneider, Carbon dioxide and climate, p. 646.

111. See, for example, Kahn, H., 1962, *Thinking About the Unthinkable* (New York: Horizon); or Kahn, H., 1969, *On Thermonuclear War,* 2d ed. (New York: Free Press).

112. Ehrlich. P. R., Ehrlich, A. H., and Holdren, J. P., 1977, *Ecoscience: Population, Resources, Environment* (San Francisco: Freeman), p. 701.

113. *Proceedings of the Symposium on Post-Attack Recovery from Nuclear War,* 1968, (Washington, D.C.: National Academy of Sciences–National Academy of Engineering–National Research Council).

114. Committee to Study the Long-term Worldwide Effect of Multiple Nuclear Weapon Detonations, 1975, *Long-term Worldwide Effect of Multiple Nuclear Weapon Detonations* (Washington, D.C.: National Academy of Sciences), p. 54.

115. Ibid.

116. Schneider with Mesirow, *The Genesis Strategy,* p. 204.

117. Ehrlich, Ehrlich, and Holdren, *Ecoscience,* p. 690–691. A similar point was later made by Lewis, K. N., 1979, The prompt and delayed effects of a nuclear war, *Scientific American 24* No. 1 (July):35–47.

118. Crutzen, P. J., and Birks, J. W., 1982, The atmosphere after a nuclear war: Twilight at noon, *Ambio 11* (2–3):114–125. See also this entire issue of *Ambio,* which is devoted to nuclear war assessments.

119. Turco, R. P., Toon, O. B., Ackerman, T., Pollack, J. B., and Sagan, C., 1983, Long-term atmospheric and climatic consequences of a nuclear exchange, Manuscript prepared for the Conference on the Long-term Worldwide Biological Consequences of Nuclear War, Cambridge, Mass., April 22–23, 1983. A shorter version of this conference manuscript has been prepared by these authors and submitted to *Science* for formal publication.

120. Barnaby, F., 1983, The effects of a global nuclear war: The arsenals, in *Nuclear War: The Aftermath* (Oxford: Pergamon Press), pp. 1–14; and Ambio Advisory Group, 1983, Reference Scenario: How a nuclear war might be fought, pp. 37–48. Sections of this book are a reprint of a special issue of *Ambio* (Vol. 11) devoted to nuclear war.

121. Report of the Committee on Atmospheric Effects of Nuclear Explosions, 1983 (Washington, D.C.: National Academy of Sciences), in

press. Covey, C., Schneider, S. H., and Thompson, S. L., 1984, Atmospheric and Surface Temperature Effects of a Massive Soot Injection in the Aftermath of a Nuclear War (Manuscript in preparation). See also Ehrlich, P. R. et al., 1983, The long-term biological consequences of nuclear war, *Science* (in press). A book tentatively titled *The Cold and the Dark: The World After Nuclear War* (New York: Norton) will follow.

122. Schneider, S. H., and Morton, L., 1981, *The Primordial Bond: Exploring Connections Between Man and Nature Through the Humanities and Sciences* (New York: Plenum), p. 279.

123. Schneider, S. H., and Chen, R. S., 1980, Carbon dioxide warming and coastline flooding: Physical factors and climatic impact, in Hollander, J. M., Simmons, M. K., and Wood, D. O. (eds.), *Annual Reviews of Energy 5:*107–140.

124. See, for example, the article by E. Lemon in Workshop on Global Effects of Carbon Dioxide from Fossil Fuels; Wittwer, S. H., 1980, Carbon dioxide change: An agricultural perspective, *Journal of Soil and Water Conservation 35:*116; or Rosenberg, N., 1981, The increasing CO_2 concentration in the atmosphere and its implication on agricultural productivity. I. Effects on photosynthesis, transpiration and water use efficiency, *Climatic Change 3:*265–280.

9. Food, Water, Health, and Climate

1. Colson, E., 1979, In good years and in bad: Food strategies of self-reliant societies, *Journal of Anthropological Research 35:*18–29; the quotation is from p. 20.

2. Mokyr, J., 1980, Industrialization and poverty in Ireland and the Netherlands, *Journal of Interdisciplinary History 10,* No. 3, 429–458.

3. Bryson, R. A., and Murray, T. J., 1977, *Climates of Hunger* (Madison: University of Wisconsin Press).

4. Hare, F. K., 1979, Food, climate and man, in Biswas, A. K., and Biswas, M. R. (eds.), *Food, Climate and Man* (New York: Wiley), p. 7.

5. Landsberg, H. E., 1979, The effect of man's activities on climate, in Biswas and Biswas (eds.), *Food, Climate and Man,* pp. 187–236.

6. Glantz, M. H., 1977, Nine fallacies of a natural disaster: The case of the Sahel, *Climatic Change 1:*69–84.

7. Lappé, F. M., Collins, J., and Fowler, C., 1978, *Food First: Beyond the Myth of Scarcity* (New York: Ballantine). For example, see pages 89–92.

8. Garcia, R. V., 1981, *Nature Pleads Not Guilty* (Oxford: Pergamon Press). See for example Chapter 7; our quote is from p. 195.

9. Wortman, S., and Cummings, R. W., Jr., 1978, *To Feed This World: The Challenge and the Strategy* (Baltimore: Johns Hopkins Press). For exam-

ple, on p. 7 they argue that "one objective of agricultural development must be to allow individual families to produce a surplus for sale so that the total output of a locality exceeds total local requirements and permits sales to urban centers, other rural regions or international markets. Imports required for higher productivity must be purchased and markets for products must be established. In short, traditional farmers must be brought into the market economy."

10. McQuigg, J., et al., 1973, The influence of weather and climate on United States grain yield: Bumper crops or drought. Report to the National Oceanic and Atmospheric Administration (NOAA), U.S. Department of Commerce (Washington, D.C.: Government Printing Office), December 1973. See also Thompson, L. M., 1975, Weather variability, climatic change, and grain production, *Science 188:*535–549.

11. See the discussion in Chapter 4 of Schneider, S. H., with Mesirow, L. E., 1976, *The Genesis Strategy: Climate and Global Survival* (New York: Plenum).

12. Hare, Food, climate and man, p. 7.

13. Robertson, G. W., 1975, *Rice and Weather* (Geneva: World Meteorological Organization), Tech. Note No. 144, WMO No. 423, p. 5.

14. Baier, W., 1977, *Crop-Weather Models and Their Use in Yield Assessments* (Geneva: World Meteorological Organization), Tech. Note No. 151, WMO No. 458, p. 36.

15. For example, see the discussion in Wortmann and Cummings, *To Feed This World,* p. 154.

16. For a set of essays on this subject see Pimentel, D. (ed.), 1978, *World Food, Pest Losses, and the Environment* (Boulder: Westview Press).

17. Pons, L. J., 1982, Climate and the soil, in Blaxter, K., and Fowden, L. (eds.), *Food, Nutrition and Climate* (Barking, Essex, England: Applied Science Publishers), pp. 3–37.

18. For example, see Bark, L. D., 1978, History of American droughts, in Rosenberg, N. J. (ed.), *North American Droughts* (Boulder: Westview Press), pp. 9–23.

19. See, for example, Newman, J. E., 1978, Drought impacts on American agricultural productivity, in Rosenberg (ed.), *North American Droughts,* pp. 43–62 for data relevant to yield variability issues; see also Schneider with Mesirow, *The Genesis Strategy,* pp. 262–264.

20. Data taken from various tables in U.S. Department of Agriculture, *World Grain Situation and Outlook: Foreign Agriculture Circular* (Washington, D.C.: Government Printing Office), August 1982.

21. Rosenberg, N. J., 1981, Technologies and strategies in weather-proofing crop production, in Slater, L. E., and Levin, S. K. (eds.), *Climate's Impact on Food Supplies: Strategies and Technologies for Climate-Defensive Food Production* (Boulder: Westview Press), pp. 157–180; the quotation is from p. 163.

22. Newman, Drought impacts.

23. Warrick, R. A., 1980, Drought in the Great Plains: A case study of research on climate and society in the U.S.A., in Ausubel, J., and Biswas, A. K. (eds.), *Climatic Constraints and Human Activities* (Oxford: Pergamon Press), Vol. 10 of the International Institute of Applied Systems Analysis Proceedings Series, pp. 98–123.

24. Brown, L. R., 1970, *Seeds of Change* (New York: Praeger). For example, see also the biography of Green Revolution pioneer Norman Borlaug by Bickel, L., 1974, *Facing Starvation: Norman Borlaug and the Fight Against Hunger* (New York: Readers Digest Press).

25. Brown, L. R., 1978, *The Twenty-Ninth Day* (New York: Norton), pp. 86–92.

26. Among these are Reid Bryson (see Bryson and Murray, *Climates of Hunger*) and Hubert Lamb [see Lamb, H. H., 1975, The current trend of world climate—a report on the early 1970s and a perspective (Norwich: Climatic Research Unit, School of Environmental Sciences, University of East Anglia), CRU RP3]. An even more alarming report warning of massive climatic disruption to world food security was published by, of all people, the U.S. Central Intelligence Agency. The Agency's report then became fodder for several climatic potboilers, such as Ponte, L., 1976, *The Cooling* (Englewood Cliffs, N.J.: Prentice Hall); or an "instant book" by the so-called "Impact Team", 1977, *The Weather Conspiracy: The Coming of the New Ice Age* (New York: Ballantine). For a rather negative discussion of these sorts of publications, see Schneider, S. H., 1977, Against instant books, *Nature 270:*650.

27. For a wide-ranging discussion of fishing and fish farming, including the Peruvian situation, see Bardach, J. E., and Santerre, R. M., 1981, Climate and aquatic food production, in Bach, W., Pankrath, J., and Schneider, S. H. (eds.), *Food-Climate Interactions* (Dordrecht: Reidel), pp. 187–233.

28. For a thorough discussion of coastal upwelling fisheries from physical, biological, and societal points of view, see Glantz, M. H., and Thompson, J. D. (eds.), 1981, *Resource Management and Environmental Uncertainty: Lessons from Coastal Upwelling Fisheries* (New York: Wiley Interscience).

29. A good example of the volumes it takes to describe the many aspects of world food systems is the 1975 publication of the U.S. National Academy of Sciences World Food Nutrition Study. In addition to a 192-page summary volume, five separate volumes of several hundred pages each discuss subjects such as crop productivity, aquatic food sources, weather and climate, nutrition, institutions, policies and social science research, information systems, and so on.

30. Hopper, W. D., 1976, The development of agriculture in developing countries, *Scientific American 235,* no. 3:196–205.

31. Norse, D., 1979, Natural resources, development strategies, and the

world food problem, in Biswas and Biswas (eds.), *Food, Climate and Man,* p. 19.

32. Ibid., p. 16 (1975 estimate); Wortmann and Cummings, *To Feed This World,* p. 59 (1965 estimate).

33. One early account of some of the formidable ecological and health obstacles to opening up some potentially arable lands in the tropics was discussed in The Institute of Ecology report: Farnworth, E. G., and Golley, F. B. (eds.), 1974, *Fragile Ecosystems* (New York: Springer-Verlag).

34. One well-known defender of technological props to growing population and food was Herman Kahn of the Hudson Institute, who suggested a world population of up to 30 billion in 2176 as a plausible scenario. See, for example, Kahn, H., Brown, W., and Martell, L., 1976, *The Next Two Hundred Years: A Scenario for America and the World* (New York: Morrow).

35. Norse, Natural resources, pp. 17–18.

36. Ehrlich, P. R., Ehrlich, A. H., and Holdren, J. P., 1977, *Ecoscience: Population, Resources, Environment* (San Francisco: W. H. Freeman), p. 250.

37. Even Herman Kahn (*The Next Two Hundred Years,* p. 123) agreed that costs of opening new land could run over one thousand dollars per hectare, but remained unconcerned, nonetheless: "It seems clear that such costs should be no great deterrent in a world of growing affluence, even if they should run as high as two thousand dollars per hectare."

38. Lindh, G., 1979, Water and food production, in Biswas and Biswas (eds.), *Food, Climate and Man,* pp. 52–72; see his Table 3-9 on page 64 for further details.

39. Norse, Natural resources, pp. 25–26.

40. Kovda, V. A., 1979, Soil reclamation and food production, in Biswas and Biswas (eds.), *Food, Climate and Man,* pp. 159–186; see especially pp. 172–175; see also Kovda, V. A., 1980, *Land Aridization and Drought Control* (Boulder: Westview) for more thorough discussions of Kovda's views on these issues.

41. See, for example, discussion of eco-farming on pp. 180–182 in Cooper, C. F., 1981, Climatic variability and sustainability of crop yield, in Bach, Pankrath, and Schneider (eds.), *Food-Climate Interactions,* pp. 167–186.

42. For example, see Farnworth and Golley (eds.), *Fragile Ecosystems.*

43. See Chapter 2 of the Report of the Study of the Critical Environmental Problems (SCEP), 1970, *Man's Impact on the Global Environment* (Cambridge: MIT Press); Stumm, W. (ed.), 1976, *Global Chemical Cycles and Their Alterations by Man,* 1976 Dahlem Conference report; or chapters 7 and 8 of Schneider, S. H., and Morton, L., 1981, *The Primordial Bond: Exploring Connections Between Man and Nature Through the Humanities and Sciences* (New York: Plenum).

537

44. Wortman and Cummings, *To Feed This World,* p. 70.

45. Steinhart, J. S., and Steinhart, C. E., 1974, Energy use in the U.S. food system, *Science 184:*307–316; see also Pimentel, D., 1981, Food, energy and climate change, in Bach, Pankrath, and Schneider, *Food-Climate Interactions,* pp. 303–323 for a more recent discussion of energy usage in the agricultural sector.

46. Ehrlich, Ehrlich, and Holdren, *Ecoscience,* p. 473.

47. Pimentel, D., 1979, Energy and agriculture, in Biswas and Biswas (eds.), *Food, Climate and Man,* pp. 73–106; see especially pp. 93–99.

48. Ehrlich, Ehrlich, and Holdren, *Ecoscience,* pp. 668–669.

49. Ibid., p. 474–475; see also Deudney, D. and Flavin, C. 1983, *Renewable Energy: The Power to Choose* (New York: W. W. Norton); see especially Chapter 7.

50. Goldemberg, J., 1979, Global options for short-range alternative energy strategies, *Energy 4:*733–744; for the case of gasohol production in Brazil see the discussion on pp. 740–742.

51. The U.S. National Academy of Sciences *World Food and Nutrition Study* admitted that "the magnitude of crop losses from pests is not precisely known" and that "the increasing resistance of pests to pesticides has seriously eroded the effectiveness of chemical control of insects, weeds, and certain plant pathogens" (pp. 80–81). The Academy study recommends "integrated control" by means of which the "burden of protection is shared by a variety of control tactics systematically combined on the basis of sound ecological principles." In the same vein analyst J. Lawrence Apple, plant pathologist and geneticist at North Carolina State University, presented a paper at the American Association for the Advancement of Science meeting in Denver, Colorado in February, 1977 at a symposium entitled World Food, Pest Losses, and the Environment, in which he argued the individual costs and benefits to a single farmer were inadequate basis for judging the costs and benefits of pesticide application: "Society cannot afford individual crop protection specialists making recommendations independently of, and in possible conflict with, actions of crop protection colleagues. . . . The complexity of crop protection tactics makes it difficult for the farmer to integrate piece-meal recommendations into a workable management tool. We must have *integrated pest management* teams that pursue research and extension activities on a coordinated, ecological basis." [Apple, J. L., 1978, Impact of plant disease on world food production, in Pimentel, D. (ed.), *World Food, Pest Losses, and the Environment* (Boulder: Praeger), p. 47.] Thus, both the agronomy and economics of pesticide use is marked by a great uncertainty and controversy.

52. Pimentel, D., and Pimentel, M., 1978, Dimensions of the world food problem and losses to pests, in Pimentel and Pimentel (eds.), *World Food, Pest Losses, and the Environment,* p. 13.

53. Ibid., p. 9. Pimentel and Pimentel quote sources that suggest some

27 metric tons of soil erodes annually per hectare of crop land, which "has resulted in removing at least one-third of the top soil of crop land in use today."

54. Eckholm, E. P., 1976, *Losing Ground: Environmental Stress and World Food Prospects* (New York: Norton).
55. Warrick, Drought in the Great Plains, p. 99.
56. Larson, W. E., Pierce, F. J., and Dowdy, R. H., The threat of soil erosion to long-term crop production, *Science 219:*458–465.
57. Pimentel, D., et al., 1976, Land degradation: Effects on food and energy resources, *Science 194:*152.
58. Meyers, N. 1981, The hamburger connection: How Central America's forests become North America's hamburgers, *Ambio 10:*3–8.
59. Wortman and Cummings, *To Feed This World,* p. 95. Also, see Trager, J., 1975, *The Great Grain Robbery* (New York: Ballantine), pp. 133–134.
60. For data on animal grain conversion efficiencies, see Pimentel, D., 1979, Energy and agriculture, in Biswas and Biswas (eds.), *Food, Climate and Man,* pp. 98–99.
61. See, for example, Borgstrom, G., 1981, Population growth, nutrition and food supply, in Bach, Pankrath, and Schneider (eds.), *Food-Climate Interactions,* pp. 69–79; and Gilland, B. 1979, *The Next Seventy Years: Population, Food and Resources* (Tunbridge Wells: Abacus); these references have different and interesting perspectives on dietary needs of and differences between various nations.
62. Paddock, W., and Paddock, P., 1967, *Famine—1975!* (Boston: Little, Brown), pp. 206–207.
63. Hardin, G., 1974, Living on a lifeboat, *Bioscience 24:*561–568.
64. Schneider with Mesirow, *The Genesis Strategy,* p. 53.
65. Ibid.
66. Roberts, W. O., and Lansford, H., 1979, *The Climate Mandate* (San Francisco: W. H. Freeman).
67. Problems and deficiencies in the application of climatic information, 1979, in *Proceedings of the World Climate Conference* (Geneva: World Meteorological Organization), WMO No. 537, pp. 730–731, lays out the framework for international action in the dissemination of climatic information.
68. Spitz, P., 1981, Economic consequences of food/climate variability, in Bach, Pankrath, and Schneider (eds.), *Food-Climate Interactions,* pp. 447–463.
69. See also Chambers, R., 1982, Health, agriculture and rural poverty: Why seasons matter, *The Journal of Development Studies 18,* No. 2:-217–238.
70. Spitz, P., Economic consequences of food/climate variability, p. 459.
71. Ibid.
72. Swindale, L. D., Virmani, S. S., and Sivakumar, M. C. K., 1981, Climatic variability and crop yields in the semi-arid tropics, in Bach, Pankrath and Schneider (eds.), *Food-Climate Interactions,* pp. 139–166;

these authors from the International Crops Research Institute for the Semi-Arid Tropics in Hyderabad, India, commenting on the high degree of year-to-year climatic variability faced by Third World farmers in this area, noted that "rain-fed farming is risky in such conditions and farmers are reluctant to invest in crop production," which often contributes to the fact that "traditional agriculture means low but stable yields, low inputs, mixed cropping, large families, low incomes and living standards and outmigration of family members, both seasonal and permanent" (p. 139).

73. The Report of Working Group A: Climate as a Hazard strongly makes the point that producers as well as consumers need protection against climatic variability (see pp. xvi–xx of Bach, Pankrath, and Schneider eds., *Food-Climate Interactions*).

74. Hodges, C. N., 1981, New options for climate-defensive food production, in Slater, L. E., and Levin, S. K. (eds.), *Climate's Impact on Food Supplies: Strategies and Technologies for Climate-Defensive Food Production* (Boulder: Westview), pp. 181–206.

75. Rosenberg, N. J., 1981, Strategies and technologies in weatherproofing crop production, in Slater and Levin (eds.), *Climate's Impact on Food Supplies*, pp. 157–180.

76. Hodges, New options, pp. 187–197; and Slater, L. E., 1981, Synthetic foods: Eliminating the climate factor, in Slater and Levin (eds.), *Climate's Impact on Food Supplies*, pp. 207–243.

77. Rosenberg, Weatherproofing crop production, p. 178.

78. Glantz, M. H., 1978, Render unto weather . . . , an editorial in *Climatic Change 1* No. 4:305–306.

79. Lindh, G., 1981, Water resources and food supply, in Bach, Pankrath and Schneider (eds.), *Food-Climate Interactions*, pp. 239–260; see especially pp. 242–245. Swedish water resource analyst Gunnar Lindh summarized world water resource availability—some 14 trillion cubic kilometers of stable runoff annually—and concluded that *if* 1200 cubic meters (1570 cubic yards) per person per year of water were the world average level of demand, then "stable runoff could allow a world population of about ten billion . . . , [which] will be reached soon after the year 2000." However, he points out, other assumptions for both water demand or supply suggest that the situation could be either more or less limiting than 10 billion—assuming the investments were made to channel the stable runoff for sustainable human use.

80. Dracup, J. A., 1977, Impact on the Colorado River Basin and Southwest water supply, in Panel on Water and Climate of the Geophysics Study Committee, *Climate, Climatic Change and Water Supply* (Washington, D.C.: National Academy of Sciences), pp. 121–132.

81. Stockton, C. W., 1977, Interpretation of past climatic variability from paleoenvironmental indicators, in Panel on Water and Change, *Climate, Climatic Change and Water Supply*, pp. 34–45.

82. Dracup, Impact on the Colorado River Basin, p. 131.
83. Panel on Water and Climate, *Climate, Climatic Change and Water Supply* contains a number of contributions that discuss the question of water rights; for example, see Frank J. Trelese, Climatic change and water law, pp. 70–84.
84. See, for example, Maier, W. L., 1977, Identification of economic and societal impacts of water shortages, climatic change, and water supply, in Panel on Water and Climate, *Climate, Climatic Change and Water Supply,* which discusses some of the problems of water sharing in a variety of regions in the United States, including the East.
85. For example, see Rosenberg, N. J., 1978, Technological options for crop production in drought, in Rosenberg, N. J. (ed.), *North American Droughts* (Boulder: Westview), pp. 123–142.
86. Committee on Climate and Weather Fluctuations in Agricultural Production, 1976, *Climate and Food* (Washington, D.C.: National Academy of Sciences), pp. 35–36.
87. Schneider, S. H., 1977, prepared statement presented to the National Water Policy Hearings of the U.S. Senate Subcommittee on Water Resources of the U.S. Senate Committee on Public Works (Washington, D.C.: Government Printing Office), 31 March, pp. 8–36.
88. The Center for Environmental Assessment Service (CEAS) of the Environmental Data and Information Service of the National Oceanic and Atmospheric Administration prepared a preliminary *Impact Assessment: U.S. Social and Economic Effects of the Great 1980 Heat Wave and Drought* (September 7, 1980) in which they estimated "the total count of fatalities related to the heat wave was estimated at 1,265, seven times the number in a near normal summer. Most of the victims were old and/or poor, living in non-air conditioned homes and apartments" (p. 12). Their estimates of economic losses were on the order of $20 billion, but unfortunately these were based upon states' own figures, which may not be objective since states' federal aid depends in part upon their dollar loss estimates. In addition to the problem of lack of independent estimates for each state, benefits (in air-conditioning sales, for example) were not figured in and thus were not subtracted from the calculated losses. Nevertheless, it seems reasonable to say that thousands of people and billions of dollars lost are reasonable rough estimates for the suffering in this 1980 heat wave.
89. Weihe, W. H., 1979, Climate, health and disease, in *Proceedings of the World Climate Conference,* pp. 313–368; see especially p. 338.
90. Momiyama, M., 1975, Seasonal variation of mortality with special reference to thermal living conditions, in Yoshimura, H., and Kobayashi, S. (eds.), *Physiological Adaptability and Nutritional Status of the Japanese, Human Adaptability 3* (Tokyo: University of Tokyo Press), pp. 136–147.
91. Weihe, Climate, health and disease, pp. 355–357.
92. Ibid., p. 361.

93. Schneider, S. H., and Temkin, R. L., 1977, Water supply and the future climate, in Panel on Water and Climates, *Climate, Climatic Change, and Water Supply,* pp. 25–33.

10. Energy and Climate

1. One highly controversial risk analysis that assumes renewable resources require vast backup systems to be reliable is Inhaber, H., 1979, Risk with energy from conventional and non-conventional sources, *Science 203:*718–723. A sharp and detailed critique of Inhaber's assumptions has been given by Holdren, J. P., Anderson, K., Gleick, P. H., Mintzer, I., Morris, G., and Smith, K. R., 1979, Risk of renewable energy sources: A critique of the Inhaber report, Energy and Resources Group Report #79-3, University of California, Berkeley; see also Gleick, P. H., and Holdren, J. P., 1981, Assessing environmental risks of energy, *American Journal of Public Health 71,* No. 9:1046–1050.
2. For example, in discussing this issue Roger Revelle noted that "the 'half-life' of buildings—the period after which half of the buildings erected in a given year have been destroyed or replaced—seems to be between 50 and 100 years. Thus, the disruptiveness of climatic change will depend strongly on the rate of change." See Revelle, R., 1982, Carbon dioxide and world climate, *Scientific American 247,* No. 2:40.
3. Kellogg, W. W., and Schneider, S. H., 1974, Climate stabilization: For better or worse? *Science 186:*1163–1172.
4. The issue of the dangers of the perception of man-induced climatic changes have been discussed for example, in Schneider, S. H., with Mesirow, L., 1976, *The Genesis Strategy: Climate and Global Survival* (New York: Plenum), p. 230; and in Perry, J., 1981, Energy and climate, today's problem, not tomorrow's, Guest editorial, *Climatic Change 3,* No. 3:223–225. Perhaps what is needed is a "global-scale superfund" to compensate losers. This could be a scaled-up version of the U.S. "super fund" that is available to help finance clean up or relocation of those affected by toxic wastes regardless of who is responsible. In essence, the super fund is a sort of no-fault hazardous waste disaster insurance.
5. See, for example, Rosenberg, N. J., 1982, The increasing CO_2 concentration in the atmosphere and its implications on agricultural productivity. II. Effects through CO_2-induced climatic change, *Climatic Change 4,* No. 3:239–254; see also National Defense University, 1980, *Crop Yields and Climatic Change to the Year 2000* (Washington: National Defense University), pp. 80–83.
6. See, for example, Lemon, E. R., 1976, The land's response to more

carbon dioxide, in Anderson, N. J., and Malahoff, A. (eds.), *The Fate of Fossil Fuel CO$_2$ in the Oceans* (New York: Plenum), pp. 97–130; Wittwer, S. H., 1982, commentary in Clark, W. C. (ed.), *Carbon Dioxide Review: 1982* (New York: Oxford University Press), pp. 320–324; and Rosenberg, N. J., 1982, in Clark (ed.), *Carbon Dioxide Review,* pp. 324–328.

7. For example, see the calculations by Chen, R. S., Risk Analysis of a Global Sea Level Rise Due to a Carbon Dioxide-induced Climate Warming, M.S. Thesis, Department of Civil Engineering, Massachusetts Institute of Technology, Cambridge, Massachusetts, January 1982 (unpublished).

8. For a brief discussion and list of references endorsing scenario analysis, see Schneider, S. H., 1981, Testimony of Stephen H. Schneider on carbon dioxide and climate: Research on potential environmental and societal impacts, in *Carbon Dioxide and Climate: The Greenhouse Effect,* Hearing before the Committee on Natural Resources, Agriculture Research and Environment and the Subcommittee on the Investigations and Oversight of the Committee on Science and Technology . . . , U.S. House of Representatives, 97th Congress, No. 45 (Washington, D.C.: U.S. Government Printing Office), 31 July, 1981, pp. 39–59; see also the commentary by Schneider in Clark (ed.) *Carbon Dioxide Review,* pp. 50–53; and Chen, R. S., and Lave, L., at the International Workshop on Resources and Environmental Applications of Scenario Analysis, held at the International Institute for Advanced Systems Analysis, Laxenburg, Austria, July, 1982.

9. *On the Assessment of the Role of CO$_2$ on Climate Variations and Their Impact,* Report of the Joint WMO/ICSU/UNEP Meeting of Experts, Villach, Austria, 1980 (Geneva: World Meteorological Organization).

10. Schneider, S. H., and Chen, R. S., 1980, Carbon dioxide warming and coastline flooding: Physical factors and climatic impact, in Hollander, J. M., Simmons, M. K., and Wood, D. O. (eds.), *Annual Reviews of Energy 5:* 107–140.

11. Meyer-Abich, K. M., 1980, Socioeconomic impacts of CO$_2$-induced climatic changes and the comparative chances of alternative political responses; Prevention, compensation and adaptation, *Climatic Change 2,* No. 4:373–385.

12. One of those frequently quoted as stating that a decade or so is ample time to research the CO$_2$ problem further before considering other actions is Lester Machta of NOAA's Air Resources Laboratory. Indeed, his views were adopted by the U.S. Department of Energy in its multiyear study of CO$_2$ assessments. For example, see Munn, R. E., and Machta, L., 1979, Human activities that affect climate, in *Proceedings of the World Climate Conference* (Geneva: World Meteorological Organization), WMO No. 537, pp. 170–209; in particular see pp. 203 and 204. Similar views have been expressed in Gribbin, J., 1981,

543

Carbon Dioxide, Climate and Man (London: Earthscan), and Wigley, T. M. L., 1983 in a book review of the same book in *Climatic Change 5:* 99.

13. Lave, L. B., 1981, Mitigating strategies for CO_2 problems (Laxenburg, Austria: International Institute for Applied Systems Analysis), IIASA Report CP-81-14, May 1981, p. vi. The general issue of vulnerability and resilience is an important theme in environmental assessment. For example, see Holling, C. S. (ed)., 1978, *Adaptive Environmental Assessment and Management* (New York: Wiley); Brown, H., 1978, *The Human Future Revisited* (New York: Norton); or Timmerman, P., 1981, Vulnerability, Resilience and the Collapse of Society (Toronto: Institute for Environmental Studies), Env. Monograph No. 1, Pub. No. Em-1. A very thoughtful essay on how societies might deal with the advent of increasing carbon dioxide has been given by Harvard University economist Thomas Schelling in *Changing Climate: Report of the Carbon Dioxide Assessment Committee*, National Research Council (Washington, D.C.: National Academy Press), 1983.

14. This notion of tie-ins was first applied to the CO_2 problem in Boulding, E. and Schneider, S. H. et al., 1980, in *Carbon Dioxide Effects, Research and Assessment Program: Workshop on Environmental and Societal Consequences of a Possible CO_2-induced Climatic Change* (Washington, D. C.: Government Printing Office), Report 009, CONF-7904143, U.S. Department of Energy, October 1980, pp. 79–103. Governments could also tax fossil fuel users, as recently proposed in *Can We Delay A Greenhouse Warming?*, 1983, U.S. Environmental Protection Agency (Washington, D.C.: Office of Policy and Resources Management).

15. Kellogg, W. W., and Mead, M. (eds.), 1977, *The Atmosphere: Endangered and Endangering*, Fogarty International Center Proceedings No. 39, Publication No. NIH 77-1065 (Washington: National Institutes of Health).

16. See, for example, the discussion in Chapters 6 and 7 of Schneider with Mesirow, *The Genesis Strategy;* see also Marchetti, C., 1977, On geoengineering and the CO_2 problem, *Climatic Change 1:*59–68.

17. Nordhaus, W. D., 1977, Strategies for the control of carbon dioxide, Cowles Foundation Discussion Paper No. 443; subsequently refined and reprinted in Nordhaus, W.D., 1977, Economic growth and climate: The carbon dioxide problem, *American Economic Review*, pp. 341–346; see also Report of the Carbon Dioxide Assessment Committee.

18. Lovins, A., 1976, Energy strategy: The road not taken, *Foreign Affairs*, October, 1976; this was Lovins' famous article on "the soft path." Also of interest is a followup book in which Lovins confronts his critics: Lovins, A., and His Critics, 1979, *The Energy Controversy: Soft Path, Questions and Answers*, Nash, H. (ed.) (San Francisco: Friends of the Earth).

544

19. The original report by MIT professor Norman Rasmussen, known as the Reactor Safety Study or the Rasmussen Report and published in 1975 by the Energy Research and Development Administration (WASH-1400), has been attacked and praised for years by nuclear critics and advocates, respectively. However, calculations suggesting that the risk of a reactor meltdown was on the order of 1 in 20,000 per reactor per year were later re-examined and the risk factor increased by a factor of nearly a hundred by Okrent, D., and Moeller, D. W., 1981, Implications for reactor safety of the accident at Three Mile Island, Unit 2, in *Annual Review of Energy 6:*43–88. Okrent and Miller noted that "in the early 1970's the point of view of the AEC [Atomic Energy Commission] regulatory staff was that the estimated frequency of an accident leading to a core melt and containment failure . . . was of the order of 10^{-7} per reactor year . . . ; when the draft of WASH-1400 report in 1974 contained an overall estimated core melt frequency of about 1 in 20,000 per reactor year, the regulatory staff's first reaction was that the stated frequency was too high. Since the issuance of the final version of the WASH-1400 report in 1975 with the same core melt frequency, a considerable number of events have occurred that tend to support the thesis that the WASH-1400 estimate of frequency of core melt . . . was too low." (p. 82). Okrent and Miller conclude that "it appears to be difficult to demonstrate with a high degree of confidence that the frequency of severe core damage or core melt for reactors in operation or under construction is less than one in a thousand or one in two thousand per year. Also, there are so many potential paths to a severe damage or core melt accident that it will be difficult to make the frequency of such an accident significantly smaller, with a high degree of confidence" (p. 83). This is five to ten *thousand* times greater risks than were assumed by the AEC in the early 1970s and ten to twenty times more risk than assumed by the Rasmussen Report in the mid-1970s.

20. For example, see Thompson, M., 1982, *Among the Energy Tribes: An Anthropologist Views the Energy Debate* (Laxenburg: International Institute for Applied Systems Analysis); see also Douglas, M., and Wildavsky, A., 1982, *Risk and Culture* (Berkeley: University of California).

21. Committee on Nuclear and Alternative Energy Systems (CONAES), 1978, Report of the Risk/Impact Panel (mimeo draft, unpublished).

22. One of the clearest discussions of both technical and moral aspects of weighing risks and benefits is contained in Fischhoff, B., Slovic, P., and Lichtenstein, S., 1979, Which risks are acceptable? *Environment 21*, No. 4:17. For another good general reference, see Lowrance, W. W., 1976, *On Acceptable Risk: Science and the Determination of Safety* (Los Altos: William Kaufman.)

23. See, for example, the data on cost per fatal accident prevented given as Figure 1 on p. 131 in Schwing, R. C., 1980, Trade-offs, in Schwing, R. C., and Albers, W. A., Jr. (eds.), *Societal Risk Assessment: How Safe*

Is Safe Enough? (New York: Plenum), p. 129–142. An alternative measure of costs of "acceptable risks" is given in a now classic paper by Starr, C., 1969, Social benefit versus technological risk, *Science 165:* 1232–1238. Starr argued that the acceptability of risk, at least based upon public spending habits, is roughly proportional to the third power (cube) of the benefits, as measured by the fatality rate per hour of exposure for some activity versus the average amount of money spent on an activity by a single person.

24. Kneese, A. V., 1977, *Economics and the Environment* (New York: Penguin); see, for example, pp. 22–24.

25. Although written in the context of CO_2, the following article contains a general discussion of transnational boundary pollution problems and includes a number of references: Weiss, E. B., 1983, International legal and institutional implications of an increase in carbon dioxide: Proposed research strategy, in Chen, R. S., Boulding, E., and Schneider, S. H. (eds.), *Social Science Research and Climate Change: An Interdisciplinary Appraisal* (Dordrecht: Reidel), pp. 148–175.

26. The Delaney clause, an amendment to the Food and Drug laws passed in 1958, bans the potential use of food additives that have been shown to cause cancer in animals or humans. An interesting discussion of opposing views regarding this issue is found on page E-79 of the well-written textbook by Miller, G. Tyler, Jr., 1982, *Living in the Environment,* 3d ed. (Belmont: Wadsworth).

27. For a brief discussion and several references to the question of risk perception see Fischhoff, Slovic, and Lichtenstein, Which risks are acceptable?

28. Ben-David, S., Kneese, A. V., Schulze, W. D., 1979, *A Study of the Ethical Foundations of Benefit-Cost Analysis Techniques,* Report to the Ethics and Values in Science and Technology Program of the National Science Foundation, August 1979.

29. The Committee on Nuclear Alternative Energy Systems (CONAES) Risk Panel Report had still not been published five years after the completion of the study. These tables, gleaned from the deliberations of the panel, were published, however, by one of the panel members: Schneider, S. H., 1979, Comparative risk assessment of energy systems, *Energy 4:*919–931.

30. Lovins, A. H., Lovins, L. H., Krause, F., and Bach, W., 1982, *Least-Cost Energy: Solving the CO_2 Problem* (Andover: Brick House).

31. Krenz, J. H., 1978, Minimizing the environmental impact by more effective energy utilization, *Climatic Change 1,* No. 4:312.

32. Schipper, L., and Lichtenberg, A. J., 1976, Efficient energy use and wellbeing: The Swedish example, *Science 194:*1001–1013.

33. For example, see Griffin, S., 1980, Waste equals grist for the mill as Swiss take up recycling, *Smithsonian 11,* No. 8:143–147.

34. For example, see Krenz, J., 1980, *From Opulence to Sufficiency* (Washing-

ton: Hemisphere); or Lovins, Lovins, Krause, and Bach, *Least-Cost Energy;* or Stobaugh, R., and Yergin, D., 1979, After the second shock: Pragmatic energy strategies, *Foreign Affairs 57:*836–871.

35. For example, see the discussion in Chapter 12 of Ehrlich, P. R., Ehrlich, A. H., and Holdren, J. P., 1977, *Ecoscience: Population, Resources, Environment* (San Francisco: W. H. Freeman).

36. For an interesting account of the views of Indian villagers on population planning see Mamdami, M., 1972, *The Myth Population Control: Family, Caste and Class in an Indian Village* (New York: Monthly Review Press).

37. For a general discussion of the theory of demographic transition, illustrative examples, and references to classical literature, see Ehrlich, Ehrlich, and Holdren, *Ecoscience;* or Miller, *Living in the Environment.*

38. For example, see Grant, J. P., 1973, Development: The end of trickle down? *Foreign Policy* No. 12, Fall, pp. 43–65.

39. Ehrlich, Ehrlich, and Holdren, *Ecoscience,* pp. 780–783.

40. Morris, M. D., and Liser, F. B., 1977, The PQLI: Preliminary progress in meeting human needs, in *Communique on Development Issues,* Overseas Development Council, No. 32; see also Morris, M. D., 1979, *Measuring the Condition of the World's Poor: The Physical Quality of Life Index* (New York: Pergamon).

41. Once again, see the discussions in Ehrlich, Ehrlich, and Holdren, *Ecoscience;* and Miller, *Living in the Environment.*

42. Schneider with Mesirow, *The Genesis Strategy,* p. 56.

43. Brown, L. R., 1981, *Building a Sustainable Society* (New York: Norton).

11. Society Permitting: The Future of Climate and Life

1. Colson, E., 1979, In good years and in bad: Food strategies of self-reliant societies, *Journal of Anthropological Research 35:*18–29; passage quoted is from p. 28; see also Schneider, S. H., 1982, Interdisciplinary research: A hedge against wavering public support of science— An editorial, *Climatic Change 4:*3–4.

2. Burton, I., Kates, R. W., and White, G. F., 1978, *The Environment as Hazard* (New York: Oxford University Press), p. 4.

3. Ibid., pp. 11–12.

4. For example, see Torry, W. I., 1979, Anthropological studies in hazardous environments: Past trends and new horizons, *Current Anthropology 20:*517–540; Timmerman, P. 1981, Vulnerability, Resilience and the Collapse of Society (Toronto: Institute for Environmental

Studies), Env. Monograph No. 1, Pub. No. Em-1; and Petak, William J., and Atkisson, A. A., 1982, *Natural Hazard Risk Assessment and Public Policy* (New York: Springer-Verlag).

5. Sakamoto, C., LeDuc, S., Strommen, N., and Steyaert, L., 1980, Climate and global grain yield variability, *Climatic Change 2:*349–361.

6. Schneider, S. H., and Temkin, R. L., 1978, Climatic changes and human affairs, in Gribbin, J. (ed.), *Climatic Change* (Cambridge: Cambridge University Press), pp. 228–246; passage quoted from pp. 235–236.

7. Wells, H. G., 1921, *The Outlines of Human History 2* (New York: Macmillan), p. 594.

8. Schneider, S. H., and Morton, L., 1981, *The Primordial Bond: Exploring Connections Between Man and Nature Through the Humanities and Sciences,* (New York: Plenum), p. 296.

9. This quote appeared on p. 1 of Lapp, R. E., 1965, *The New Priesthood* (New York: Harper & Row).

10. Samuelson, P. A., 1958, *Economics and Introductory Analysis* (New York: McGraw-Hill), p. 38.

11. Ibid.; also, see Chapter 1 of Kneese, A. V., 1977, *Economics and the Environment* (Middlesex, England: Penguin).

12. Silk, L., and Vogel, D., 1976, *Ethics and Profits: The Crisis of Confidence in American Business* (New York: Simon and Schuster), p. 233.

13. Ibid., p. 234–235.

14. Ibid., p. 236.

15. Schumacher, E. F., 1975, *Small Is Beautiful: Economics As If People Mattered* (New York: Harper & Row), p. 294.

16. Evans, D. D., and Adler, L. N., 1979, *Appropriate Technology for Development: A Discussion and Case Histories* (Boulder: Westview Press) is an example.

17. Daly, H. E., 1977, *Steady-State Economics: The Economics of Biophysical Equilibrium and Moral Growth* (San Francisco: W. H. Freeman), pp. 1–4.

18. Ibid., p. 8.

19. Ibid., p. 17.

20. Ibid., p. 177.

21. Ibid., p. 3.

22. Lippmann, W., 1955, *The Public Philosophy* (New York: New American Library), p. 15.

23. Typical examples of optimistic and pessimistic writings over the "problematique" are: Heilbroner, R. L., 1974, *An Inquiry into the Human Prospect* (New York: Norton); or Ehrlich, P. R., and Ehrlich, A. H., 1974, *The End of Affluence* (New York: Ballantine), on the pessimistic side; and Kahn, H., Brown, W., and Martell, L., 1976, *The Next Two Hundred Years* (New York: Morrow); or Maddox, J., 1973, *The Doomsday Syndrome* (New York: McGraw-Hill), on the optimistic side.

Index

553

557